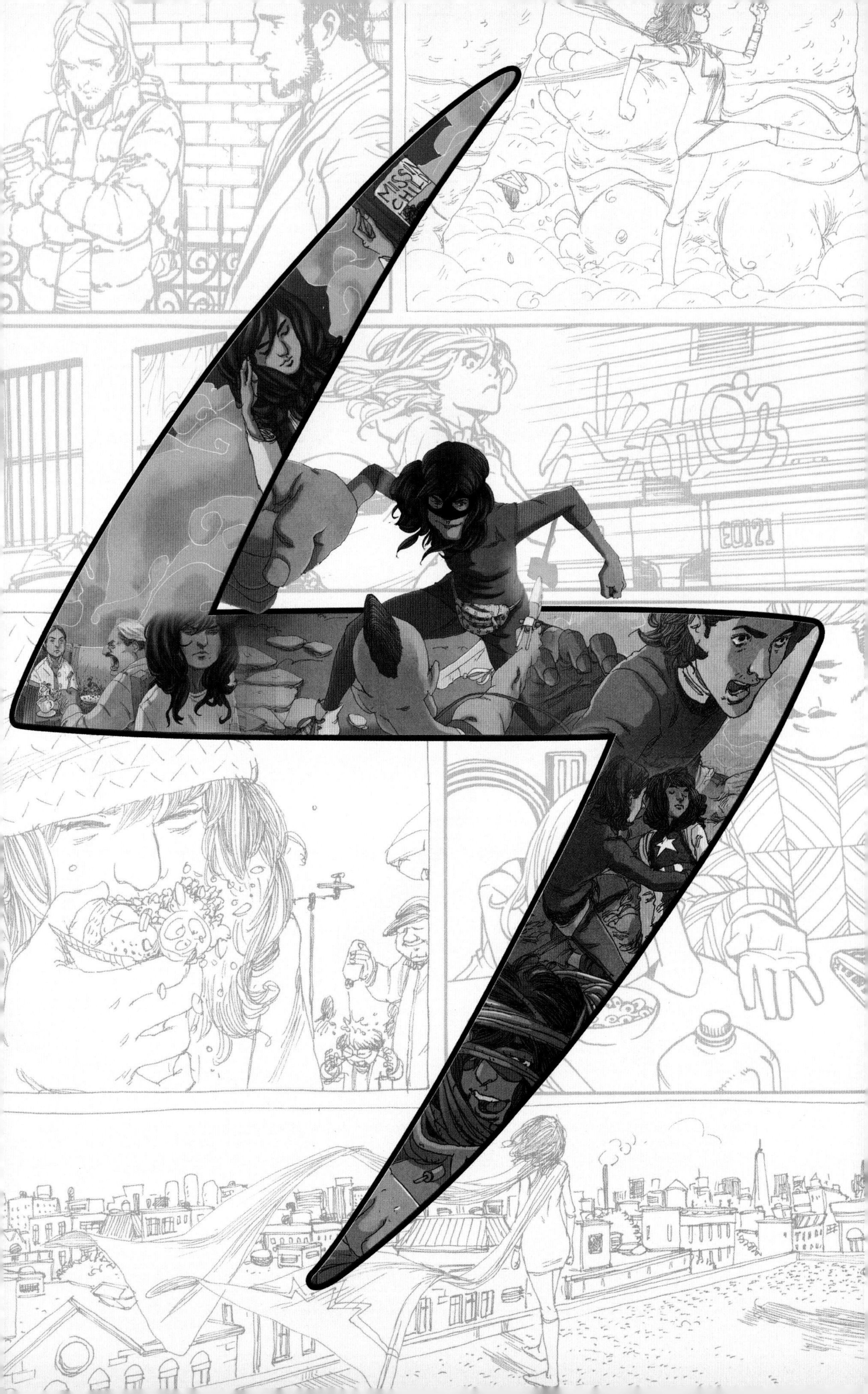

collection editor JENNIFER GRÜNWALD • assistant editor SARAH BRUNSTAD
associate managing editor ALEX STARBUCK • editor, special projects MARK D. BEAZLEY
senior editor, special projects JEFF YOUNGQUIST • svp print, sales & marketing DAVID GABRIEL

editor in chief AXEL ALONSO • chief creative officer JOE QUESADA
publisher DAN BUCKLEY • executive producer ALAN FINE

MS. MARVEL VOL. 2. Contains material originally published in magazine form as MS. MARVEL #12-19, S.H.I.E.L.D. #2 and AMAZING SPIDER-MAN #7-8. First printing 2016. ISBN# 978-0-7851-9836-9. Published by MARVEL WORLDWIDE, INC., a subsidiary of MARVEL ENTERTAINMENT, LLC. OFFICE OF PUBLICATION: 135 West 50th Street, New York, NY 10020. Copyright © 2016 MARVEL No similarity between any of the names, characters, persons, and/or institutions in this magazine with those of any living or dead person or institution is intended, and any such similarity which may exist is purely coincidental. ALAN FINE, President, Marvel Entertainment; DAN BUCKLEY, President, TV, Publishing and Brand Management; JOE QUESADA, Chief Creative Officer; TOM BREVOORT, SVP of Publishing; DAVID BOGART, SVP of Operations & Procurement, Publishing; C.B. CEBULSKI, VP of International Development & Brand Management; DAVID GABRIEL, SVP Print, Sales & Marketing; JIM O'KEEFE, VP of Operations & Logistics; DAN CARR, Executive Director of Publishing Technology; SUSAN CRESPI, Editorial Operations Manager; ALEX MORALES, Publishing Operations Manager; STAN LEE, Chairman Emeritus. For information regarding advertising in Marvel Comics or on Marvel.com, please contact Jonathan Rheingold, VP of Custom Solutions & Ad Sales, at jrheingold@marvel.com. For Marvel subscription inquiries, please call 800-217-9158. **Manufactured between 12/4/2015 and 2/15/2016 by R.R. DONNELLEY ASIA PRINTING SOLUTIONS, CHINA.**

10 9 8 7 6 5 4 3 2 1

MS. MARVEL

writer
G. WILLOW WILSON

artists
ELMO BONDOC (#12),
TAKESHI MIYAZAWA (#13-15) &
ADRIAN ALPHONA (#16-19) &

color artist
IAN HERRING WITH IRMA KNIIVILA (#13)

letterer
VC'S JOE CARAMAGNA

cover art
KRIS ANKA (#12 & #15-19),
MARGUERITE SAUVAGE (#13),
& **JAKE WYATT** (#14)

assistant editors
CHARLES BEACHAM & DEVIN LEWIS

editor
SANA AMANAT

senior editor
NICK LOWE

S.H.I.E.L.D. #2
writer **MARK WAID**
penciler **HUMBERTO RAMOS**
inker **VICTOR OLAZABA**
colorist **EDGAR DELGADO**
letterer **VC'S JOE CARAMAGNA**
cover art **JULIAN TOTINO TEDESCO**
assistant editor **JON MOISAN**
editors **TOM BREVOORT** with **ELLIE PYLE**

AMAZING SPIDER-MAN #7-8
"MS. MARVEL TEAM-UP" & "ADVENTURES IN BABYSITTING"
plot **DAN SLOTT**
script **CHRISTOS GAGE**
penciler **GIUSEPPE CAMUNCOLI**
inker **CAM SMITH**
colorist **ANTONIO FABELA**
letterer **CHRIS ELIOPOULOS**
cover art **GIUSEPPE CAMUNCOLI,
CAM SMITH & ANTONIO FABELA**
associate editor **ELLIE PYLE**
editor **NICK LOWE**

PREVIOUSLY

AFTER A STRANGE TERRIGEN MIST DESCENDED UPON JERSEY CITY,
KAMALA KHAN GOT POLYMORPH POWERS AND BECAME THE ALL-NEW...

MS.MARVEL

WITH STRICT PARENTS ON HER CASE, HER BEST FRIEND BRUNO BY HER
SIDE AND A WHOLE LOT OF WEIRD ENSNARING JERSEY CITY EVERY DAY,
KAMALA SOON REALIZED THAT BEING A SUPER HERO IS...COMPLICATED.

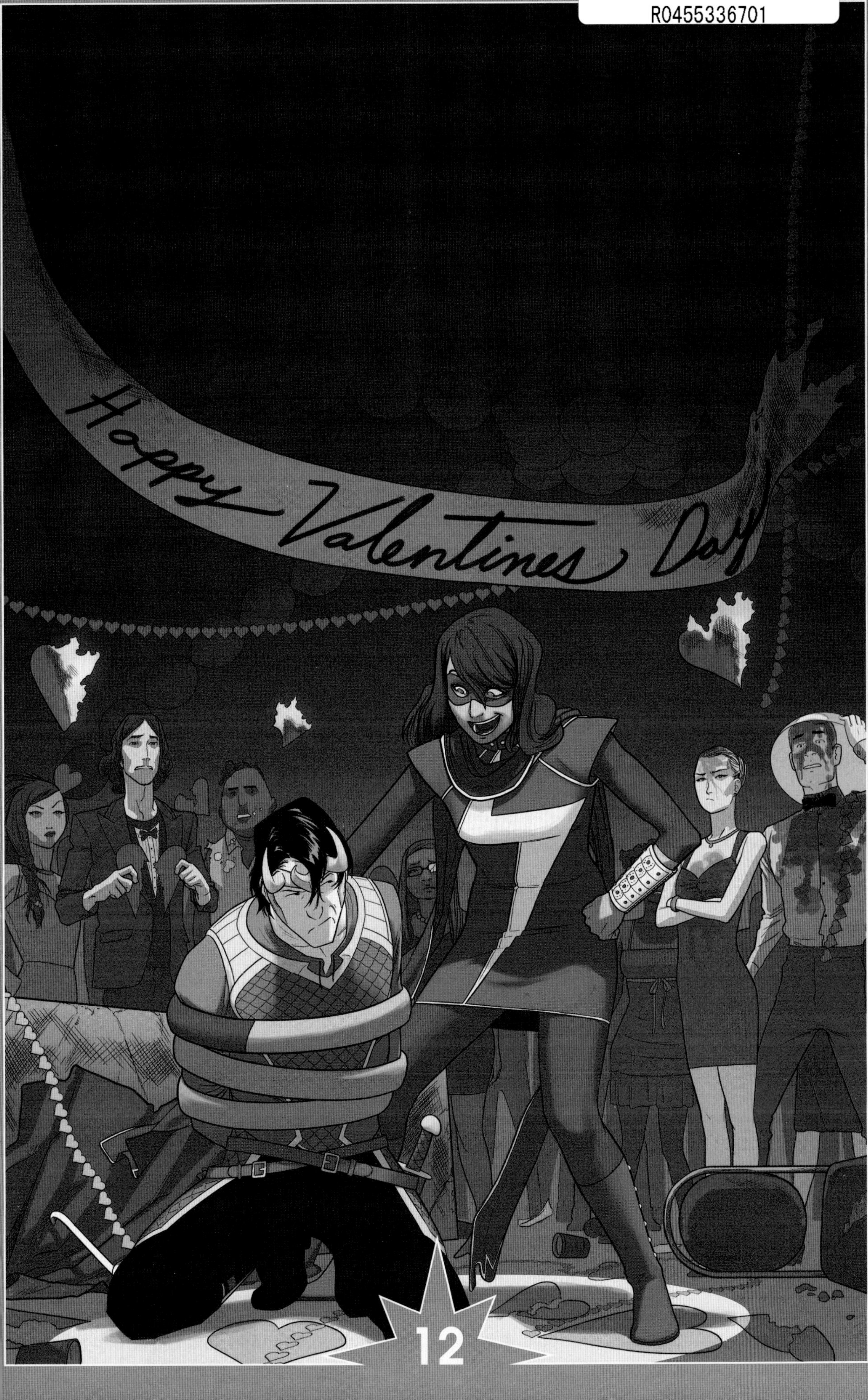
Happy Valentines Day
12

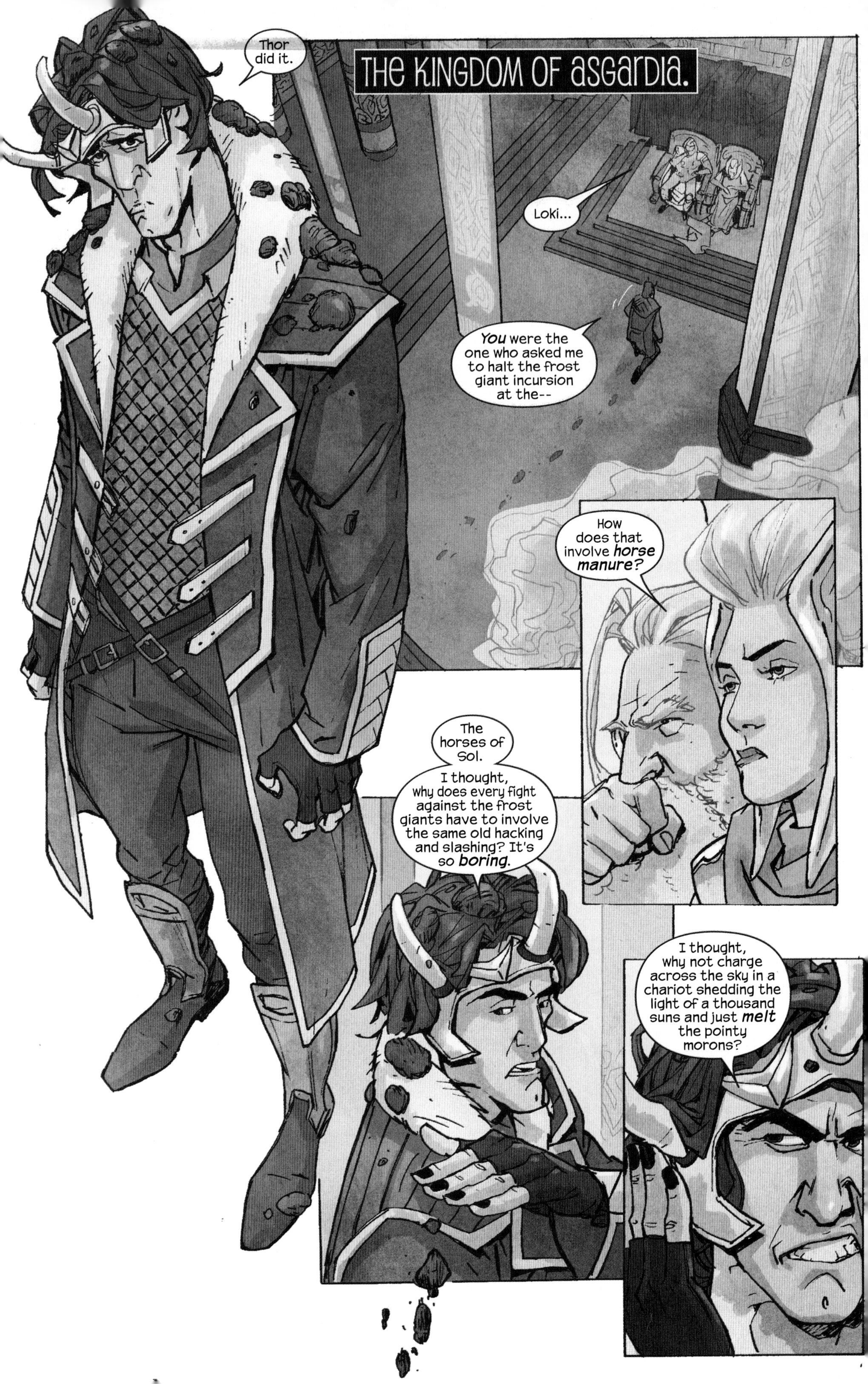
THE KINGDOM OF ASGARDIA.
Thor did it.
Loki...
You were the one who asked me to halt the frost giant incursion at the--
How does that involve ***horse manure?***
The horses of Sol.
I thought, why does every fight against the frost giants have to involve the same old hacking and slashing? It's so ***boring***.
I thought, why not charge across the sky in a chariot shedding the light of a thousand suns and just ***melt*** the pointy morons?

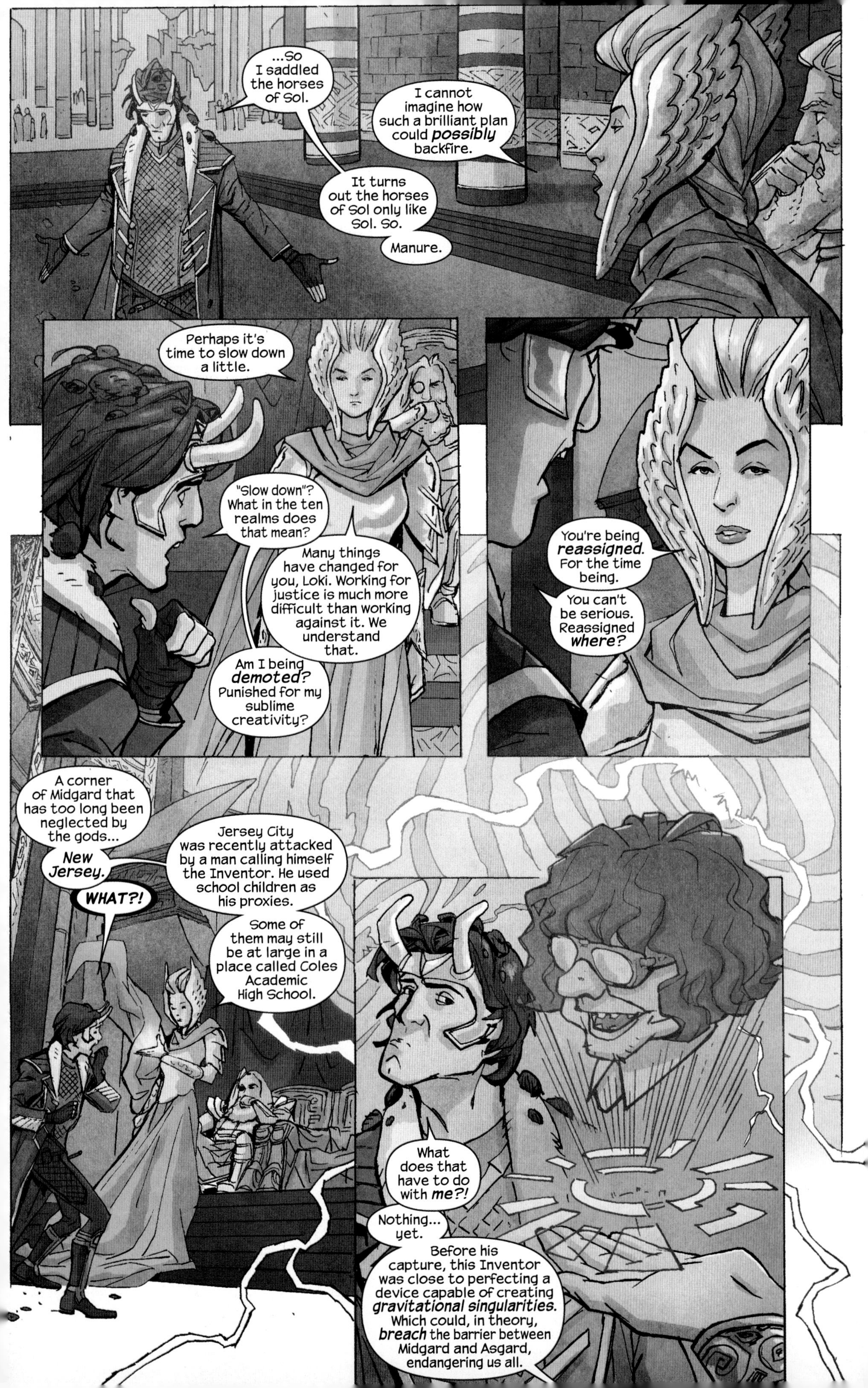
...So I saddled the horses of Sol.
I cannot imagine how such a brilliant plan could *possibly* backfire.
It turns out the horses of Sol only like Sol. So.
Manure.
Perhaps it's time to slow down a little.
"Slow down"? What in the ten realms does that mean?
Many things have changed for you, Loki. Working for justice is much more difficult than working against it. We understand that.
Am I being *demoted?* Punished for my sublime creativity?
You're being *reassigned*. For the time being.
You can't be serious. Reassigned *where?*
A corner of Midgard that has too long been neglected by the gods...
New Jersey.
WHAT?!
Jersey City was recently attacked by a man calling himself the Inventor. He used school children as his proxies.
Some of them may still be at large in a place called Coles Academic High School.
What does that have to do with *me?!*
Nothing... yet.
Before his capture, this Inventor was close to perfecting a device capable of creating *gravitational singularities.* Which could, in theory, *breach* the barrier between Midgard and Asgard, endangering us all.

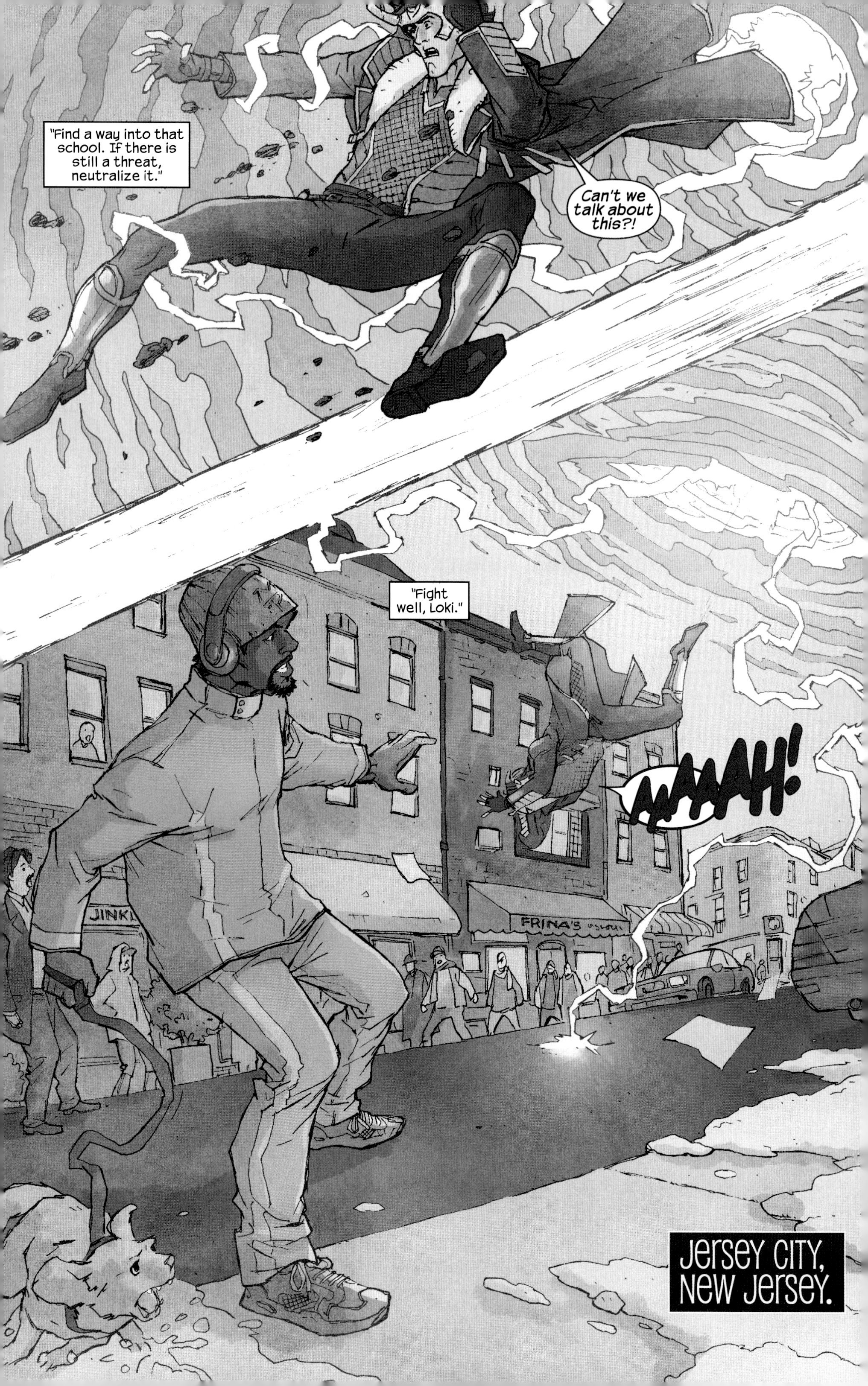
"Find a way into that school. If there is still a threat, neutralize it."
Can't we talk about this?!
"Fight well, Loki."
AAAAAH!
JINK
FRINA'S
Jersey City, New Jersey.

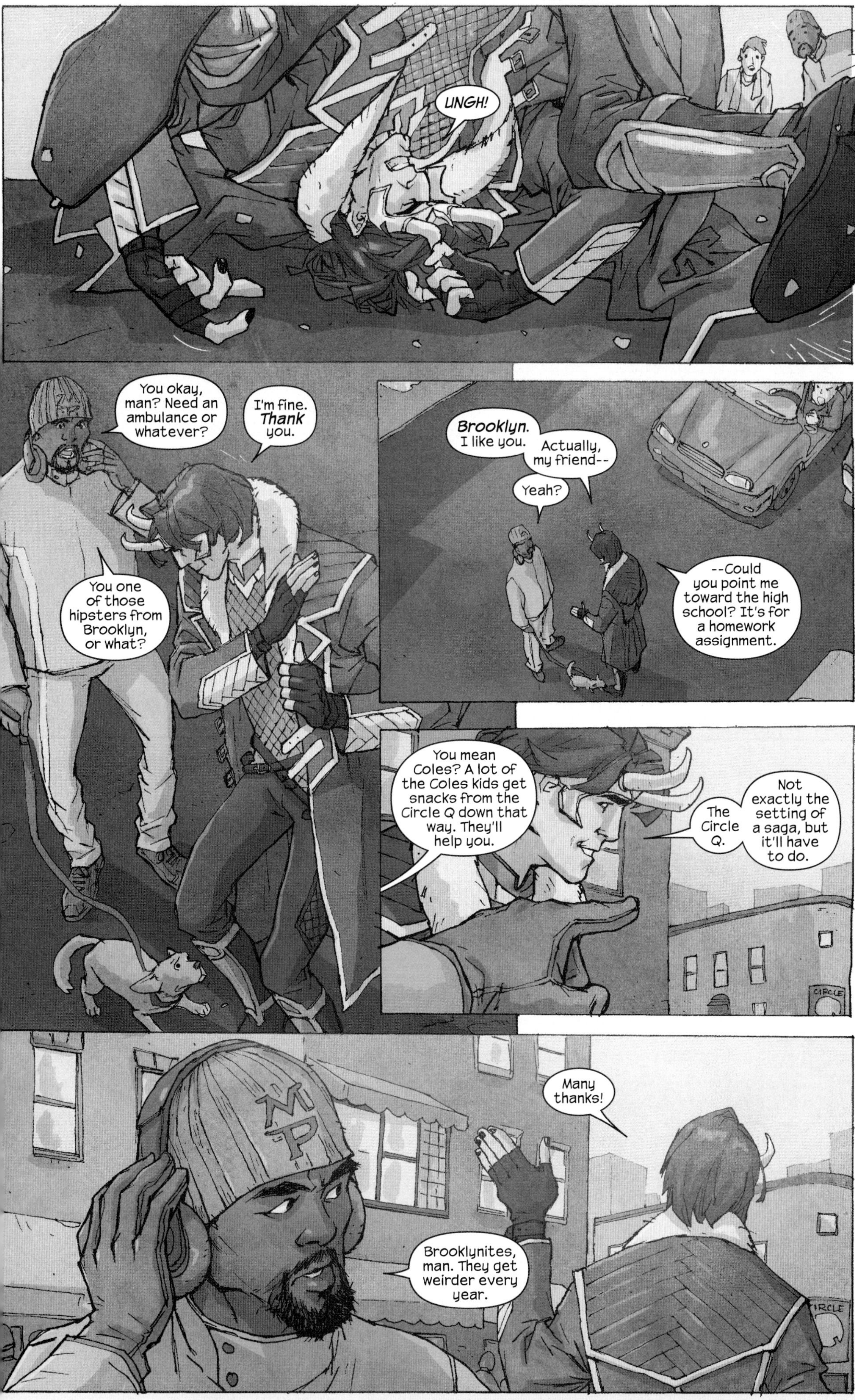
UNGH!
You okay, man? Need an ambulance or whatever?
I'm fine. *Thank* you.
You one of those hipsters from Brooklyn, or what?
Brooklyn. I like you.
Actually, my friend--
Yeah?
--Could you point me toward the high school? It's for a homework assignment.
You mean Coles? A lot of the Coles kids get snacks from the Circle Q down that way. They'll help you.
The Circle Q.
Not exactly the setting of a saga, but it'll have to do.
CIRCLE
Many thanks!
Brooklynites, man. They get weirder every year.

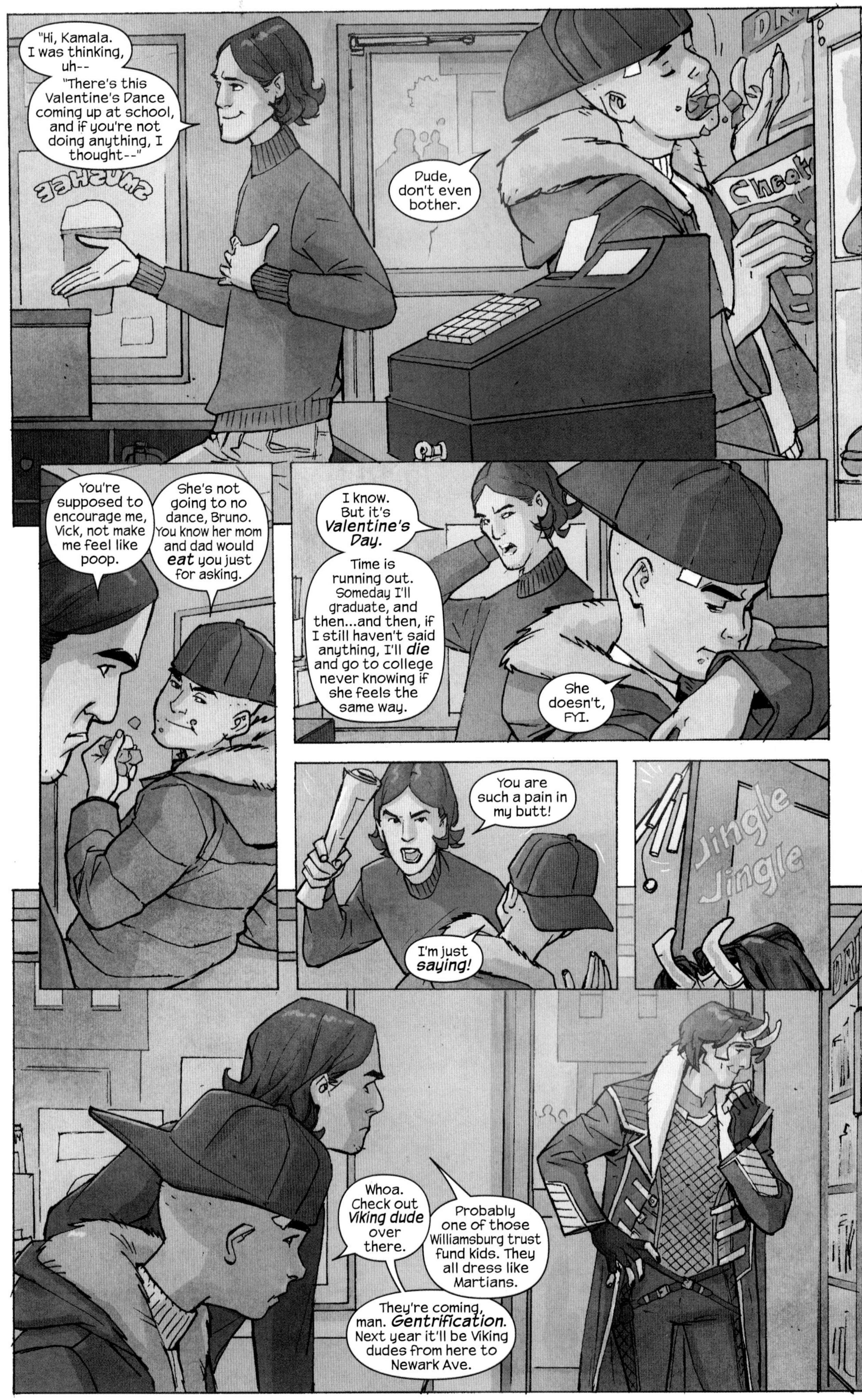
"Hi, Kamala. I was thinking, uh--
"There's this Valentine's Dance coming up at school, and if you're not doing anything, I thought--"
Dude, don't even bother.
You're supposed to encourage me, Vick, not make me feel like poop.
She's not going to no dance, Bruno. You know her mom and dad would *eat* you just for asking.
I know. But it's *Valentine's Day.*
Time is running out. Someday I'll graduate, and then...and then, if I still haven't said anything, I'll *die* and go to college never knowing if she feels the same way.
She doesn't, FYI.
You are such a pain in my butt!
I'm just *saying!*
Jingle Jingle
Whoa. Check out *Viking dude* over there.
Probably one of those Williamsburg trust fund kids. They all dress like Martians.
They're coming, man. *Gentrification.* Next year it'll be Viking dudes from here to Newark Ave.

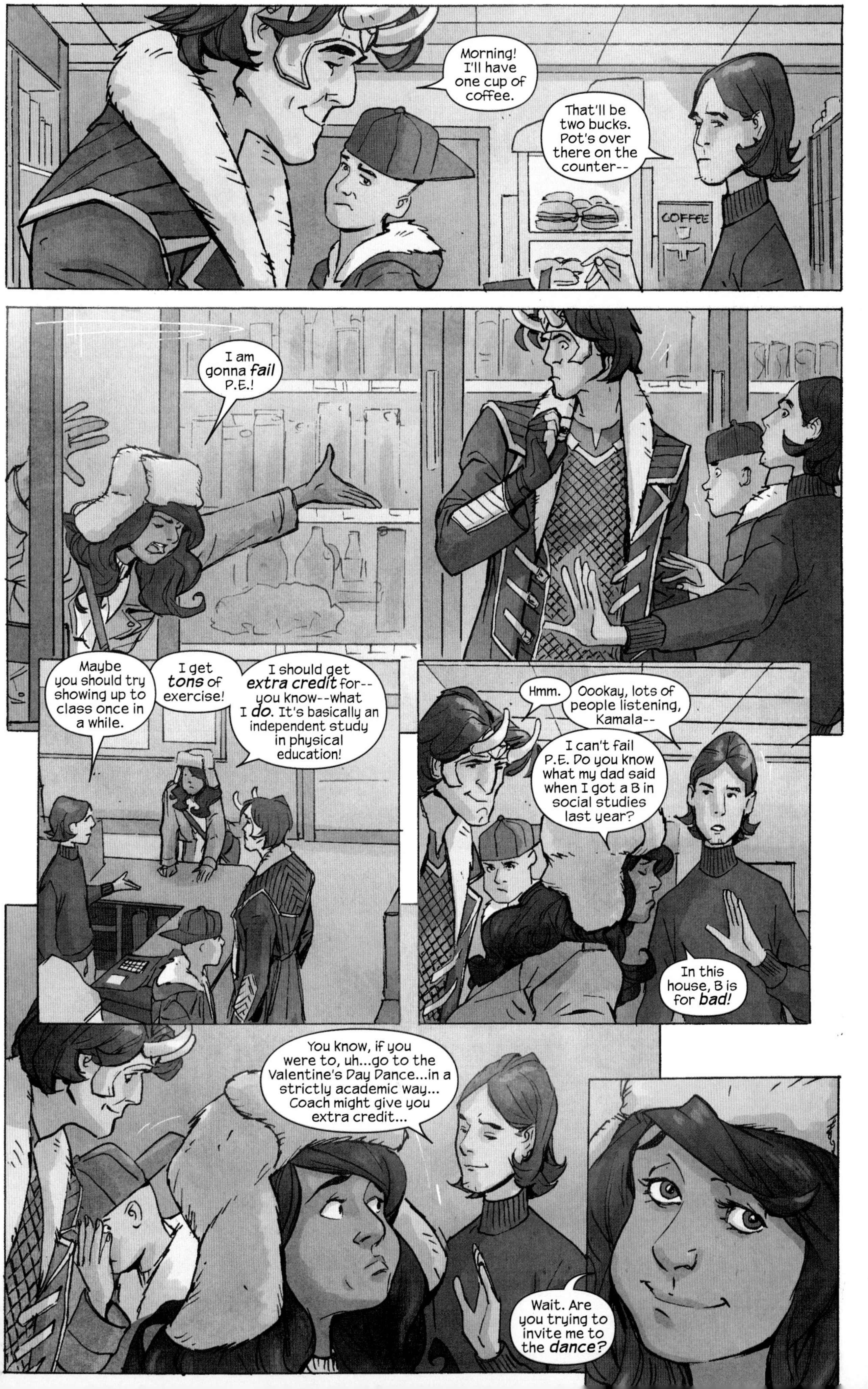
Morning! I'll have one cup of coffee.
That'll be two bucks. Pot's over there on the counter--
COFFEE
I am gonna *fail* P.E.!
Maybe you should try showing up to class once in a while.
I get *tons* of exercise!
I should get *extra credit* for--you know--what I *do*. It's basically an independent study in physical education!
Hmm.
Oookay, lots of people listening, Kamala--
I can't fail P.E. Do you know what my dad said when I got a B in social studies last year?
In this house, B is for *bad!*
You know, if you were to, uh...go to the Valentine's Day Dance...in a strictly academic way... Coach might give you extra credit...
Wait. Are you trying to invite me to the *dance?*

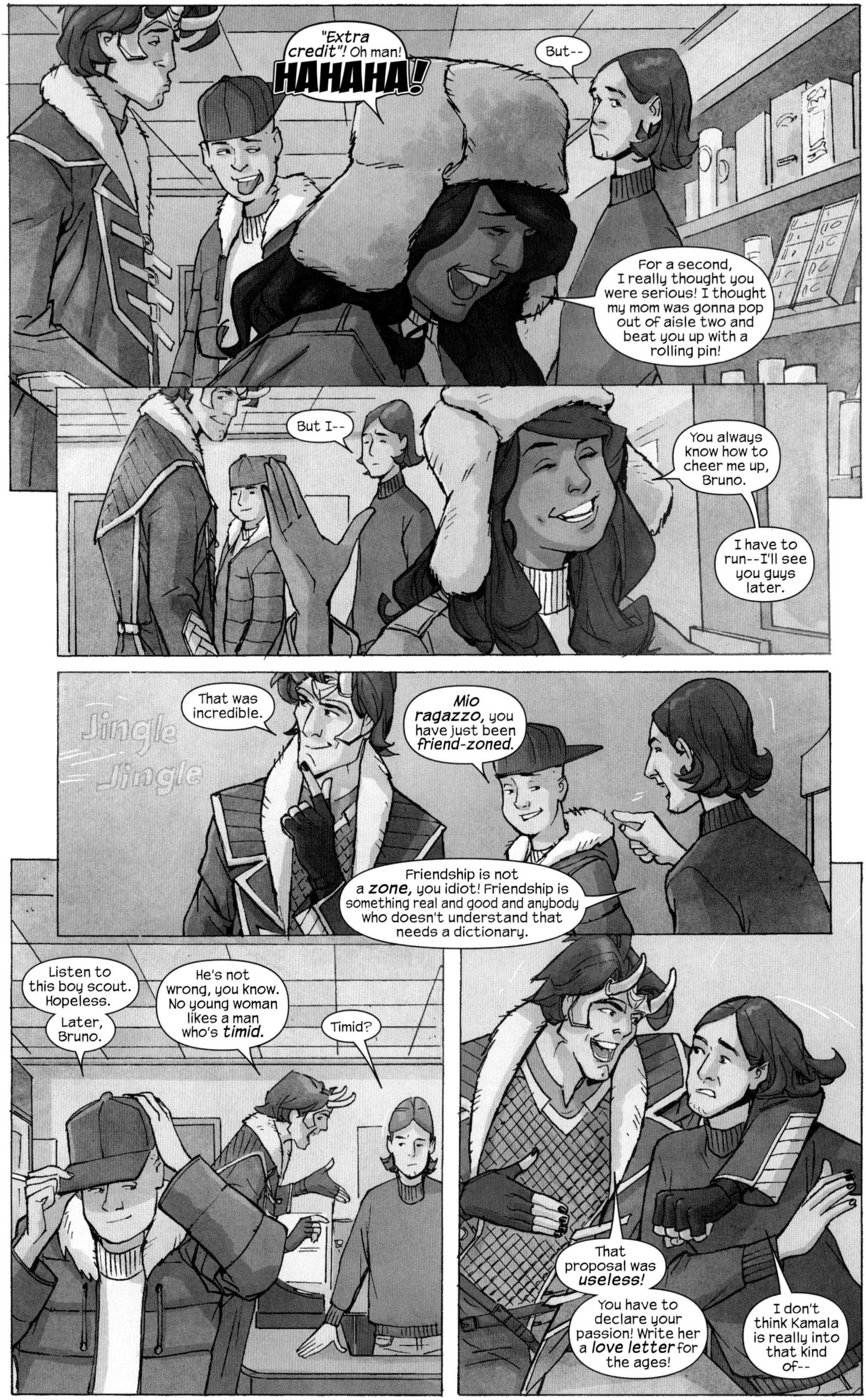
"Extra credit"! Oh man! HAHAHA!
But--
For a second, I really thought you were serious! I thought my mom was gonna pop out of aisle two and beat you up with a rolling pin!
But I--
You always know how to cheer me up, Bruno.
I have to run--I'll see you guys later.
Jingle Jingle
That was incredible.
Mio ragazzo, you have just been friend-zoned.
Friendship is not a zone, you idiot! Friendship is something real and good and anybody who doesn't understand that needs a dictionary.
Listen to this boy scout. Hopeless.
Later, Bruno.
He's not wrong, you know. No young woman likes a man who's timid.
Timid?
That proposal was useless!
You have to declare your passion! Write her a love letter for the ages!
I don't think Kamala is really into that kind of--

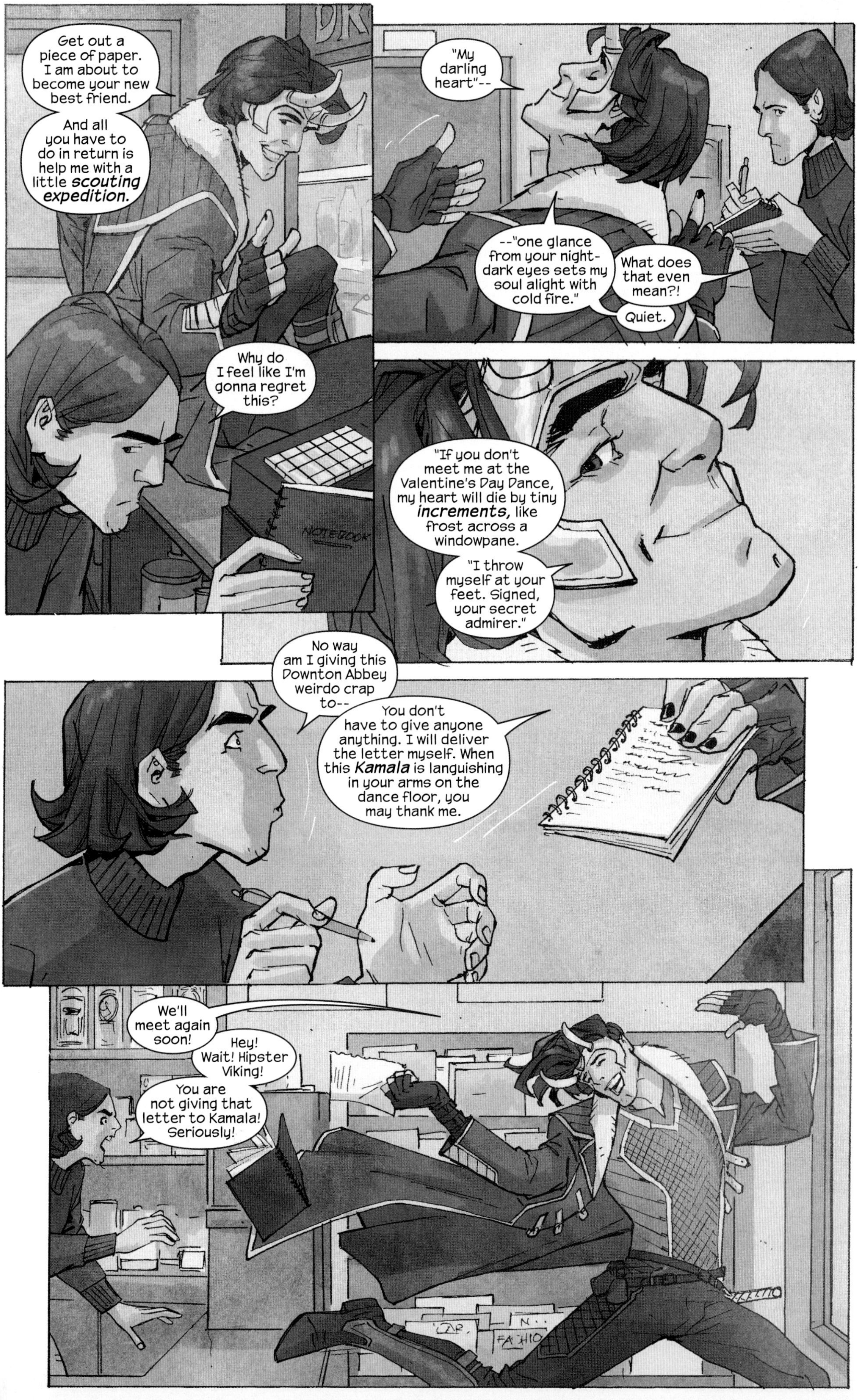

Get out a piece of paper. I am about to become your new best friend.
And all you have to do in return is help me with a little *scouting expedition.*
Why do I feel like I'm gonna regret this?
"My darling heart"--
--"one glance from your night-dark eyes sets my soul alight with cold fire."
What does that even mean?!
Quiet.
"If you don't meet me at the Valentine's Day Dance, my heart will die by tiny *increments,* like frost across a windowpane.
"I throw myself at your feet. Signed, your secret admirer."
No way am I giving this Downton Abbey weirdo crap to--
You don't have to give anyone anything. I will deliver the letter myself. When this *Kamala* is languishing in your arms on the dance floor, you may thank me.
We'll meet again soon!
Hey! Wait! Hipster Viking!
You are not giving that letter to Kamala! Seriously!

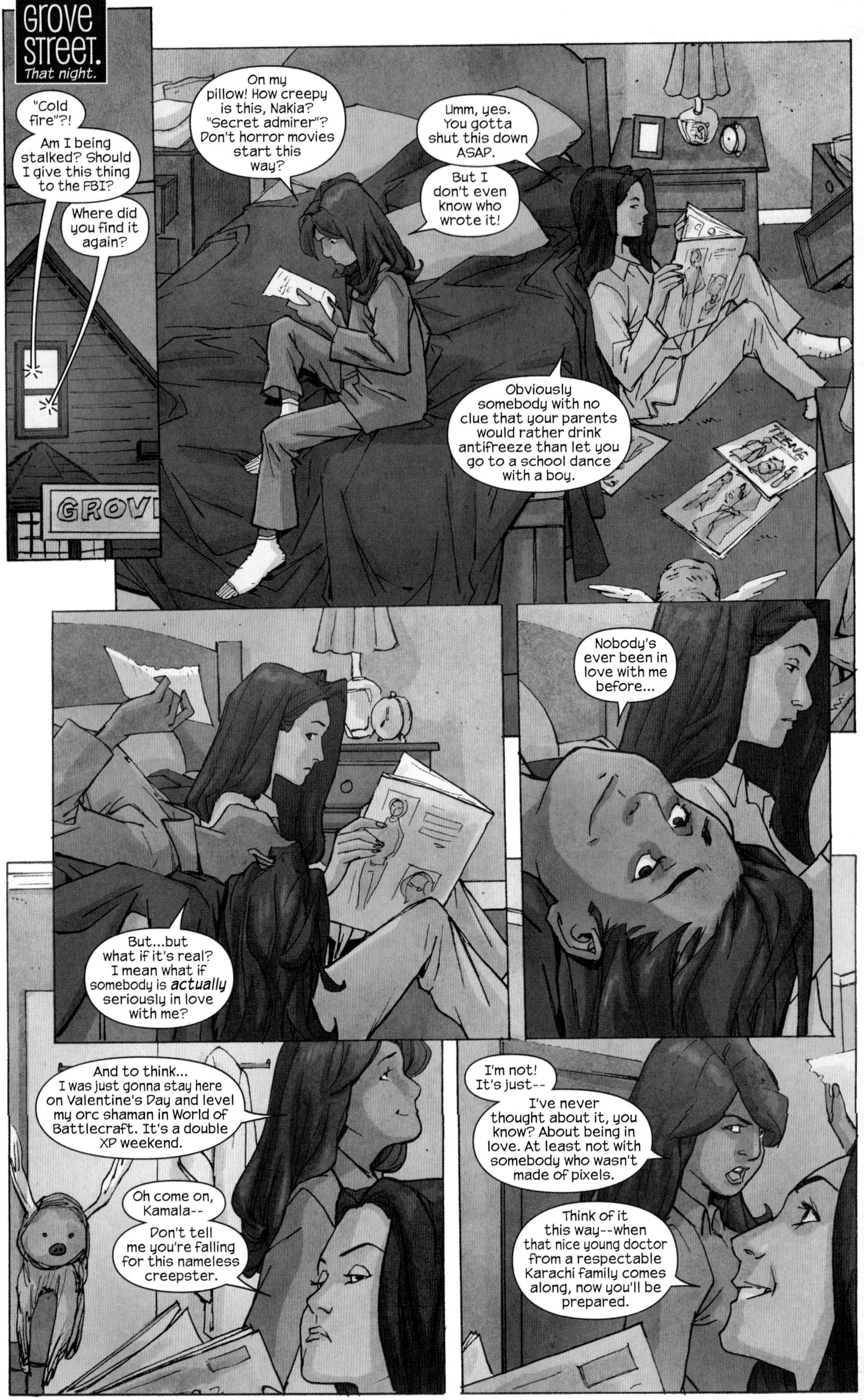

GROVE STREET. That night.
"Cold fire"?!
Am I being stalked? Should I give this thing to the FBI?
Where did you find it again?
GROV
On my pillow! How creepy is this, Nakia? "Secret admirer"? Don't horror movies start this way?
Umm, yes. You gotta shut this down ASAP.
But I don't even know who wrote it!
Obviously somebody with no clue that your parents would rather drink antifreeze than let you go to a school dance with a boy.
But...but what if it's real? I mean what if somebody is *actually* seriously in love with me?
Nobody's ever been in love with me before...
And to think... I was just gonna stay here on Valentine's Day and level my orc shaman in World of Battlecraft. It's a double XP weekend.
Oh come on, Kamala--
Don't tell me you're falling for this nameless creepster.
I'm not! It's just--
I've never thought about it, you know? About being in love. At least not with somebody who wasn't made of pixels.
Think of it this way--when that nice young doctor from a respectable Karachi family comes along, now you'll be prepared.

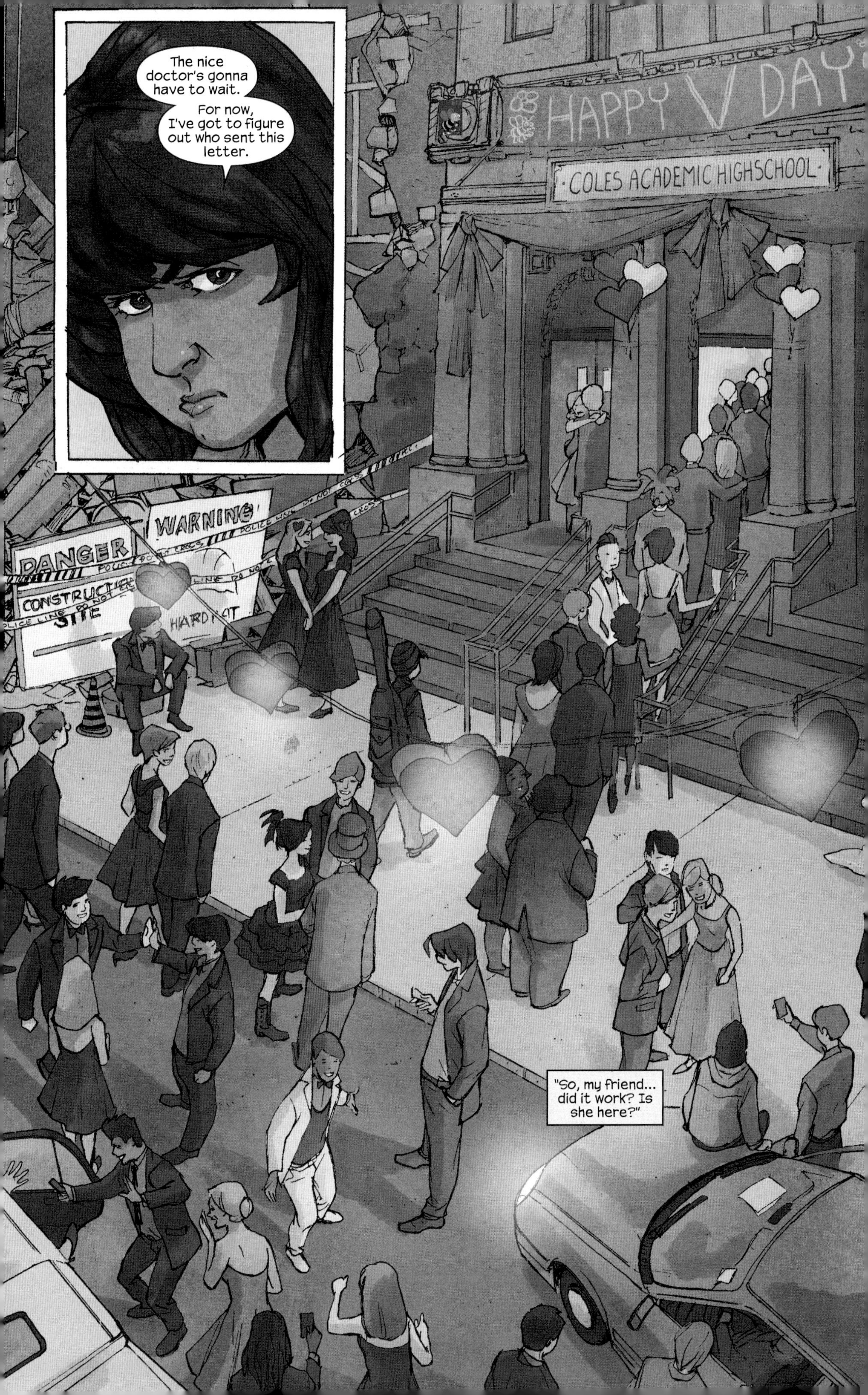
The nice doctor's gonna have to wait.
For now, I've got to figure out who sent this letter.
HAPPY V DAY
COLES ACADEMIC HIGHSCHOOL
WARNING
DANGER
CONSTRUCTION SITE
HARD HAT
POLICE LINE DO NOT CROSS
"So, my friend... did it work? Is she here?"

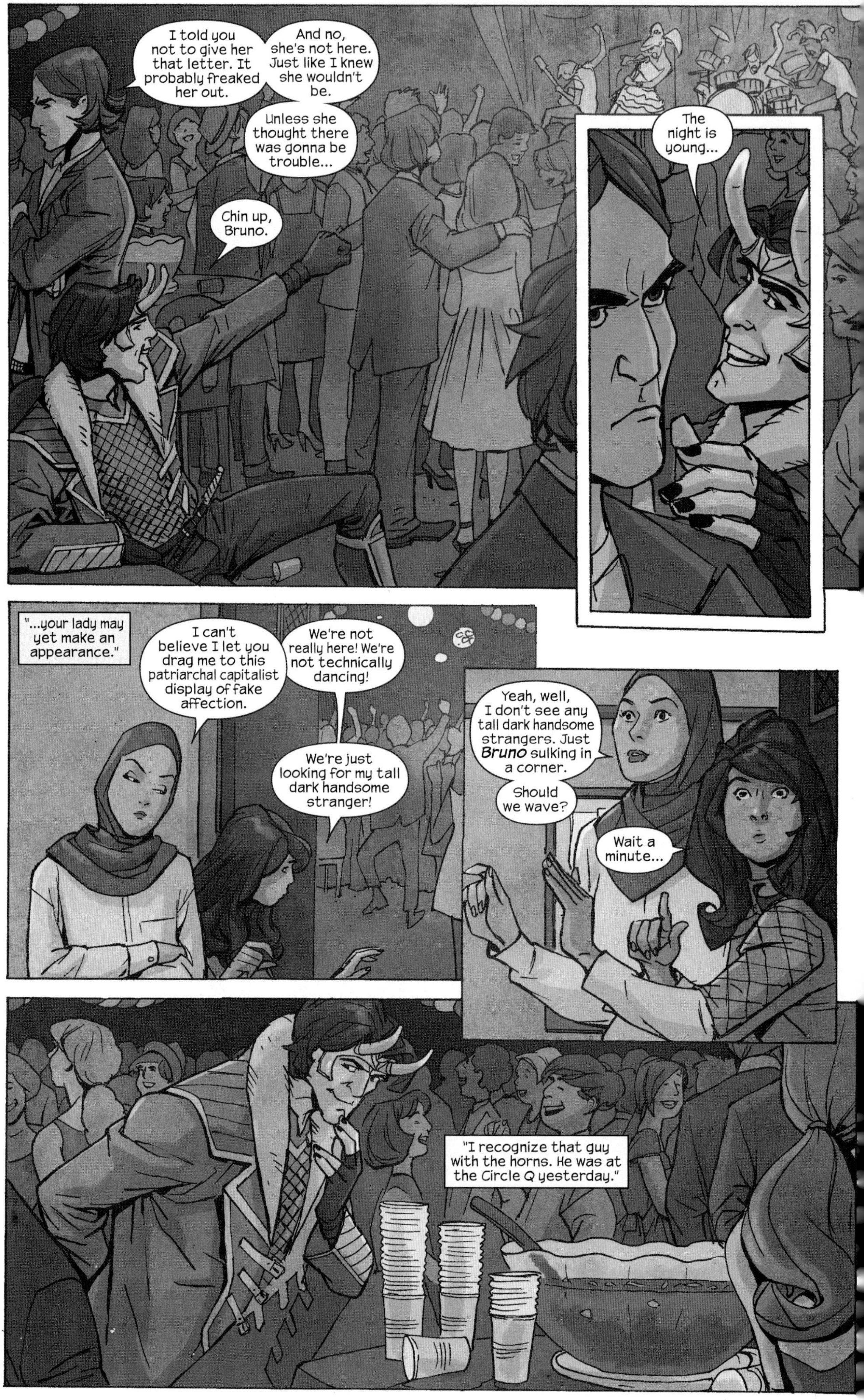
I told you not to give her that letter. It probably freaked her out.
And no, she's not here. Just like I knew she wouldn't be.
Unless she thought there was gonna be trouble...
Chin up, Bruno.
The night is young...
"...your lady may yet make an appearance."
I can't believe I let you drag me to this patriarchal capitalist display of fake affection.
We're not really here! We're not technically dancing!
We're just looking for my tall dark handsome stranger!
Yeah, well, I don't see any tall dark handsome strangers. Just *Bruno* sulking in a corner.
Should we wave?
Wait a minute...
"I recognize that guy with the horns. He was at the Circle Q yesterday."

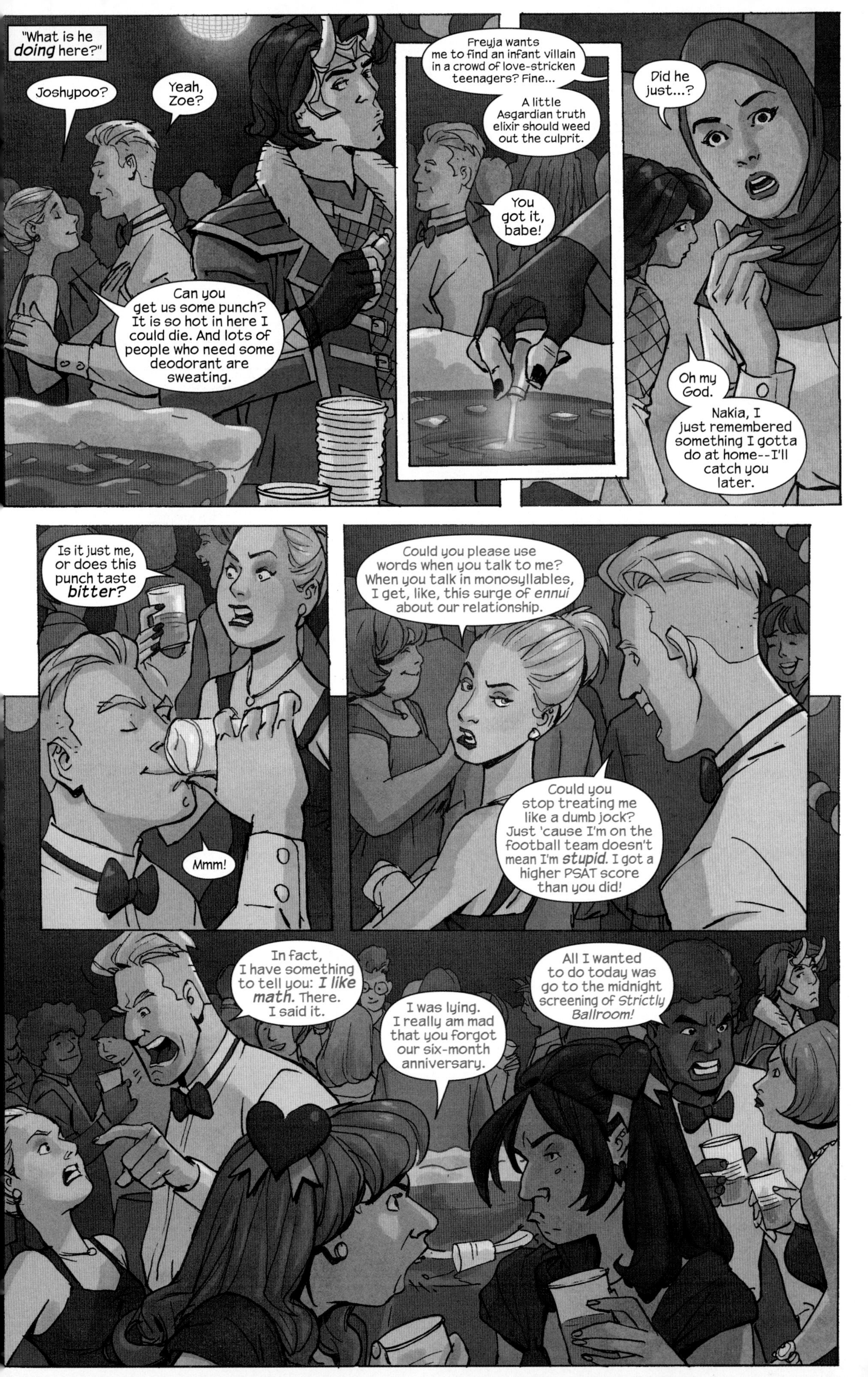
"What is he *doing* here?"
Joshypoo?
Yeah, Zoe?
Can you get us some punch? It is so hot in here I could die. And lots of people who need some deodorant are sweating.
Freyja wants me to find an infant villain in a crowd of love-stricken teenagers? Fine...
A little Asgardian truth elixir should weed out the culprit.
You got it, babe!
Did he just...?
Oh my God.
Nakia, I just remembered something I gotta do at home--I'll catch you later.
Is it just me, or does this punch taste *bitter*?
Mmm!
Could you please use words when you talk to me? When you talk in monosyllables, I get, like, this surge of *ennui* about our relationship.
Could you stop treating me like a dumb jock? Just 'cause I'm on the football team doesn't mean I'm *stupid*. I got a higher PSAT score than you did!
In fact, I have something to tell you: *I like math.* There. I said it.
I was lying. I really am mad that you forgot our six-month anniversary.
All I wanted to do today was go to the midnight screening of *Strictly Ballroom!*

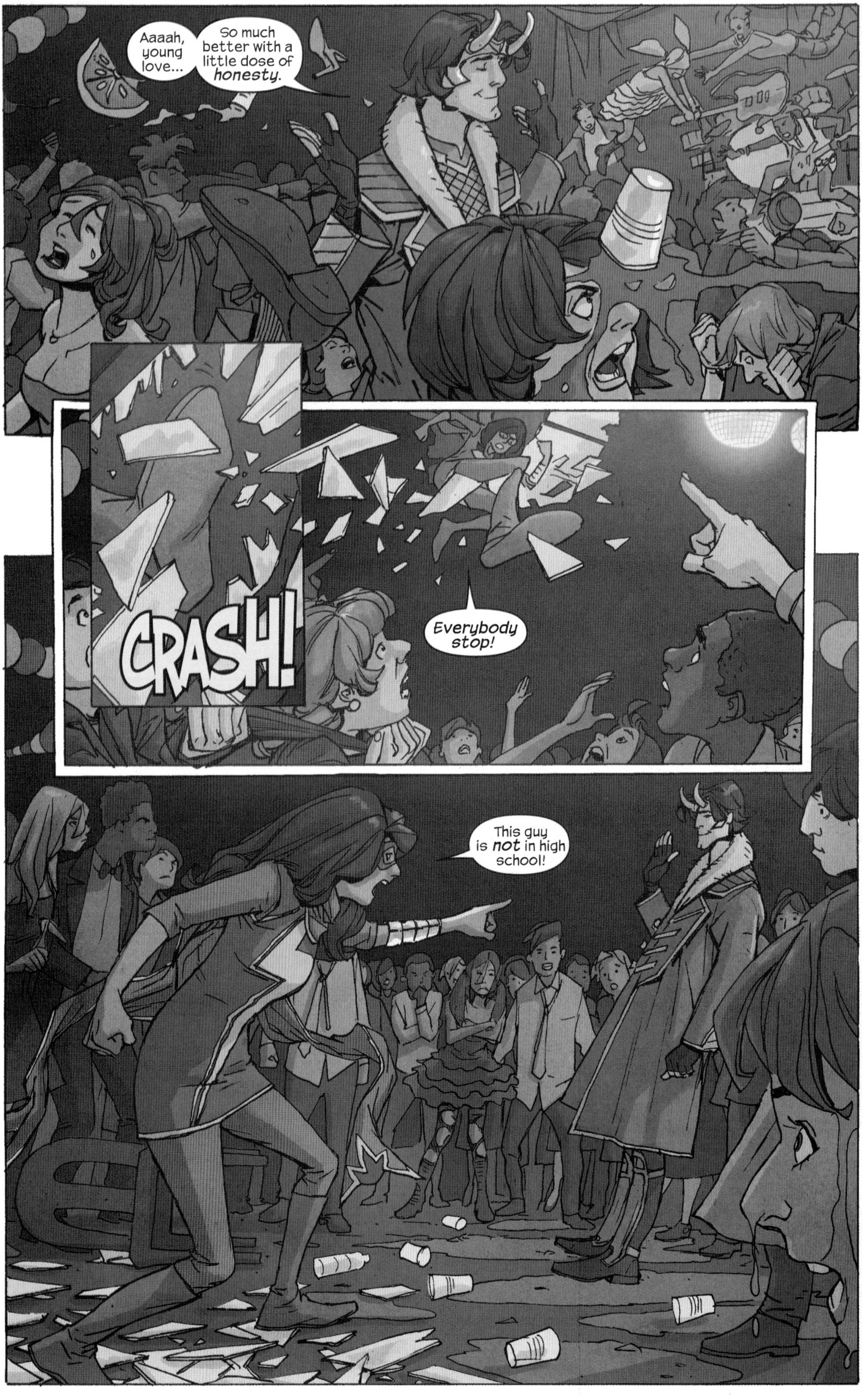
Aaaah, young love...
So much better with a little dose of *honesty*.
CRASH!
Everybody stop!
This guy is **not** in high school!

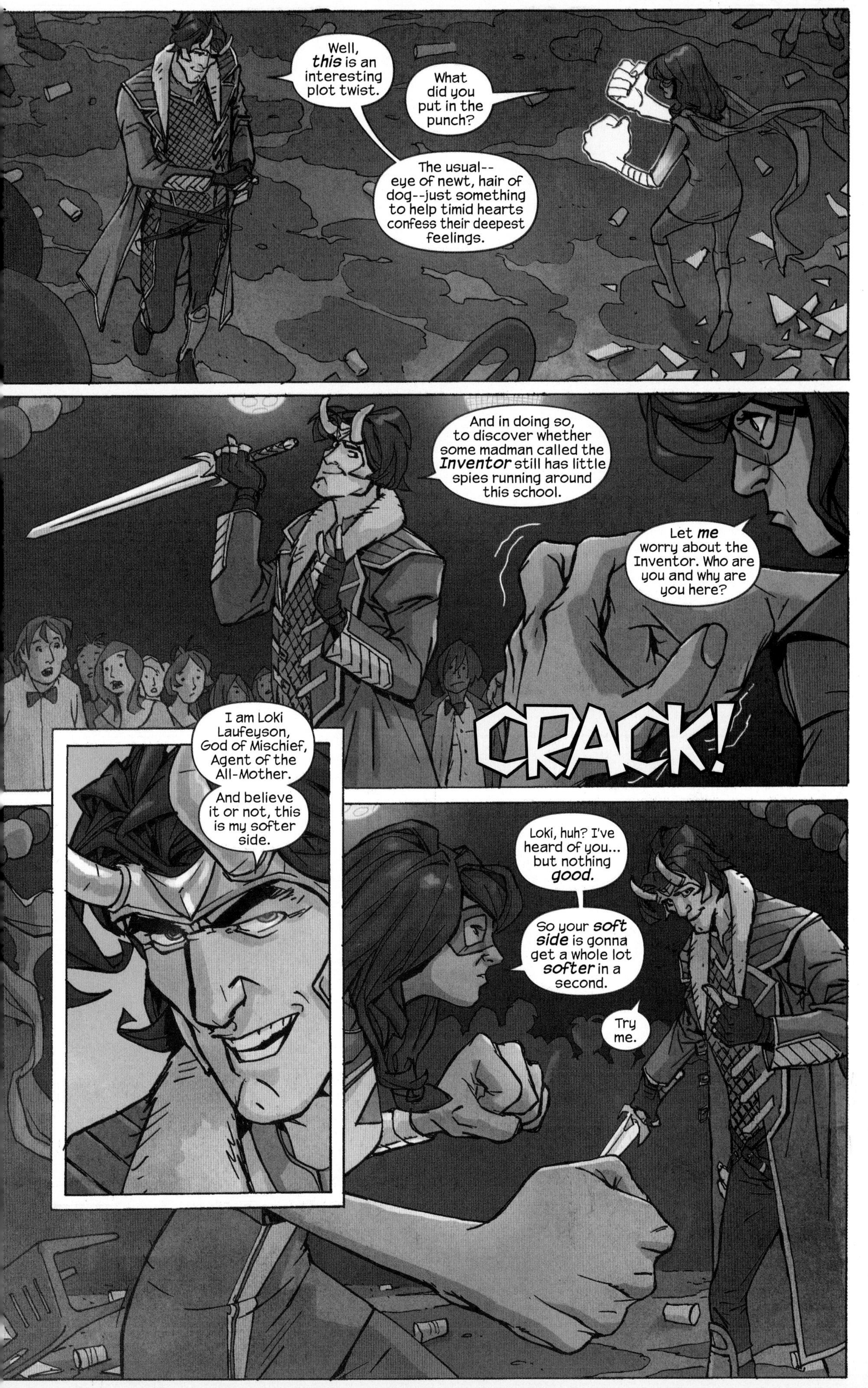
Well, *this* is an interesting plot twist.
What did you put in the punch?
The usual-- eye of newt, hair of dog--just something to help timid hearts confess their deepest feelings.
And in doing so, to discover whether some madman called the *Inventor* still has little spies running around this school.
Let *me* worry about the Inventor. Who are you and why are you here?
CRACK!
I am Loki Laufeyson, God of Mischief, Agent of the All-Mother.
And believe it or not, this is my softer side.
Loki, huh? I've heard of you... but nothing *good.*
So your *soft side* is gonna get a whole lot *softer* in a second.
Try me.

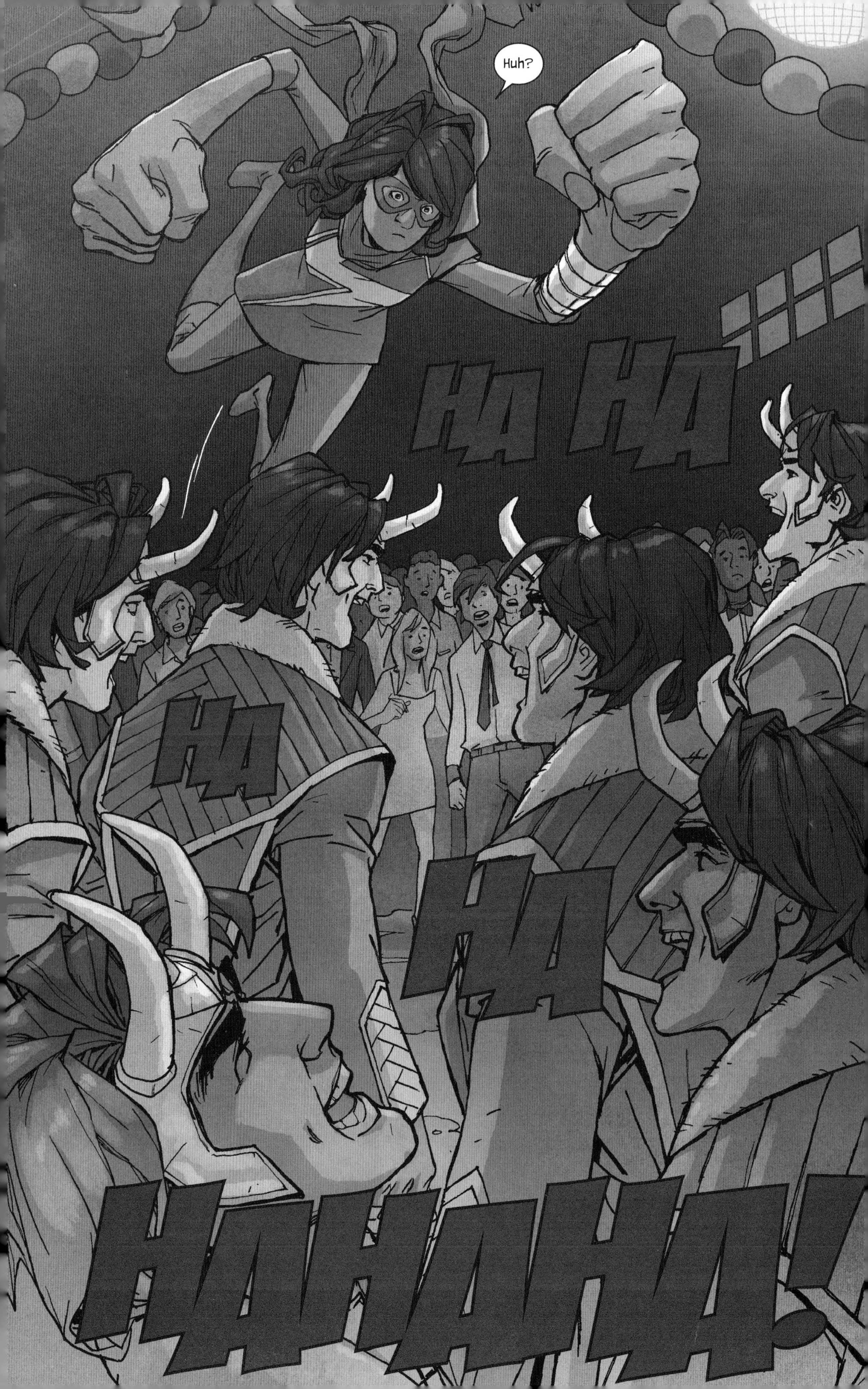
Huh?
HA HA
HA
HA
HAHAHA!

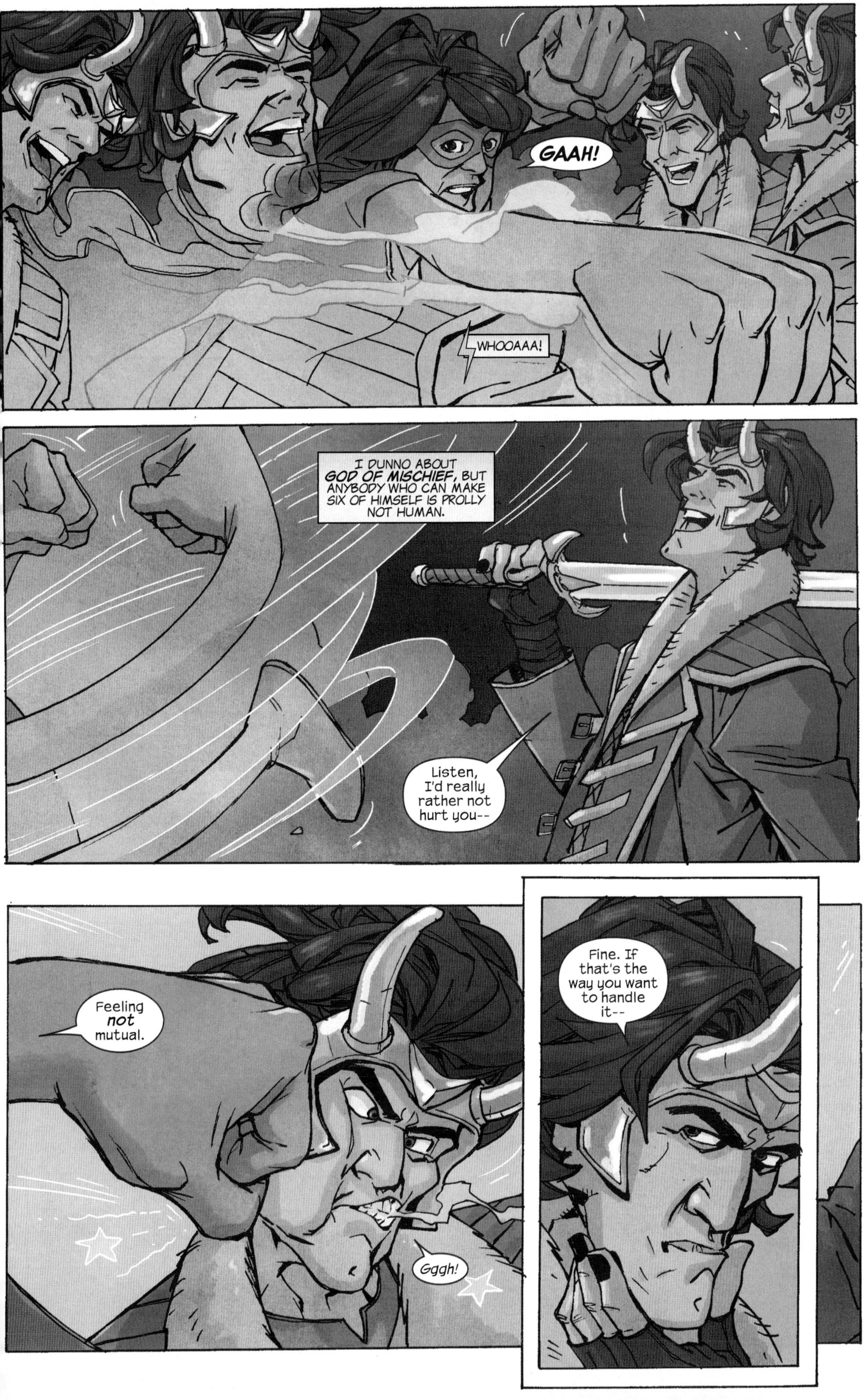
GAAH!
WHOOAAA!
I DUNNO ABOUT GOD OF MISCHIEF, BUT ANYBODY WHO CAN MAKE SIX OF HIMSELF IS PROLLY NOT HUMAN.
Listen, I'd really rather not hurt you--
Feeling not mutual.
Gggh!
Fine. If that's the way you want to handle it--

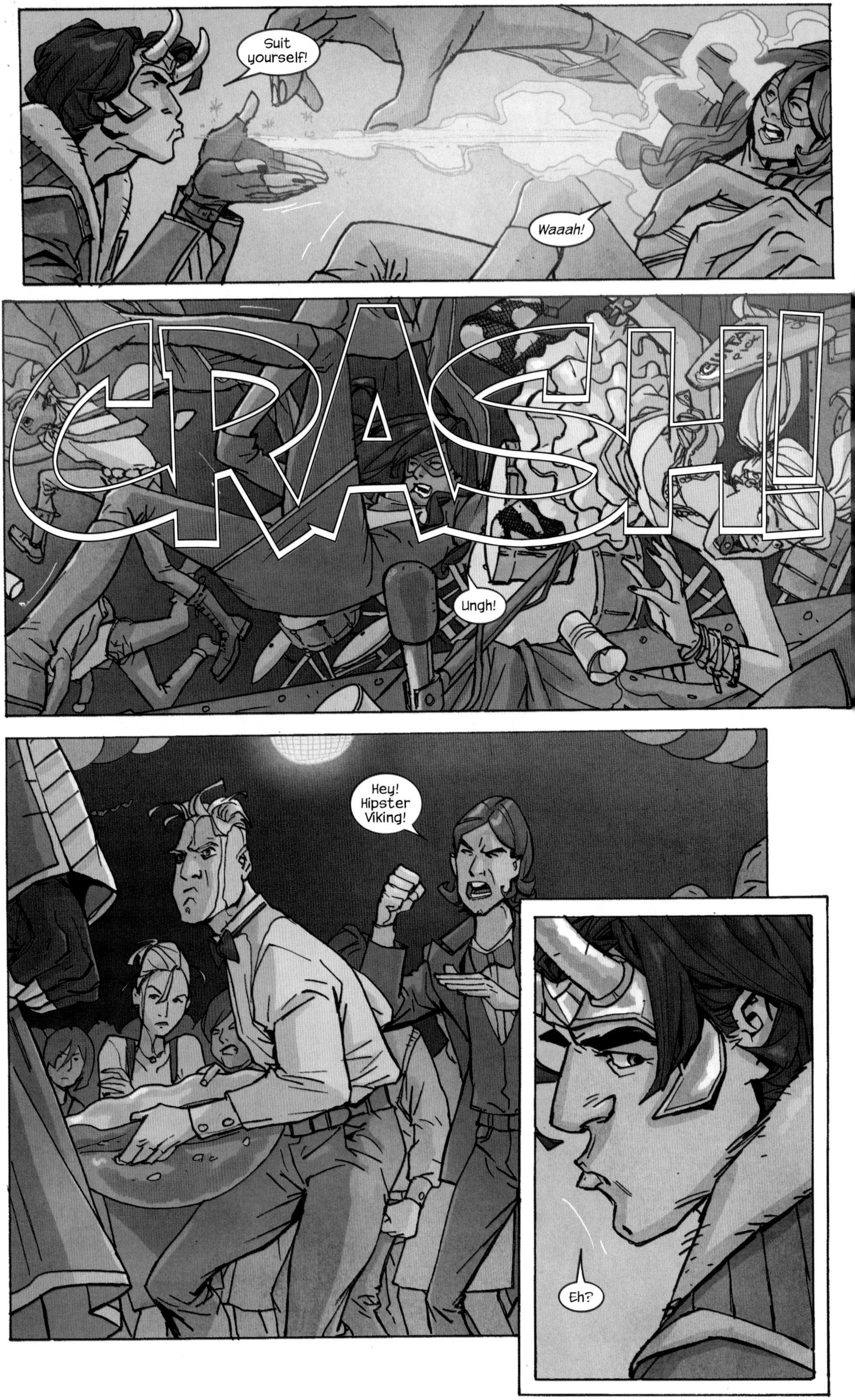
Suit yourself!
Waaah!
CRASH!
Ungh!
Hey! Hipster Viking!
Eh?

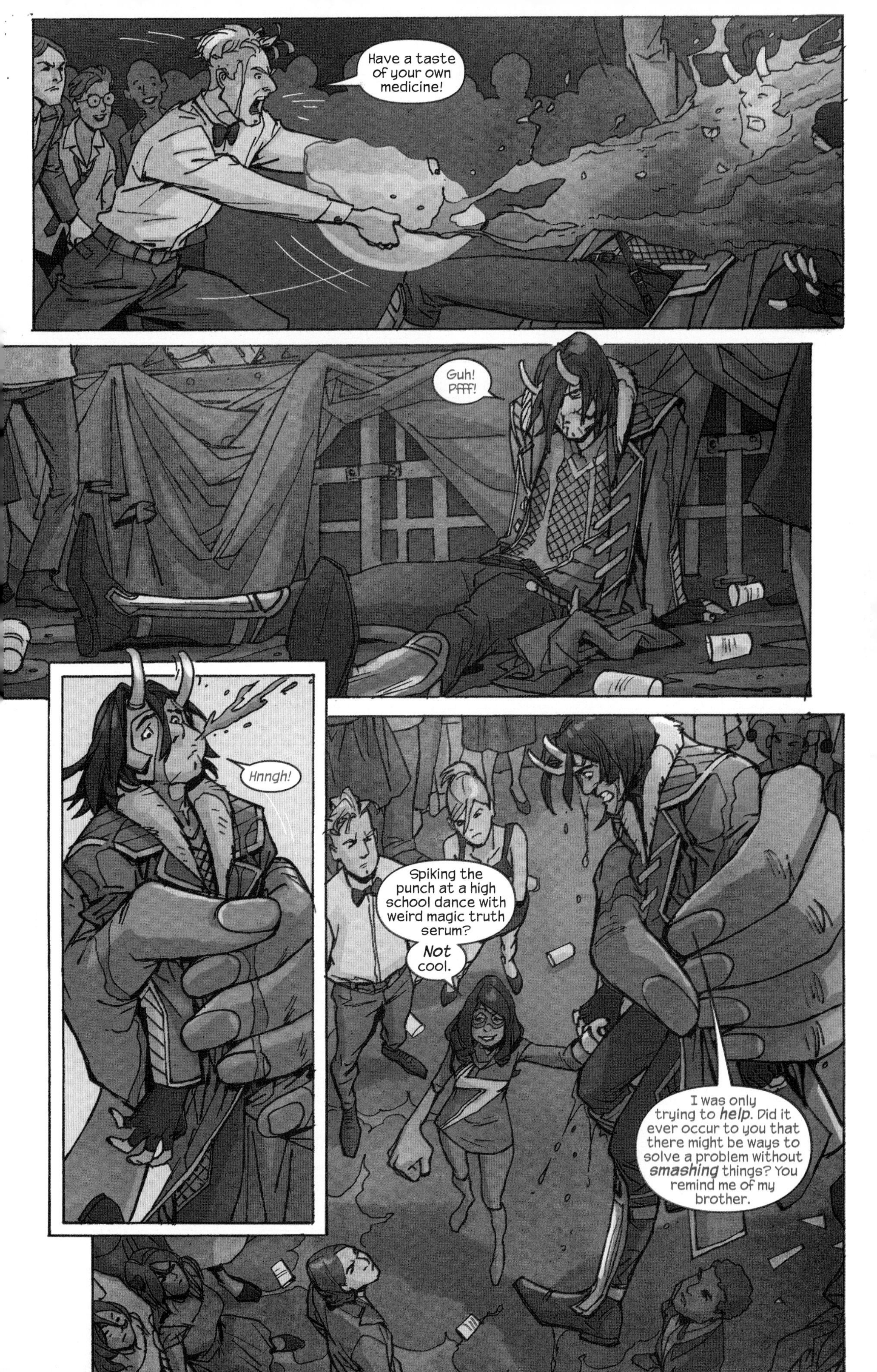
Have a taste of your own medicine!
Guh! Pfff!
Hnngh!
Spiking the punch at a high school dance with weird magic truth serum?
Not cool.
I was only trying to ***help***. Did it ever occur to you that there might be ways to solve a problem without ***smashing*** things? You remind me of my brother.

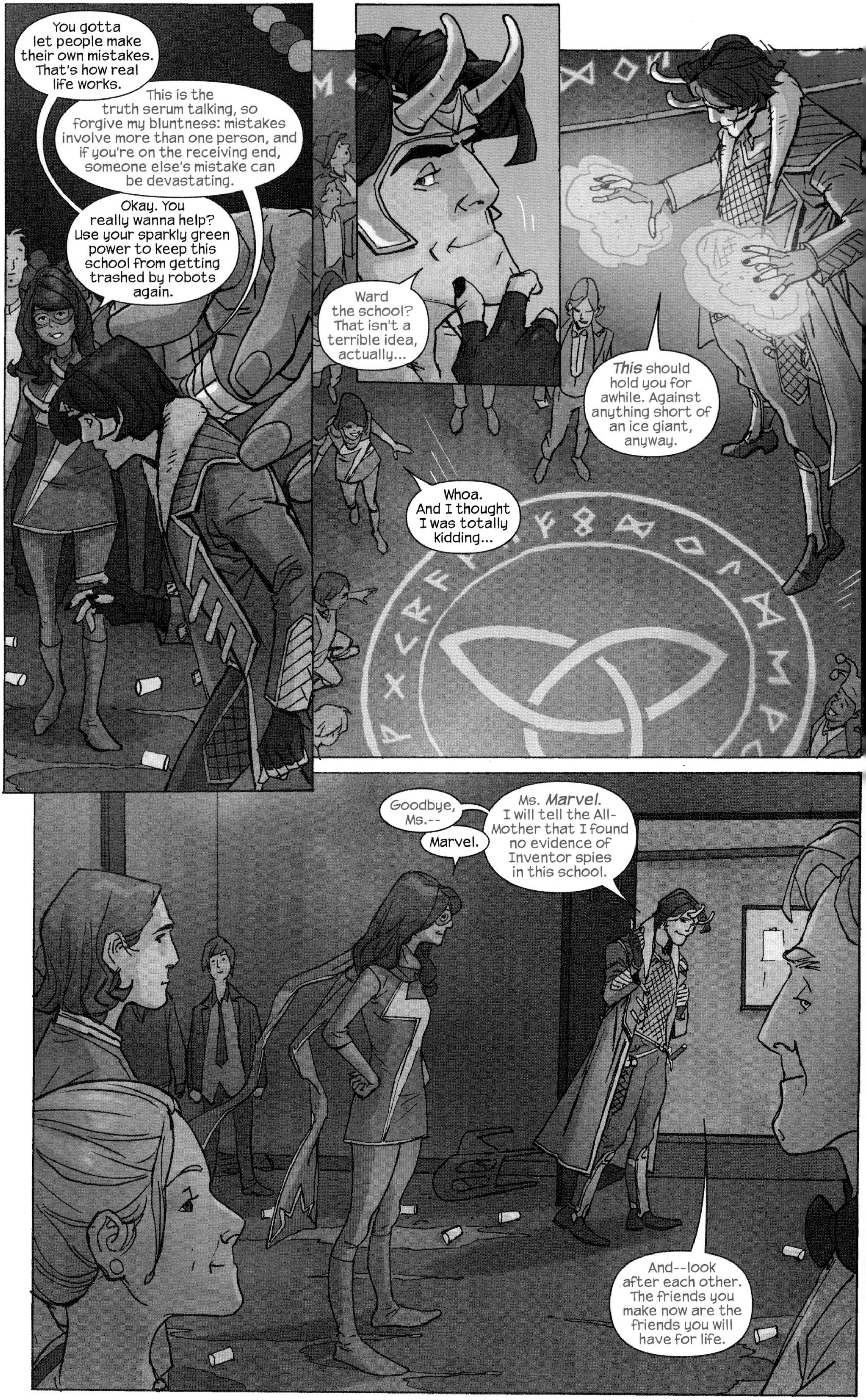

You gotta let people make their own mistakes. That's how real life works.
This is the truth serum talking, so forgive my bluntness: mistakes involve more than one person, and if you're on the receiving end, someone else's mistake can be devastating.
Okay. You really wanna help? Use your sparkly green power to keep this school from getting trashed by robots again.
Ward the school? That isn't a terrible idea, actually...
This should hold you for awhile. Against anything short of an ice giant, anyway.
Whoa. And I thought I was totally kidding...
Goodbye, Ms.--
Marvel.
Ms. Marvel. I will tell the All-Mother that I found no evidence of Inventor spies in this school.
And--look after each other. The friends you make now are the friends you will have for life.

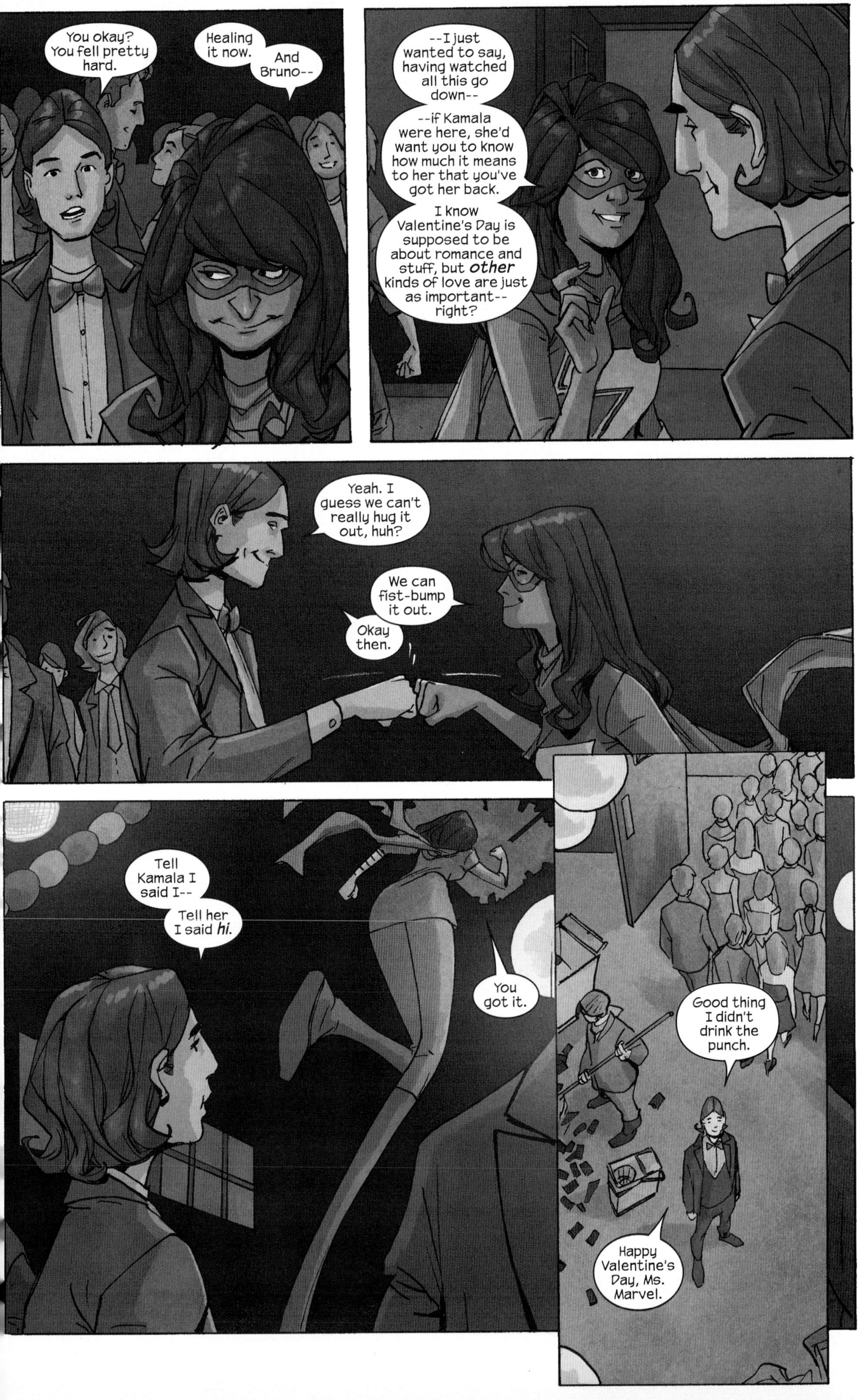
You okay? You fell pretty hard.
Healing it now.
And Bruno--
--I just wanted to say, having watched all this go down--
--if Kamala were here, she'd want you to know how much it means to her that you've got her back.
I know Valentine's Day is supposed to be about romance and stuff, but *other* kinds of love are just as important-- right?
Yeah. I guess we can't really hug it out, huh?
We can fist-bump it out.
Okay then.
Tell Kamala I said I--
Tell her I said *hi*.
You got it.
Good thing I didn't drink the punch.
Happy Valentine's Day, Ms. Marvel.

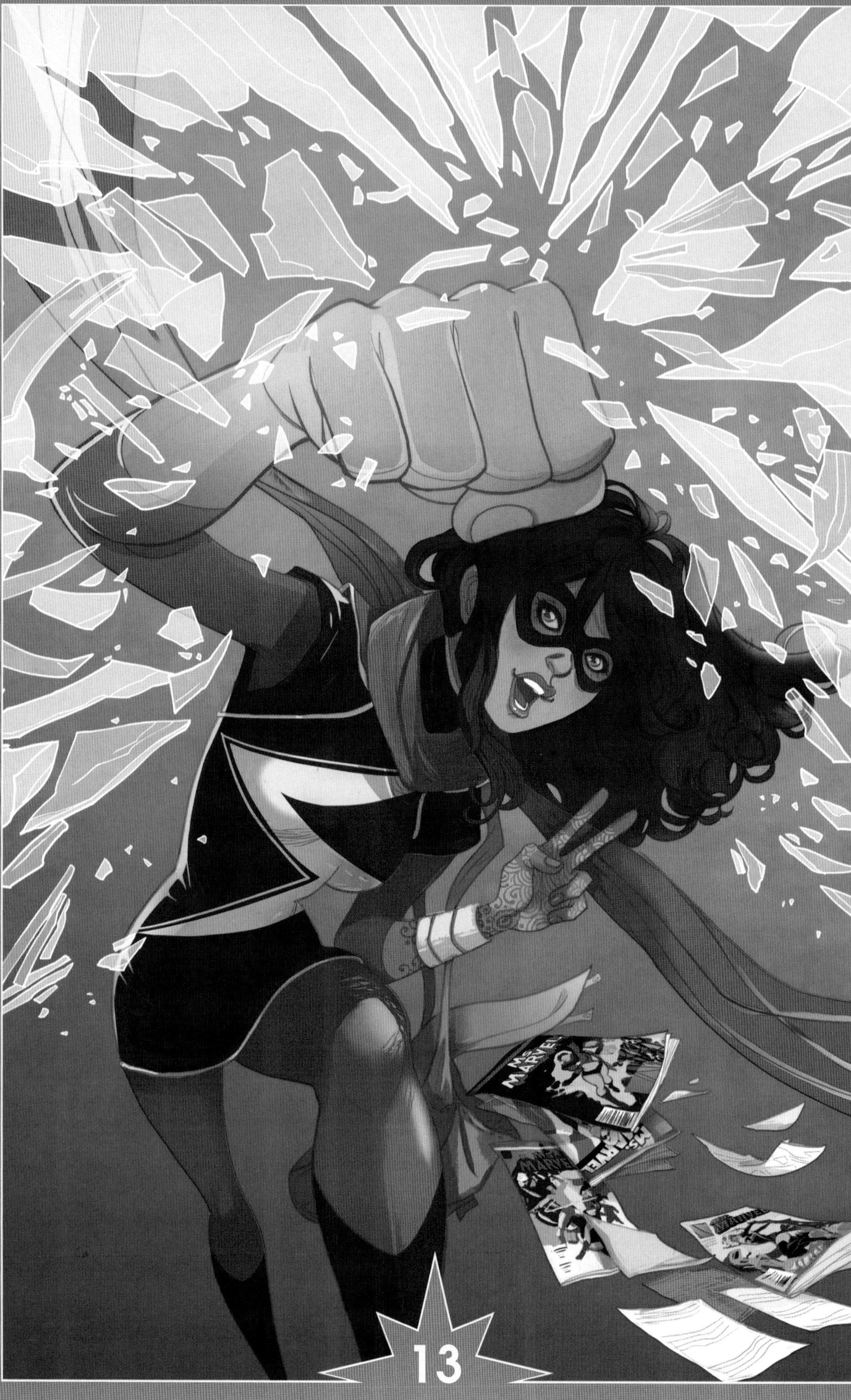
MS. MARVEL
13

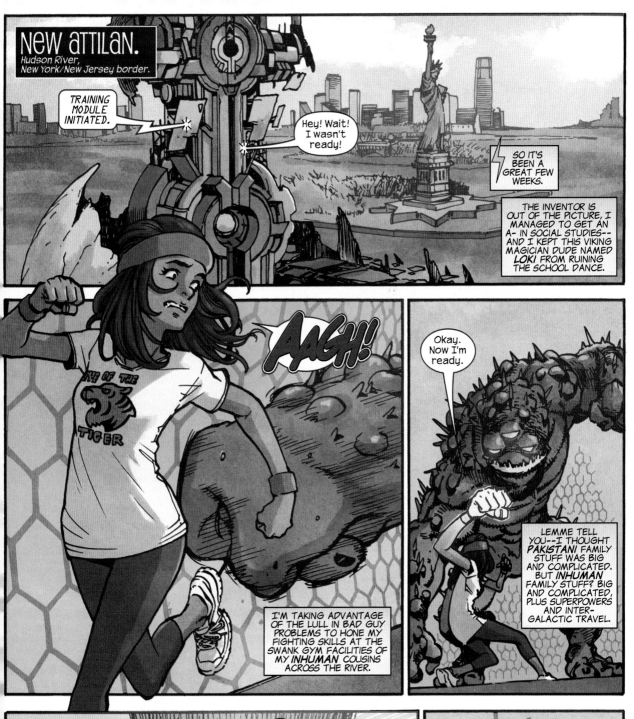

NEW ATTILAN.
Hudson River, New York/New Jersey border.

TRAINING MODULE INITIATED.

Hey! Wait! I wasn't ready!

SO IT'S BEEN A GREAT FEW WEEKS.

THE INVENTOR IS OUT OF THE PICTURE, I MANAGED TO GET AN A- IN SOCIAL STUDIES-- AND I KEPT THIS VIKING MAGICIAN DUDE NAMED *LOKI* FROM RUINING THE SCHOOL DANCE.

AAGH!

I'M TAKING ADVANTAGE OF THE LULL IN BAD GUY PROBLEMS TO HONE MY FIGHTING SKILLS AT THE SWANK GYM FACILITIES OF MY *INHUMAN* COUSINS ACROSS THE RIVER.

Okay. Now I'm ready.

LEMME TELL YOU--I THOUGHT *PAKISTANI* FAMILY STUFF WAS BIG AND COMPLICATED. BUT *INHUMAN* FAMILY STUFF? BIG AND COMPLICATED, PLUS SUPERPOWERS AND INTER-GALACTIC TRAVEL.

THOOM!

THE PERKS ARE PRETTY GREAT, THOUGH.

NORMAL MODULE COMPLETE. LEGENDARY MODULE INITIATED.

Legendary module?!

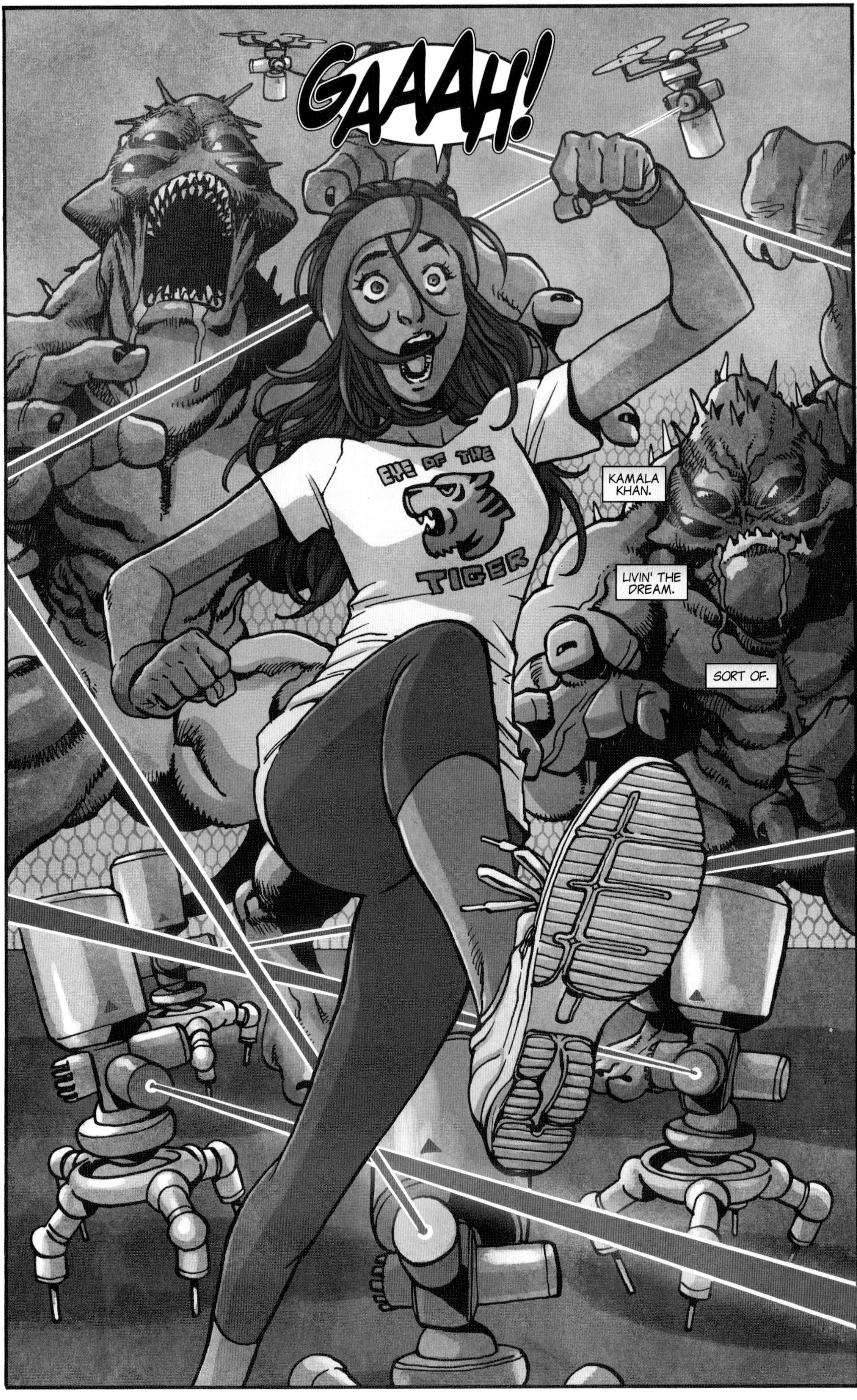
GAAAH!
EYE OF THE TIGER
KAMALA KHAN.
LIVIN' THE DREAM.
SORT OF.

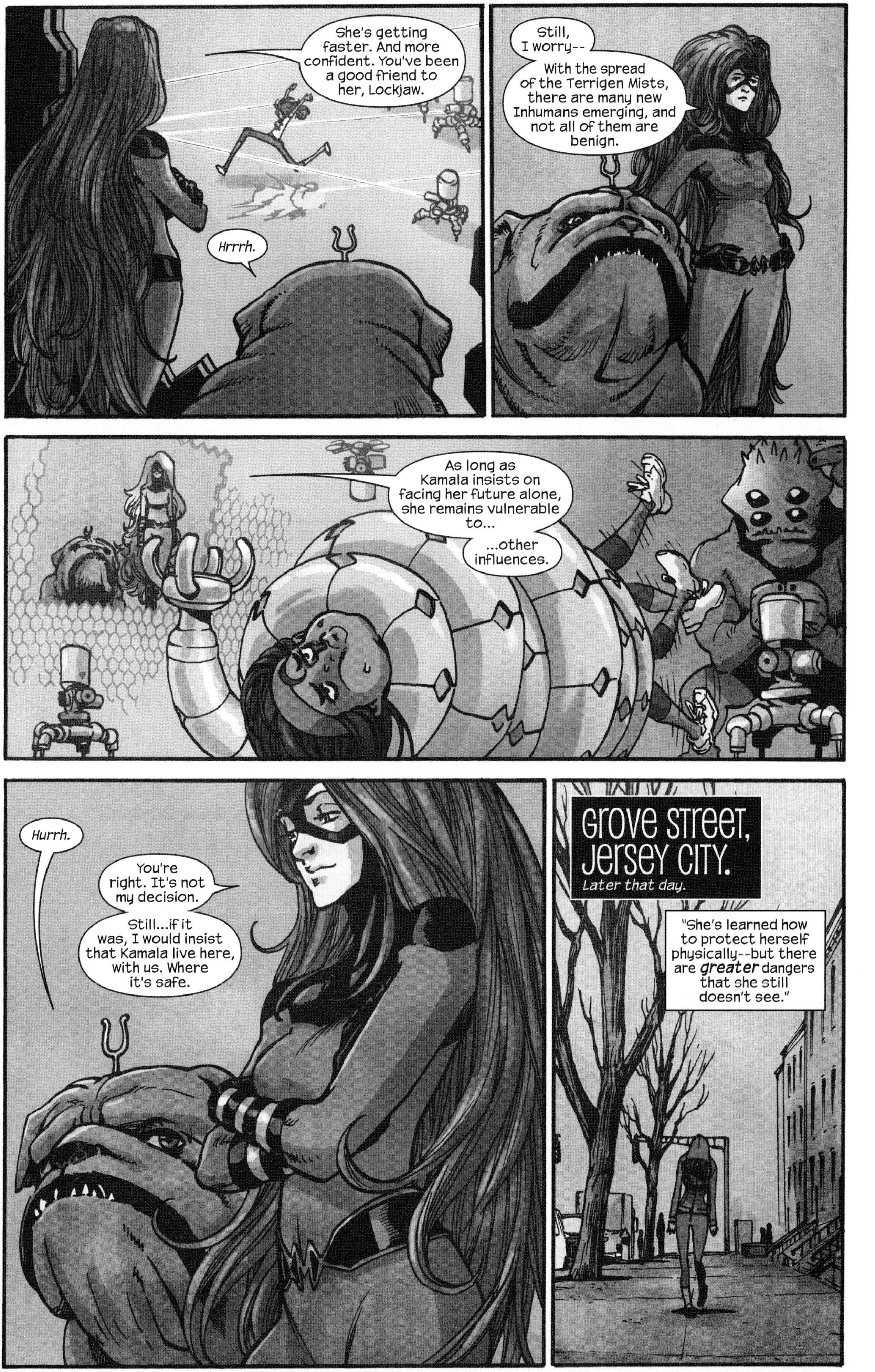
She's getting faster. And more confident. You've been a good friend to her, Lockjaw.
Hrrrh.
Still, I worry--
With the spread of the Terrigen Mists, there are many new Inhumans emerging, and not all of them are benign.
As long as Kamala insists on facing her future alone, she remains vulnerable to...
...other influences.
Hurrh.
You're right. It's not my decision.
Still...if it was, I would insist that Kamala live here, with us. Where it's safe.
GROVE STREET, JERSEY CITY.
Later that day.
"She's learned how to protect herself physically--but there are *greater* dangers that she still doesn't see."

How was your jogging, *beta?*

Hnngh.

I still don't like the idea of you running around in the street, puffing and sweating. It's not *decent.*

Don't worry, Ammi. I only sweat when nobody's looking.

Acha. Eat your breakfast and get cleaned up-- we're having visitors today.

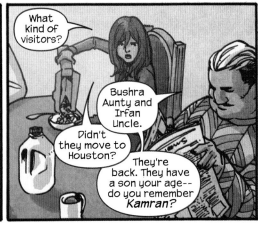

What kind of visitors?

Bushra Aunty and Irfan Uncle.

Didn't they move to Houston?

They're back. They have a son your age-- do you remember *Kamran?*

That kid who used to pick his nose?!

He was five years old then, *beta.* He's almost grown up now.

Bushra tells me he's at the top of his class in math and science! Applying to MIT, early admission!

Great. An overachiever *and* a nosepicker.

Do I have to hang around here all afternoon making small talk? I was planning to meet Nakia and Bruno at Funtimes Arcade--

Would it be so hard to put on a nice *shalwar* and humor your old abu for once?

These are our oldest friends in the US, and we haven't seen them in years!

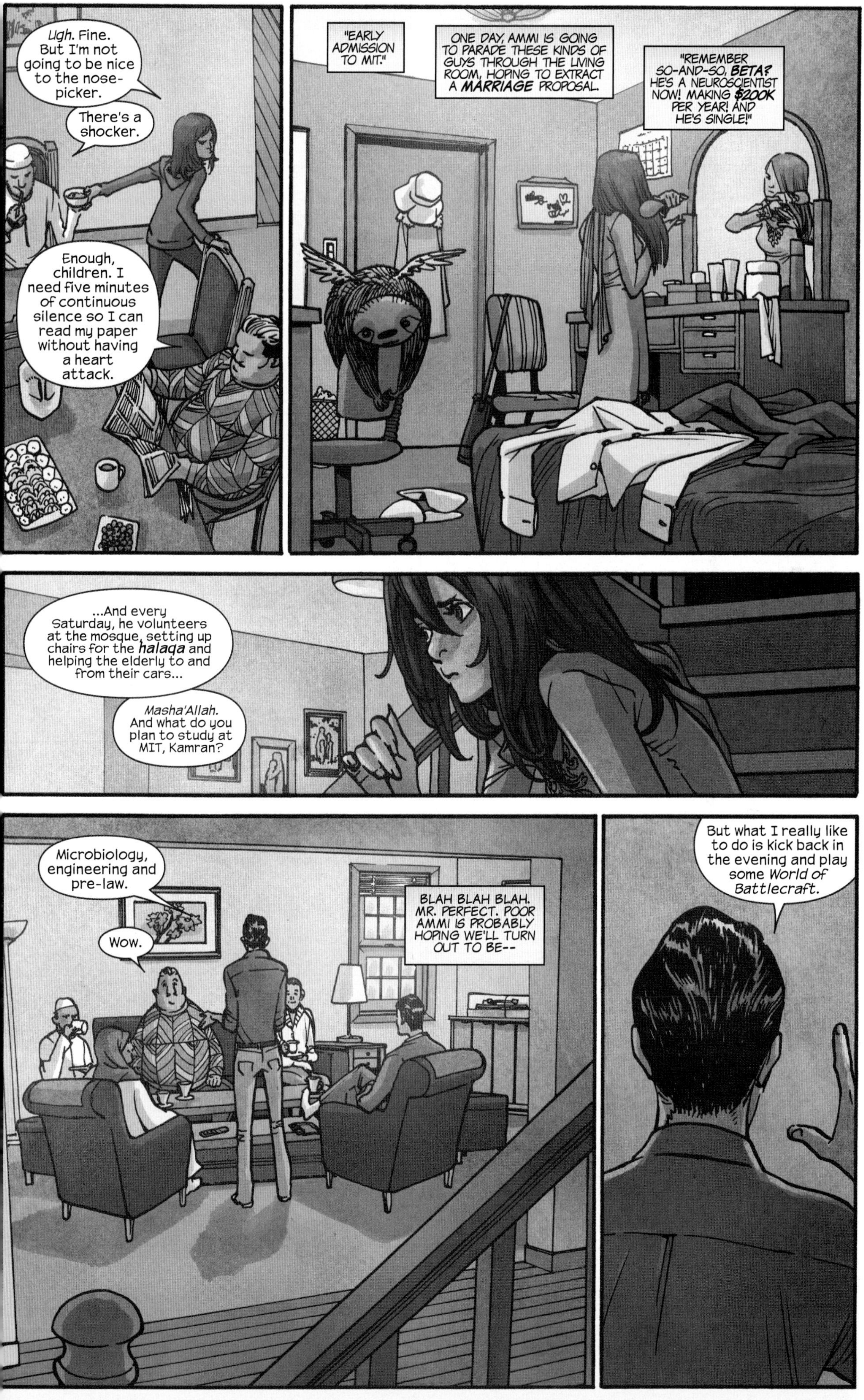
Ugh. Fine. But I'm not going to be nice to the nose-picker.
There's a shocker.
Enough, children. I need five minutes of continuous silence so I can read my paper without having a heart attack.
"EARLY ADMISSION TO MIT."
ONE DAY, AMMI IS GOING TO PARADE THESE KINDS OF GUYS THROUGH THE LIVING ROOM, HOPING TO EXTRACT A MARRIAGE PROPOSAL.
"REMEMBER SO-AND-SO, BETA? HE'S A NEUROSCIENTIST NOW! MAKING $200K PER YEAR! AND HE'S SINGLE!"
...And every Saturday, he volunteers at the mosque, setting up chairs for the halaqa and helping the elderly to and from their cars...
Masha'Allah. And what do you plan to study at MIT, Kamran?
Microbiology, engineering and pre-law.
Wow.
BLAH BLAH BLAH. MR. PERFECT. POOR AMMI IS PROBABLY HOPING WE'LL TURN OUT TO BE--
But what I really like to do is kick back in the evening and play some World of Battlecraft.

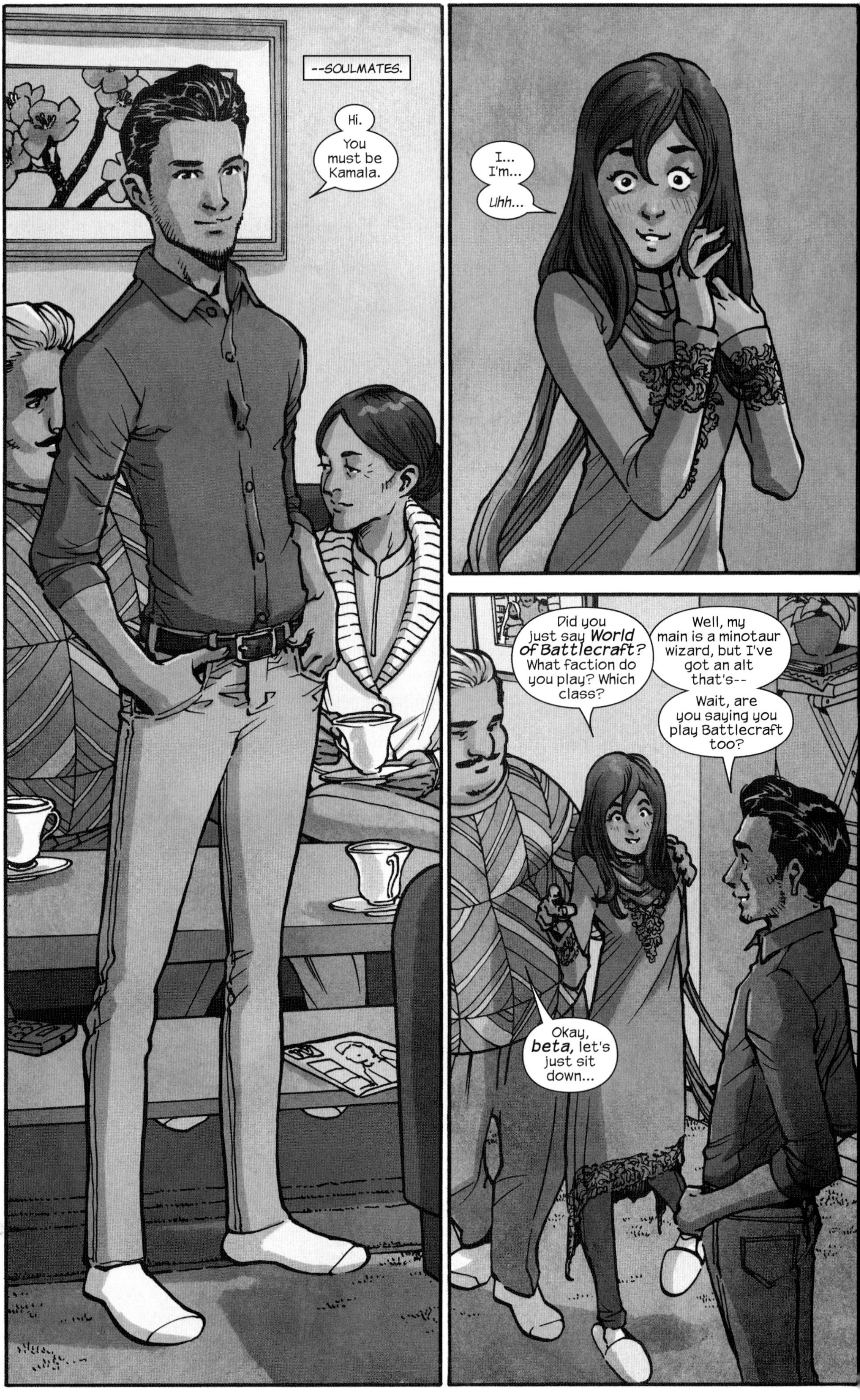
--SOULMATES.
Hi.
You must be Kamala.
I... I'm...
Uhh...
Did you just say *World of Battlecraft*? What faction do you play? Which class?
Well, my main is a minotaur wizard, but I've got an alt that's--
Wait, are you saying you play Battlecraft too?
Okay, **beta,** let's just sit down...

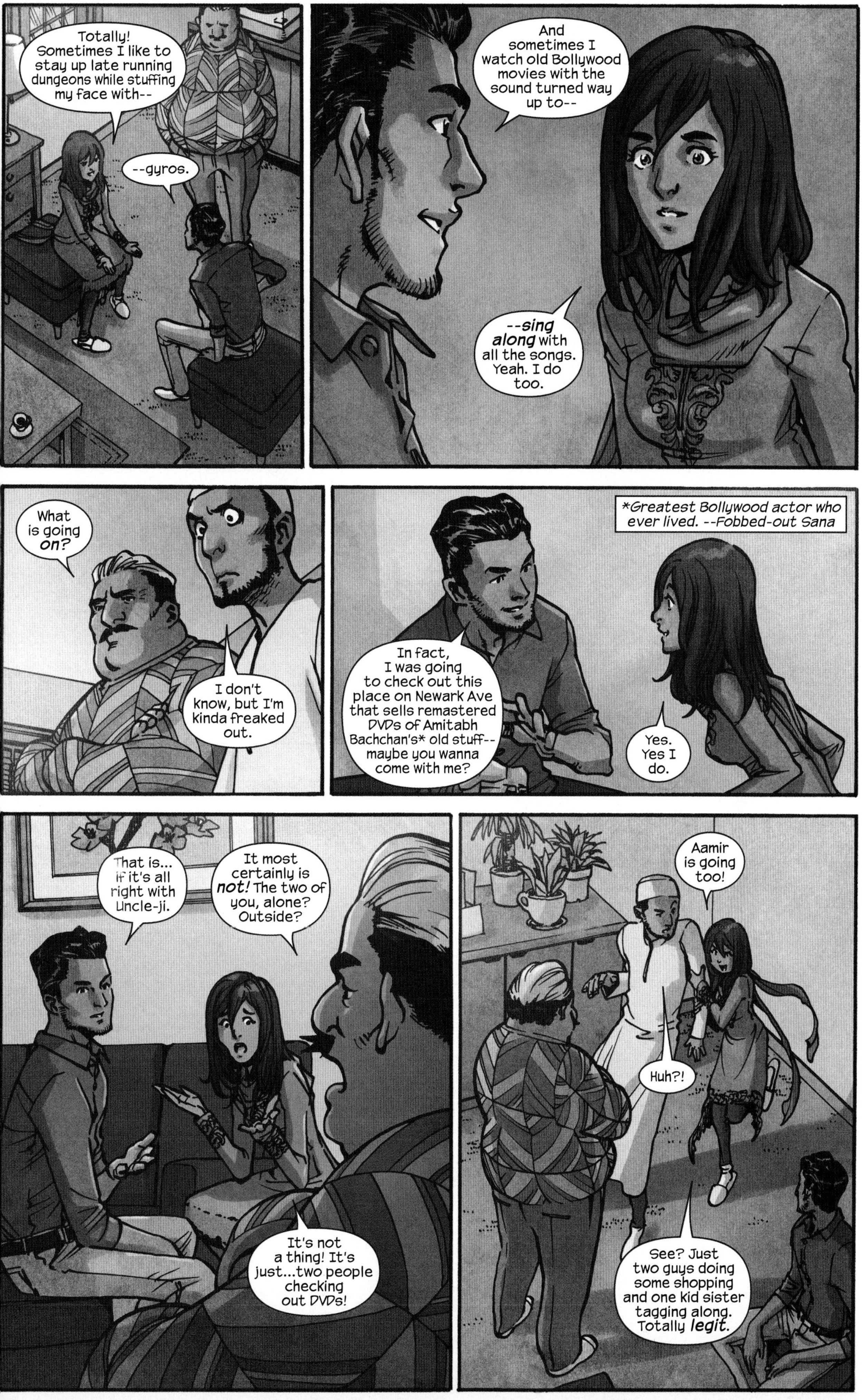
Totally! Sometimes I like to stay up late running dungeons while stuffing my face with--
--gyros.
And sometimes I watch old Bollywood movies with the sound turned way up to--
--*sing along* with all the songs. Yeah. I do too.
What is going *on*?
I don't know, but I'm kinda freaked out.
*Greatest Bollywood actor who ever lived. --Fobbed-out Sana
In fact, I was going to check out this place on Newark Ave that sells remastered DVDs of Amitabh Bachchan's* old stuff-- maybe you wanna come with me?
Yes. Yes I do.
That is... if it's all right with Uncle-ji.
It most certainly is *not!* The two of you, alone? Outside?
It's not a thing! It's just...two people checking out DVDs!
Aamir is going too!
Huh?!
See? Just two guys doing some shopping and one kid sister tagging along. Totally *legit*.

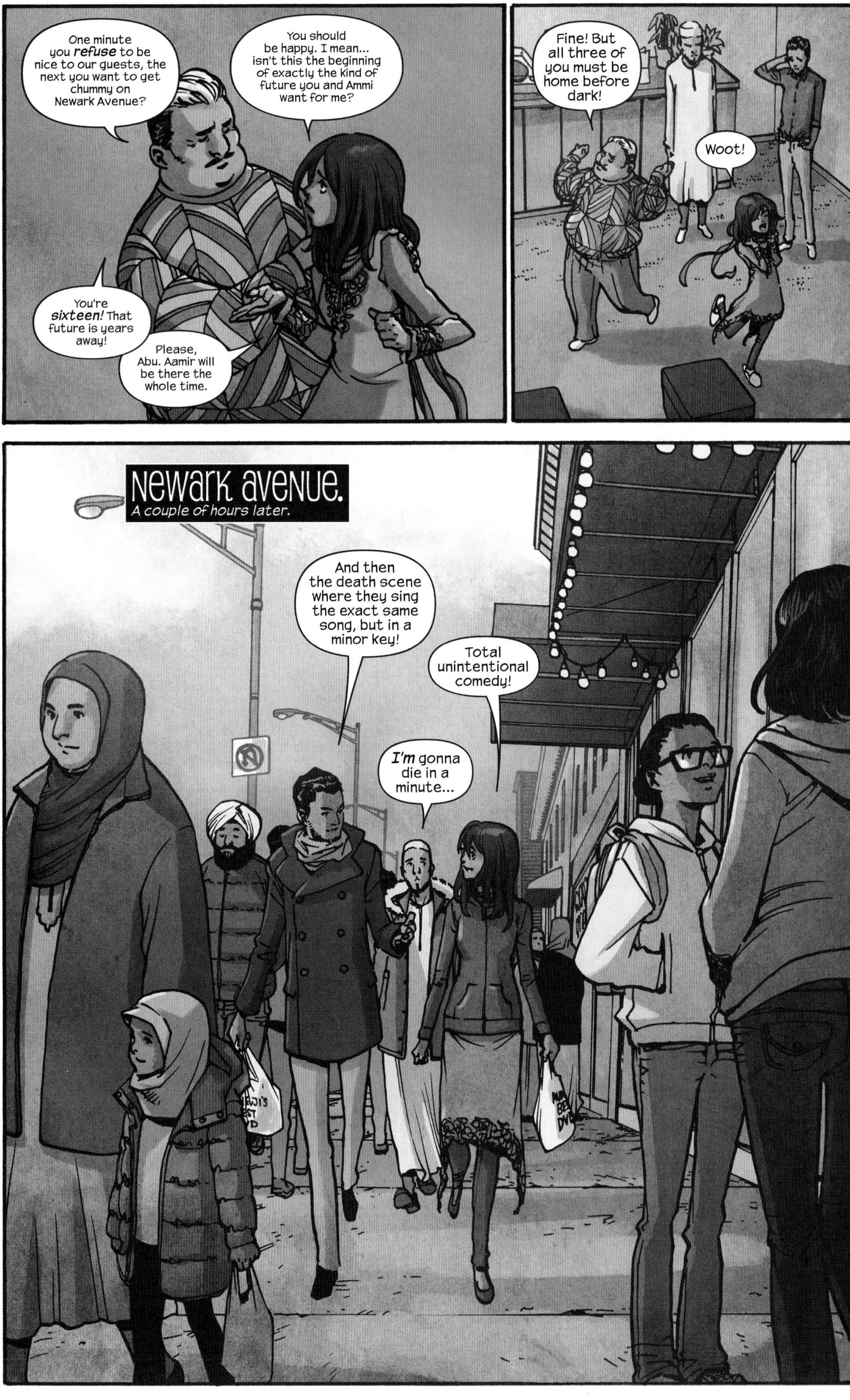

One minute you *refuse* to be nice to our guests, the next you want to get chummy on Newark Avenue?
You should be happy. I mean... isn't this the beginning of exactly the kind of future you and Ammi want for me?
You're *sixteen!* That future is years away!
Please, Abu. Aamir will be there the whole time.
Fine! But all three of you must be home before dark!
Woot!
Newark avenue.
A couple of hours later.
And then the death scene where they sing the exact same song, but in a minor key!
Total unintentional comedy!
I'm gonna die in a minute...

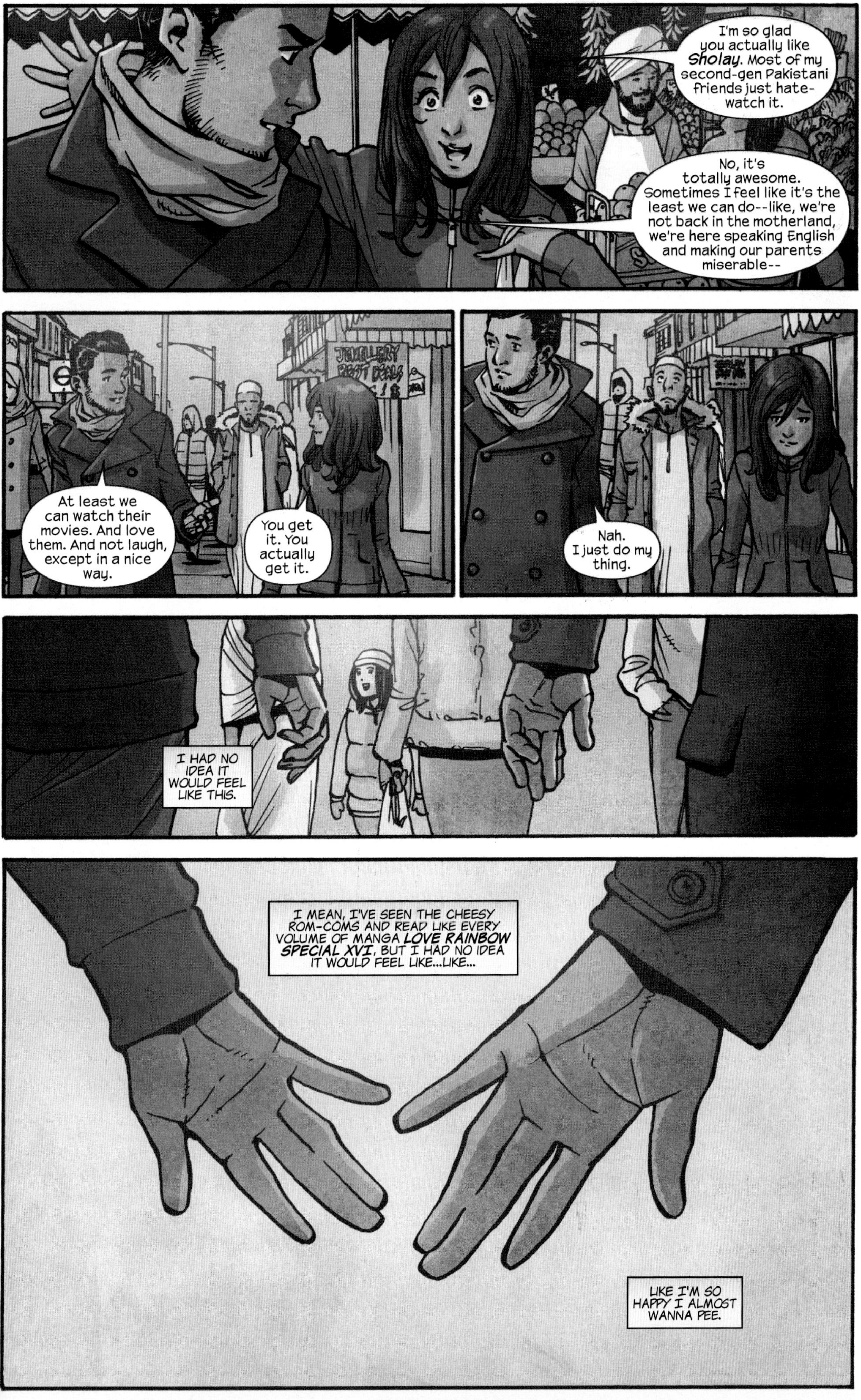
I'm so glad you actually like *Sholay*. Most of my second-gen Pakistani friends just hate-watch it.
No, it's totally awesome. Sometimes I feel like it's the least we can do--like, we're not back in the motherland, we're here speaking English and making our parents miserable--
JEWELLERY BEST DEALS
At least we can watch their movies. And love them. And not laugh, except in a nice way.
You get it. You actually get it.
Nah. I just do my thing.
I HAD NO IDEA IT WOULD FEEL LIKE THIS.
I MEAN, I'VE SEEN THE CHEESY ROM-COMS AND READ LIKE EVERY VOLUME OF MANGA *LOVE RAINBOW SPECIAL XVI*, BUT I HAD NO IDEA IT WOULD FEEL LIKE...LIKE...
LIKE I'M SO HAPPY I ALMOST WANNA PEE.

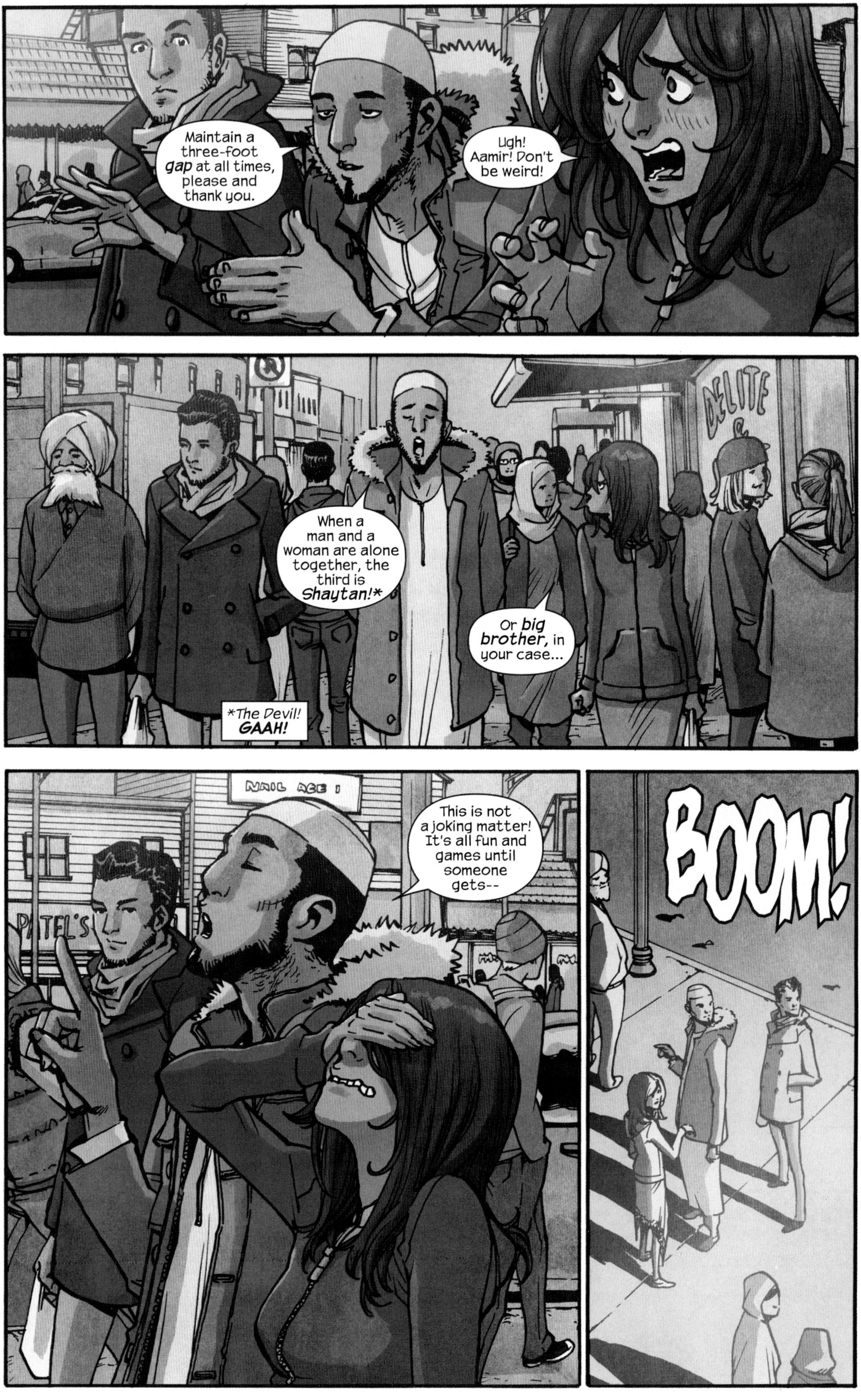

Maintain a three-foot gap at all times, please and thank you.
Ugh! Aamir! Don't be weird!
When a man and a woman are alone together, the third is Shaytan!*
Or big brother, in your case...
*The Devil! GAAH!
DELITE
NAIL AGE
PATEL'S
This is not a joking matter! It's all fun and games until someone gets--
BOOM!

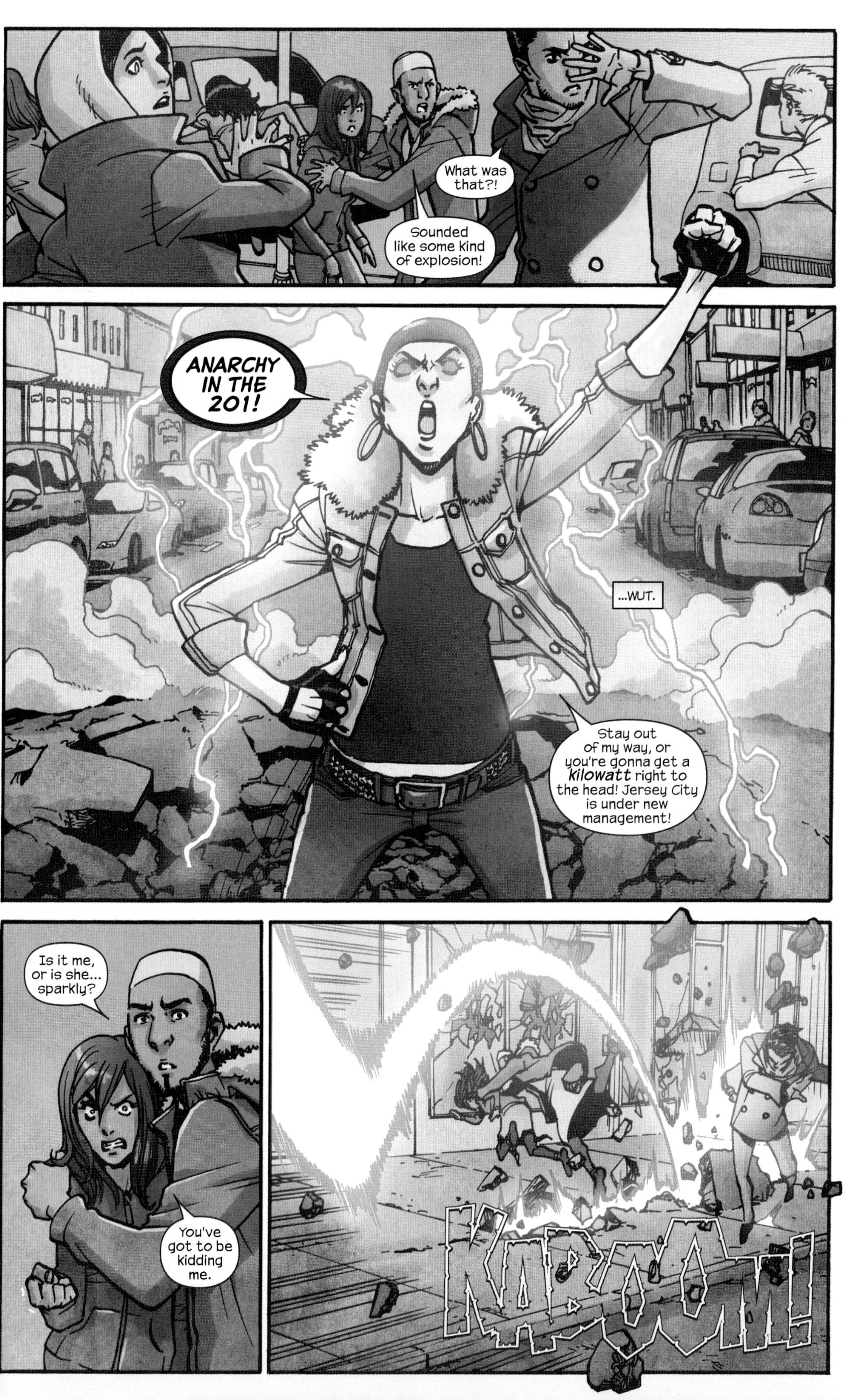
What was that?!
Sounded like some kind of explosion!
ANARCHY IN THE 201!
...WUT.
Stay out of my way, or you're gonna get a **kilowatt** right to the head! Jersey City is under new management!
Is it me, or is she... sparkly?
You've got to be kidding me.
KA-BOOM!

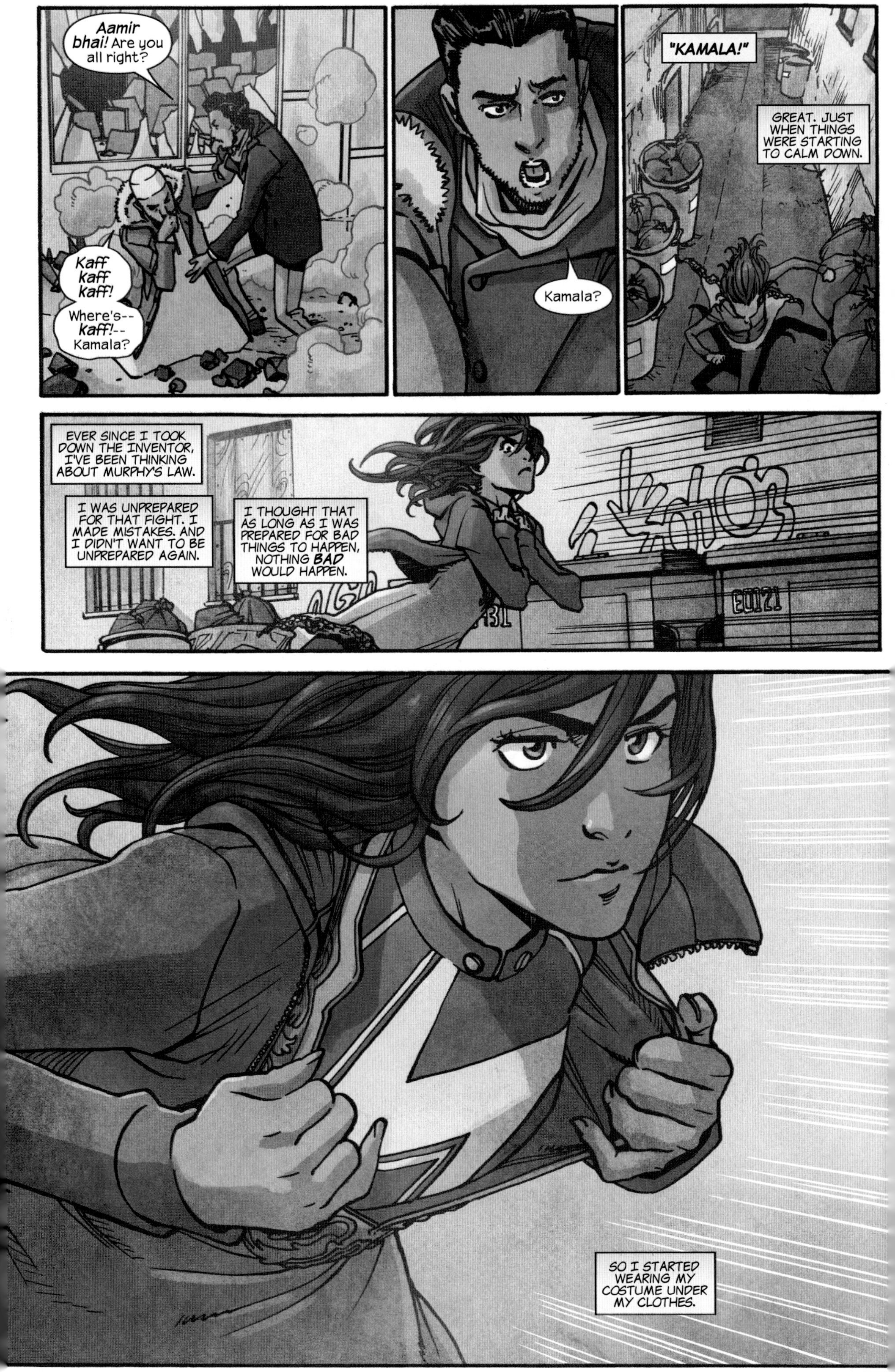
Aamir bhai! Are you all right?
Kaff kaff kaff!
Where's-- kaff!-- Kamala?
Kamala?
"KAMALA!"
GREAT. JUST WHEN THINGS WERE STARTING TO CALM DOWN.
EVER SINCE I TOOK DOWN THE INVENTOR, I'VE BEEN THINKING ABOUT MURPHY'S LAW.
I WAS UNPREPARED FOR THAT FIGHT. I MADE MISTAKES. AND I DIDN'T WANT TO BE UNPREPARED AGAIN.
I THOUGHT THAT AS LONG AS I WAS PREPARED FOR BAD THINGS TO HAPPEN, NOTHING BAD WOULD HAPPEN.
SO I STARTED WEARING MY COSTUME UNDER MY CLOTHES.

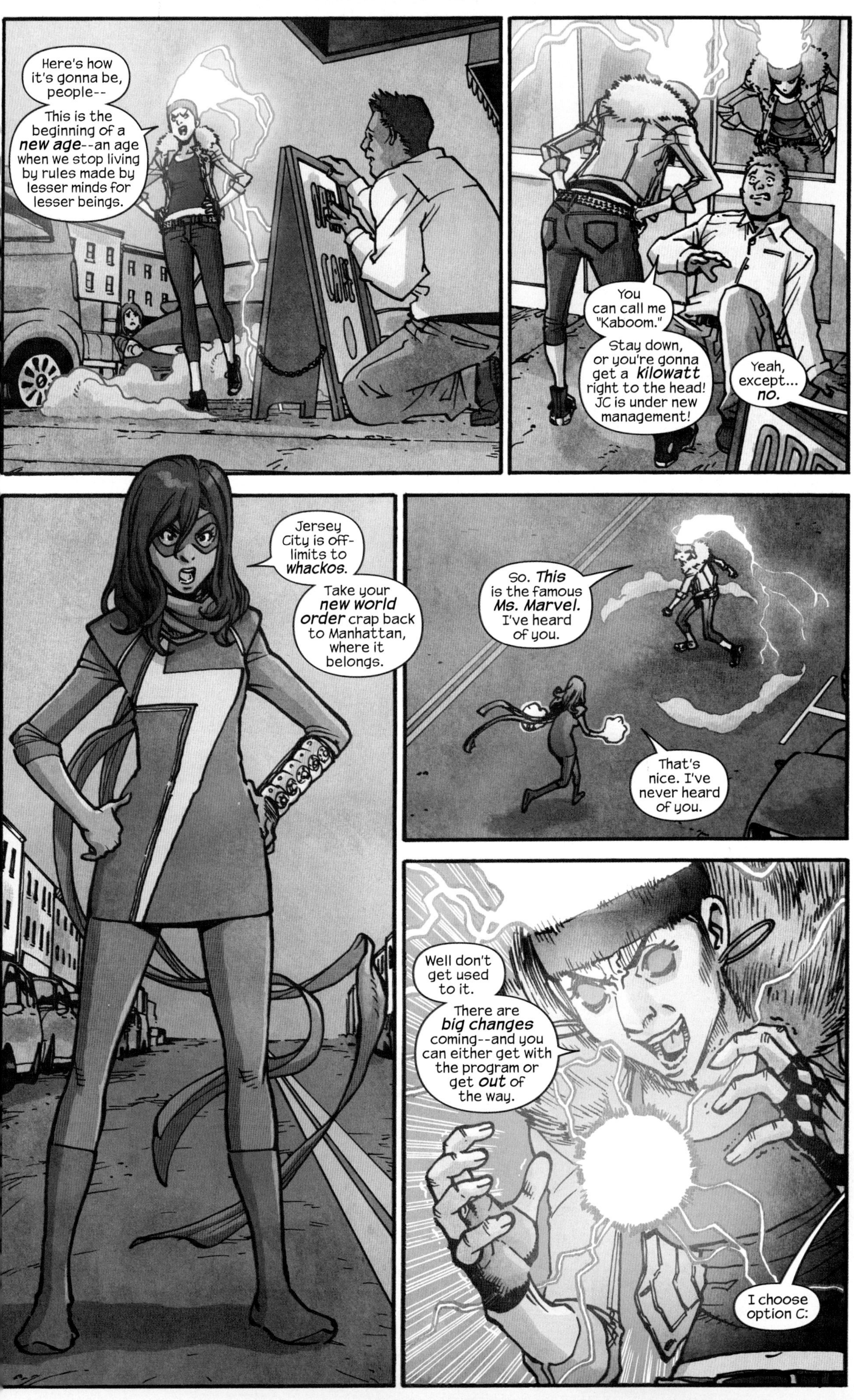

Here's how it's gonna be, people--
This is the beginning of a **new age**--an age when we stop living by rules made by lesser minds for lesser beings.
You can call me "Kaboom."
Stay down, or you're gonna get a **kilowatt** right to the head! JC is under new management!
Yeah, except... **no.**
Jersey City is off-limits to **whackos**.
Take your **new world order** crap back to Manhattan, where it belongs.
So. **This** is the famous **Ms. Marvel.** I've heard of you.
That's nice. I've never heard of you.
Well don't get used to it.
There are **big changes** coming--and you can either get with the program or get **out** of the way.
I choose option C:

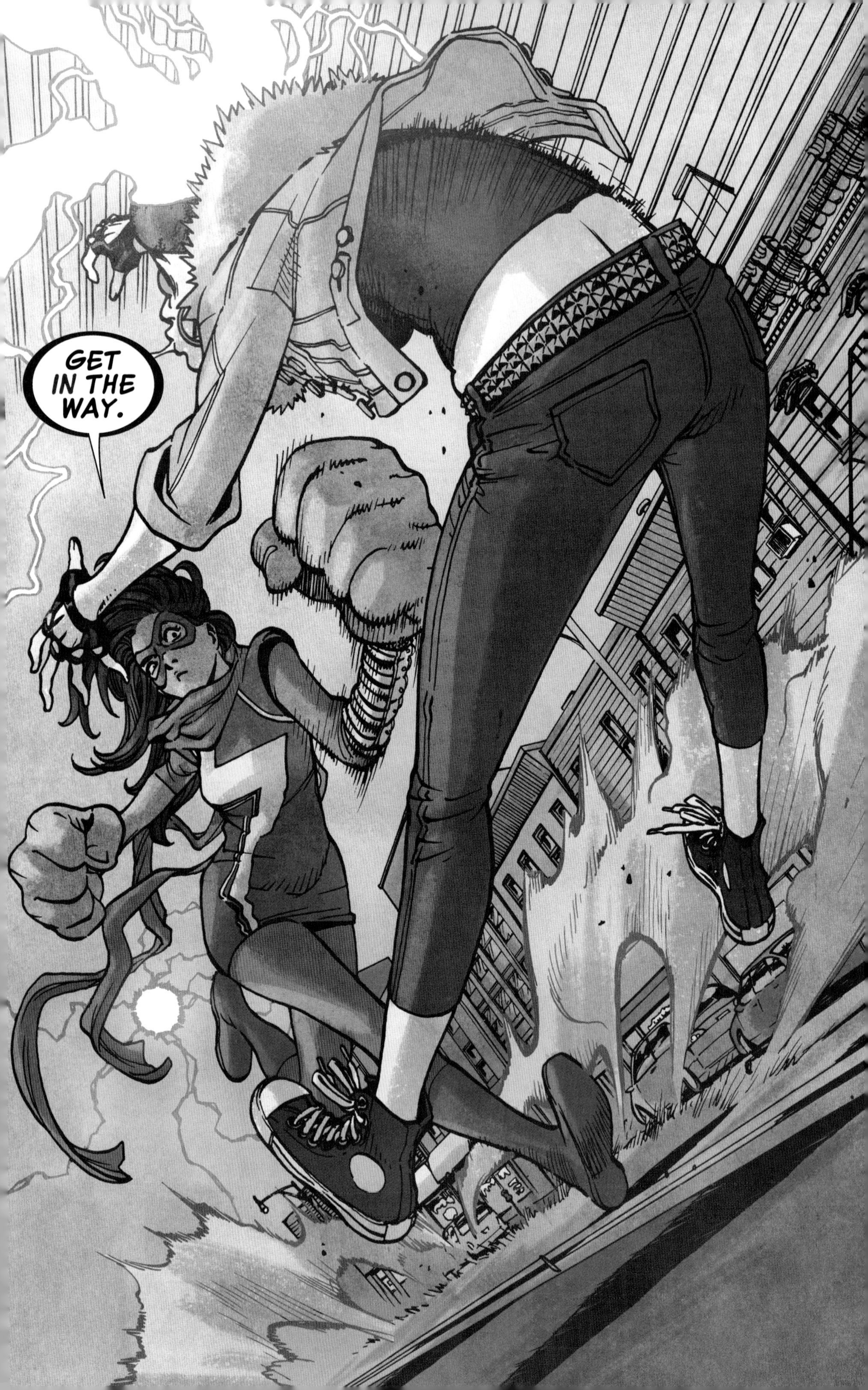
GET IN THE WAY.

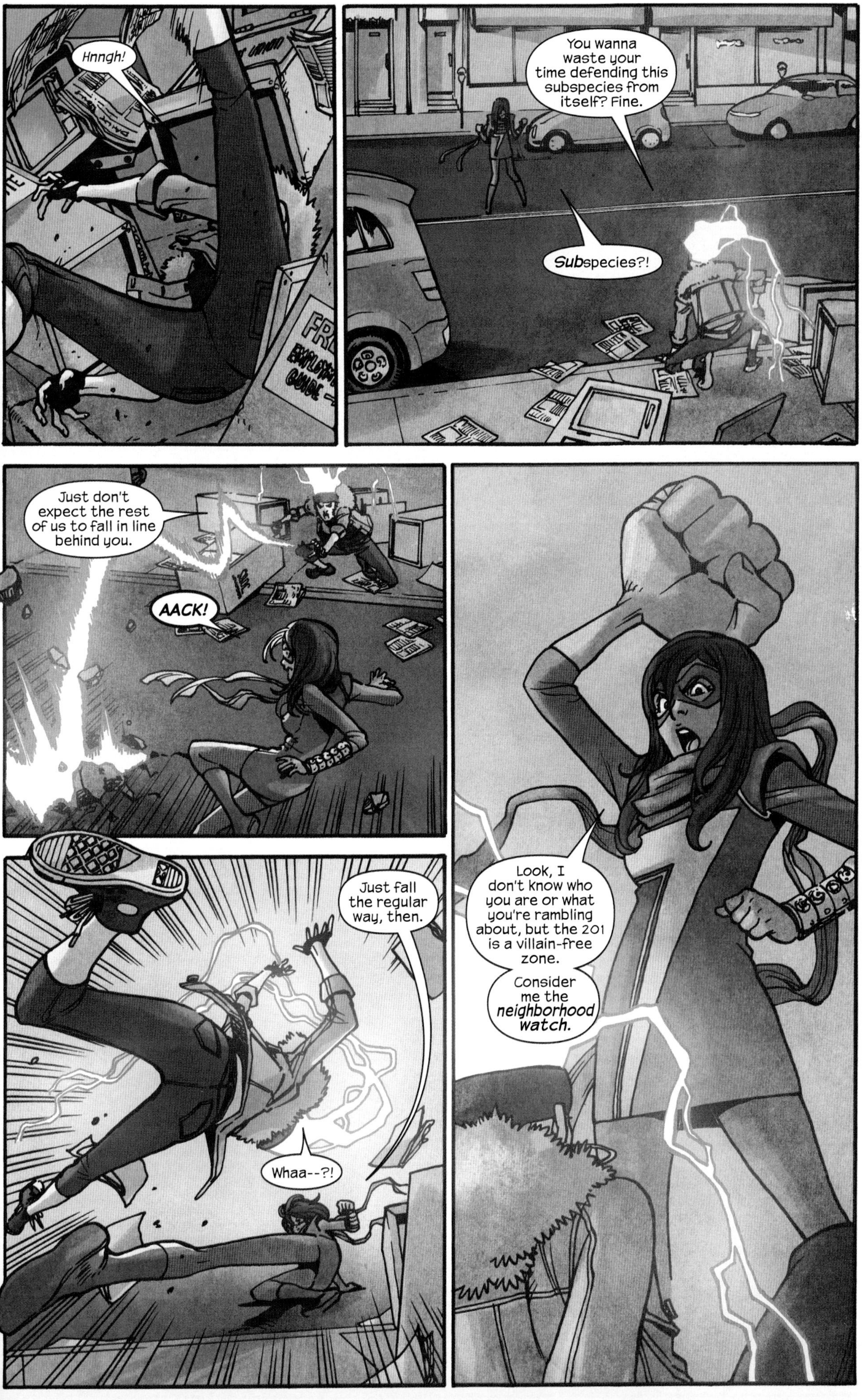
Hnngh!
You wanna waste your time defending this subspecies from itself? Fine.
*Sub*species?!
Just don't expect the rest of us to fall in line behind you.
AACK!
Look, I don't know who you are or what you're rambling about, but the 201 is a villain-free zone.
Consider me the *neighborhood watch.*
Just fall the regular way, then.
Whaa--?!

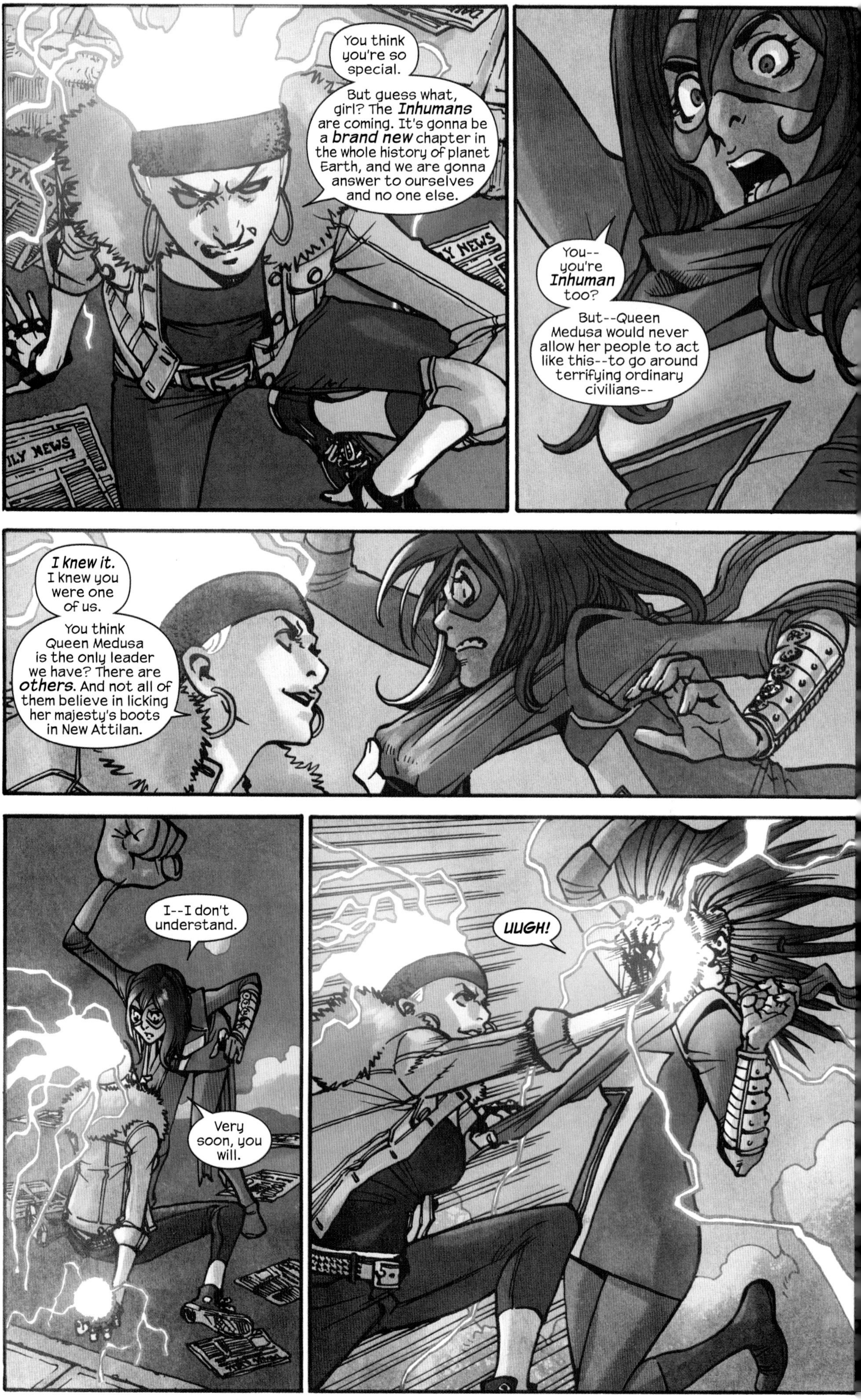

You think you're so special.
But guess what, girl? The *Inhumans* are coming. It's gonna be a ***brand new*** chapter in the whole history of planet Earth, and we are gonna answer to ourselves and no one else.
DAILY NEWS
You-- you're *Inhuman* too?
But--Queen Medusa would never allow her people to act like this--to go around terrifying ordinary civilians--
I knew it. I knew you were one of us.
You think Queen Medusa is the only leader we have? There are ***others***. And not all of them believe in licking her majesty's boots in New Attilan.
I--I don't understand.
Very soon, you will.
UUGH!

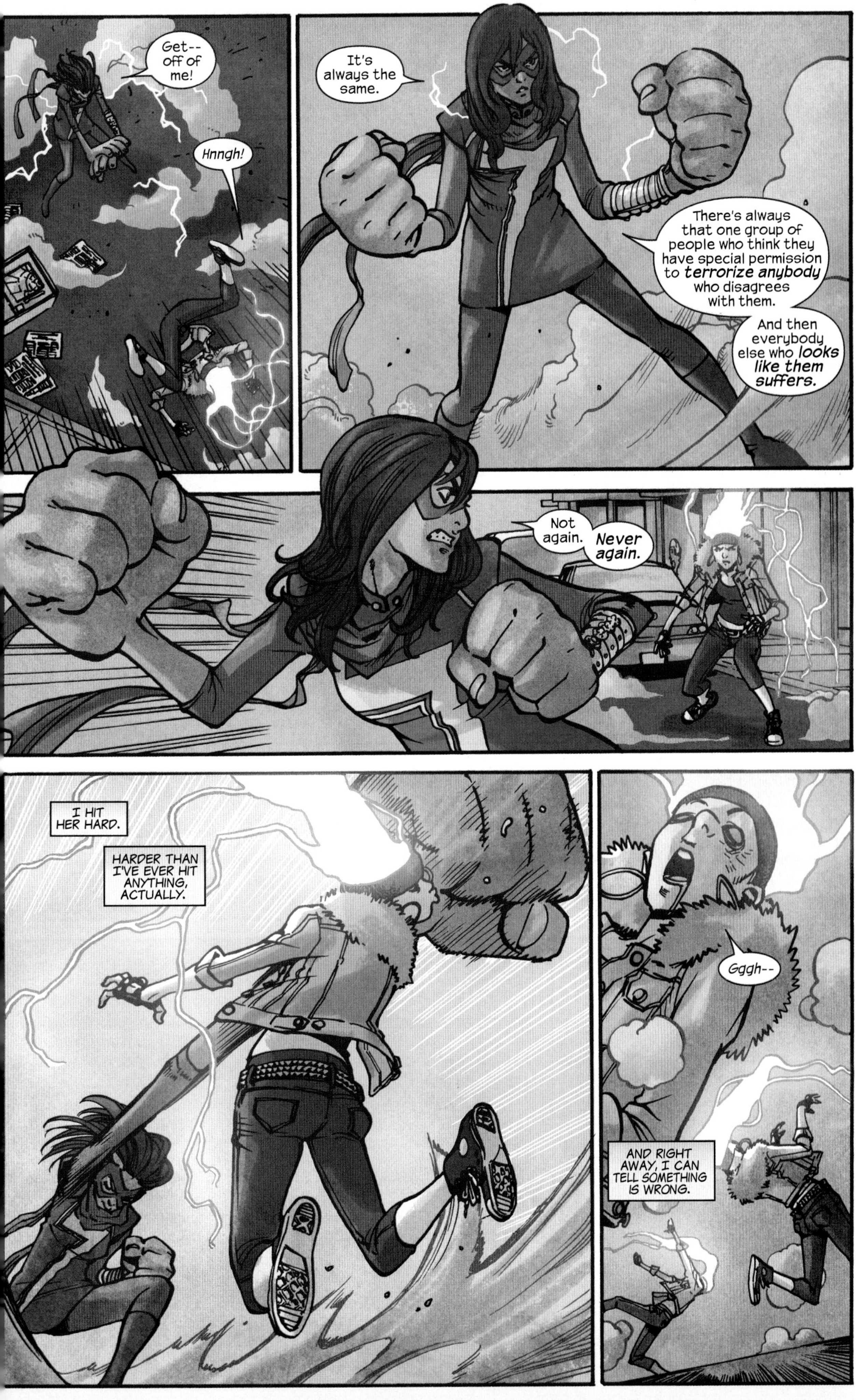
Get-- off of me!
Hnngh!
It's always the same.
There's always that one group of people who think they have special permission to *terrorize anybody* who disagrees with them.
And then everybody else who *looks like them suffers.*
Not again.
Never again.
I HIT HER HARD.
HARDER THAN I'VE EVER HIT ANYTHING, ACTUALLY.
Gggh--
AND RIGHT AWAY, I CAN TELL SOMETHING IS WRONG.

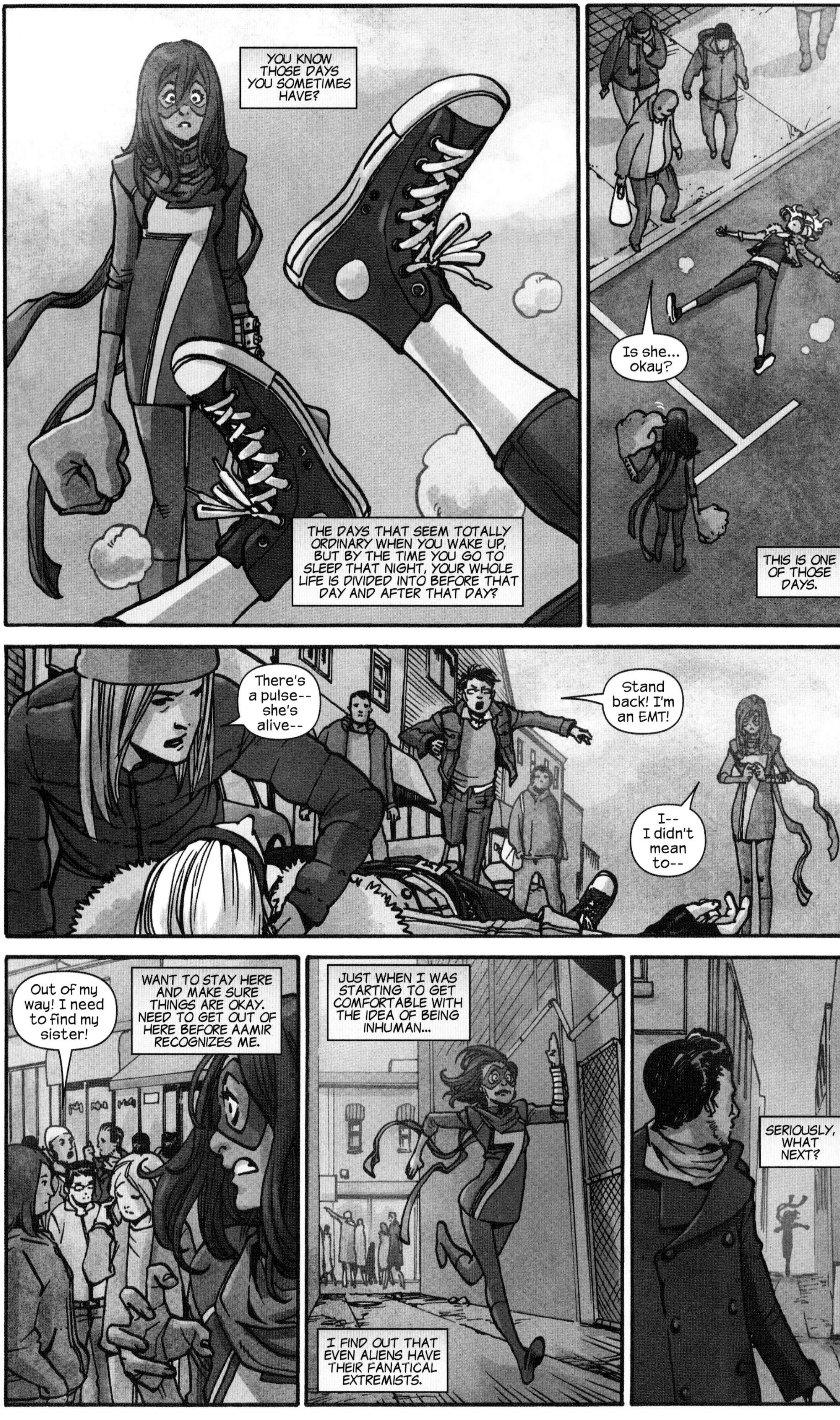
YOU KNOW THOSE DAYS YOU SOMETIMES HAVE?
THE DAYS THAT SEEM TOTALLY ORDINARY WHEN YOU WAKE UP, BUT BY THE TIME YOU GO TO SLEEP THAT NIGHT, YOUR WHOLE LIFE IS DIVIDED INTO BEFORE THAT DAY AND AFTER THAT DAY?
Is she... okay?
THIS IS ONE OF THOSE DAYS.
There's a pulse-- she's alive--
Stand back! I'm an EMT!
I-- I didn't mean to--
Out of my way! I need to find my sister!
WANT TO STAY HERE AND MAKE SURE THINGS ARE OKAY. NEED TO GET OUT OF HERE BEFORE AAMIR RECOGNIZES ME.
JUST WHEN I WAS STARTING TO GET COMFORTABLE WITH THE IDEA OF BEING INHUMAN...
I FIND OUT THAT EVEN ALIENS HAVE THEIR FANATICAL EXTREMISTS.
SERIOUSLY, WHAT NEXT?

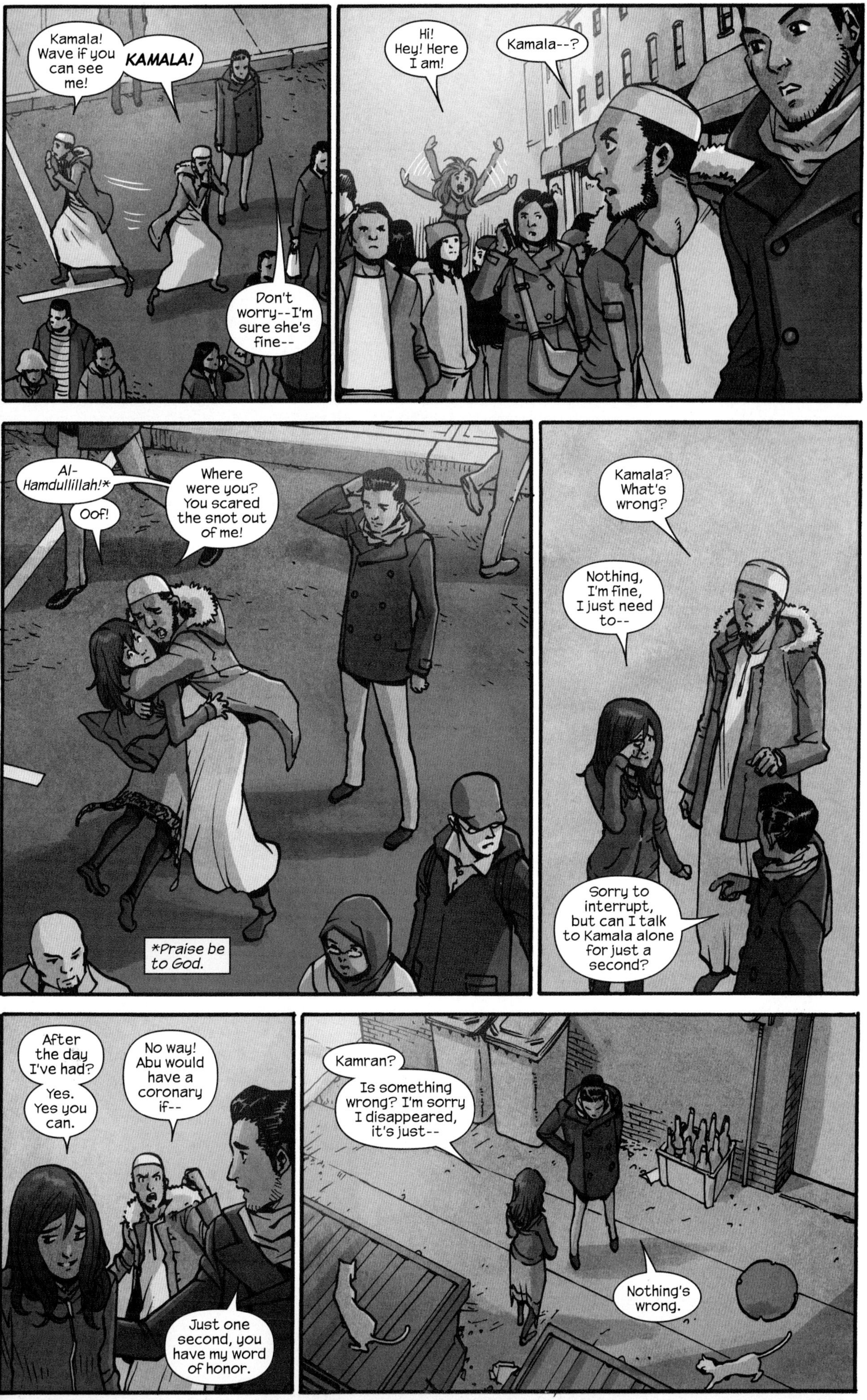

Kamala! Wave if you can see me!
KAMALA!
Don't worry--I'm sure she's fine--
Hi! Hey! Here I am!
Kamala--?
Al-Hamdullillah!*
Oof!
Where were you? You scared the snot out of me!
*Praise be to God.
Kamala? What's wrong?
Nothing, I'm fine, I just need to--
Sorry to interrupt, but can I talk to Kamala alone for just a second?
After the day I've had?
Yes. Yes you can.
No way! Abu would have a coronary if--
Just one second, you have my word of honor.
Kamran?
Is something wrong? I'm sorry I disappeared, it's just--
Nothing's wrong.

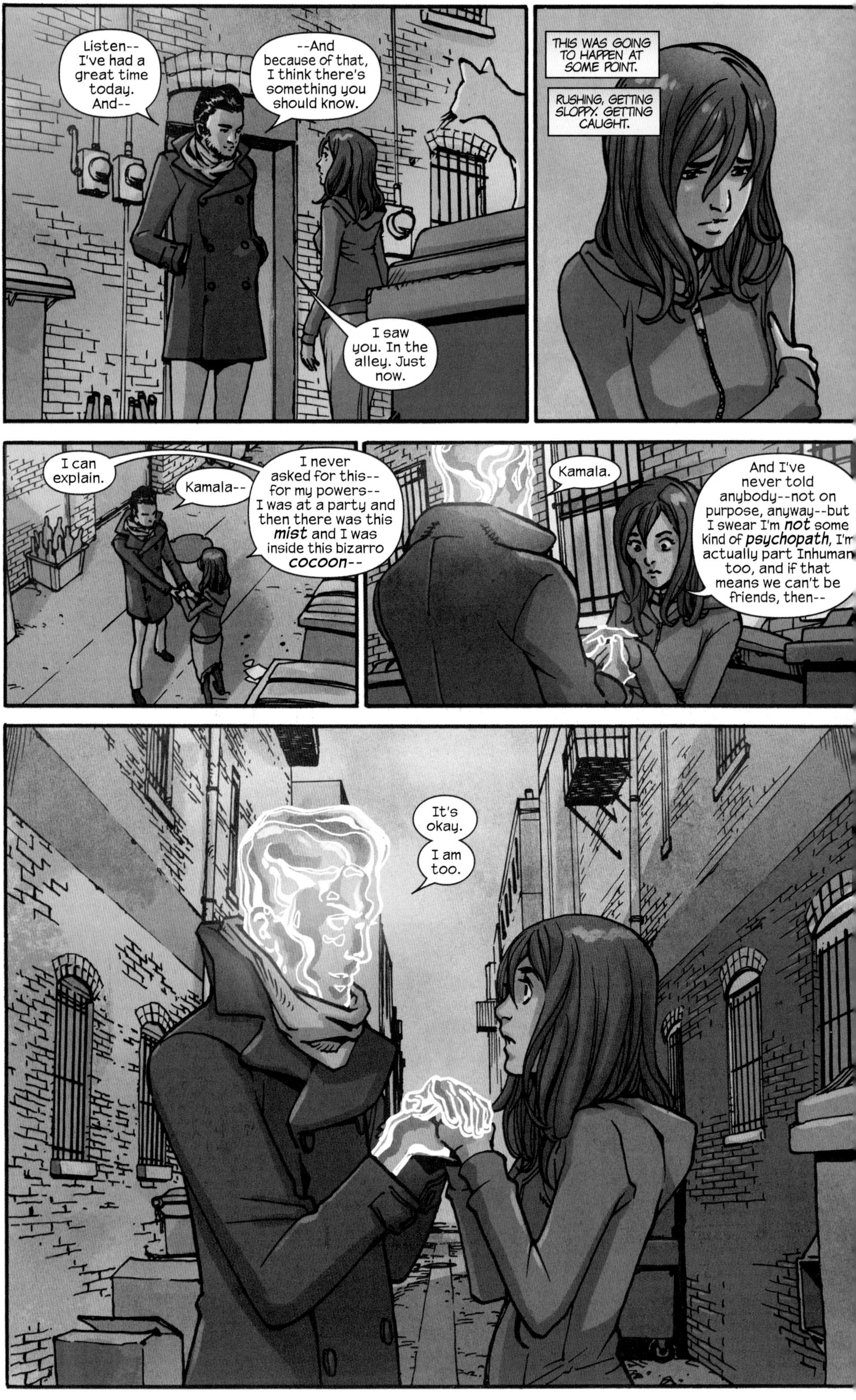
Listen-- I've had a great time today. And--
--And because of that, I think there's something you should know.
I saw you. In the alley. Just now.
THIS WAS GOING TO HAPPEN AT SOME POINT.
RUSHING, GETTING SLOPPY. GETTING CAUGHT.
I can explain.
Kamala--
I never asked for this-- for my powers-- I was at a party and then there was this *mist* and I was inside this bizarro *cocoon*--
Kamala.
And I've never told anybody--not on purpose, anyway--but I swear I'm *not* some kind of *psychopath*, I'm actually part Inhuman too, and if that means we can't be friends, then--
It's okay.
I am too.

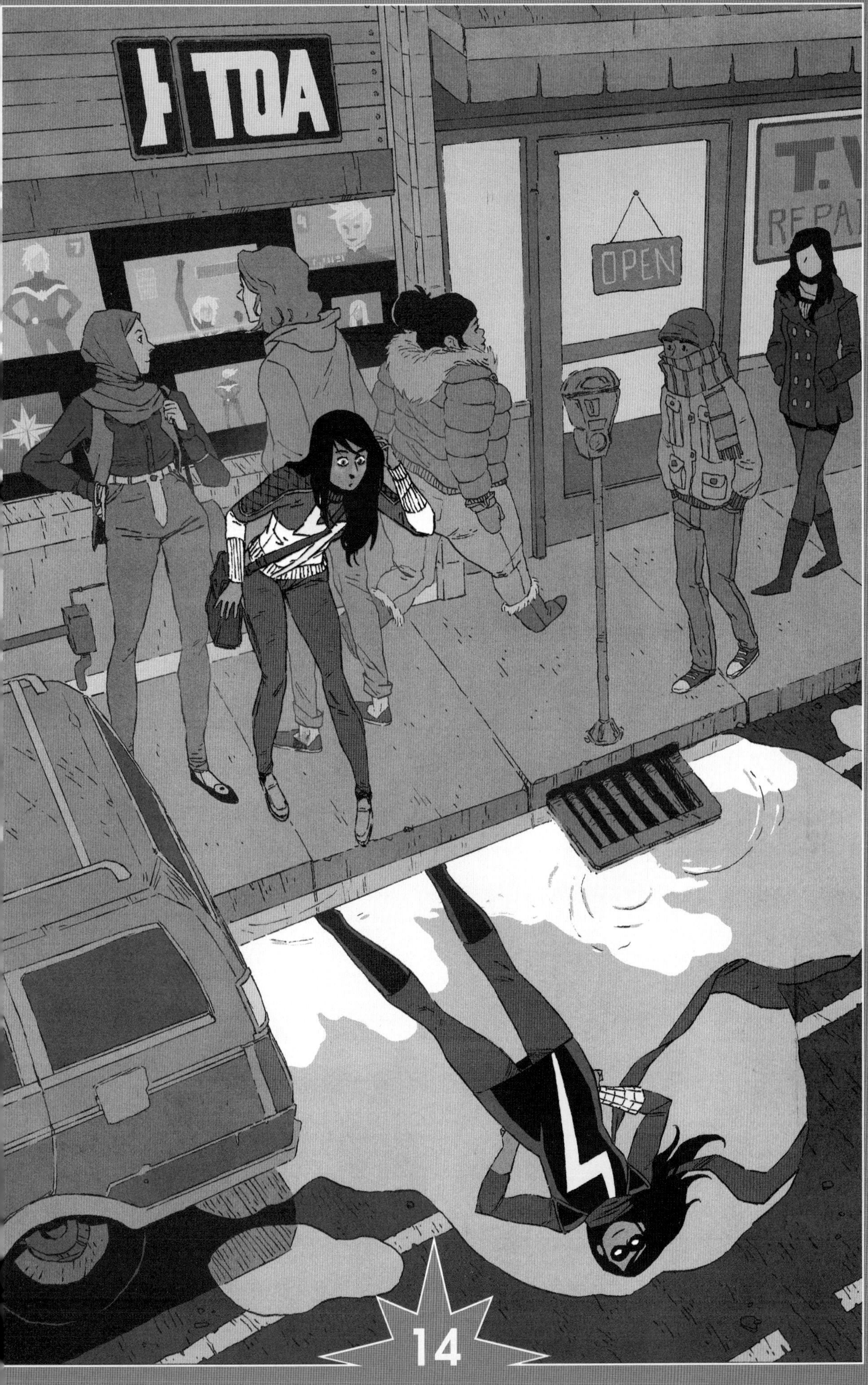
OPEN
14

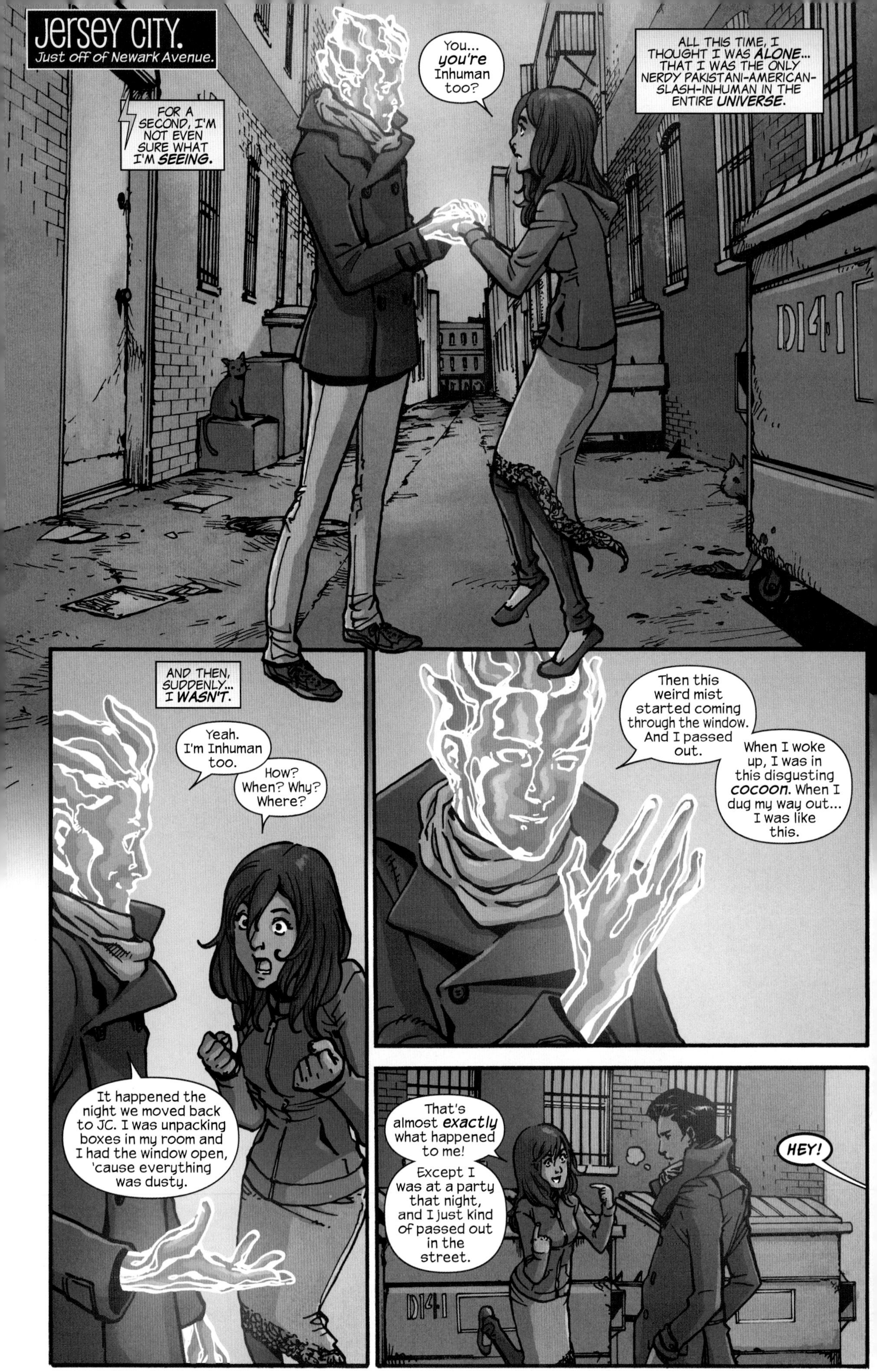
JERSEY CITY.
Just off of Newark Avenue.
FOR A SECOND, I'M NOT EVEN SURE WHAT I'M SEEING.
You... you're Inhuman too?
ALL THIS TIME, I THOUGHT I WAS ALONE... THAT I WAS THE ONLY NERDY PAKISTANI-AMERICAN-SLASH-INHUMAN IN THE ENTIRE UNIVERSE.
D141
AND THEN, SUDDENLY... I WASN'T.
Yeah. I'm Inhuman too.
How? When? Why? Where?
It happened the night we moved back to JC. I was unpacking boxes in my room and I had the window open, 'cause everything was dusty.
Then this weird mist started coming through the window. And I passed out.
When I woke up, I was in this disgusting cocoon. When I dug my way out... I was like this.
That's almost exactly what happened to me!
Except I was at a party that night, and I just kind of passed out in the street.
HEY!
D141

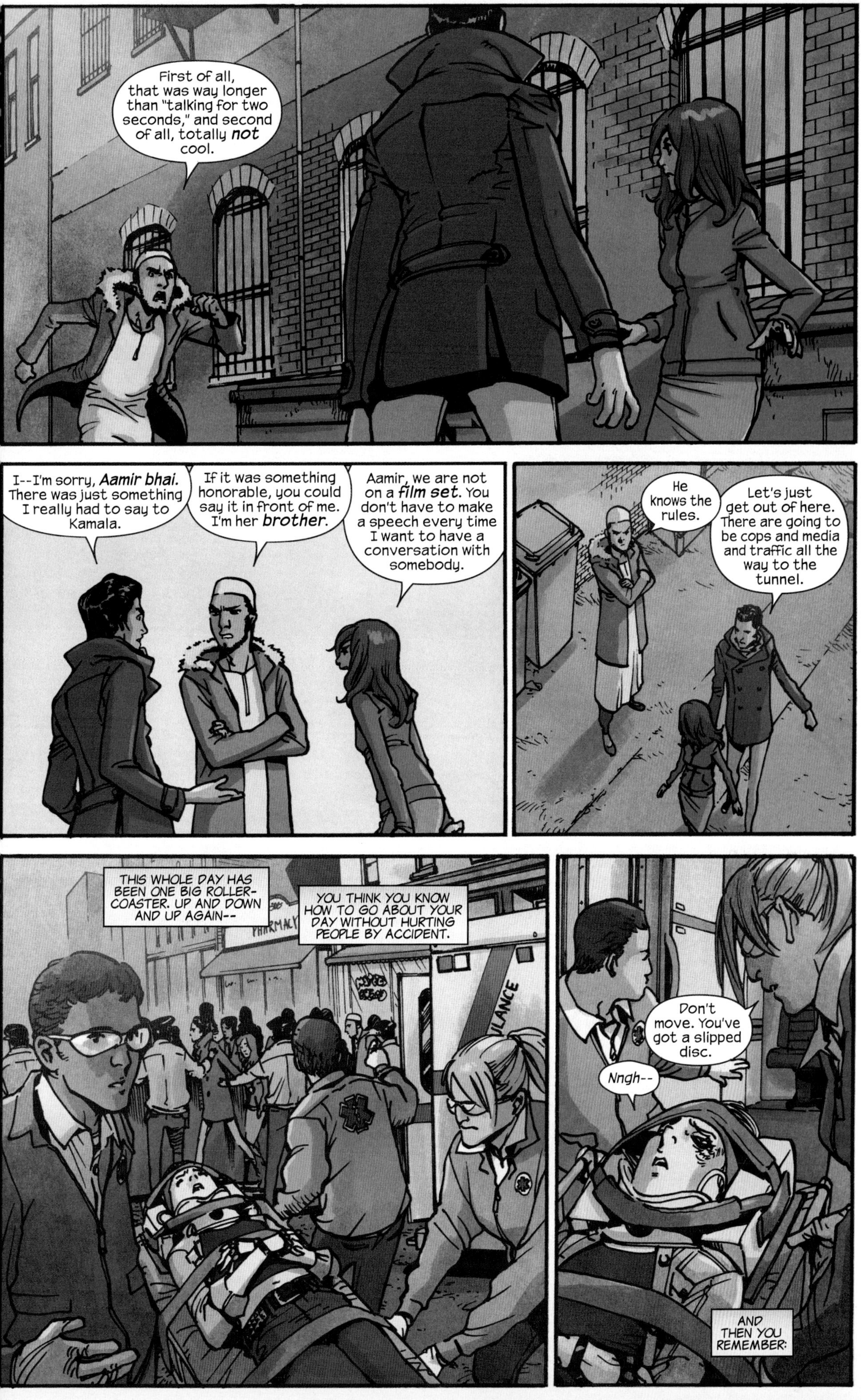
First of all, that was way longer than "talking for two seconds," and second of all, totally *not* cool.
I--I'm sorry, *Aamir bhai.* There was just something I really had to say to Kamala.
If it was something honorable, you could say it in front of me. I'm her *brother*.
Aamir, we are not on a *film set*. You don't have to make a speech every time I want to have a conversation with somebody.
He knows the rules.
Let's just get out of here. There are going to be cops and media and traffic all the way to the tunnel.
THIS WHOLE DAY HAS BEEN ONE BIG ROLLER-COASTER. UP AND DOWN AND UP AGAIN--
YOU THINK YOU KNOW HOW TO GO ABOUT YOUR DAY WITHOUT HURTING PEOPLE BY ACCIDENT.
PHARMACY
Don't move. You've got a slipped disc.
Nngh--
AND THEN YOU REMEMBER:

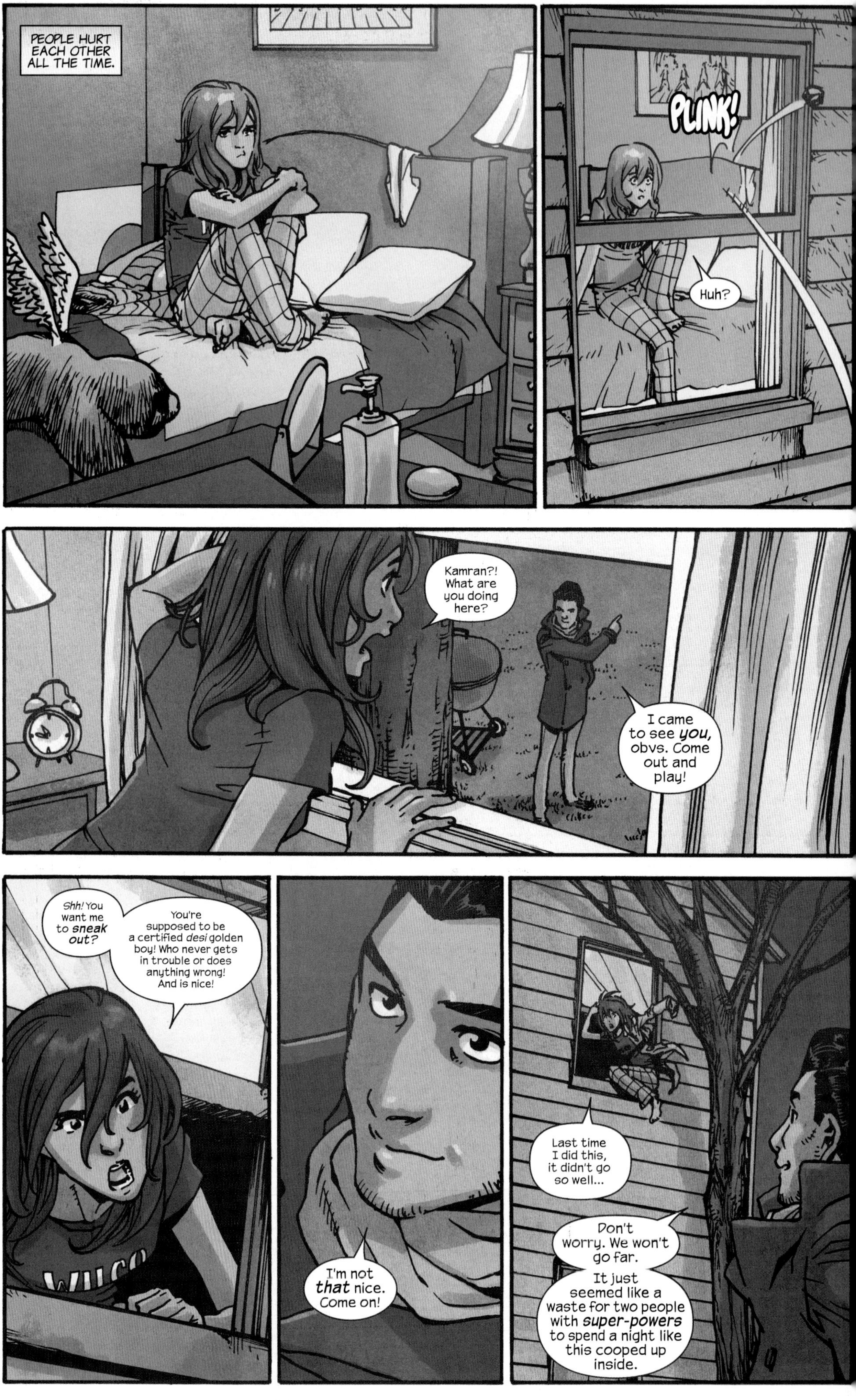
PEOPLE HURT EACH OTHER ALL THE TIME.
PLINK!
Huh?
Kamran?! What are you doing here?
I came to see *you,* obvs. Come out and play!
Shh! You want me to ***sneak out?***
You're supposed to be a certified *desi* golden boy! Who never gets in trouble or does anything wrong! And is nice!
I'm not ***that*** nice. Come on!
Last time I did this, it didn't go so well...
Don't worry. We won't go far.
It just seemed like a waste for two people with ***super-powers*** to spend a night like this cooped up inside.
WILCO

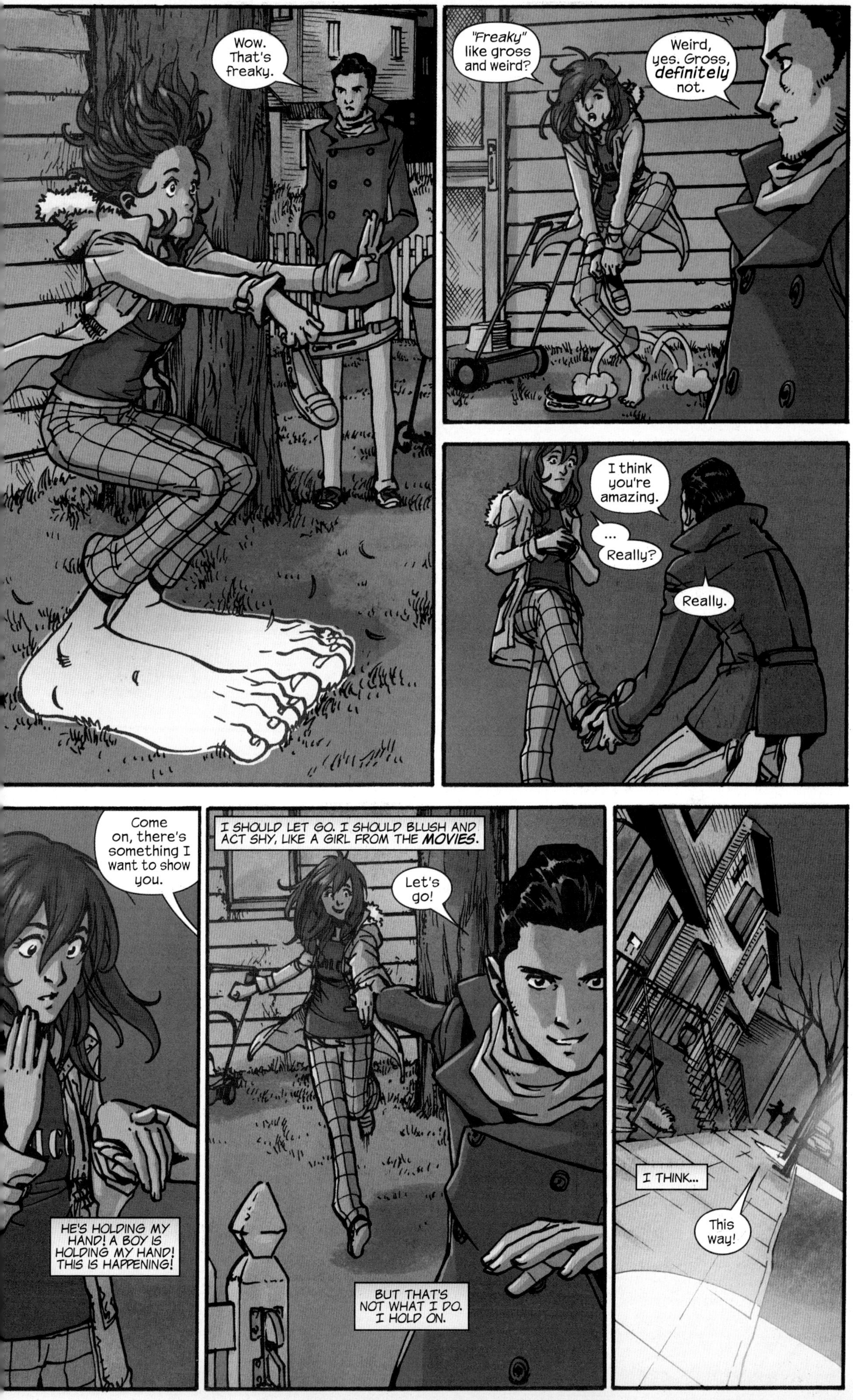
Wow. That's freaky.
"Freaky" like gross and weird?
Weird, yes. Gross, definitely not.
I think you're amazing.
... Really?
Really.
Come on, there's something I want to show you.
HE'S HOLDING MY HAND! A BOY IS HOLDING MY HAND! THIS IS HAPPENING!
I SHOULD LET GO. I SHOULD BLUSH AND ACT SHY, LIKE A GIRL FROM THE MOVIES.
Let's go!
BUT THAT'S NOT WHAT I DO. I HOLD ON.
I THINK...
This way!

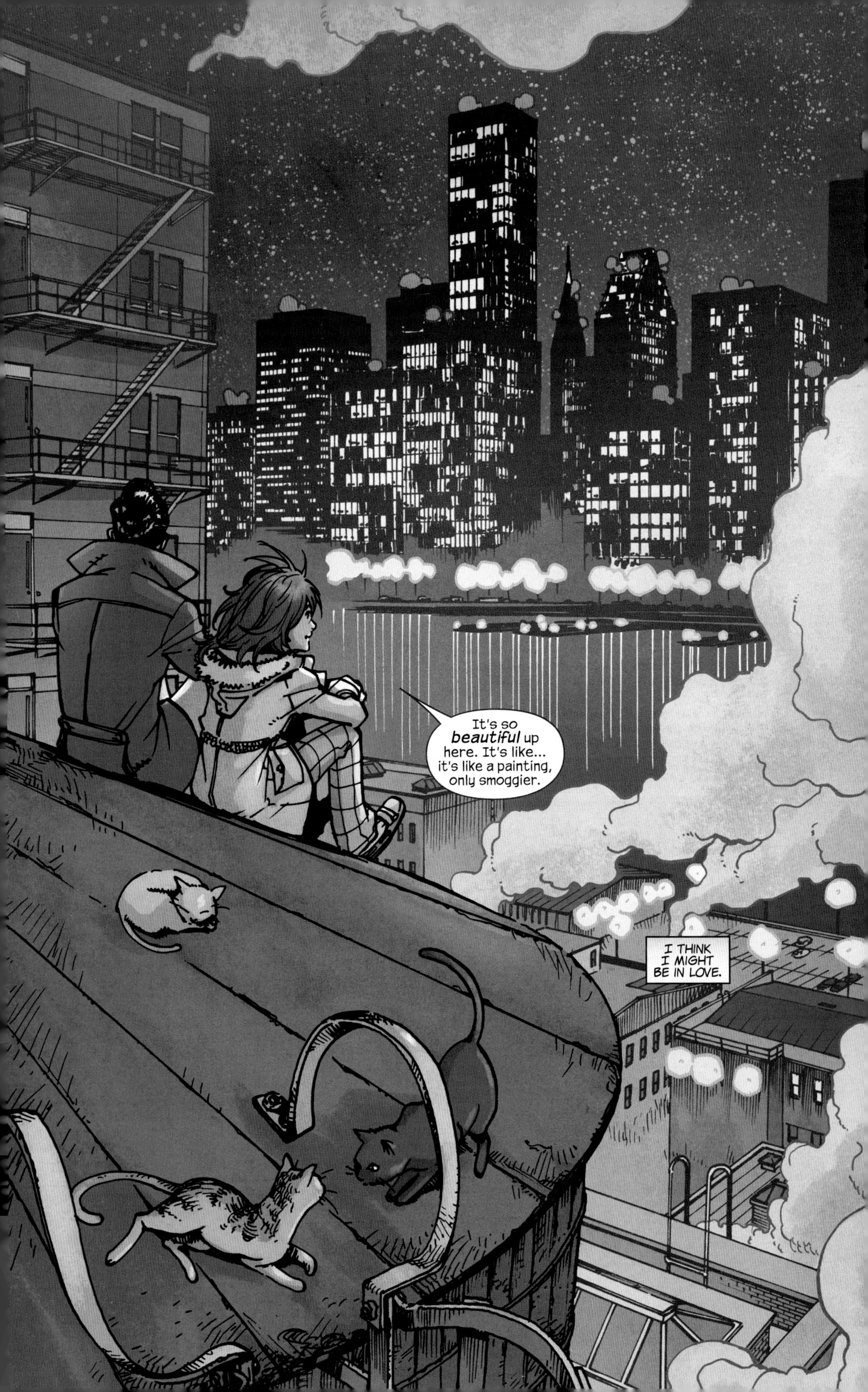
It's so beautiful up here. It's like... it's like a painting, only smoggier.
I THINK I MIGHT BE IN LOVE.

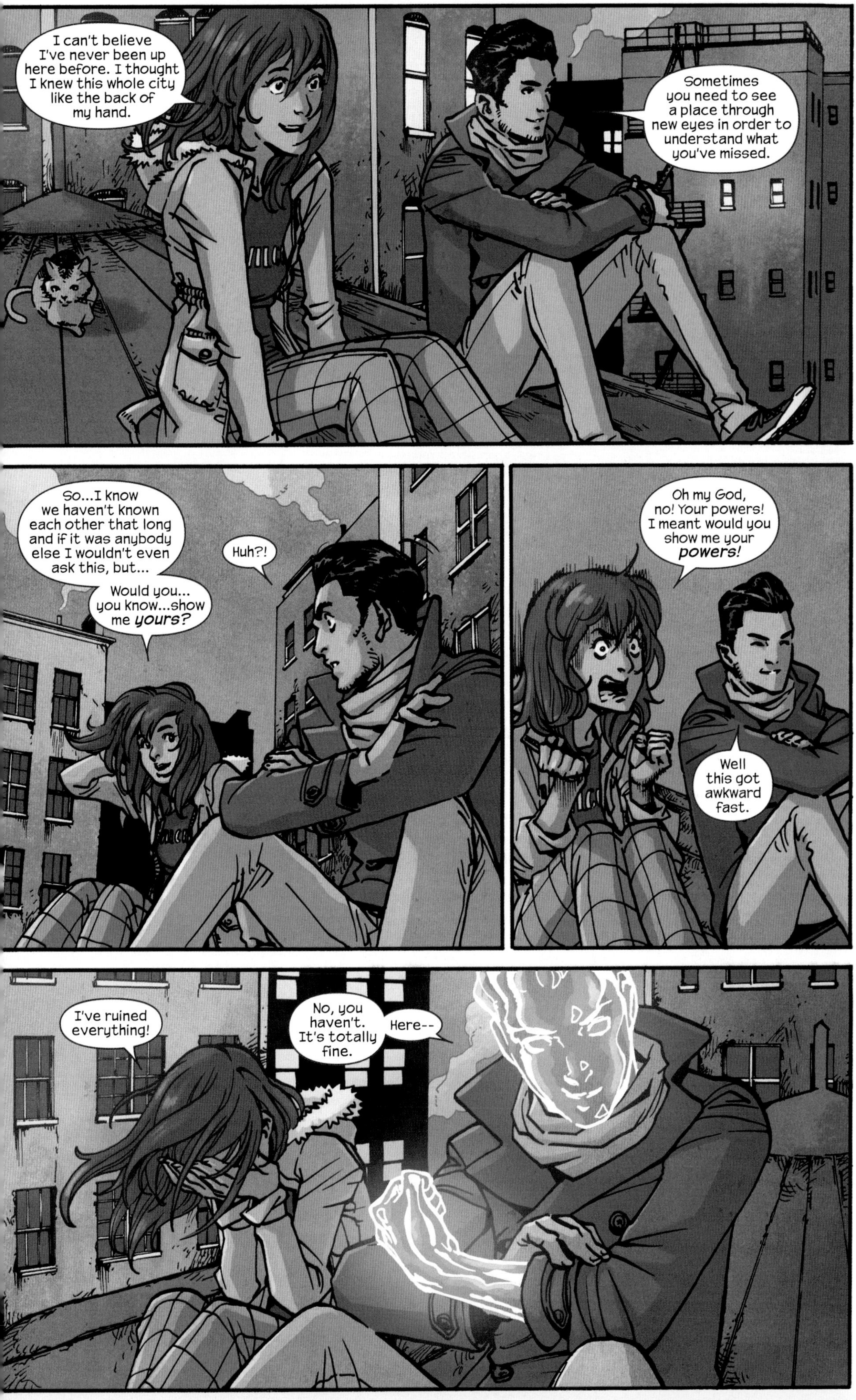
I can't believe I've never been up here before. I thought I knew this whole city like the back of my hand.
Sometimes you need to see a place through new eyes in order to understand what you've missed.
So...I know we haven't known each other that long and if it was anybody else I wouldn't even ask this, but...
Would you... you know...show me *yours?*
Huh?!
Oh my God, no! Your powers! I meant would you show me your *powers!*
Well this got awkward fast.
I've ruined everything!
No, you haven't. It's totally fine.
Here--

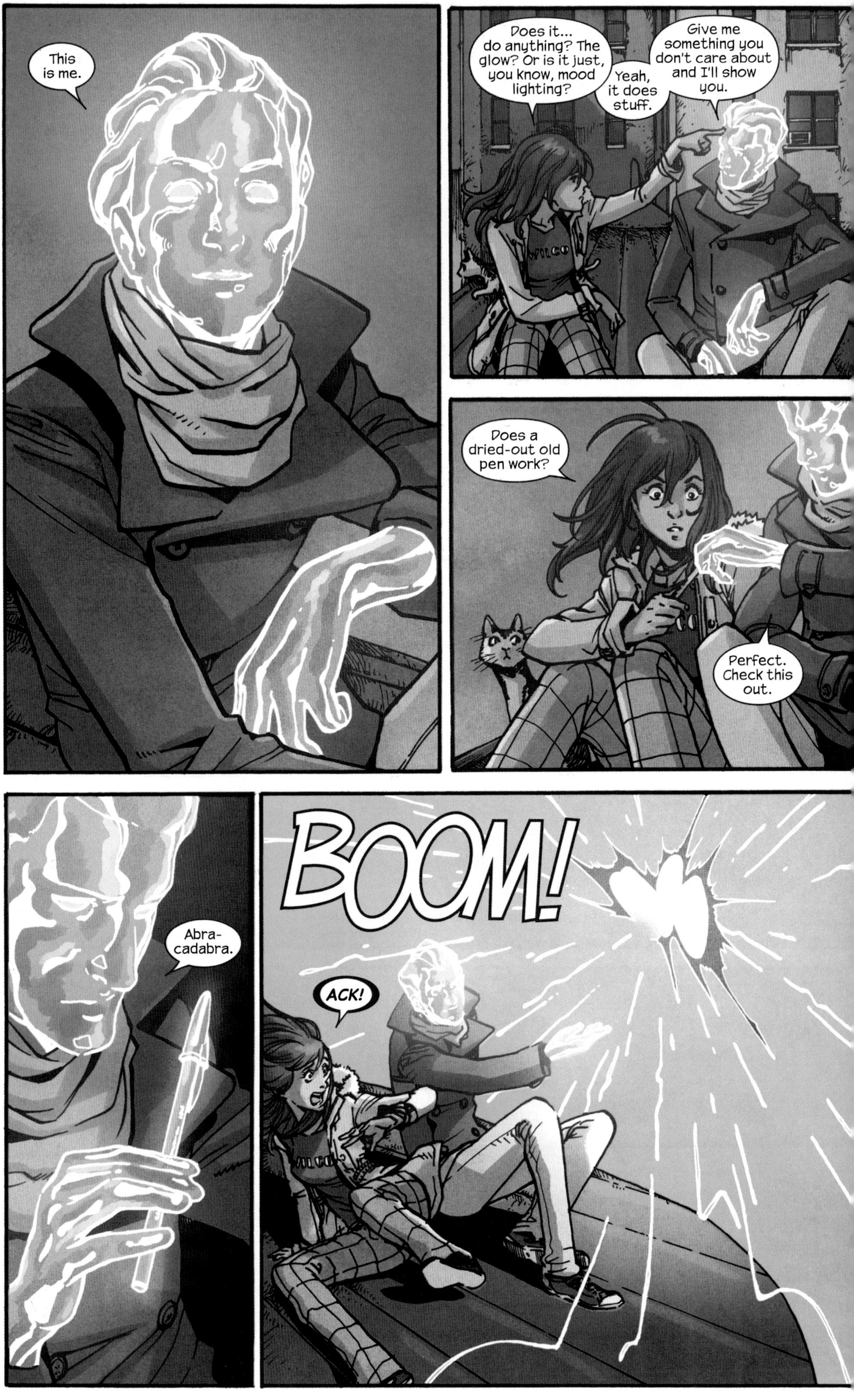
This is me.
Does it... do anything? The glow? Or is it just, you know, mood lighting?
Yeah, it does stuff.
Give me something you don't care about and I'll show you.
WILCO
Does a dried-out old pen work?
Perfect. Check this out.
Abra-cadabra.
BOOM!
ACK!

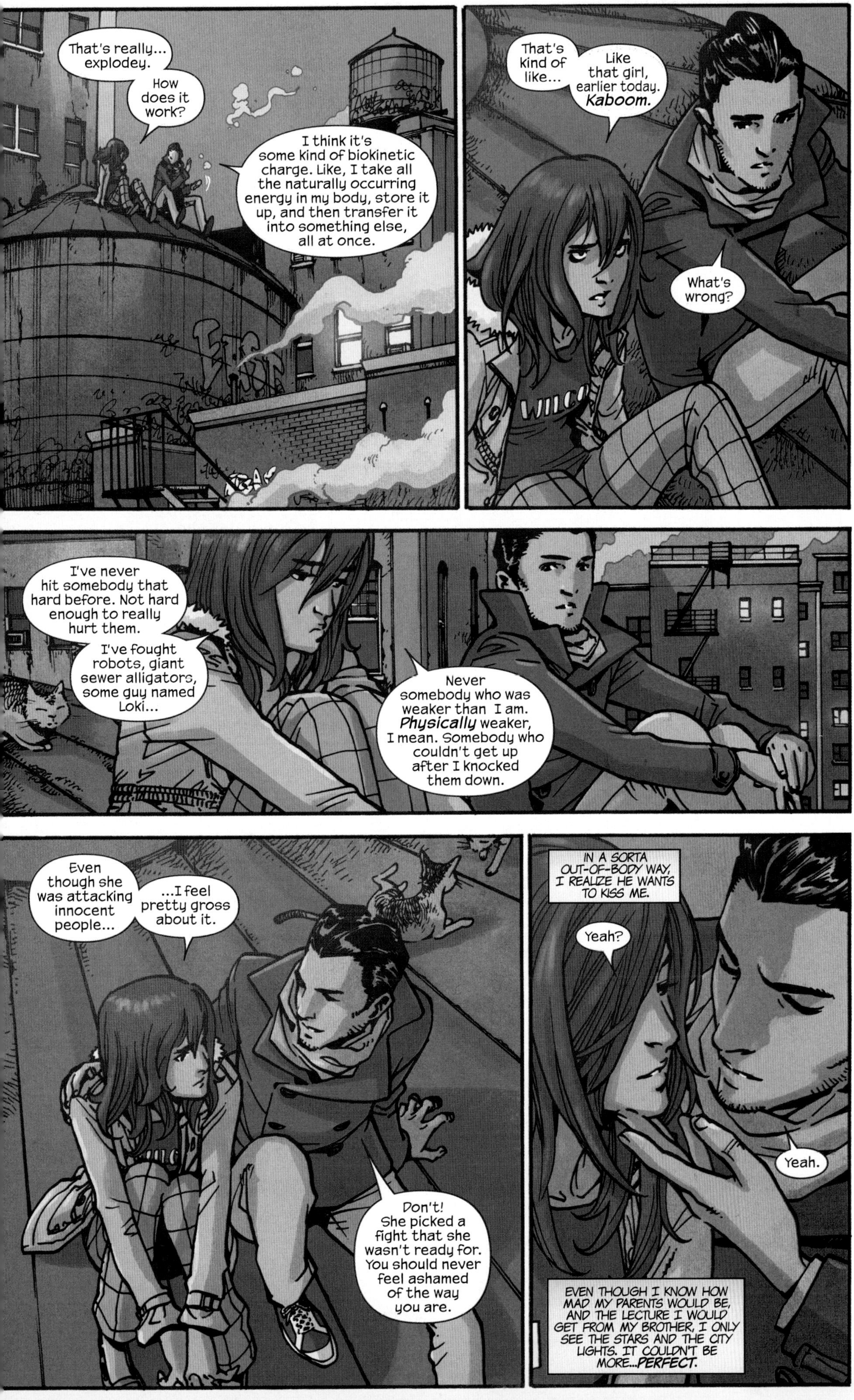

That's really... explodey.
How does it work?
I think it's some kind of biokinetic charge. Like, I take all the naturally occurring energy in my body, store it up, and then transfer it into something else, all at once.
That's kind of like...
Like that girl, earlier today. *Kaboom.*
What's wrong?
I've never hit somebody that hard before. Not hard enough to really hurt them.
I've fought robots, giant sewer alligators, some guy named Loki...
Never somebody who was weaker than I am. *Physically* weaker, I mean. Somebody who couldn't get up after I knocked them down.
Even though she was attacking innocent people...
...I feel pretty gross about it.
Don't! She picked a fight that she wasn't ready for. You should never feel ashamed of the way you are.
IN A SORTA OUT-OF-BODY WAY, I REALIZE HE WANTS TO KISS ME.
Yeah?
Yeah.
EVEN THOUGH I KNOW HOW MAD MY PARENTS WOULD BE, AND THE LECTURE I WOULD GET FROM MY BROTHER, I ONLY SEE THE STARS AND THE CITY LIGHTS. IT COULDN'T BE MORE...*PERFECT.*

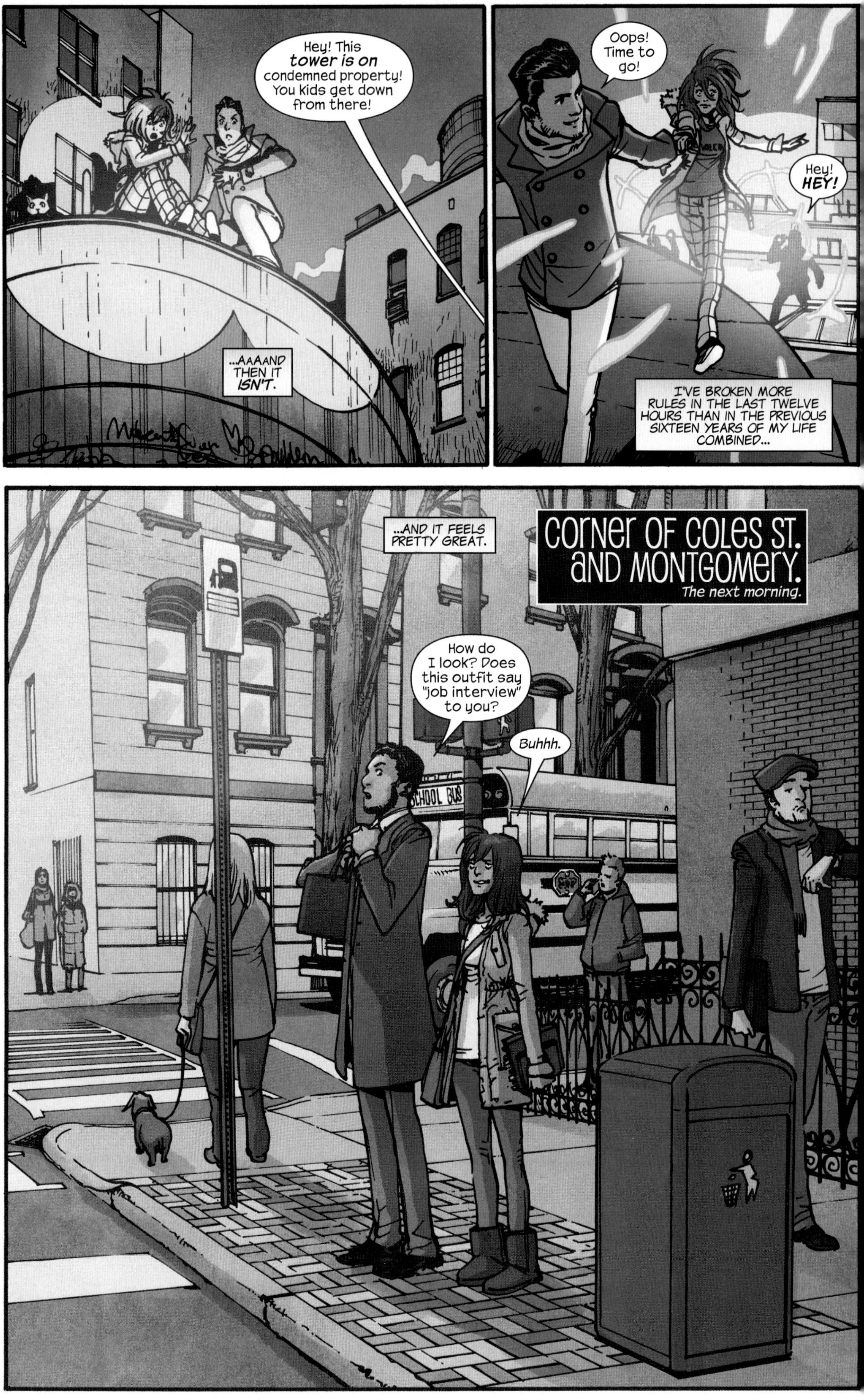
Hey! This tower is on condemned property! You kids get down from there!
...AAAAND THEN IT ISN'T.
Oops! Time to go!
Hey! HEY!
I'VE BROKEN MORE RULES IN THE LAST TWELVE HOURS THAN IN THE PREVIOUS SIXTEEN YEARS OF MY LIFE COMBINED...
...AND IT FEELS PRETTY GREAT.
CORNER OF COLES ST. AND MONTGOMERY.
The next morning.
How do I look? Does this outfit say "job interview" to you?
Buhhh.
SCHOOL BUS

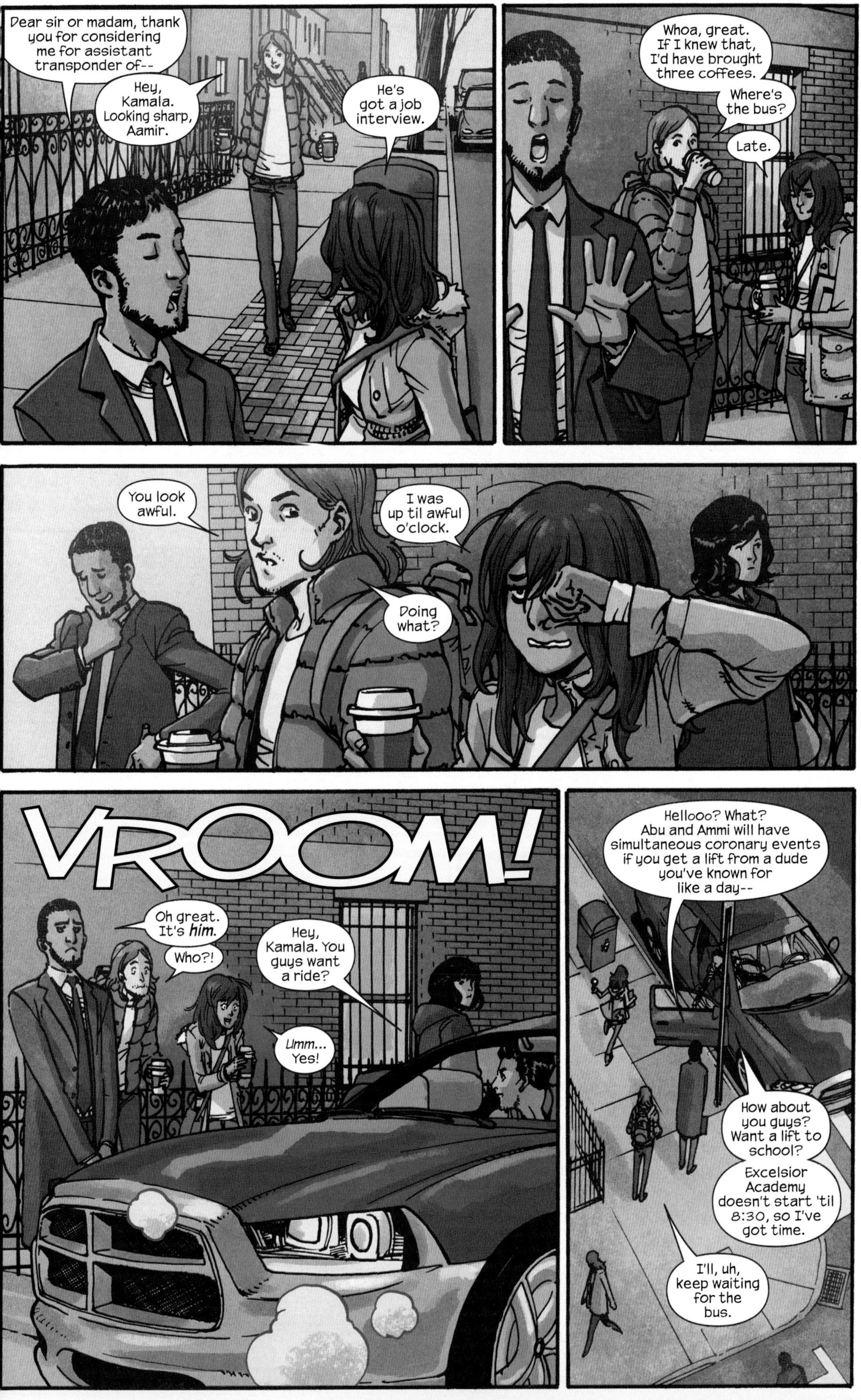
Dear sir or madam, thank you for considering me for assistant transponder of--
Hey, Kamala. Looking sharp, Aamir.
He's got a job interview.
Whoa, great. If I knew that, I'd have brought three coffees.
Where's the bus?
Late.
You look awful.
I was up til awful o'clock.
Doing what?
VROOM!
Oh great. It's *him.*
Who?!
Hey, Kamala. You guys want a ride?
Umm... Yes!
Hellooo? What? Abu and Ammi will have simultaneous coronary events if you get a lift from a dude you've known for like a day--
How about you guys? Want a lift to school?
Excelsior Academy doesn't start 'til 8:30, so I've got time.
I'll, uh, keep waiting for the bus.

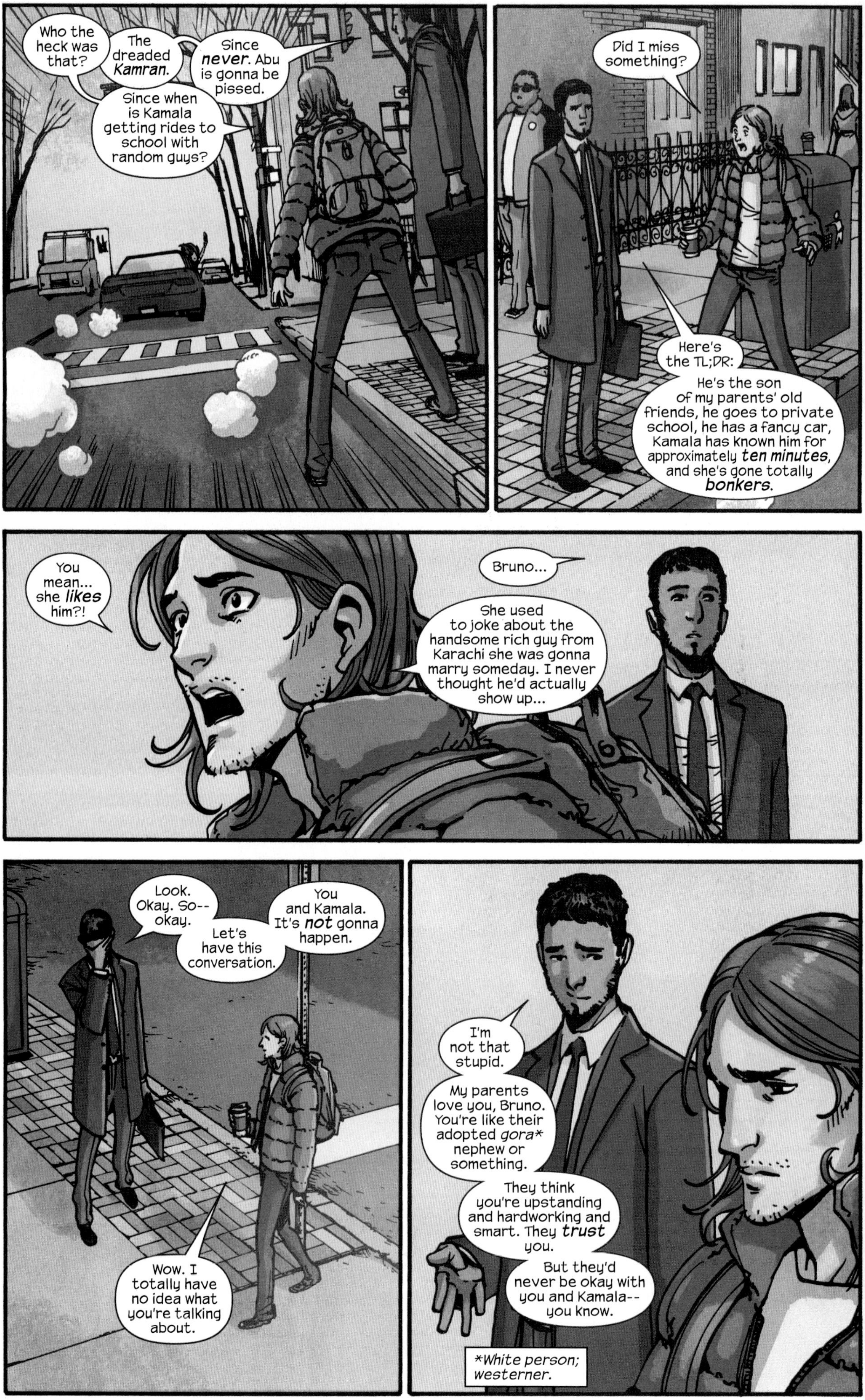
Who the heck was that?
The dreaded *Kamran*.
Since when is Kamala getting rides to school with random guys?
Since ***never***. Abu is gonna be pissed.
Did I miss something?
Here's the TL;DR:
He's the son of my parents' old friends, he goes to private school, he has a fancy car, Kamala has known him for approximately ***ten minutes***, and she's gone totally **bonkers**.
You mean... she ***likes*** him?!
Bruno...
She used to joke about the handsome rich guy from Karachi she was gonna marry someday. I never thought he'd actually show up...
Look. Okay. So-- okay.
Let's have this conversation.
You and Kamala. It's ***not*** gonna happen.
Wow. I totally have no idea what you're talking about.
I'm not that stupid.
My parents love you, Bruno. You're like their adopted *gora** nephew or something.
They think you're upstanding and hardworking and smart. They ***trust*** you.
But they'd never be okay with you and Kamala-- you know.
*White person; westerner.

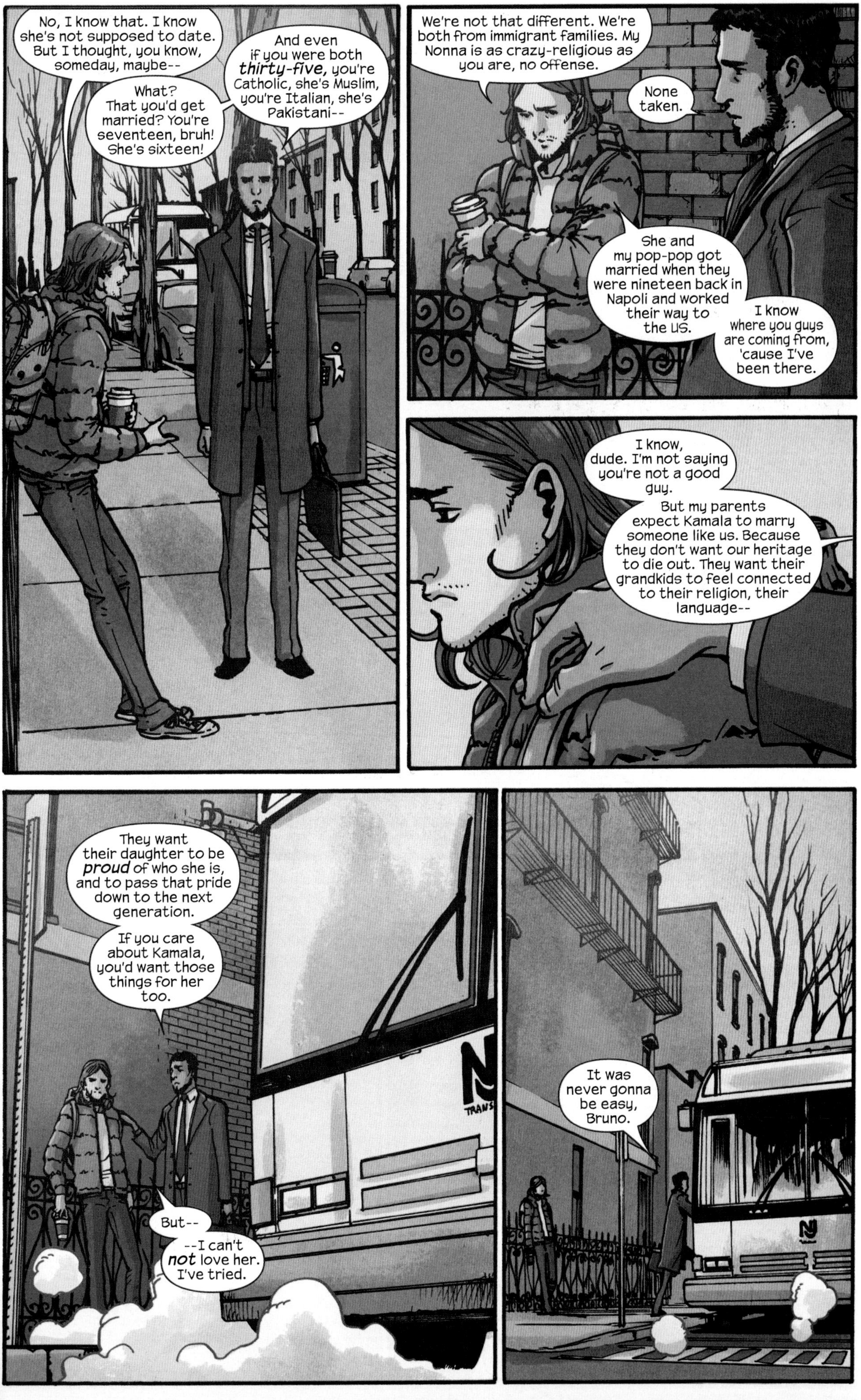
No, I know that. I know she's not supposed to date. But I thought, you know, someday, maybe--
What? That you'd get married? You're seventeen, bruh! She's sixteen!
And even if you were both *thirty-five,* you're Catholic, she's Muslim, you're Italian, she's Pakistani--
We're not that different. We're both from immigrant families. My Nonna is as crazy-religious as you are, no offense.
None taken.
She and my pop-pop got married when they were nineteen back in Napoli and worked their way to the US.
I know where you guys are coming from, 'cause I've been there.
I know, dude. I'm not saying you're not a good guy.
But my parents expect Kamala to marry someone like us. Because they don't want our heritage to die out. They want their grandkids to feel connected to their religion, their language--
They want their daughter to be *proud* of who she is, and to pass that pride down to the next generation.
If you care about Kamala, you'd want those things for her too.
But--
--I can't *not* love her. I've tried.
It was never gonna be easy, Bruno.

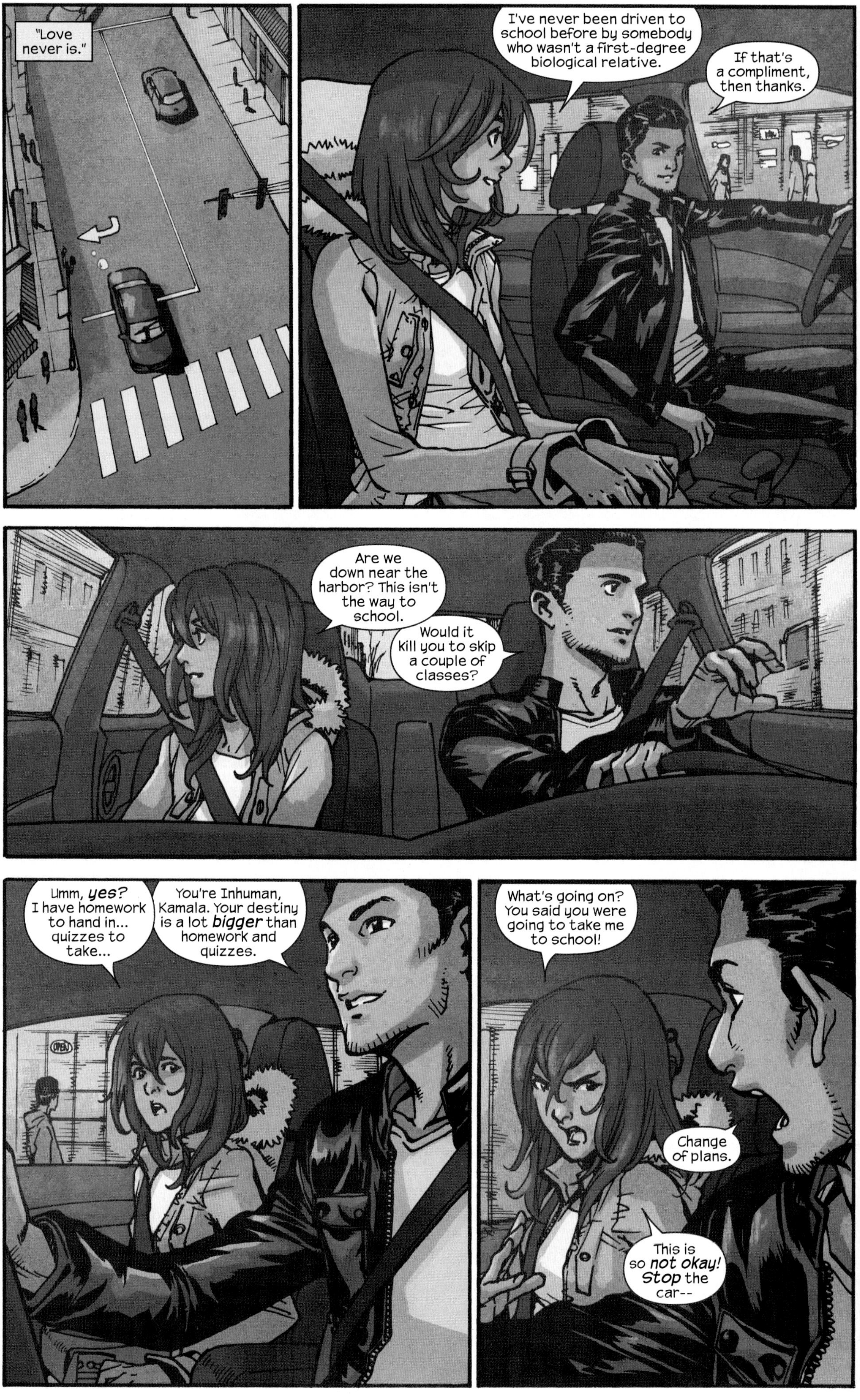
"Love never is."
I've never been driven to school before by somebody who wasn't a first-degree biological relative.
If that's a compliment, then thanks.
Are we down near the harbor? This isn't the way to school.
Would it kill you to skip a couple of classes?
Umm, *yes?* I have homework to hand in... quizzes to take...
You're Inhuman, Kamala. Your destiny is a lot *bigger* than homework and quizzes.
OPEN
What's going on? You said you were going to take me to school!
Change of plans.
This is so *not okay! Stop* the car--

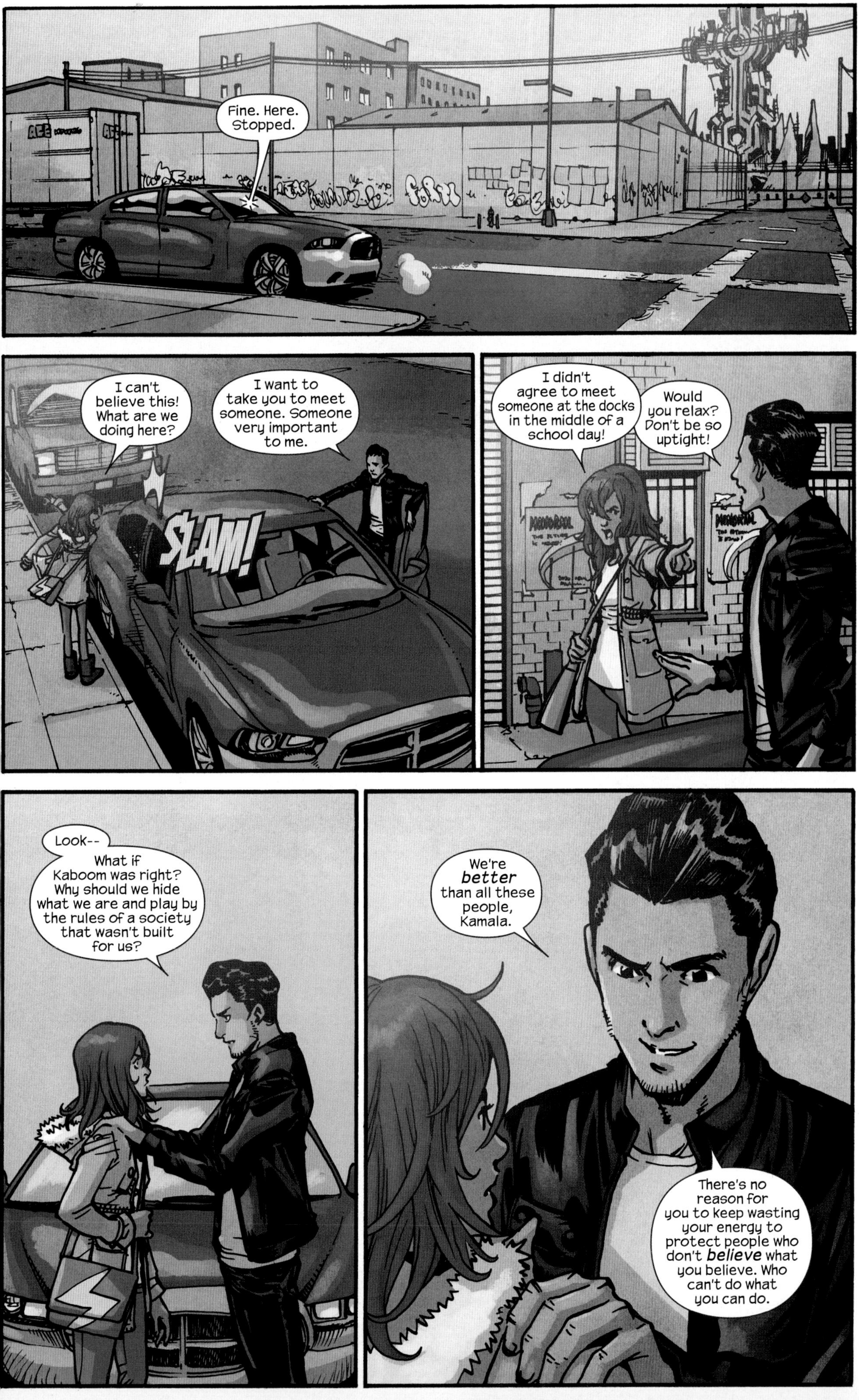
Fine. Here. Stopped.
I can't believe this! What are we doing here?
SLAM!
I want to take you to meet someone. Someone very important to me.
I didn't agree to meet someone at the docks in the middle of a school day!
Would you relax? Don't be so uptight!
Look--
What if Kaboom was right? Why should we hide what we are and play by the rules of a society that wasn't built for us?
We're *better* than all these people, Kamala.
There's no reason for you to keep wasting your energy to protect people who don't *believe* what you believe. Who can't do what you can do.

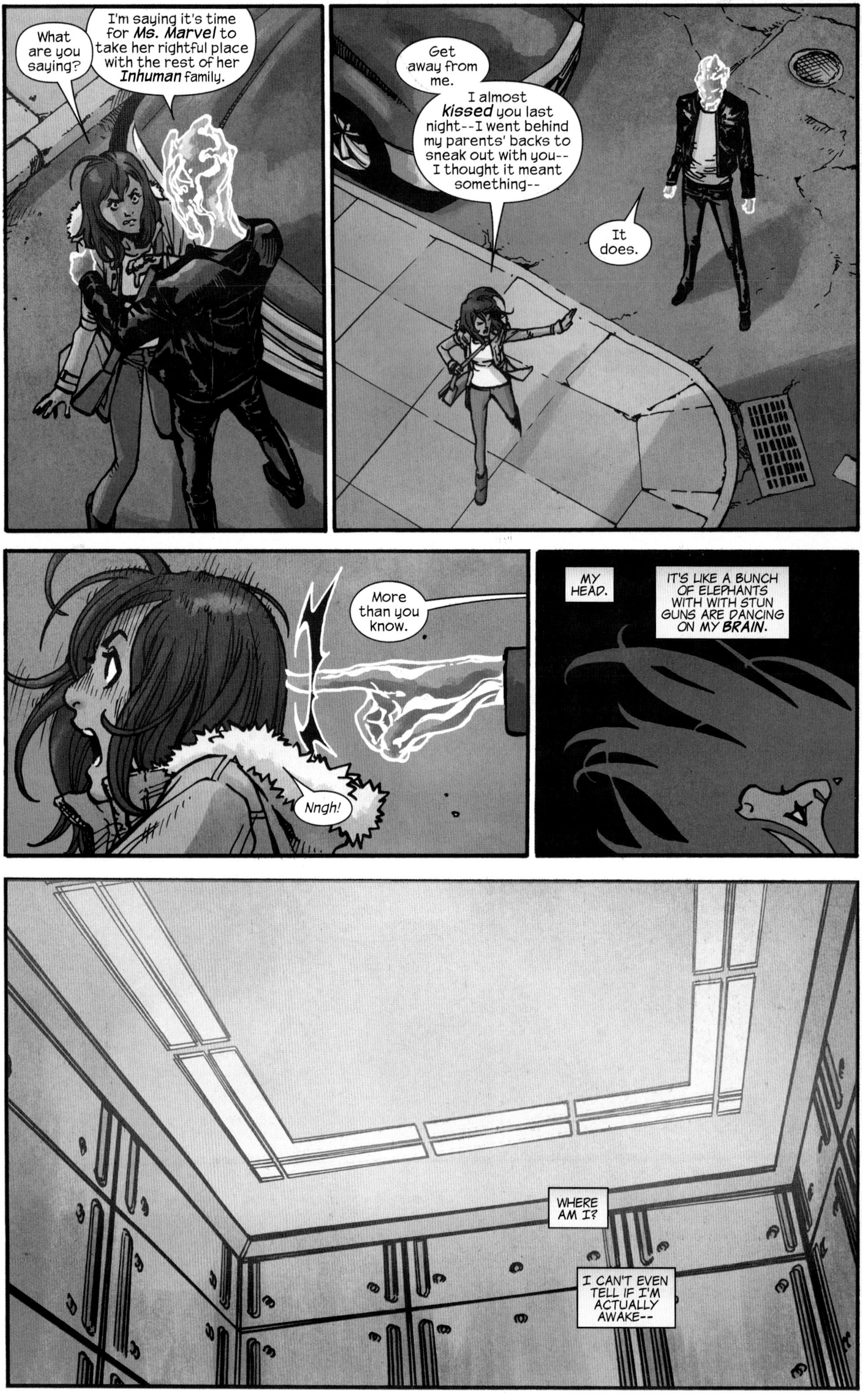
What are you saying?
I'm saying it's time for *Ms. Marvel* to take her rightful place with the rest of her *Inhuman* family.
Get away from me.
I almost *kissed* you last night--I went behind my parents' backs to sneak out with you--I thought it meant something--
It does.
More than you know.
Nngh!
MY HEAD.
IT'S LIKE A BUNCH OF ELEPHANTS WITH WITH STUN GUNS ARE DANCING ON MY *BRAIN*.
WHERE AM I?
I CAN'T EVEN TELL IF I'M ACTUALLY AWAKE--

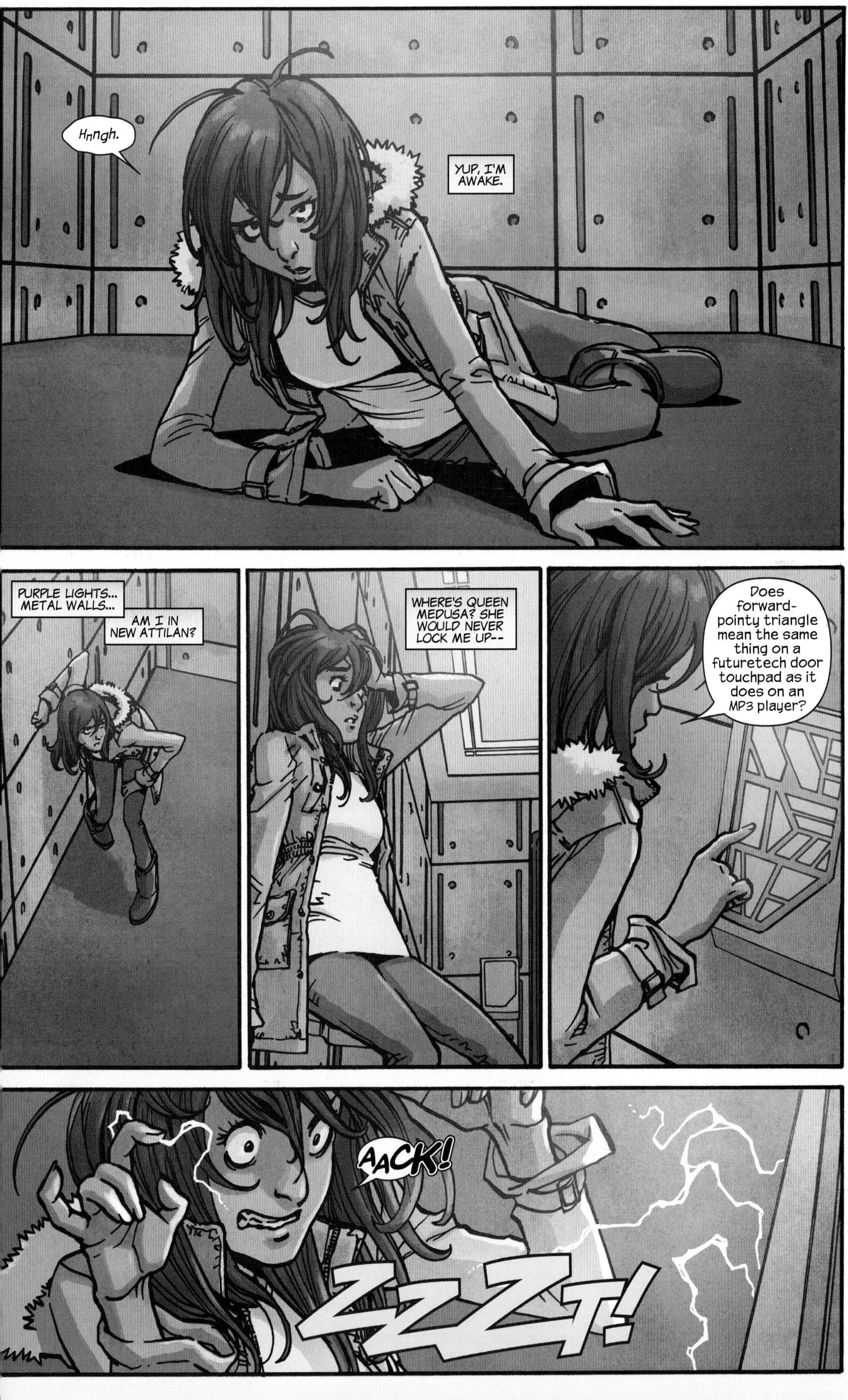
Hnngh.
YUP, I'M AWAKE.
PURPLE LIGHTS... METAL WALLS...
AM I IN NEW ATTILAN?
WHERE'S QUEEN MEDUSA? SHE WOULD NEVER LOCK ME UP--
Does forward-pointy triangle mean the same thing on a futuretech door touchpad as it does on an MP3 player?
AACK!
ZZZT!

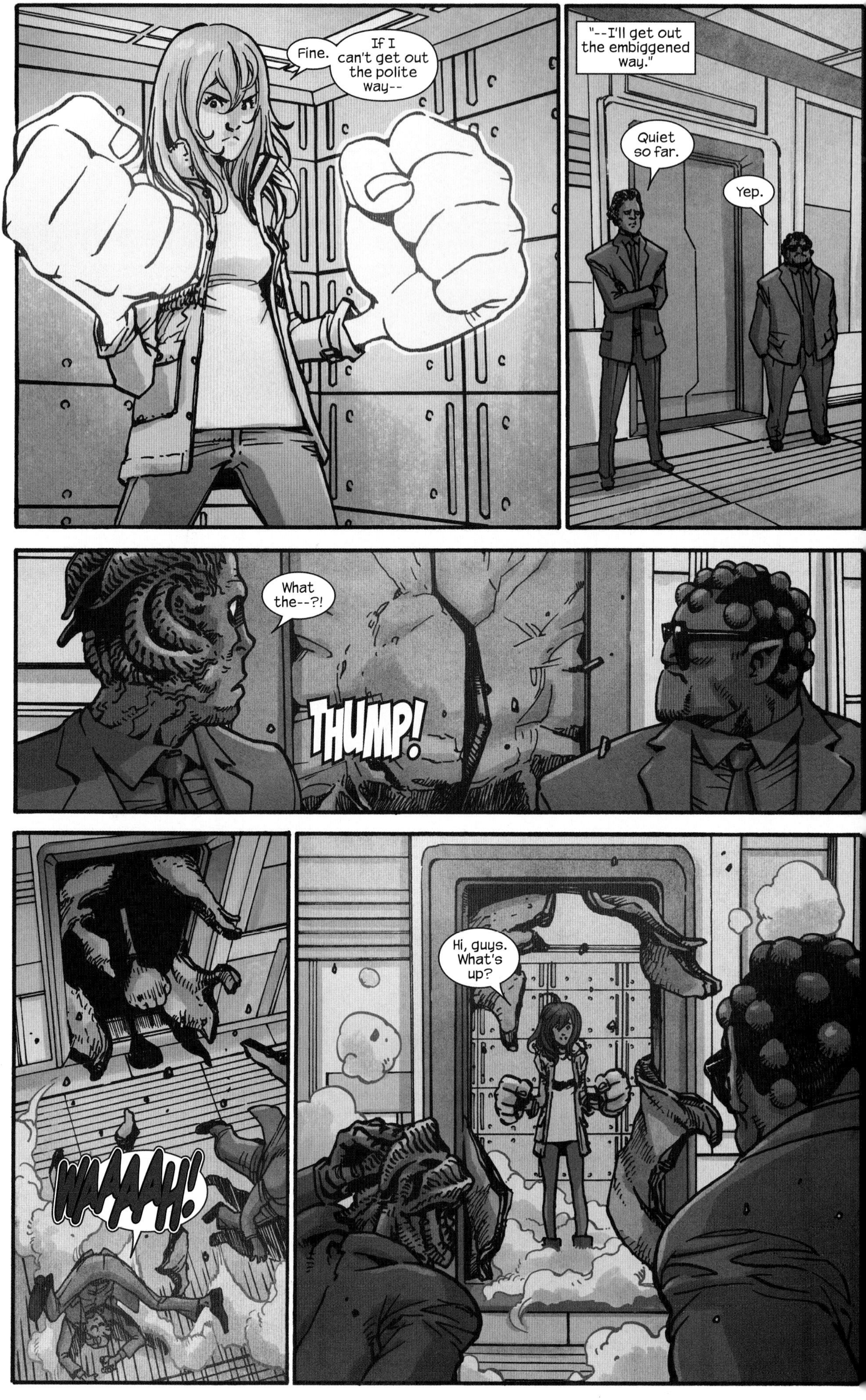
Fine.
If I can't get out the polite way--
"--I'll get out the embiggened way."
Quiet so far.
Yep.
What the--?!
THUMP!
WAAAAH!
Hi, guys. What's up?

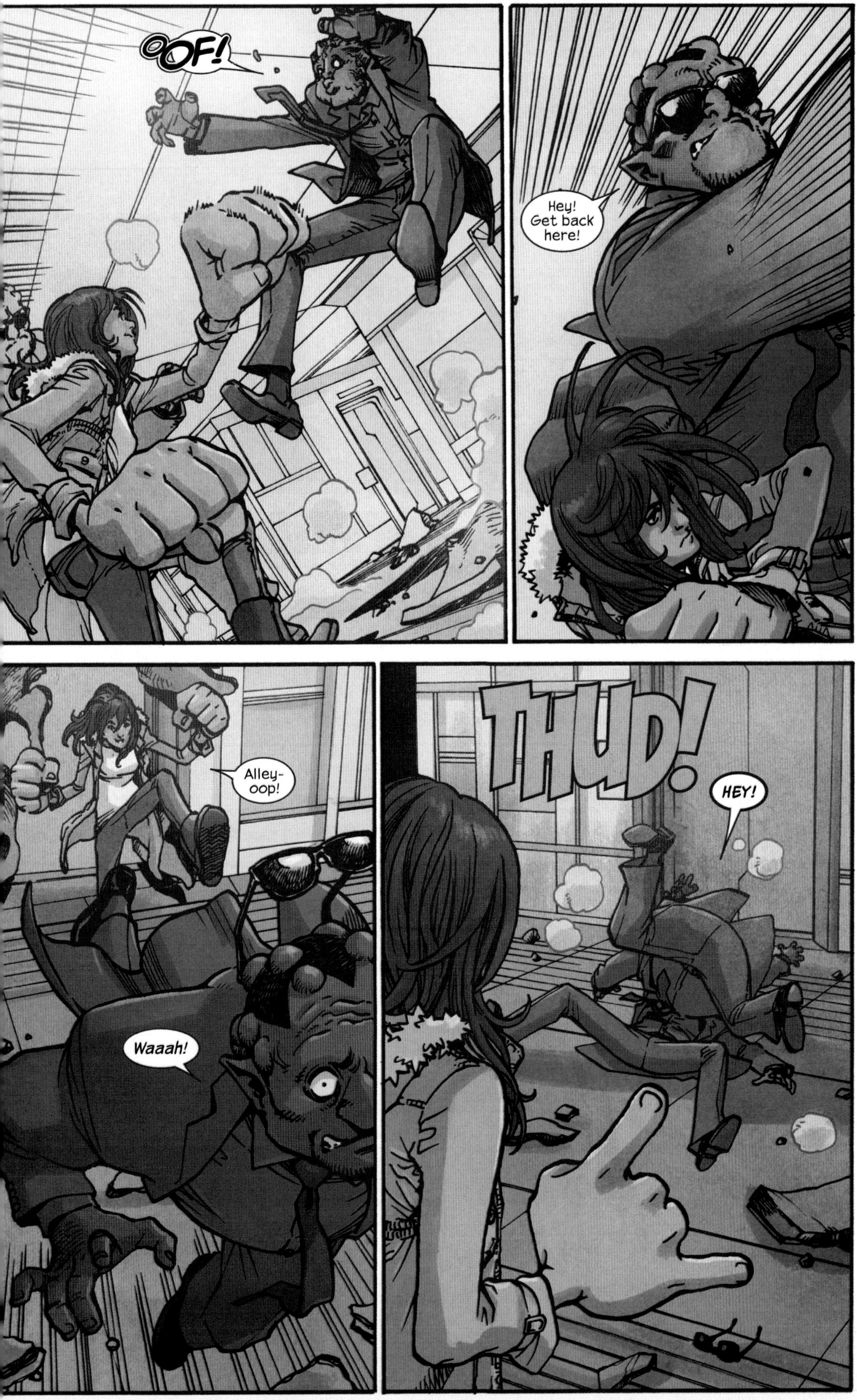
OOF!
Hey! Get back here!
Alley-oop!
Waaah!
THUD!
HEY!

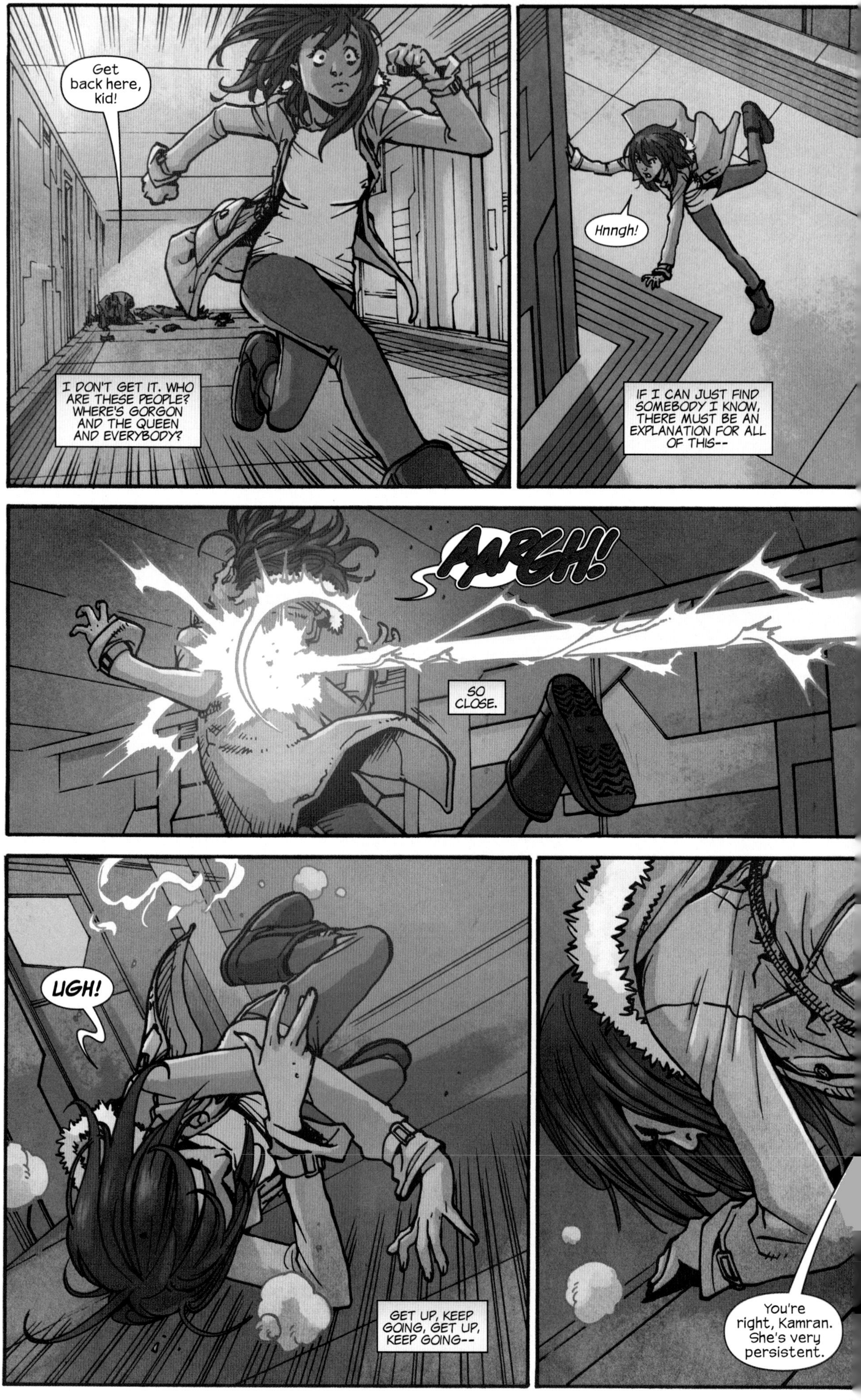
Get back here, kid!
I DON'T GET IT. WHO ARE THESE PEOPLE? WHERE'S GORGON AND THE QUEEN AND EVERYBODY?
Hnngh!
IF I CAN JUST FIND SOMEBODY I KNOW, THERE MUST BE AN EXPLANATION FOR ALL OF THIS--
AARGH!
SO CLOSE.
UGH!
GET UP, KEEP GOING, GET UP, KEEP GOING--
You're right, Kamran. She's very persistent.

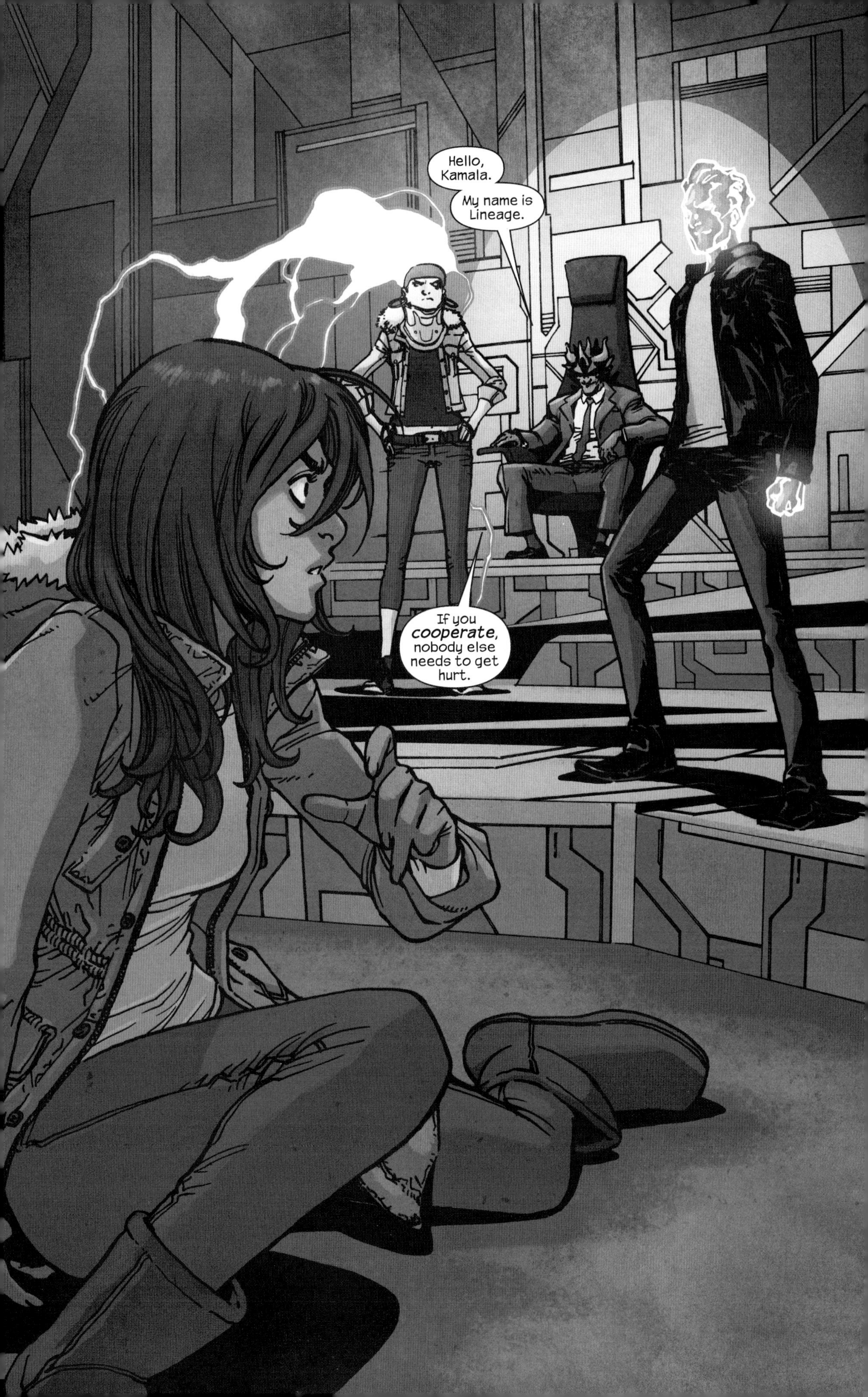
Hello, Kamala.
My name is Lineage.
If you *cooperate*, nobody else needs to get hurt.

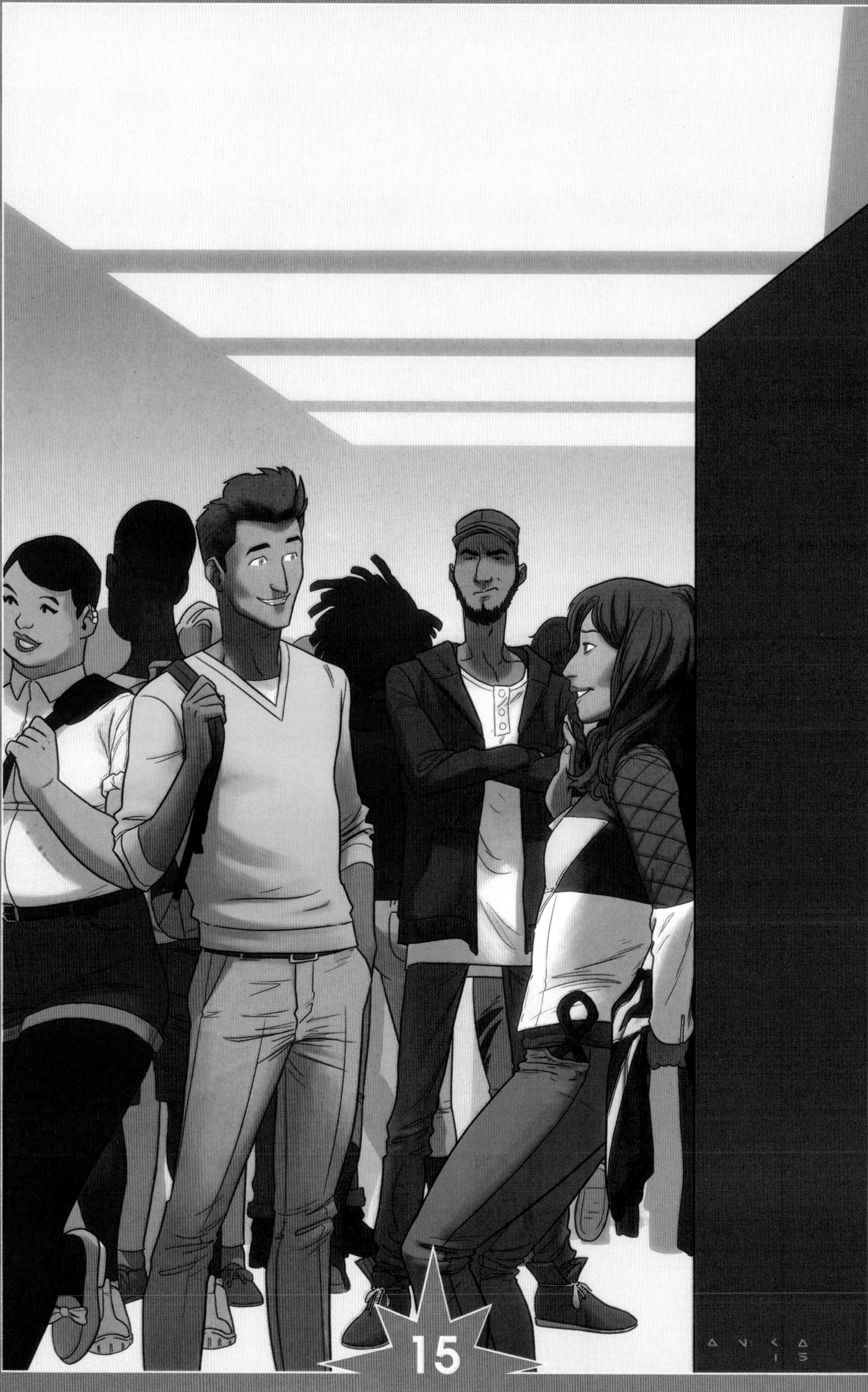
15

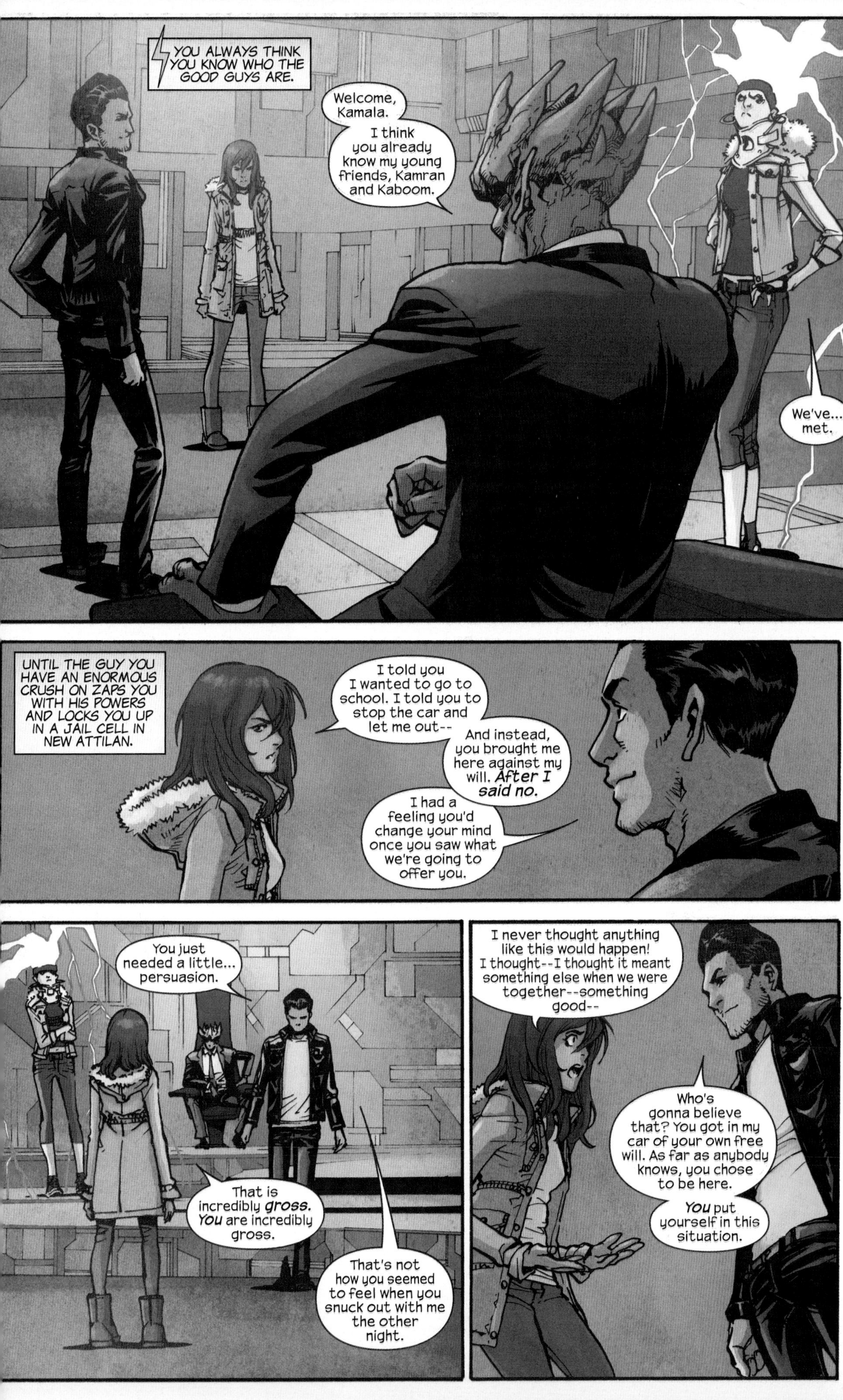
YOU ALWAYS THINK YOU KNOW WHO THE GOOD GUYS ARE.
Welcome, Kamala.
I think you already know my young friends, Kamran and Kaboom.
We've... met.
UNTIL THE GUY YOU HAVE AN ENORMOUS CRUSH ON ZAPS YOU WITH HIS POWERS AND LOCKS YOU UP IN A JAIL CELL IN NEW ATTILAN.
I told you I wanted to go to school. I told you to stop the car and let me out--
And instead, you brought me here against my will. After I said no.
I had a feeling you'd change your mind once you saw what we're going to offer you.
You just needed a little... persuasion.
That is incredibly gross. You are incredibly gross.
That's not how you seemed to feel when you snuck out with me the other night.
I never thought anything like this would happen! I thought--I thought it meant something else when we were together--something good--
Who's gonna believe that? You got in my car of your own free will. As far as anybody knows, you chose to be here.
You put yourself in this situation.

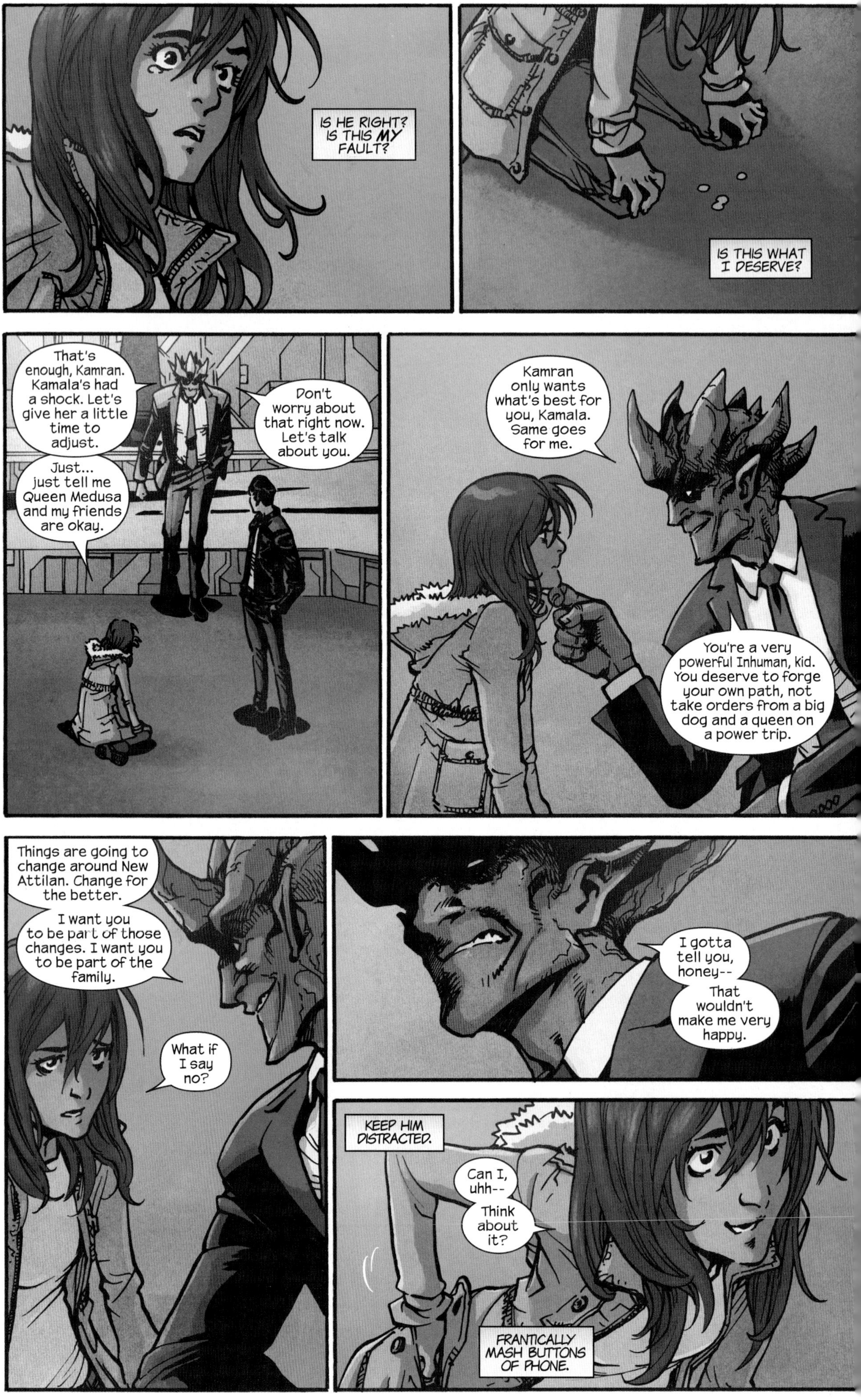
IS HE RIGHT? IS THIS MY FAULT?
IS THIS WHAT I DESERVE?
That's enough, Kamran. Kamala's had a shock. Let's give her a little time to adjust.
Just... just tell me Queen Medusa and my friends are okay.
Don't worry about that right now. Let's talk about you.
Kamran only wants what's best for you, Kamala. Same goes for me.
You're a very powerful Inhuman, kid. You deserve to forge your own path, not take orders from a big dog and a queen on a power trip.
Things are going to change around New Attilan. Change for the better.
I want you to be part of those changes. I want you to be part of the family.
What if I say no?
I gotta tell you, honey--
That wouldn't make me very happy.
KEEP HIM DISTRACTED.
Can I, uhh--
Think about it?
FRANTICALLY MASH BUTTONS OF PHONE.

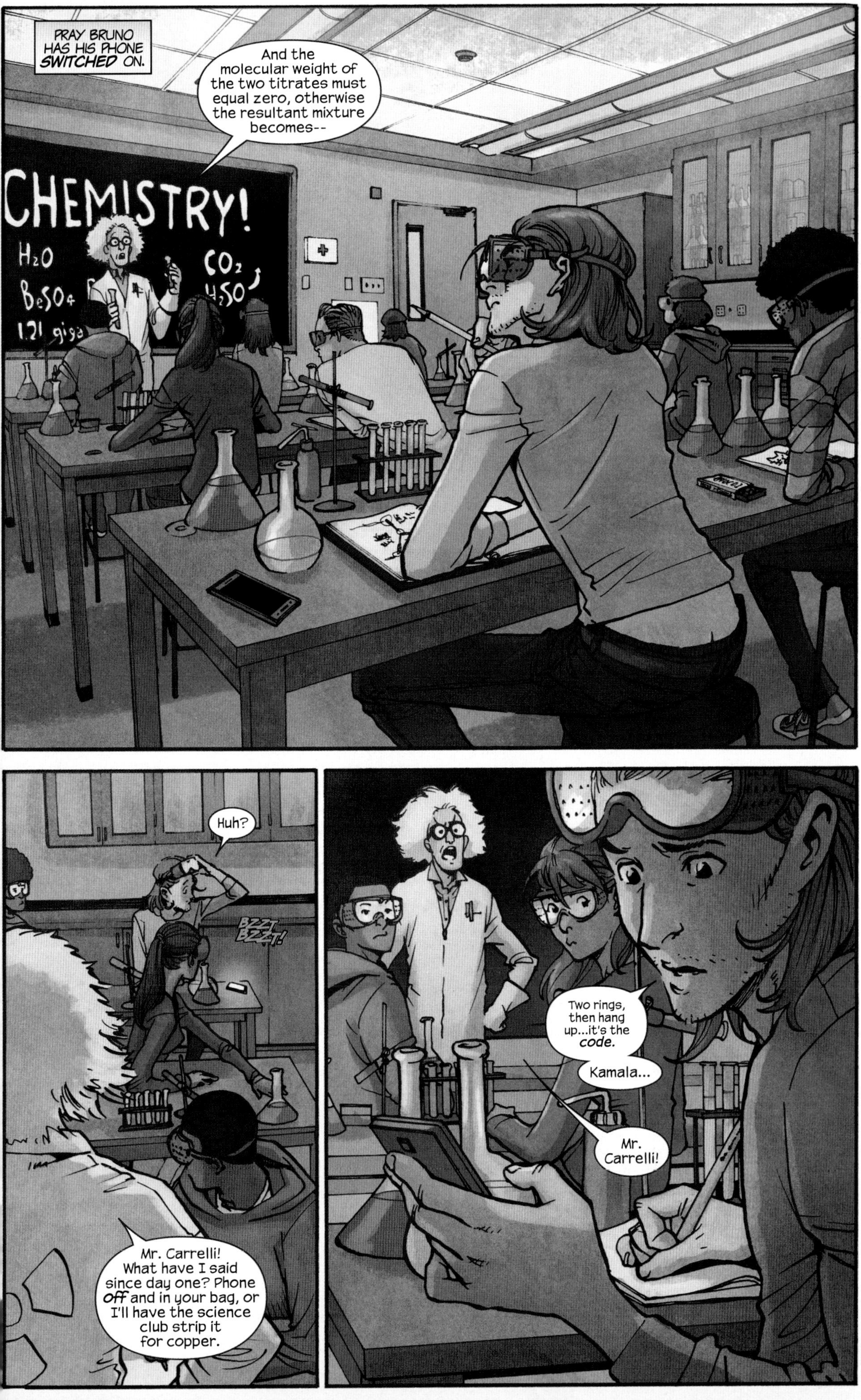
PRAY BRUNO HAS HIS PHONE *SWITCHED* ON.
And the molecular weight of the two titrates must equal zero, otherwise the resultant mixture becomes--
CHEMISTRY!
H2O
CO2
BeSO4
H2SO
1.21 giga
Huh?
BZZT BZZT!
Mr. Carrelli! What have I said since day one? Phone *off* and in your bag, or I'll have the science club strip it for copper.
Two rings, then hang up...it's the *code.*
Kamala...
Mr. Carrelli!

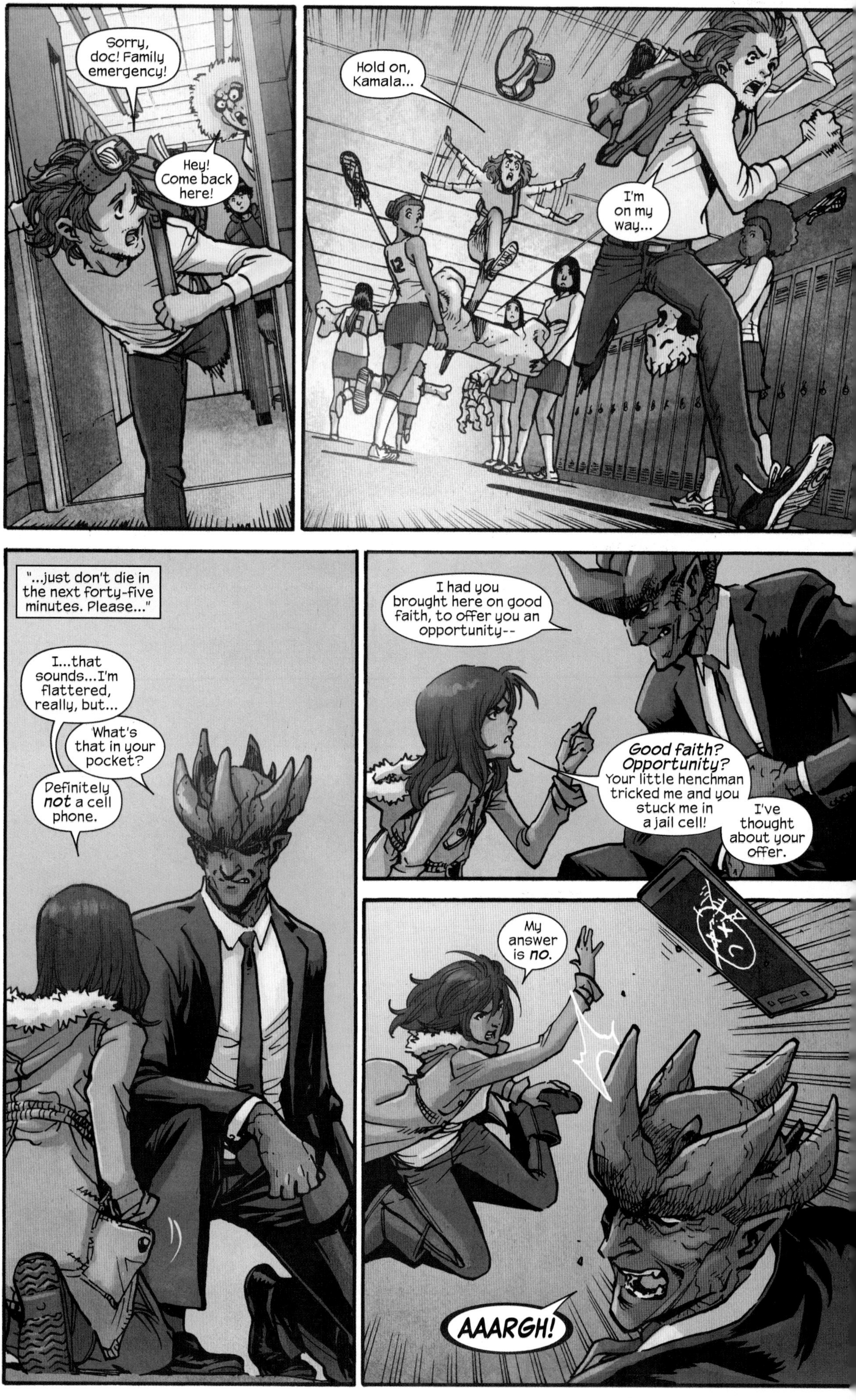
Sorry, doc! Family emergency!
Hey! Come back here!
Hold on, Kamala...
I'm on my way...
"...just don't die in the next forty-five minutes. Please..."
I...that sounds...I'm flattered, really, but...
What's that in your pocket?
Definitely *not* a cell phone.
I had you brought here on good faith, to offer you an opportunity--
Good faith? Opportunity? Your little henchman tricked me and you stuck me in a jail cell!
I've thought about your offer.
My answer is *no*.
AAARGH!

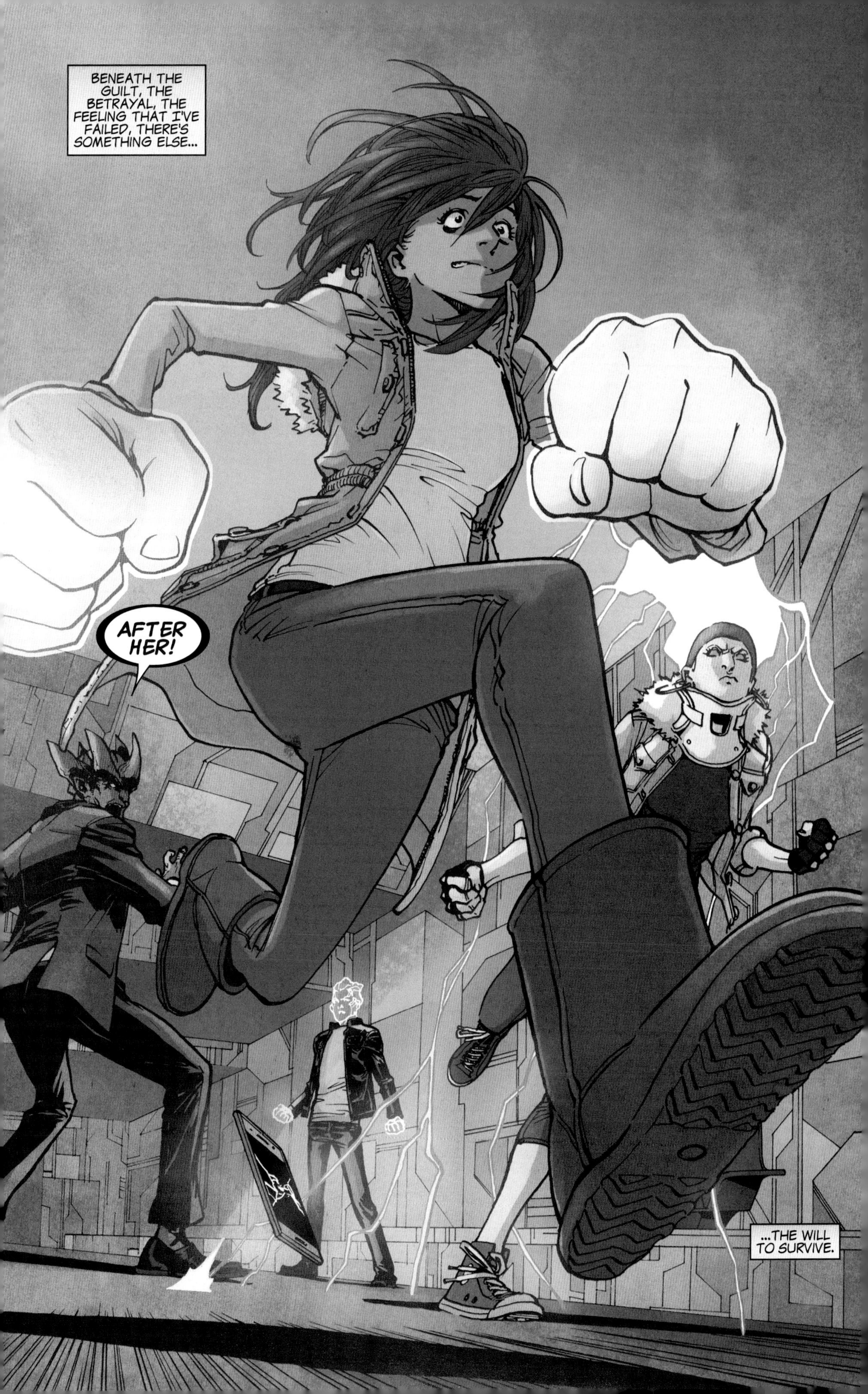
BENEATH THE GUILT, THE BETRAYAL, THE FEELING THAT I'VE FAILED, THERE'S SOMETHING ELSE...
AFTER HER!
...THE WILL TO SURVIVE.

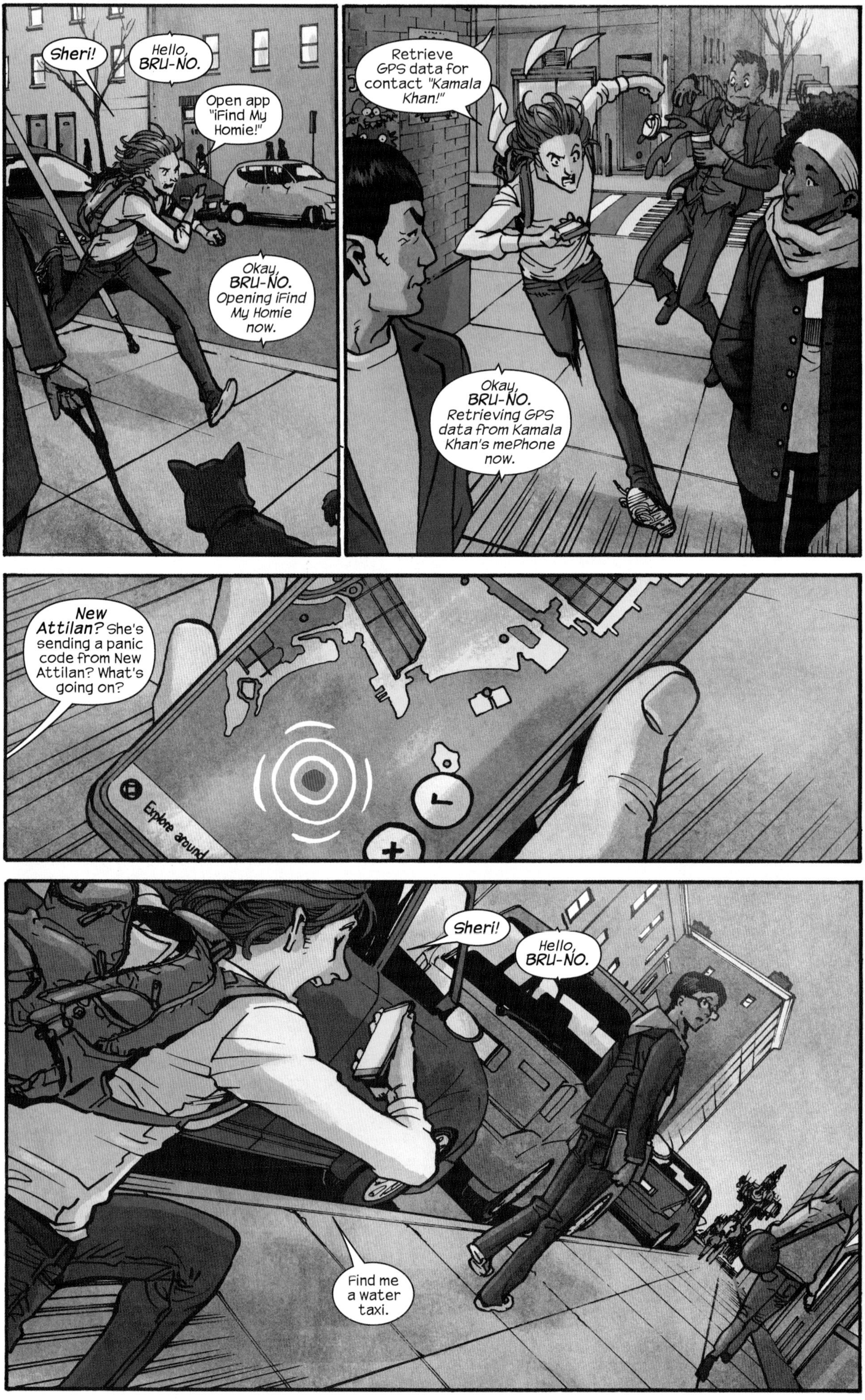
Sheri!
Hello, BRU-NO.
Open app "iFind My Homie!"
Okay, BRU-NO. Opening iFind My Homie now.
Retrieve GPS data for contact "Kamala Khan!"
Okay, BRU-NO. Retrieving GPS data from Kamala Khan's mePhone now.
New Attilan? She's sending a panic code from New Attilan? What's going on?
Explore around
Sheri!
Hello, BRU-NO.
Find me a water taxi.

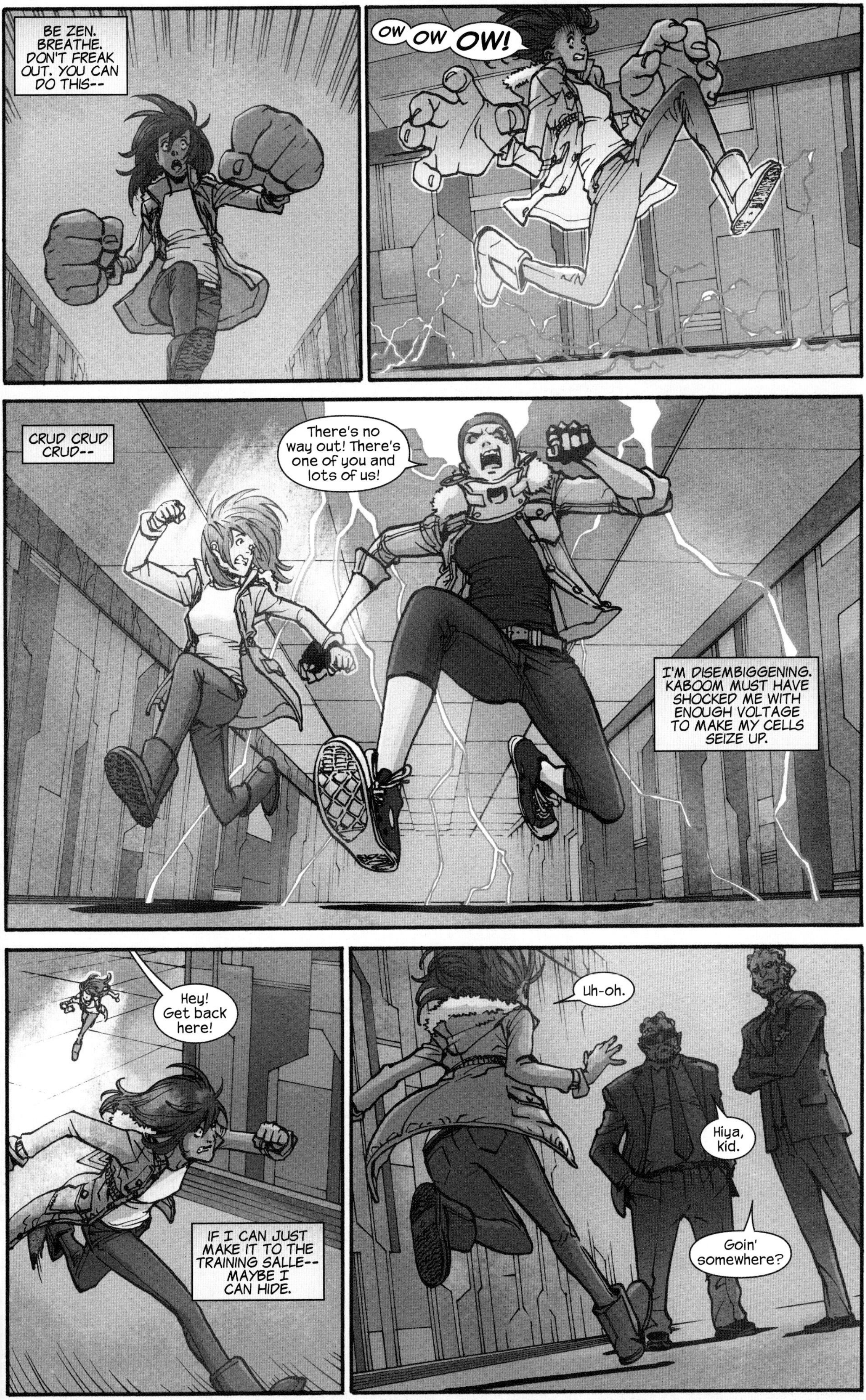

BE ZEN. BREATHE. DON'T FREAK OUT. YOU CAN DO THIS--
OW OW OW!
CRUD CRUD CRUD--
There's no way out! There's one of you and lots of us!
I'M DISEMBIGGENING. KABOOM MUST HAVE SHOCKED ME WITH ENOUGH VOLTAGE TO MAKE MY CELLS SEIZE UP.
Hey! Get back here!
IF I CAN JUST MAKE IT TO THE TRAINING SALLE-- MAYBE I CAN HIDE.
Uh-oh.
Hiya, kid.
Goin' somewhere?

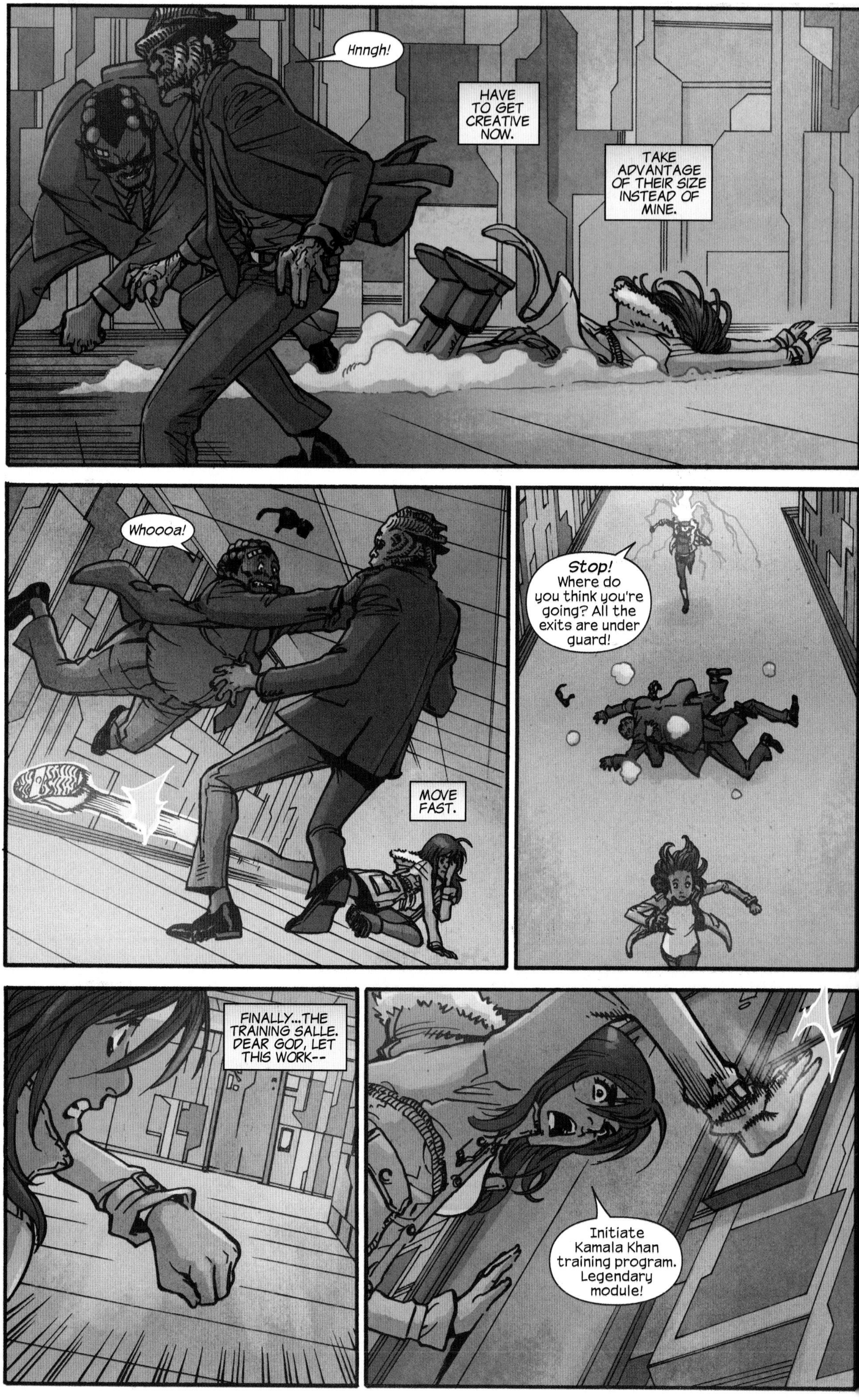
Hnngh!
HAVE TO GET CREATIVE NOW.
TAKE ADVANTAGE OF THEIR SIZE INSTEAD OF MINE.
Whoooa!
MOVE FAST.
Stop! Where do you think you're going? All the exits are under guard!
FINALLY...THE TRAINING SALLE. DEAR GOD, LET THIS WORK--
Initiate Kamala Khan training program. Legendary module!

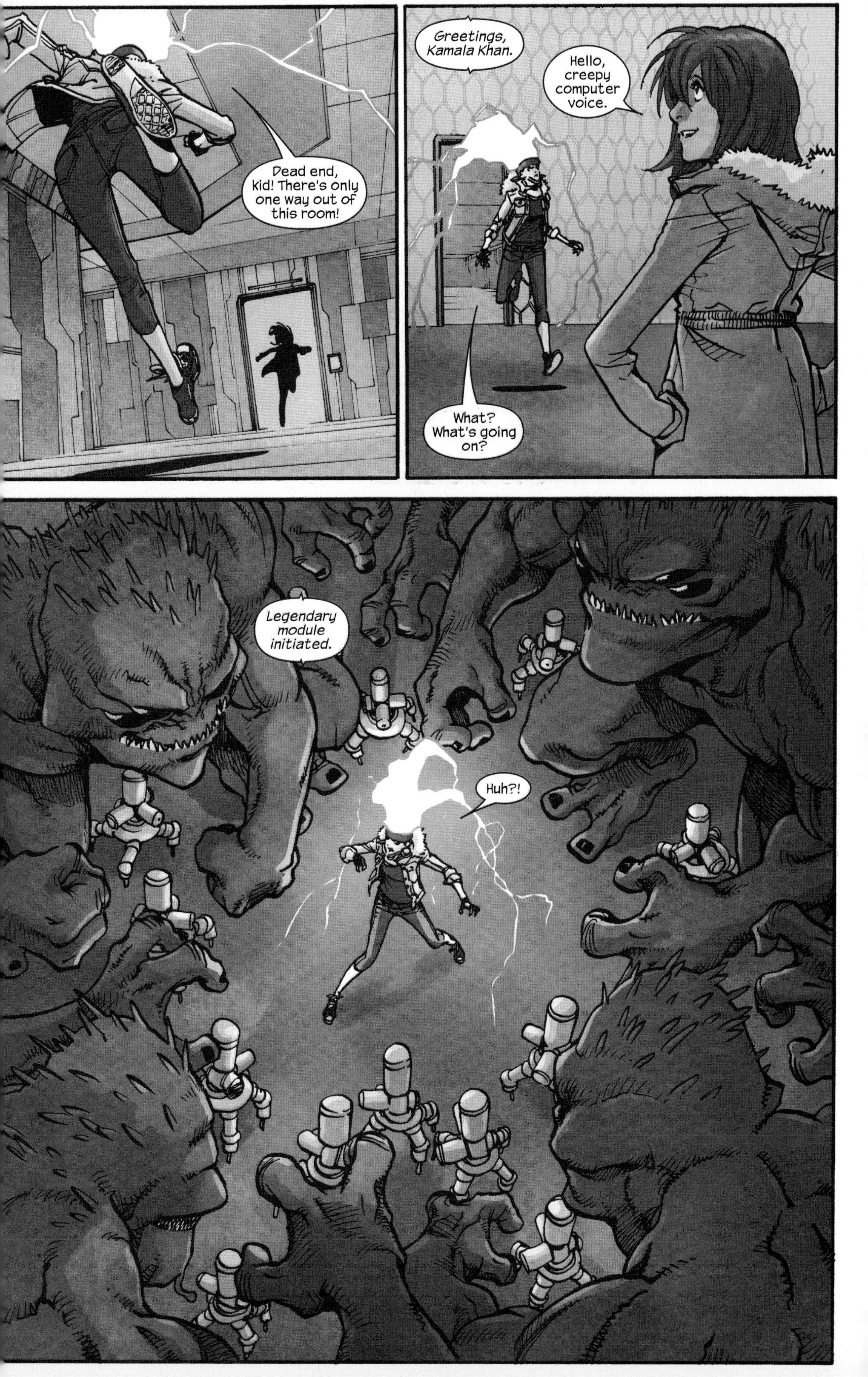
Dead end, kid! There's only one way out of this room!
Greetings, Kamala Khan.
Hello, creepy computer voice.
What? What's going on?
Legendary module initiated.
Huh?!

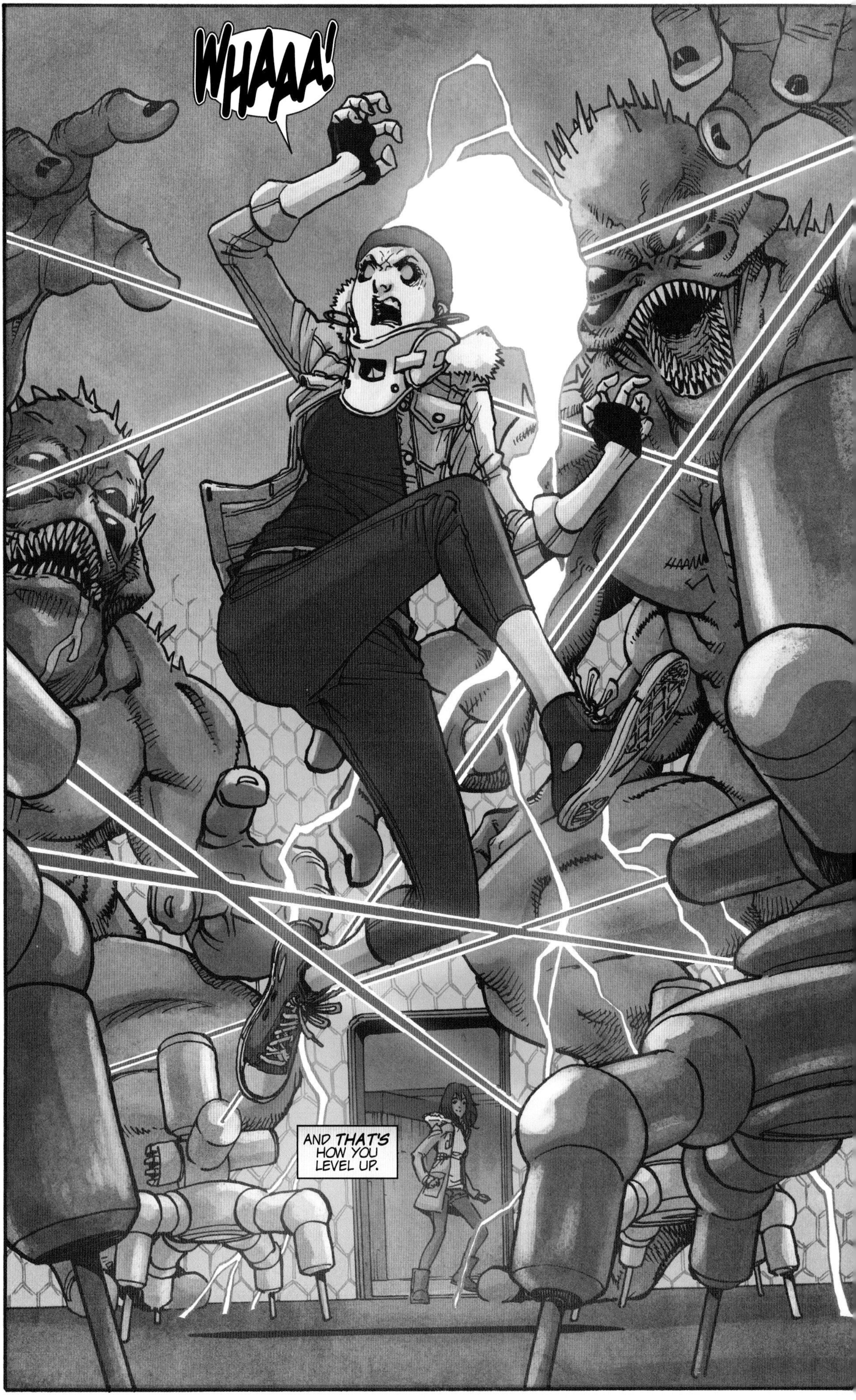
WHAAA!
AND THAT'S HOW YOU LEVEL UP.

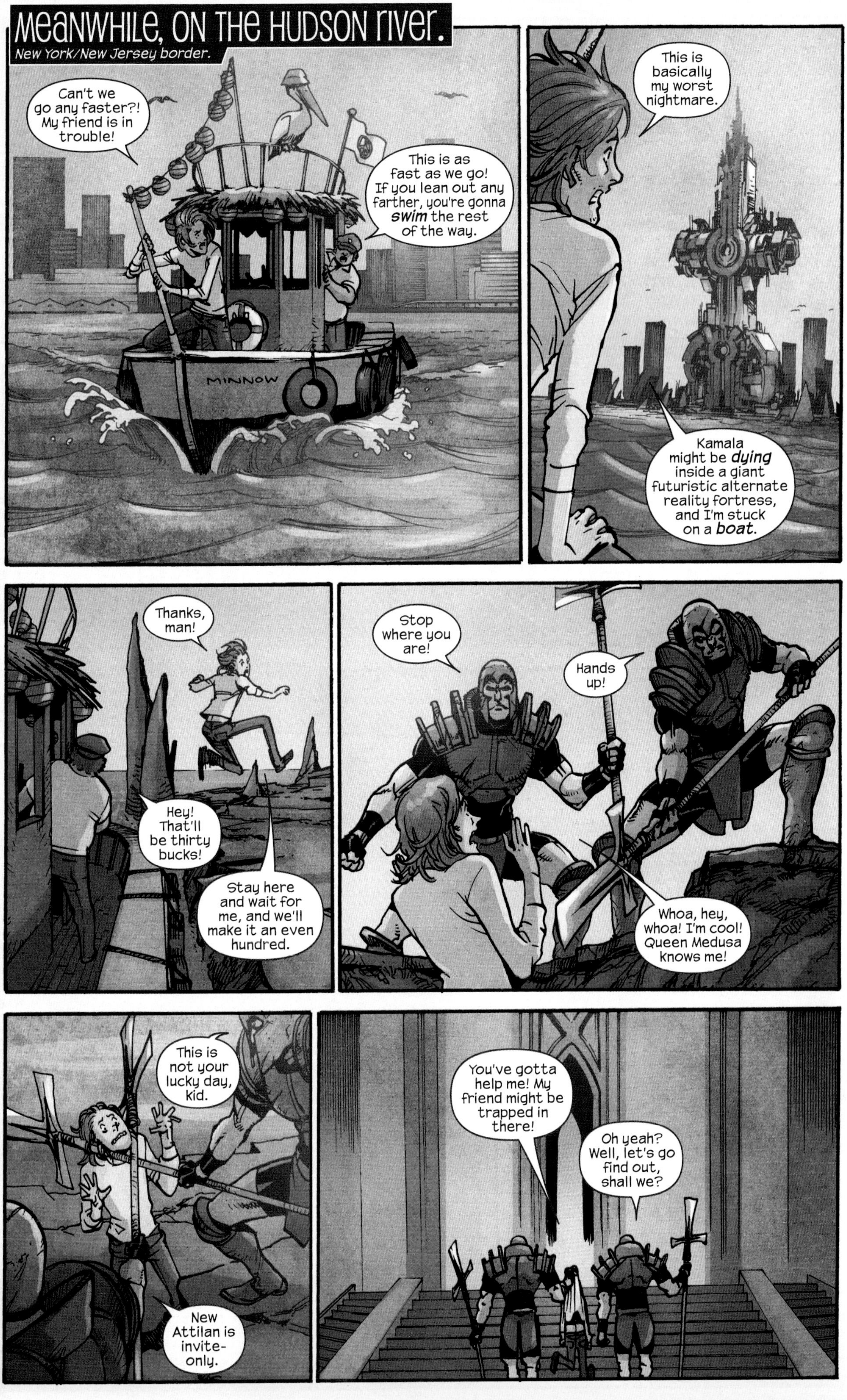
MEANWHILE, ON THE HUDSON RIVER.
New York/New Jersey border.
Can't we go any faster?! My friend is in trouble!
This is as fast as we go! If you lean out any farther, you're gonna *swim* the rest of the way.
MINNOW
This is basically my worst nightmare.
Kamala might be *dying* inside a giant futuristic alternate reality fortress, and I'm stuck on a *boat*.
Thanks, man!
Hey! That'll be thirty bucks!
Stay here and wait for me, and we'll make it an even hundred.
Stop where you are!
Hands up!
Whoa, hey, whoa! I'm cool! Queen Medusa knows me!
This is not your lucky day, kid.
New Attilan is invite-only.
You've gotta help me! My friend might be trapped in there!
Oh yeah? Well, let's go find out, shall we?

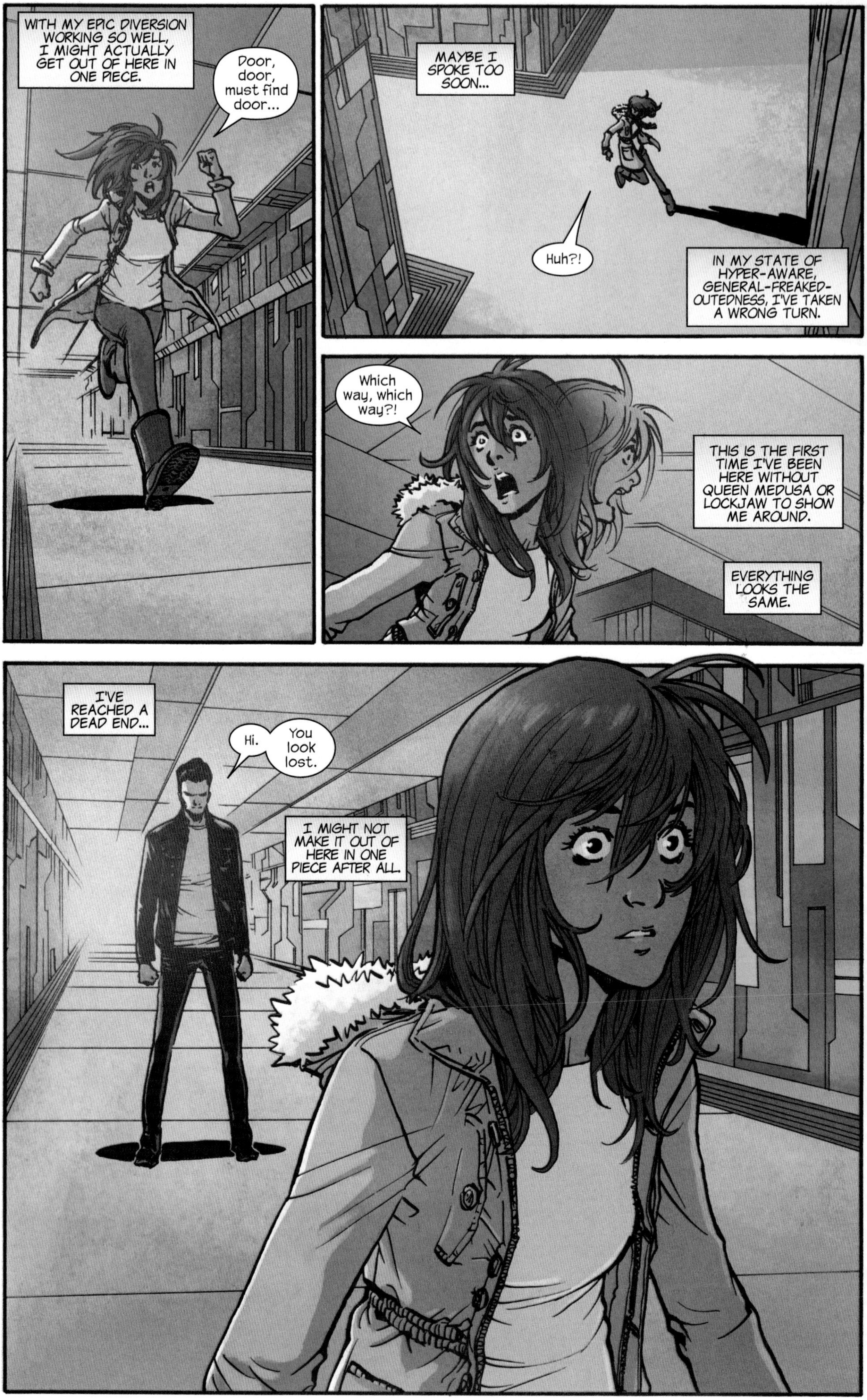
WITH MY EPIC DIVERSION WORKING SO WELL, I MIGHT ACTUALLY GET OUT OF HERE IN ONE PIECE.
Door, door, must find door...
MAYBE I SPOKE TOO SOON...
Huh?!
IN MY STATE OF HYPER-AWARE, GENERAL-FREAKED-OUTEDNESS, I'VE TAKEN A WRONG TURN.
Which way, which way?!
THIS IS THE FIRST TIME I'VE BEEN HERE WITHOUT QUEEN MEDUSA OR LOCKJAW TO SHOW ME AROUND.
EVERYTHING LOOKS THE SAME.
I'VE REACHED A DEAD END...
Hi.
You look lost.
I MIGHT NOT MAKE IT OUT OF HERE IN ONE PIECE AFTER ALL.

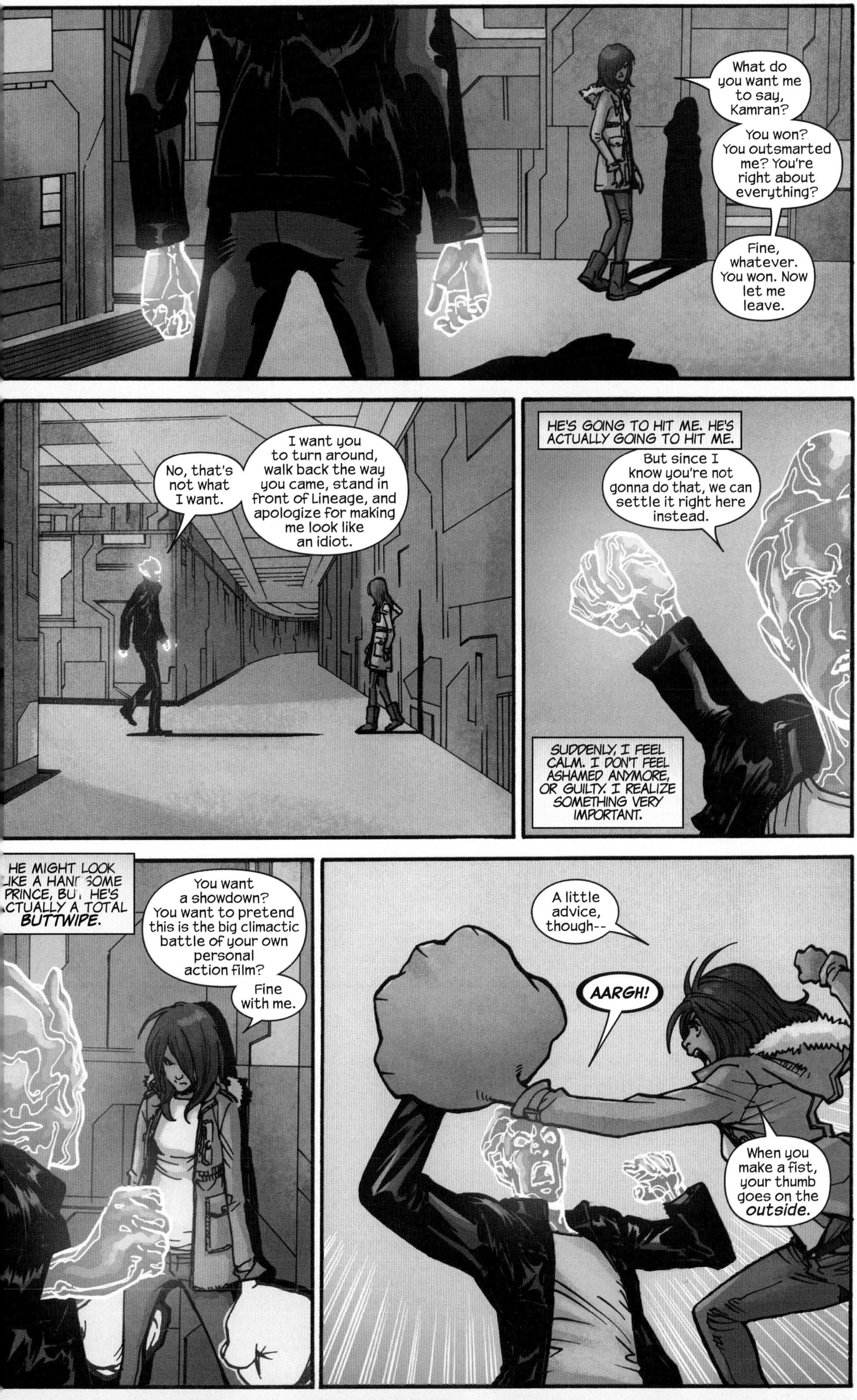
What do you want me to say, Kamran?
You won? You outsmarted me? You're right about everything?
Fine, whatever. You won. Now let me leave.
No, that's not what I want.
I want you to turn around, walk back the way you came, stand in front of Lineage, and apologize for making me look like an idiot.
HE'S GOING TO HIT ME. HE'S ACTUALLY GOING TO HIT ME.
But since I know you're not gonna do that, we can settle it right here instead.
SUDDENLY, I FEEL CALM. I DON'T FEEL ASHAMED ANYMORE, OR GUILTY. I REALIZE SOMETHING VERY IMPORTANT.
HE MIGHT LOOK LIKE A HANDSOME PRINCE, BUT HE'S ACTUALLY A TOTAL BUTTWIPE.
You want a showdown? You want to pretend this is the big climactic battle of your own personal action film?
Fine with me.
A little advice, though--
AARGH!
When you make a fist, your thumb goes on the outside.

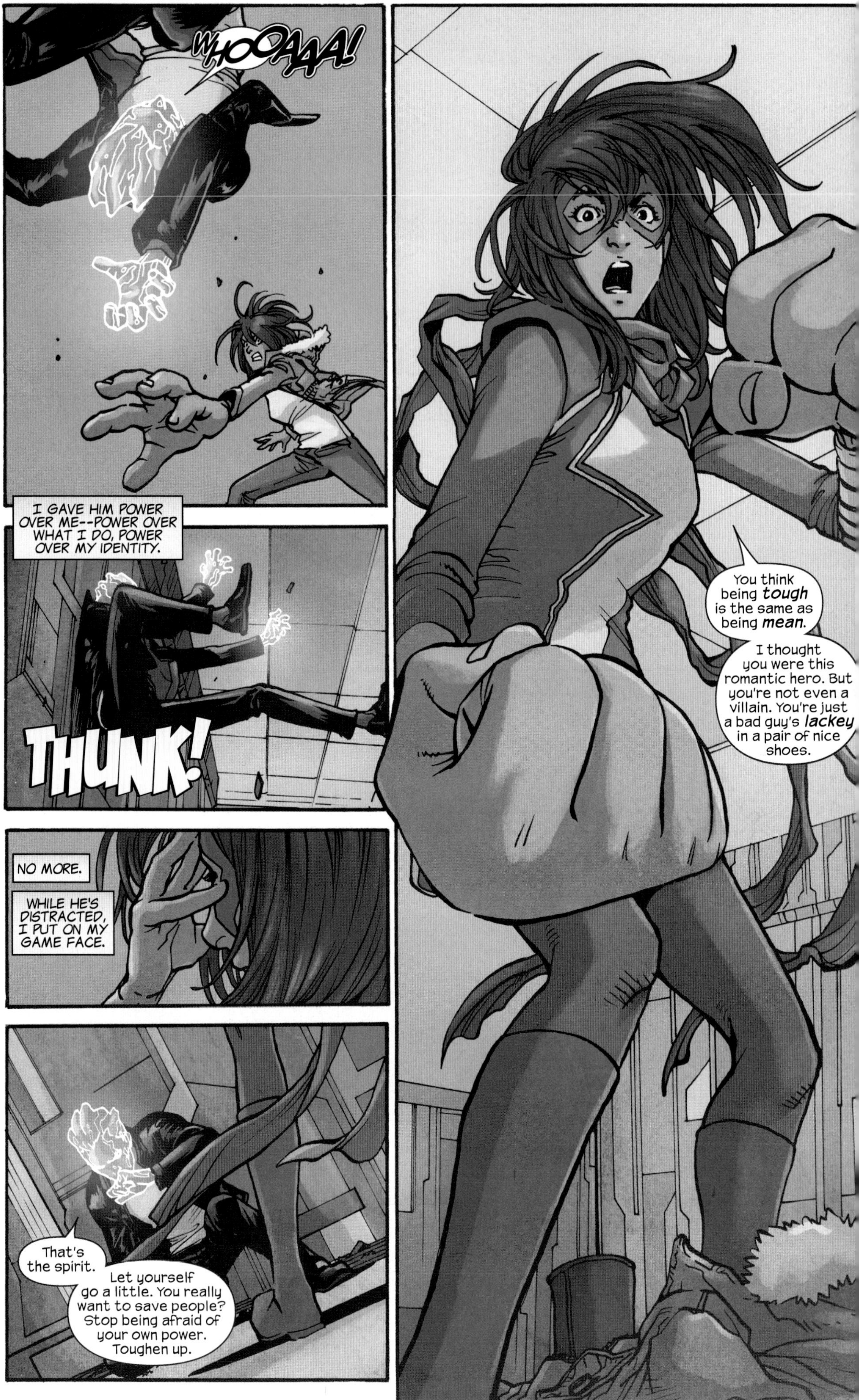
WHOOAAA!
I GAVE HIM POWER OVER ME--POWER OVER WHAT I DO, POWER OVER MY IDENTITY.
THUNK!
NO MORE.
WHILE HE'S DISTRACTED, I PUT ON MY GAME FACE.
That's the spirit.
Let yourself go a little. You really want to save people? Stop being afraid of your own power. Toughen up.
You think being tough is the same as being mean.
I thought you were this romantic hero. But you're not even a villain. You're just a bad guy's lackey in a pair of nice shoes.

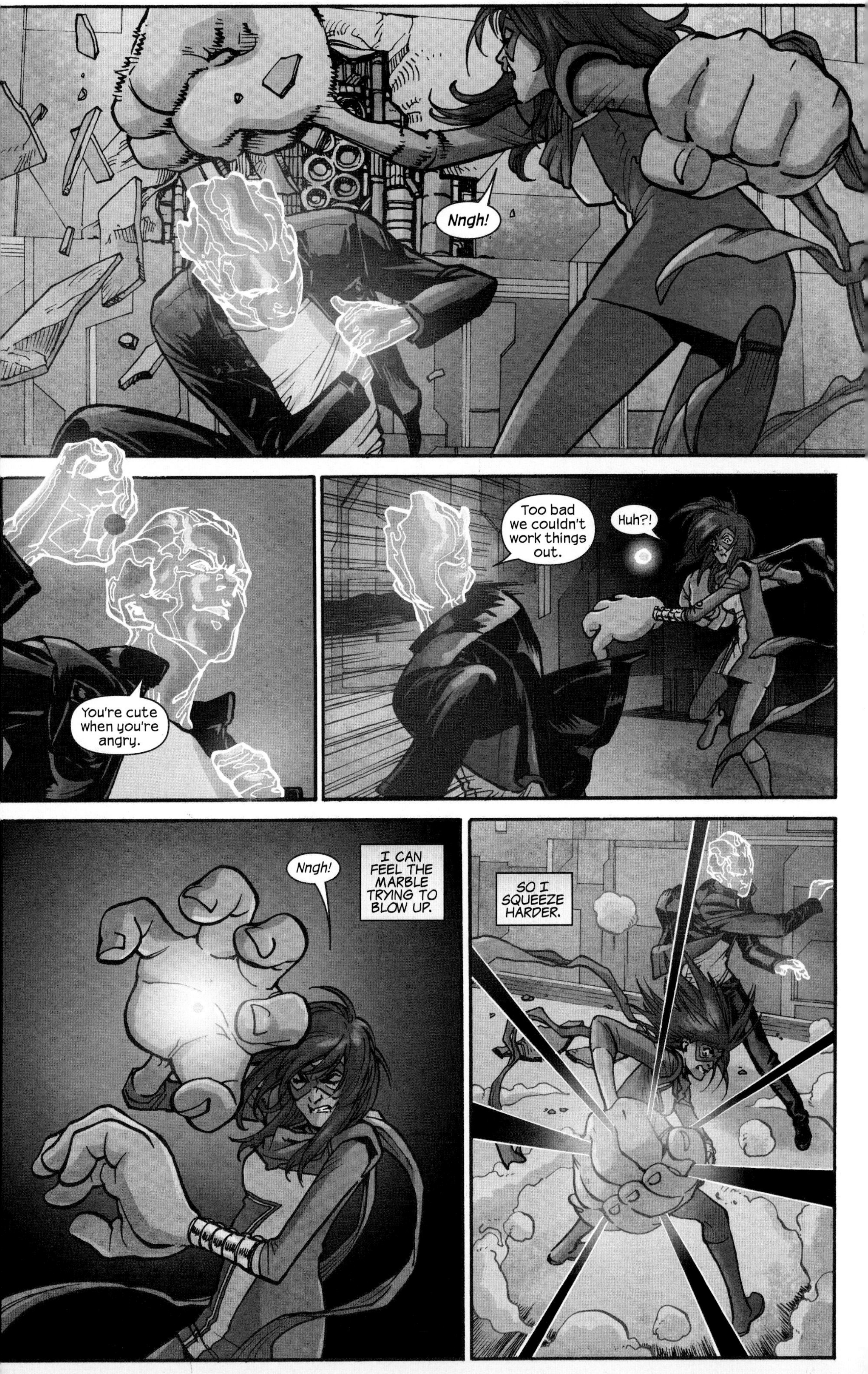
Nngh!
You're cute when you're angry.
Too bad we couldn't work things out.
Huh?!
Nngh!
I CAN FEEL THE MARBLE TRYING TO BLOW UP.
SO I SQUEEZE HARDER.

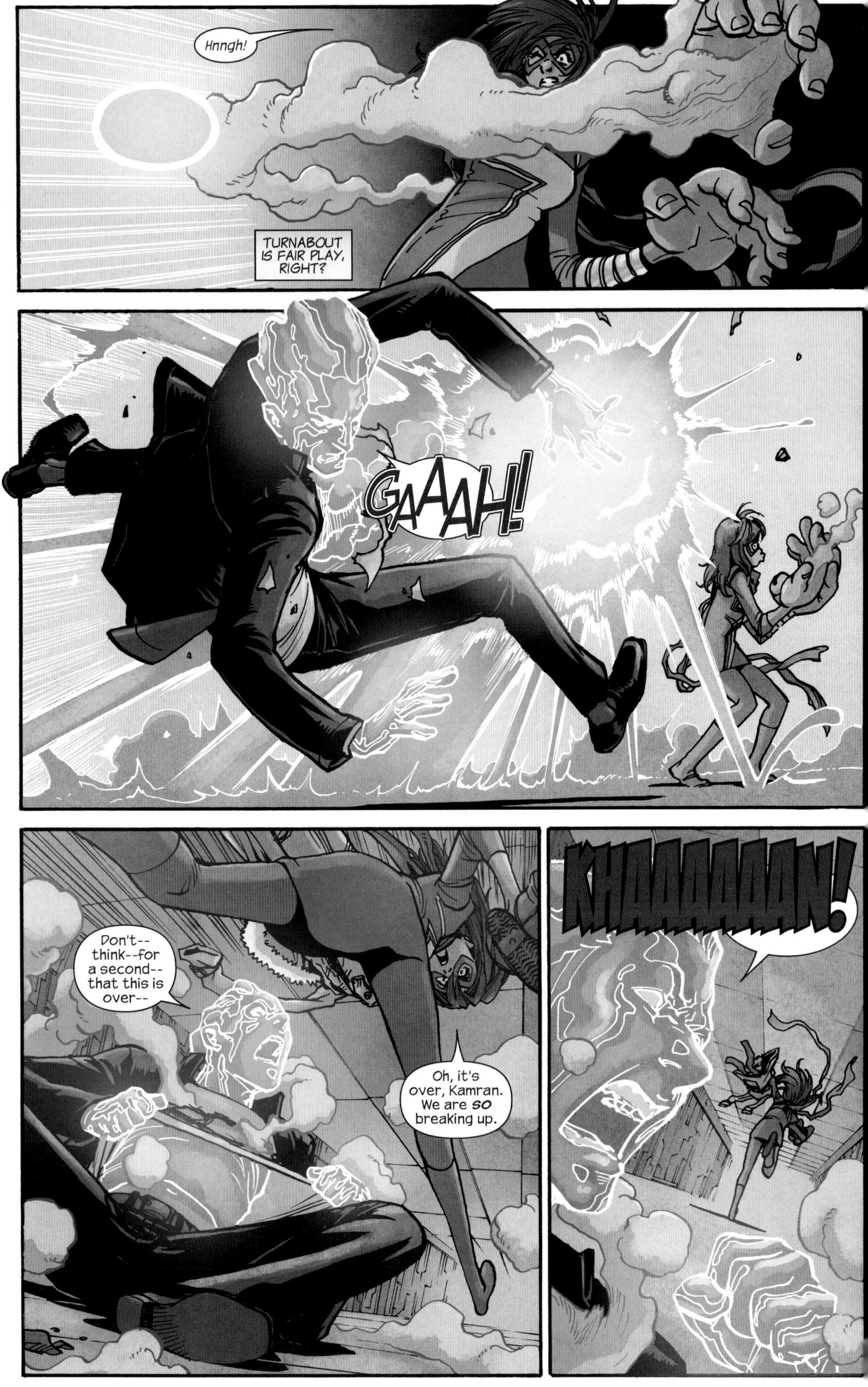
Hnngh!
TURNABOUT IS FAIR PLAY, RIGHT?
GAAAH!
Don't--think--for a second--that this is over--
Oh, it's over, Kamran. We are *SO* breaking up.
KHAAAAAAN!

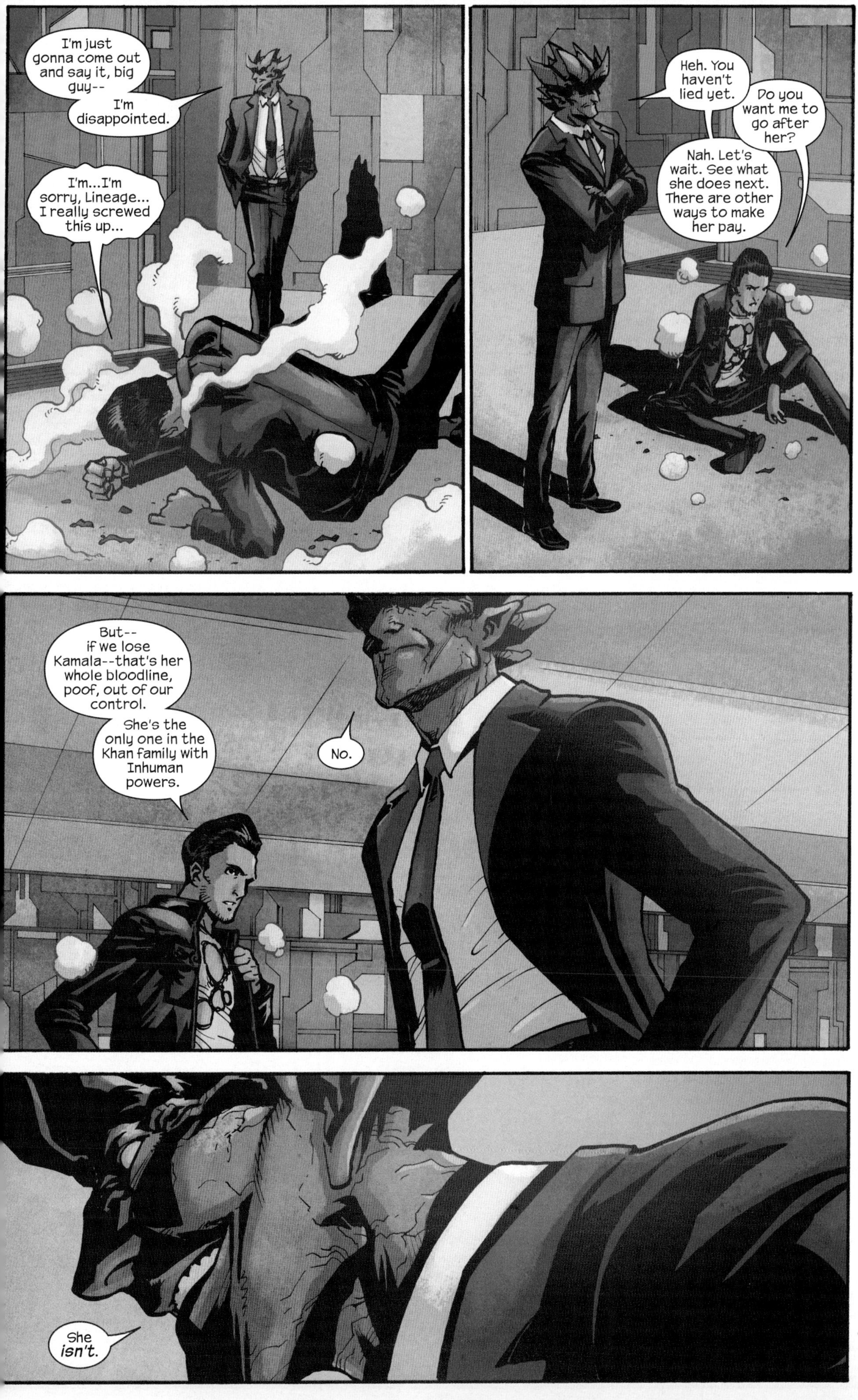
I'm just gonna come out and say it, big guy--
I'm disappointed.
I'm...I'm sorry, Lineage... I really screwed this up...
Heh. You haven't lied yet.
Do you want me to go after her?
Nah. Let's wait. See what she does next. There are other ways to make her pay.
But-- if we lose Kamala--that's her whole bloodline, poof, out of our control.
She's the only one in the Khan family with Inhuman powers.
No.
She *isn't*.

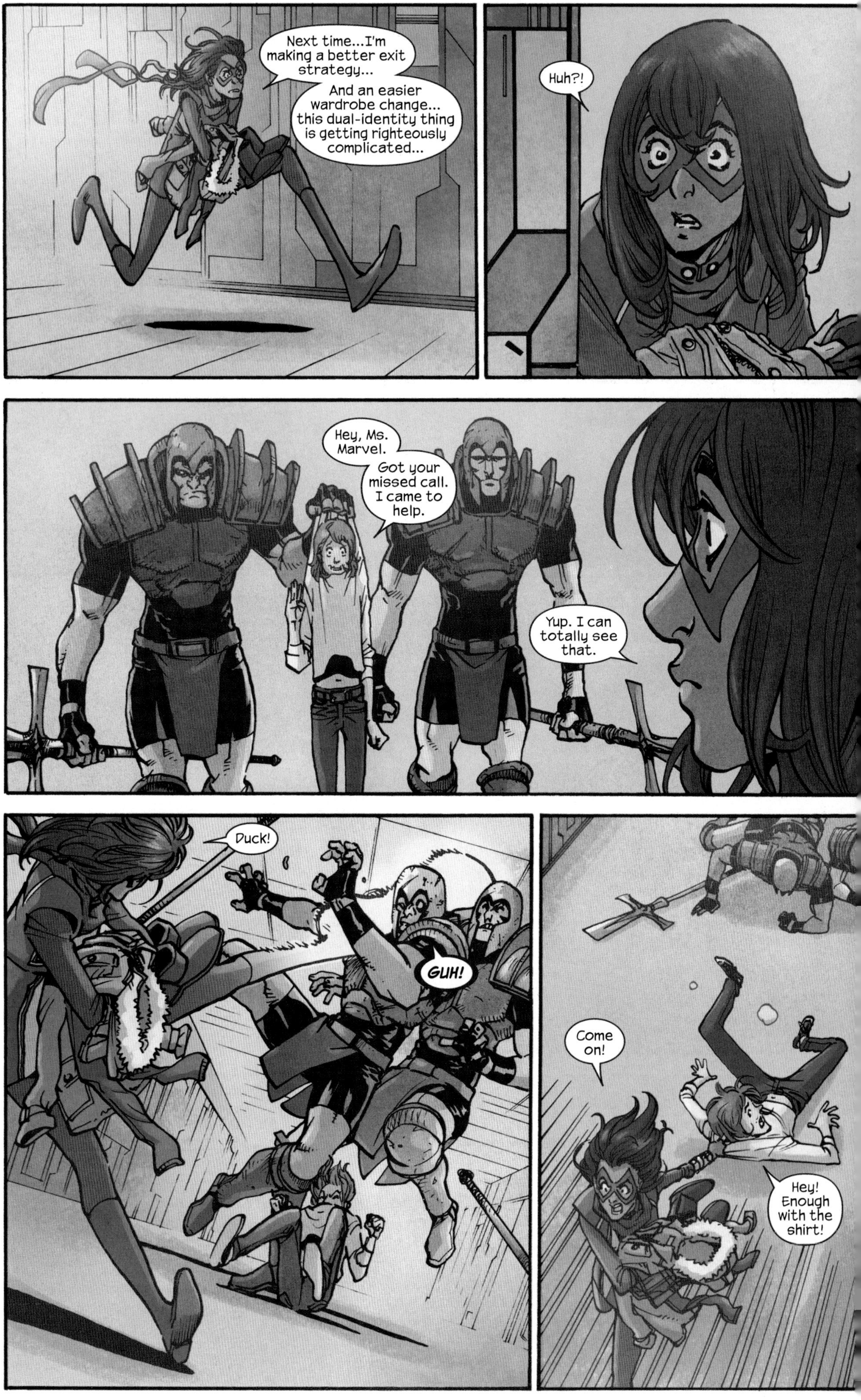
Next time...I'm making a better exit strategy...
And an easier wardrobe change... this dual-identity thing is getting righteously complicated...
Huh?!
Hey, Ms. Marvel.
Got your missed call. I came to help.
Yup. I can totally see that.
Duck!
GUH!
Come on!
Hey! Enough with the shirt!

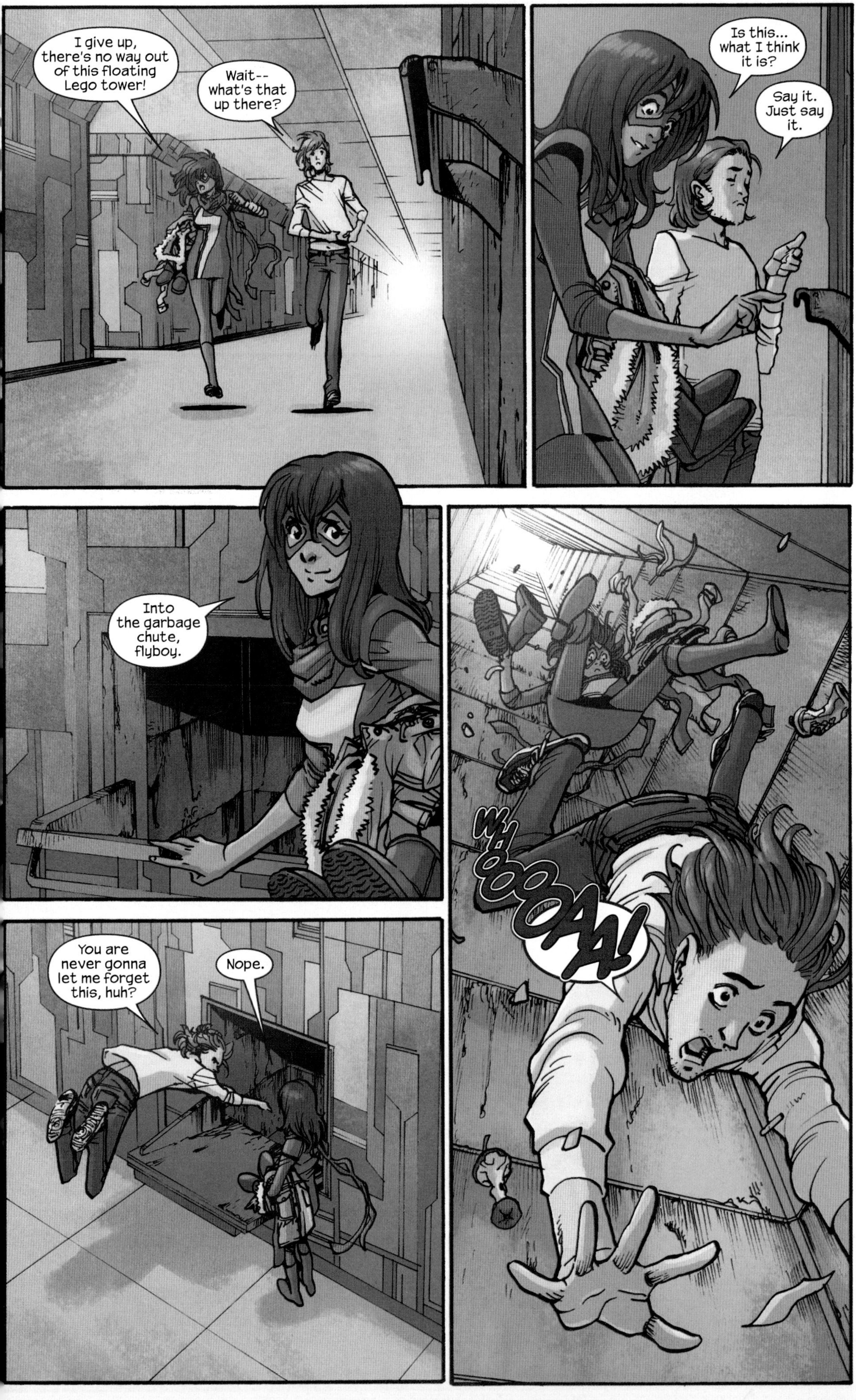
I give up, there's no way out of this floating Lego tower!
Wait-- what's that up there?
Is this... what I think it is?
Say it. Just say it.
Into the garbage chute, flyboy.
WHOOOOAA!
You are never gonna let me forget this, huh?
Nope.

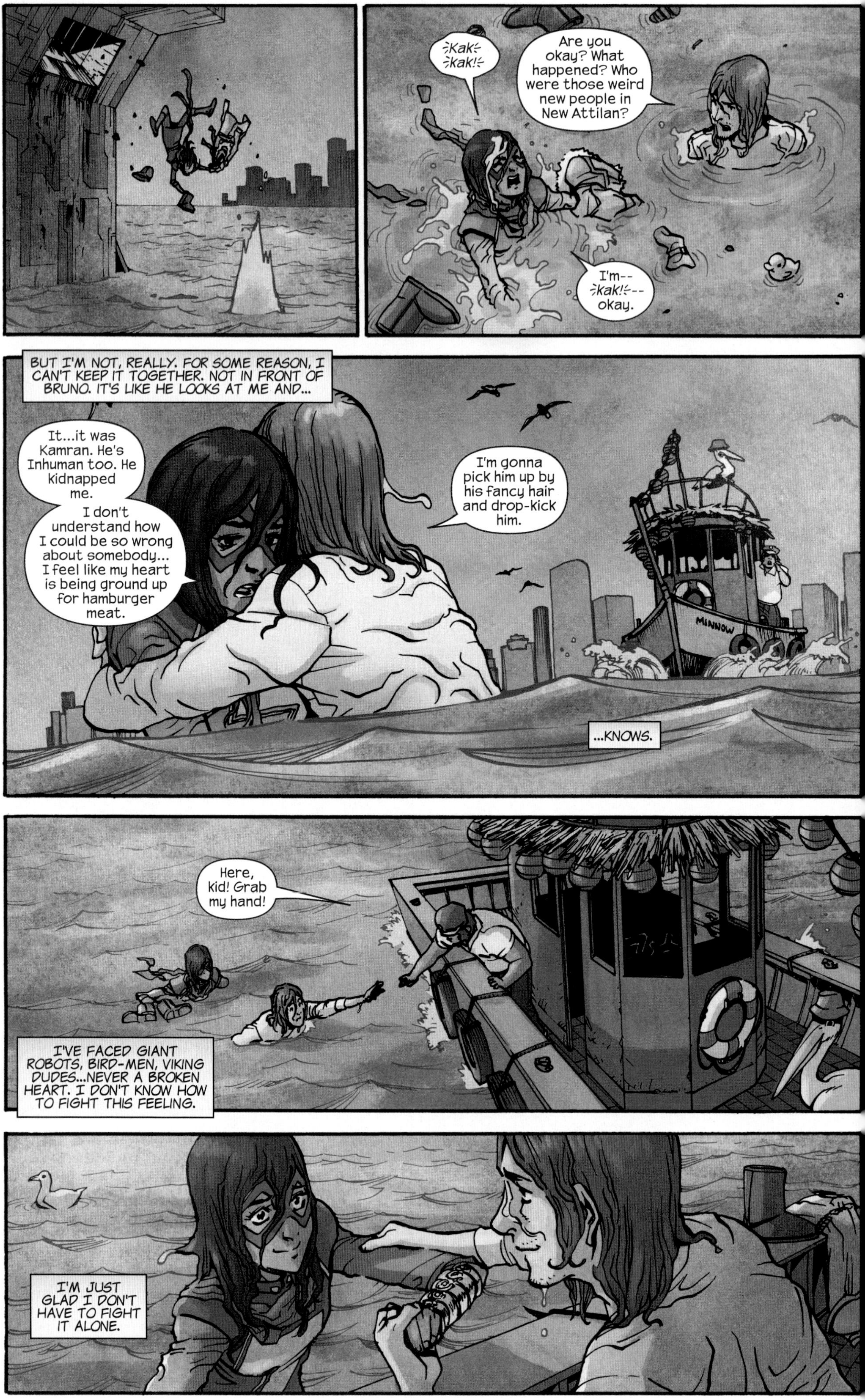

-Kak-
-kak!-
Are you okay? What happened? Who were those weird new people in New Attilan?
I'm-- -kak!- -- okay.
BUT I'M NOT, REALLY. FOR SOME REASON, I CAN'T KEEP IT TOGETHER. NOT IN FRONT OF BRUNO. IT'S LIKE HE LOOKS AT ME AND...
It...it was Kamran. He's Inhuman too. He kidnapped me.
I don't understand how I could be so wrong about somebody... I feel like my heart is being ground up for hamburger meat.
I'm gonna pick him up by his fancy hair and drop-kick him.
MINNOW
...KNOWS.
Here, kid! Grab my hand!
I'VE FACED GIANT ROBOTS, BIRD-MEN, VIKING DUDES...NEVER A BROKEN HEART. I DON'T KNOW HOW TO FIGHT THIS FEELING.
I'M JUST GLAD I DON'T HAVE TO FIGHT IT ALONE.

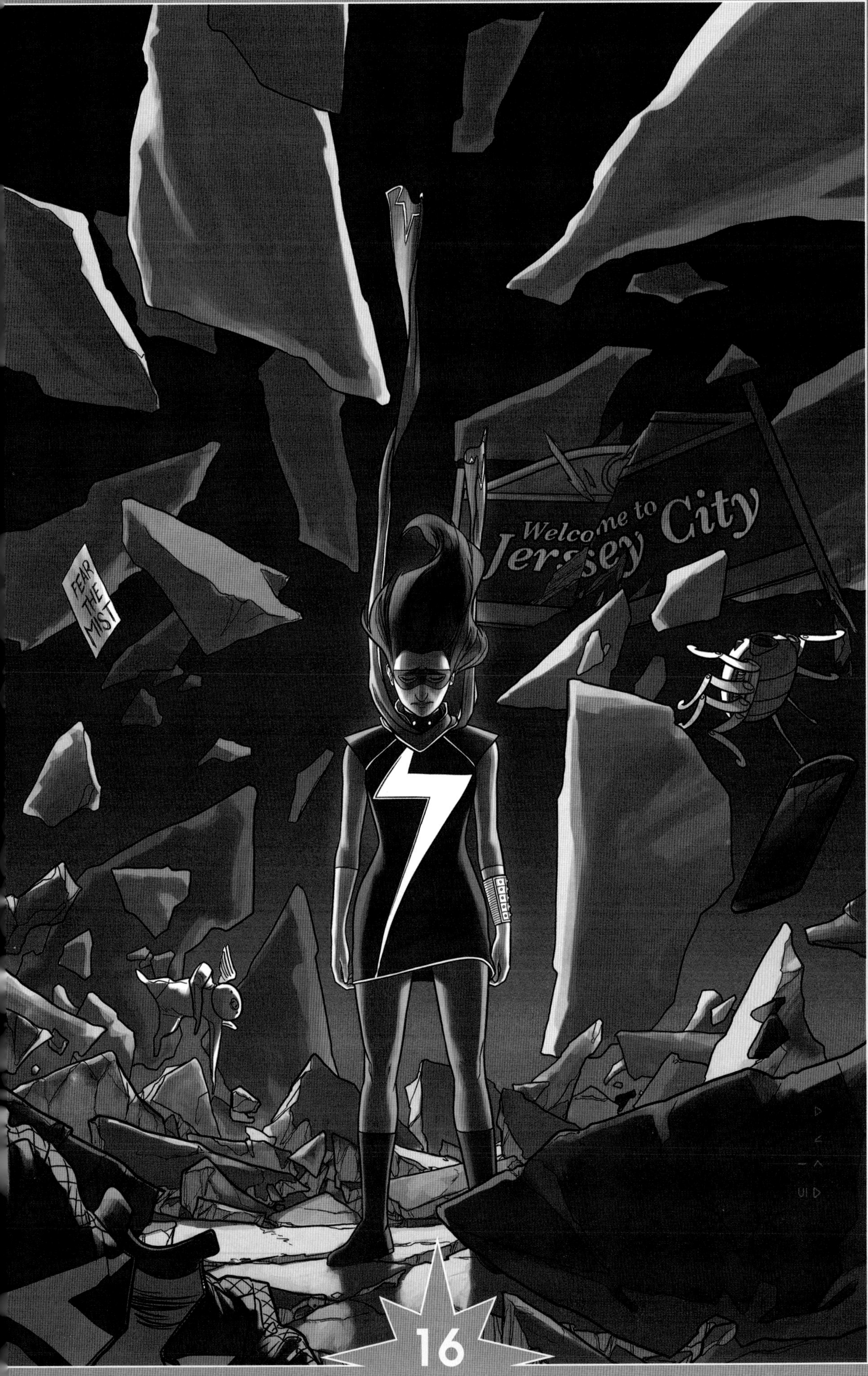
Welcome to Jersey City
FEAR THE MIST
16

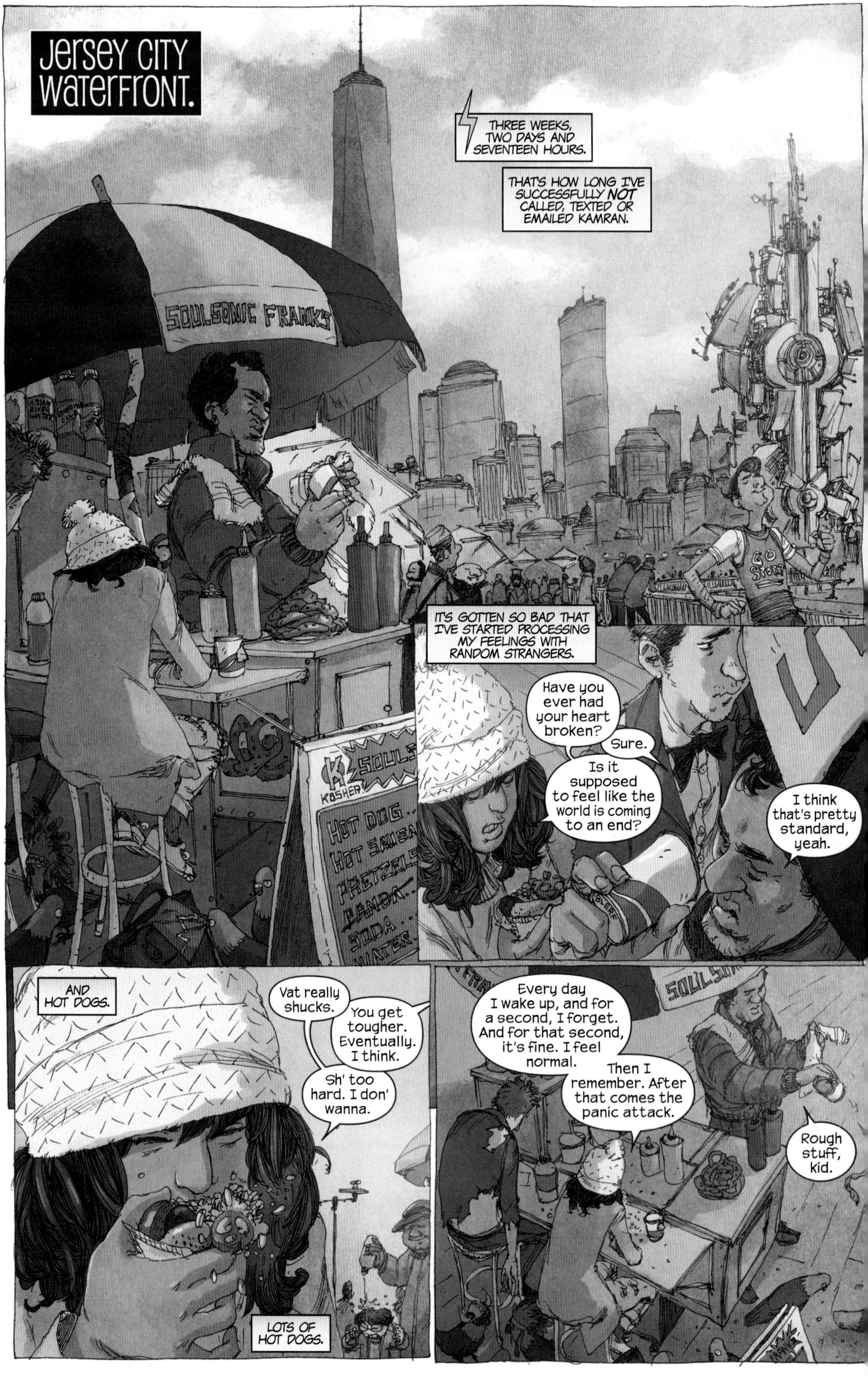
Jersey City Waterfront.
THREE WEEKS, TWO DAYS AND SEVENTEEN HOURS.
THAT'S HOW LONG I'VE SUCCESSFULLY NOT CALLED, TEXTED OR EMAILED KAMRAN.
SOULSONIC FRANKS
GO SPORT
IT'S GOTTEN SO BAD THAT I'VE STARTED PROCESSING MY FEELINGS WITH RANDOM STRANGERS.
Have you ever had your heart broken?
Sure.
Is it supposed to feel like the world is coming to an end?
I think that's pretty standard, yeah.
KOSHER
HOT DOG..
PRETZELS
SODA
AND HOT DOGS.
Vat really shucks.
You get tougher. Eventually. I think.
Sh' too hard. I don' wanna.
LOTS OF HOT DOGS.
Every day I wake up, and for a second, I forget. And for that second, it's fine. I feel normal.
Then I remember. After that comes the panic attack.
Rough stuff, kid.

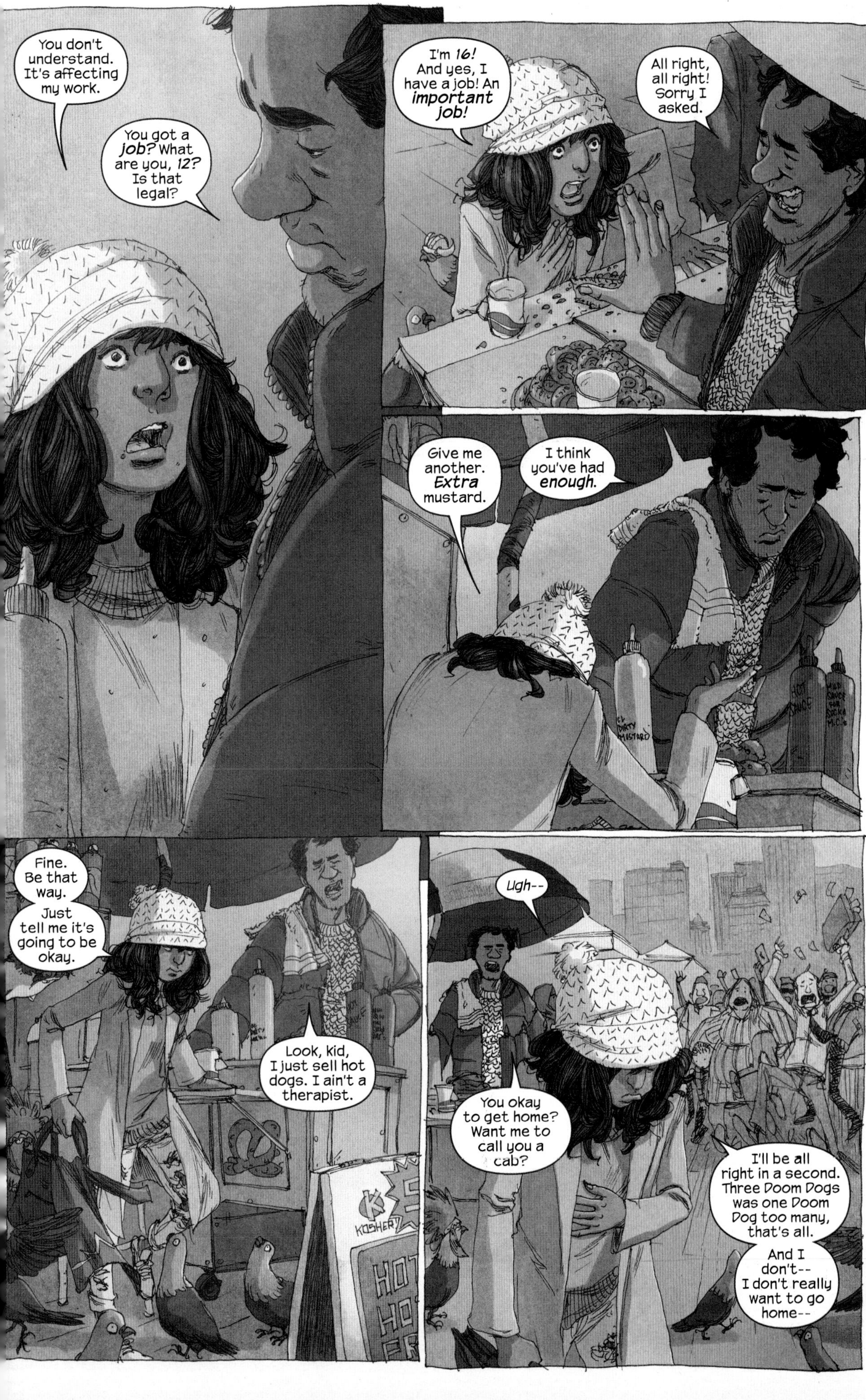
You don't understand. It's affecting my work.
You got a job? What are you, 12? Is that legal?
I'm 16! And yes, I have a job! An important job!
All right, all right! Sorry I asked.
Give me another. Extra mustard.
I think you've had enough.
DIRTY MUSTARD
HOT SAUCE
Fine. Be that way.
Just tell me it's going to be okay.
Look, kid, I just sell hot dogs. I ain't a therapist.
KOSHER
Ugh--
You okay to get home? Want me to call you a cab?
I'll be all right in a second. Three Doom Dogs was one Doom Dog too many, that's all.
And I don't-- I don't really want to go home--

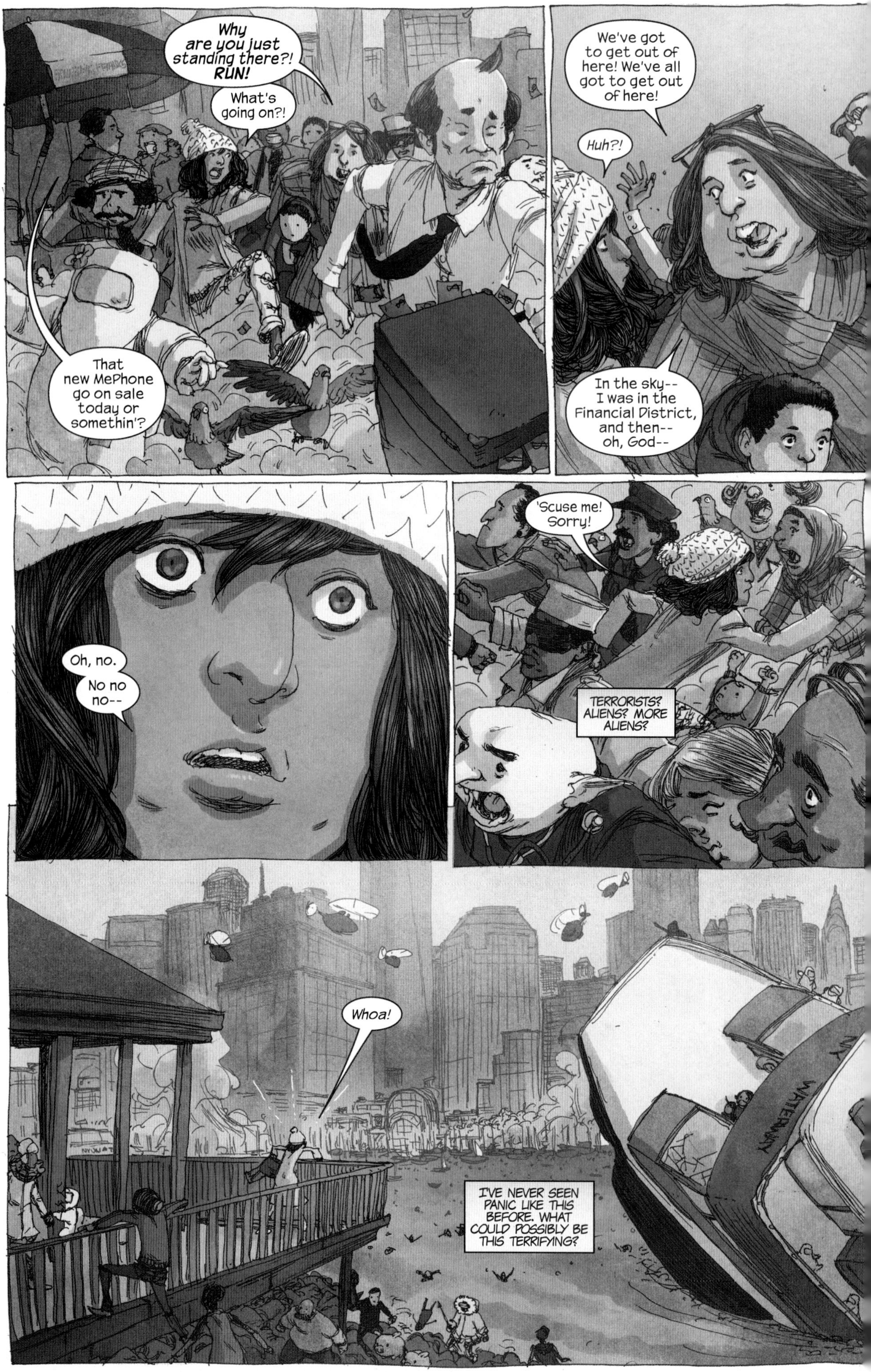

Why are you just standing there?! RUN!
What's going on?!
That new MePhone go on sale today or somethin'?
We've got to get out of here! We've all got to get out of here!
Huh?!
In the sky-- I was in the Financial District, and then-- oh, God--
Oh, no.
No no no--
'Scuse me! Sorry!
TERRORISTS? ALIENS? MORE ALIENS?
Whoa!
I'VE NEVER SEEN PANIC LIKE THIS BEFORE. WHAT COULD POSSIBLY BE THIS TERRIFYING?

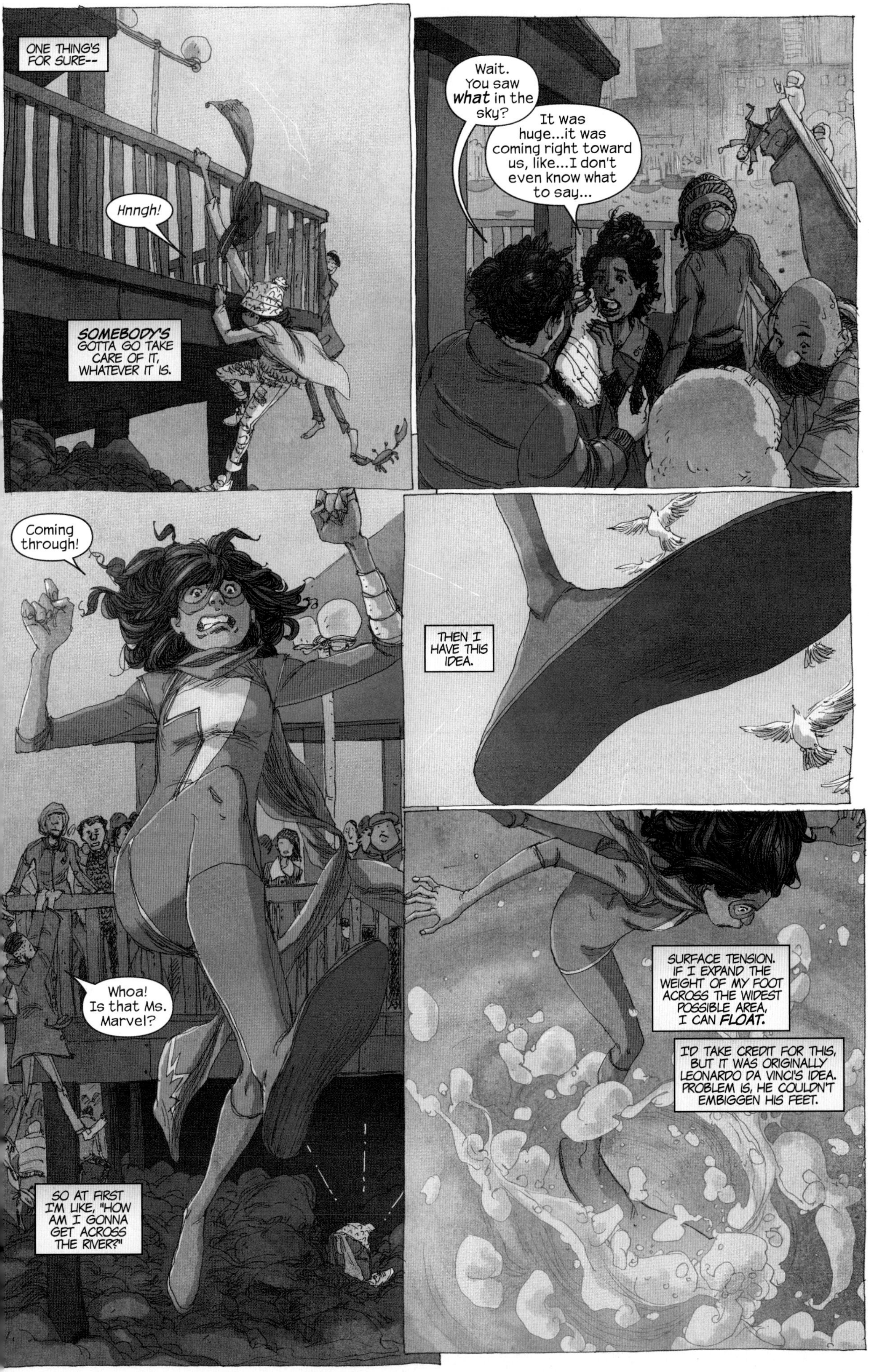
ONE THING'S FOR SURE--
Hnngh!
SOMEBODY'S GOTTA GO TAKE CARE OF IT, WHATEVER IT IS.
Wait. You saw what in the sky?
It was huge...it was coming right toward us, like...I don't even know what to say...
Coming through!
Whoa! Is that Ms. Marvel?
SO AT FIRST I'M LIKE, "HOW AM I GONNA GET ACROSS THE RIVER?"
THEN I HAVE THIS IDEA.
SURFACE TENSION. IF I EXPAND THE WEIGHT OF MY FOOT ACROSS THE WIDEST POSSIBLE AREA, I CAN FLOAT.
I'D TAKE CREDIT FOR THIS, BUT IT WAS ORIGINALLY LEONARDO DA VINCI'S IDEA. PROBLEM IS, HE COULDN'T EMBIGGEN HIS FEET.

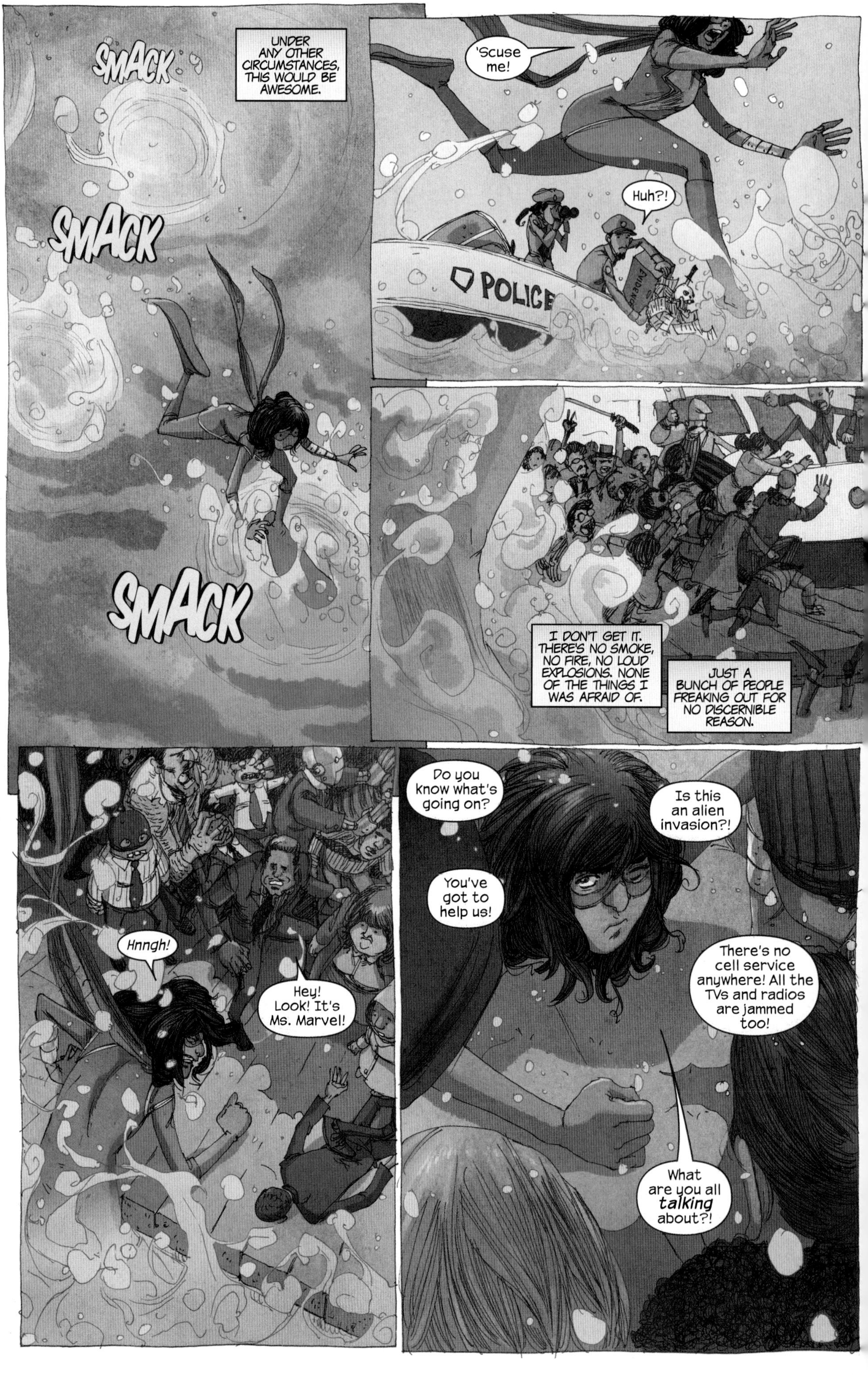
SMACK
UNDER ANY OTHER CIRCUMSTANCES, THIS WOULD BE AWESOME.
SMACK
SMACK
'Scuse me!
Huh?!
POLICE
EVIDENCE
I DON'T GET IT. THERE'S NO SMOKE, NO FIRE, NO LOUD EXPLOSIONS. NONE OF THE THINGS I WAS AFRAID OF.
JUST A BUNCH OF PEOPLE FREAKING OUT FOR NO DISCERNIBLE REASON.
Hnngh!
Hey! Look! It's Ms. Marvel!
Do you know what's going on?
Is this an alien invasion?!
You've got to help us!
There's no cell service anywhere! All the TVs and radios are jammed too!
What are you all *talking* about?!

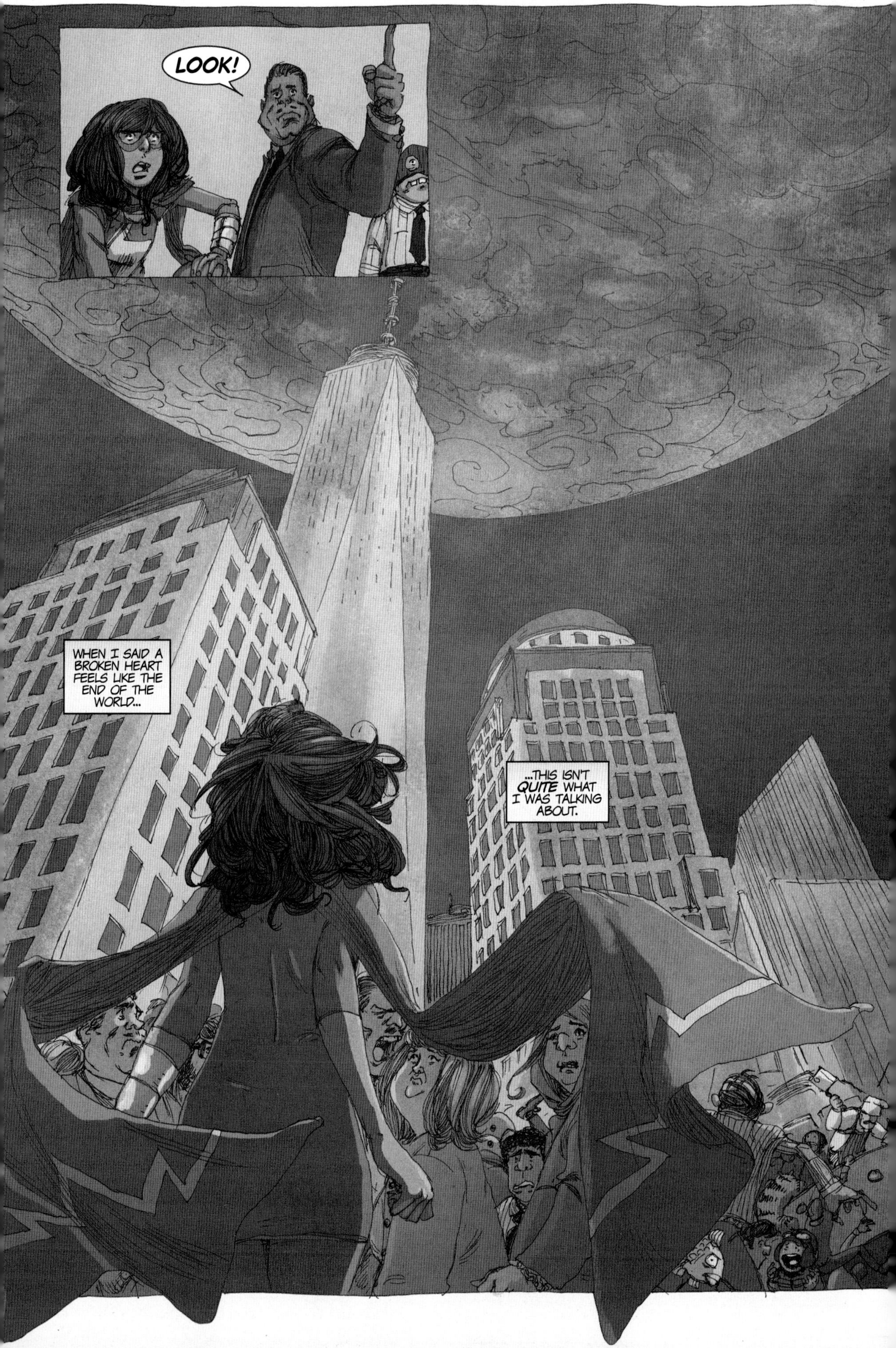
LOOK!
WHEN I SAID A BROKEN HEART FEELS LIKE THE END OF THE WORLD...
...THIS ISN'T QUITE WHAT I WAS TALKING ABOUT.

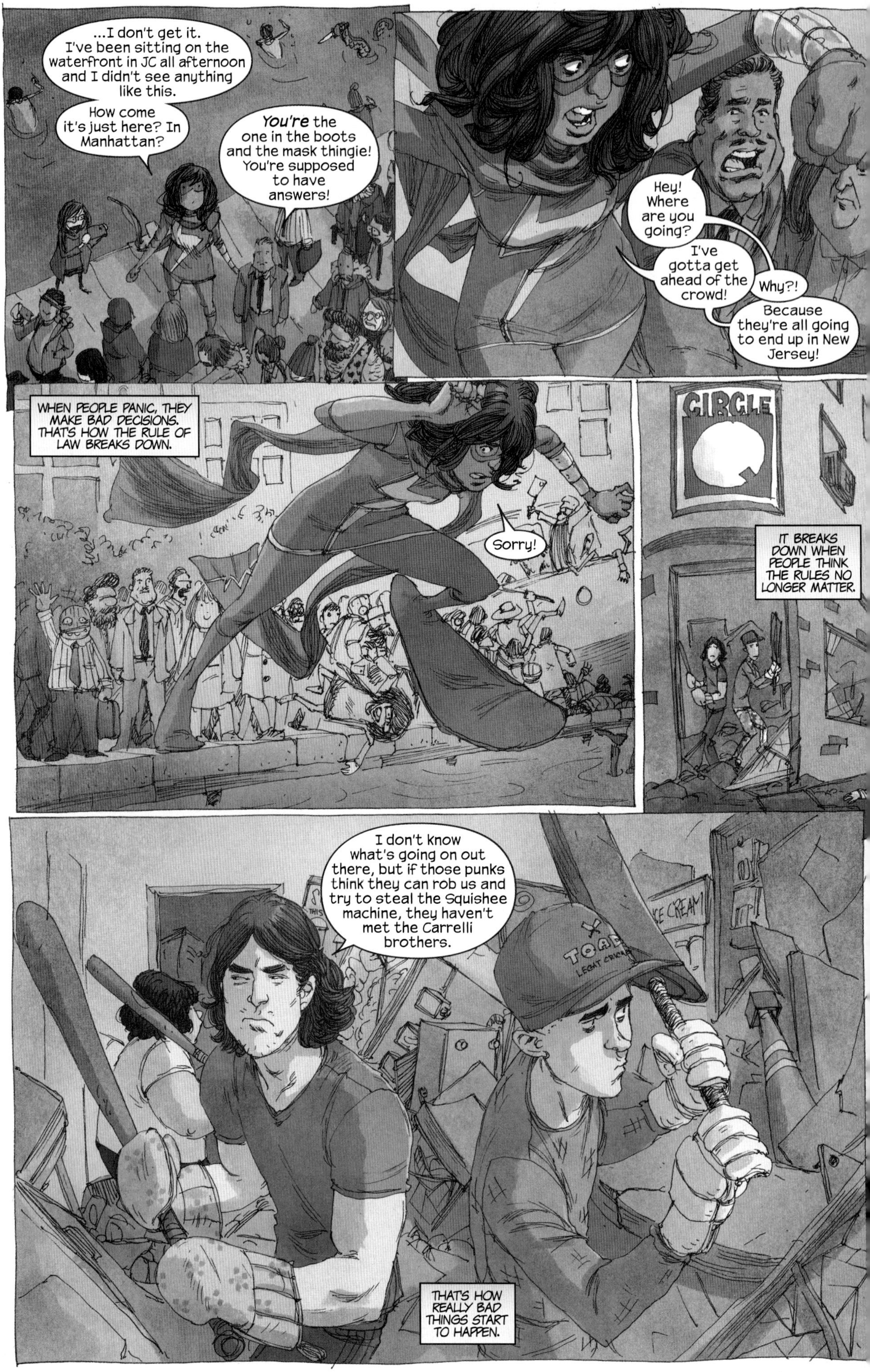

...I don't get it. I've been sitting on the waterfront in JC all afternoon and I didn't see anything like this.
How come it's just here? In Manhattan?
You're the one in the boots and the mask thingie! You're supposed to have answers!
Hey! Where are you going?
I've gotta get ahead of the crowd!
Why?!
Because they're all going to end up in New Jersey!
WHEN PEOPLE PANIC, THEY MAKE BAD DECISIONS. THAT'S HOW THE RULE OF LAW BREAKS DOWN.
Sorry!
CIRCLE
IT BREAKS DOWN WHEN PEOPLE THINK THE RULES NO LONGER MATTER.
I don't know what's going on out there, but if those punks think they can rob us and try to steal the Squishee machine, they haven't met the Carrelli brothers.
THAT'S HOW REALLY BAD THINGS START TO HAPPEN.

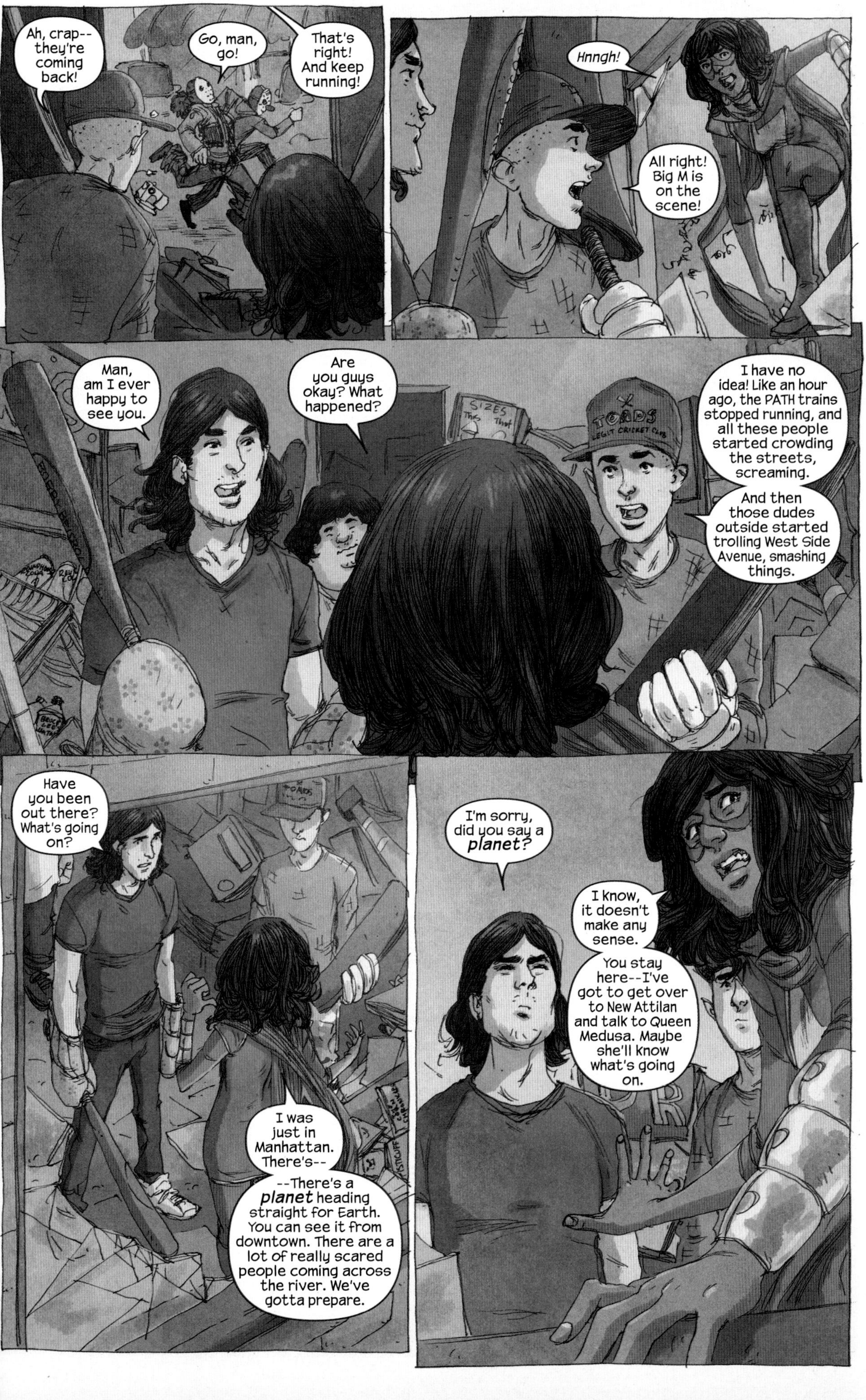
Ah, crap--they're coming back!
Go, man, go!
That's right! And keep running!
Hnngh!
All right! Big M is on the scene!
Man, am I ever happy to see you.
Are you guys okay? What happened?
SIZES
TOADS
LEGIT CRICKET CLUB
I have no idea! Like an hour ago, the PATH trains stopped running, and all these people started crowding the streets, screaming.
And then those dudes outside started trolling West Side Avenue, smashing things.
Have you been out there? What's going on?
I was just in Manhattan. There's--
--There's a *planet* heading straight for Earth. You can see it from downtown. There are a lot of really scared people coming across the river. We've gotta prepare.
I'm sorry, did you say a *planet*?
I know, it doesn't make any sense.
You stay here--I've got to get over to New Attilan and talk to Queen Medusa. Maybe she'll know what's going on.

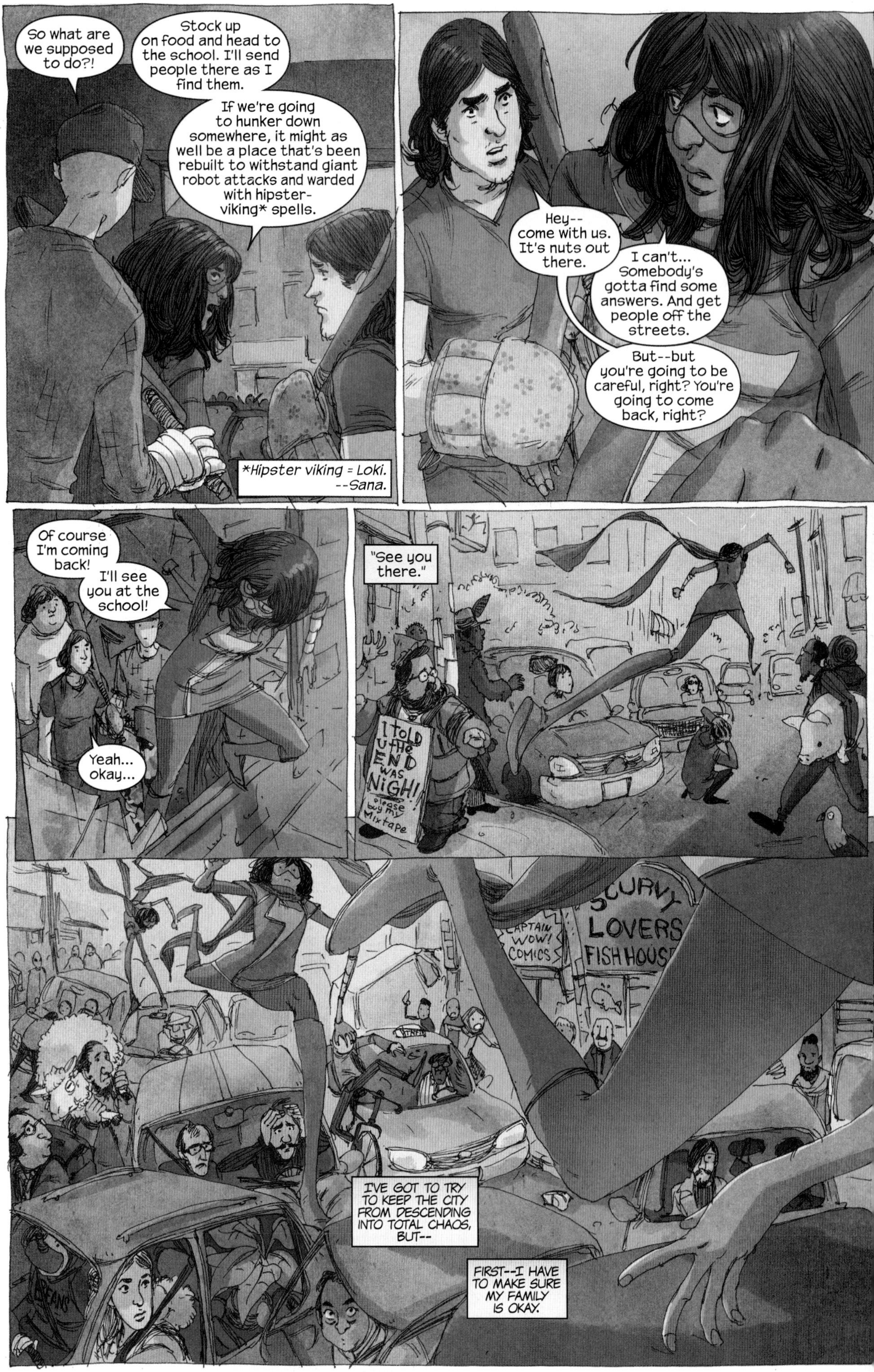
So what are we supposed to do?!
Stock up on food and head to the school. I'll send people there as I find them.
If we're going to hunker down somewhere, it might as well be a place that's been rebuilt to withstand giant robot attacks and warded with hipster-viking* spells.
*Hipster viking = Loki. --Sana.
Hey-- come with us. It's nuts out there.
I can't... Somebody's gotta find some answers. And get people off the streets.
But--but you're going to be careful, right? You're going to come back, right?
Of course I'm coming back!
I'll see you at the school!
Yeah... okay...
"See you there."
I TOLD U the END WAS NIGH! please buy my Mixtape
CAPTAIN WOW! COMICS
SCURVY LOVERS FISH HOUS
I'VE GOT TO TRY TO KEEP THE CITY FROM DESCENDING INTO TOTAL CHAOS, BUT--
FIRST--I HAVE TO MAKE SURE MY FAMILY IS OKAY.

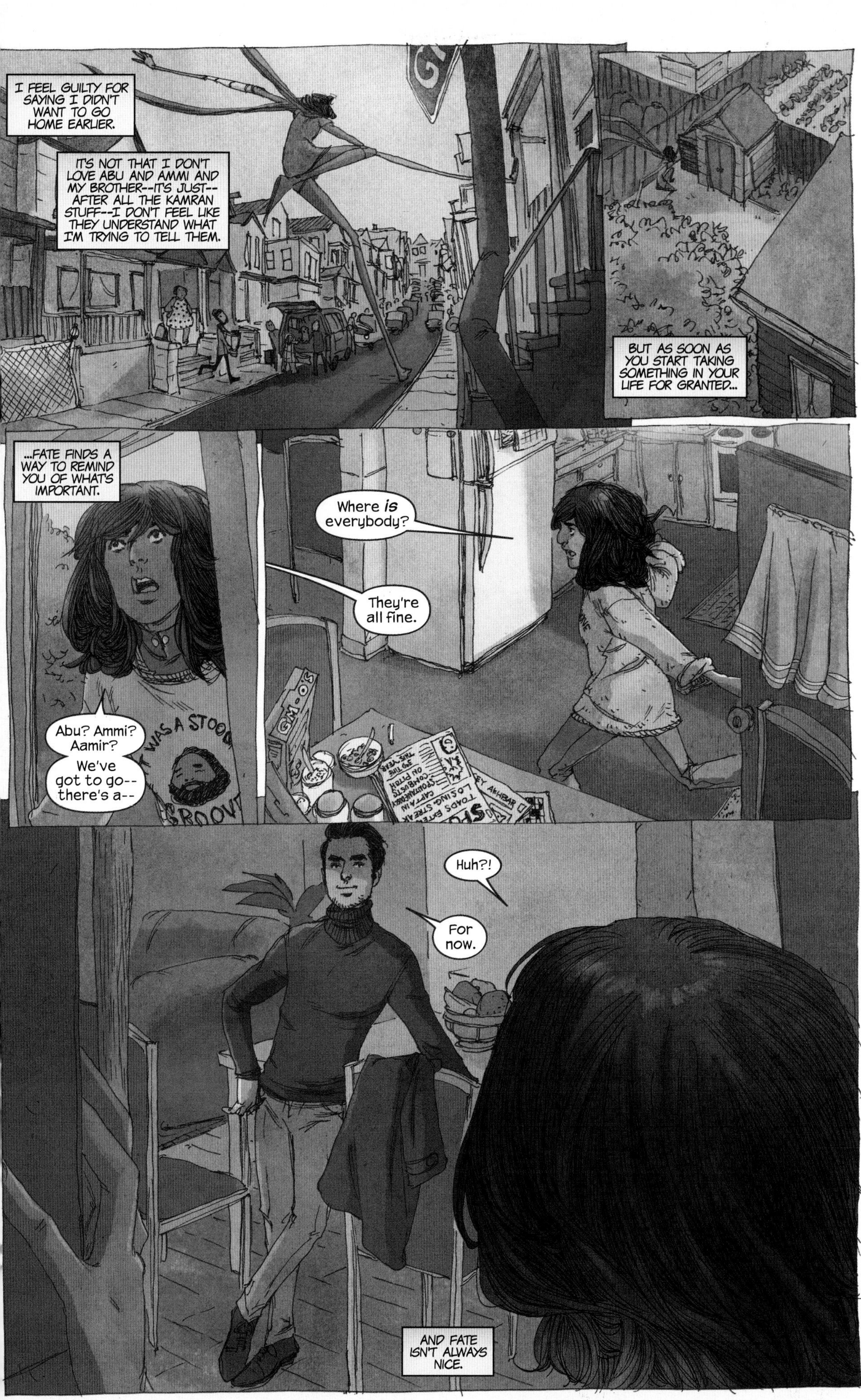

I FEEL GUILTY FOR SAYING I DIDN'T WANT TO GO HOME EARLIER.
IT'S NOT THAT I DON'T LOVE ABU AND AMMI AND MY BROTHER--IT'S JUST--AFTER ALL THE KAMRAN STUFF--I DON'T FEEL LIKE THEY UNDERSTAND WHAT I'M TRYING TO TELL THEM.
BUT AS SOON AS YOU START TAKING SOMETHING IN YOUR LIFE FOR GRANTED...
...FATE FINDS A WAY TO REMIND YOU OF WHAT'S IMPORTANT.
Where *is* everybody?
They're all fine.
Abu? Ammi? Aamir?
We've got to go--there's a--
Huh?!
For now.
AND FATE ISN'T ALWAYS NICE.

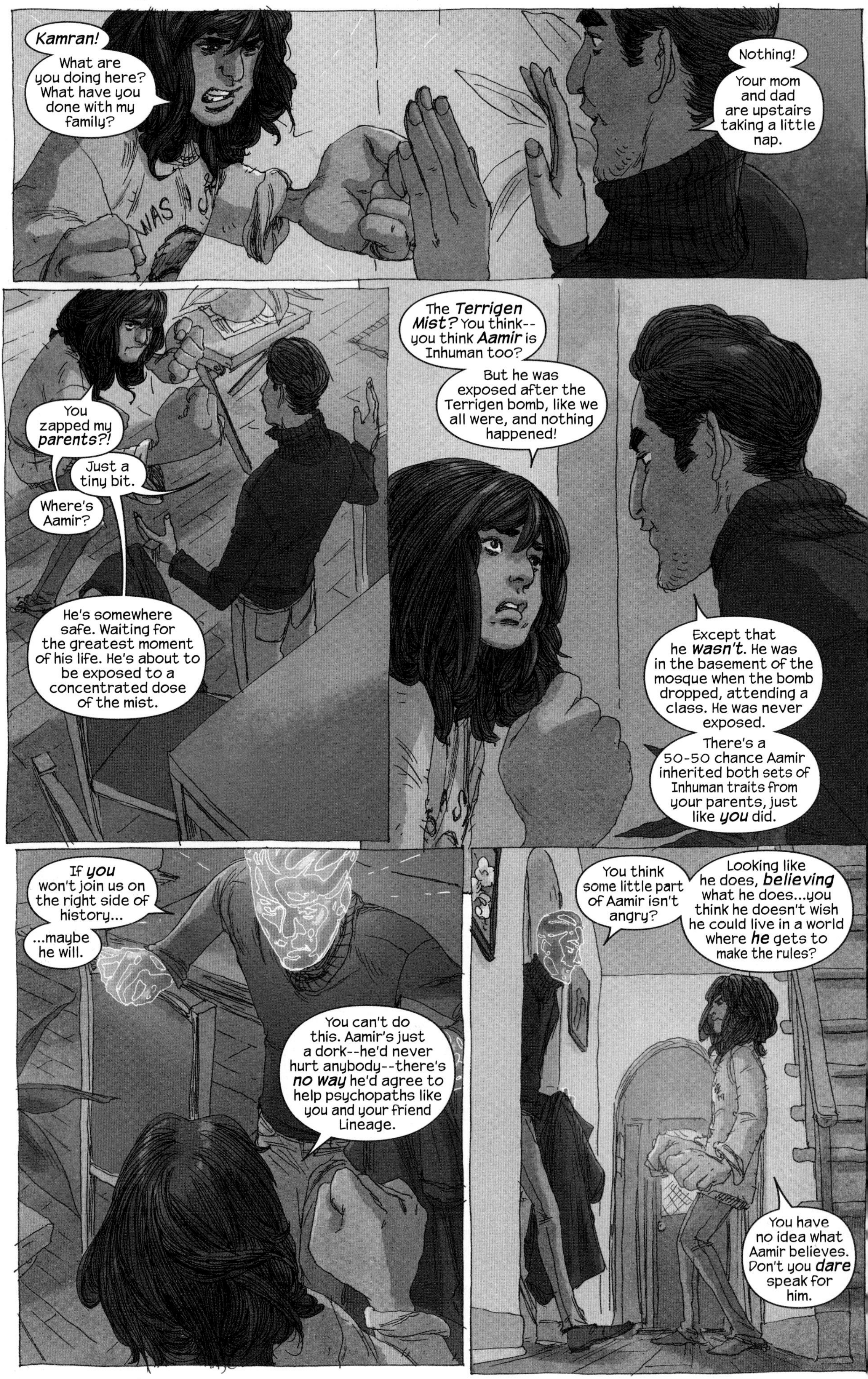
Kamran! What are you doing here? What have you done with my family?
Nothing! Your mom and dad are upstairs taking a little nap.
You zapped my parents?!
Just a tiny bit.
Where's Aamir?
He's somewhere safe. Waiting for the greatest moment of his life. He's about to be exposed to a concentrated dose of the mist.
The Terrigen Mist? You think--you think Aamir is Inhuman too?
But he was exposed after the Terrigen bomb, like we all were, and nothing happened!
Except that he wasn't. He was in the basement of the mosque when the bomb dropped, attending a class. He was never exposed.
There's a 50-50 chance Aamir inherited both sets of Inhuman traits from your parents, just like you did.
If you won't join us on the right side of history...
...maybe he will.
You can't do this. Aamir's just a dork--he'd never hurt anybody--there's no way he'd agree to help psychopaths like you and your friend Lineage.
You think some little part of Aamir isn't angry?
Looking like he does, believing what he does...you think he doesn't wish he could live in a world where he gets to make the rules?
You have no idea what Aamir believes. Don't you dare speak for him.

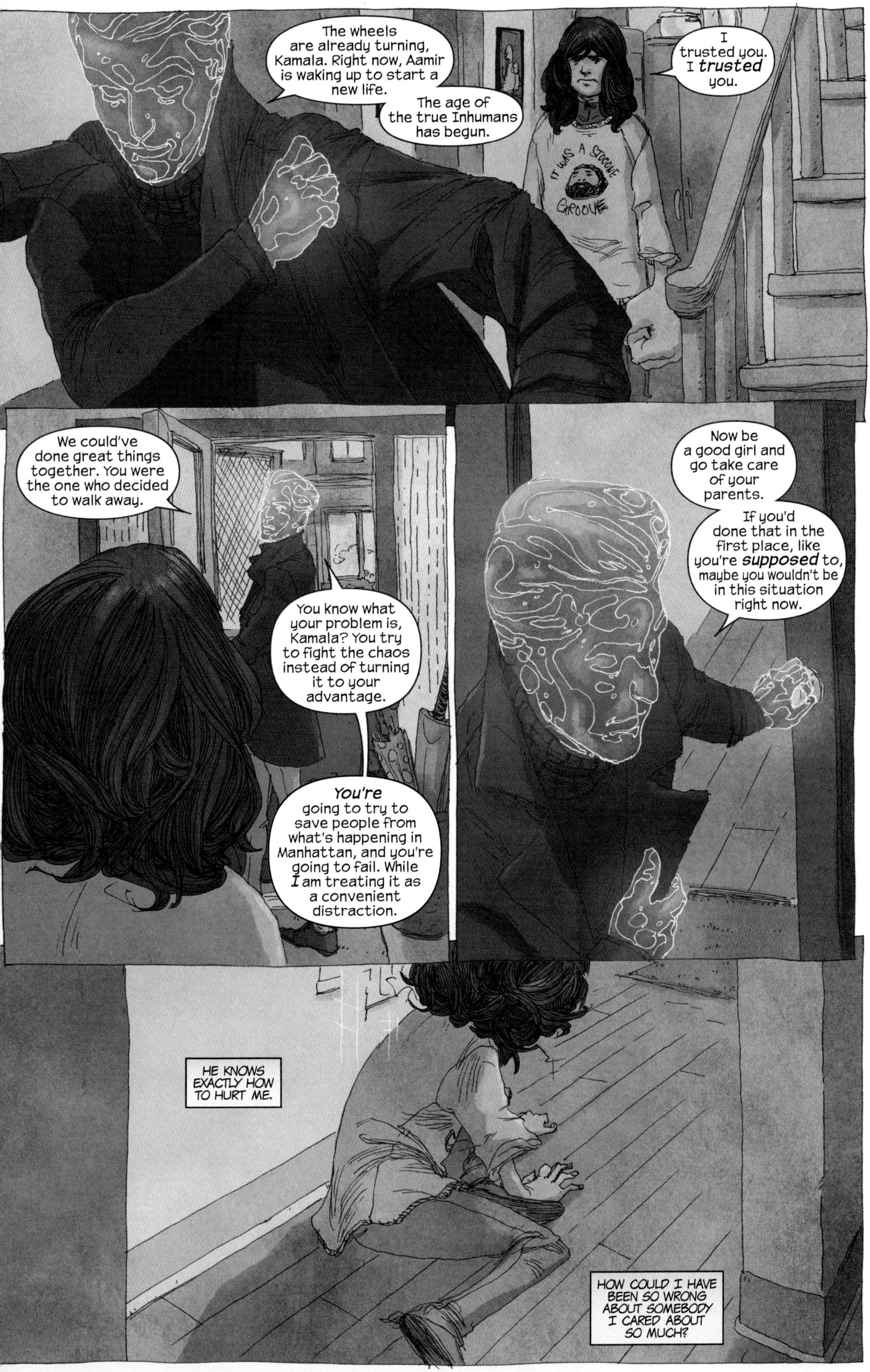
The wheels are already turning, Kamala. Right now, Aamir is waking up to start a new life.
The age of the true Inhumans has begun.
I trusted you. I *trusted* you.
We could've done great things together. You were the one who decided to walk away.
You know what your problem is, Kamala? You try to fight the chaos instead of turning it to your advantage.
You're going to try to save people from what's happening in Manhattan, and you're going to fail. While *I* am treating it as a convenient distraction.
Now be a good girl and go take care of your parents.
If you'd done that in the first place, like you're *supposed* to, maybe you wouldn't be in this situation right now.
HE KNOWS EXACTLY HOW TO HURT ME.
HOW COULD I HAVE BEEN SO WRONG ABOUT SOMEBODY I CARED ABOUT SO MUCH?

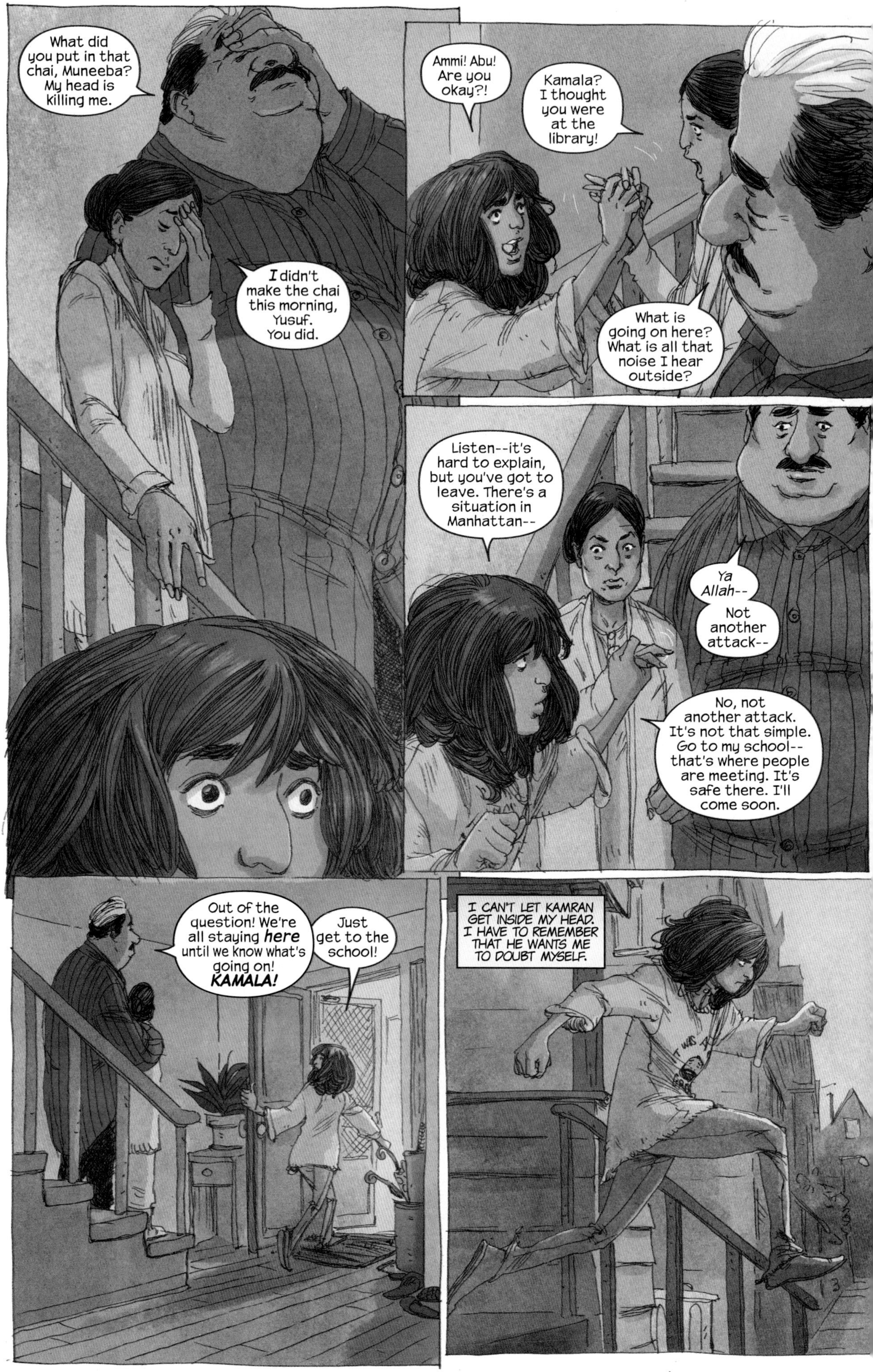

What did you put in that chai, Muneeba? My head is killing me.
I didn't make the chai this morning, Yusuf. You did.
Ammi! Abu! Are you okay?!
Kamala? I thought you were at the library!
What is going on here? What is all that noise I hear outside?
Listen--it's hard to explain, but you've got to leave. There's a situation in Manhattan--
Ya Allah--
Not another attack--
No, not another attack. It's not that simple. Go to my school--that's where people are meeting. It's safe there. I'll come soon.
Out of the question! We're all staying ***here*** until we know what's going on! ***KAMALA!***
Just get to the school!
I CAN'T LET KAMRAN GET INSIDE MY HEAD. I HAVE TO REMEMBER THAT HE WANTS ME TO DOUBT MYSELF.

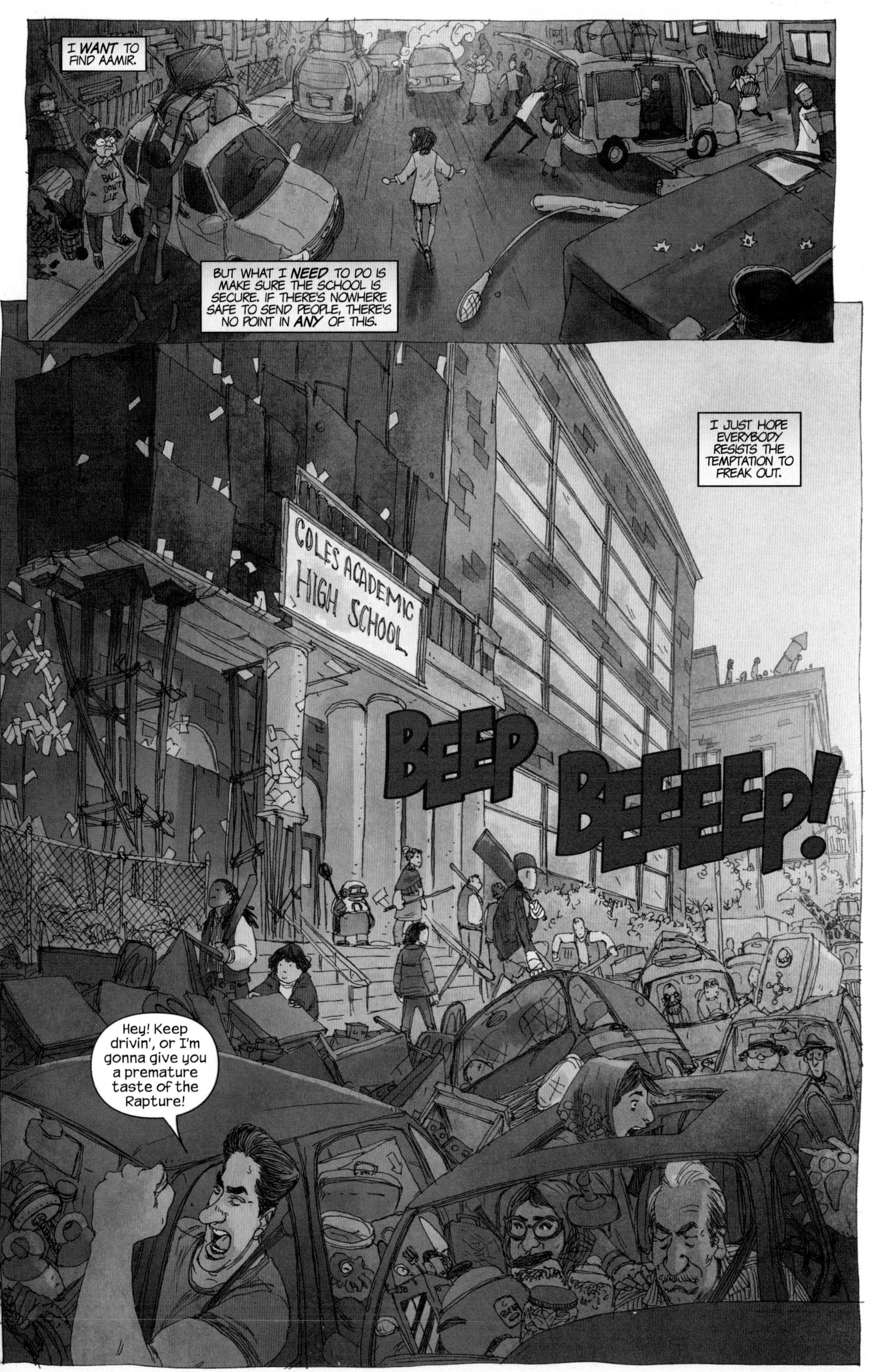

I WANT TO FIND AAMIR.
BALL DON'T LIE
BUT WHAT I NEED TO DO IS MAKE SURE THE SCHOOL IS SECURE. IF THERE'S NOWHERE SAFE TO SEND PEOPLE, THERE'S NO POINT IN ANY OF THIS.
I JUST HOPE EVERYBODY RESISTS THE TEMPTATION TO FREAK OUT.
COLES ACADEMIC HIGH SCHOOL
BEEP
BEEEEP!
Hey! Keep drivin', or I'm gonna give you a premature taste of the Rapture!

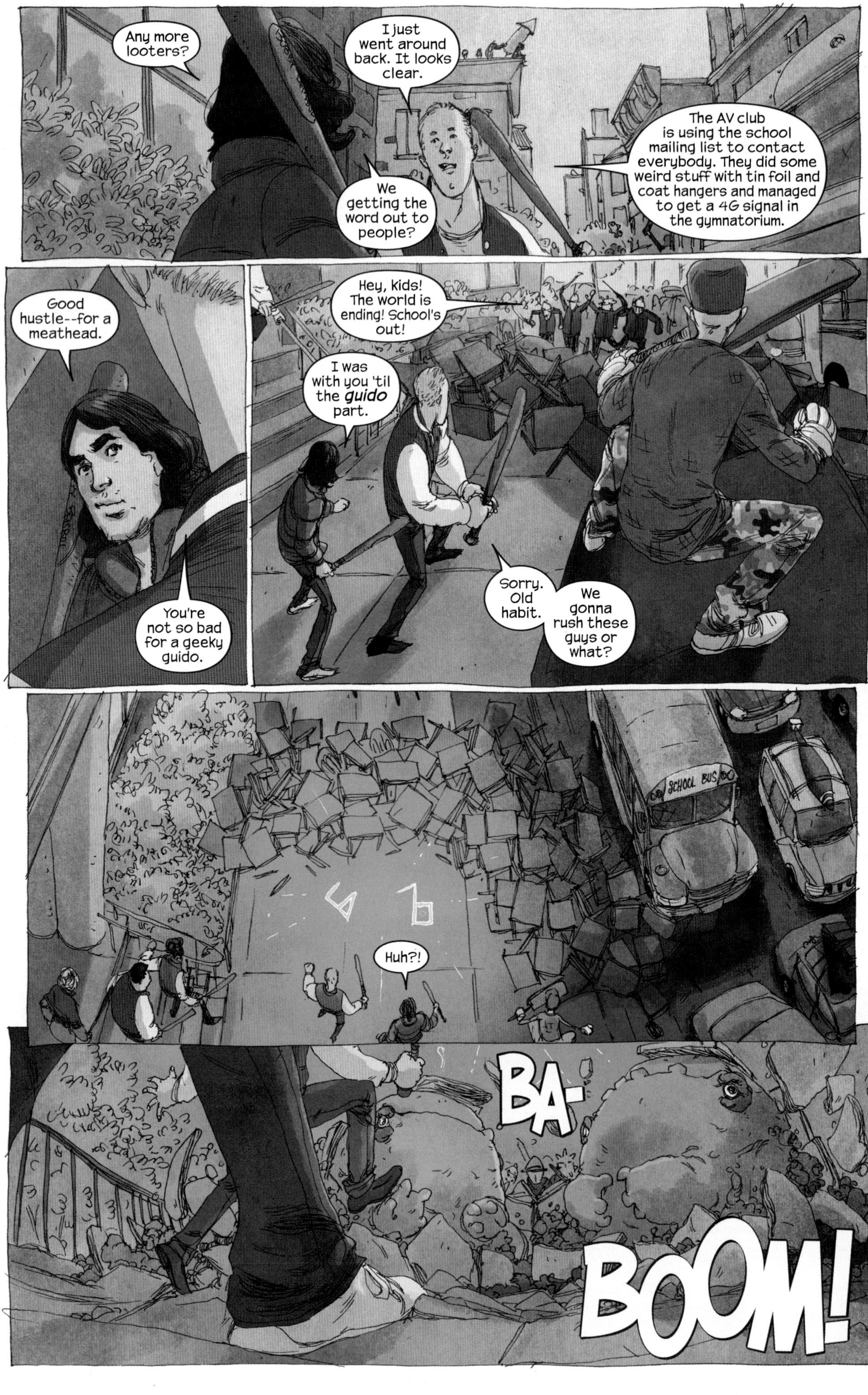
Any more looters?
I just went around back. It looks clear.
We getting the word out to people?
The AV club is using the school mailing list to contact everybody. They did some weird stuff with tin foil and coat hangers and managed to get a 4G signal in the gymnatorium.
Good hustle--for a meathead.
You're not so bad for a geeky guido.
Hey, kids! The world is ending! School's out!
I was with you 'til the *guido* part.
Sorry. Old habit.
We gonna rush these guys or what?
SCHOOL BUS
Huh?!
BA-
BOOM!

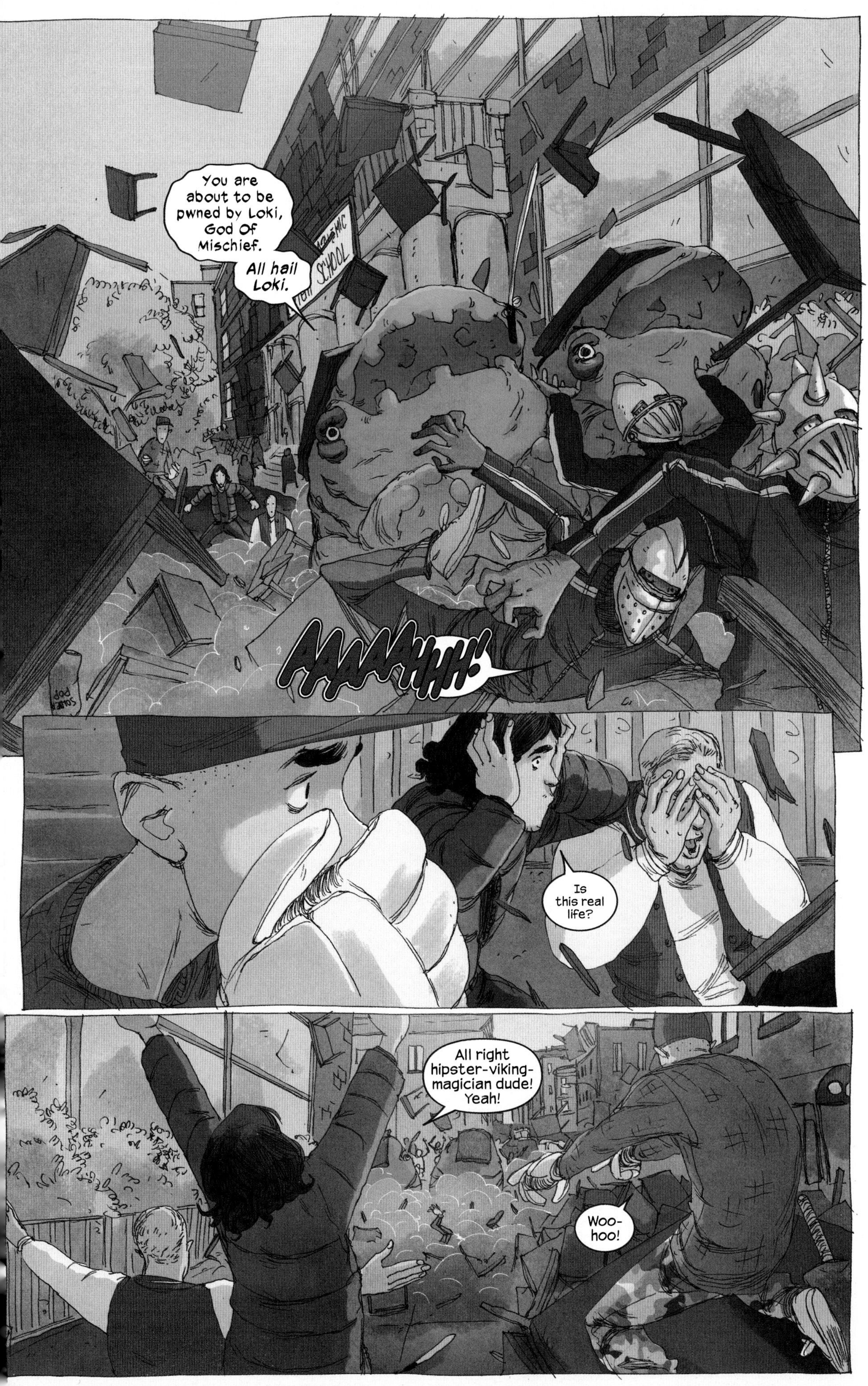
You are about to be pwned by Loki, God Of Mischief.
All hail Loki.
SCHOOL
AAAAAHHH!
Is this real life?
All right hipster-viking-magician dude! Yeah!
Woo-hoo!

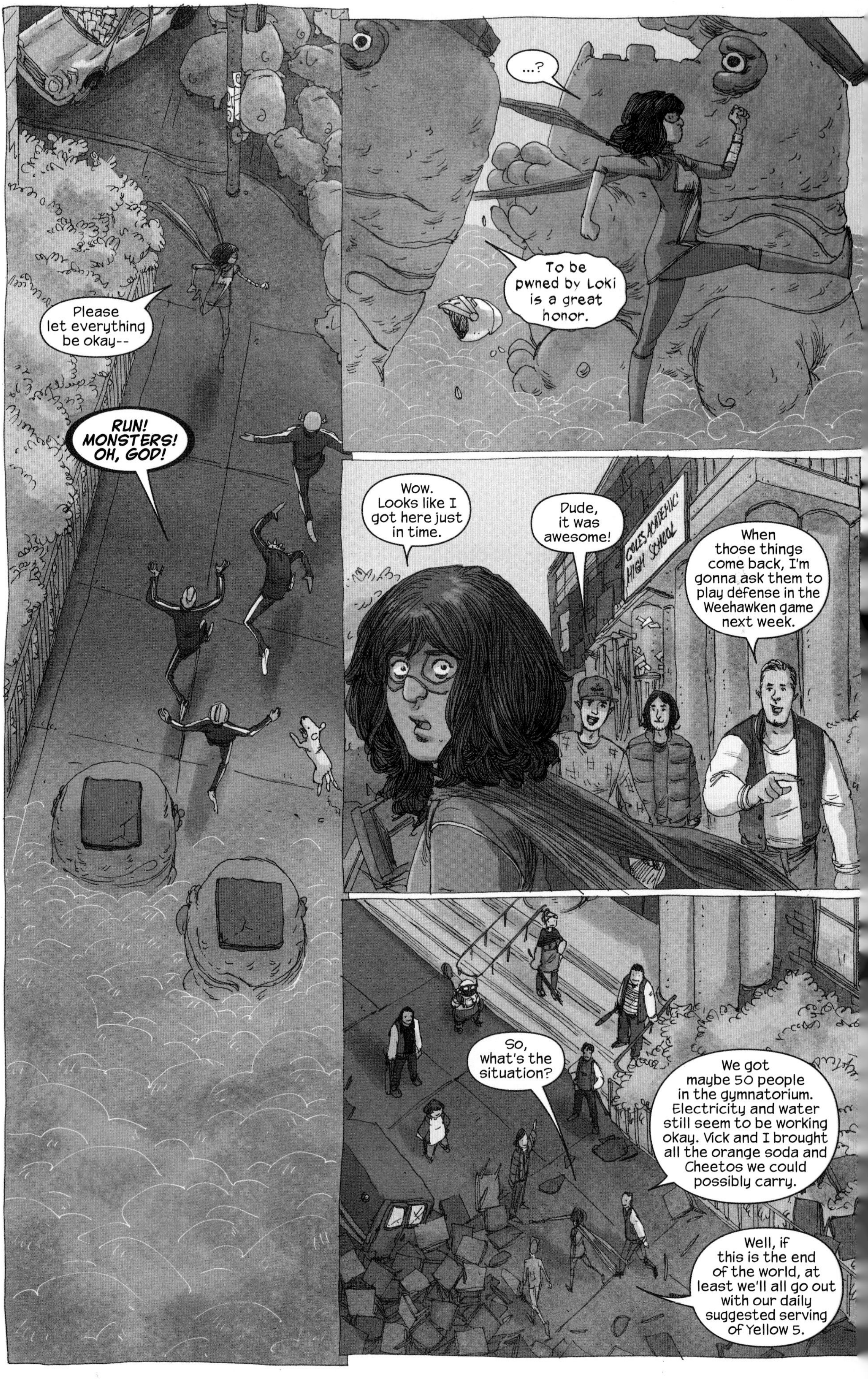
Please let everything be okay--
RUN! MONSTERS! OH, GOD!
...?
To be pwned by Loki is a great honor.
Wow. Looks like I got here just in time.
Dude, it was awesome!
COLES ACADEMIC HIGH SCHOOL
When those things come back, I'm gonna ask them to play defense in the Weehawken game next week.
So, what's the situation?
We got maybe 50 people in the gymnatorium. Electricity and water still seem to be working okay. Vick and I brought all the orange soda and Cheetos we could possibly carry.
Well, if this is the end of the world, at least we'll all go out with our daily suggested serving of Yellow 5.

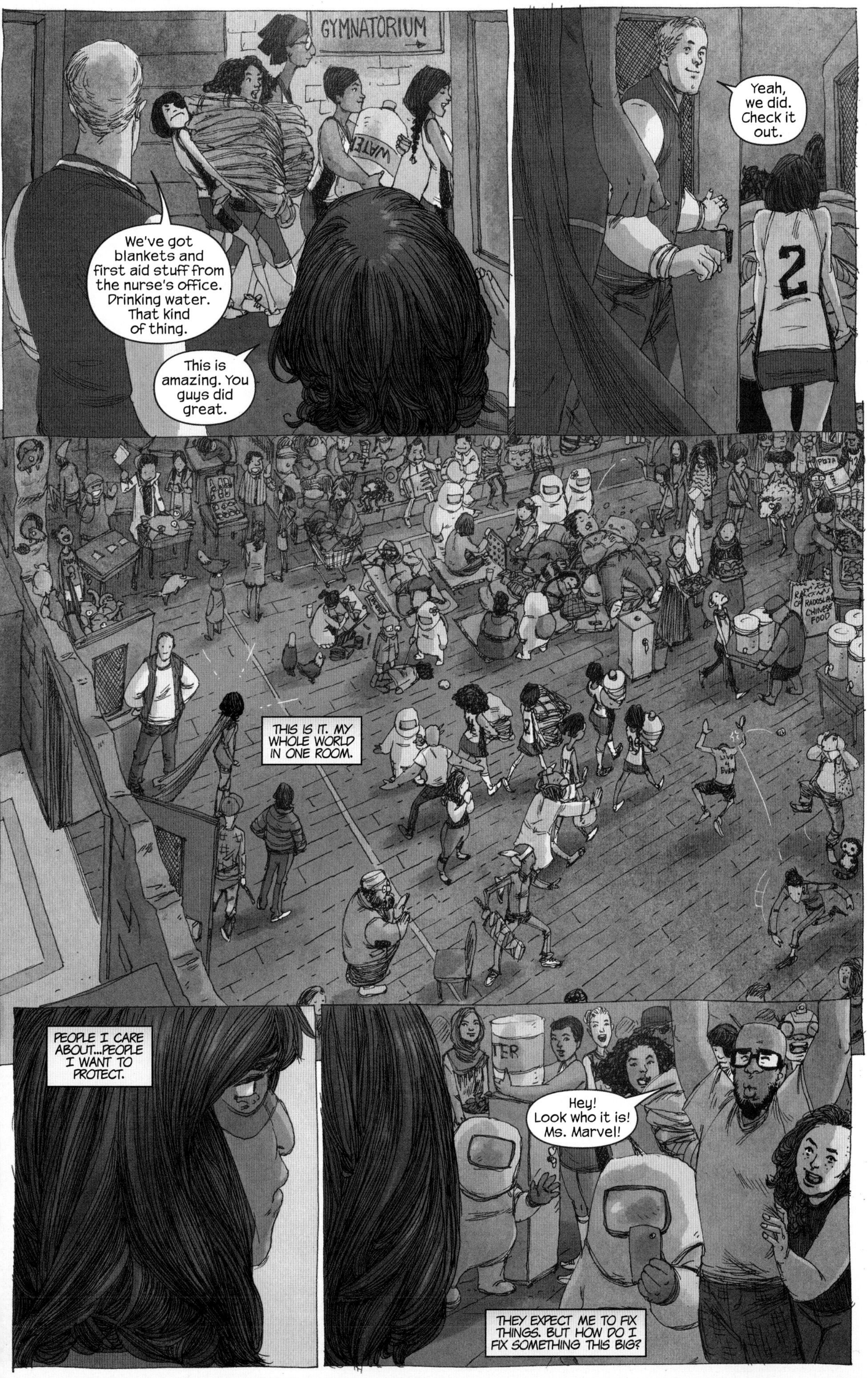
GYMNATORIUM
WATER
We've got blankets and first aid stuff from the nurse's office. Drinking water. That kind of thing.
This is amazing. You guys did great.
Yeah, we did. Check it out.
2
RADOSLAW CHINESE FOOD
THIS IS IT. MY WHOLE WORLD IN ONE ROOM.
PEOPLE I CARE ABOUT...PEOPLE I WANT TO PROTECT.
TER
Hey! Look who it is! Ms. Marvel!
THEY EXPECT ME TO FIX THINGS. BUT HOW DO I FIX SOMETHING THIS BIG?

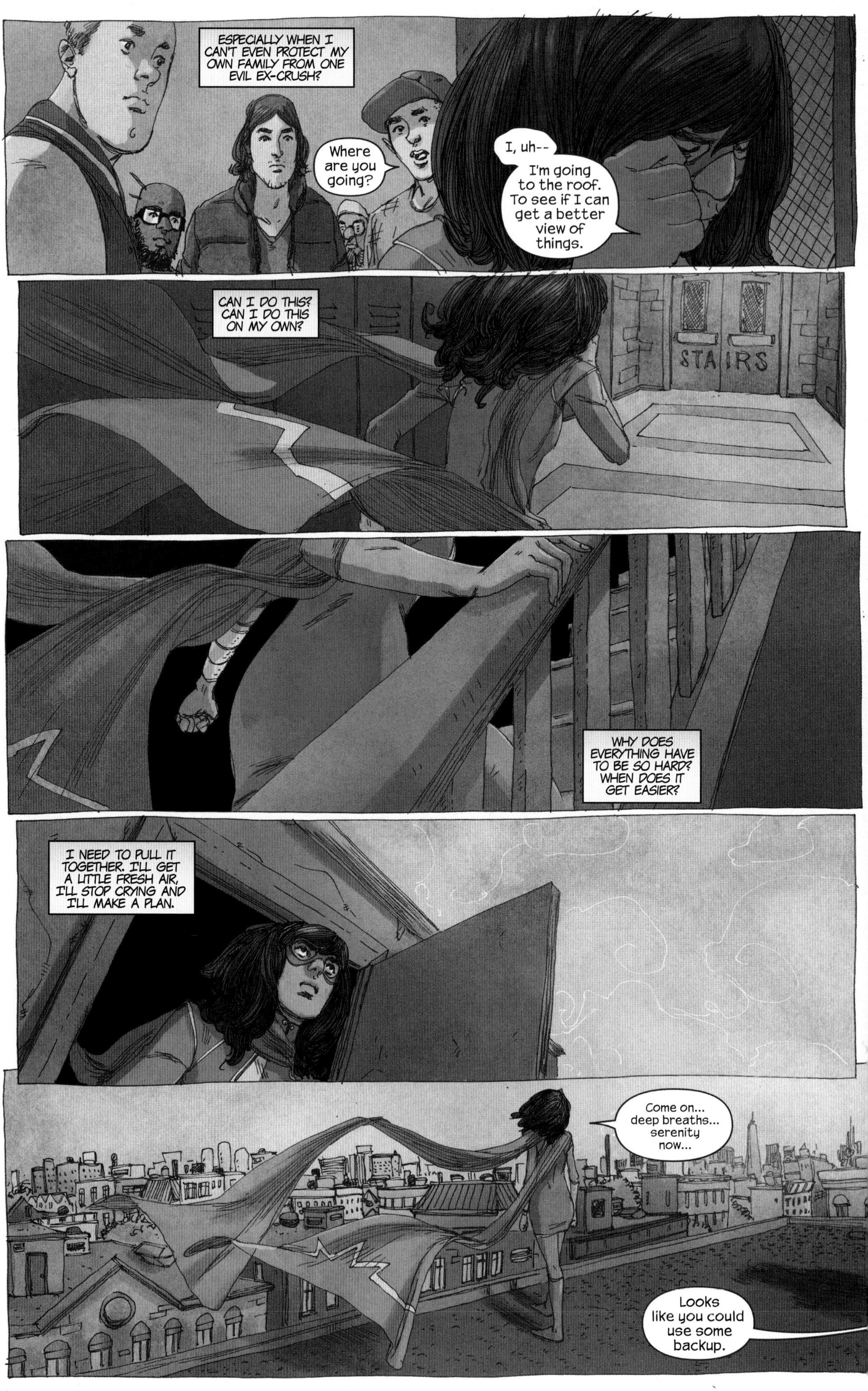
ESPECIALLY WHEN I CAN'T EVEN PROTECT MY OWN FAMILY FROM ONE EVIL EX-CRUSH?
Where are you going?
I, uh--
I'm going to the roof. To see if I can get a better view of things.
CAN I DO THIS? CAN I DO THIS ON MY OWN?
STAIRS
WHY DOES EVERYTHING HAVE TO BE SO HARD? WHEN DOES IT GET EASIER?
I NEED TO PULL IT TOGETHER. I'LL GET A LITTLE FRESH AIR, I'LL STOP CRYING AND I'LL MAKE A PLAN.
Come on... deep breaths... serenity now...
Looks like you could use some backup.

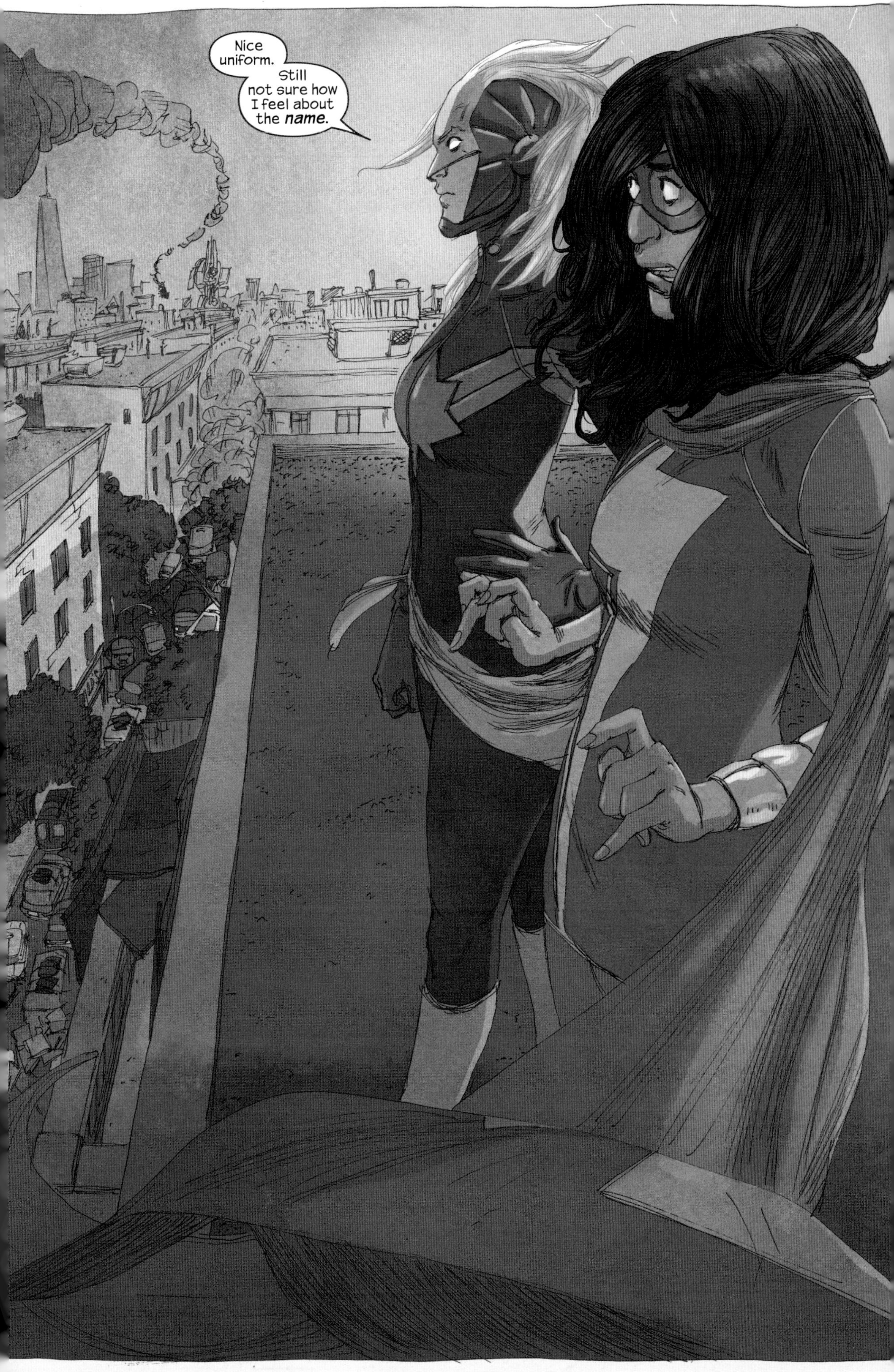
Nice uniform.
Still not sure how I feel about the *name*.

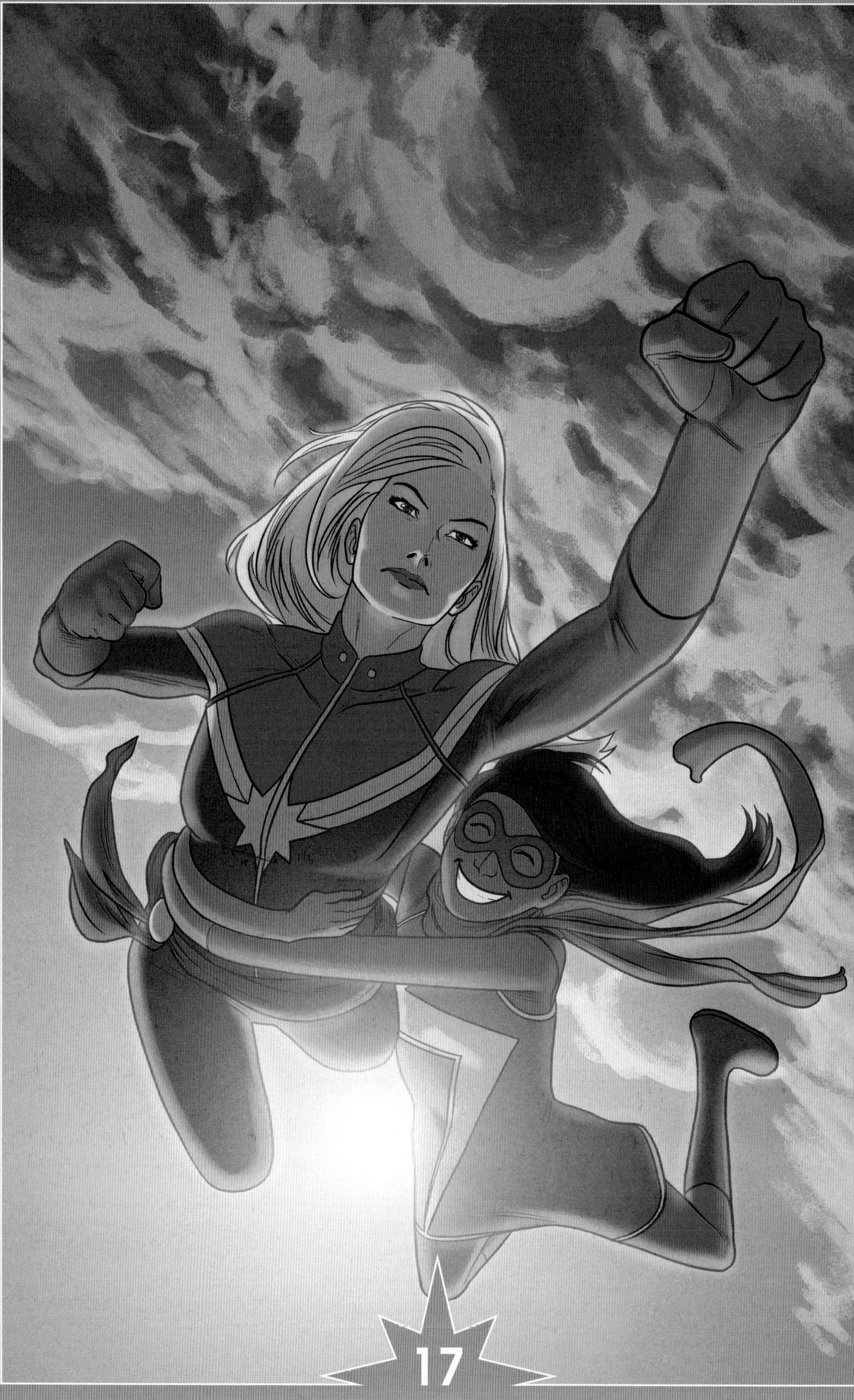

17

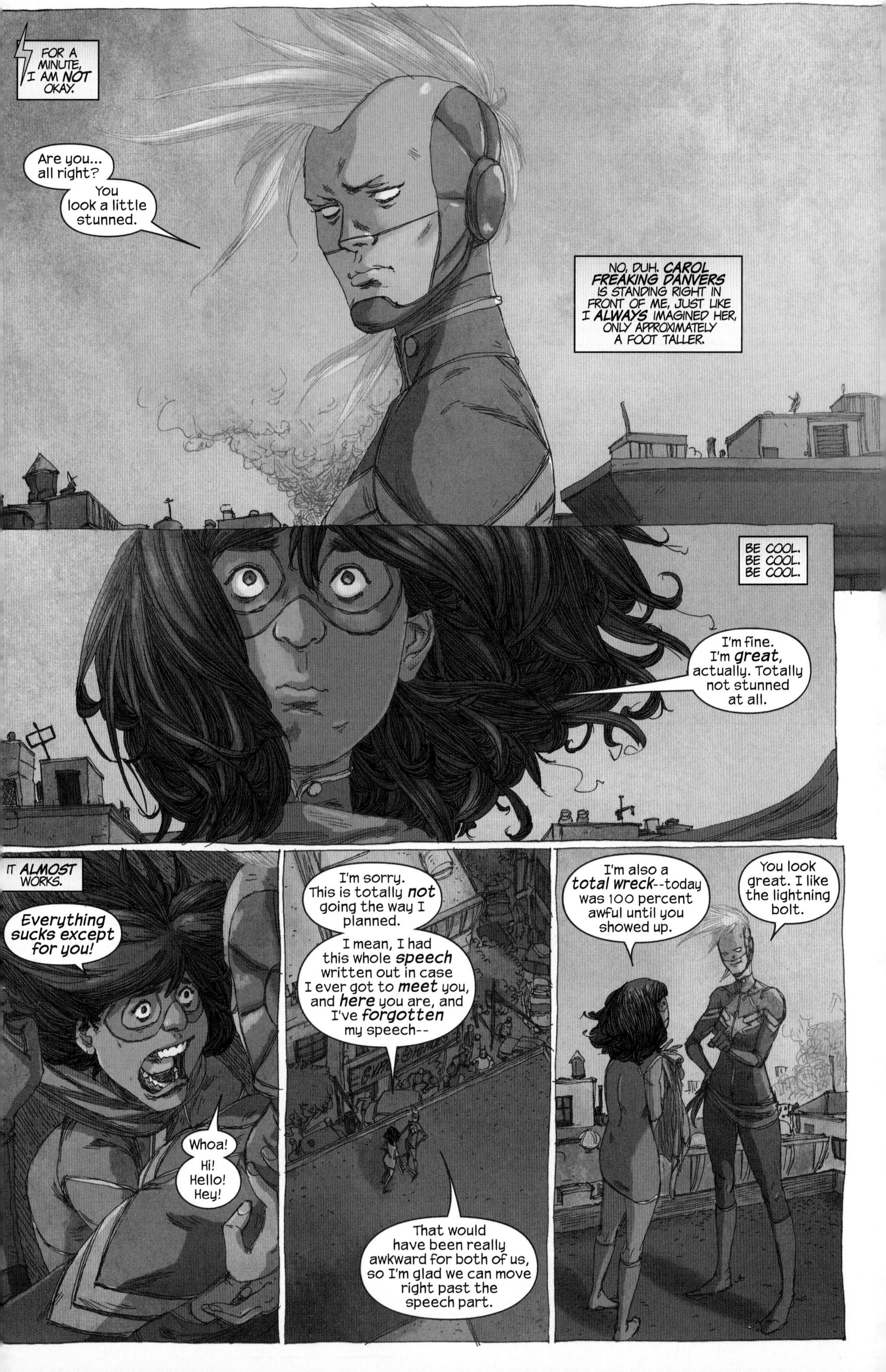
FOR A MINUTE, I AM NOT OKAY.
Are you... all right?
You look a little stunned.
NO, DUH. CAROL FREAKING DANVERS IS STANDING RIGHT IN FRONT OF ME, JUST LIKE I ALWAYS IMAGINED HER, ONLY APPROXIMATELY A FOOT TALLER.
BE COOL. BE COOL. BE COOL.
I'm fine. I'm great, actually. Totally not stunned at all.
IT ALMOST WORKS.
Everything sucks except for you!
Whoa! Hi! Hello! Hey!
I'm sorry. This is totally not going the way I planned.
I mean, I had this whole speech written out in case I ever got to meet you, and here you are, and I've forgotten my speech--
That would have been really awkward for both of us, so I'm glad we can move right past the speech part.
I'm also a total wreck--today was 100 percent awful until you showed up.
You look great. I like the lightning bolt.

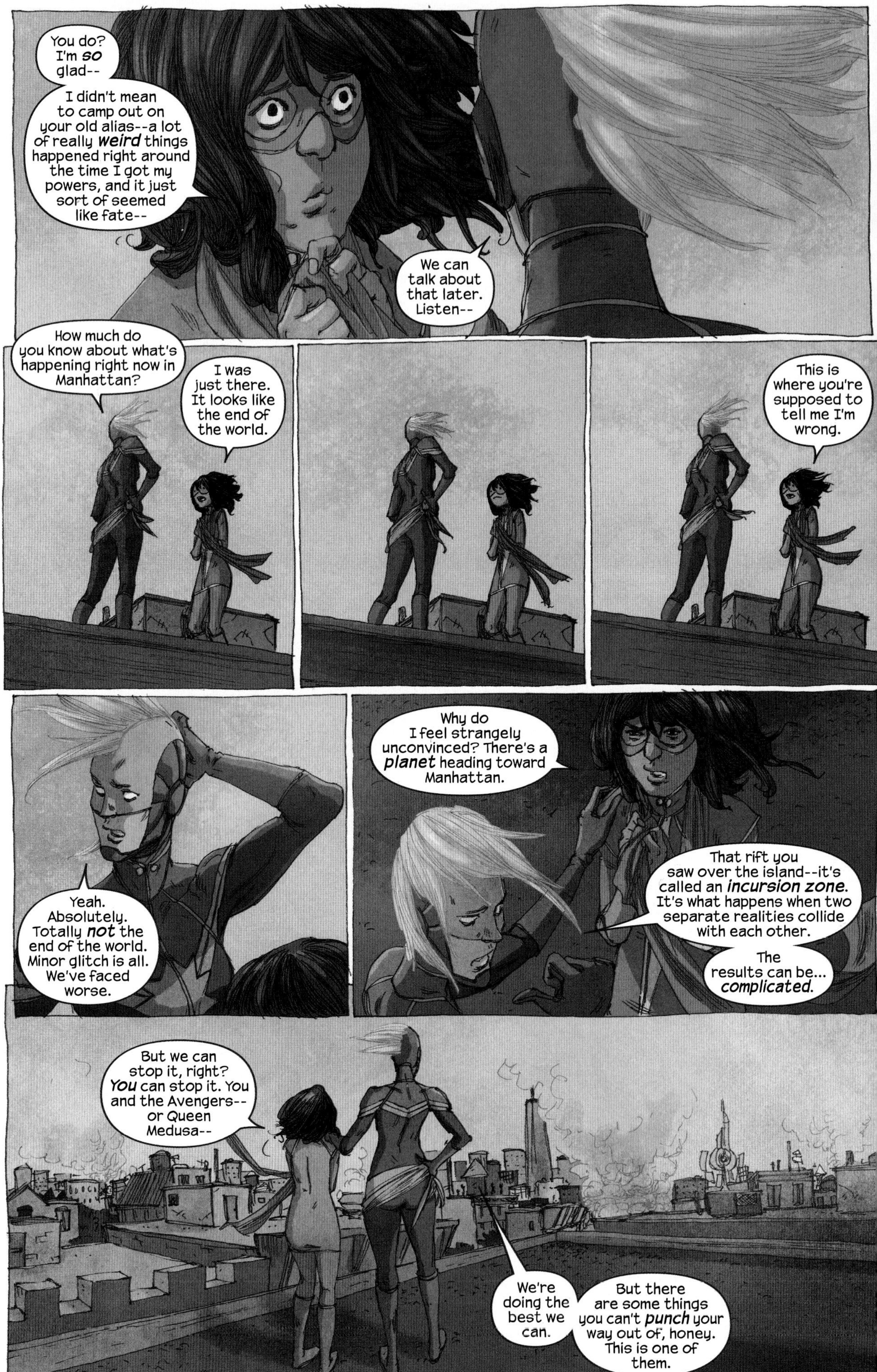

You do? I'm SO glad--
I didn't mean to camp out on your old alias--a lot of really weird things happened right around the time I got my powers, and it just sort of seemed like fate--
We can talk about that later. Listen--
How much do you know about what's happening right now in Manhattan?
I was just there. It looks like the end of the world.
This is where you're supposed to tell me I'm wrong.
Yeah. Absolutely. Totally not the end of the world. Minor glitch is all. We've faced worse.
Why do I feel strangely unconvinced? There's a planet heading toward Manhattan.
That rift you saw over the island--it's called an incursion zone. It's what happens when two separate realities collide with each other.
The results can be... complicated.
But we can stop it, right? You can stop it. You and the Avengers--or Queen Medusa--
We're doing the best we can.
But there are some things you can't punch your way out of, honey. This is one of them.

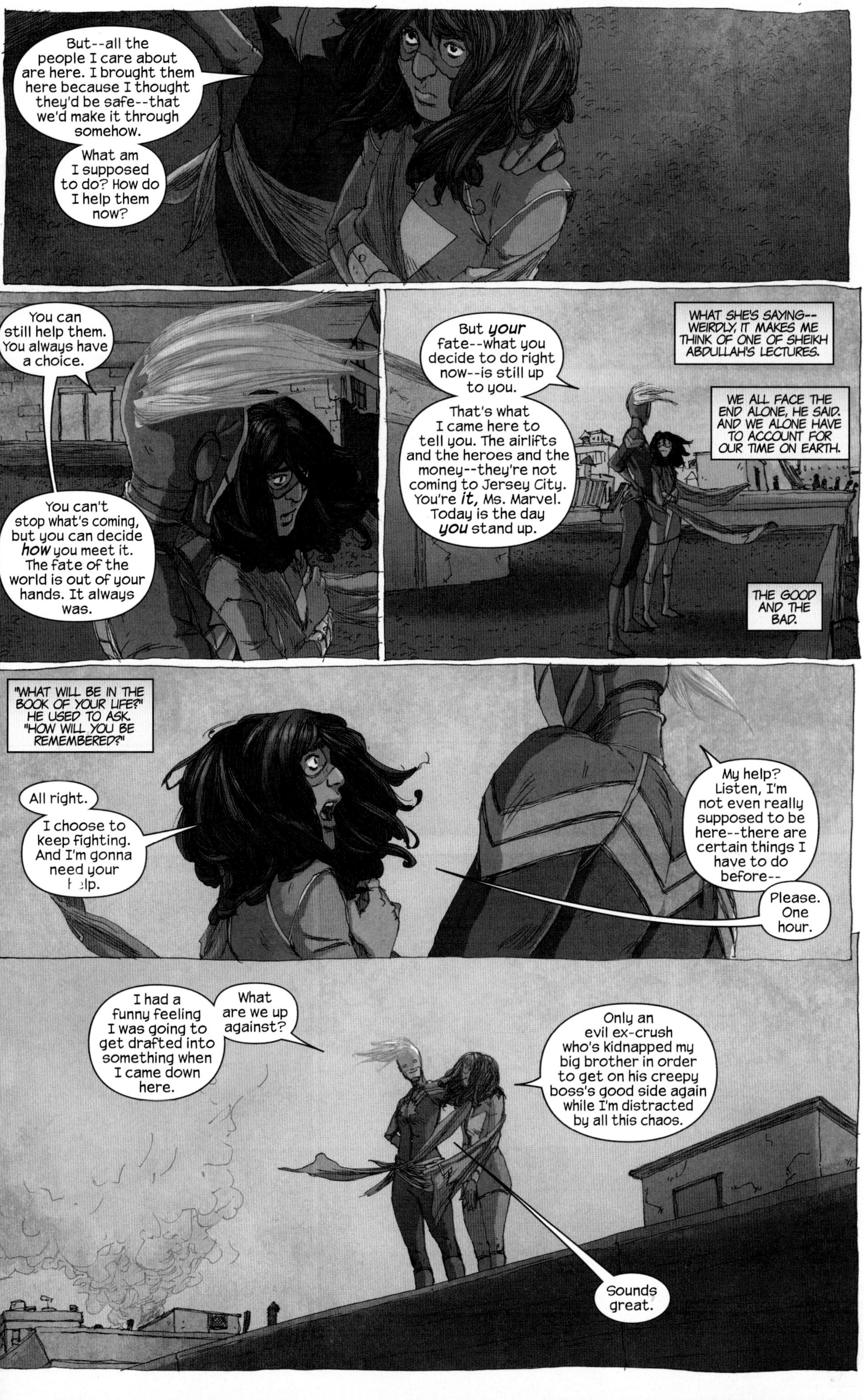
But--all the people I care about are here. I brought them here because I thought they'd be safe--that we'd make it through somehow.
What am I supposed to do? How do I help them now?
You can still help them. You always have a choice.
You can't stop what's coming, but you can decide *how* you meet it. The fate of the world is out of your hands. It always was.
But *your* fate--what you decide to do right now--is still up to you.
That's what I came here to tell you. The airlifts and the heroes and the money--they're not coming to Jersey City. You're *it,* Ms. Marvel. Today is the day *you* stand up.
WHAT SHE'S SAYING--WEIRDLY, IT MAKES ME THINK OF ONE OF SHEIKH ABDULLAH'S LECTURES.
WE ALL FACE THE END ALONE, HE SAID. AND WE ALONE HAVE TO ACCOUNT FOR OUR TIME ON EARTH.
THE GOOD AND THE BAD.
"WHAT WILL BE IN THE BOOK OF YOUR LIFE?" HE USED TO ASK. "HOW WILL YOU BE REMEMBERED?"
All right.
I choose to keep fighting. And I'm gonna need your help.
My help? Listen, I'm not even really supposed to be here--there are certain things I have to do before--
Please. One hour.
I had a funny feeling I was going to get drafted into something when I came down here.
What are we up against?
Only an evil ex-crush who's kidnapped my big brother in order to get on his creepy boss's good side again while I'm distracted by all this chaos.
Sounds great.

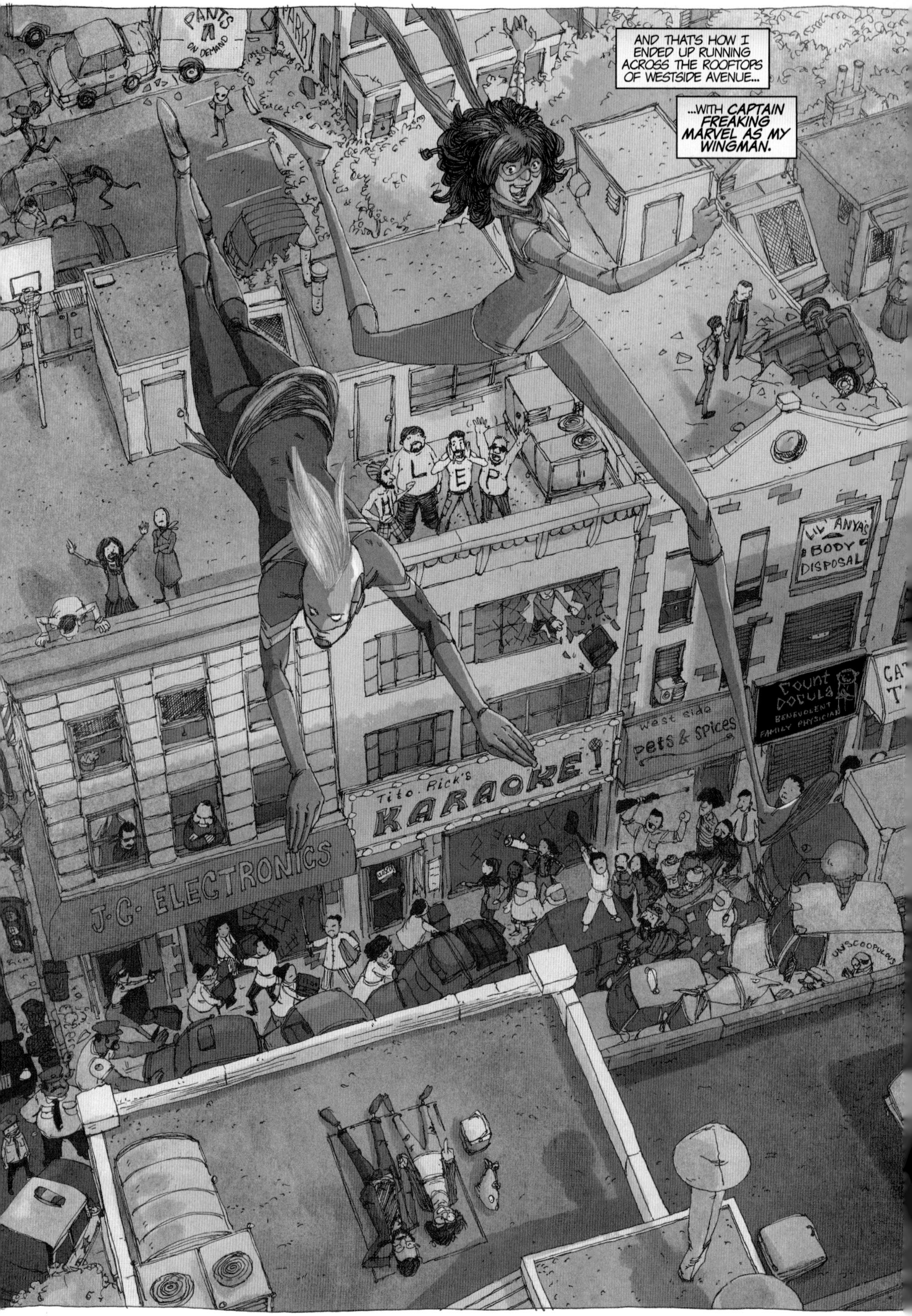
AND THAT'S HOW I ENDED UP RUNNING ACROSS THE ROOFTOPS OF WESTSIDE AVENUE...
...WITH CAPTAIN FREAKING MARVEL AS MY WINGMAN.
PANTS ON DEMAND
LIL' ANYA'S BODY DISPOSAL
Count Docula BENEVOLENT FAMILY PHYSICIAN
west side pets & spices
Tito Rick's KARAOKE
J.C. ELECTRONICS
UNSCOOPULOUS

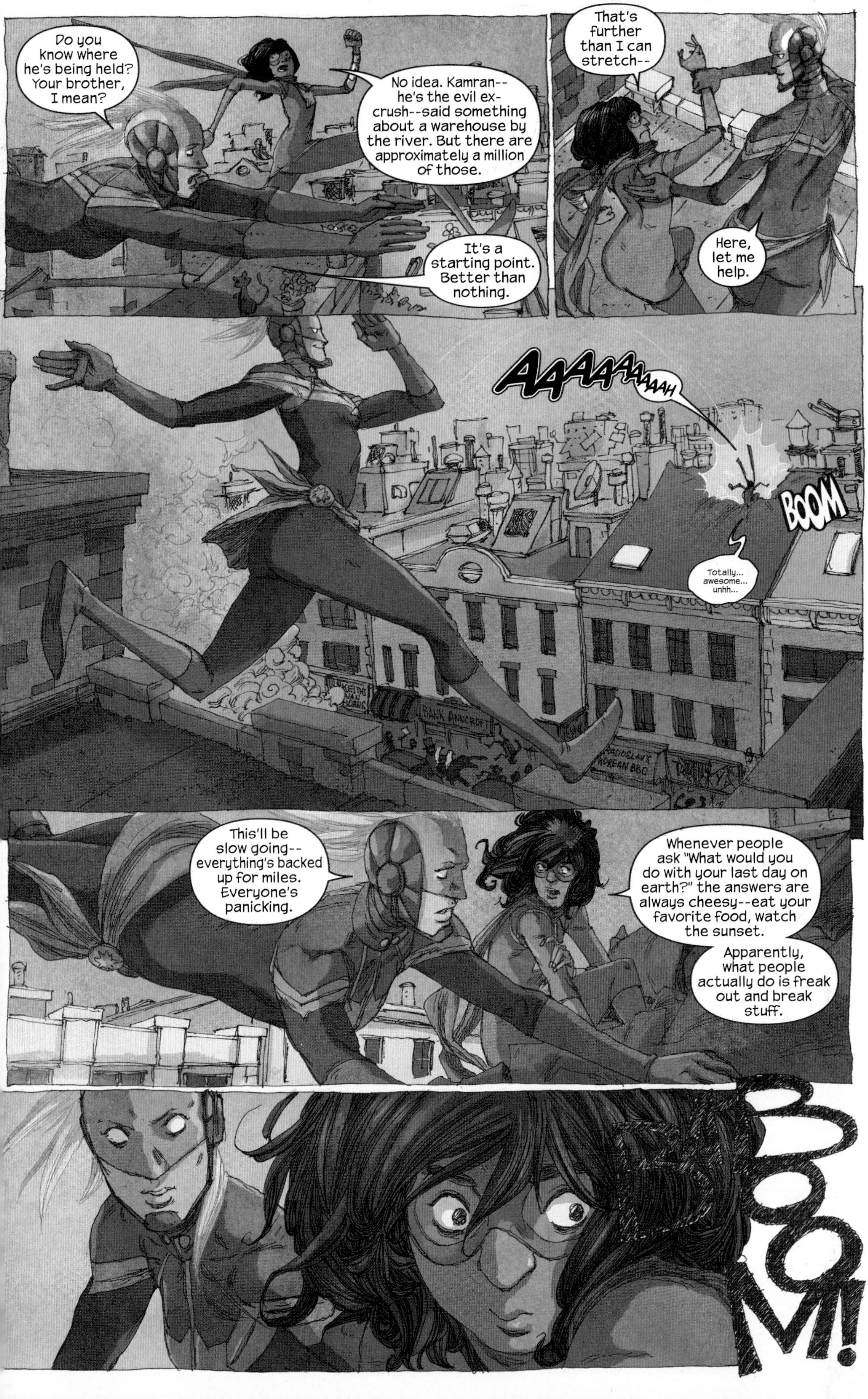

Do you know where he's being held? Your brother, I mean?
No idea. Kamran--he's the evil ex-crush--said something about a warehouse by the river. But there are approximately a million of those.
It's a starting point. Better than nothing.
That's further than I can stretch--
Here, let me help.
AAAAAAAAAH
BOOM
Totally... awesome... unhh...
RADOSLAV'S KOREAN BBQ
This'll be slow going--everything's backed up for miles. Everyone's panicking.
Whenever people ask "What would you do with your last day on earth?" the answers are always cheesy--eat your favorite food, watch the sunset.
Apparently, what people actually do is freak out and break stuff.
BOOOM!

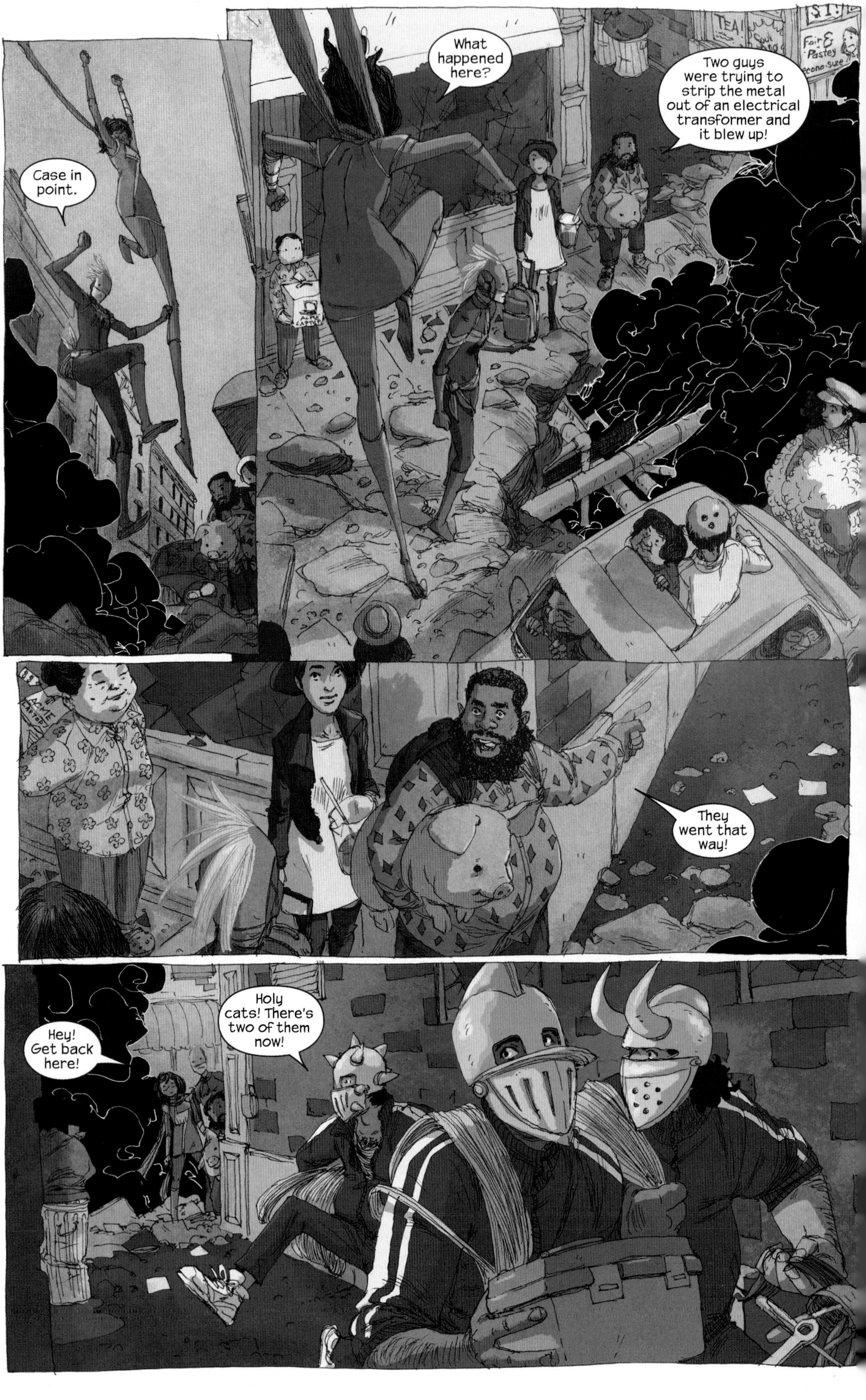
Case in point.
What happened here?
TEA!
Two guys were trying to strip the metal out of an electrical transformer and it blew up!
They went that way!
Hey! Get back here!
Holy cats! There's two of them now!

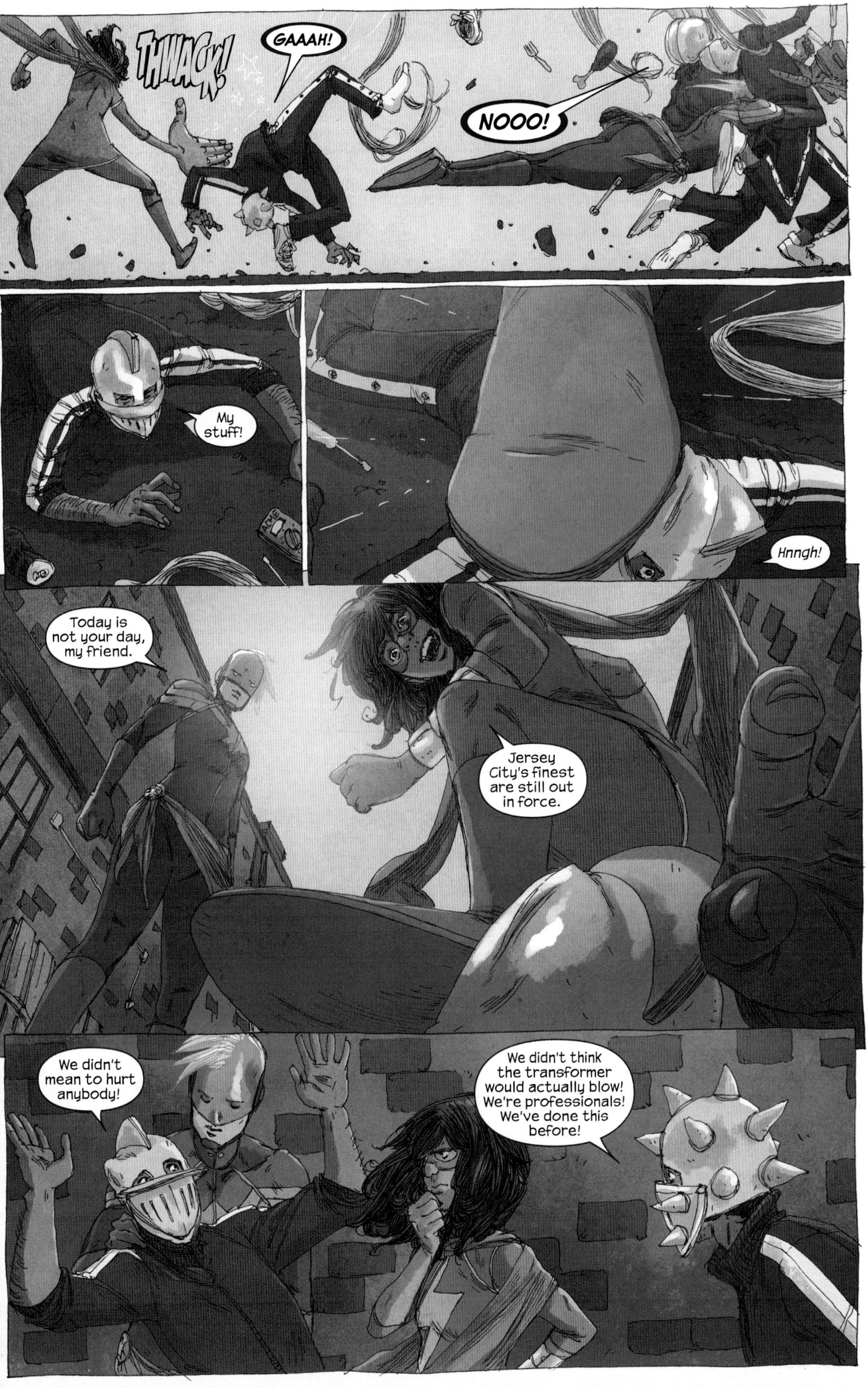
THWACK!
GAAAH!
NOOO!
My stuff!
Hnngh!
Today is not your day, my friend.
Jersey City's finest are still out in force.
We didn't mean to hurt anybody!
We didn't think the transformer would actually blow! We're professionals! We've done this before!

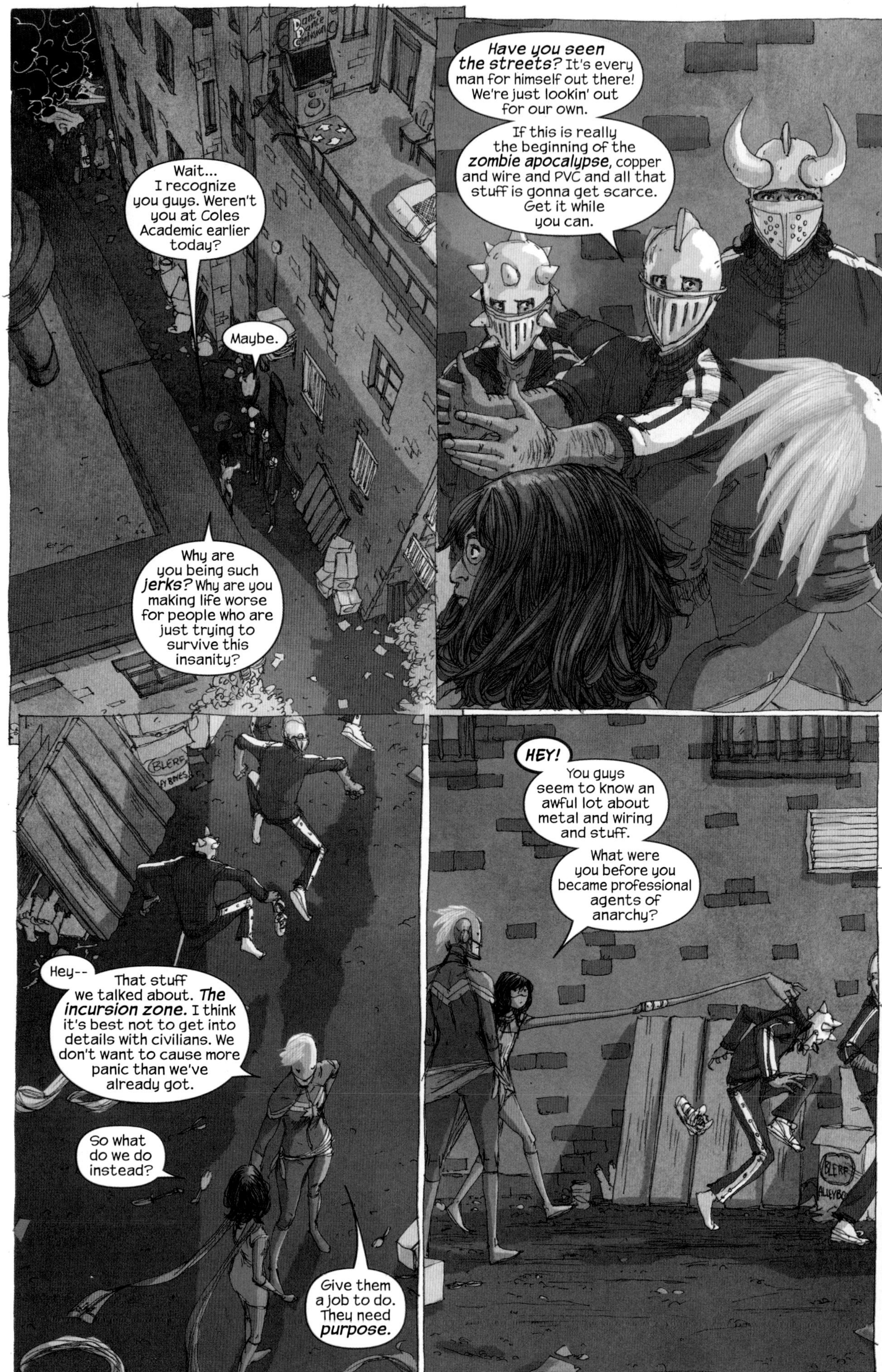
Wait... I recognize you guys. Weren't you at Coles Academic earlier today?
Maybe.
Why are you being such *jerks?* Why are you making life worse for people who are just trying to survive this insanity?
Have you seen the streets? It's every man for himself out there! We're just lookin' out for our own.
If this is really the beginning of the *zombie apocalypse*, copper and wire and PVC and all that stuff is gonna get scarce. Get it while you can.
Hey--
That stuff we talked about. *The incursion zone.* I think it's best not to get into details with civilians. We don't want to cause more panic than we've already got.
So what do we do instead?
Give them a job to do. They need *purpose.*
HEY!
You guys seem to know an awful lot about metal and wiring and stuff.
What were you before you became professional agents of anarchy?

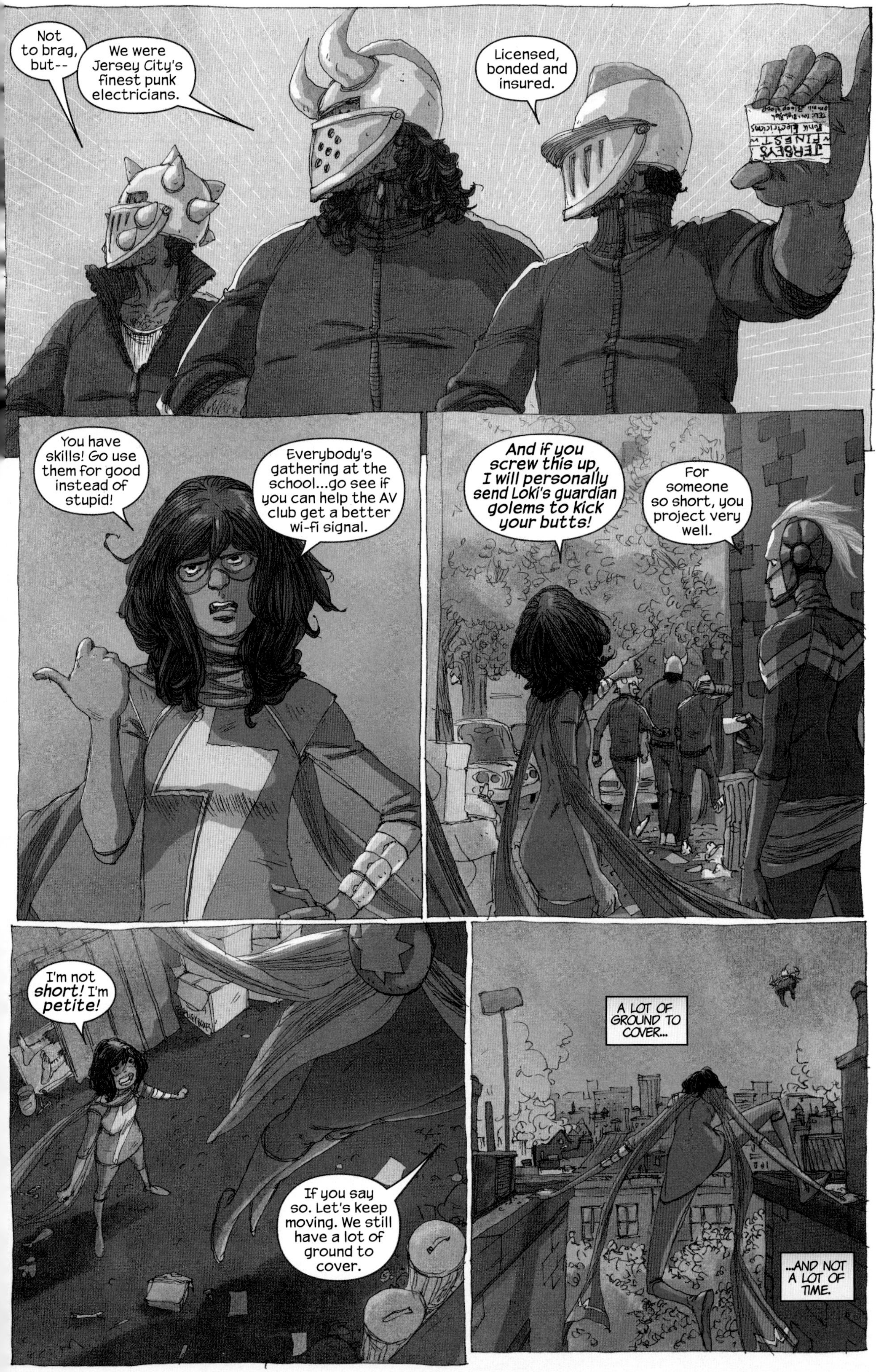

Not to brag, but--
We were Jersey City's finest punk electricians.
Licensed, bonded and insured.
JERSEY'S FINEST Punk electricians
You have skills! Go use them for good instead of stupid!
Everybody's gathering at the school...go see if you can help the AV club get a better wi-fi signal.
And if you screw this up, I will personally send Loki's guardian golems to kick your butts!
For someone so short, you project very well.
I'm not short! I'm petite!
If you say so. Let's keep moving. We still have a lot of ground to cover.
A LOT OF GROUND TO COVER...
...AND NOT A LOT OF TIME.

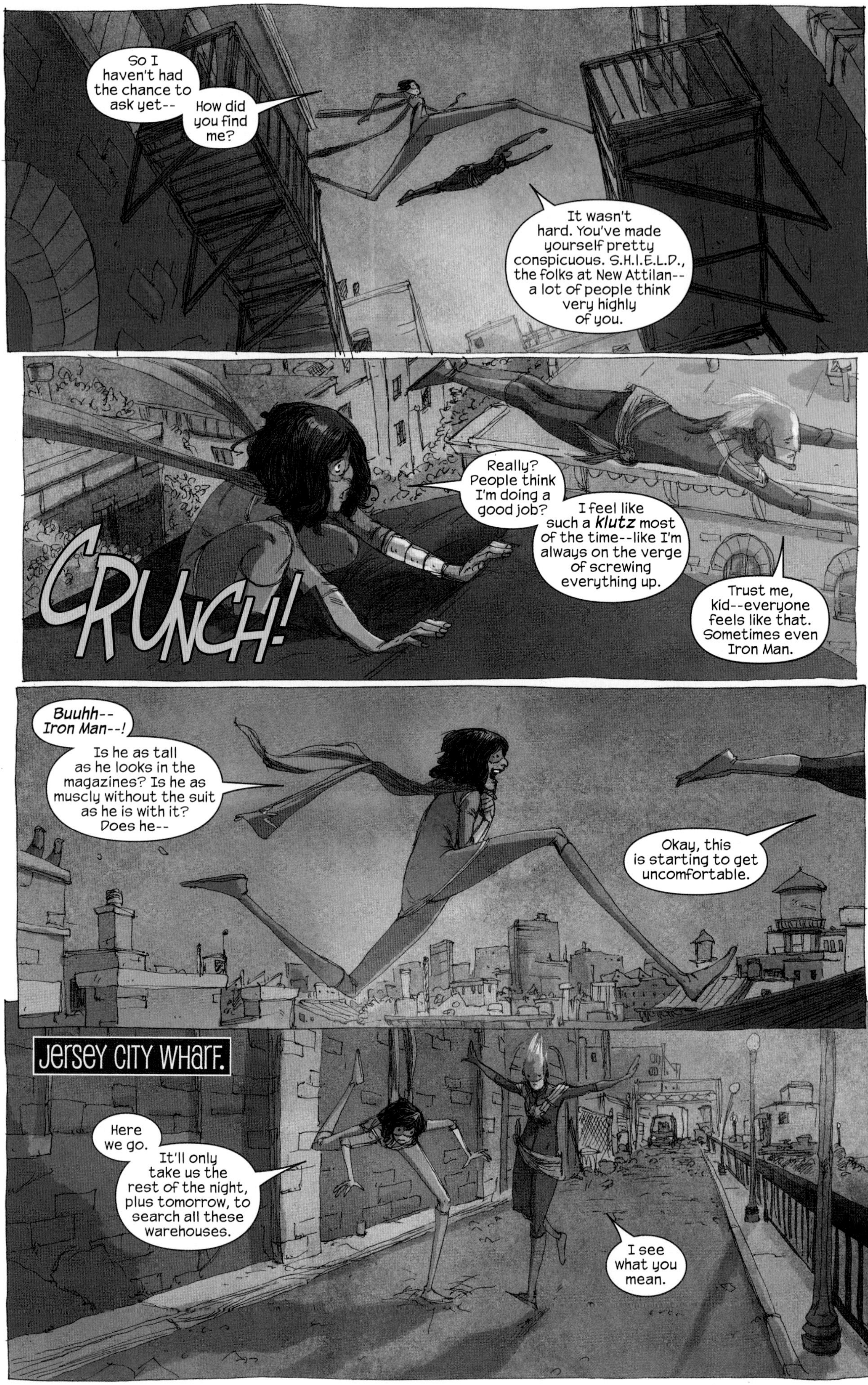
So I haven't had the chance to ask yet--
How did you find me?
It wasn't hard. You've made yourself pretty conspicuous. S.H.I.E.L.D., the folks at New Attilan--a lot of people think very highly of you.
Really? People think I'm doing a good job?
I feel like such a *klutz* most of the time--like I'm always on the verge of screwing everything up.
CRUNCH!
Trust me, kid--everyone feels like that. Sometimes even Iron Man.
Buuhh-- Iron Man--!
Is he as tall as he looks in the magazines? Is he as muscly without the suit as he is with it? Does he--
Okay, this is starting to get uncomfortable.
Jersey City Wharf.
Here we go.
It'll only take us the rest of the night, plus tomorrow, to search all these warehouses.
I see what you mean.

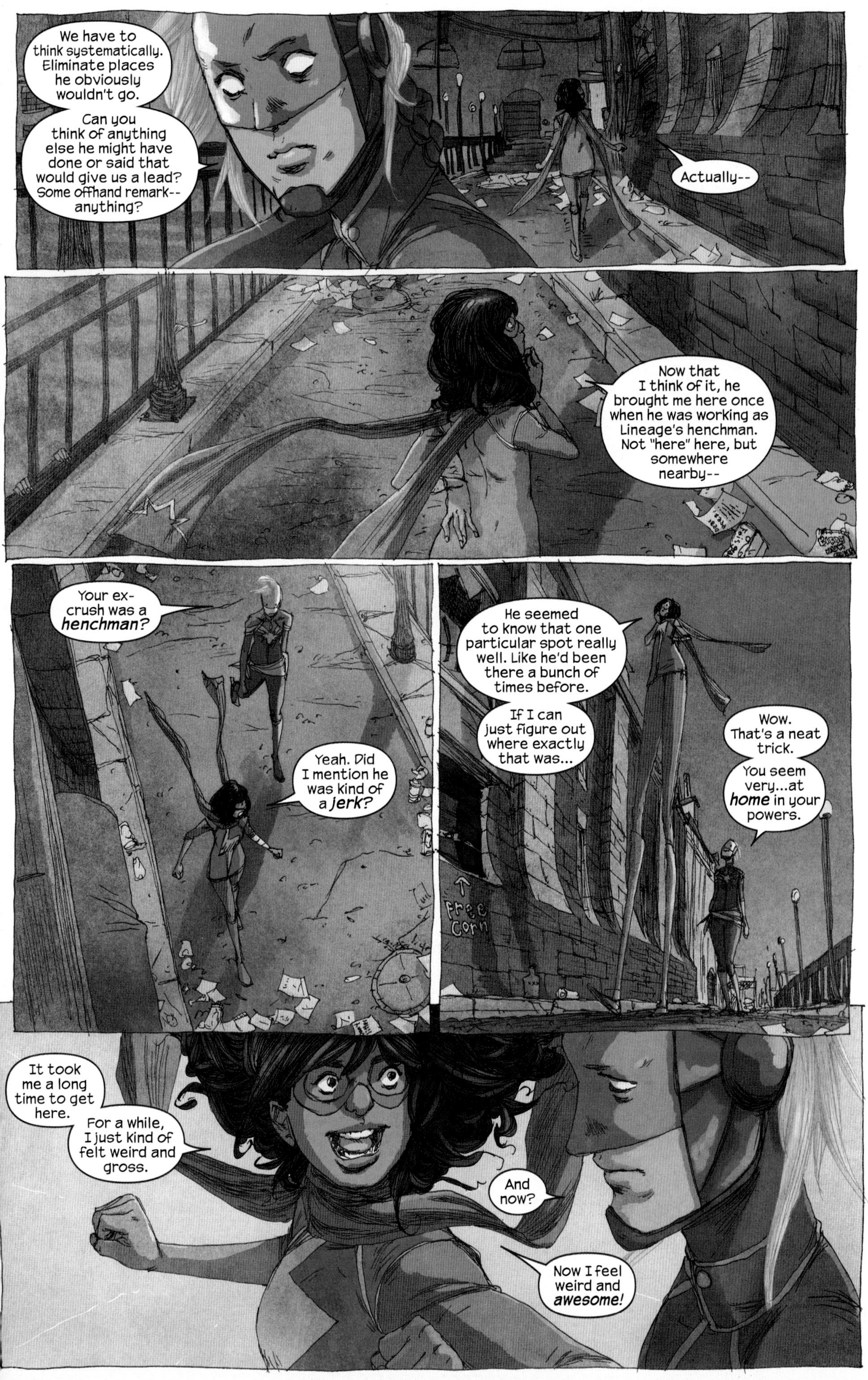
We have to think systematically. Eliminate places he obviously wouldn't go.
Can you think of anything else he might have done or said that would give us a lead? Some offhand remark--anything?
Actually--
Now that I think of it, he brought me here once when he was working as Lineage's henchman. Not "here" here, but somewhere nearby--
Your ex-crush was a *henchman*?
Yeah. Did I mention he was kind of a *jerk?*
He seemed to know that one particular spot really well. Like he'd been there a bunch of times before.
If I can just figure out where exactly that was...
Wow. That's a neat trick.
You seem very...at *home* in your powers.
Free Corn
It took me a long time to get here.
For a while, I just kind of felt weird and gross.
And now?
Now I feel weird and *awesome!*

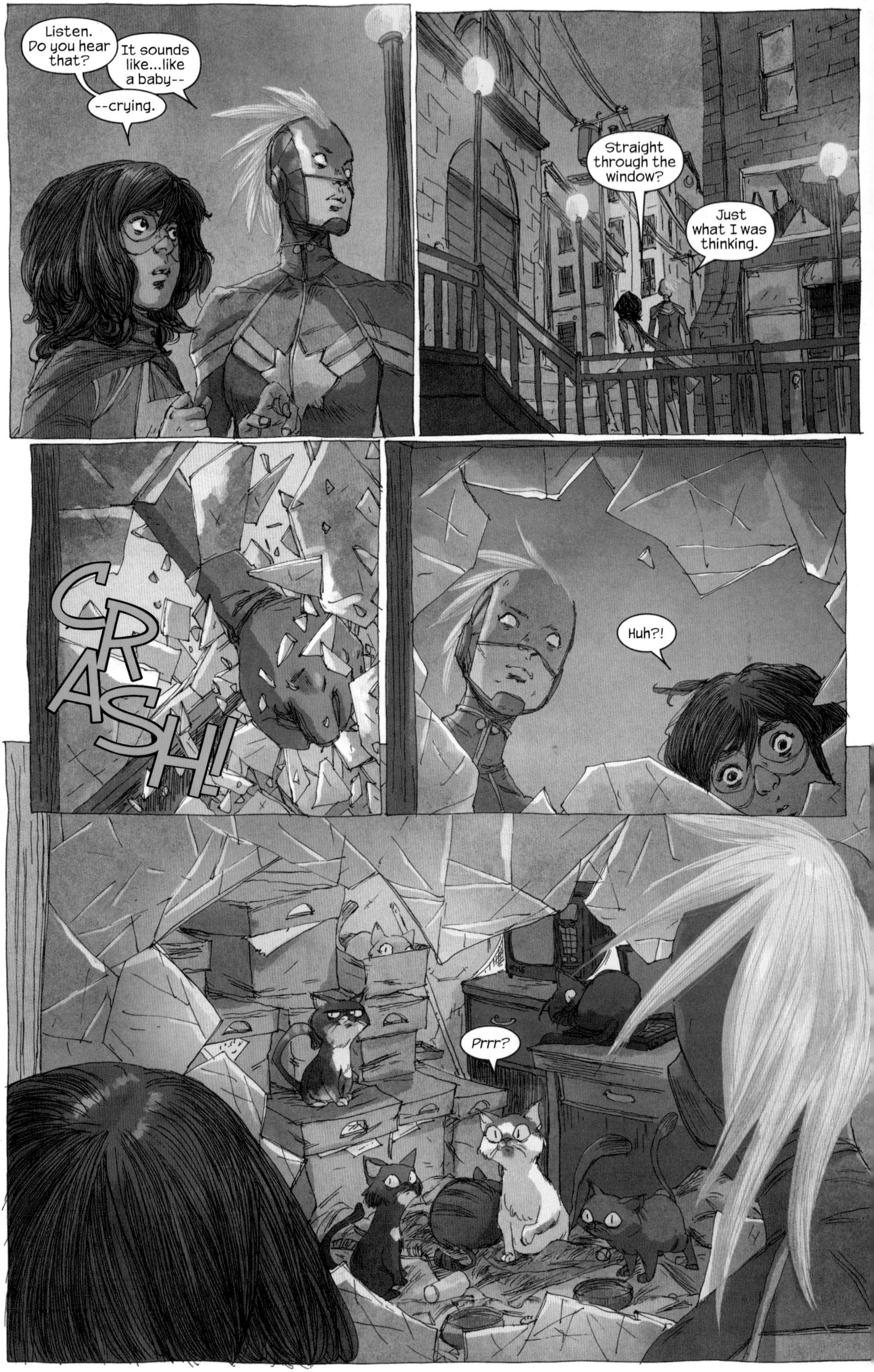
Listen. Do you hear that?
It sounds like...like a baby--
--crying.
Straight through the window?
Just what I was thinking.
CRASH!
Huh?!
Prrr?

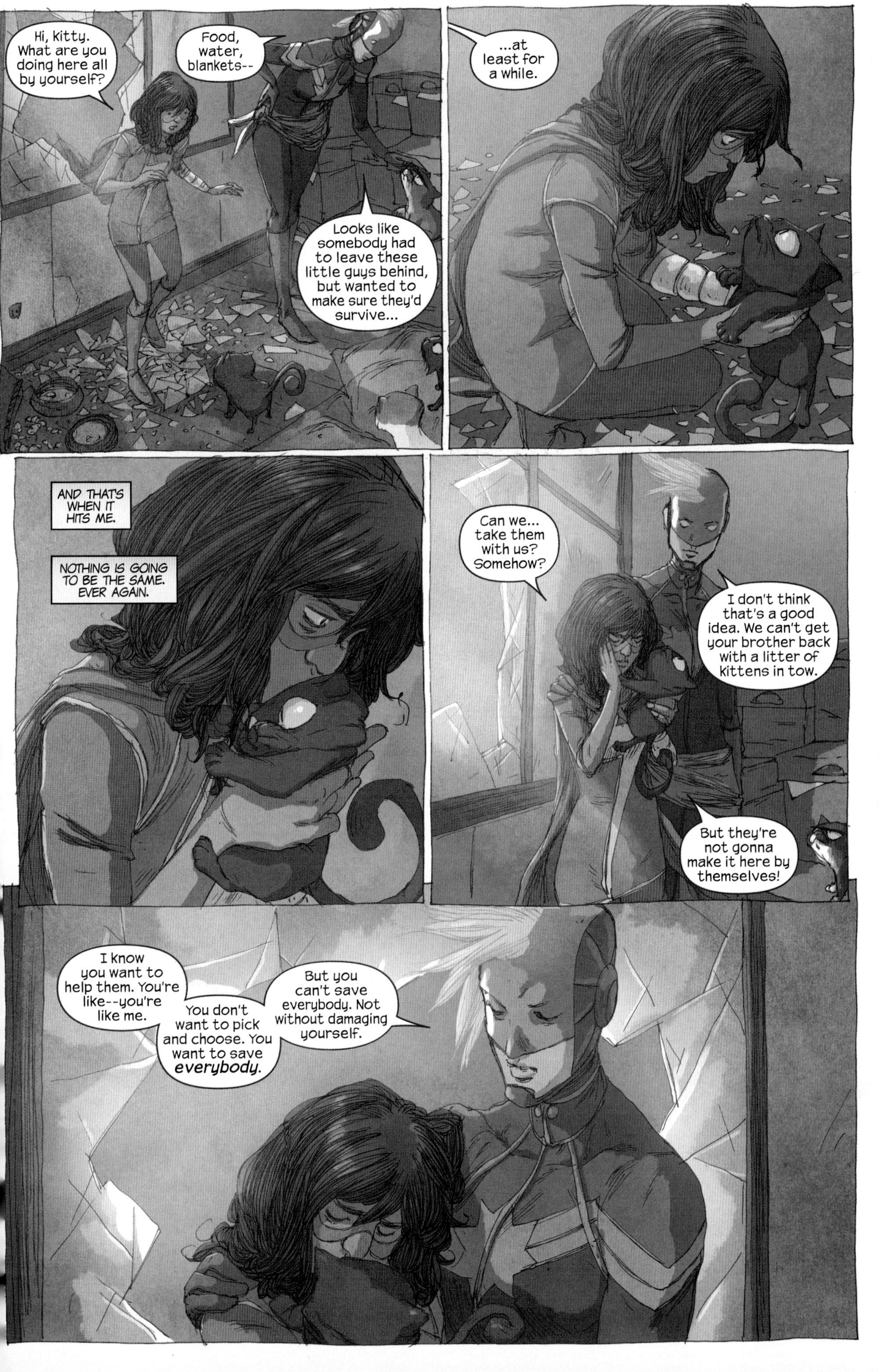
Hi, kitty. What are you doing here all by yourself?
Food, water, blankets--
Looks like somebody had to leave these little guys behind, but wanted to make sure they'd survive...
...at least for a while.
AND THAT'S WHEN IT HITS ME.
NOTHING IS GOING TO BE THE SAME. EVER AGAIN.
Can we... take them with us? Somehow?
I don't think that's a good idea. We can't get your brother back with a litter of kittens in tow.
But they're not gonna make it here by themselves!
I know you want to help them. You're like--you're like me.
You don't want to pick and choose. You want to save *everybody*.
But you can't save everybody. Not without damaging yourself.

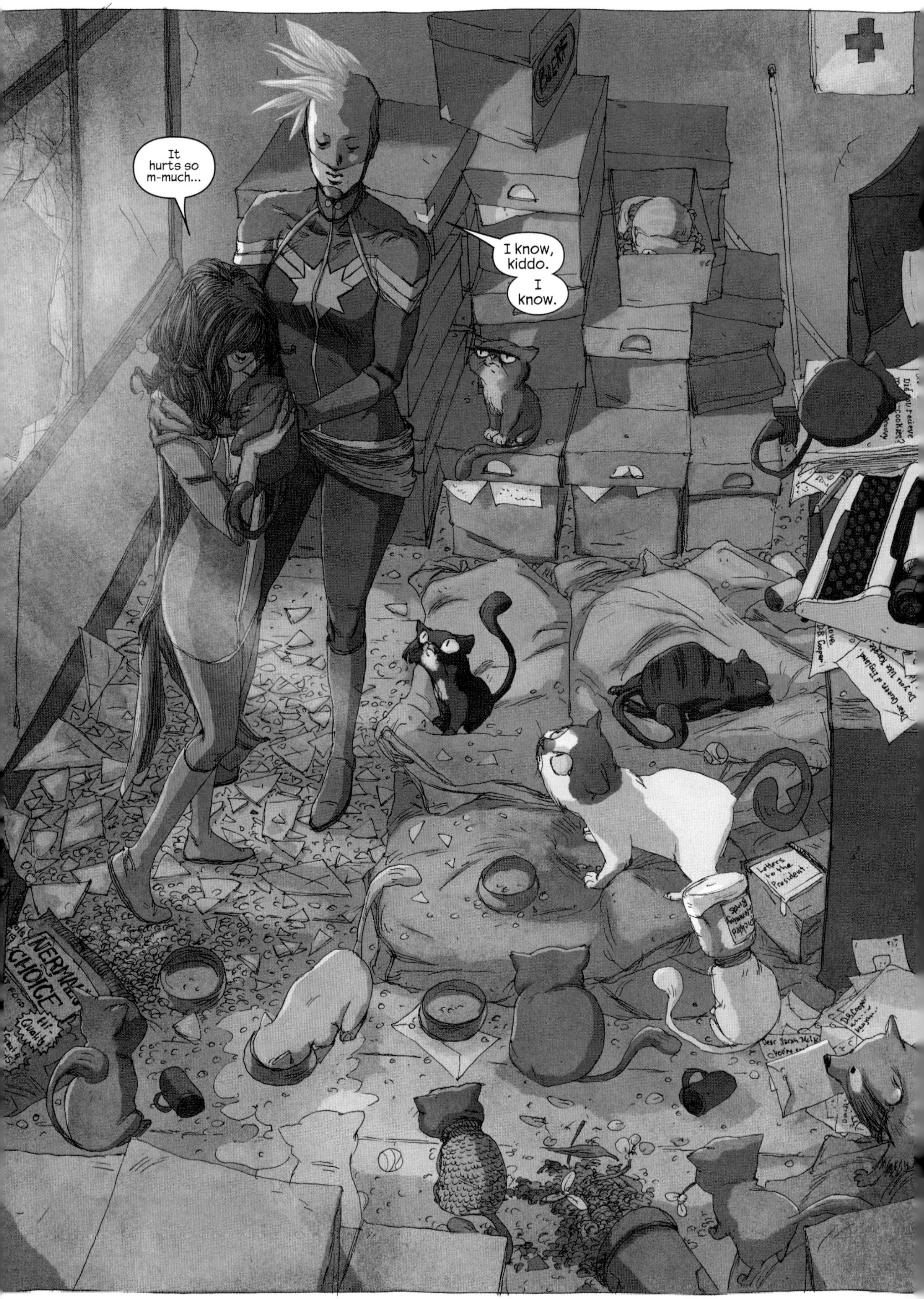
It hurts so m-much...
I know, kiddo.
I know.
Letters to the President

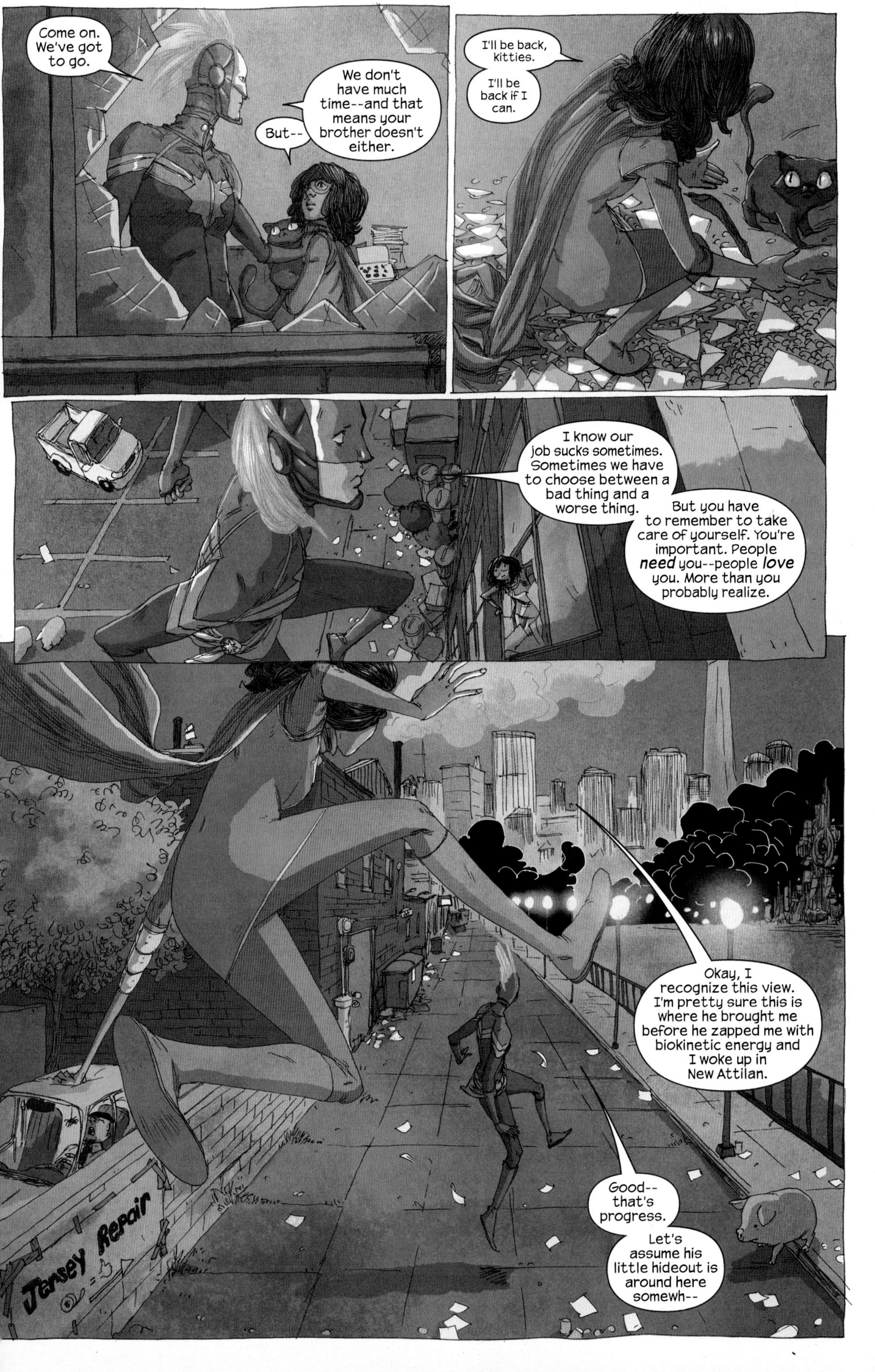
Come on. We've got to go.
But--
We don't have much time--and that means your brother doesn't either.
I'll be back, kitties.
I'll be back if I can.
I know our job sucks sometimes. Sometimes we have to choose between a bad thing and a worse thing.
But you have to remember to take care of yourself. You're important. People *need* you--people *love* you. More than you probably realize.
Okay, I recognize this view. I'm pretty sure this is where he brought me before he zapped me with biokinetic energy and I woke up in New Attilan.
Good--that's progress.
Let's assume his little hideout is around here somewh--
Jersey Repair

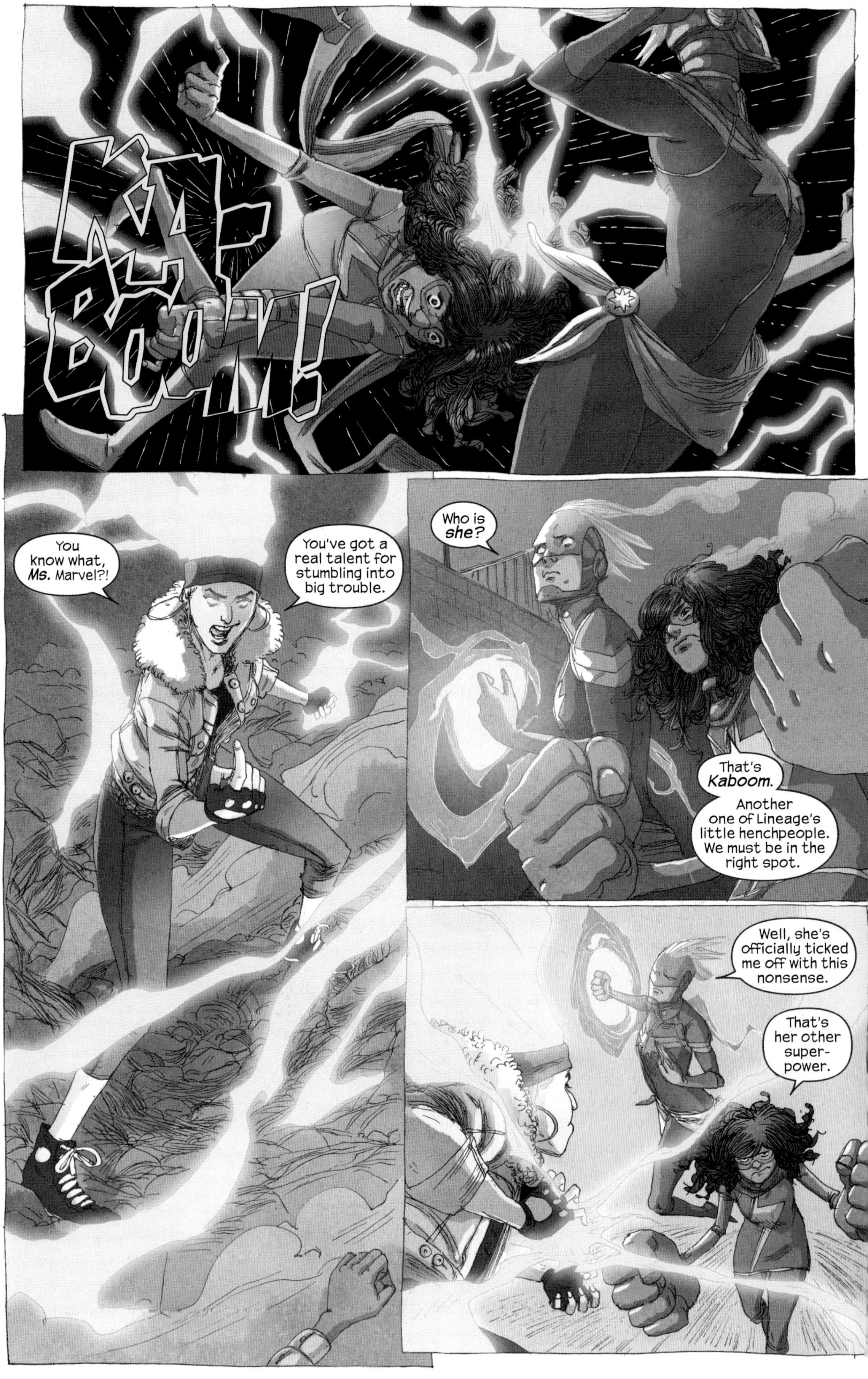
KA-BOOM!
You know what, Ms. Marvel?!
You've got a real talent for stumbling into big trouble.
Who is she?
That's Kaboom.
Another one of Lineage's little henchpeople. We must be in the right spot.
Well, she's officially ticked me off with this nonsense.
That's her other super-power.

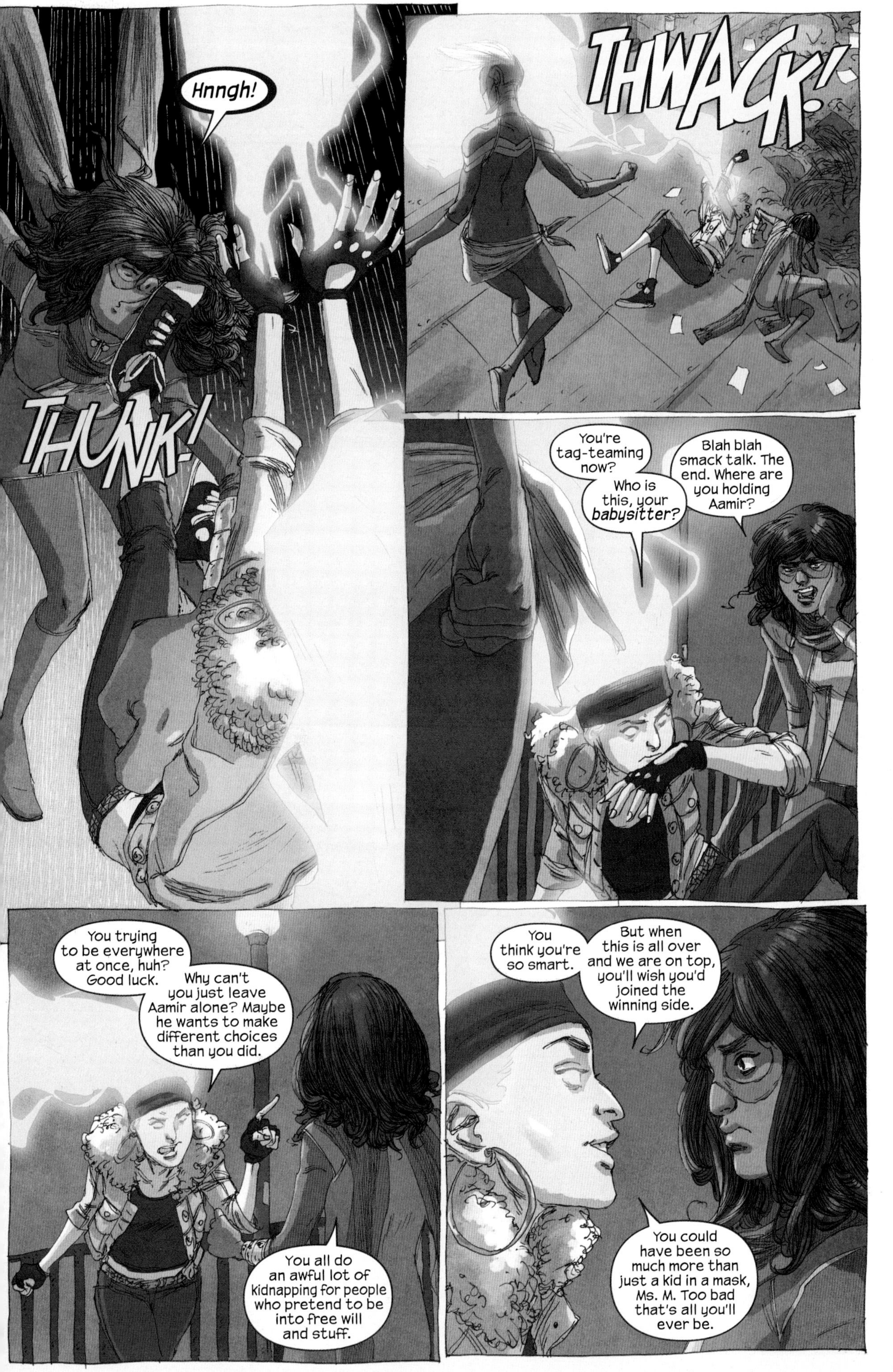
Hnngh!
THUNK!
THWACK!
You're tag-teaming now? Who is this, your *babysitter*?
Blah blah smack talk. The end. Where are you holding Aamir?
You trying to be everywhere at once, huh? Good luck.
Why can't you just leave Aamir alone? Maybe he wants to make different choices than you did.
You all do an awful lot of kidnapping for people who pretend to be into free will and stuff.
You think you're so smart.
But when this is all over and we are on top, you'll wish you'd joined the winning side.
You could have been so much more than just a kid in a mask, Ms. M. Too bad that's all you'll ever be.

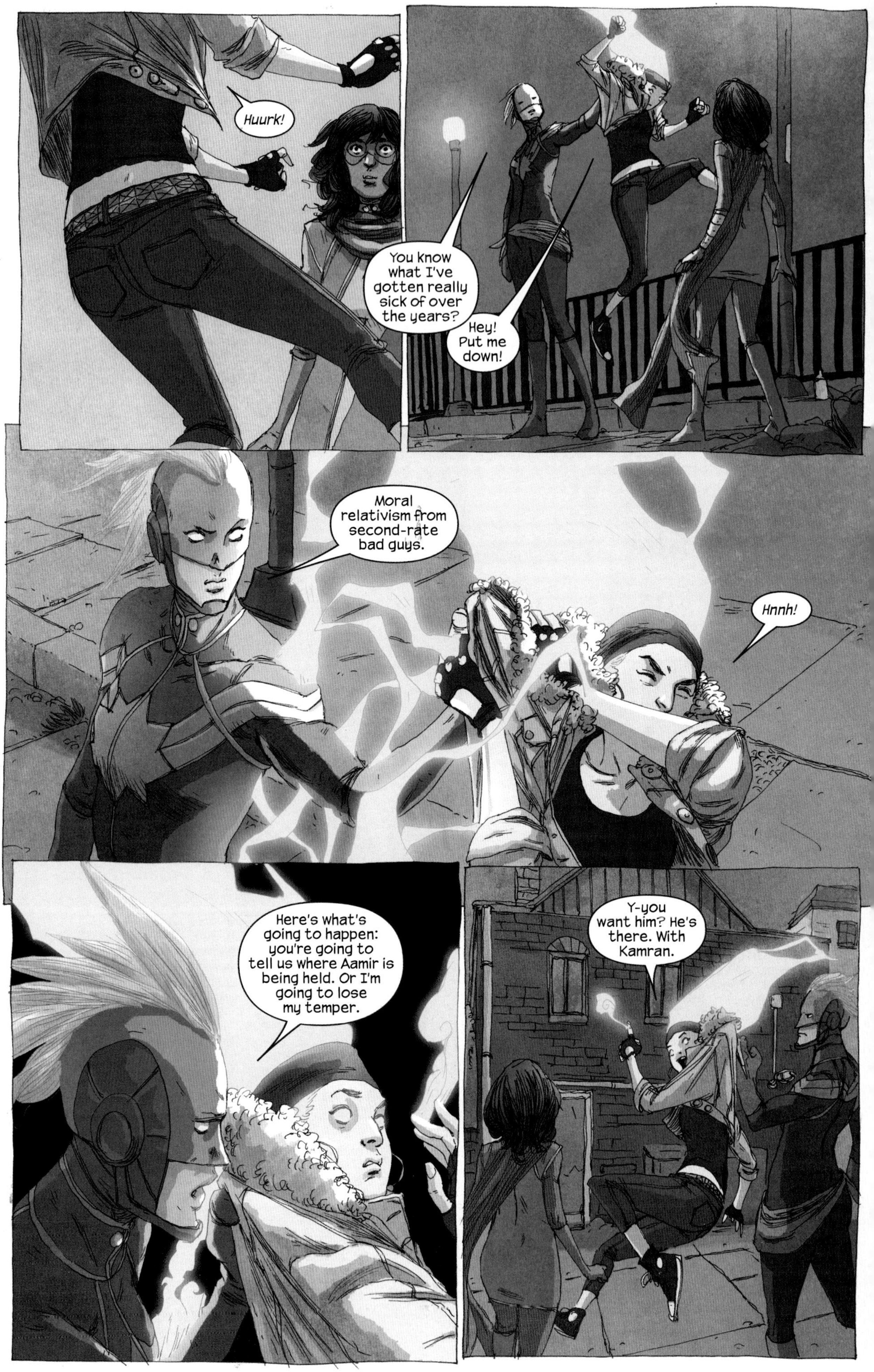
Huurk!
You know what I've gotten really sick of over the years?
Hey! Put me down!
Moral relativism from second-rate bad guys.
Hnnh!
Here's what's going to happen: you're going to tell us where Aamir is being held. Or I'm going to lose my temper.
Y-you want him? He's there. With Kamran.

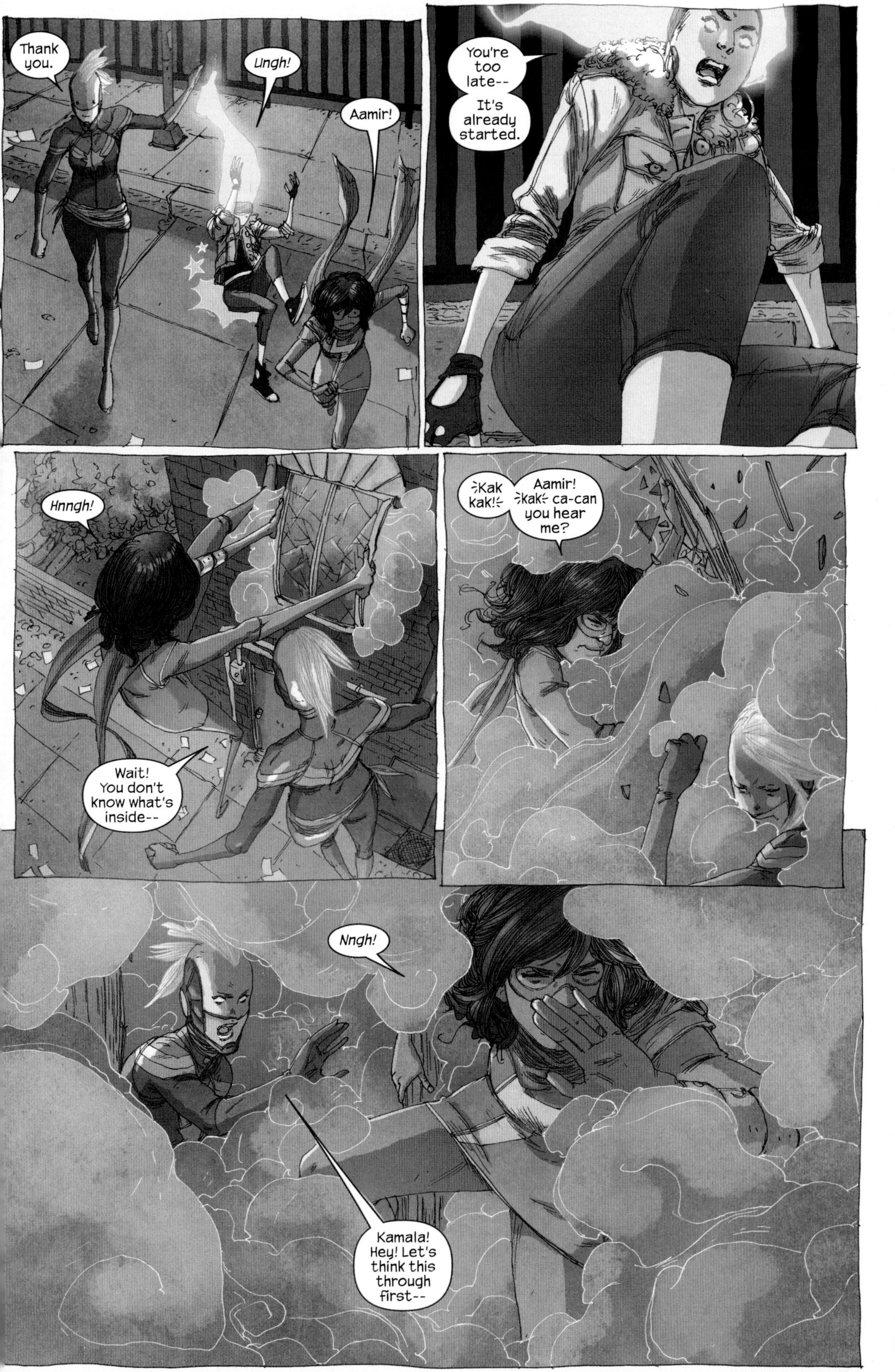

Thank you.
Ungh!
Aamir!
You're too late--
It's already started.
Hnngh!
Wait! You don't know what's inside--
Kak kak!
Aamir! *kak* ca-can you hear me?
Nngh!
Kamala! Hey! Let's think this through first--

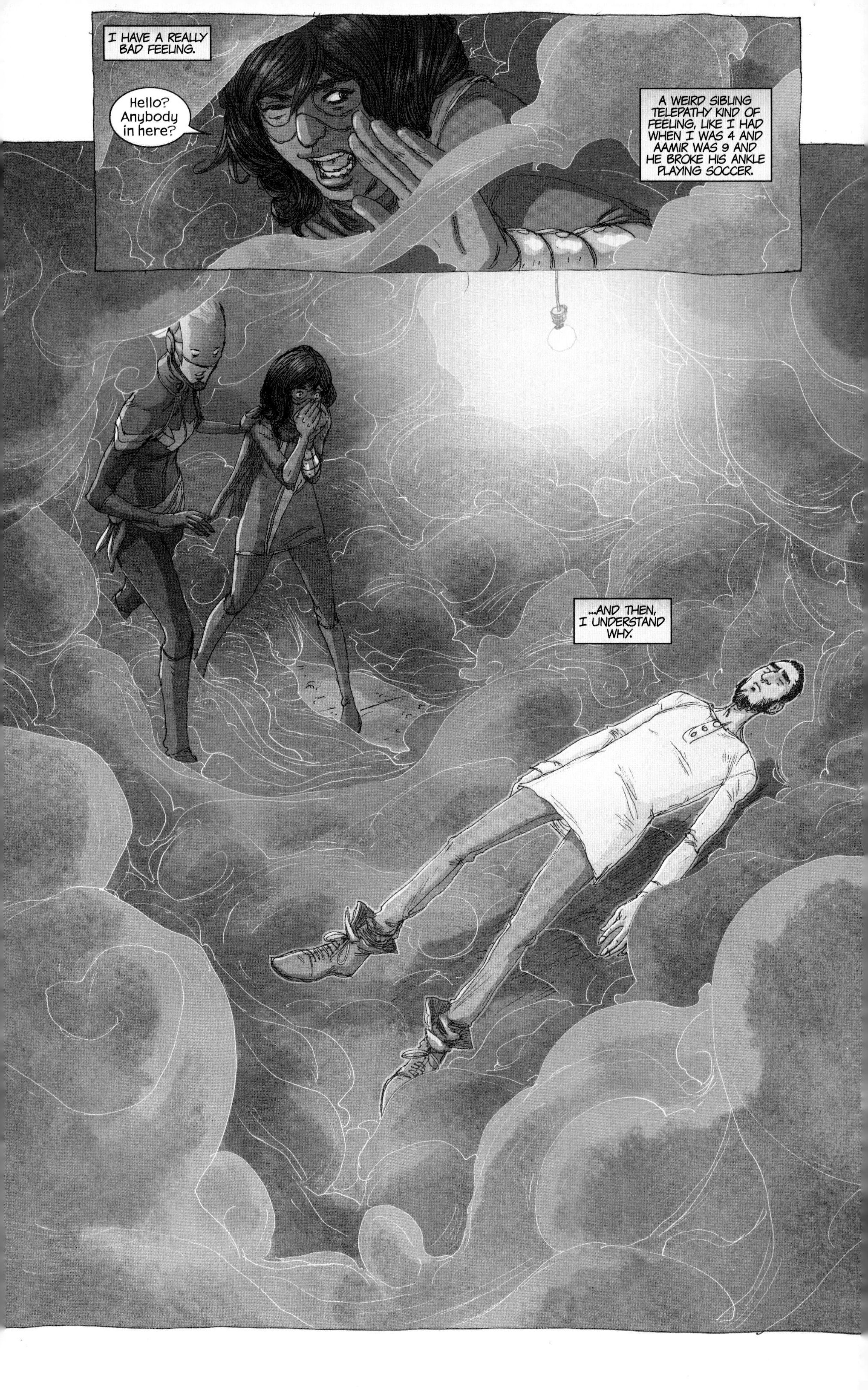
I HAVE A REALLY BAD FEELING.
Hello? Anybody in here?
A WEIRD SIBLING TELEPATHY KIND OF FEELING, LIKE I HAD WHEN I WAS 4 AND AAMIR WAS 9 AND HE BROKE HIS ANKLE PLAYING SOCCER.
...AND THEN, I UNDERSTAND WHY.

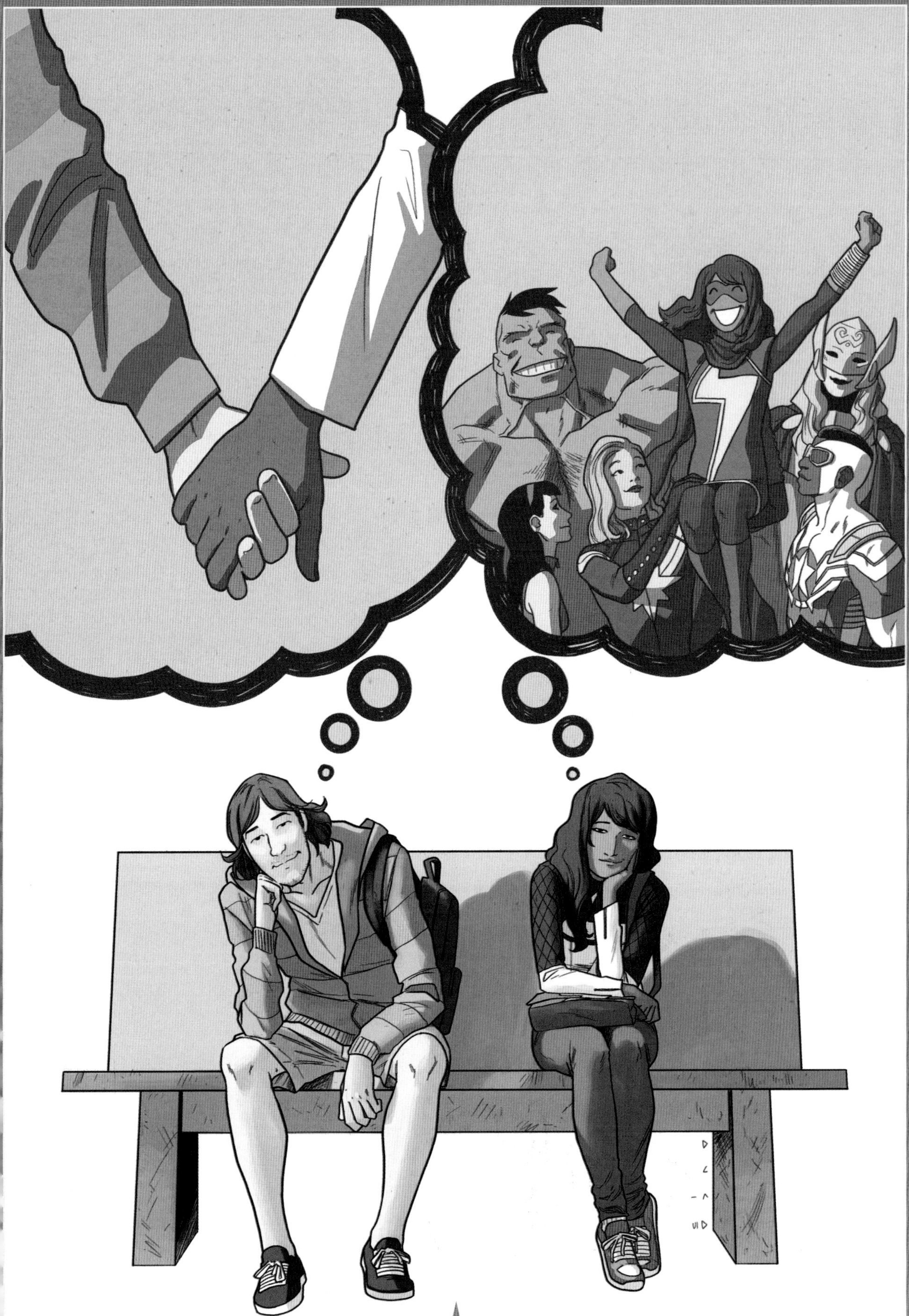

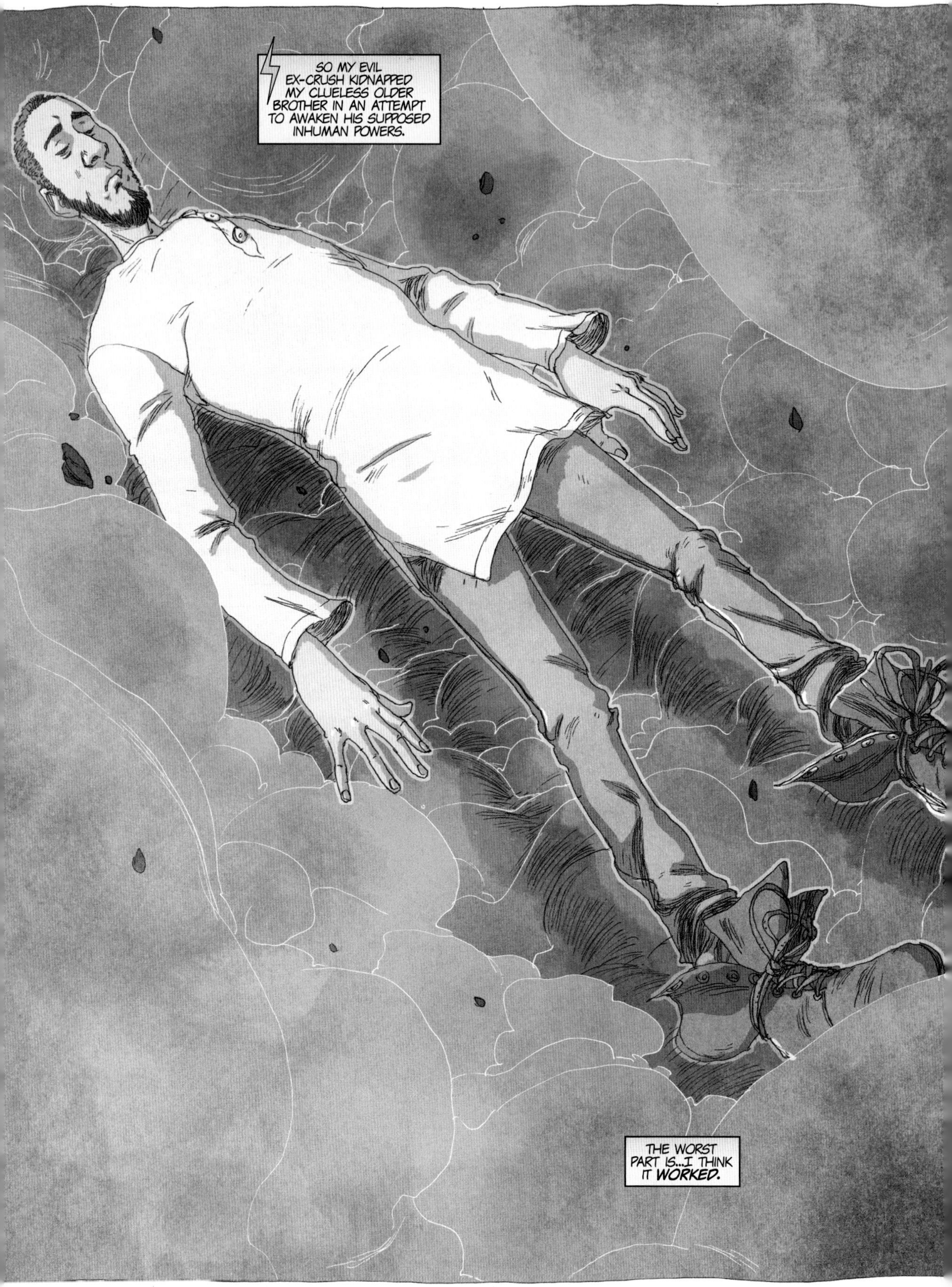
SO MY EVIL EX-CRUSH KIDNAPPED MY CLUELESS OLDER BROTHER IN AN ATTEMPT TO AWAKEN HIS SUPPOSED INHUMAN POWERS.
THE WORST PART IS...I THINK IT WORKED.

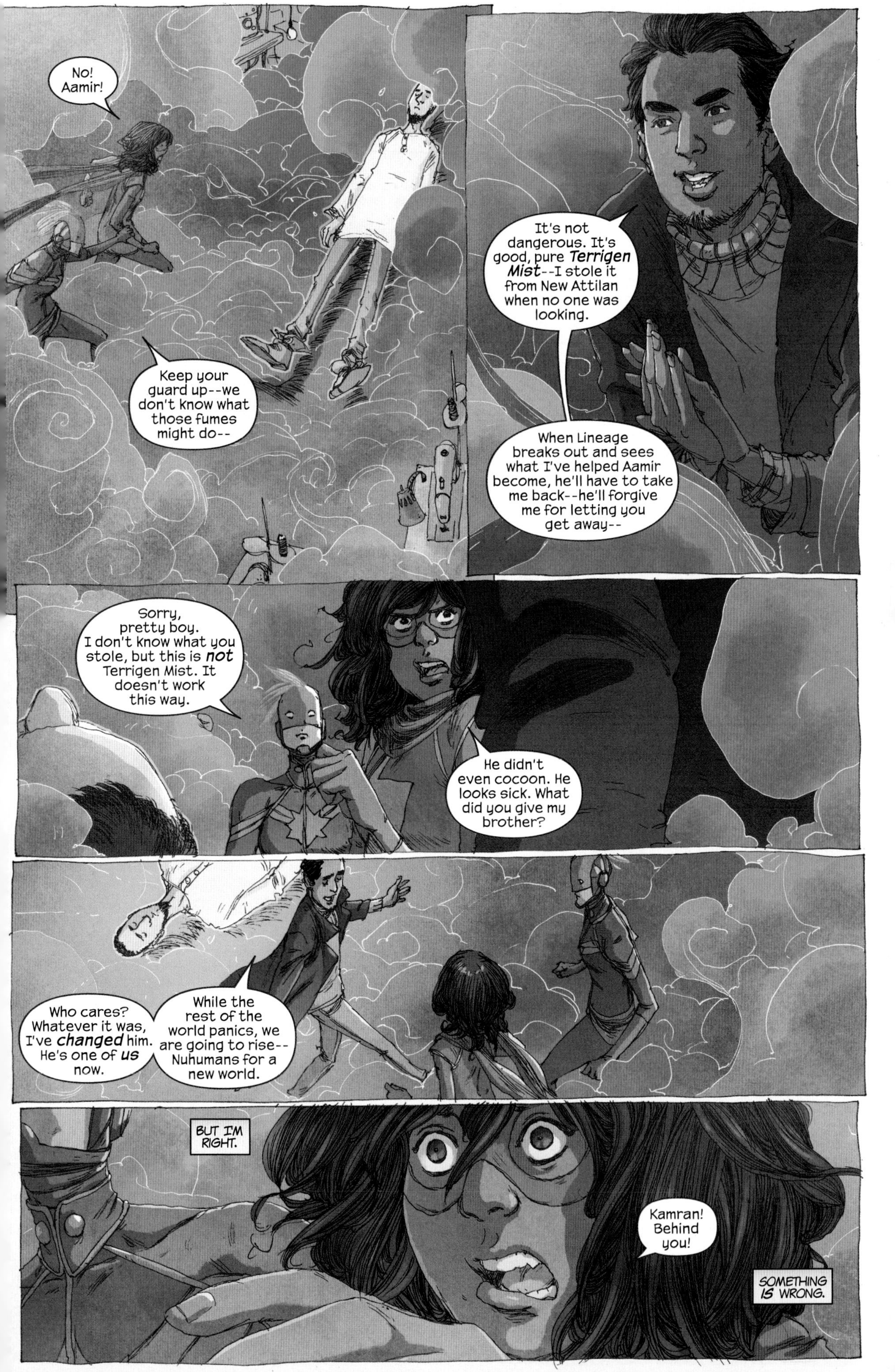
No! Aamir!
Keep your guard up--we don't know what those fumes might do--
It's not dangerous. It's good, pure *Terrigen Mist*--I stole it from New Attilan when no one was looking.
When Lineage breaks out and sees what I've helped Aamir become, he'll have to take me back--he'll forgive me for letting you get away--
Sorry, pretty boy. I don't know what you stole, but this is *not* Terrigen Mist. It doesn't work this way.
He didn't even cocoon. He looks sick. What did you give my brother?
Who cares? Whatever it was, I've *changed* him. He's one of *us* now.
While the rest of the world panics, we are going to rise--Nuhumans for a new world.
BUT I'M RIGHT.
Kamran! Behind you!
SOMETHING *IS* WRONG.

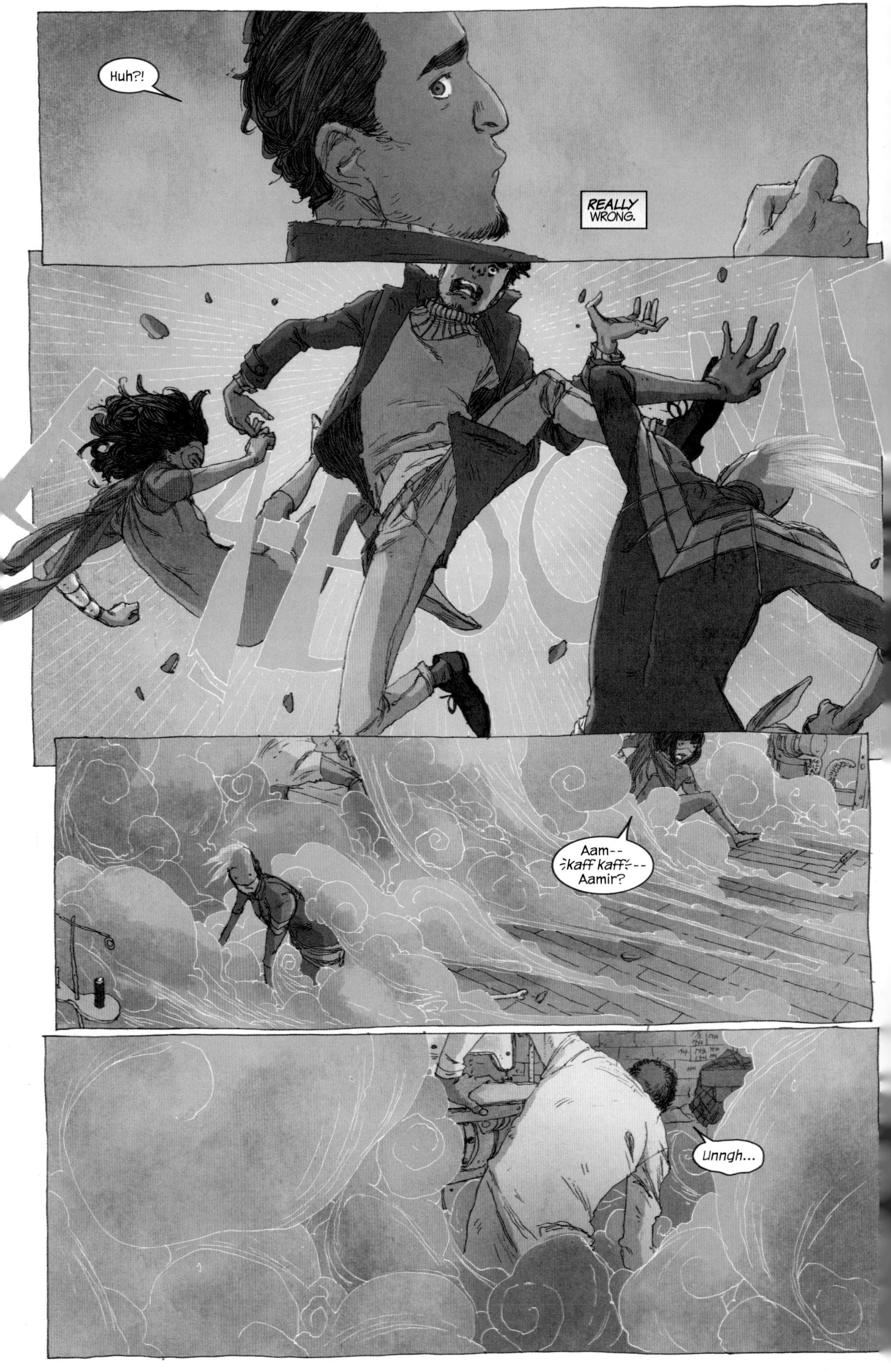
Huh?!
REALLY WRONG.
Aam-- kaff kaff-- Aamir?
Unngh...

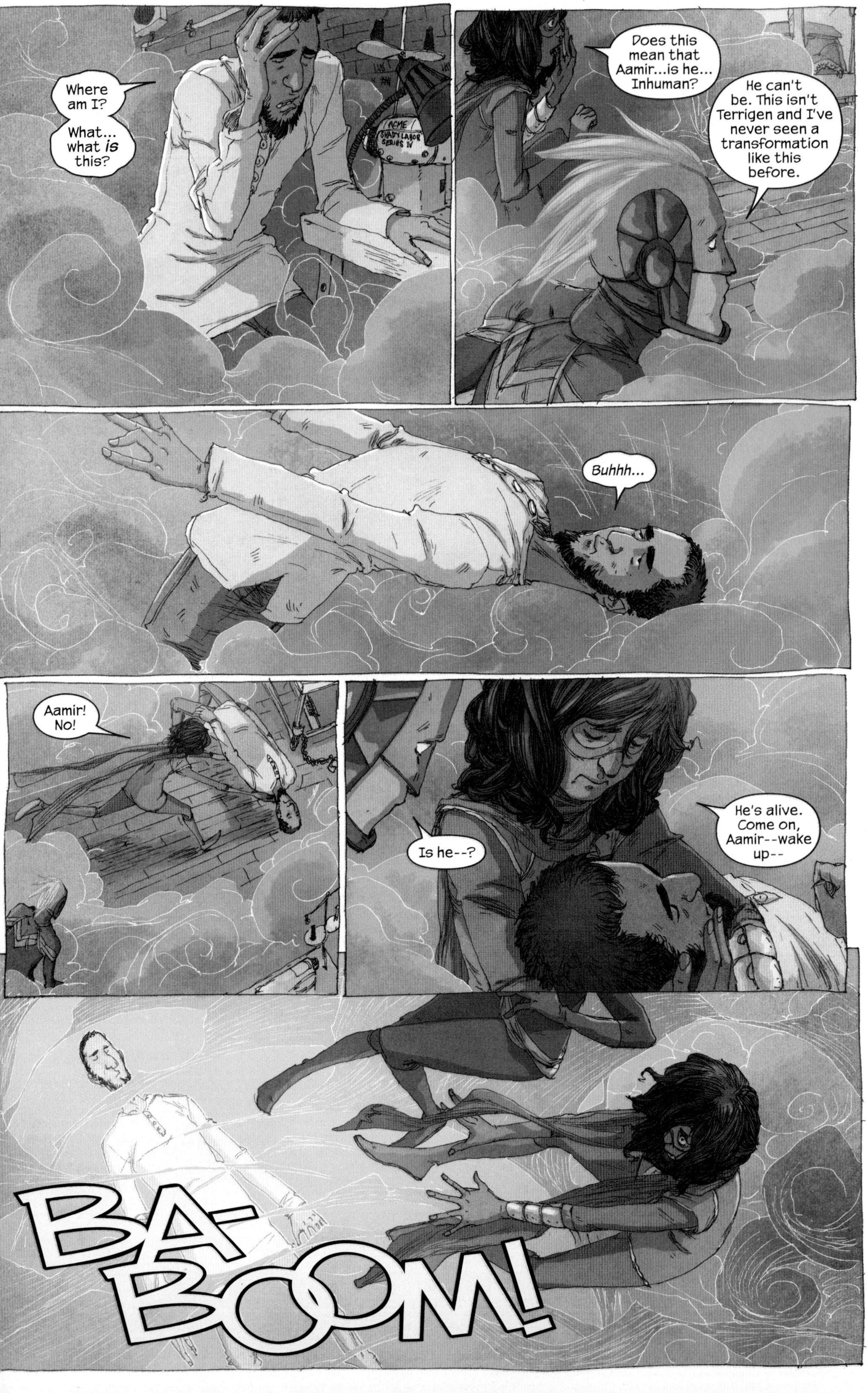
Where am I?
What... what *is* this?
ACME SHADY LABOR SERIES IV
Does this mean that Aamir...is he... Inhuman?
He can't be. This isn't Terrigen and I've never seen a transformation like this before.
Buhhh...
Aamir! No!
Is he--?
He's alive. Come on, Aamir--wake up--
BA-BOOM!

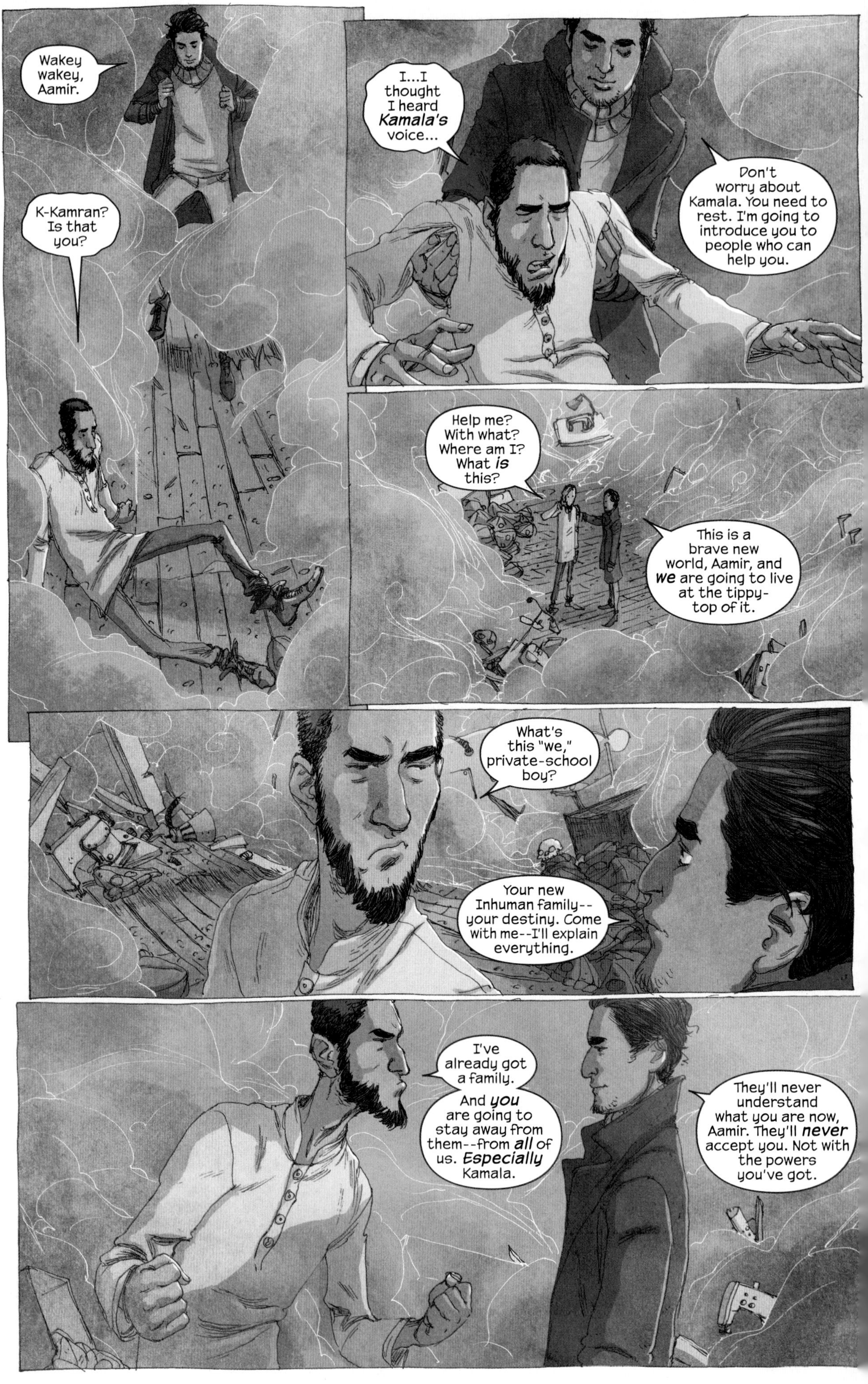
Wakey wakey, Aamir.
K-Kamran? Is that you?
I...I thought I heard *Kamala's* voice...
Don't worry about Kamala. You need to rest. I'm going to introduce you to people who can help you.
Help me? With what? Where am I? What *is* this?
This is a brave new world, Aamir, and *we* are going to live at the tippy-top of it.
What's this "we," private-school boy?
Your new Inhuman family--your destiny. Come with me--I'll explain everything.
I've already got a family.
And *you* are going to stay away from them--from *all* of us. *Especially* Kamala.
They'll never understand what you are now, Aamir. They'll *never* accept you. Not with the powers you've got.

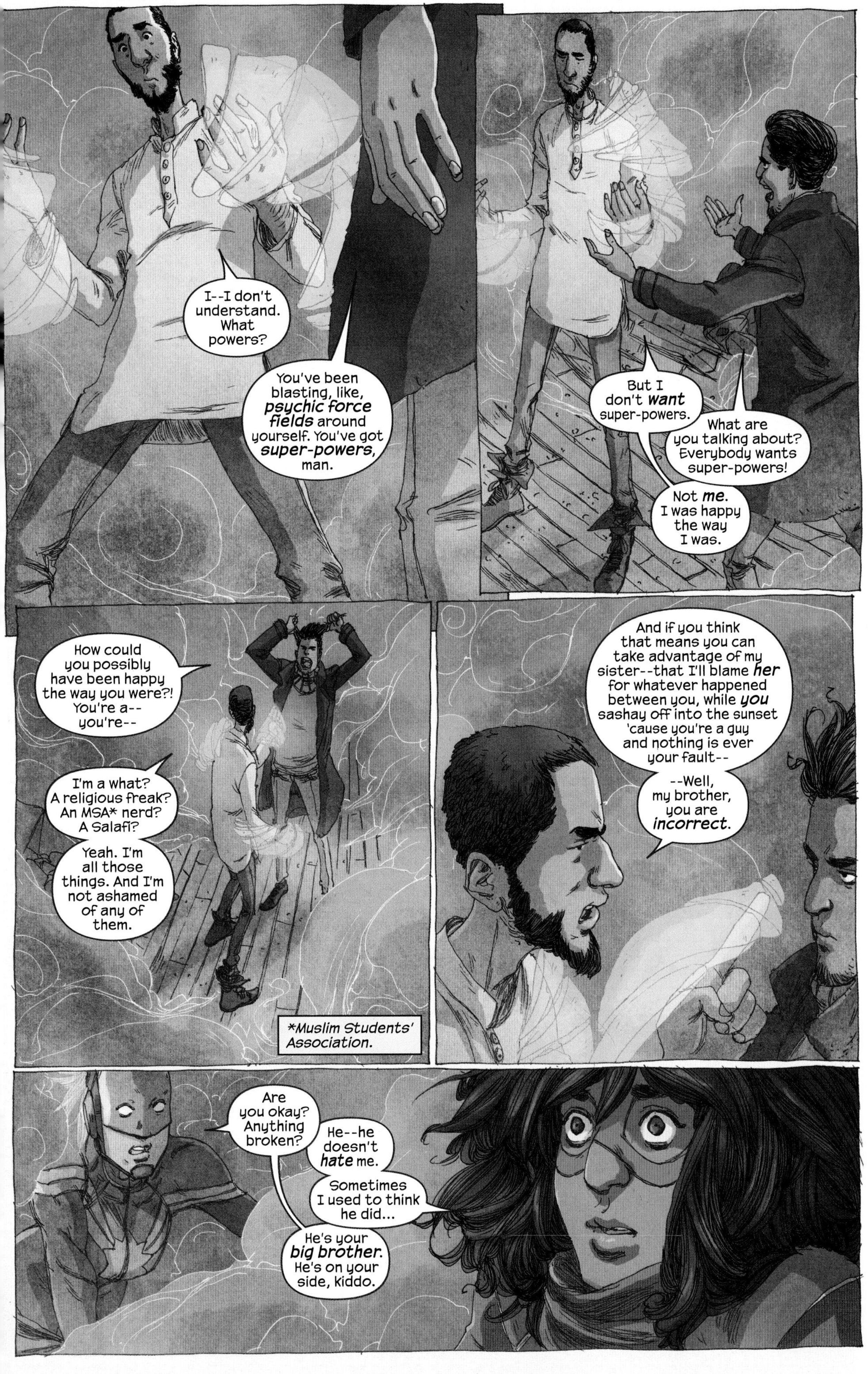

I--I don't understand. What powers?
You've been blasting, like, psychic force fields around yourself. You've got super-powers, man.
But I don't want super-powers.
What are you talking about? Everybody wants super-powers!
Not me. I was happy the way I was.
How could you possibly have been happy the way you were?! You're a-- you're--
I'm a what? A religious freak? An MSA* nerd? A Salafi?
Yeah. I'm all those things. And I'm not ashamed of any of them.
*Muslim Students' Association.
And if you think that means you can take advantage of my sister--that I'll blame her for whatever happened between you, while you sashay off into the sunset 'cause you're a guy and nothing is ever your fault--
--Well, my brother, you are incorrect.
Are you okay? Anything broken?
He--he doesn't hate me.
Sometimes I used to think he did...
He's your big brother. He's on your side, kiddo.

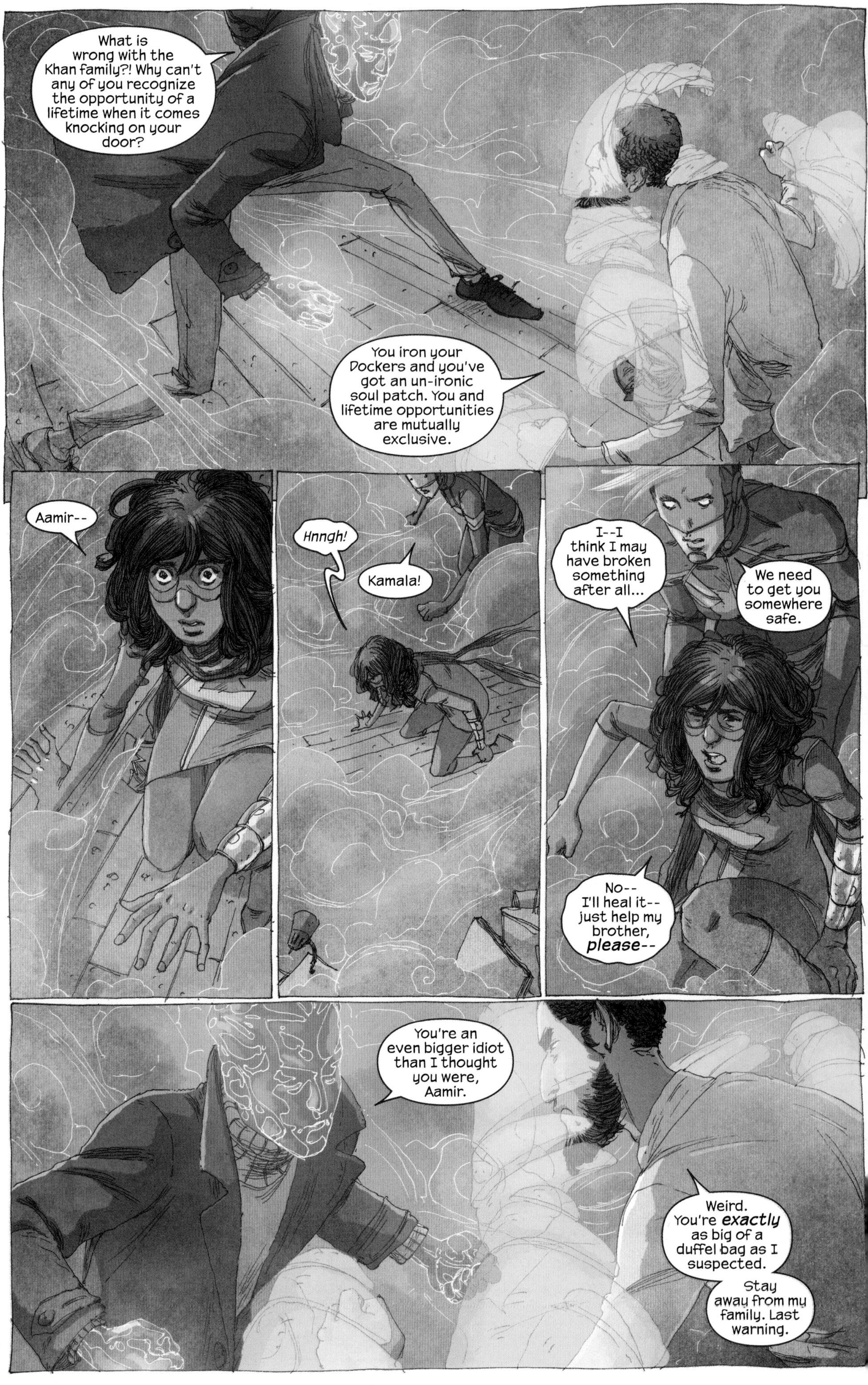
What is wrong with the Khan family?! Why can't any of you recognize the opportunity of a lifetime when it comes knocking on your door?
You iron your Dockers and you've got an un-ironic soul patch. You and lifetime opportunities are mutually exclusive.
Aamir--
Hnngh!
Kamala!
I--I think I may have broken something after all...
We need to get you somewhere safe.
No-- I'll heal it-- just help my brother, please--
You're an even bigger idiot than I thought you were, Aamir.
Weird. You're exactly as big of a duffel bag as I suspected.
Stay away from my family. Last warning.

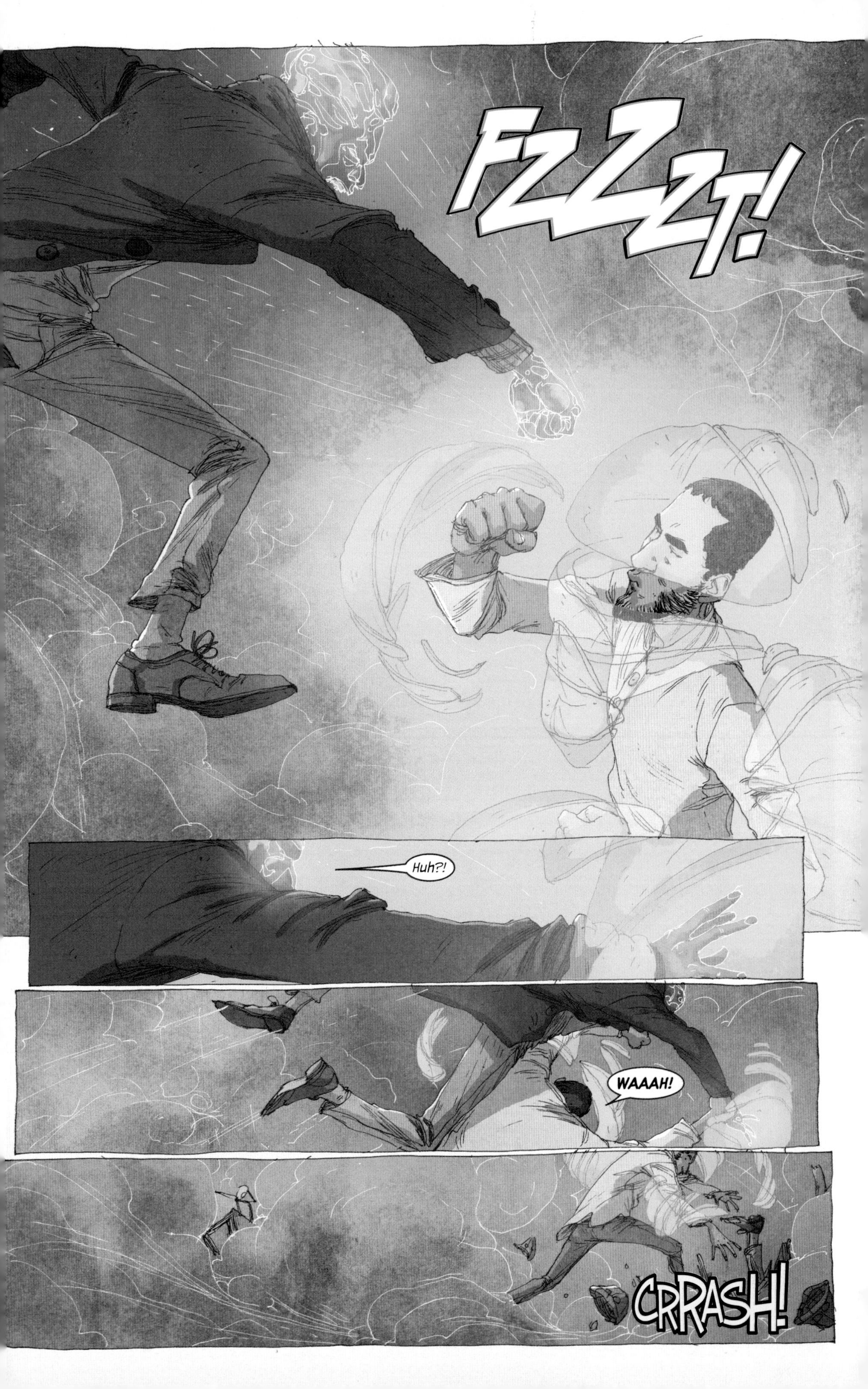
FZZZZT!
Huh?!
WAAAH!
CRRASH!

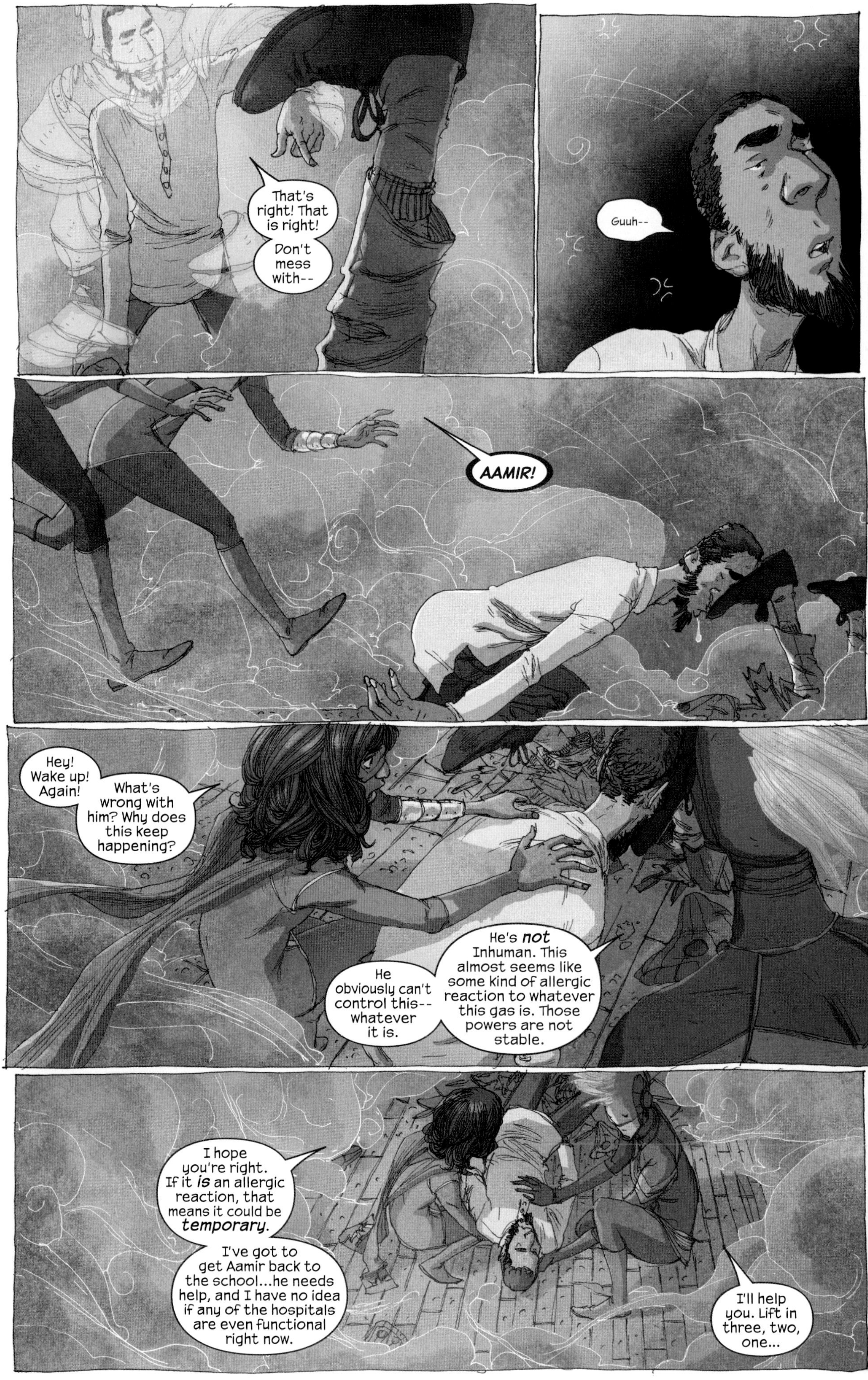
That's right! That is right!
Don't mess with--
Guuh--
AAMIR!
Hey! Wake up! Again!
What's wrong with him? Why does this keep happening?
He obviously can't control this-- whatever it is.
He's *not* Inhuman. This almost seems like some kind of allergic reaction to whatever this gas is. Those powers are not stable.
I hope you're right. If it *is* an allergic reaction, that means it could be *temporary*.
I've got to get Aamir back to the school...he needs help, and I have no idea if any of the hospitals are even functional right now.
I'll help you. Lift in three, two, one...

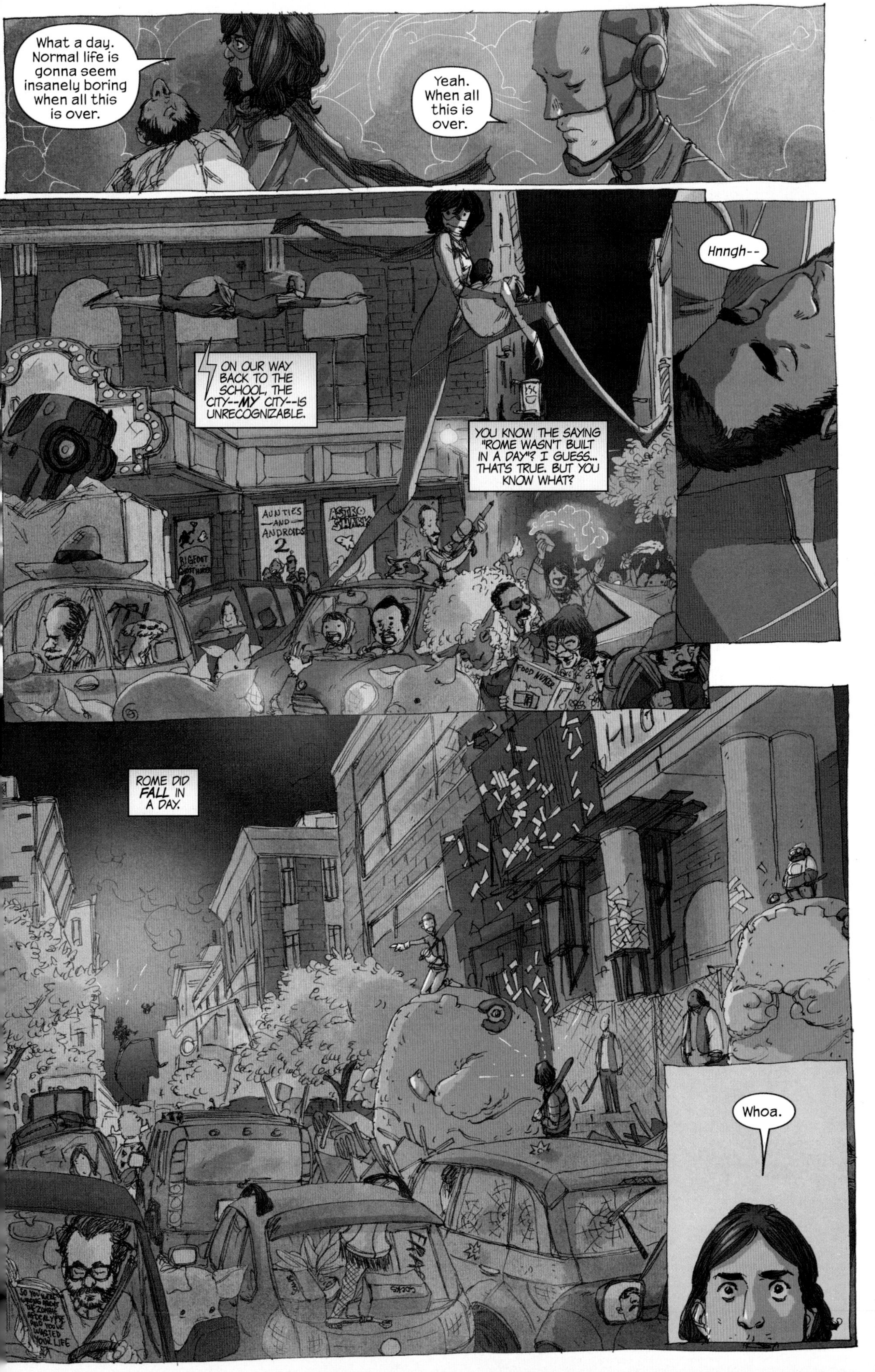
What a day. Normal life is gonna seem insanely boring when all this is over.
Yeah. When all this is over.
ON OUR WAY BACK TO THE SCHOOL, THE CITY--MY CITY--IS UNRECOGNIZABLE.
YOU KNOW THE SAYING "ROME WASN'T BUILT IN A DAY"? I GUESS... THAT'S TRUE. BUT YOU KNOW WHAT?
AUNTIES AND ANDROIDS 2
ASTRO SHARK
BIGFOOT
FOOD HUNTER
Hnngh--
ROME DID FALL IN A DAY.
Whoa.

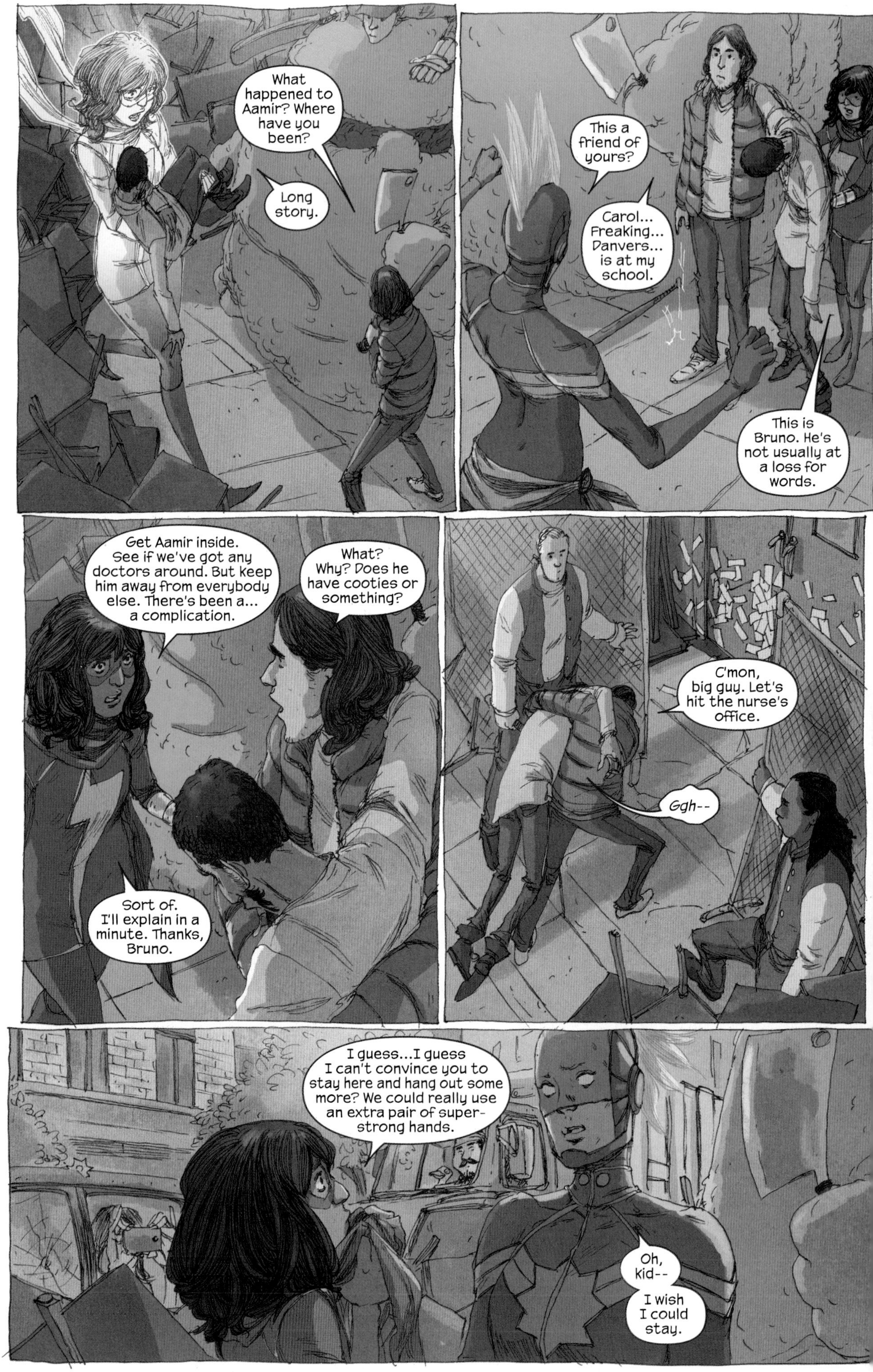
What happened to Aamir? Where have you been?
Long story.
This a friend of yours?
Carol... Freaking... Danvers... is at my school.
This is Bruno. He's not usually at a loss for words.
Get Aamir inside. See if we've got any doctors around. But keep him away from everybody else. There's been a... a complication.
What? Why? Does he have cooties or something?
Sort of. I'll explain in a minute. Thanks, Bruno.
C'mon, big guy. Let's hit the nurse's office.
Ggh--
I guess...I guess I can't convince you to stay here and hang out some more? We could really use an extra pair of super-strong hands.
Oh, kid--
I wish I could stay.

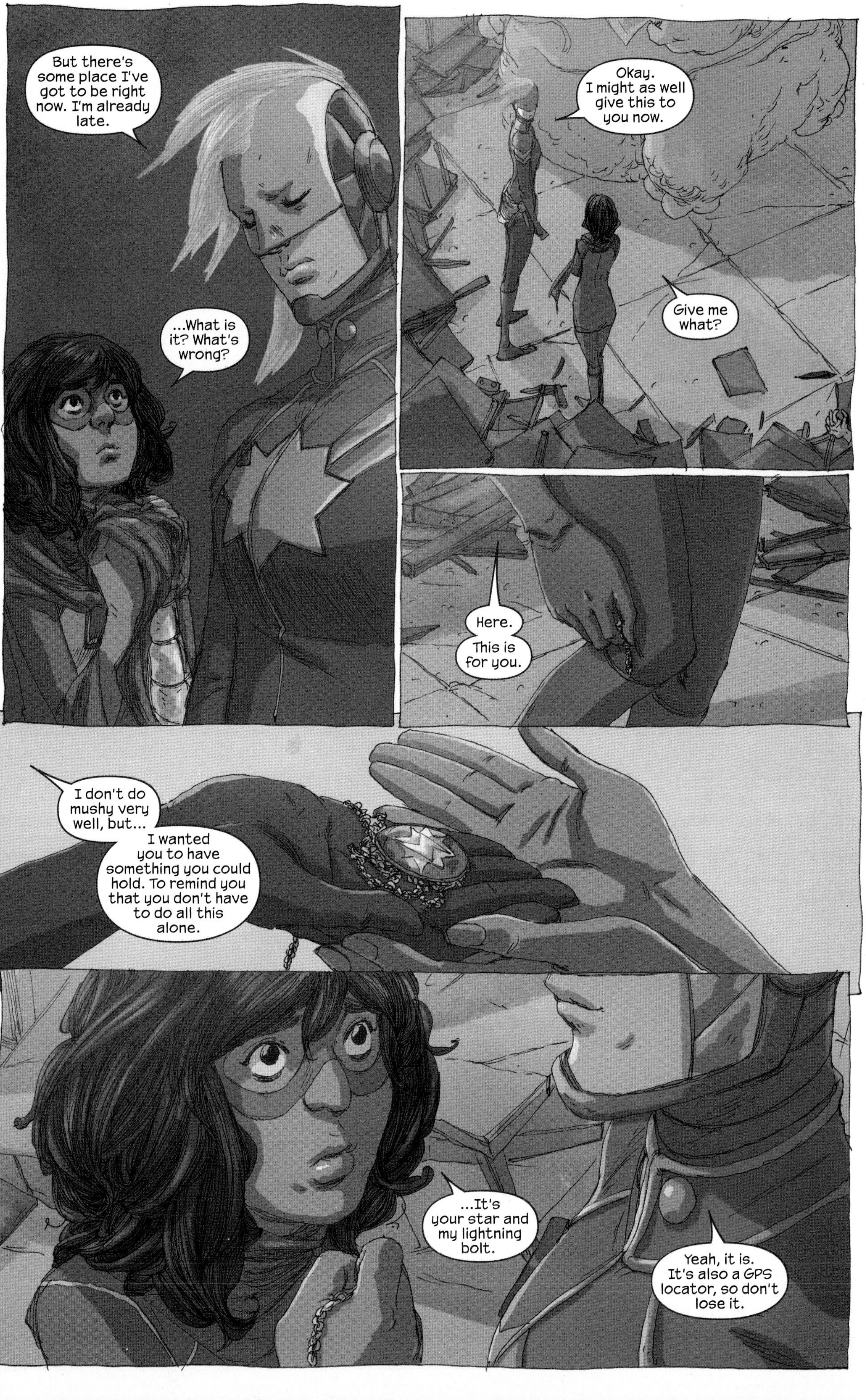
But there's some place I've got to be right now. I'm already late.
...What is it? What's wrong?
Okay. I might as well give this to you now.
Give me what?
Here. This is for you.
I don't do mushy very well, but...
I wanted you to have something you could hold. To remind you that you don't have to do all this alone.
...It's your star and my lightning bolt.
Yeah, it is. It's also a GPS locator, so don't lose it.

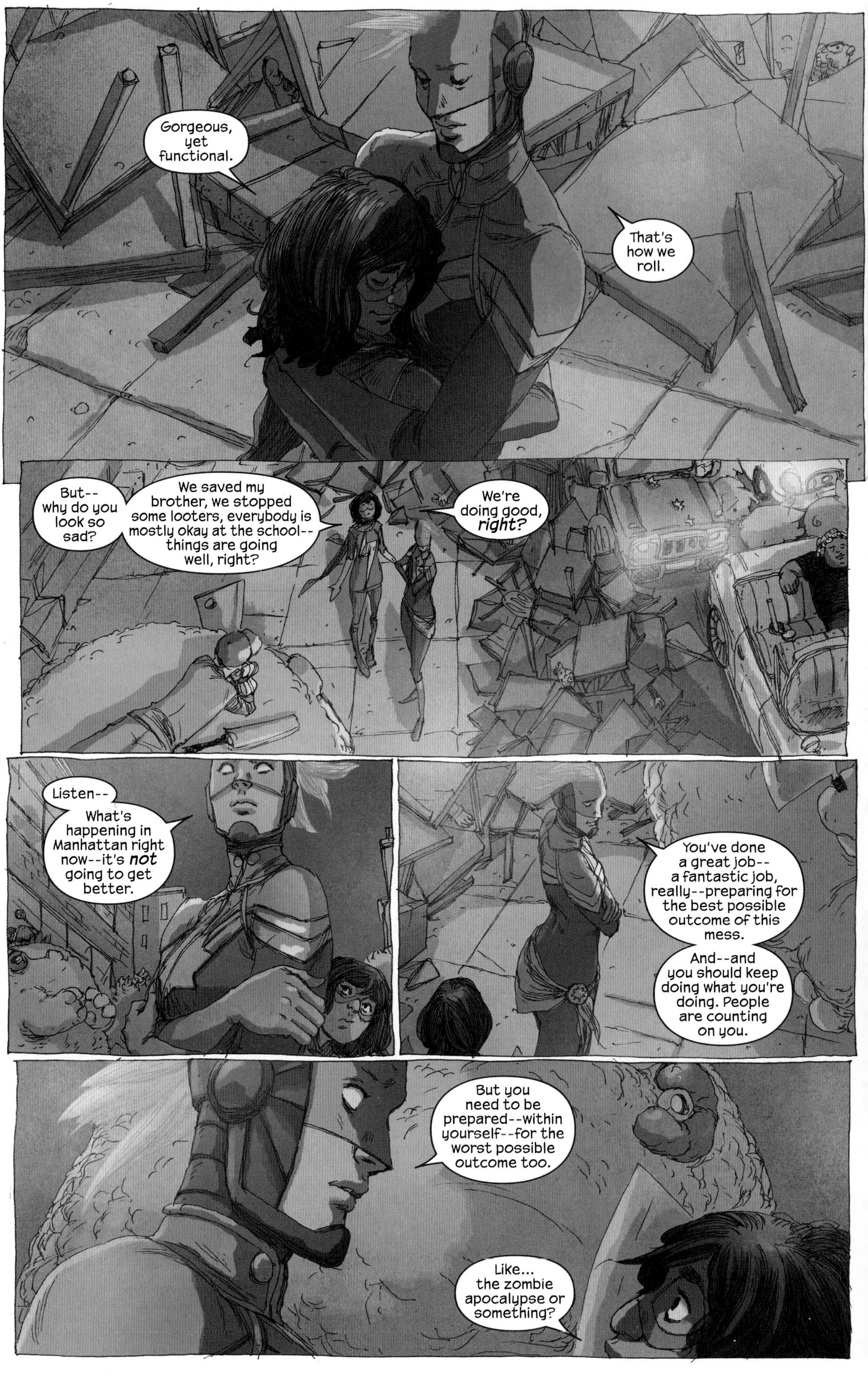
Gorgeous, yet functional.
That's how we roll.
But-- why do you look so sad?
We saved my brother, we stopped some looters, everybody is mostly okay at the school-- things are going well, right?
We're doing good, *right?*
Listen--
What's happening in Manhattan right now--it's *not* going to get better.
You've done a great job-- a fantastic job, really--preparing for the best possible outcome of this mess.
And--and you should keep doing what you're doing. People are counting on you.
But you need to be prepared--within yourself--for the worst possible outcome too.
Like... the zombie apocalypse or something?

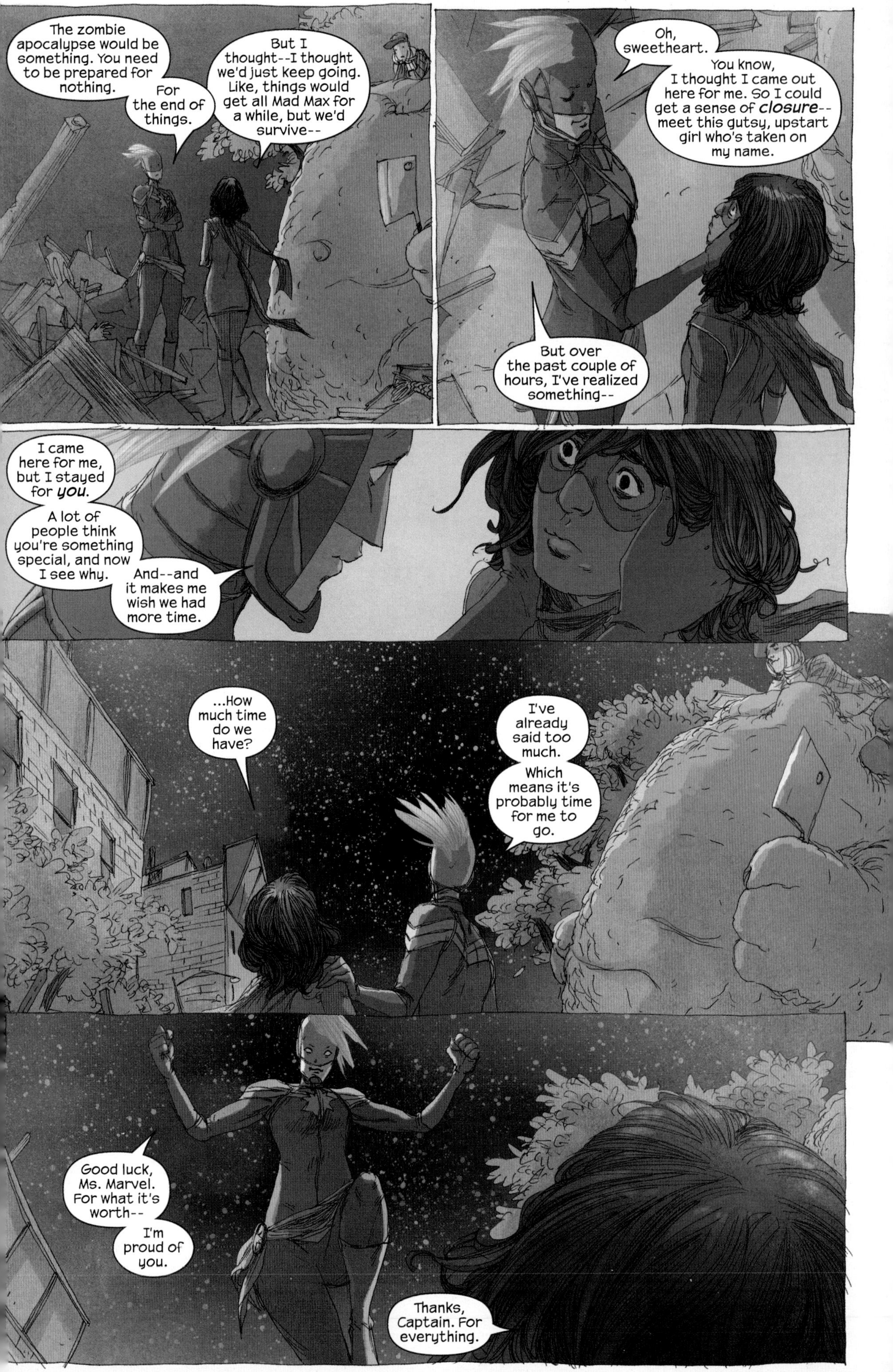
The zombie apocalypse would be something. You need to be prepared for nothing.
For the end of things.
But I thought--I thought we'd just keep going. Like, things would get all Mad Max for a while, but we'd survive--
Oh, sweetheart.
You know, I thought I came out here for me. So I could get a sense of *closure*--meet this gutsy, upstart girl who's taken on my name.
But over the past couple of hours, I've realized something--
I came here for me, but I stayed for *you*.
A lot of people think you're something special, and now I see why.
And--and it makes me wish we had more time.
...How much time do we have?
I've already said too much.
Which means it's probably time for me to go.
Good luck, Ms. Marvel. For what it's worth--
I'm proud of you.
Thanks, Captain. For everything.

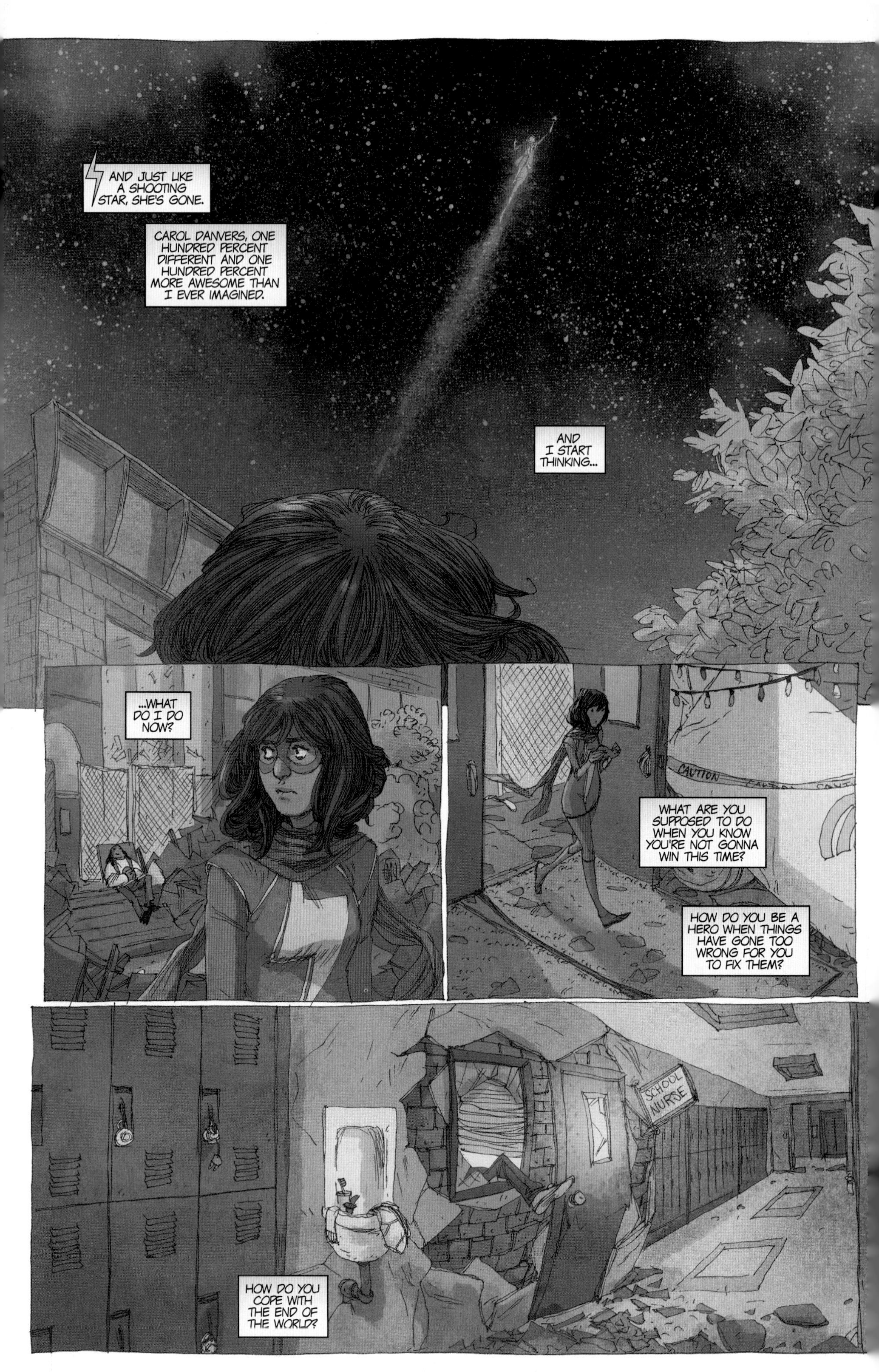
AND JUST LIKE A SHOOTING STAR, SHE'S GONE.
CAROL DANVERS, ONE HUNDRED PERCENT DIFFERENT AND ONE HUNDRED PERCENT MORE AWESOME THAN I EVER IMAGINED.
AND I START THINKING...
...WHAT DO I DO NOW?
WHAT ARE YOU SUPPOSED TO DO WHEN YOU KNOW YOU'RE NOT GONNA WIN THIS TIME?
HOW DO YOU BE A HERO WHEN THINGS HAVE GONE TOO WRONG FOR YOU TO FIX THEM?
CAUTION
SCHOOL NURSE
HOW DO YOU COPE WITH THE END OF THE WORLD?

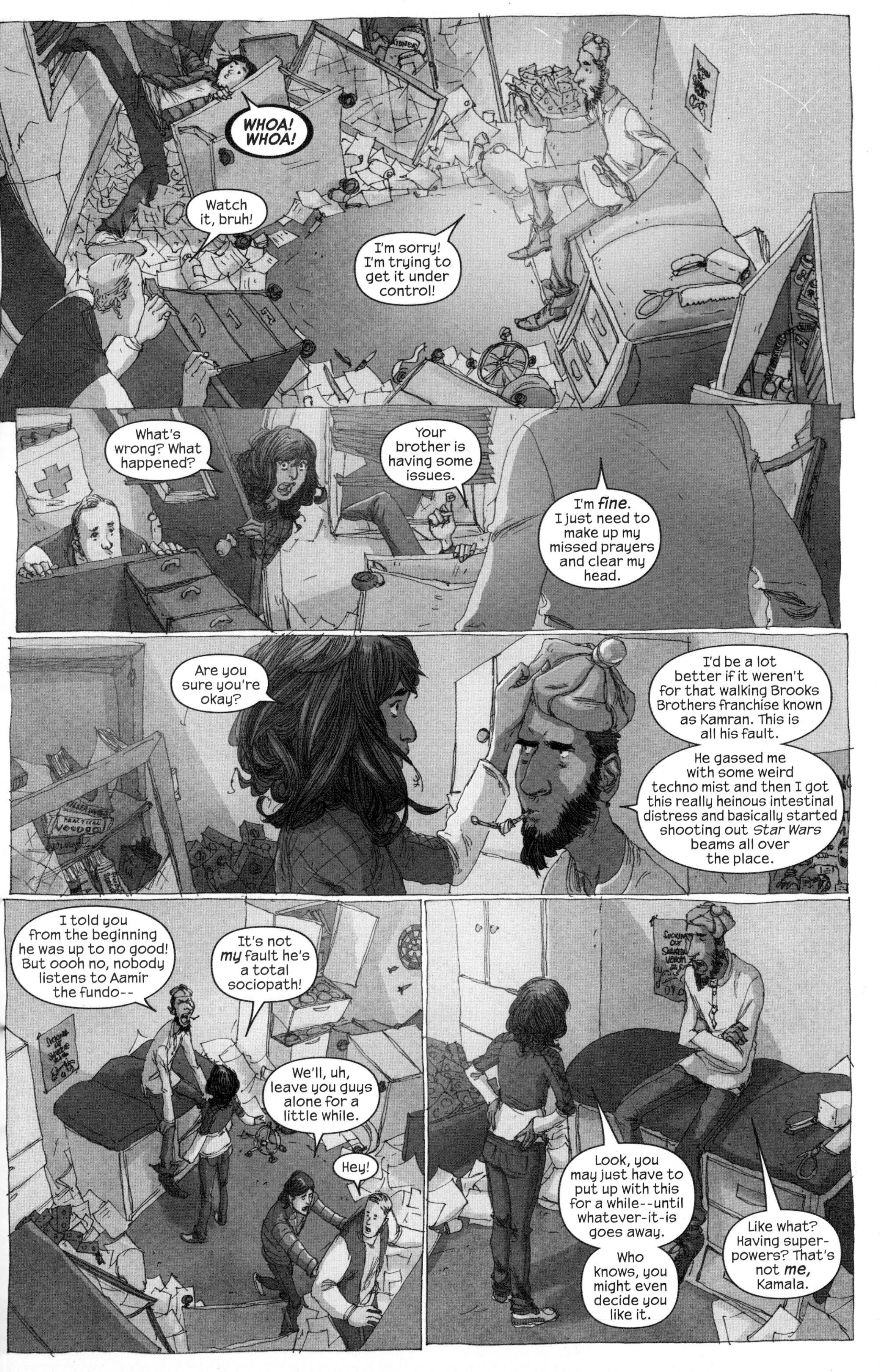
WHOA! WHOA!
Watch it, bruh!
I'm sorry! I'm trying to get it under control!
What's wrong? What happened?
Your brother is having some issues.
I'm *fine*. I just need to make up my missed prayers and clear my head.
Are you sure you're okay?
I'd be a lot better if it weren't for that walking Brooks Brothers franchise known as Kamran. This is all his fault.
He gassed me with some weird techno mist and then I got this really heinous intestinal distress and basically started shooting out *Star Wars* beams all over the place.
I told you from the beginning he was up to no good! But oooh no, nobody listens to Aamir the fundo--
It's not *my* fault he's a total sociopath!
We'll, uh, leave you guys alone for a little while.
Hey!
Look, you may just have to put up with this for a while--until whatever-it-is goes away.
Who knows, you might even decide you like it.
Like what? Having superpowers? That's not *me,* Kamala.

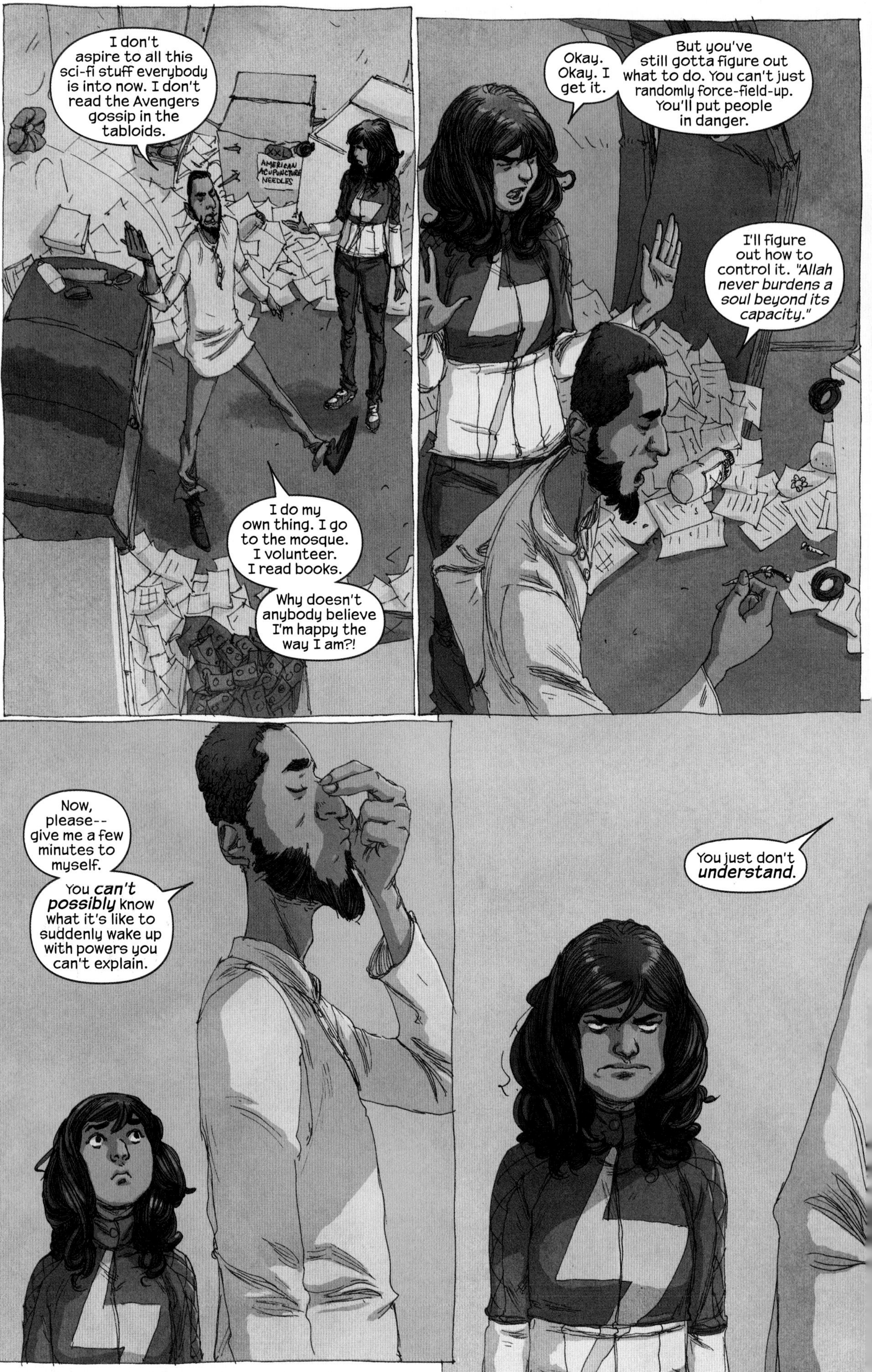
I don't aspire to all this sci-fi stuff everybody is into now. I don't read the Avengers gossip in the tabloids.
XXL
AMERICAN ACUPUNCTURE NEEDLES
I do my own thing. I go to the mosque. I volunteer. I read books.
Why doesn't anybody believe I'm happy the way I am?!
Okay. Okay. I get it.
But you've still gotta figure out what to do. You can't just randomly force-field-up. You'll put people in danger.
I'll figure out how to control it. *"Allah never burdens a soul beyond its capacity."*
Now, please-- give me a few minutes to myself.
You ***can't possibly*** know what it's like to suddenly wake up with powers you can't explain.
You just don't ***understand***.

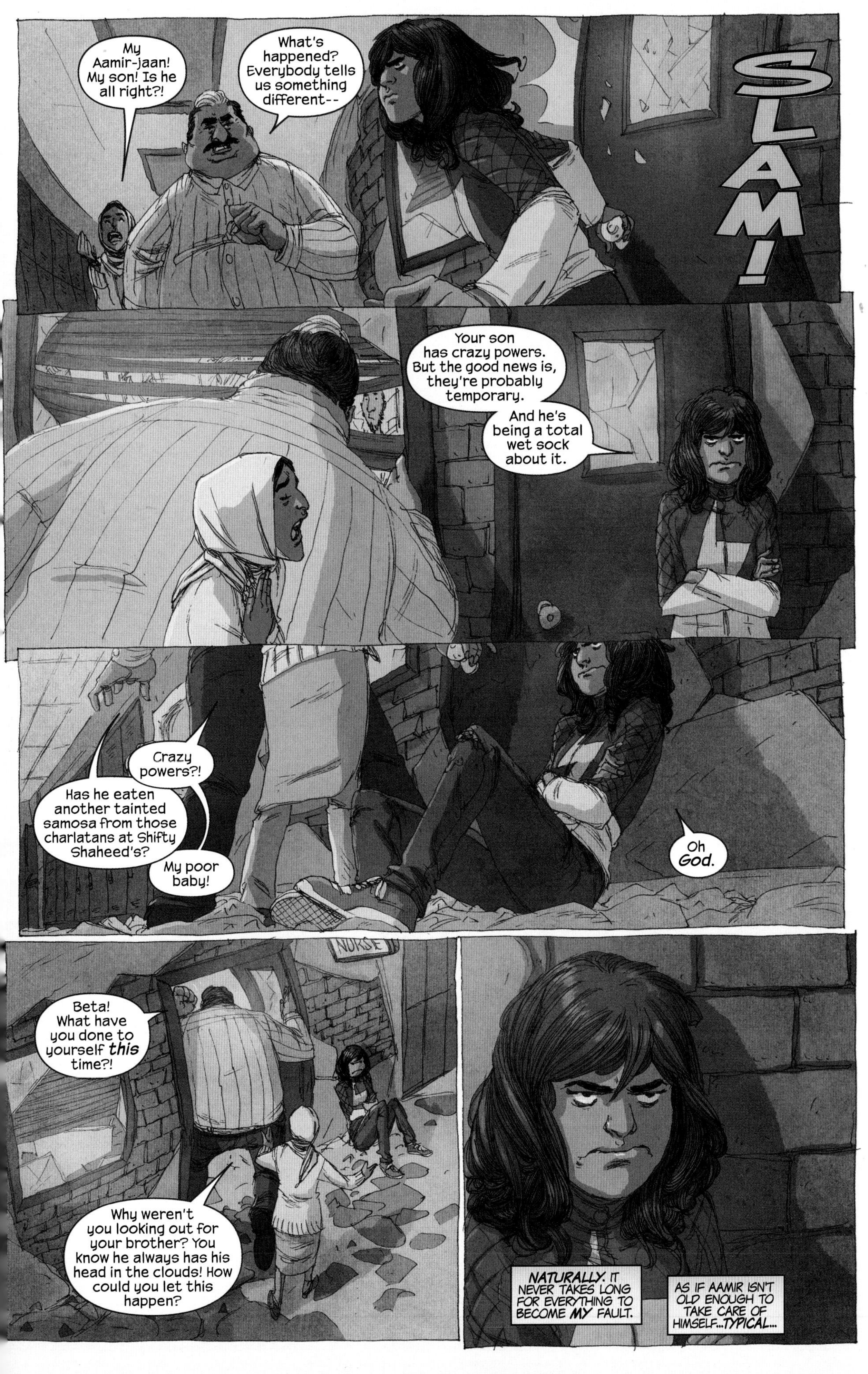

My Aamir-jaan! My son! Is he all right?!
What's happened? Everybody tells us something different--
SLAM!
Your son has crazy powers. But the good news is, they're probably temporary.
And he's being a total wet sock about it.
Crazy powers?!
Has he eaten another tainted samosa from those charlatans at Shifty Shaheed's?
My poor baby!
Oh *God*.
NURSE
Beta! What have you done to yourself *this* time?!
Why weren't you looking out for your brother? You know he always has his head in the clouds! How could you let this happen?
NATURALLY. IT NEVER TAKES LONG FOR EVERYTHING TO BECOME *MY* FAULT.
AS IF AAMIR ISN'T OLD ENOUGH TO TAKE CARE OF HIMSELF...*TYPICAL*...

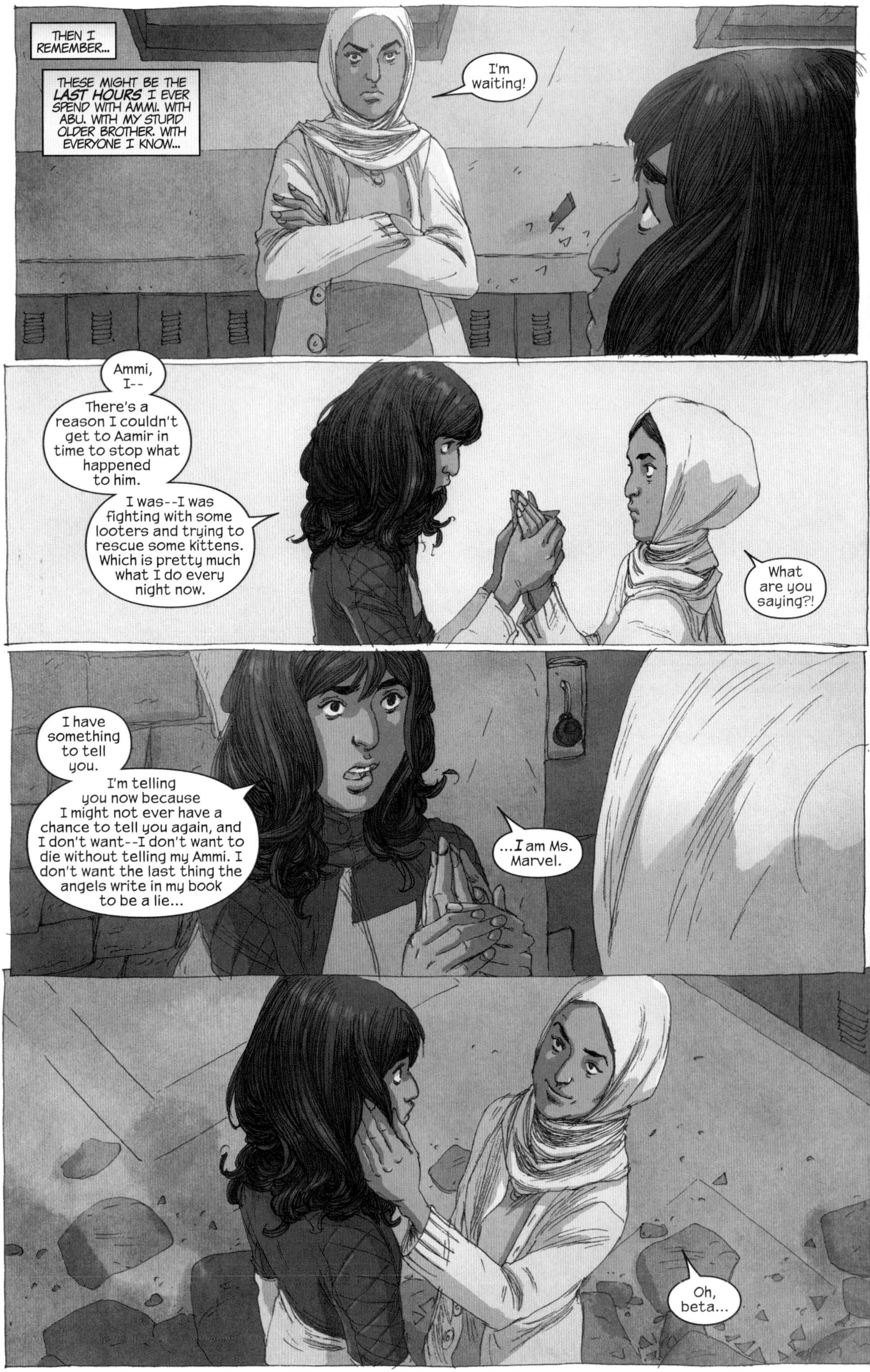
THEN I REMEMBER...
THESE MIGHT BE THE LAST HOURS I EVER SPEND WITH AMMI. WITH ABU. WITH MY STUPID OLDER BROTHER. WITH EVERYONE I KNOW...
I'm waiting!
Ammi, I--
There's a reason I couldn't get to Aamir in time to stop what happened to him.
I was--I was fighting with some looters and trying to rescue some kittens. Which is pretty much what I do every night now.
What are you saying?!
I have something to tell you.
I'm telling you now because I might not ever have a chance to tell you again, and I don't want--I don't want to die without telling my Ammi. I don't want the last thing the angels write in my book to be a lie...
...I am Ms. Marvel.
Oh, beta...

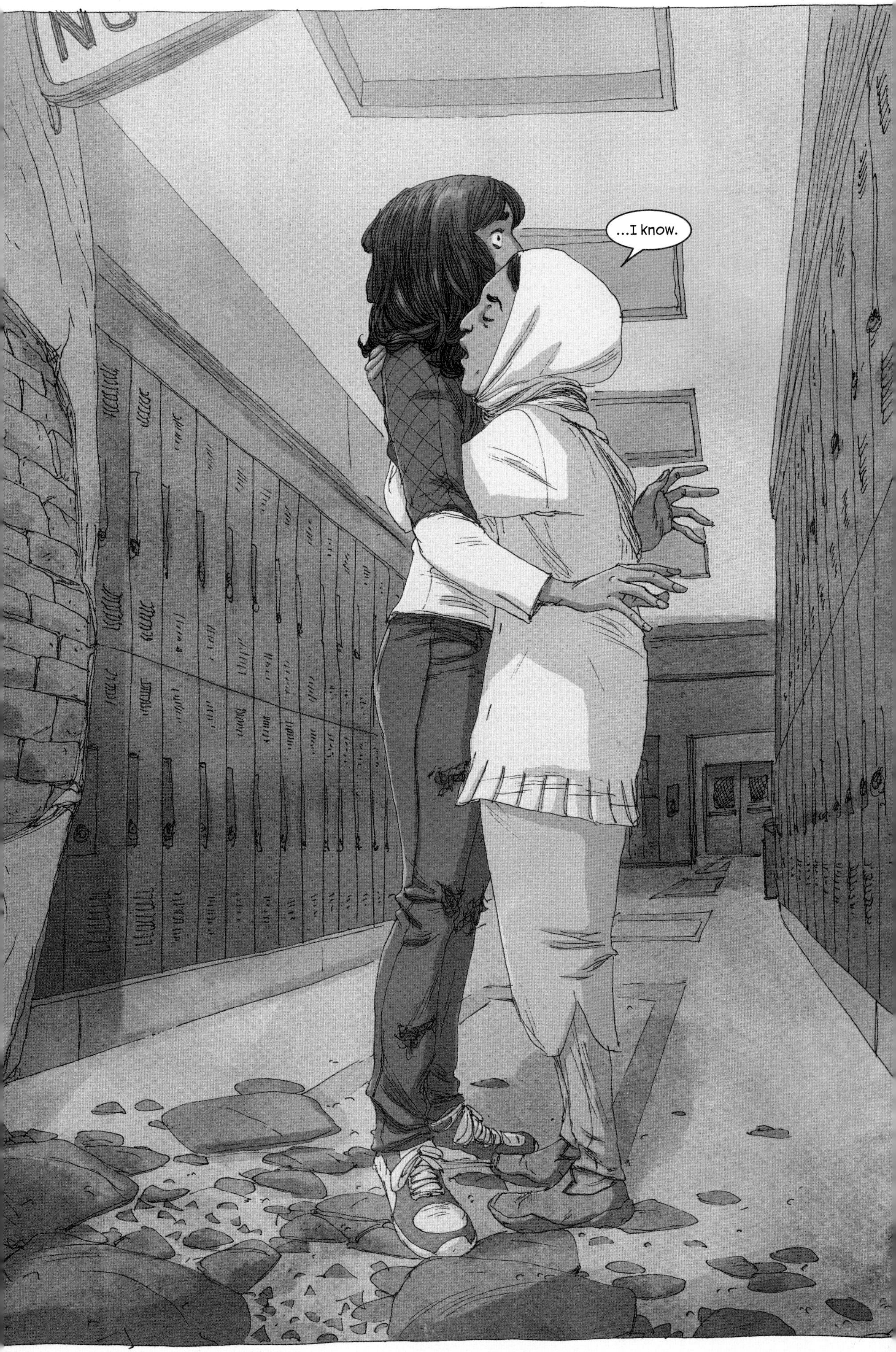
...I know.

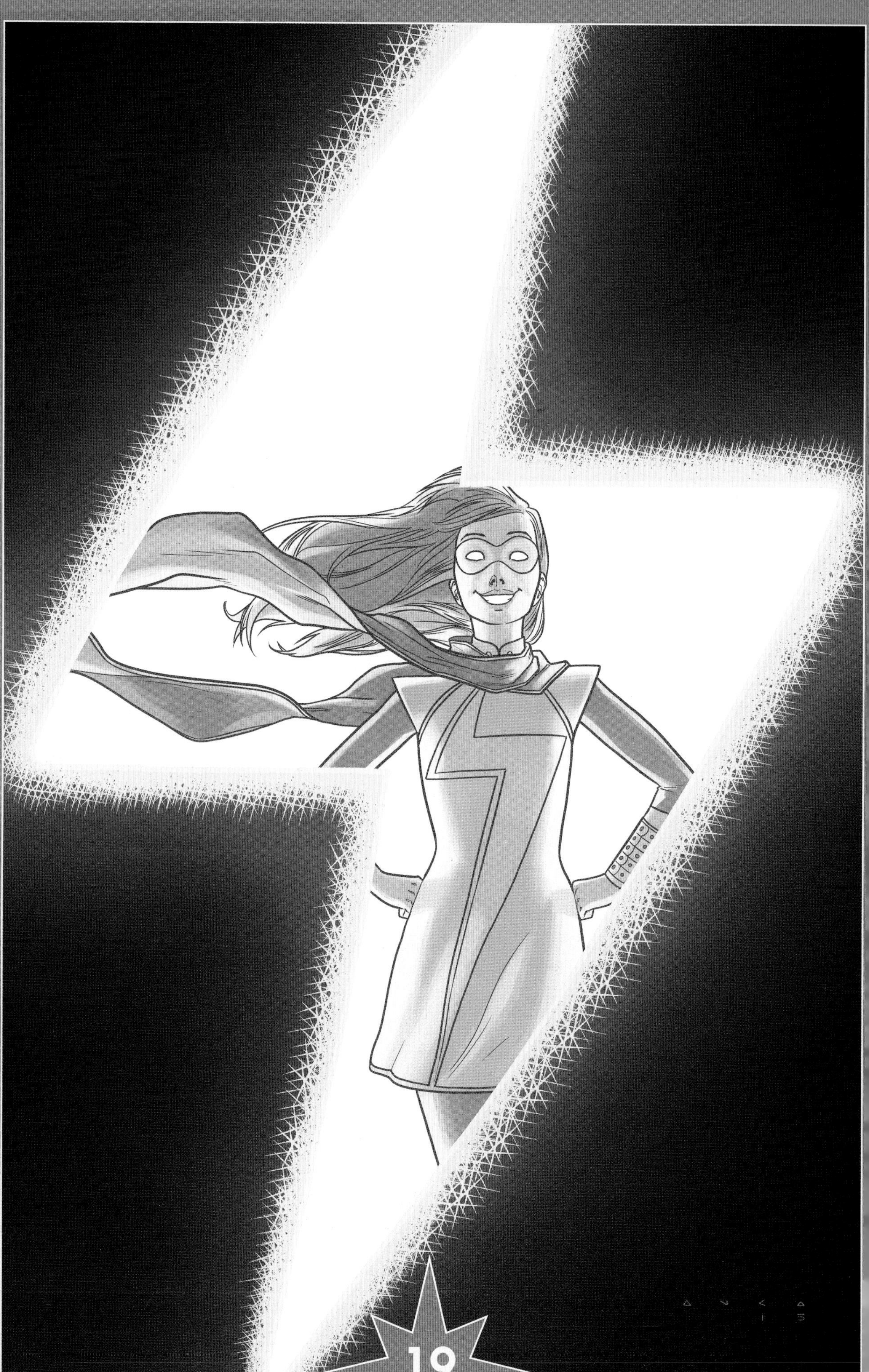
19

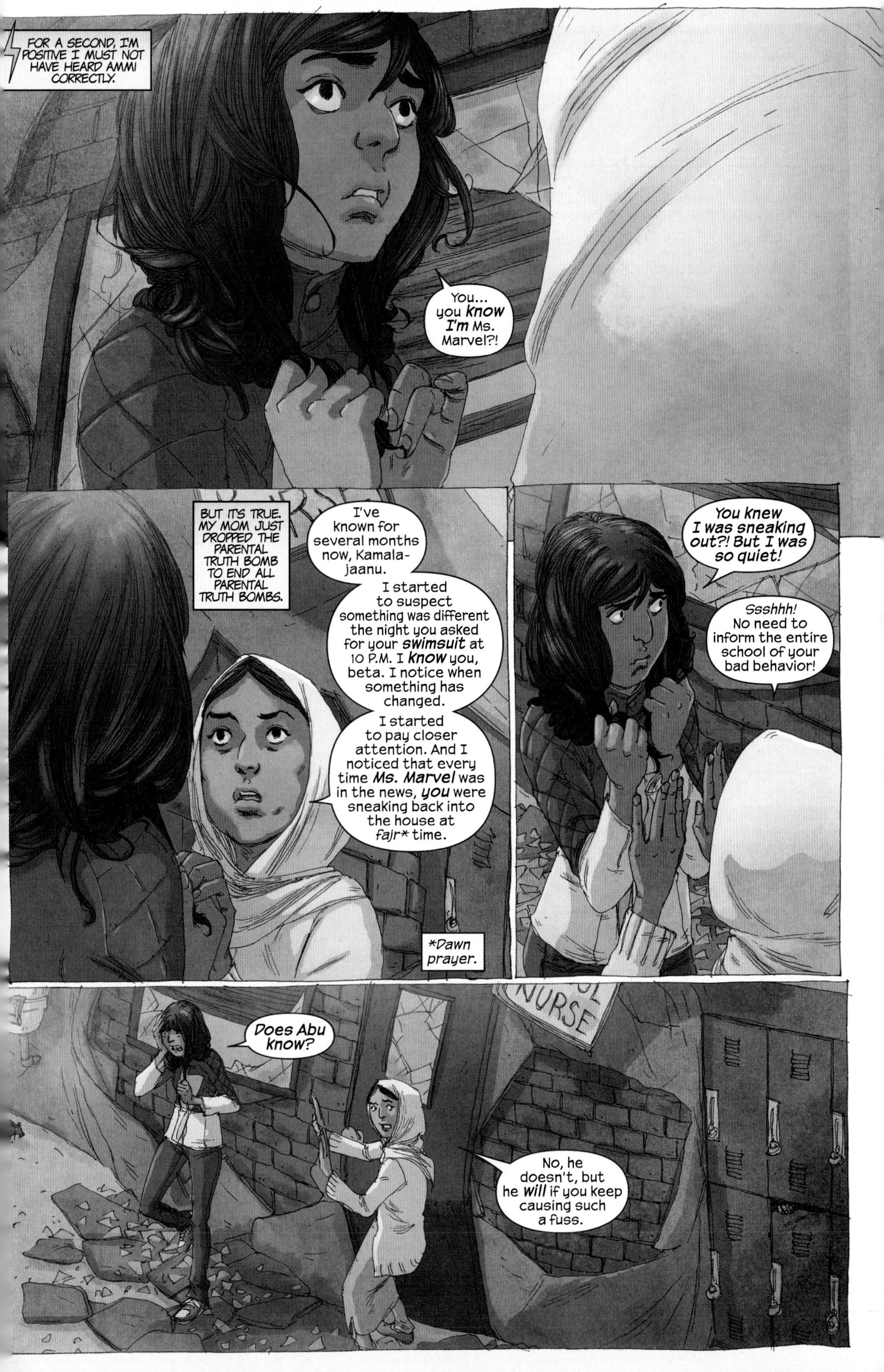
FOR A SECOND, I'M POSITIVE I MUST NOT HAVE HEARD AMMI CORRECTLY.
You... you KNOW I'm Ms. Marvel?!
BUT IT'S TRUE. MY MOM JUST DROPPED THE PARENTAL TRUTH BOMB TO END ALL PARENTAL TRUTH BOMBS.
I've known for several months now, Kamala-jaanu.
I started to suspect something was different the night you asked for your swimsuit at 10 P.M. I KNOW you, beta. I notice when something has changed.
I started to pay closer attention. And I noticed that every time Ms. Marvel was in the news, you were sneaking back into the house at fajr* time.
*Dawn prayer.
You knew I was sneaking out?! But I was so quiet!
Ssshhh! No need to inform the entire school of your bad behavior!
NURSE
Does Abu know?
No, he doesn't, but he will if you keep causing such a fuss.

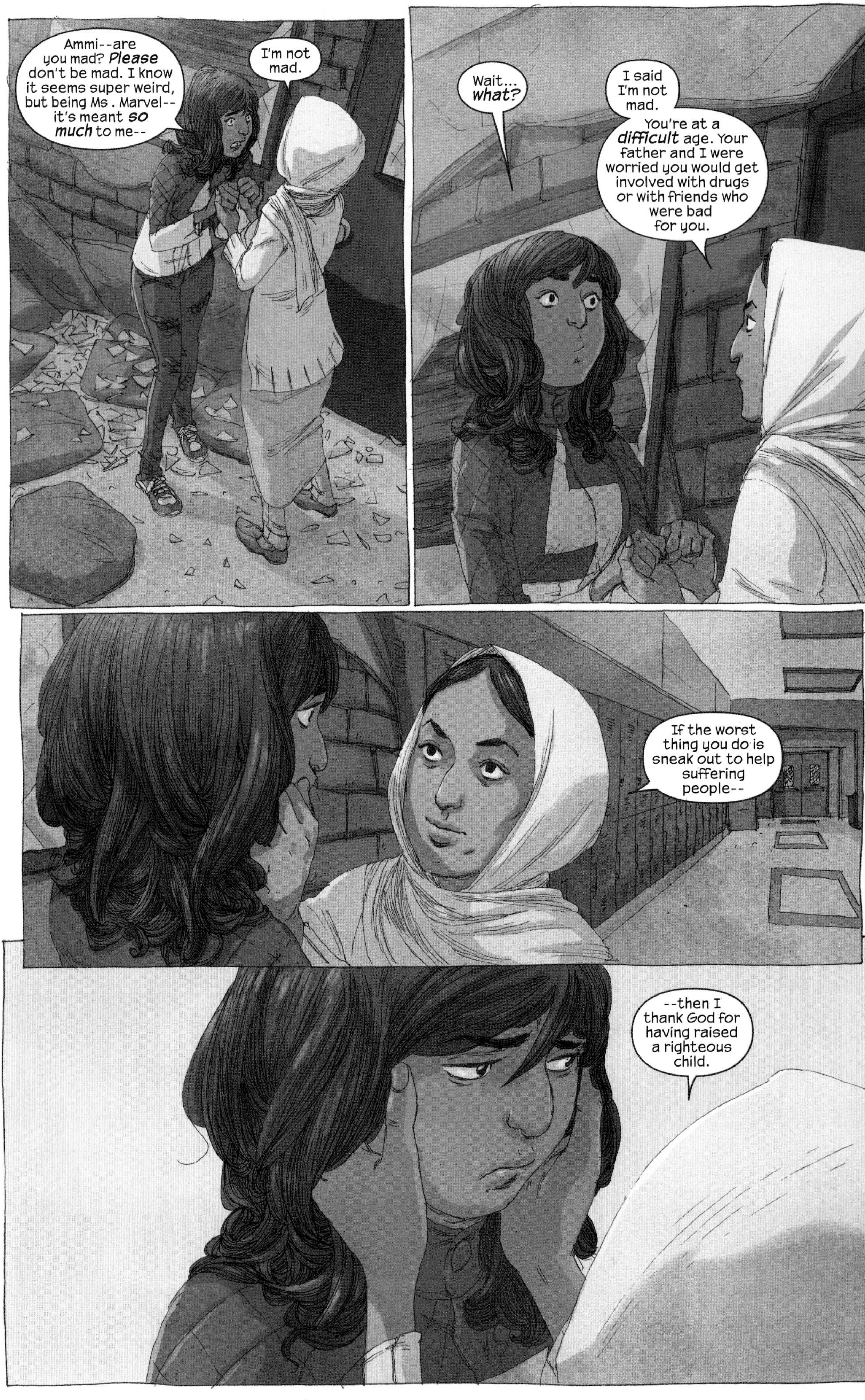
Ammi--are you mad? Please don't be mad. I know it seems super weird, but being Ms . Marvel-- it's meant so much to me--
I'm not mad.
Wait... what?
I said I'm not mad.
You're at a difficult age. Your father and I were worried you would get involved with drugs or with friends who were bad for you.
If the worst thing you do is sneak out to help suffering people--
--then I thank God for having raised a righteous child.

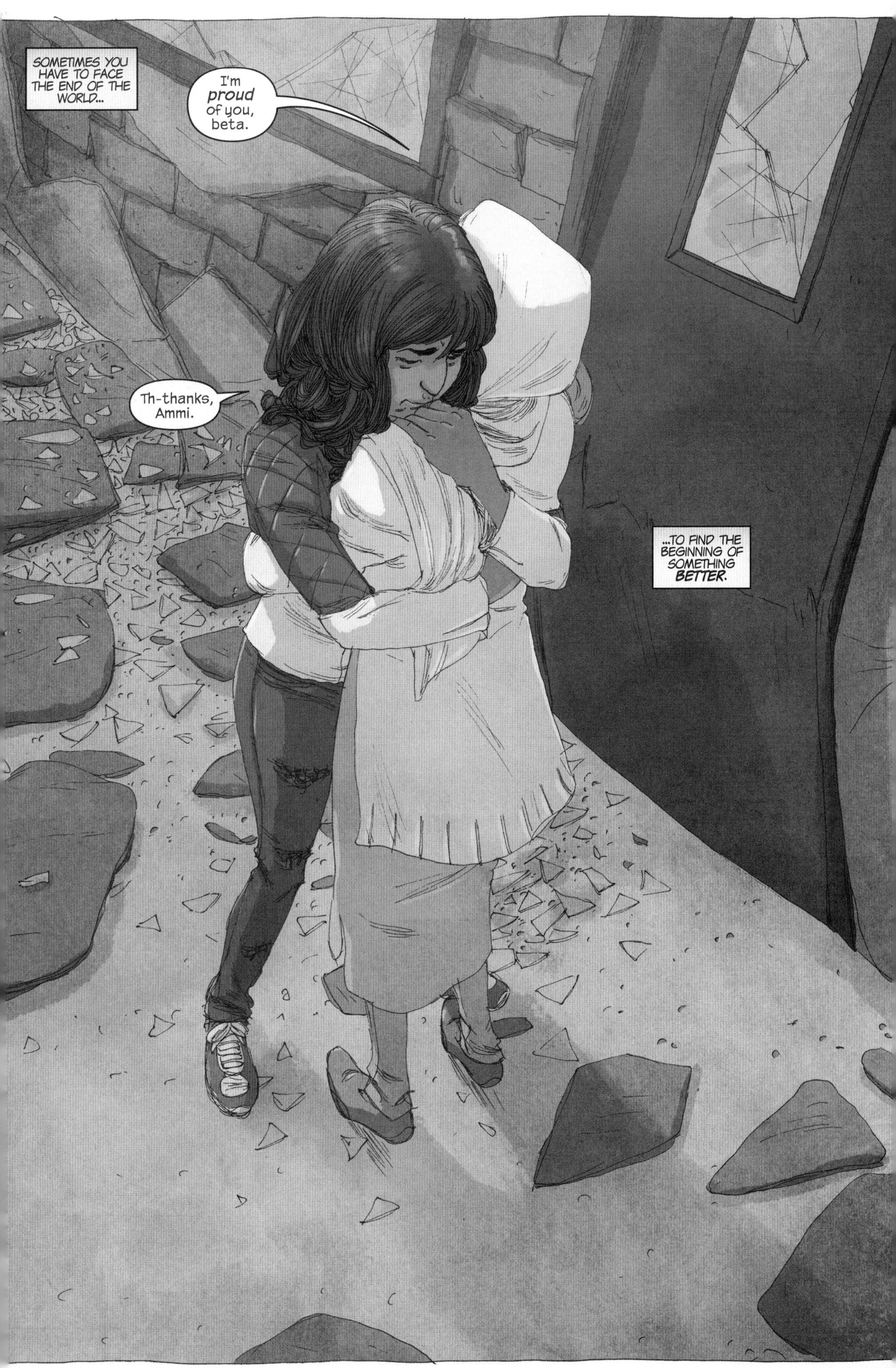
SOMETIMES YOU HAVE TO FACE THE END OF THE WORLD...
I'm proud of you, beta.
Th-thanks, Ammi.
...TO FIND THE BEGINNING OF SOMETHING BETTER.

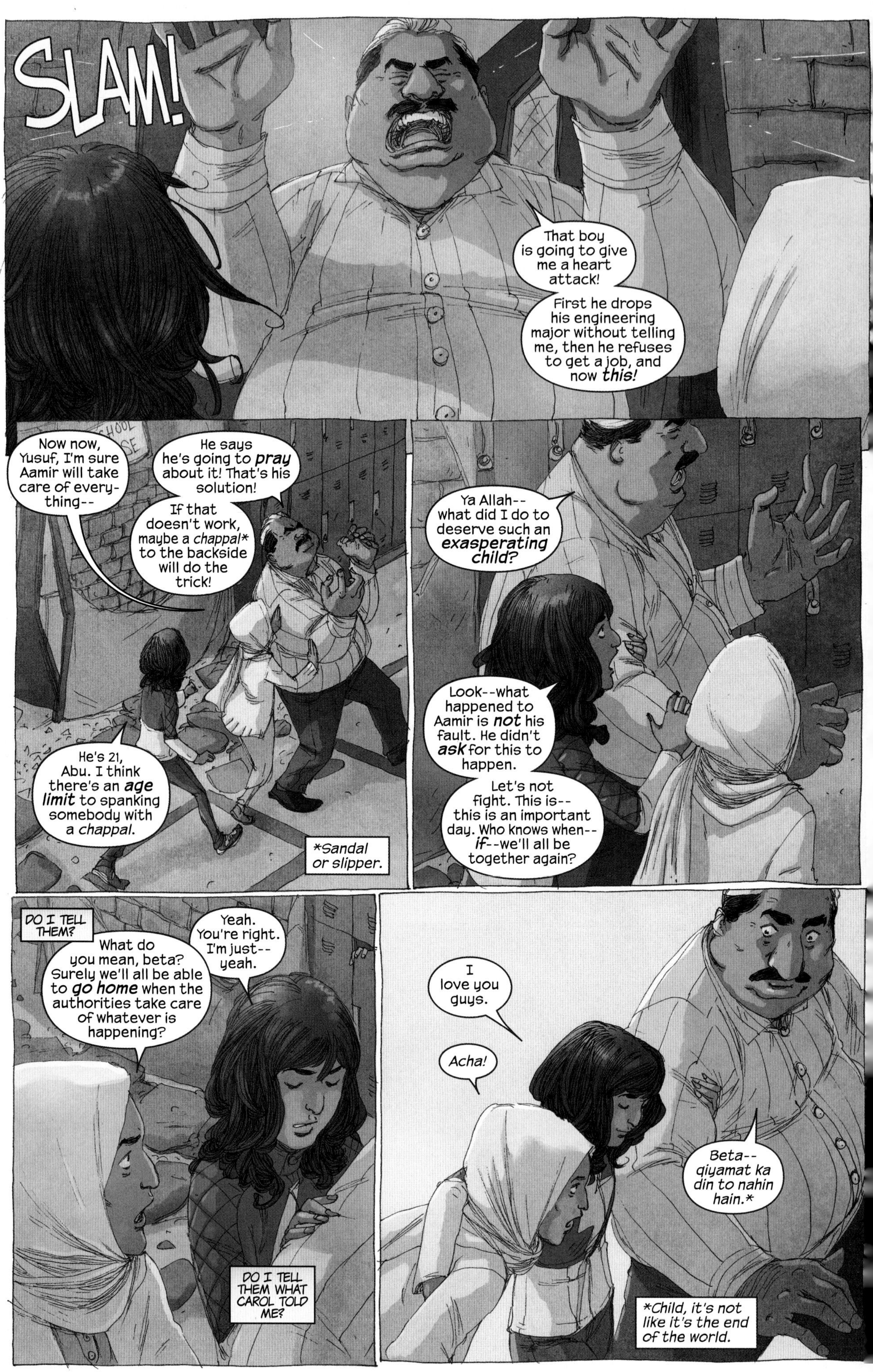
SLAM!
That boy is going to give me a heart attack!
First he drops his engineering major without telling me, then he refuses to get a job, and now this!
Now now, Yusuf, I'm sure Aamir will take care of every-thing--
He says he's going to pray about it! That's his solution!
If that doesn't work, maybe a chappal* to the backside will do the trick!
He's 21, Abu. I think there's an age limit to spanking somebody with a chappal.
*Sandal or slipper.
Ya Allah-- what did I do to deserve such an exasperating child?
Look--what happened to Aamir is not his fault. He didn't ask for this to happen.
Let's not fight. This is-- this is an important day. Who knows when-- if--we'll all be together again?
DO I TELL THEM?
What do you mean, beta? Surely we'll all be able to go home when the authorities take care of whatever is happening?
Yeah. You're right. I'm just-- yeah.
DO I TELL THEM WHAT CAROL TOLD ME?
I love you guys.
Acha!
Beta-- qiyamat ka din to nahin hain.*
*Child, it's not like it's the end of the world.

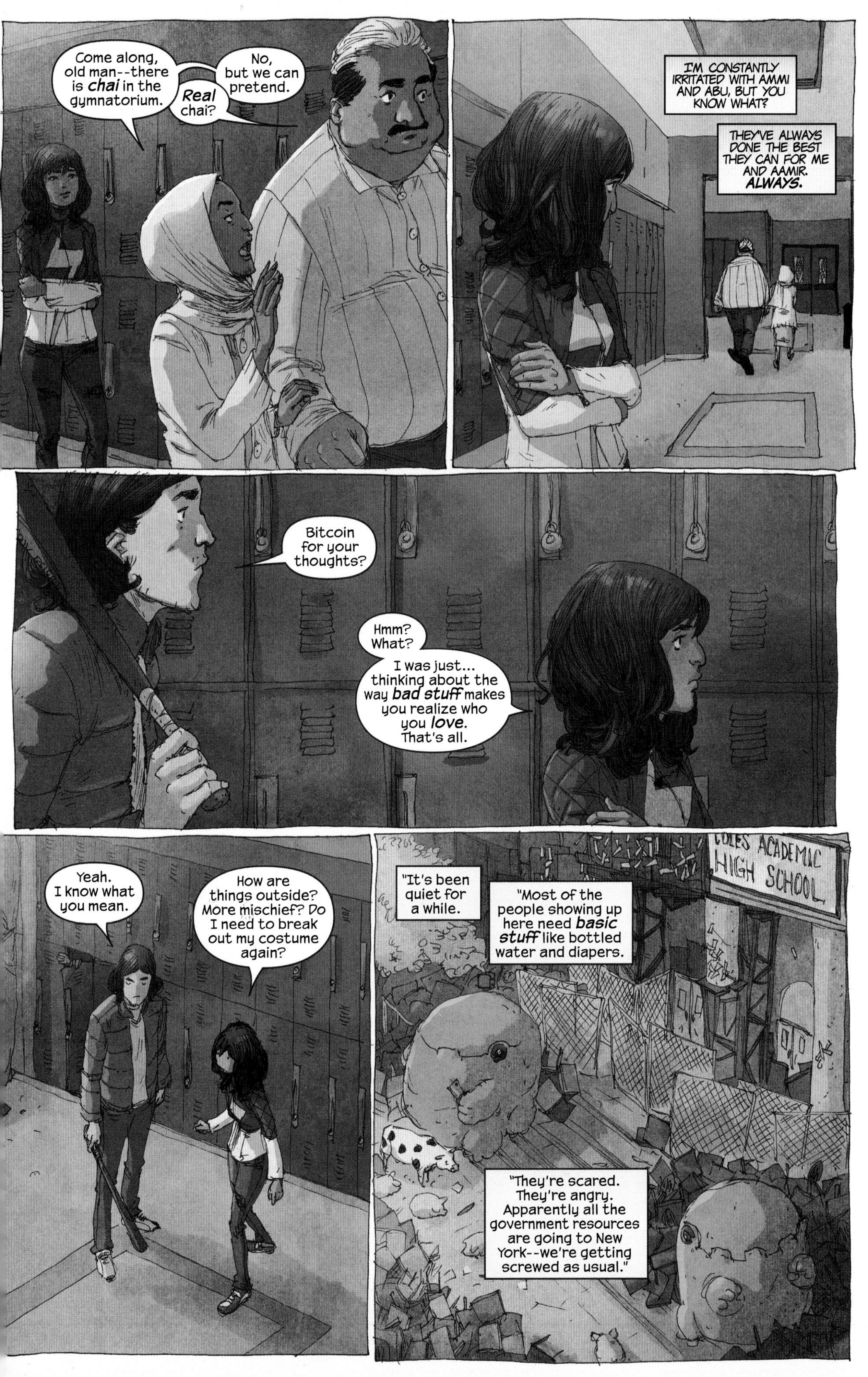

Come along, old man--there is chai in the gymnatorium.
Real chai?
No, but we can pretend.
I'M CONSTANTLY IRRITATED WITH AMMI AND ABU, BUT YOU KNOW WHAT?
THEY'VE ALWAYS DONE THE BEST THEY CAN FOR ME AND AAMIR. ALWAYS.
Bitcoin for your thoughts?
Hmm? What?
I was just... thinking about the way bad stuff makes you realize who you love. That's all.
Yeah. I know what you mean.
How are things outside? More mischief? Do I need to break out my costume again?
"It's been quiet for a while.
"Most of the people showing up here need basic stuff like bottled water and diapers.
COLES ACADEMIC HIGH SCHOOL
"They're scared. They're angry. Apparently all the government resources are going to New York--we're getting screwed as usual."

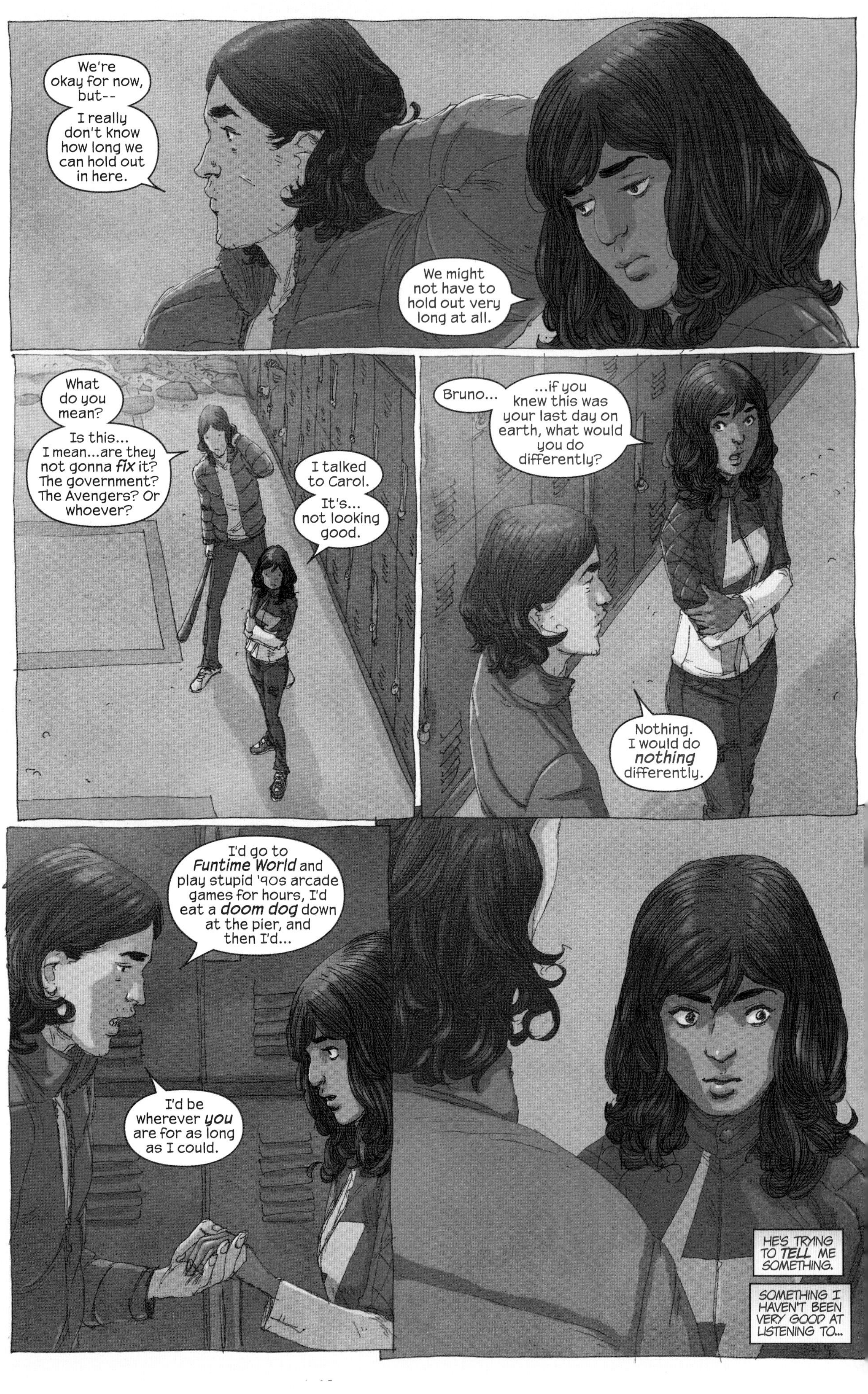
We're okay for now, but--
I really don't know how long we can hold out in here.
We might not have to hold out very long at all.
What do you mean?
Is this... I mean...are they not gonna *fix* it? The government? The Avengers? Or whoever?
I talked to Carol.
It's... not looking good.
Bruno...
...if you knew this was your last day on earth, what would you do differently?
Nothing. I would do *nothing* differently.
I'd go to *Funtime World* and play stupid '90s arcade games for hours, I'd eat a *doom dog* down at the pier, and then I'd...
I'd be wherever *you* are for as long as I could.
HE'S TRYING TO *TELL* ME SOMETHING.
SOMETHING I HAVEN'T BEEN VERY GOOD AT LISTENING TO...

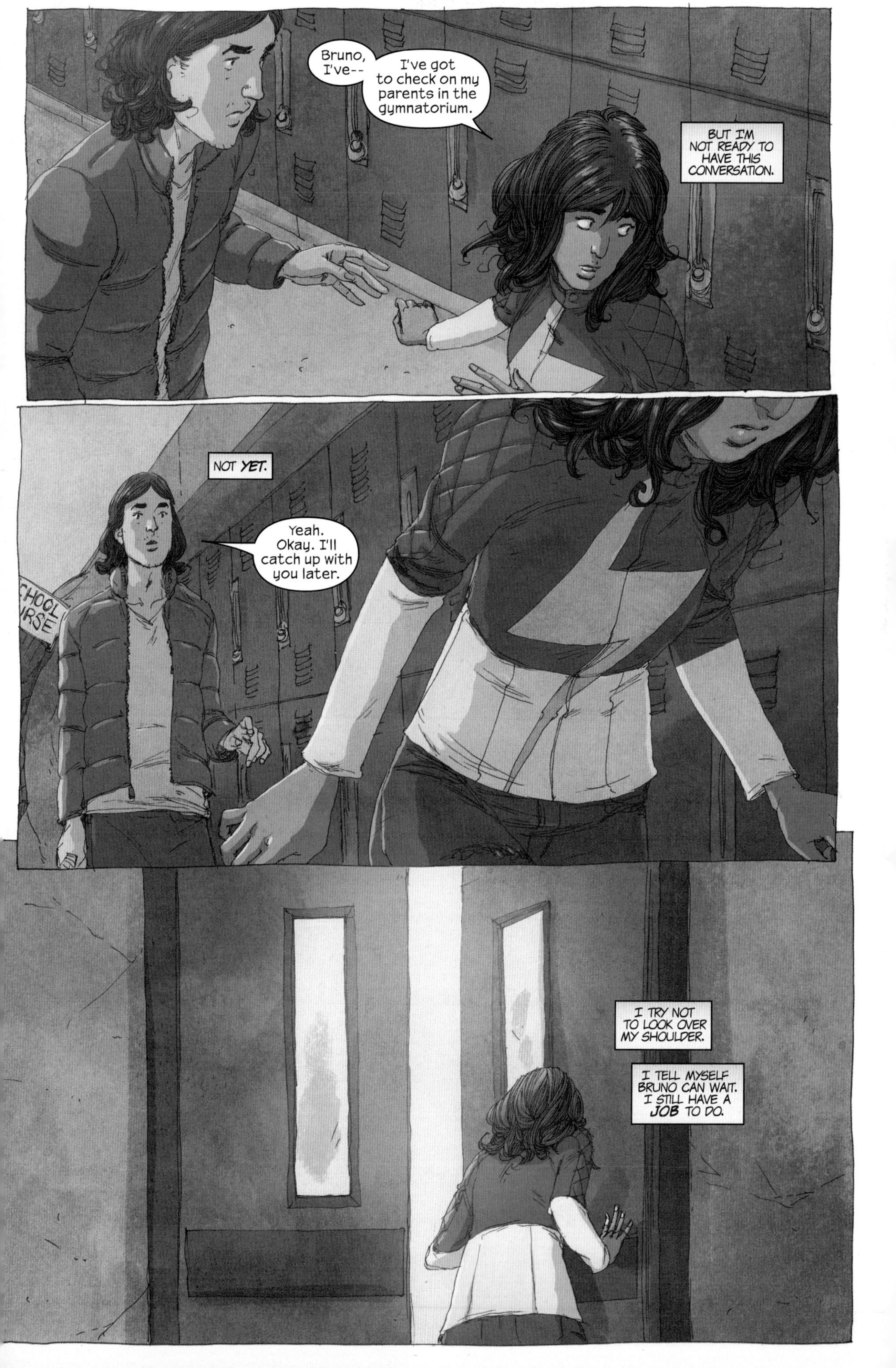
Bruno, I've--
I've got to check on my parents in the gymnatorium.
BUT I'M NOT READY TO HAVE THIS CONVERSATION.
NOT YET.
Yeah. Okay. I'll catch up with you later.
I TRY NOT TO LOOK OVER MY SHOULDER.
I TELL MYSELF BRUNO CAN WAIT. I STILL HAVE A JOB TO DO.

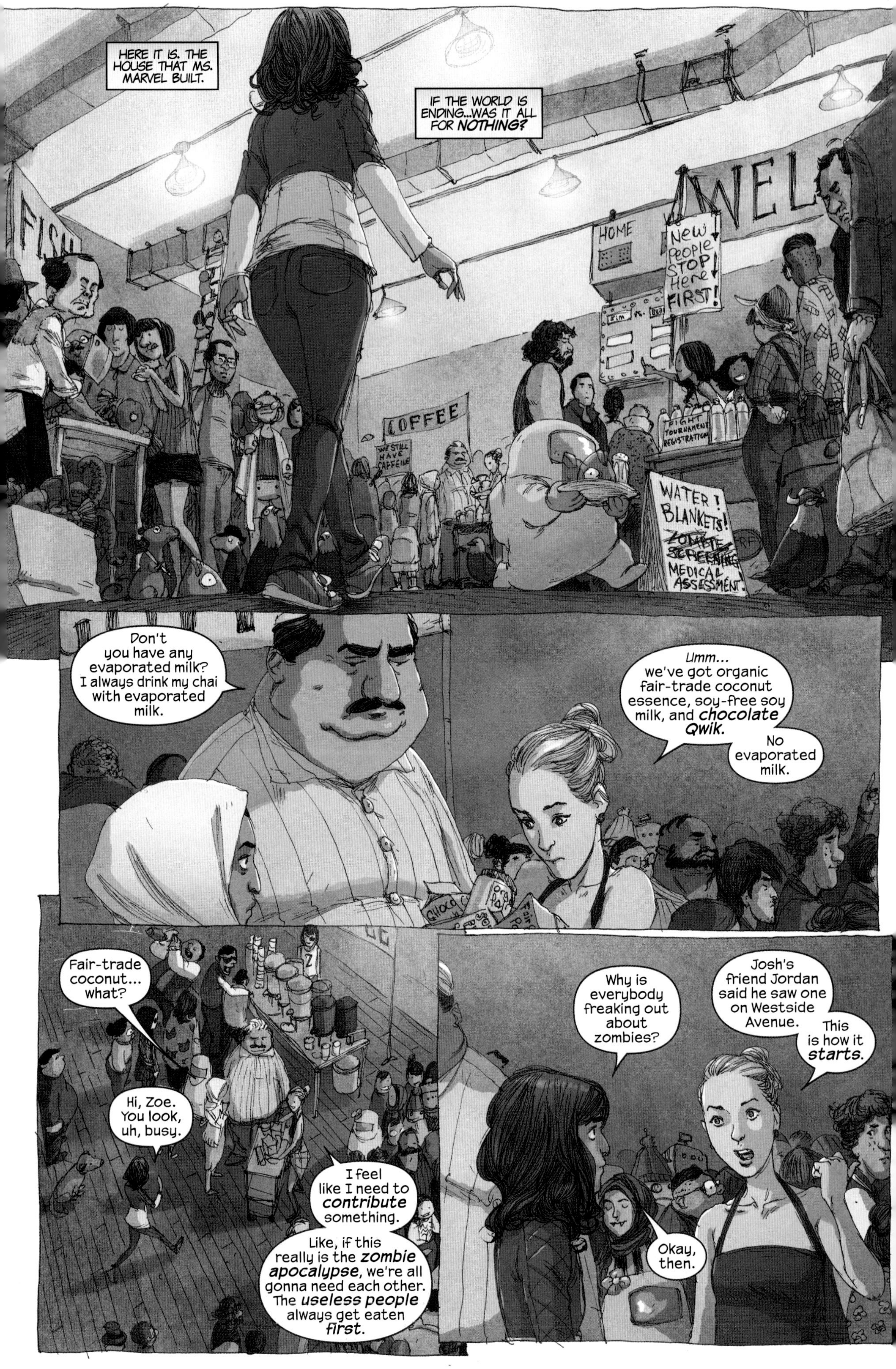
HERE IT IS. THE HOUSE THAT MS. MARVEL BUILT.
IF THE WORLD IS ENDING...WAS IT ALL FOR NOTHING?
FISH
COFFEE
WE STILL HAVE CAFFEINE
HOME
New People STOP Here FIRST!
FIGHT TOURNAMENT REGISTRATION
WATER! BLANKETS! ZOMBIE SCREENING MEDICAL ASSESSMENT
WEL
Don't you have any evaporated milk? I always drink my chai with evaporated milk.
Umm... we've got organic fair-trade coconut essence, soy-free soy milk, and chocolate Qwik.
No evaporated milk.
Fair-trade coconut... what?
Hi, Zoe. You look, uh, busy.
I feel like I need to contribute something.
Like, if this really is the zombie apocalypse, we're all gonna need each other. The useless people always get eaten first.
Why is everybody freaking out about zombies?
Josh's friend Jordan said he saw one on Westside Avenue.
This is how it starts.
Okay, then.

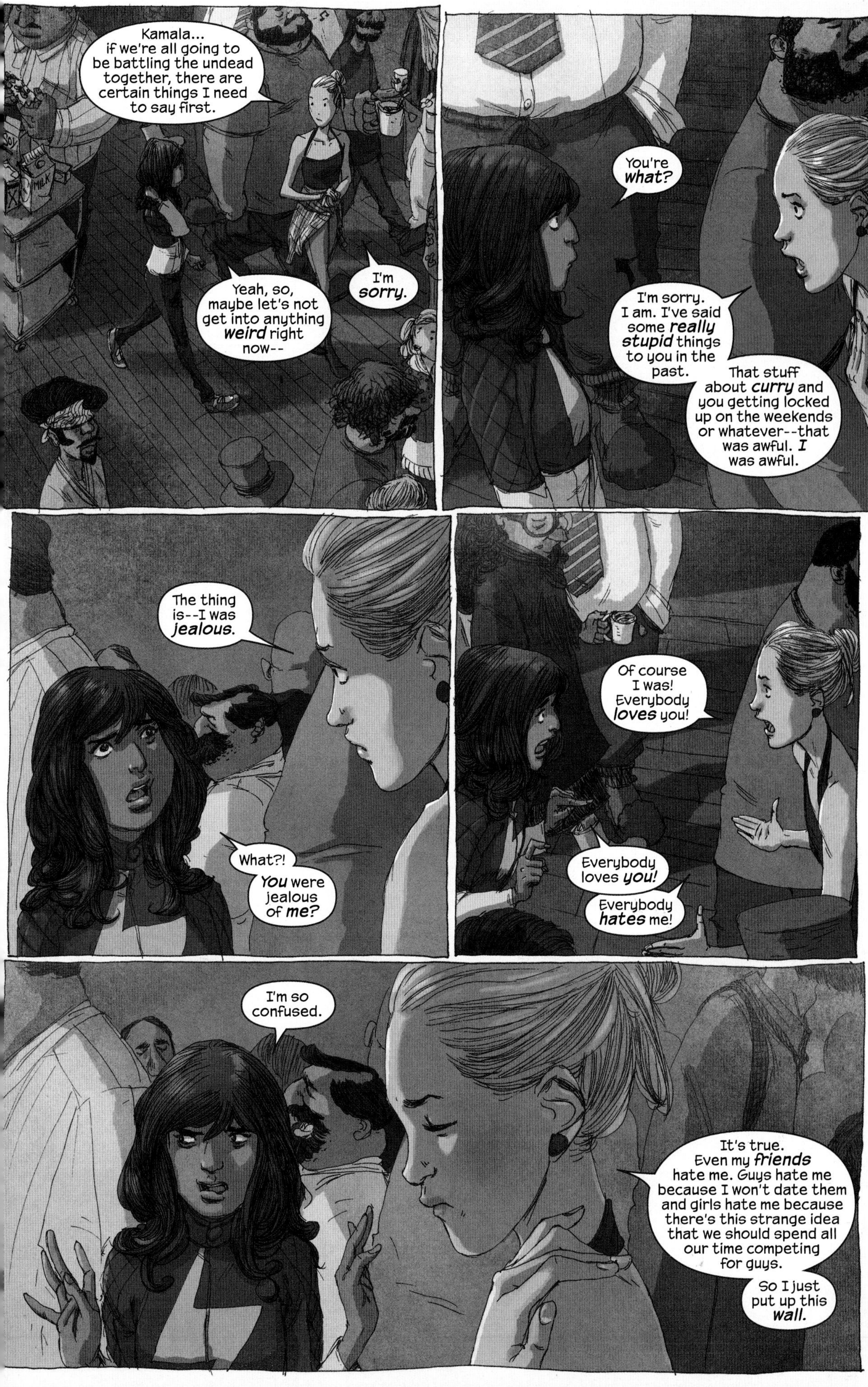
Kamala... if we're all going to be battling the undead together, there are certain things I need to say first.
Yeah, so, maybe let's not get into anything weird right now--
I'm sorry.
You're what?
I'm sorry. I am. I've said some really stupid things to you in the past.
That stuff about curry and you getting locked up on the weekends or whatever--that was awful. I was awful.
The thing is--I was jealous.
What?! You were jealous of me?
Of course I was! Everybody loves you!
Everybody loves you!
Everybody hates me!
I'm so confused.
It's true. Even my friends hate me. Guys hate me because I won't date them and girls hate me because there's this strange idea that we should spend all our time competing for guys.
So I just put up this wall.

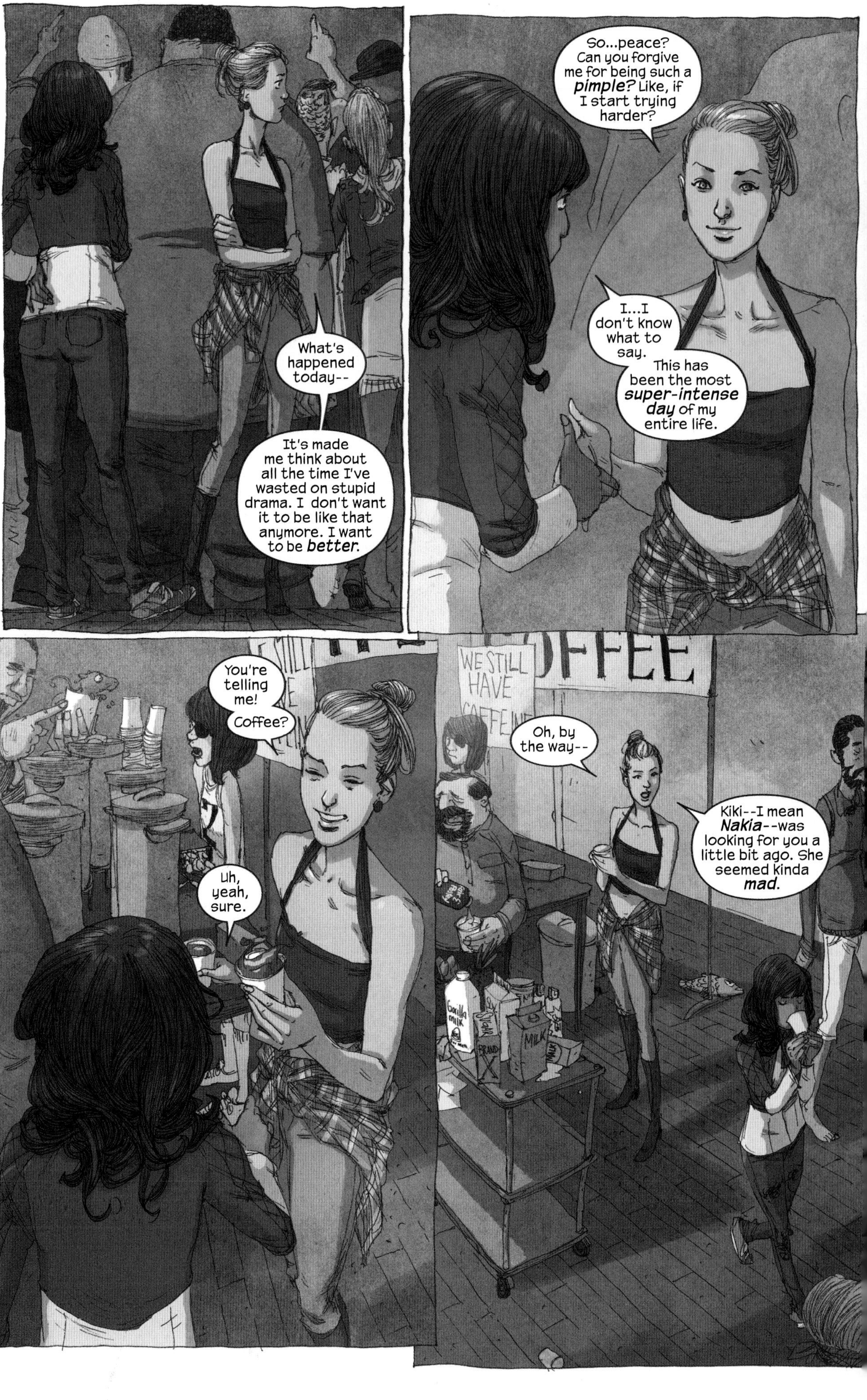

What's happened today--
It's made me think about all the time I've wasted on stupid drama. I don't want it to be like that anymore. I want to be *better*.
So...peace? Can you forgive me for being such a *pimple?* Like, if I start trying harder?
I...I don't know what to say.
This has been the most *super-intense day* of my entire life.
You're telling me!
Coffee?
Uh, yeah, sure.
WE STILL HAVE
Oh, by the way--
Kiki--I mean *Nakia*--was looking for you a little bit ago. She seemed kinda *mad*.

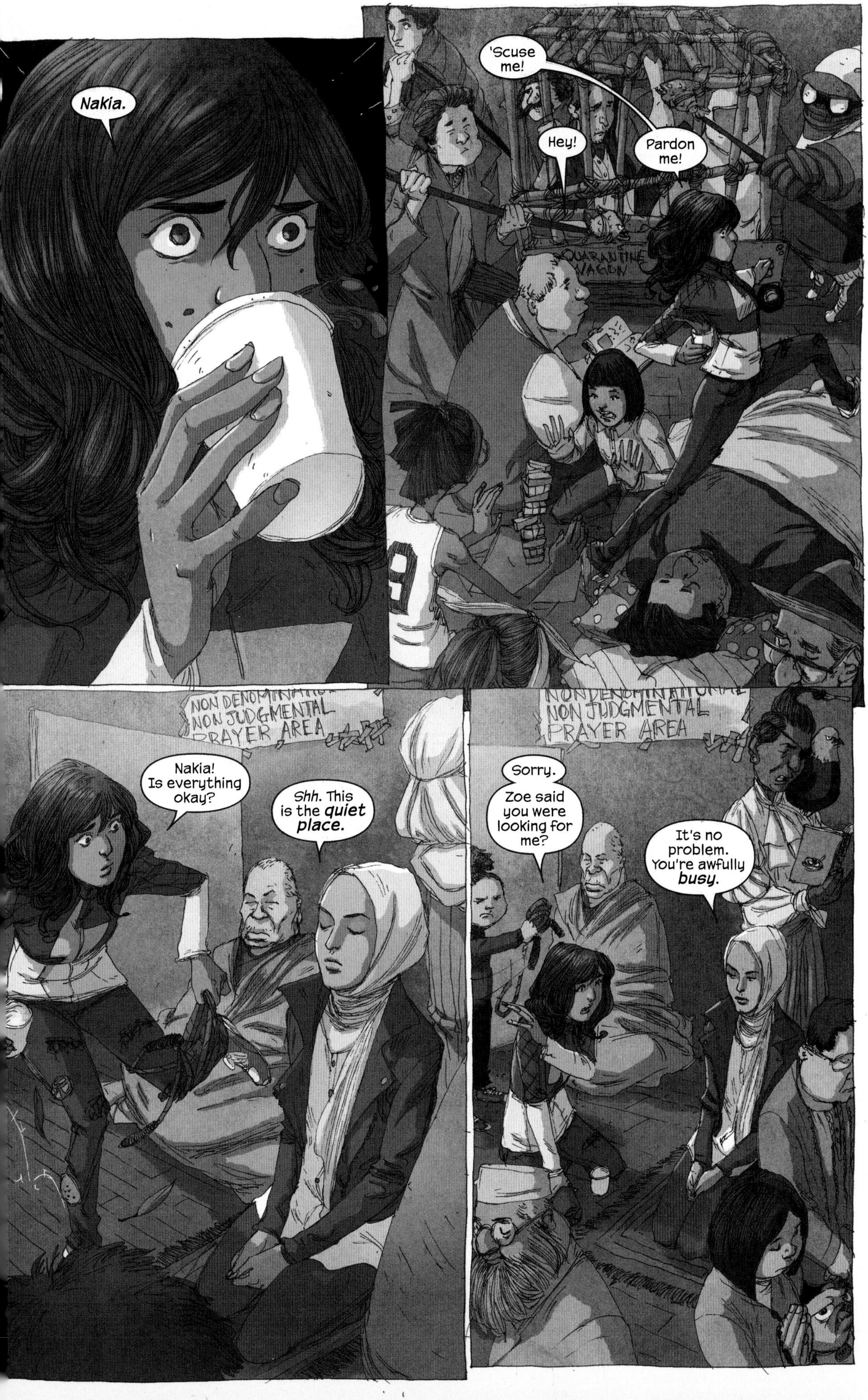
Nakia.
'Scuse me!
Hey!
Pardon me!
QUARANTINE WAGON
NON DENOMINATIONAL NON JUDGMENTAL PRAYER AREA
Nakia! Is everything okay?
Shh. This is the quiet place.
Sorry.
Zoe said you were looking for me?
It's no problem. You're awfully busy.

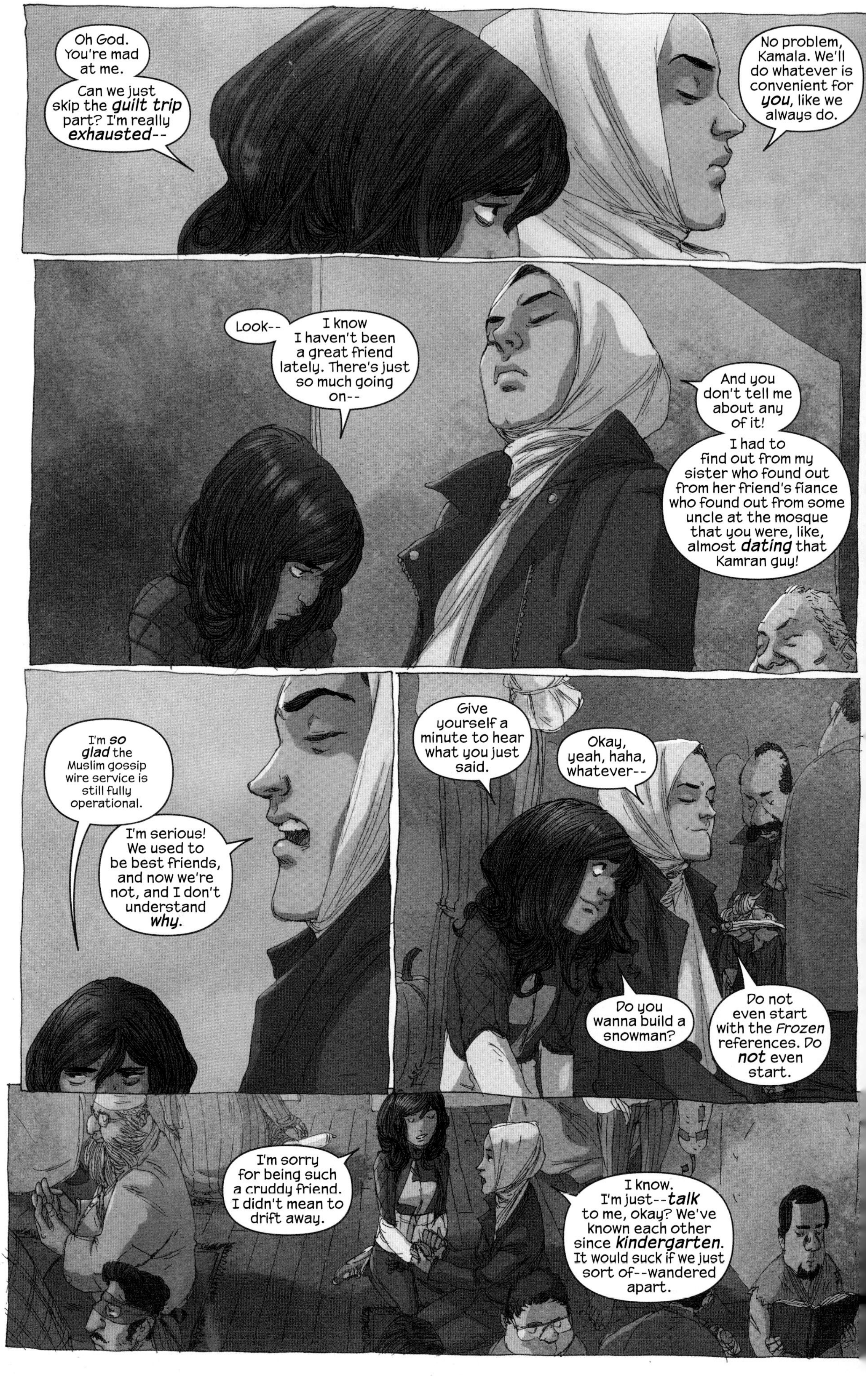
Oh God. You're mad at me.
Can we just skip the guilt trip part? I'm really exhausted--
No problem, Kamala. We'll do whatever is convenient for you, like we always do.
Look--
I know I haven't been a great friend lately. There's just so much going on--
And you don't tell me about any of it!
I had to find out from my sister who found out from her friend's fiance who found out from some uncle at the mosque that you were, like, almost dating that Kamran guy!
I'm so glad the Muslim gossip wire service is still fully operational.
I'm serious! We used to be best friends, and now we're not, and I don't understand why.
Give yourself a minute to hear what you just said.
Okay, yeah, haha, whatever--
Do you wanna build a snowman?
Do not even start with the Frozen references. Do not even start.
I'm sorry for being such a cruddy friend. I didn't mean to drift away.
I know. I'm just--talk to me, okay? We've known each other since kindergarten. It would suck if we just sort of--wandered apart.

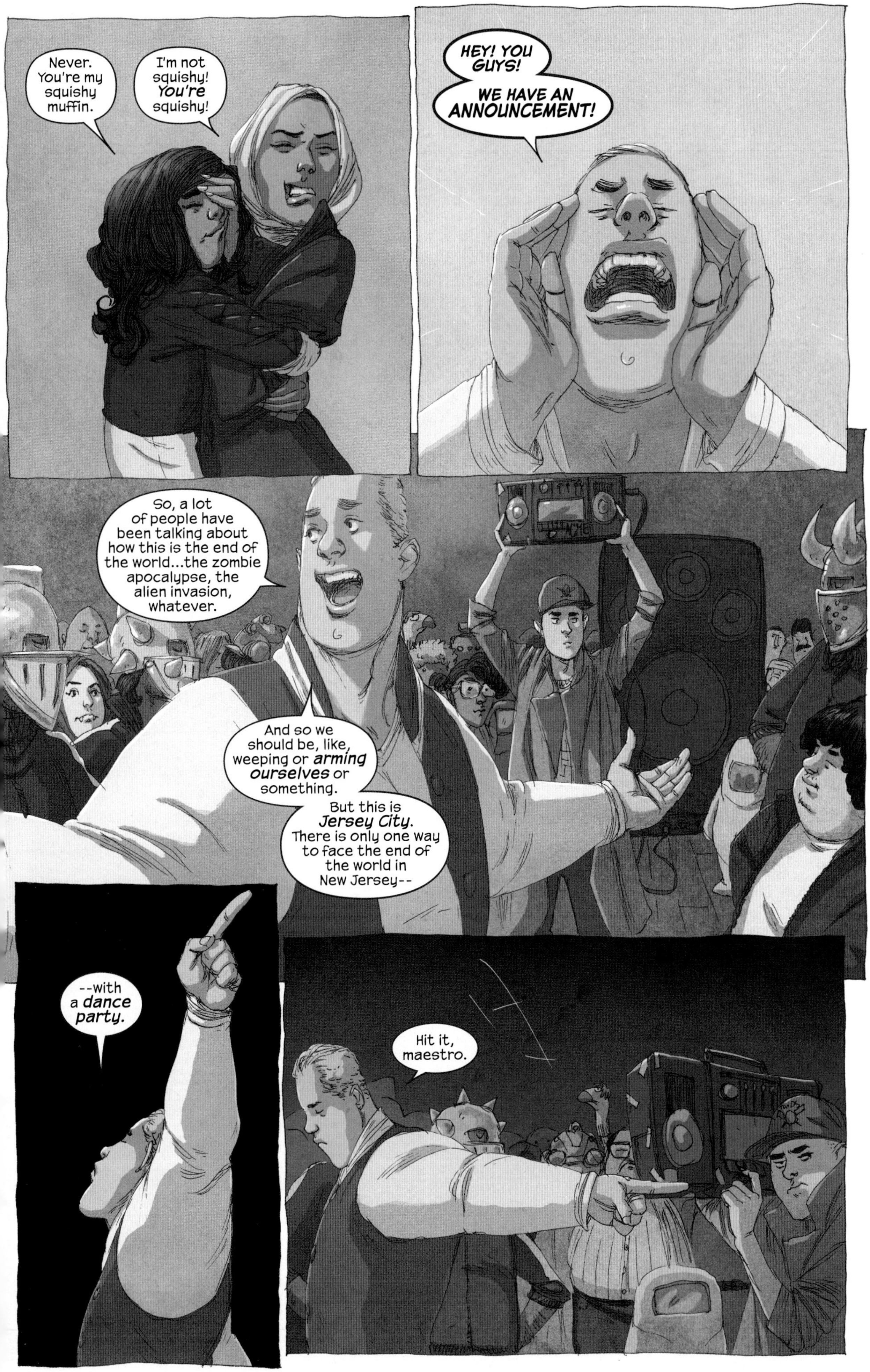

Never. You're my squishy muffin.
I'm not squishy! You're squishy!
HEY! YOU GUYS!
WE HAVE AN ANNOUNCEMENT!
So, a lot of people have been talking about how this is the end of the world...the zombie apocalypse, the alien invasion, whatever.
And so we should be, like, weeping or arming ourselves or something.
But this is Jersey City. There is only one way to face the end of the world in New Jersey--
--with a dance party.
Hit it, maestro.

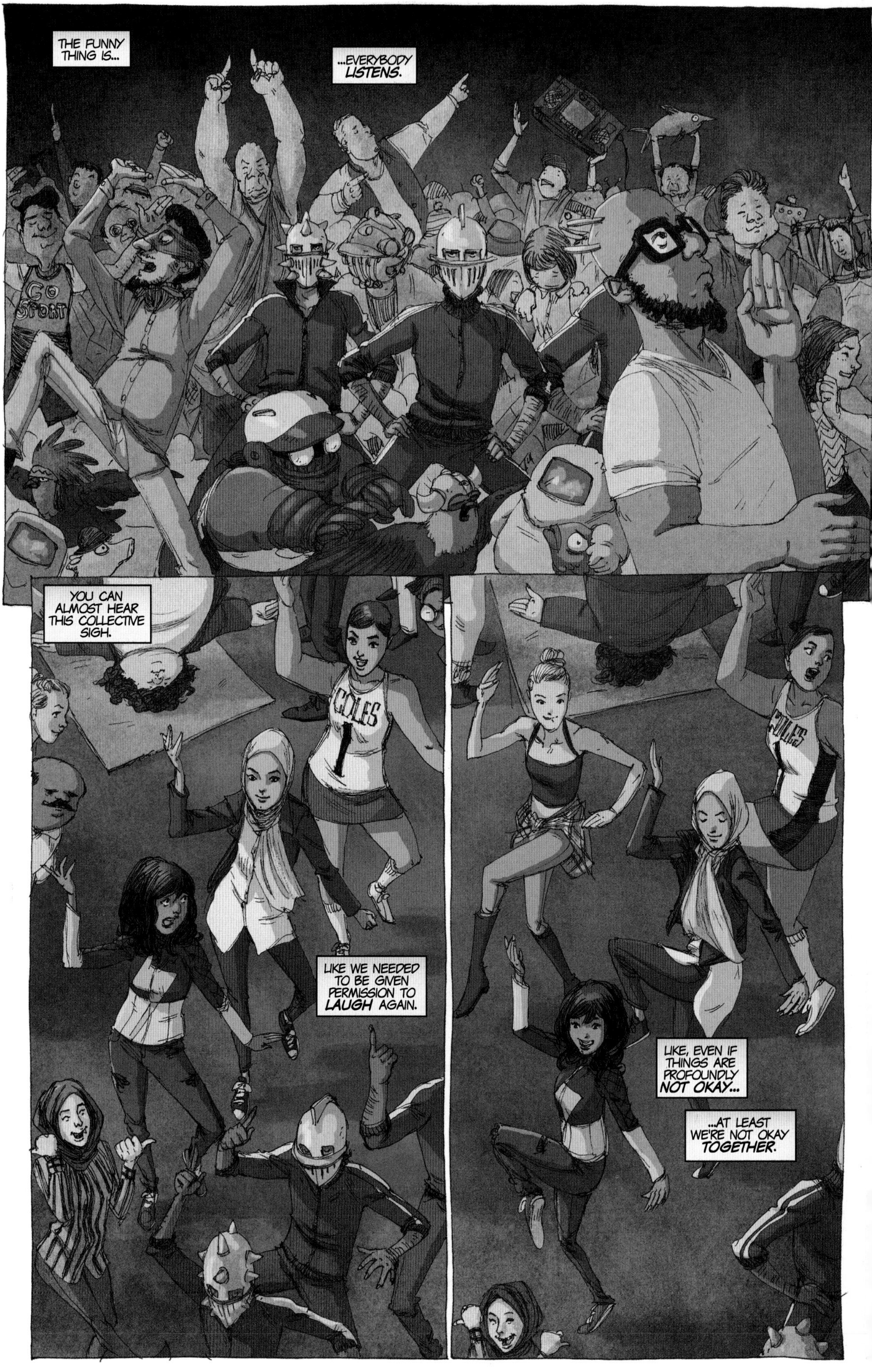
THE FUNNY THING IS...
...EVERYBODY LISTENS.
GO SPORT
YOU CAN ALMOST HEAR THIS COLLECTIVE SIGH.
COLES 1
LIKE WE NEEDED TO BE GIVEN PERMISSION TO LAUGH AGAIN.
LIKE, EVEN IF THINGS ARE PROFOUNDLY NOT OKAY...
...AT LEAST WE'RE NOT OKAY TOGETHER.

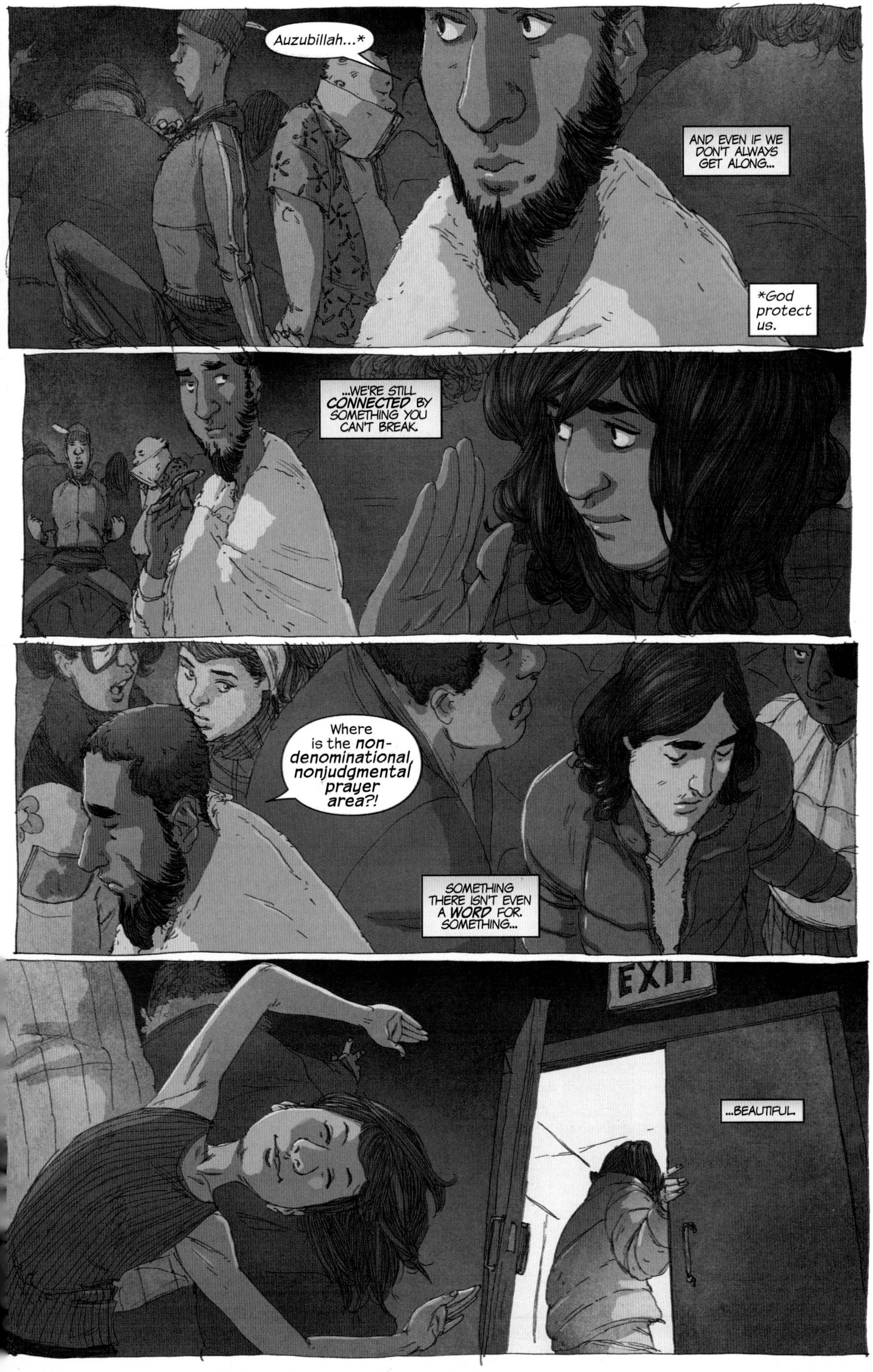
Auzubillah...*
AND EVEN IF WE DON'T ALWAYS GET ALONG...
*God protect us.
...WE'RE STILL CONNECTED BY SOMETHING YOU CAN'T BREAK.
Where is the non-denominational, nonjudgmental prayer area?!
SOMETHING THERE ISN'T EVEN A WORD FOR. SOMETHING...
EXIT
...BEAUTIFUL.

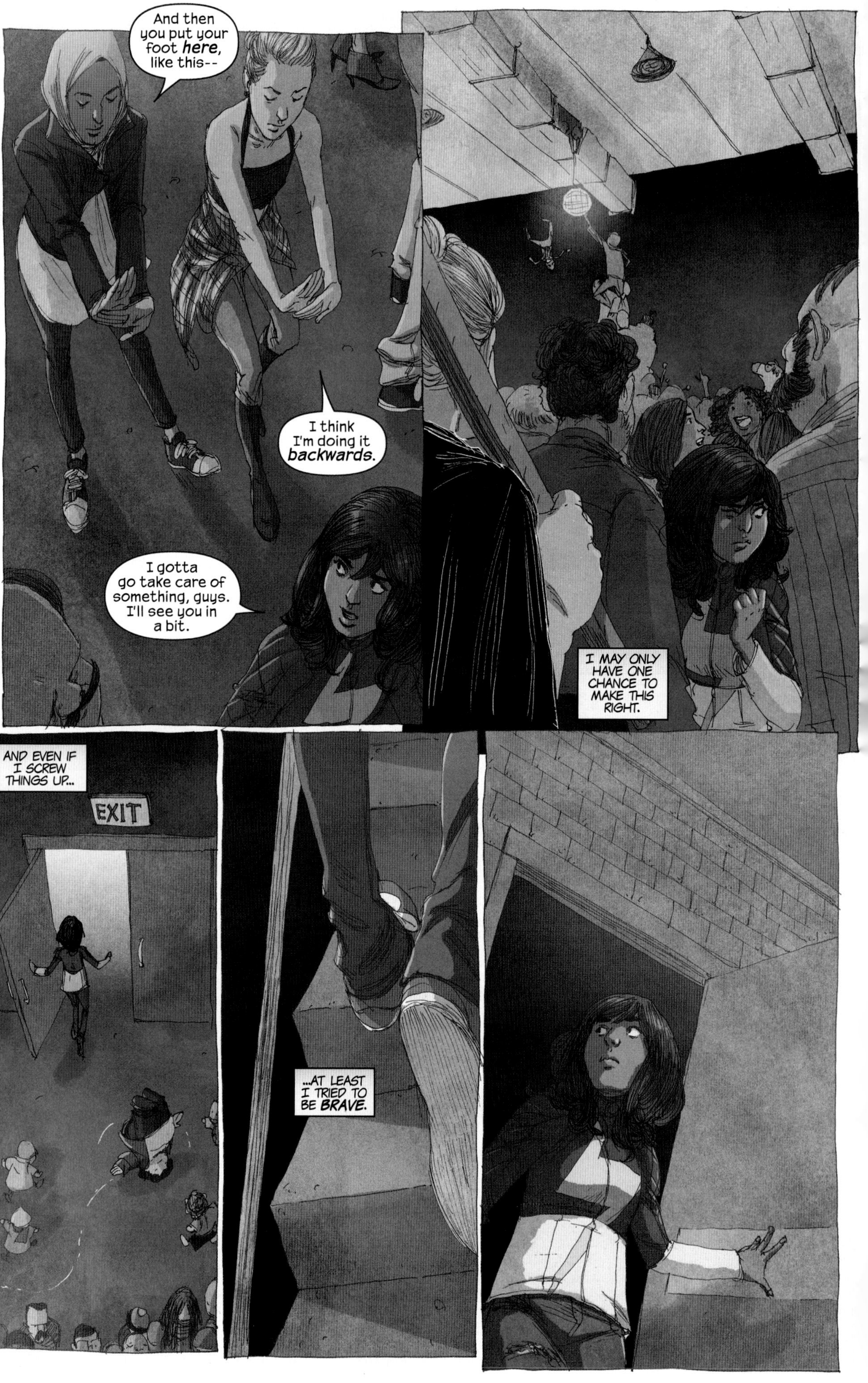
And then you put your foot *here*, like this--
I think I'm doing it *backwards*.
I gotta go take care of something, guys. I'll see you in a bit.
I MAY ONLY HAVE ONE CHANCE TO MAKE THIS RIGHT.
AND EVEN IF I SCREW THINGS UP...
EXIT
...AT LEAST I TRIED TO BE *BRAVE*.

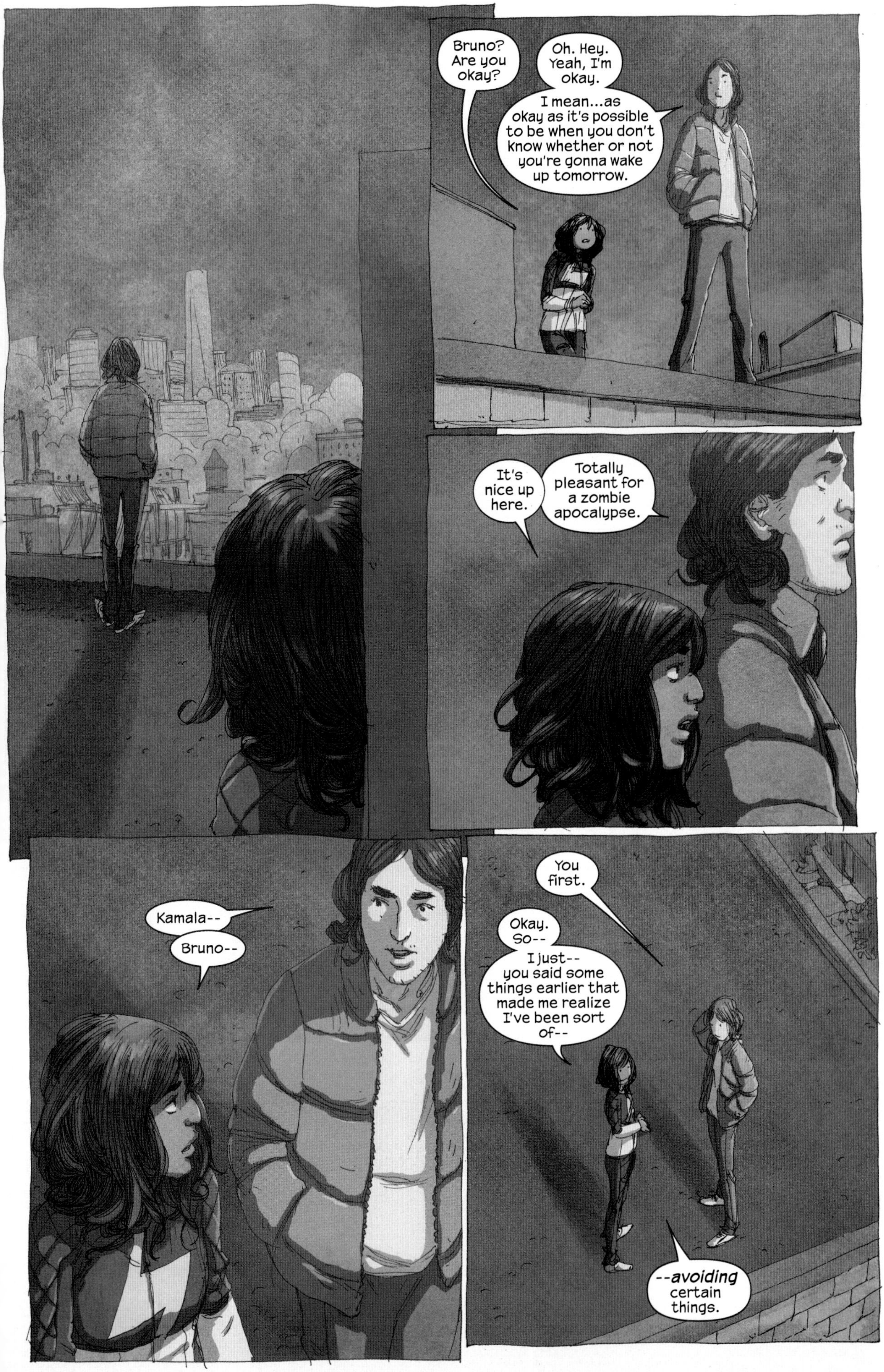
Bruno? Are you okay?
Oh. Hey. Yeah, I'm okay.
I mean...as okay as it's possible to be when you don't know whether or not you're gonna wake up tomorrow.
It's nice up here.
Totally pleasant for a zombie apocalypse.
Kamala--
Bruno--
You first.
Okay. So--
I just-- you said some things earlier that made me realize I've been sort of--
--*avoiding* certain things.

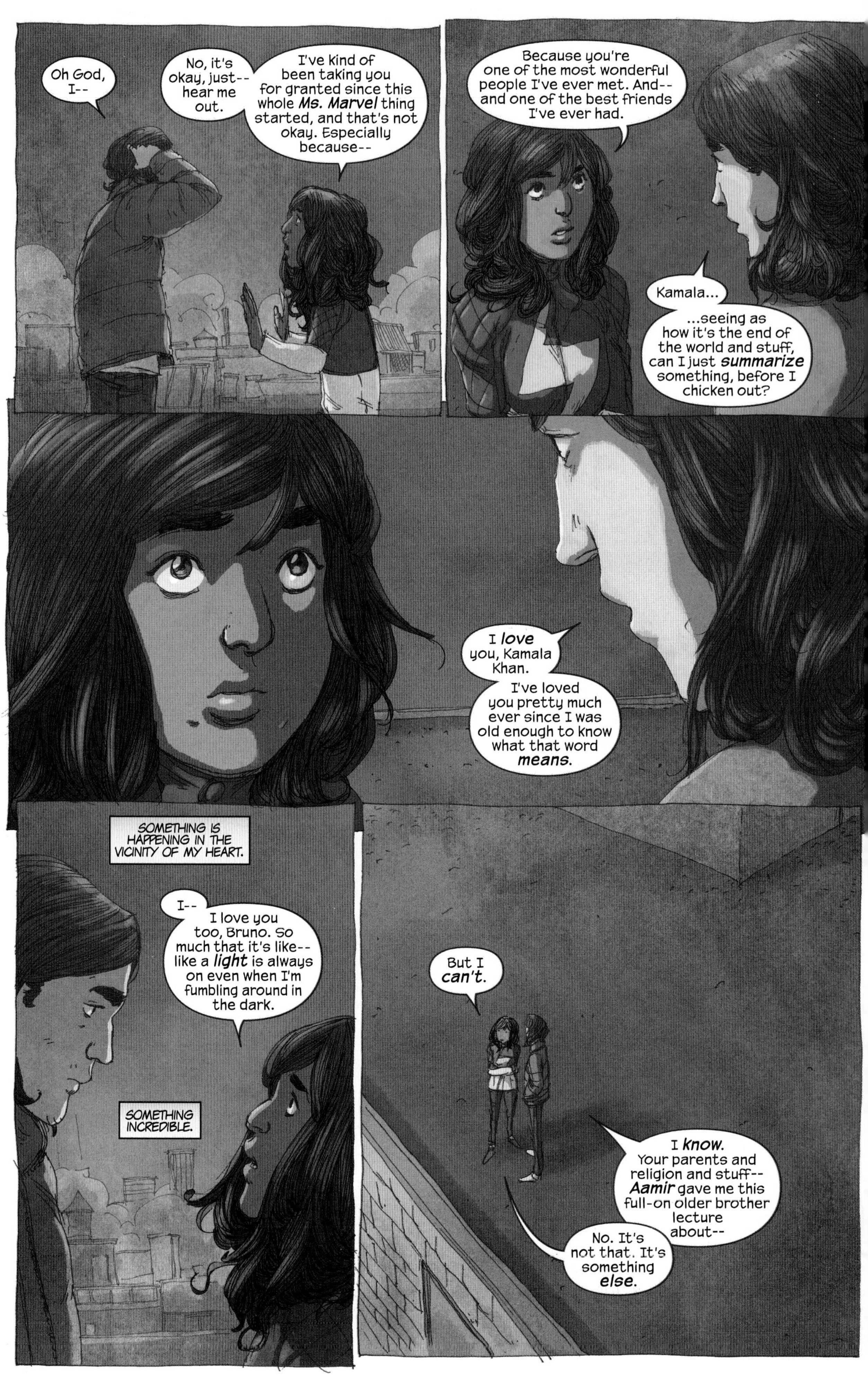
Oh God, I--
No, it's okay, just-- hear me out.
I've kind of been taking you for granted since this whole *Ms. Marvel* thing started, and that's not okay. Especially because--
Because you're one of the most wonderful people I've ever met. And-- and one of the best friends I've ever had.
Kamala...
...seeing as how it's the end of the world and stuff, can I just **summarize** something, before I chicken out?
I *love* you, Kamala Khan.
I've loved you pretty much ever since I was old enough to know what that word **means**.
SOMETHING IS HAPPENING IN THE VICINITY OF MY HEART.
I--
I love you too, Bruno. So much that it's like-- like a *light* is always on even when I'm fumbling around in the dark.
SOMETHING INCREDIBLE.
But I **can't**.
I *know*. Your parents and religion and stuff-- *Aamir* gave me this full-on older brother lecture about--
No. It's not that. It's something **else**.

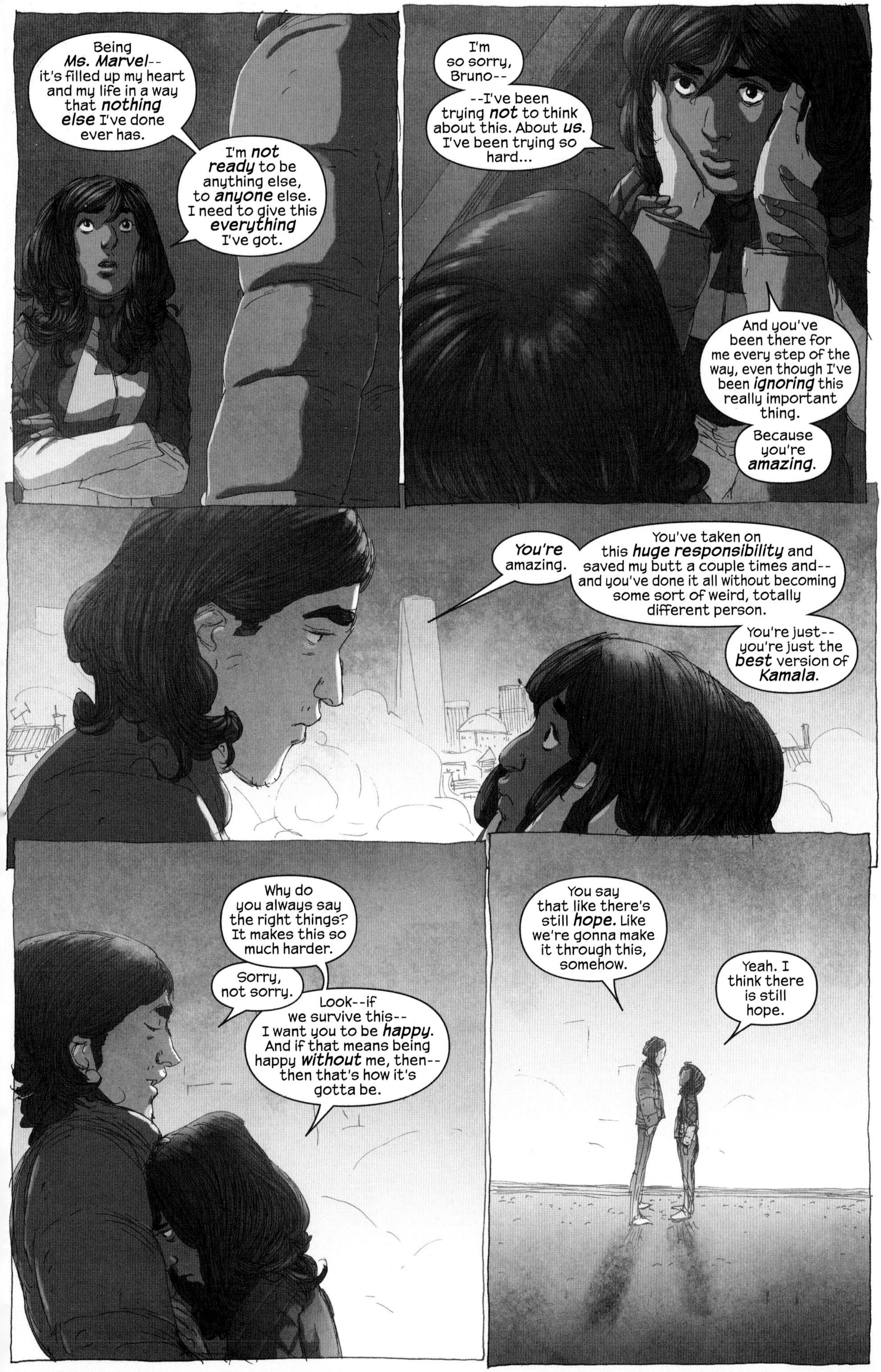
Being *Ms. Marvel*-- it's filled up my heart and my life in a way that *nothing else* I've done ever has.
I'm *not ready* to be anything else, to *anyone* else. I need to give this *everything* I've got.
I'm so sorry, Bruno--
--I've been trying *not* to think about this. About *us*. I've been trying so hard...
And you've been there for me every step of the way, even though I've been *ignoring* this really important thing.
Because you're *amazing*.
You're amazing.
You've taken on this *huge responsibility* and saved my butt a couple times and-- and you've done it all without becoming some sort of weird, totally different person.
You're just-- you're just the *best* version of *Kamala*.
Why do you always say the right things? It makes this so much harder.
Sorry, not sorry.
Look--if we survive this-- I want you to be *happy*. And if that means being happy *without* me, then-- then that's how it's gotta be.
You say that like there's still *hope*. Like we're gonna make it through this, somehow.
Yeah. I think there is still hope.

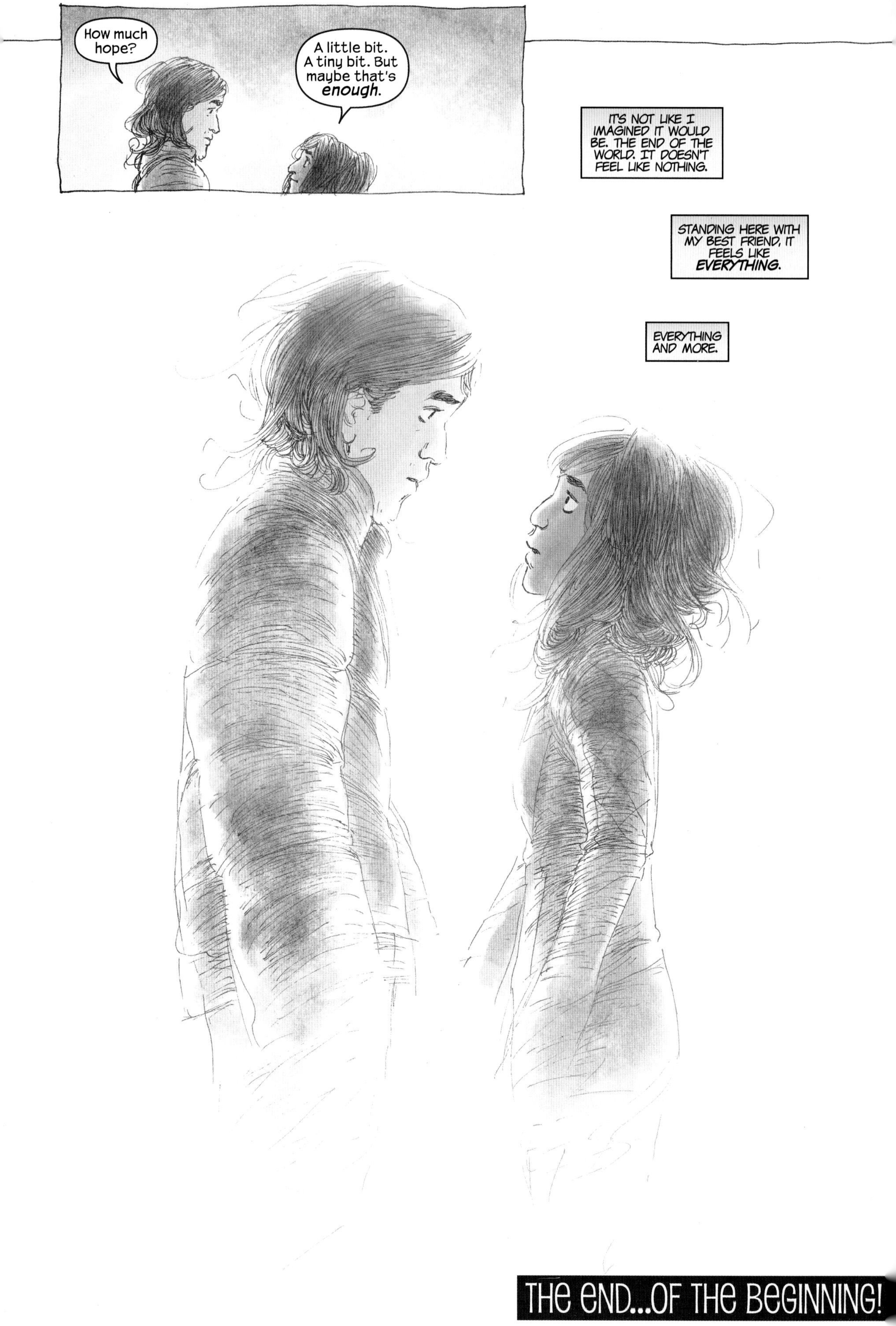
How much hope?
A little bit. A tiny bit. But maybe that's *enough*.
IT'S NOT LIKE I IMAGINED IT WOULD BE. THE END OF THE WORLD. IT DOESN'T FEEL LIKE NOTHING.
STANDING HERE WITH MY BEST FRIEND, IT FEELS LIKE ***EVERYTHING***.
EVERYTHING AND MORE.
THE END...OF THE BEGINNING!

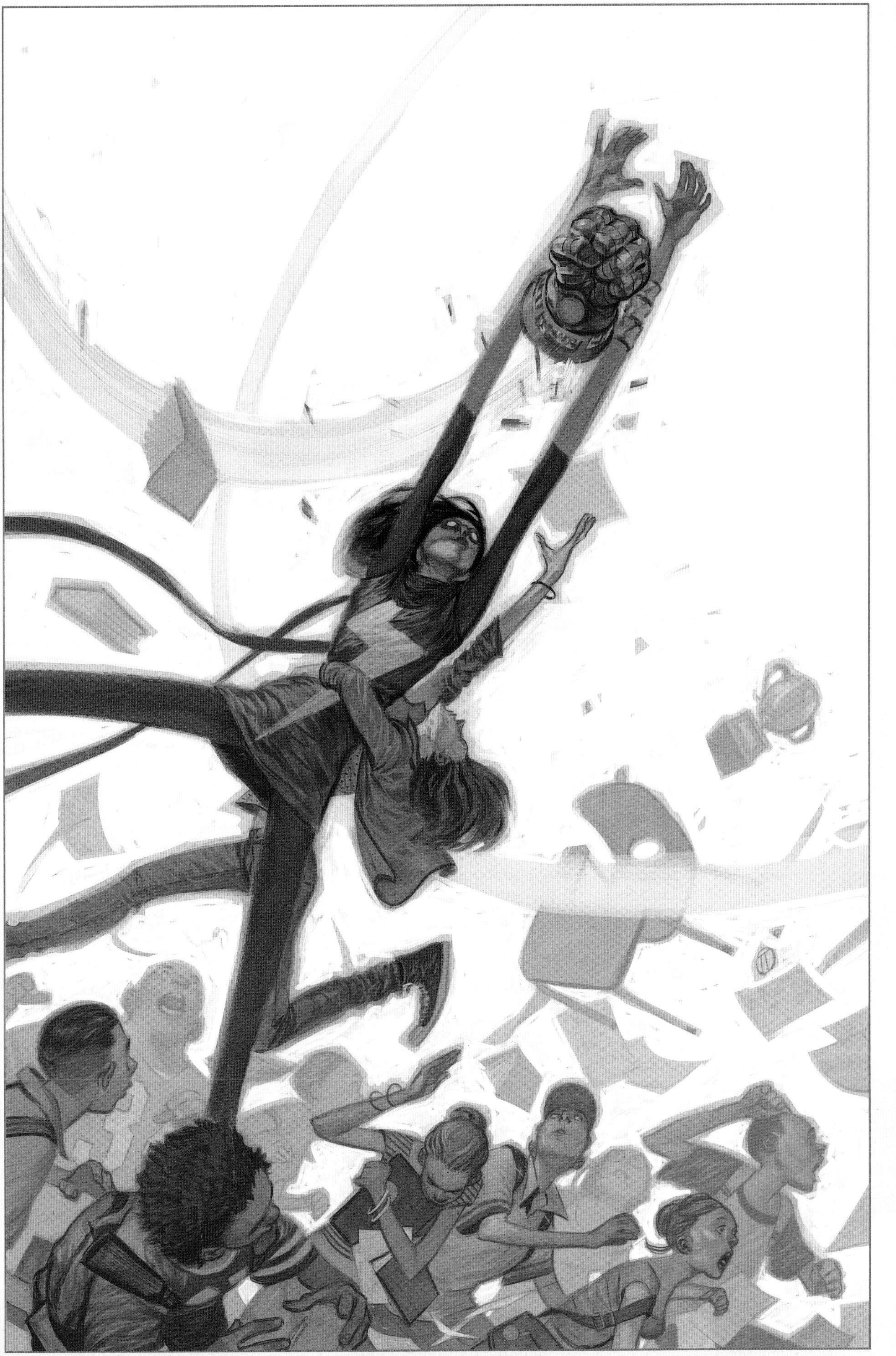

S.H.I.E.L.D. #2

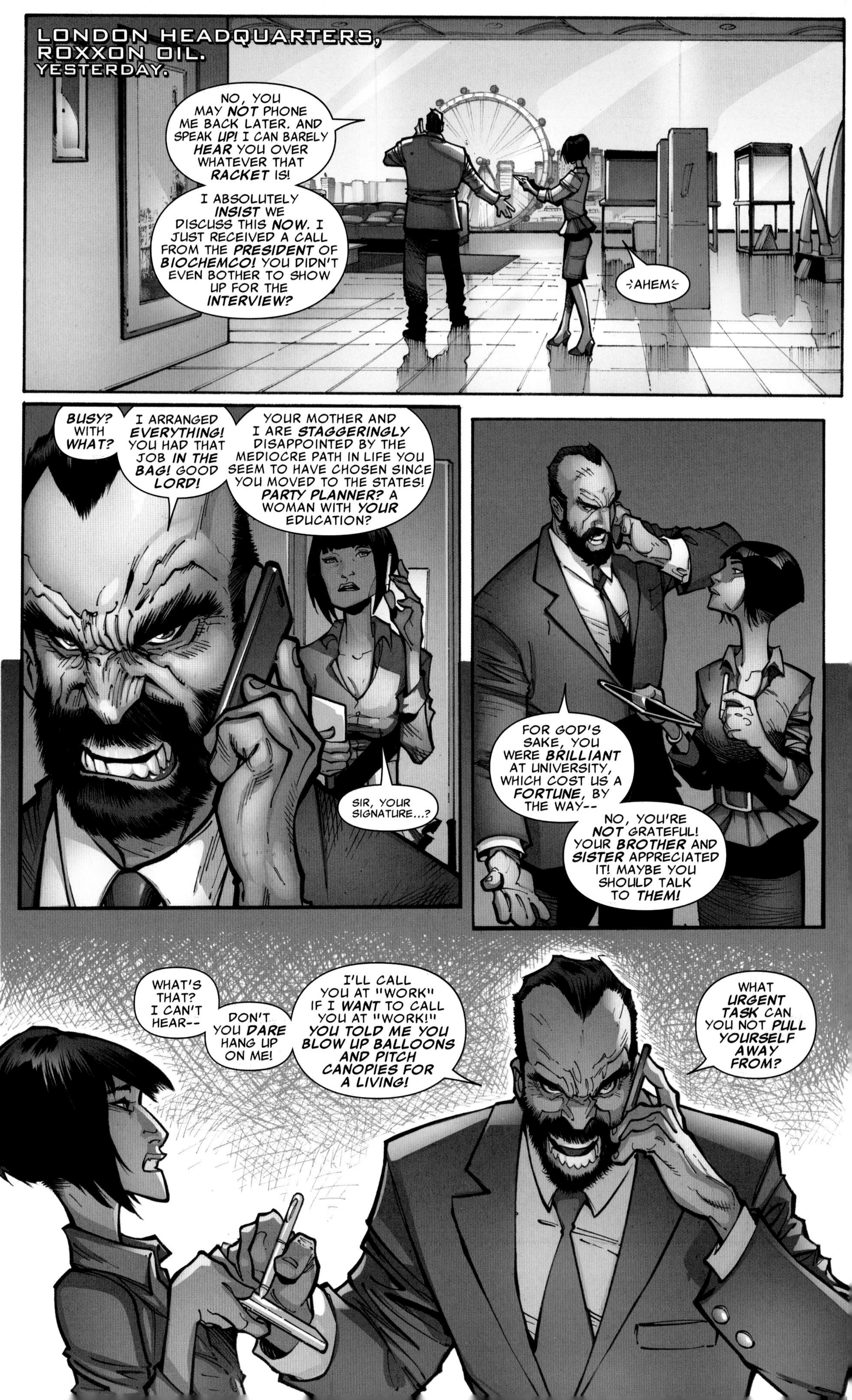
LONDON HEADQUARTERS, ROXXON OIL. YESTERDAY.
NO, YOU MAY NOT PHONE ME BACK LATER. AND SPEAK UP! I CAN BARELY HEAR YOU OVER WHATEVER THAT RACKET IS!
I ABSOLUTELY INSIST WE DISCUSS THIS NOW. I JUST RECEIVED A CALL FROM THE PRESIDENT OF BIOCHEMCO! YOU DIDN'T EVEN BOTHER TO SHOW UP FOR THE INTERVIEW?
AHEM
BUSY? WITH WHAT?
I ARRANGED EVERYTHING! YOU HAD THAT JOB IN THE BAG! GOOD LORD!
YOUR MOTHER AND I ARE STAGGERINGLY DISAPPOINTED BY THE MEDIOCRE PATH IN LIFE YOU SEEM TO HAVE CHOSEN SINCE YOU MOVED TO THE STATES! PARTY PLANNER? A WOMAN WITH YOUR EDUCATION?
SIR, YOUR SIGNATURE...?
FOR GOD'S SAKE, YOU WERE BRILLIANT AT UNIVERSITY, WHICH COST US A FORTUNE, BY THE WAY--
NO, YOU'RE NOT GRATEFUL! YOUR BROTHER AND SISTER APPRECIATED IT! MAYBE YOU SHOULD TALK TO THEM!
WHAT'S THAT? I CAN'T HEAR--
DON'T YOU DARE HANG UP ON ME!
I'LL CALL YOU AT "WORK" IF I WANT TO CALL YOU AT "WORK!" YOU TOLD ME YOU BLOW UP BALLOONS AND PITCH CANOPIES FOR A LIVING!
WHAT URGENT TASK CAN YOU NOT PULL YOURSELF AWAY FROM?

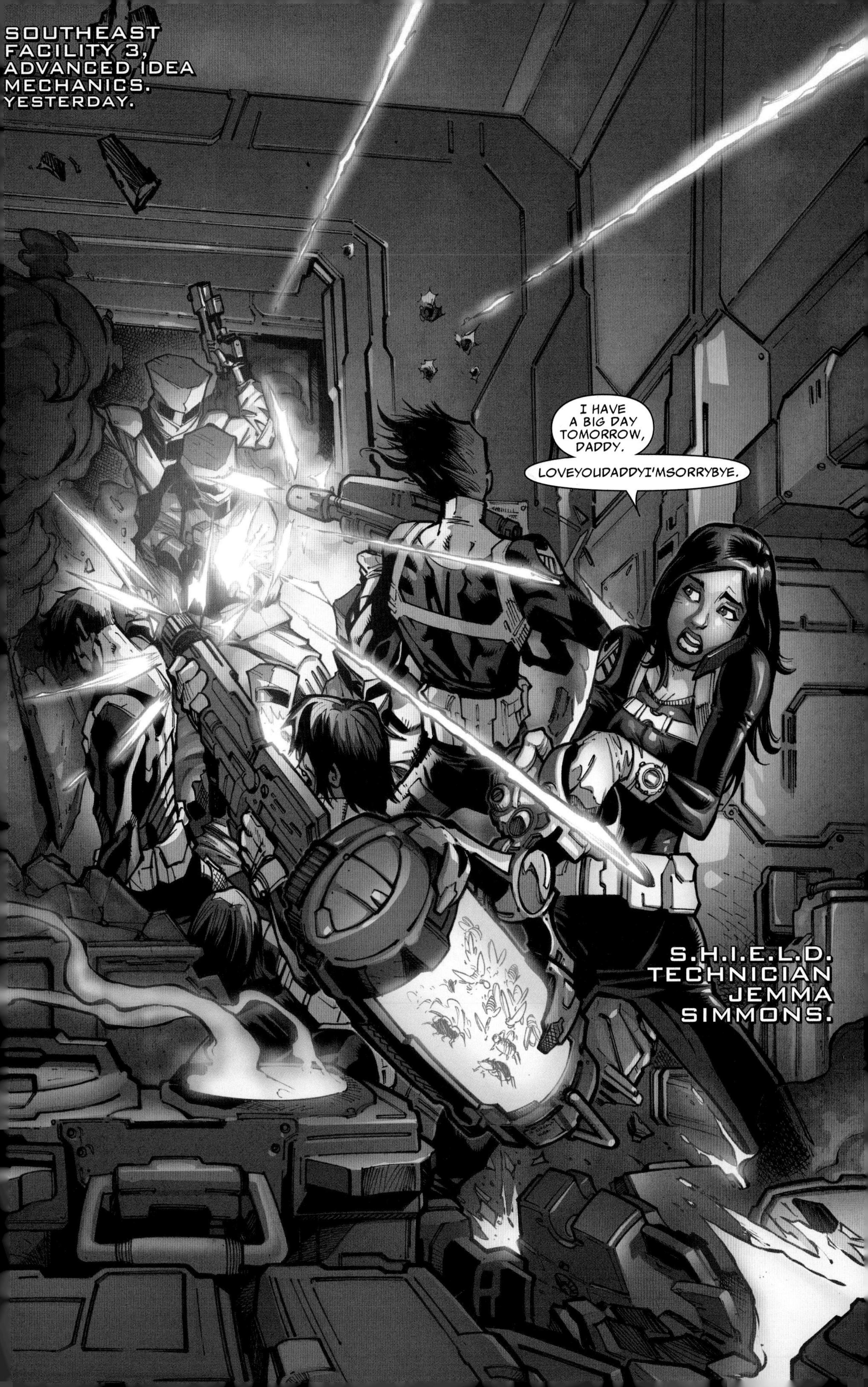
SOUTHEAST FACILITY 3, ADVANCED IDEA MECHANICS. YESTERDAY.
I HAVE A BIG DAY TOMORROW, DADDY.
LOVEYOUDADDYI'MSORRYBYE.
S.H.I.E.L.D. TECHNICIAN JEMMA SIMMONS.

ACCESS GRANTED...

ACTIVE MISSION:
THE ANIMATOR

STRATEGIC HOMELAND INTERVENTION ENFORCEMENT LOGISTICS DIVISION

S.H.I.E.L.D.

PAST MISSION:

S.H.I.E.L.D., the Strategic Homeland Intervention, Enforcement and Logistics Division, mitigates and confronts threats to the security of the Earth and its people. Its highly trained agents detect and defend against any menace that might rear its ugly head against us. Among these agents are Phil Coulson–cool-headed, mild-mannered, and singularly dedicated to his work–and xenobiologist Jemma Simmons, calmly collected, wildly intelligent, and surprisingly sentimental. Coulson, Simmons, and their fellow S.H.I.E.L.D. agents encounter mutants, monsters, villains, gods, and the best and worst of humanity on a daily basis as they endeavor to carry out S.H.I.E.L.D.'s mission.

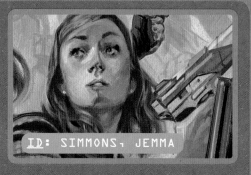

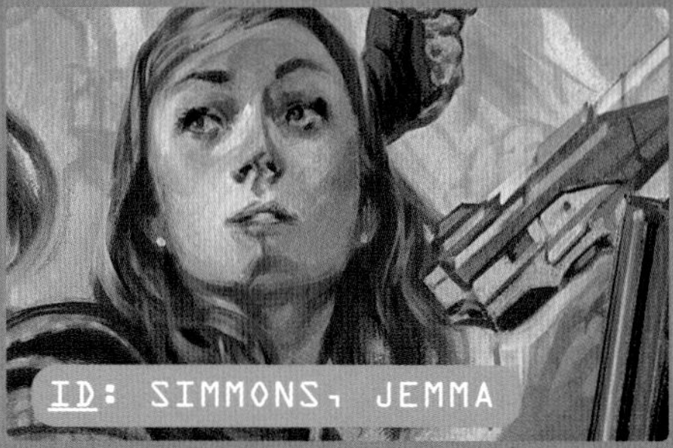
ID: SIMMONS, JEMMA

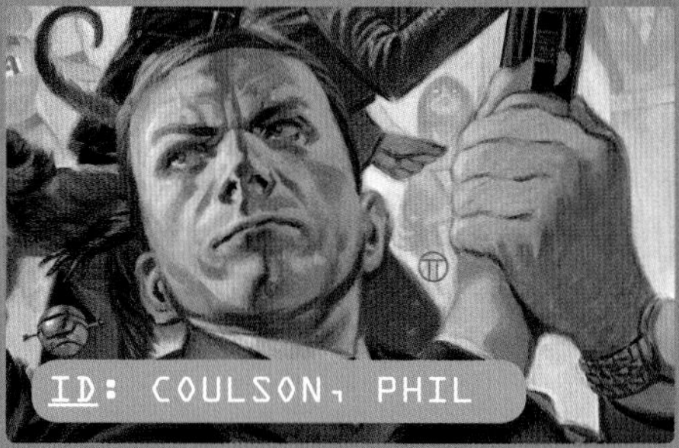
ID: COULSON, PHIL

KNOWN AGENTS:

MARK WAID
WRITER
HUMBERTO RAMOS
PENCILER
VICTOR OLAZABA
INKER
EDGAR DELGADO
COLORIST
VC'S JOE CARAMAGNA
LETTERER
JESSICA PIZARRO
DESIGNER

JULIAN TOTINO TEDESCO
COVER ARTIST
HUMBERTO RAMOS & EDGAR DELGADO;
SALVADOR LARROCA & ISRAEL SILVA
VARIANT COVER ARTISTS

JON MOISAN
ASSISTANT EDITOR
TOM BREVOORT
WITH ELLIE PYLE
(K.I.A.)
EDITORS
AXEL ALONSO
EDITOR IN CHIEF

JOE QUESADA
CHIEF CREATIVE
OFFICER
DAN BUCKLEY
PUBLISHER
ALAN FINE
EXECUTIVE PRODUCER

FITZ AND H.E.N.R.Y. STRIPS BY JOE QUESADA
S.H.I.E.L.D. CREATED BY STAN LEE AND JACK KIRBY

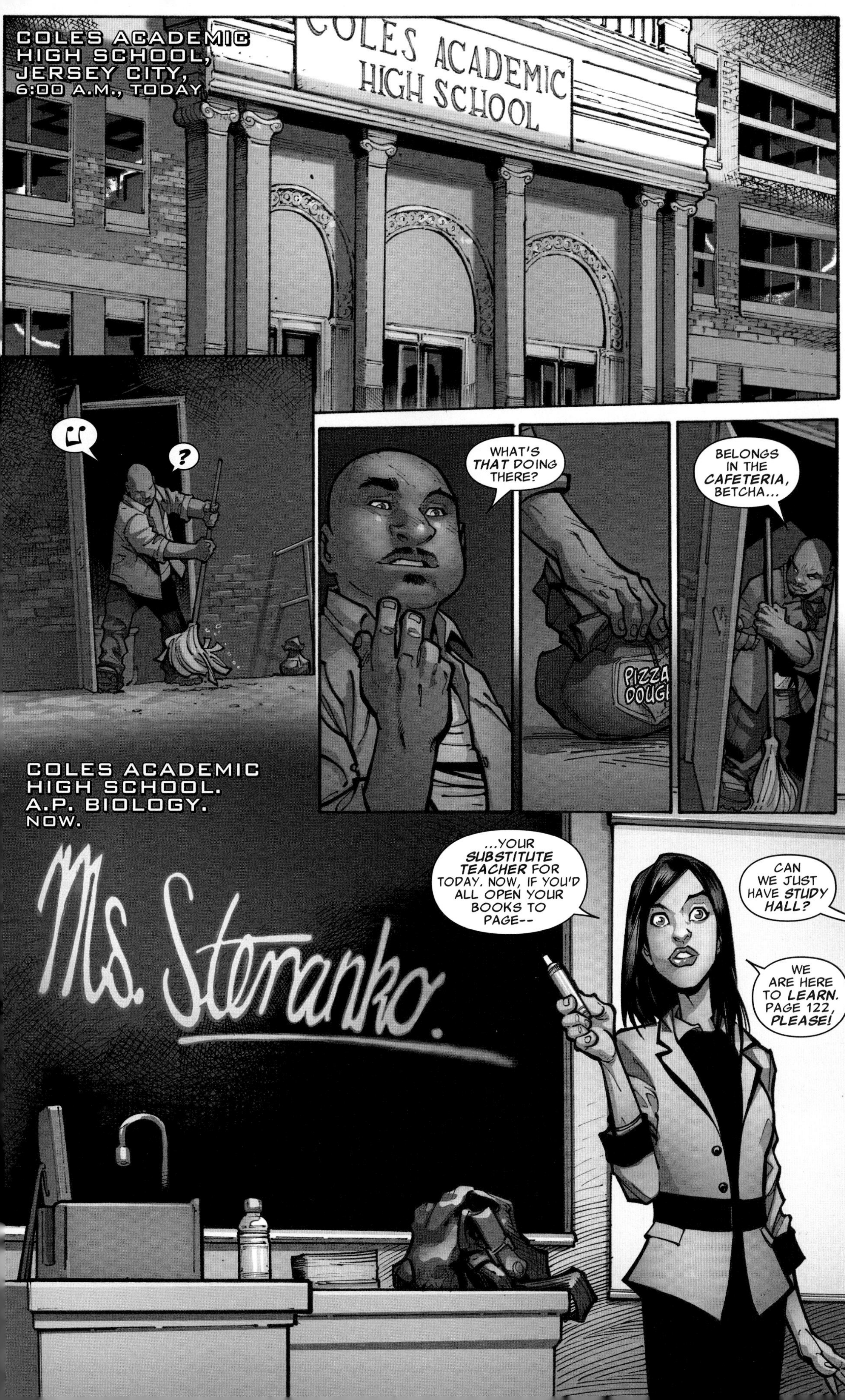

COLES ACADEMIC HIGH SCHOOL, JERSEY CITY, 6:00 A.M., TODAY
COLES ACADEMIC HIGH SCHOOL
?
WHAT'S THAT DOING THERE?
PIZZA DOUGH
BELONGS IN THE CAFETERIA, BETCHA...
COLES ACADEMIC HIGH SCHOOL. A.P. BIOLOGY. NOW.
Ms. Steranko.
...YOUR SUBSTITUTE TEACHER FOR TODAY. NOW, IF YOU'D ALL OPEN YOUR BOOKS TO PAGE--
CAN WE JUST HAVE STUDY HALL?
WE ARE HERE TO LEARN. PAGE 122, PLEASE!

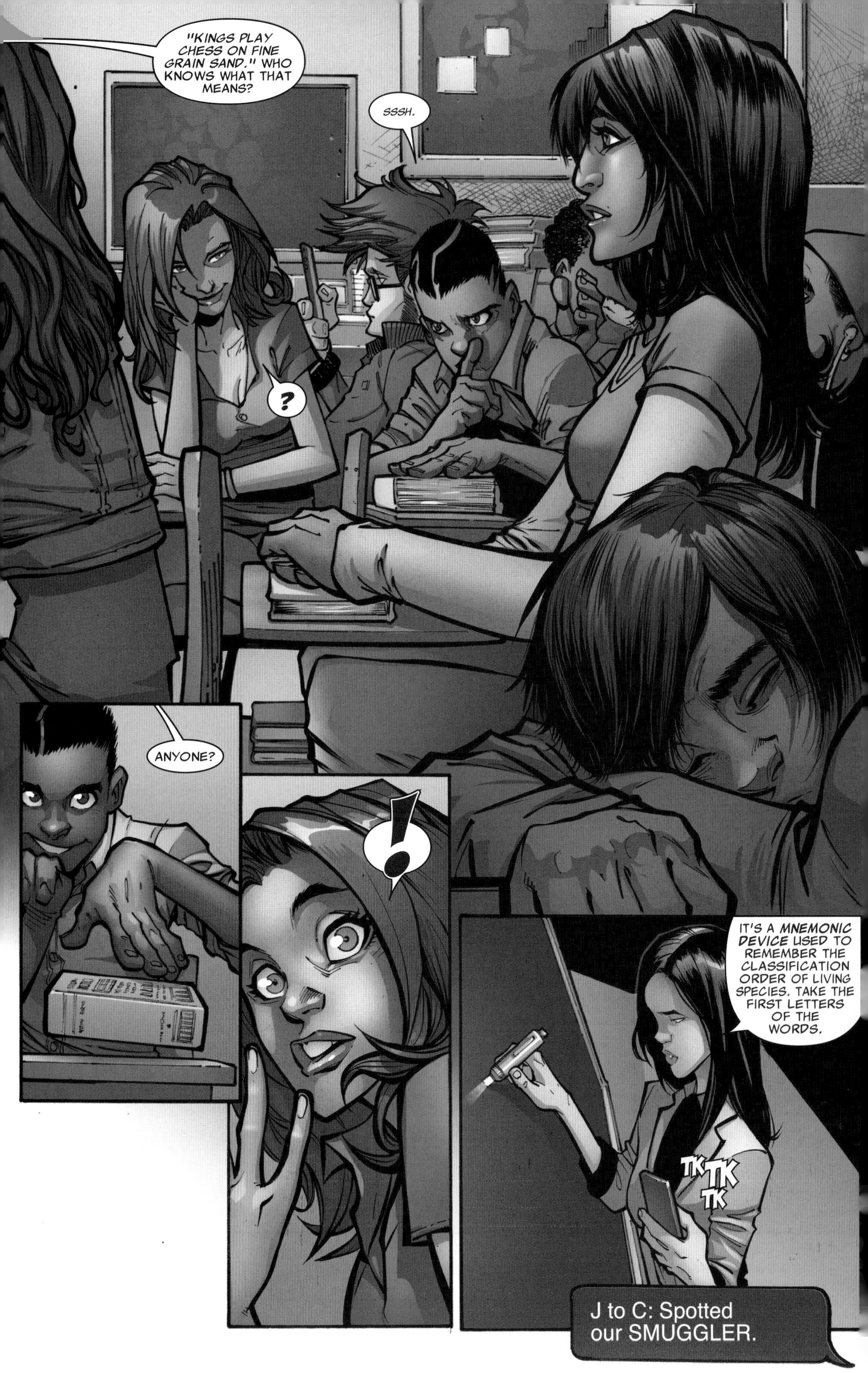
"KINGS PLAY CHESS ON FINE GRAIN SAND." WHO KNOWS WHAT THAT MEANS?
SSSH.
?
ANYONE?
!
IT'S A MNEMONIC DEVICE USED TO REMEMBER THE CLASSIFICATION ORDER OF LIVING SPECIES. TAKE THE FIRST LETTERS OF THE WORDS.
TK TK TK
J to C: Spotted our SMUGGLER.

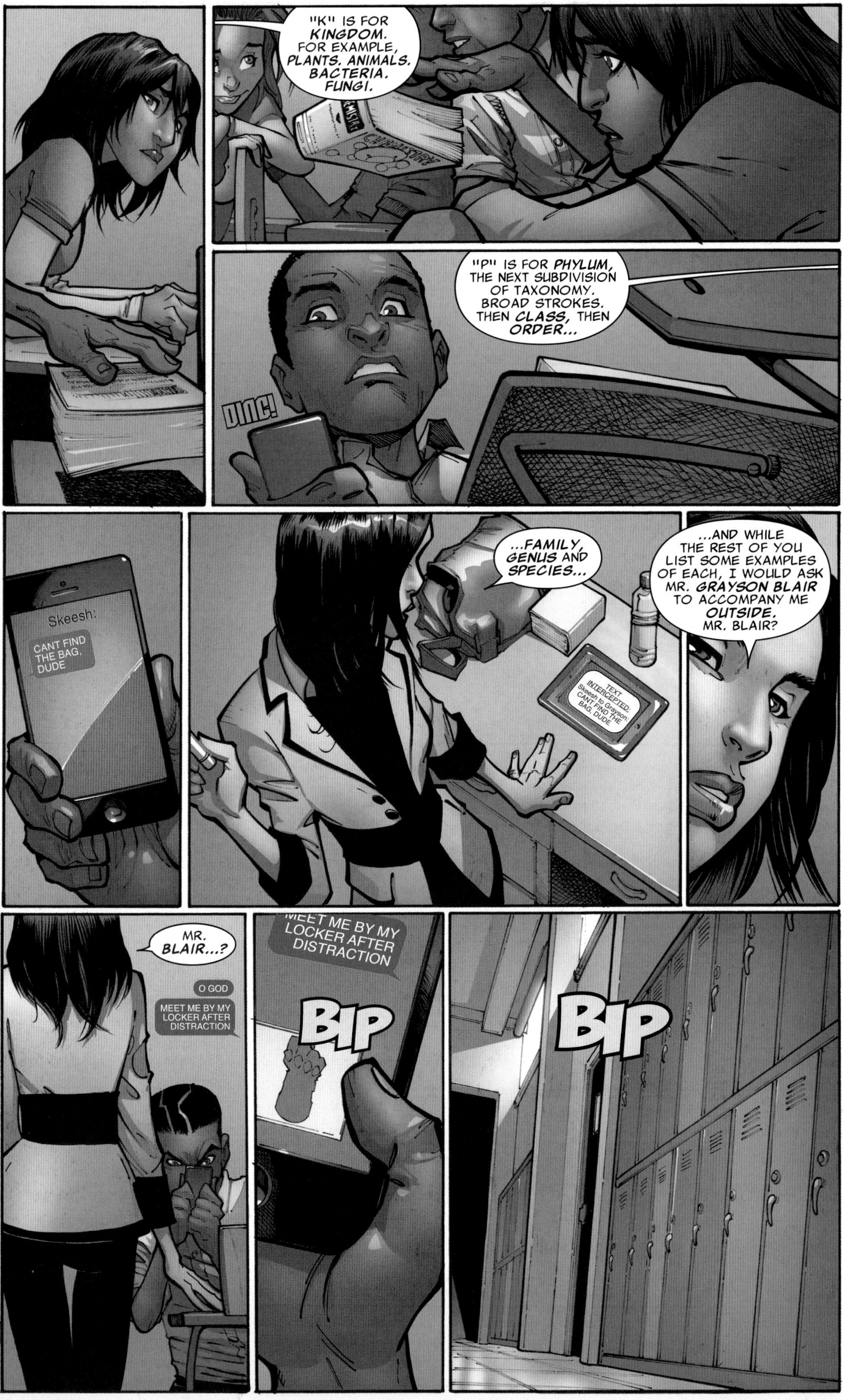
"K" IS FOR KINGDOM. FOR EXAMPLE, PLANTS. ANIMALS. BACTERIA. FUNGI.
"P" IS FOR PHYLUM, THE NEXT SUBDIVISION OF TAXONOMY. BROAD STROKES. THEN CLASS, THEN ORDER...
DING!
Skeesh:
CANT FIND THE BAG, DUDE
...FAMILY, GENUS AND SPECIES...
TEXT INTERCEPTED: Skeesh to Grayson: CANT FIND THE BAG, DUDE
...AND WHILE THE REST OF YOU LIST SOME EXAMPLES OF EACH, I WOULD ASK MR. GRAYSON BLAIR TO ACCOMPANY ME OUTSIDE. MR. BLAIR?
MR. BLAIR...?
O GOD
MEET ME BY MY LOCKER AFTER DISTRACTION
MEET ME BY MY LOCKER AFTER DISTRACTION
BIP
BIP

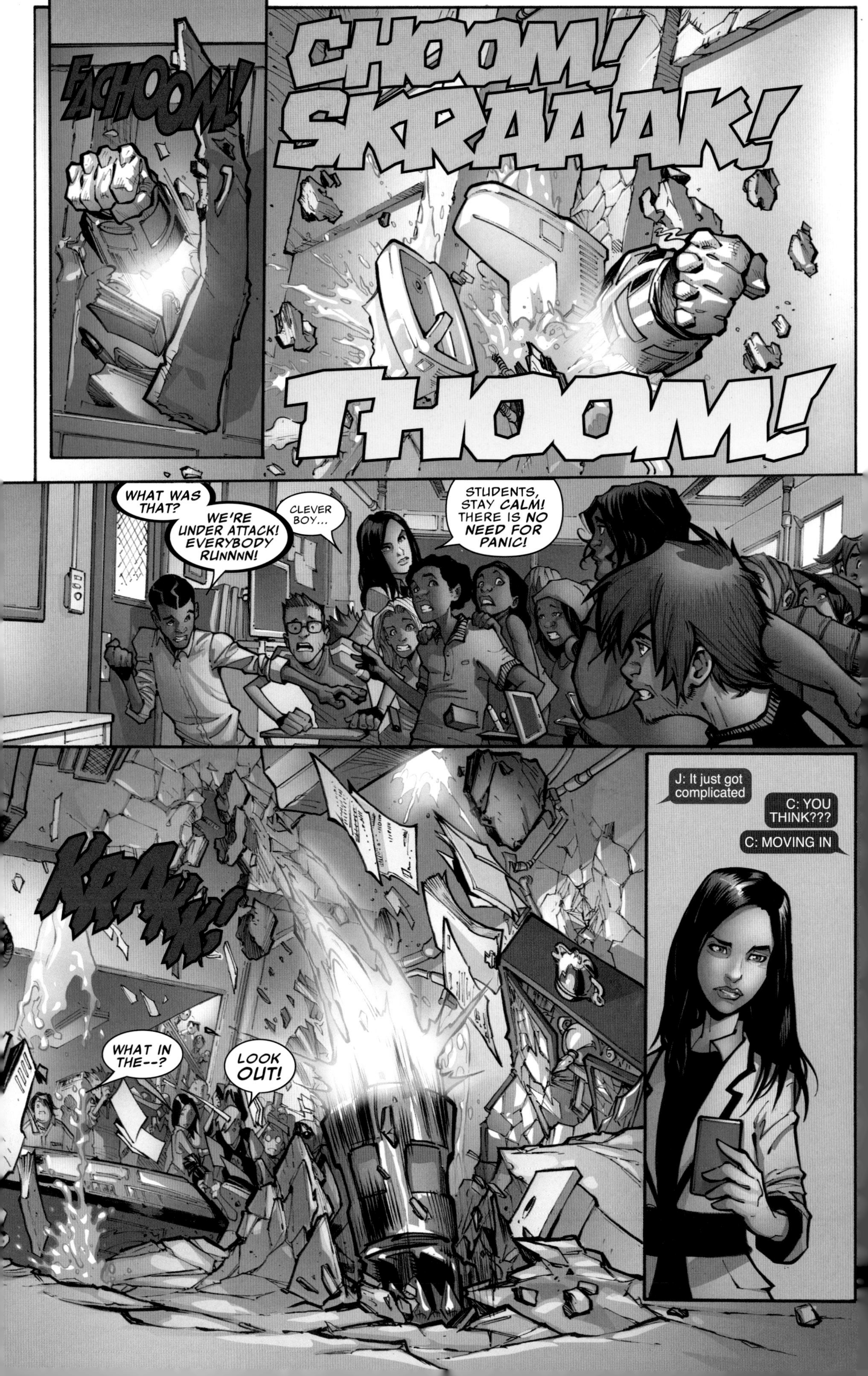
FACHOOM!
CHOOM!
SKRAAAK!
THOOM!
WHAT WAS THAT?
WE'RE UNDER ATTACK! EVERYBODY RUNNNN!
CLEVER BOY...
STUDENTS, STAY CALM! THERE IS NO NEED FOR PANIC!
KRAKK!
WHAT IN THE--?
LOOK OUT!
J: It just got complicated
C: YOU THINK???
C: MOVING IN

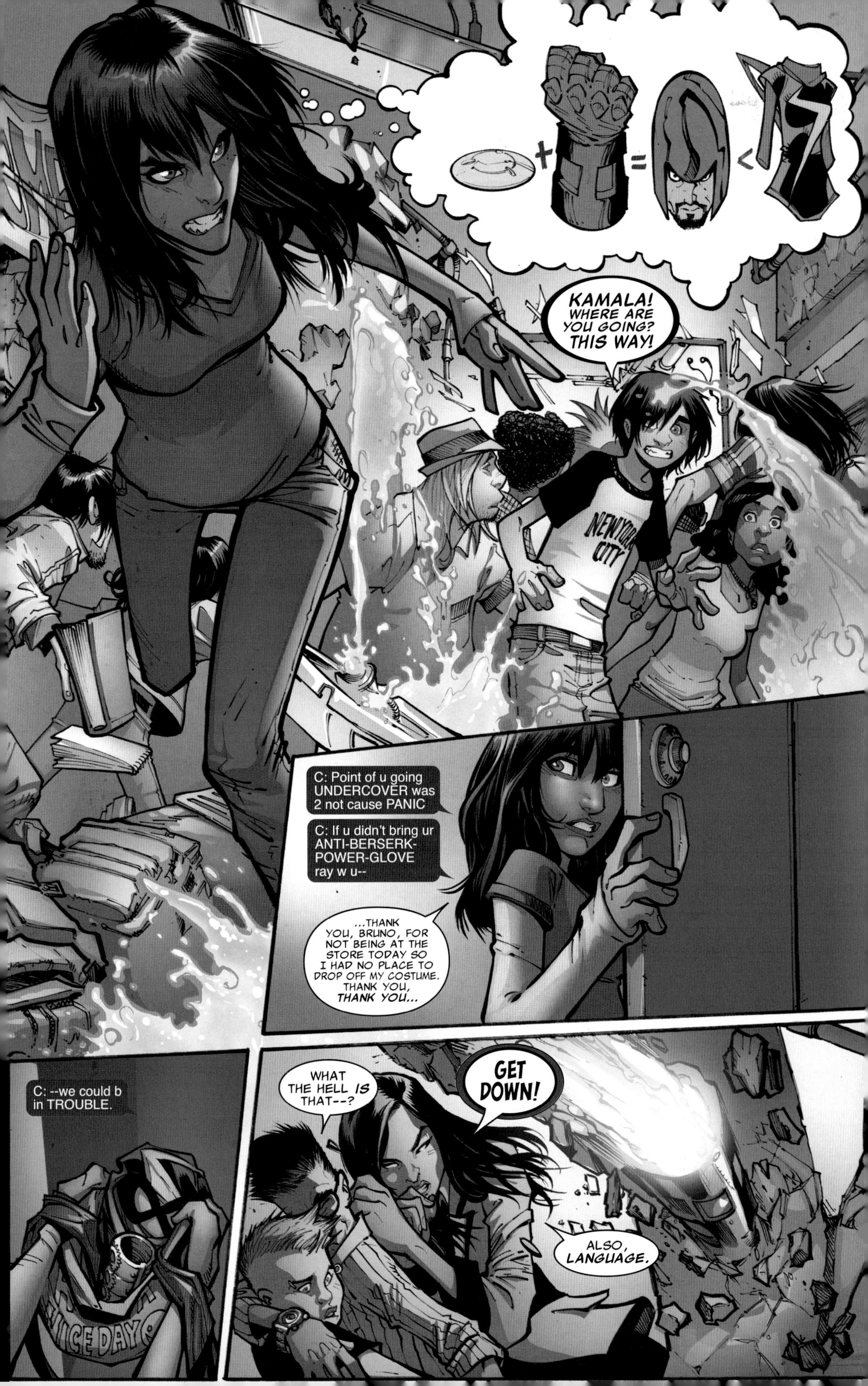
KAMALA! WHERE ARE YOU GOING? THIS WAY!
NEW YORK CITY
C: Point of u going UNDERCOVER was 2 not cause PANIC
C: If u didn't bring ur ANTI-BERSERK-POWER-GLOVE ray w u--
...THANK YOU, BRUNO, FOR NOT BEING AT THE STORE TODAY SO I HAD NO PLACE TO DROP OFF MY COSTUME. THANK YOU, THANK YOU...
C: --we could b in TROUBLE.
WHAT THE HELL IS THAT--?
GET DOWN!
ALSO, LANGUAGE.

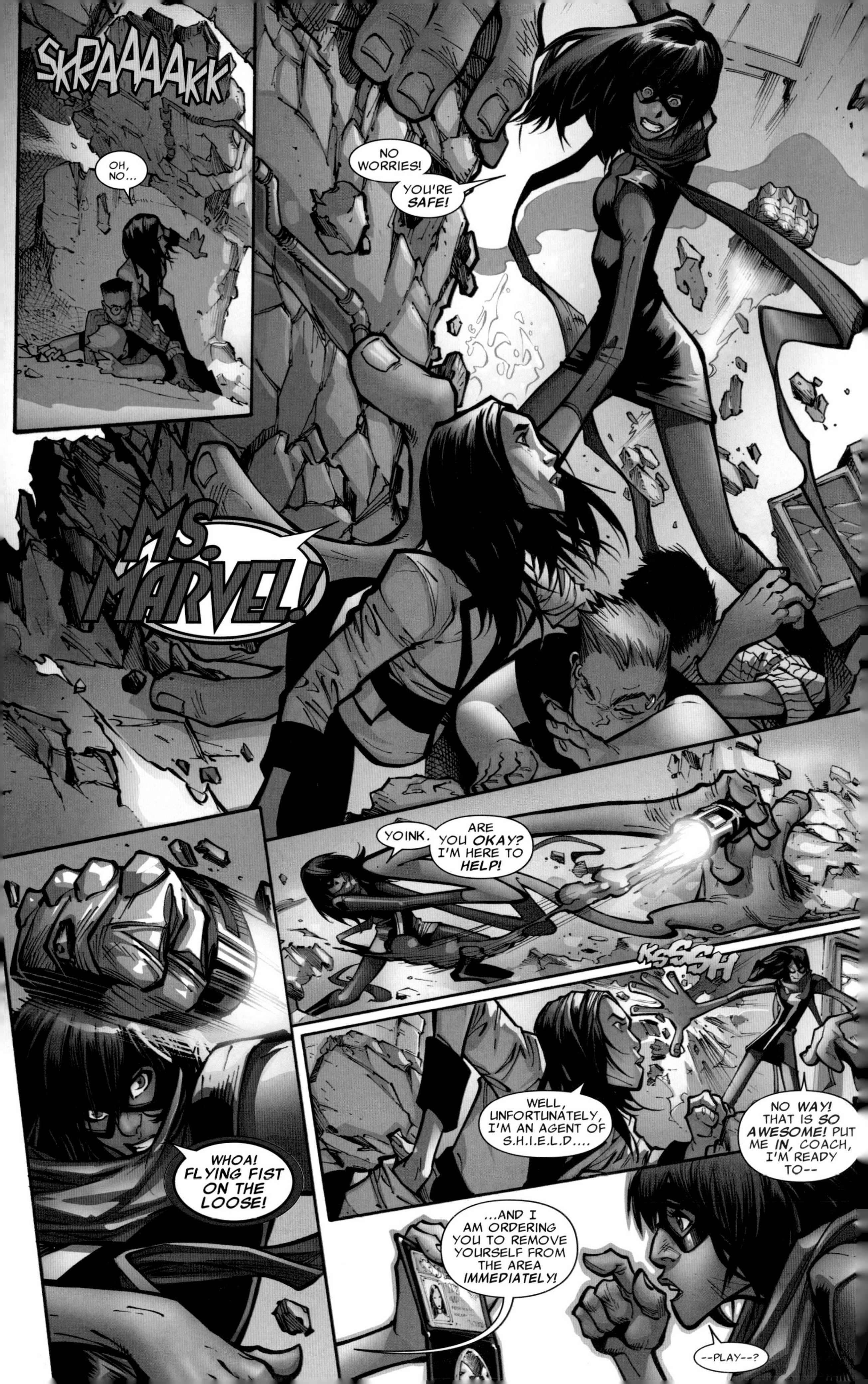
SKRAAAAKK
OH, NO...
NO WORRIES!
YOU'RE SAFE!
MS. MARVEL!
YOINK.
ARE YOU OKAY? I'M HERE TO HELP!
WHOA! FLYING FIST ON THE LOOSE!
KSSSH
WELL, UNFORTUNATELY, I'M AN AGENT OF S.H.I.E.L.D....
NO WAY! THAT IS SO AWESOME! PUT ME IN, COACH, I'M READY TO--
...AND I AM ORDERING YOU TO REMOVE YOURSELF FROM THE AREA IMMEDIATELY!
--PLAY--?

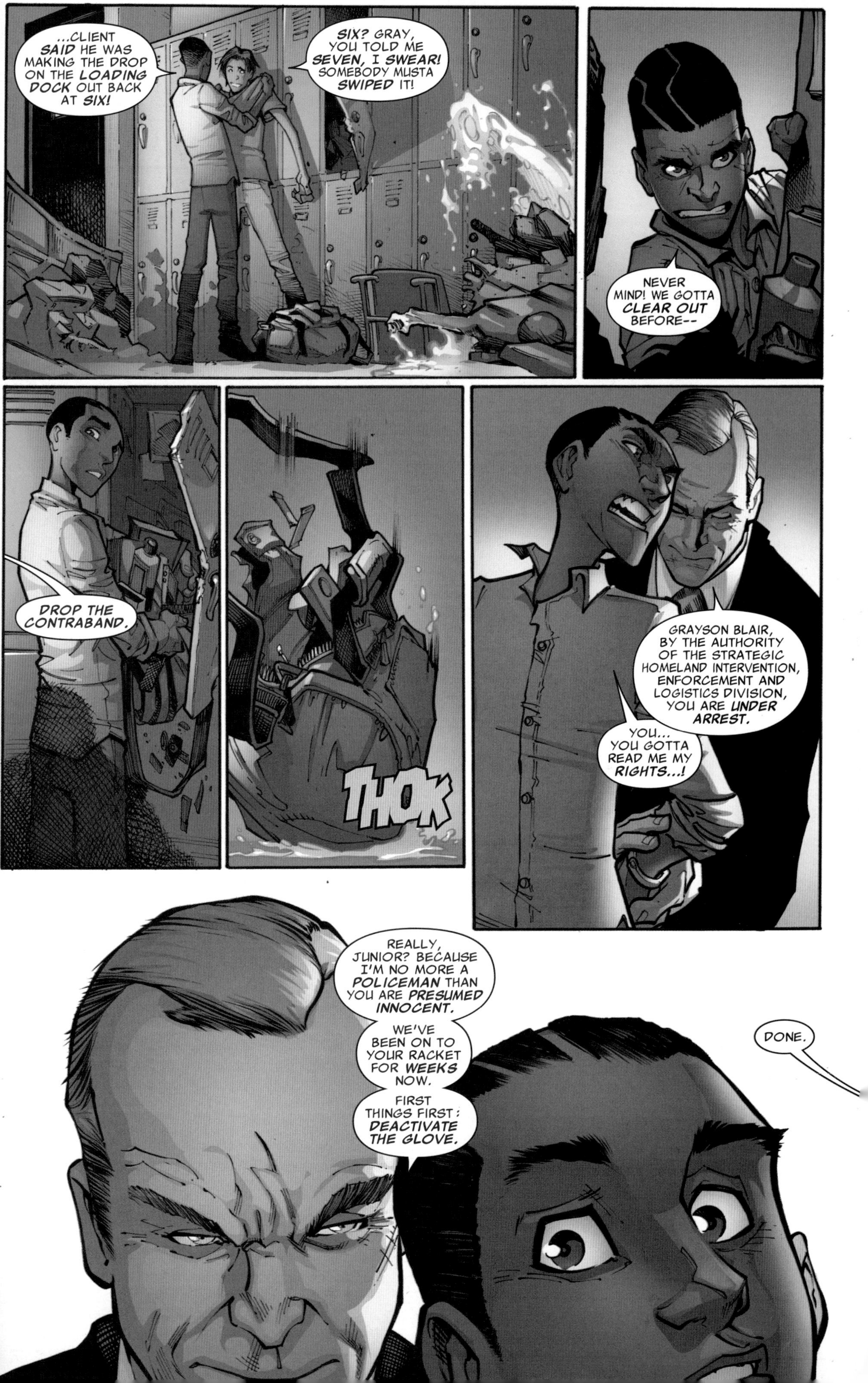
...CLIENT SAID HE WAS MAKING THE DROP ON THE LOADING DOCK OUT BACK AT SIX!
SIX? GRAY, YOU TOLD ME SEVEN, I SWEAR! SOMEBODY MUSTA SWIPED IT!
NEVER MIND! WE GOTTA CLEAR OUT BEFORE--
DROP THE CONTRABAND.
THOK
GRAYSON BLAIR, BY THE AUTHORITY OF THE STRATEGIC HOMELAND INTERVENTION, ENFORCEMENT AND LOGISTICS DIVISION, YOU ARE UNDER ARREST.
YOU... YOU GOTTA READ ME MY RIGHTS...!
REALLY, JUNIOR? BECAUSE I'M NO MORE A POLICEMAN THAN YOU ARE PRESUMED INNOCENT.
WE'VE BEEN ON TO YOUR RACKET FOR WEEKS NOW.
FIRST THINGS FIRST: DEACTIVATE THE GLOVE.
DONE.

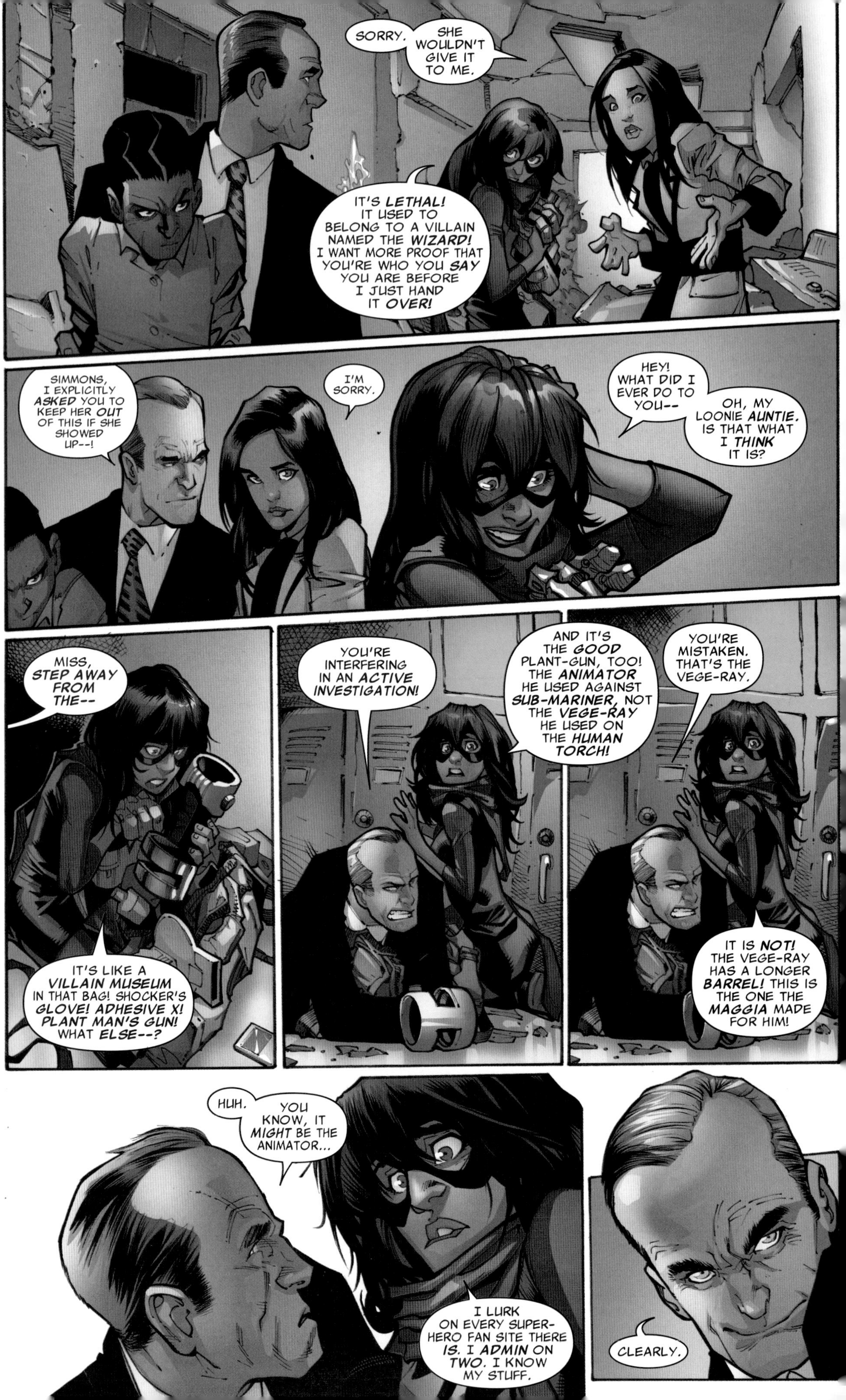
SORRY.
SHE WOULDN'T GIVE IT TO ME.
IT'S LETHAL! IT USED TO BELONG TO A VILLAIN NAMED THE WIZARD! I WANT MORE PROOF THAT YOU'RE WHO YOU SAY YOU ARE BEFORE I JUST HAND IT OVER!
SIMMONS, I EXPLICITLY ASKED YOU TO KEEP HER OUT OF THIS IF SHE SHOWED UP--!
I'M SORRY.
HEY! WHAT DID I EVER DO TO YOU--
OH, MY LOONIE AUNTIE. IS THAT WHAT I THINK IT IS?
MISS, STEP AWAY FROM THE--
IT'S LIKE A VILLAIN MUSEUM IN THAT BAG! SHOCKER'S GLOVE! ADHESIVE X! PLANT MAN'S GUN! WHAT ELSE--?
YOU'RE INTERFERING IN AN ACTIVE INVESTIGATION!
AND IT'S THE GOOD PLANT-GUN, TOO! THE ANIMATOR HE USED AGAINST SUB-MARINER, NOT THE VEGE-RAY HE USED ON THE HUMAN TORCH!
YOU'RE MISTAKEN. THAT'S THE VEGE-RAY.
IT IS NOT! THE VEGE-RAY HAS A LONGER BARREL! THIS IS THE ONE THE MAGGIA MADE FOR HIM!
HUH.
YOU KNOW, IT MIGHT BE THE ANIMATOR...
I LURK ON EVERY SUPER-HERO FAN SITE THERE IS. I ADMIN ON TWO. I KNOW MY STUFF.
CLEARLY.

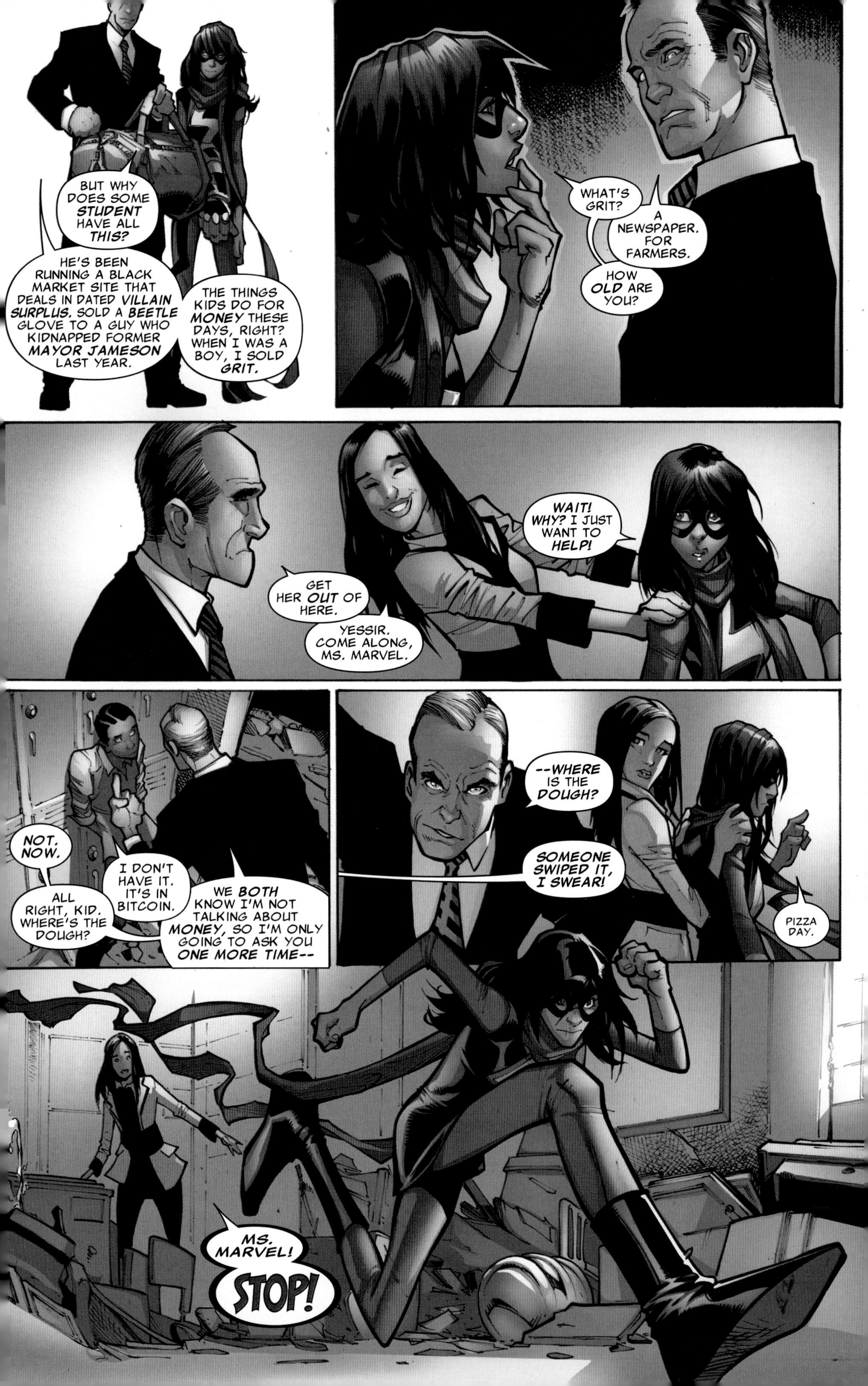
BUT WHY DOES SOME STUDENT HAVE ALL THIS?
HE'S BEEN RUNNING A BLACK MARKET SITE THAT DEALS IN DATED VILLAIN SURPLUS. SOLD A BEETLE GLOVE TO A GUY WHO KIDNAPPED FORMER MAYOR JAMESON LAST YEAR.
THE THINGS KIDS DO FOR MONEY THESE DAYS, RIGHT? WHEN I WAS A BOY, I SOLD GRIT.
WHAT'S GRIT?
A NEWSPAPER. FOR FARMERS.
HOW OLD ARE YOU?
WAIT! WHY? I JUST WANT TO HELP!
GET HER OUT OF HERE.
YESSIR. COME ALONG, MS. MARVEL.
NOT. NOW.
ALL RIGHT, KID. WHERE'S THE DOUGH?
I DON'T HAVE IT. IT'S IN BITCOIN.
WE BOTH KNOW I'M NOT TALKING ABOUT MONEY, SO I'M ONLY GOING TO ASK YOU ONE MORE TIME--
--WHERE IS THE DOUGH?
SOMEONE SWIPED IT, I SWEAR!
PIZZA DAY.
MS. MARVEL!
STOP!

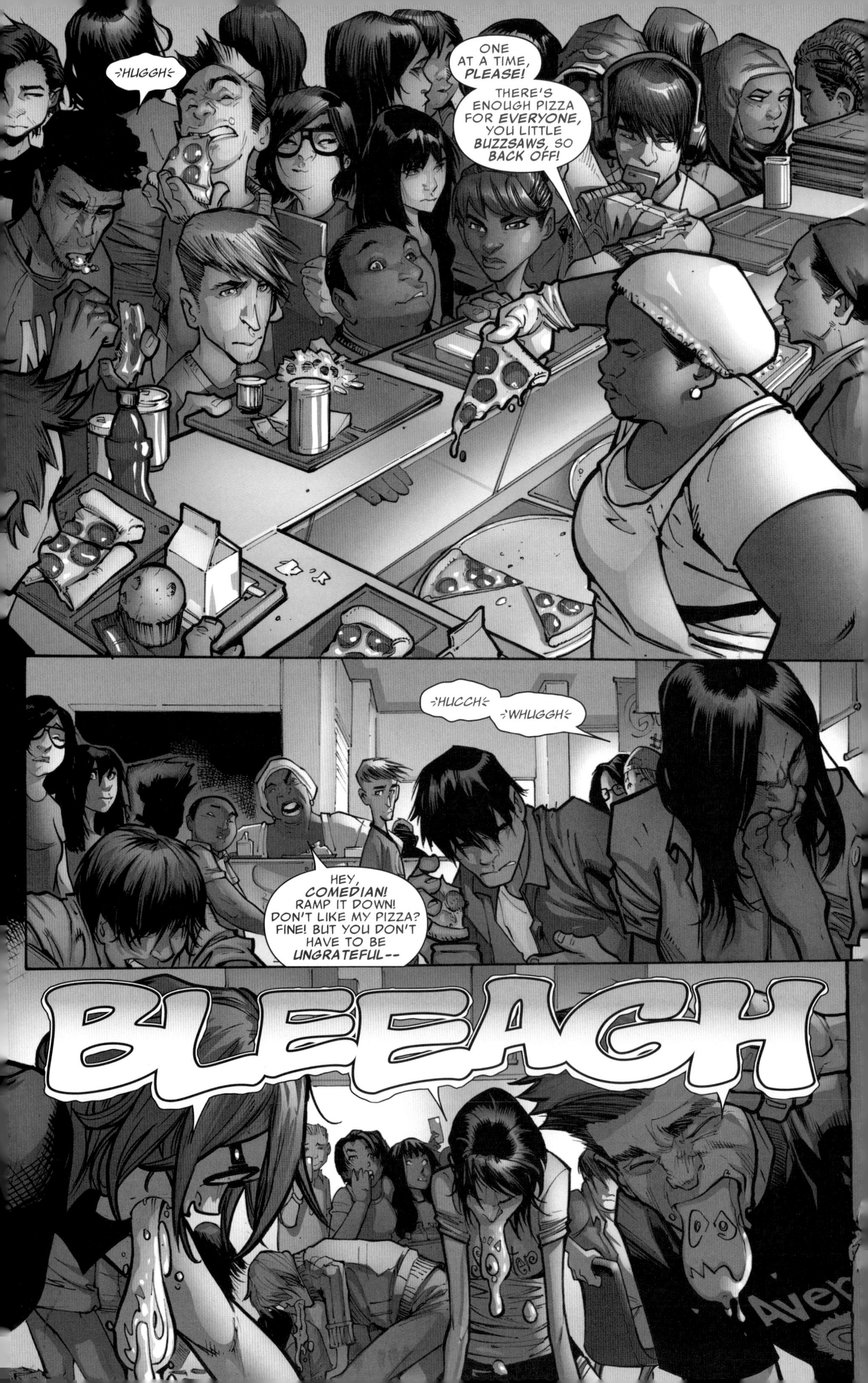

HUGGH
ONE AT A TIME, PLEASE!
THERE'S ENOUGH PIZZA FOR EVERYONE, YOU LITTLE BUZZSAWS, SO BACK OFF!
HUCCH
WHUGGH
HEY, COMEDIAN! RAMP IT DOWN! DON'T LIKE MY PIZZA? FINE! BUT YOU DON'T HAVE TO BE UNGRATEFUL--
BLEEACH

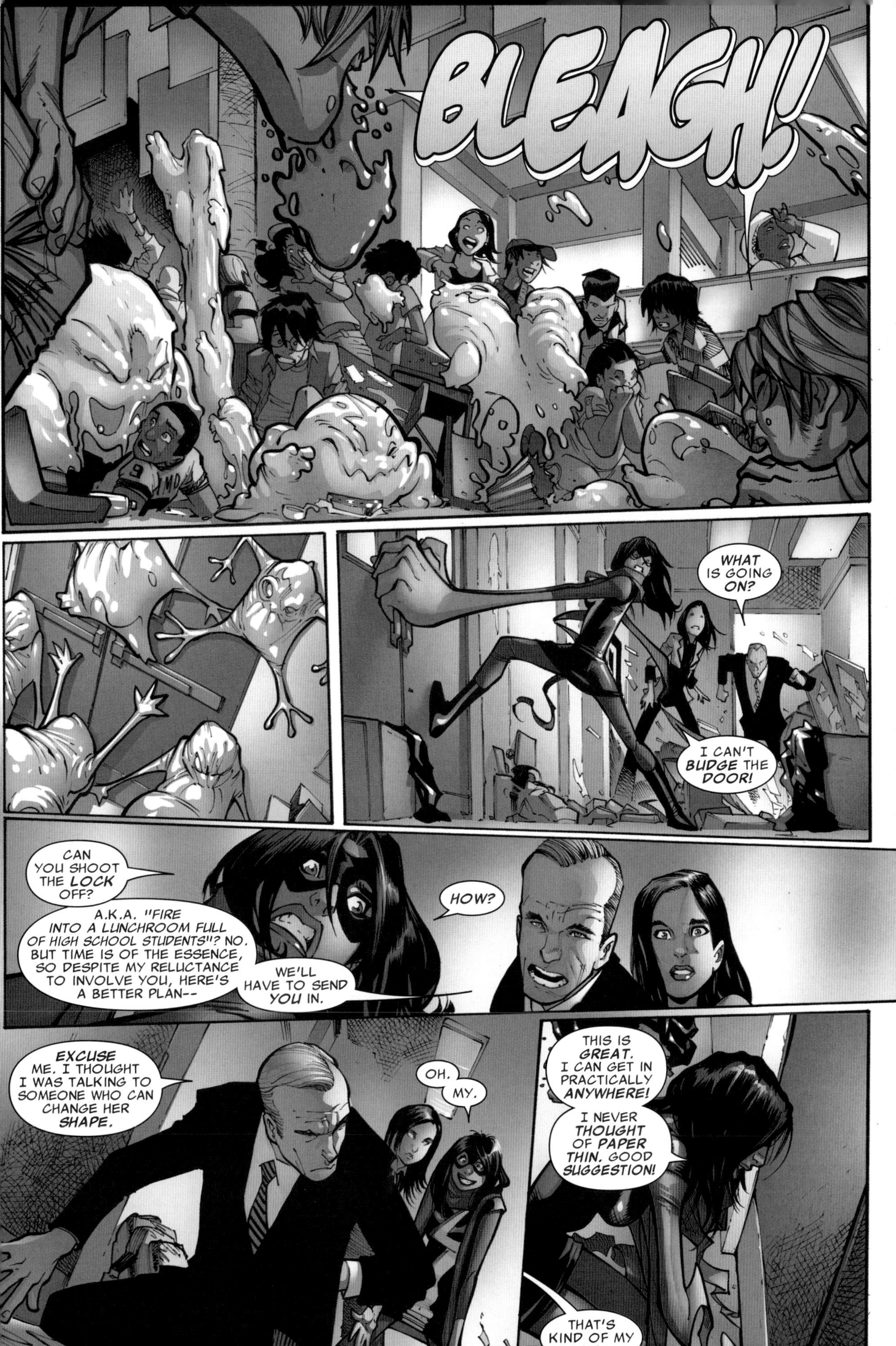
BLEACH!
WHAT IS GOING ON?
I CAN'T BUDGE THE DOOR!
CAN YOU SHOOT THE LOCK OFF?
A.K.A. "FIRE INTO A LUNCHROOM FULL OF HIGH SCHOOL STUDENTS"? NO. BUT TIME IS OF THE ESSENCE, SO DESPITE MY RELUCTANCE TO INVOLVE YOU, HERE'S A BETTER PLAN--
WE'LL HAVE TO SEND YOU IN.
HOW?
EXCUSE ME. I THOUGHT I WAS TALKING TO SOMEONE WHO CAN CHANGE HER SHAPE.
OH.
MY.
THIS IS GREAT. I CAN GET IN PRACTICALLY ANYWHERE!
I NEVER THOUGHT OF PAPER THIN. GOOD SUGGESTION!
THAT'S KIND OF MY THING.
DON'T MESS AROUND IN THERE. OPEN THAT DOOR STRAIGHT AWAY!

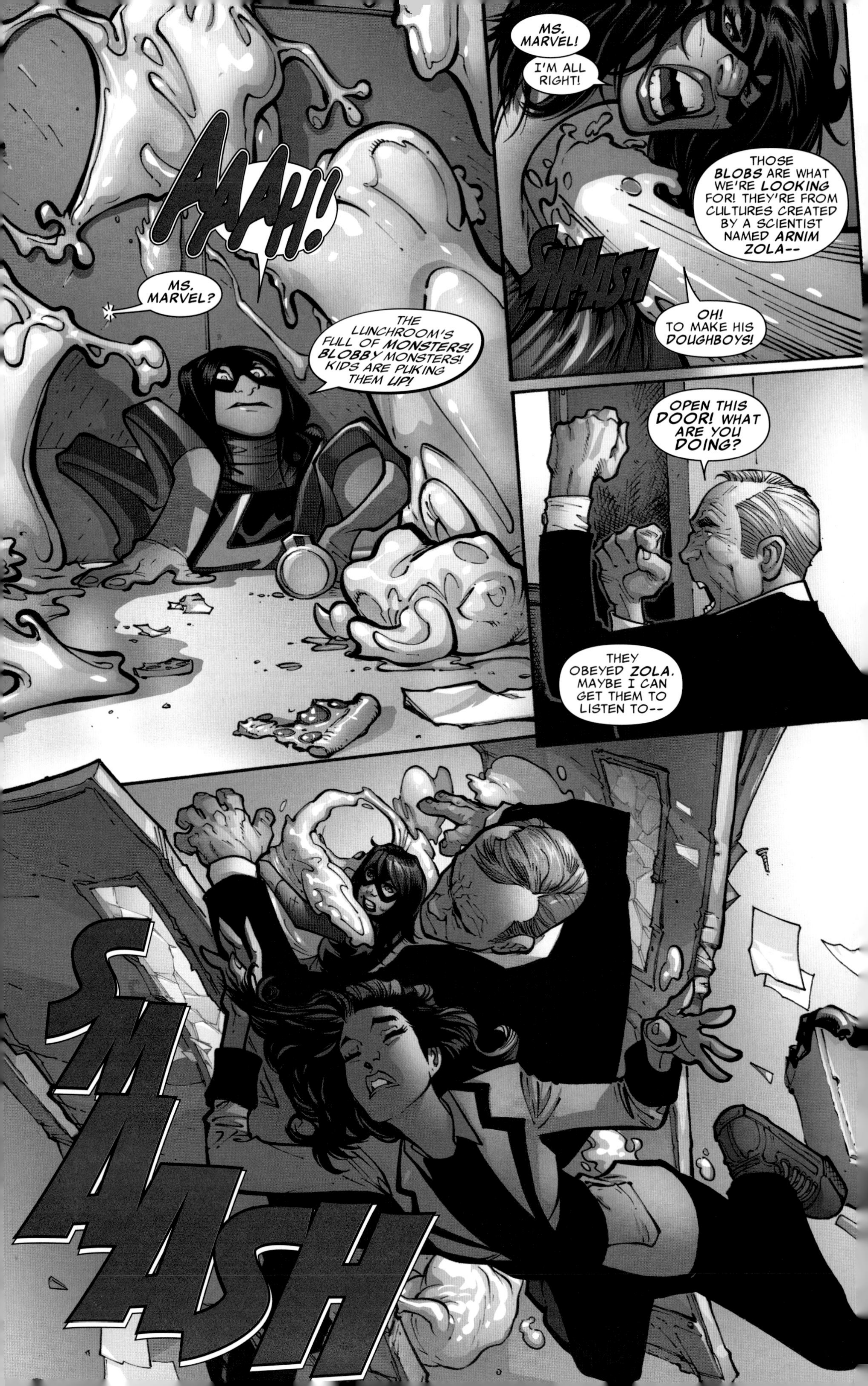
AAAH!
MS. MARVEL?
THE LUNCHROOM'S FULL OF MONSTERS! BLOBBY MONSTERS! KIDS ARE PUKING THEM UP!
MS. MARVEL!
I'M ALL RIGHT!
SHHASH
THOSE BLOBS ARE WHAT WE'RE LOOKING FOR! THEY'RE FROM CULTURES CREATED BY A SCIENTIST NAMED ARNIM ZOLA--
OH! TO MAKE HIS DOUGHBOYS!
OPEN THIS DOOR! WHAT ARE YOU DOING?
THEY OBEYED ZOLA. MAYBE I CAN GET THEM TO LISTEN TO--
SMASH

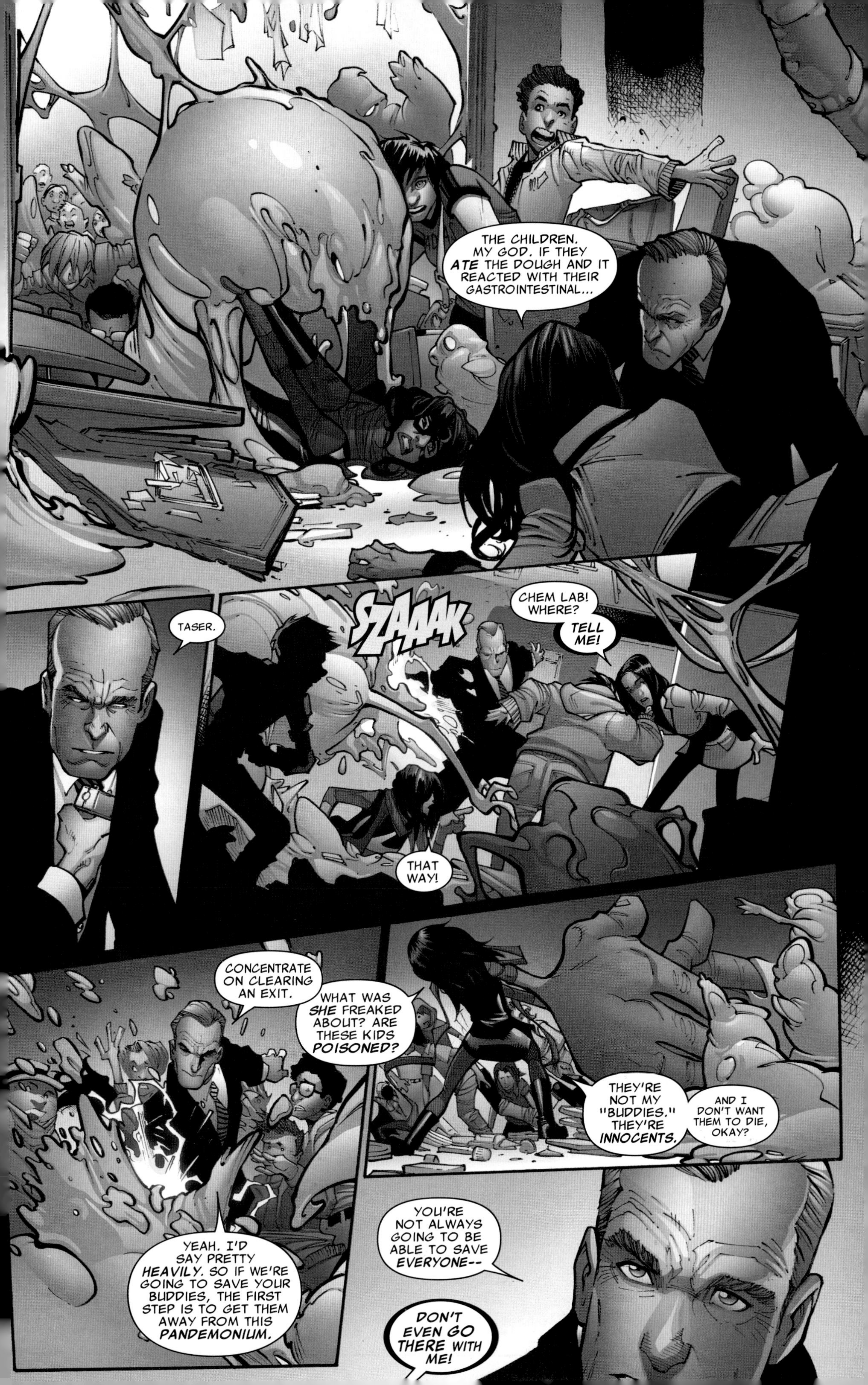

THE CHILDREN. MY GOD. IF THEY ATE THE DOUGH AND IT REACTED WITH THEIR GASTROINTESTINAL...
TASER.
SZAAAK
CHEM LAB! WHERE? TELL ME!
THAT WAY!
CONCENTRATE ON CLEARING AN EXIT.
WHAT WAS SHE FREAKED ABOUT? ARE THESE KIDS POISONED?
YEAH. I'D SAY PRETTY HEAVILY. SO IF WE'RE GOING TO SAVE YOUR BUDDIES, THE FIRST STEP IS TO GET THEM AWAY FROM THIS PANDEMONIUM.
THEY'RE NOT MY "BUDDIES." THEY'RE INNOCENTS.
AND I DON'T WANT THEM TO DIE, OKAY?
YOU'RE NOT ALWAYS GOING TO BE ABLE TO SAVE EVERYONE--
DON'T EVEN GO THERE WITH ME!

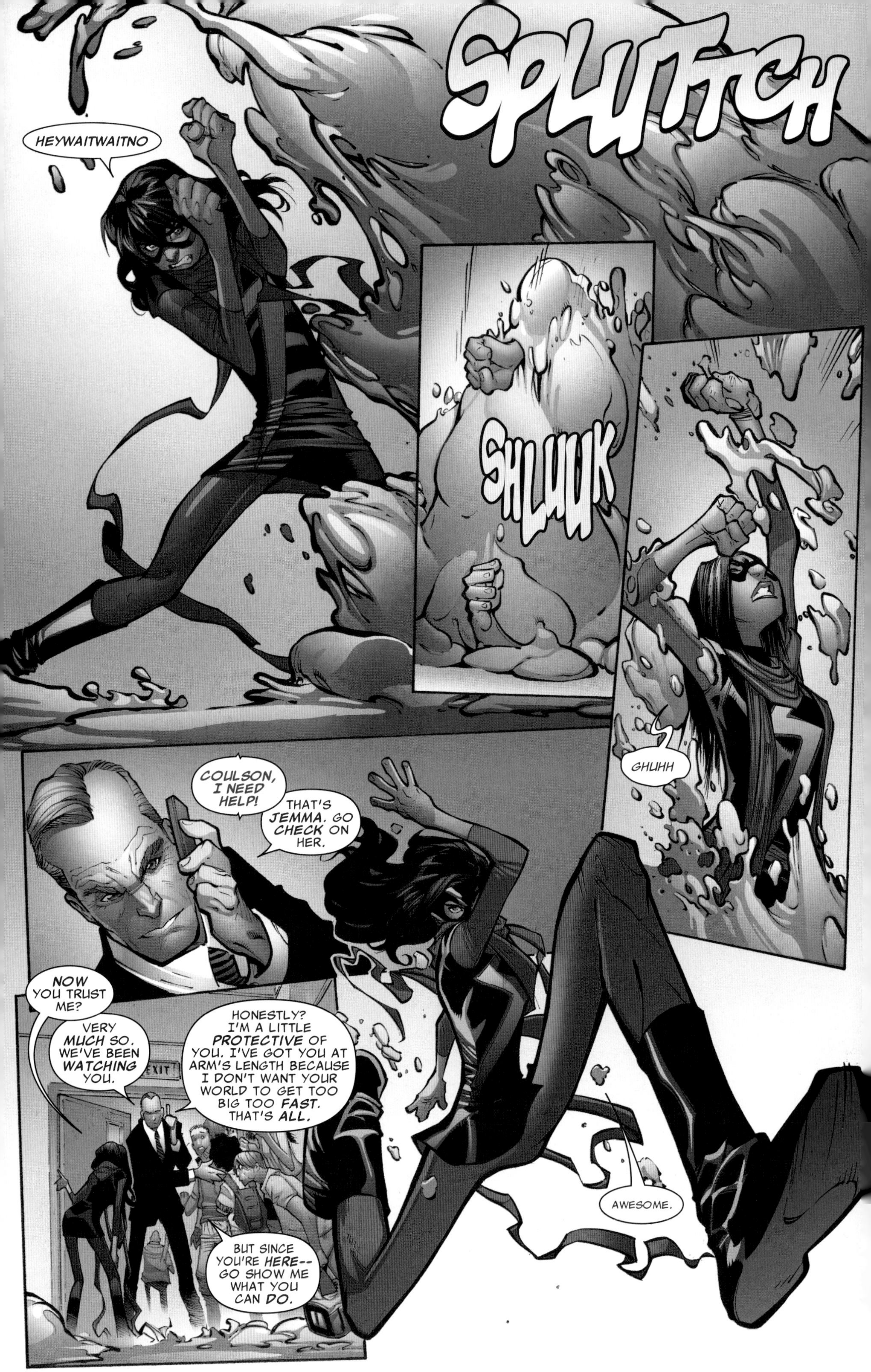
SPLUTCH
HEYWAITWAITNO
SHLUUK
GHUHH
COULSON, I NEED HELP!
THAT'S JEMMA. GO CHECK ON HER.
NOW YOU TRUST ME?
VERY MUCH SO. WE'VE BEEN WATCHING YOU.
HONESTLY? I'M A LITTLE PROTECTIVE OF YOU. I'VE GOT YOU AT ARM'S LENGTH BECAUSE I DON'T WANT YOUR WORLD TO GET TOO BIG TOO FAST. THAT'S ALL.
EXIT
BUT SINCE YOU'RE HERE--GO SHOW ME WHAT YOU CAN DO.
AWESOME.

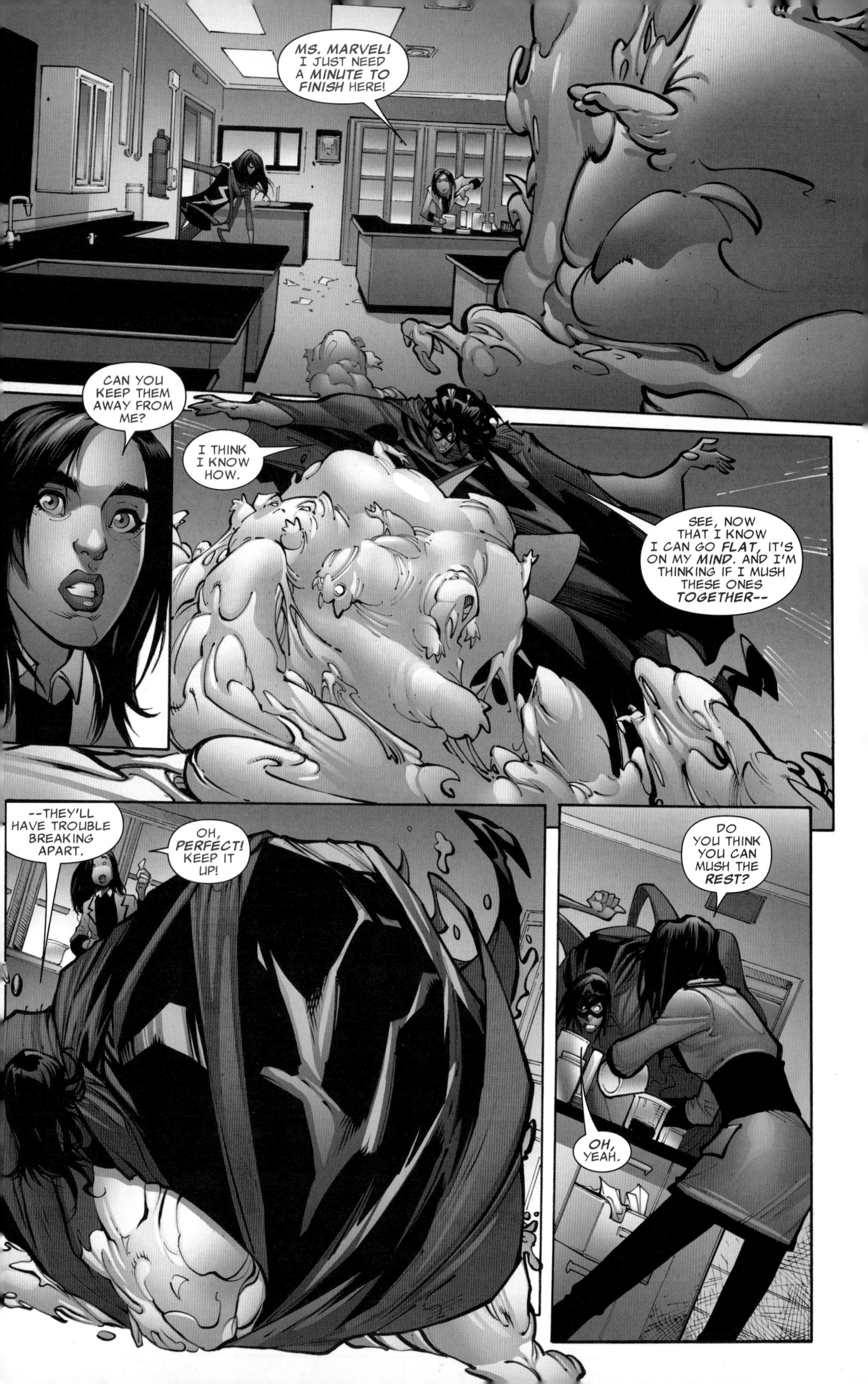
MS. MARVEL! I JUST NEED A MINUTE TO FINISH HERE!
CAN YOU KEEP THEM AWAY FROM ME?
I THINK I KNOW HOW.
SEE, NOW THAT I KNOW I CAN GO FLAT, IT'S ON MY MIND. AND I'M THINKING IF I MUSH THESE ONES TOGETHER--
--THEY'LL HAVE TROUBLE BREAKING APART.
OH, PERFECT! KEEP IT UP!
DO YOU THINK YOU CAN MUSH THE REST?
OH, YEAH.

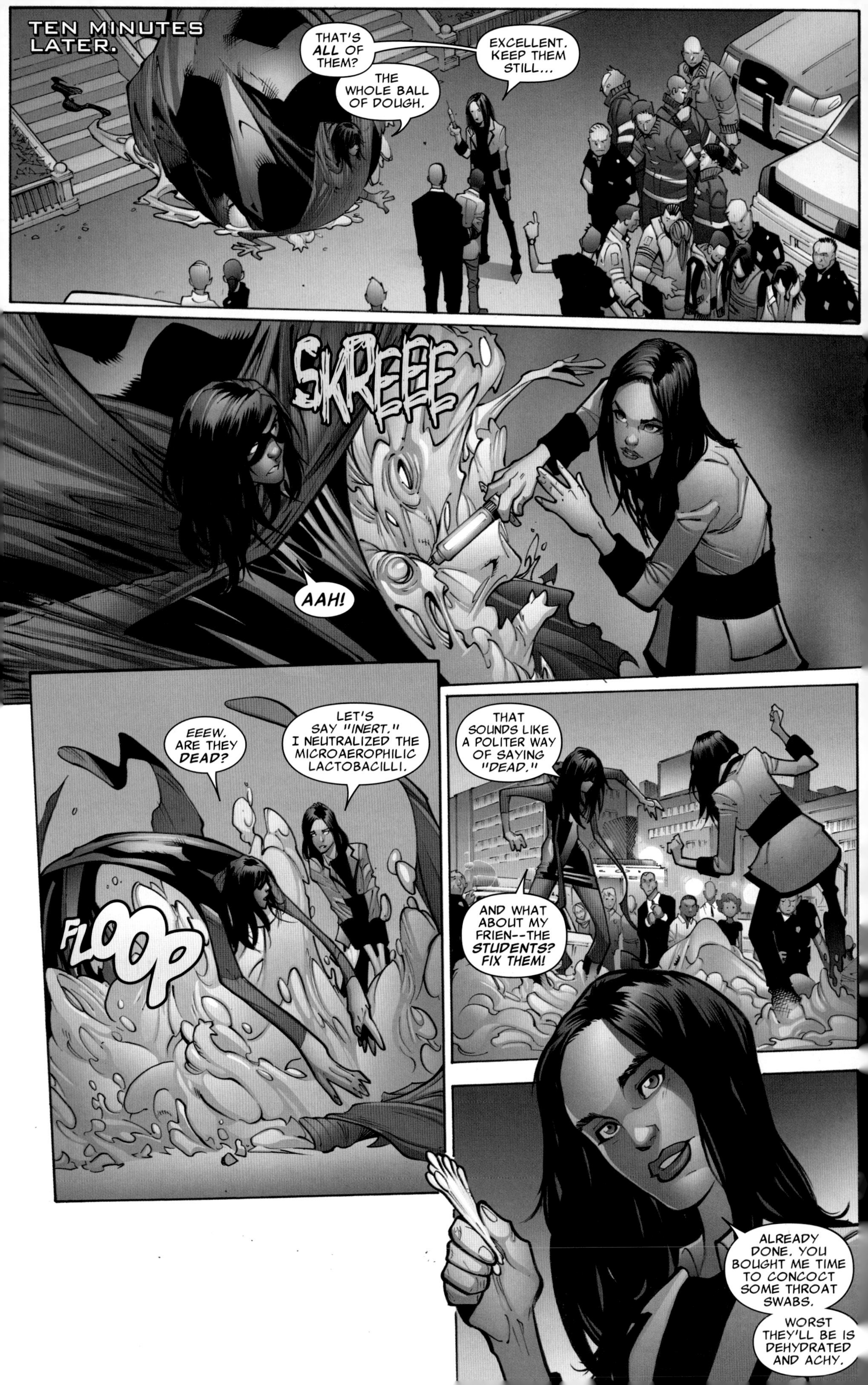
TEN MINUTES LATER.
THAT'S ALL OF THEM?
THE WHOLE BALL OF DOUGH.
EXCELLENT. KEEP THEM STILL...
SKREEE
AAH!
EEEW. ARE THEY DEAD?
LET'S SAY "INERT." I NEUTRALIZED THE MICROAEROPHILIC LACTOBACILLI.
FLOOP
THAT SOUNDS LIKE A POLITER WAY OF SAYING "DEAD."
AND WHAT ABOUT MY FRIEN--THE STUDENTS? FIX THEM!
ALREADY DONE. YOU BOUGHT ME TIME TO CONCOCT SOME THROAT SWABS.
WORST THEY'LL BE IS DEHYDRATED AND ACHY.

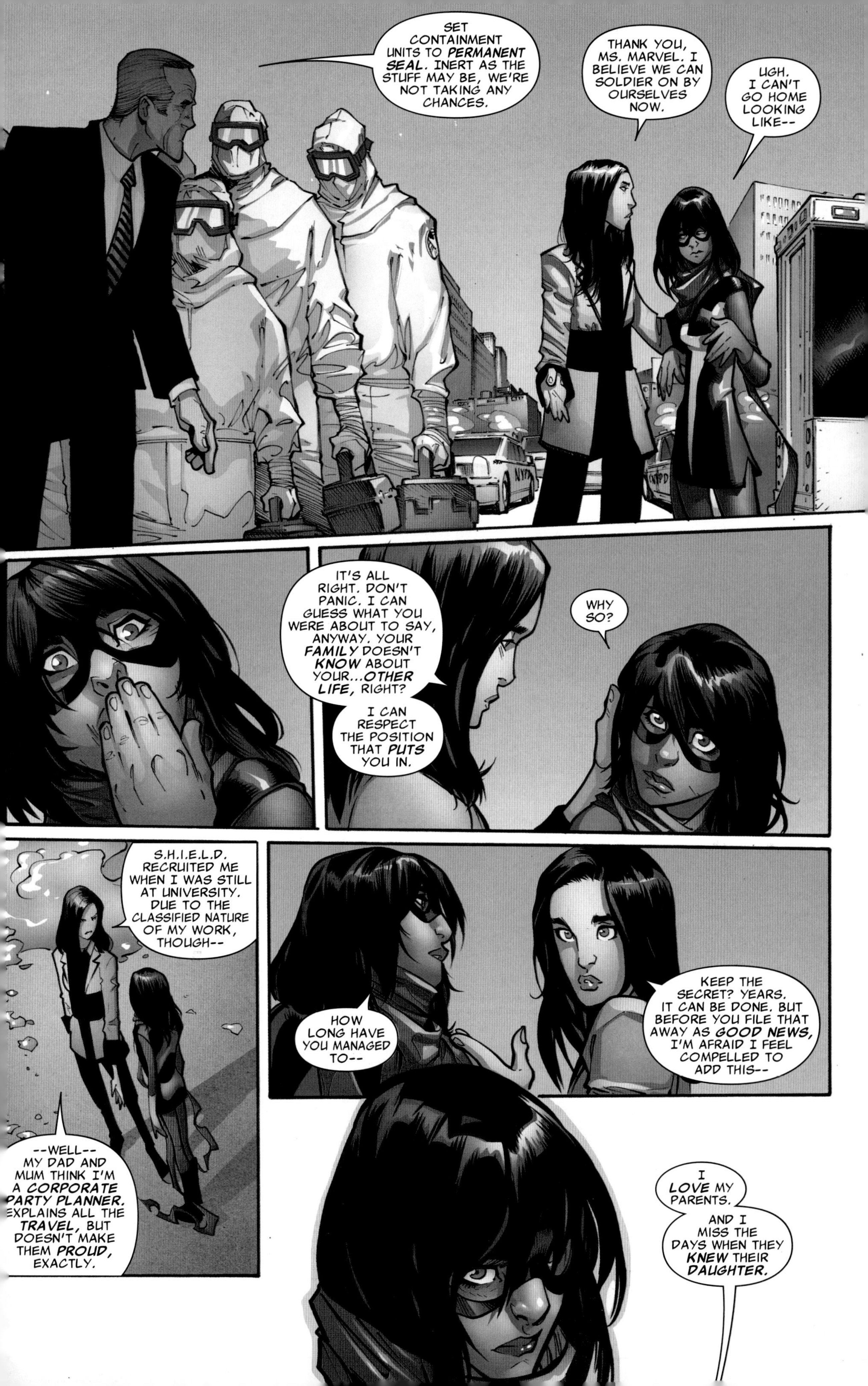
SET CONTAINMENT UNITS TO PERMANENT SEAL. INERT AS THE STUFF MAY BE, WE'RE NOT TAKING ANY CHANCES.
THANK YOU, MS. MARVEL. I BELIEVE WE CAN SOLDIER ON BY OURSELVES NOW.
UGH. I CAN'T GO HOME LOOKING LIKE--
IT'S ALL RIGHT. DON'T PANIC. I CAN GUESS WHAT YOU WERE ABOUT TO SAY, ANYWAY. YOUR FAMILY DOESN'T KNOW ABOUT YOUR...OTHER LIFE, RIGHT?
I CAN RESPECT THE POSITION THAT PUTS YOU IN.
WHY SO?
S.H.I.E.L.D. RECRUITED ME WHEN I WAS STILL AT UNIVERSITY. DUE TO THE CLASSIFIED NATURE OF MY WORK, THOUGH--
--WELL-- MY DAD AND MUM THINK I'M A CORPORATE PARTY PLANNER. EXPLAINS ALL THE TRAVEL, BUT DOESN'T MAKE THEM PROUD, EXACTLY.
HOW LONG HAVE YOU MANAGED TO--
KEEP THE SECRET? YEARS. IT CAN BE DONE. BUT BEFORE YOU FILE THAT AWAY AS GOOD NEWS, I'M AFRAID I FEEL COMPELLED TO ADD THIS--
I LOVE MY PARENTS.
AND I MISS THE DAYS WHEN THEY KNEW THEIR DAUGHTER.

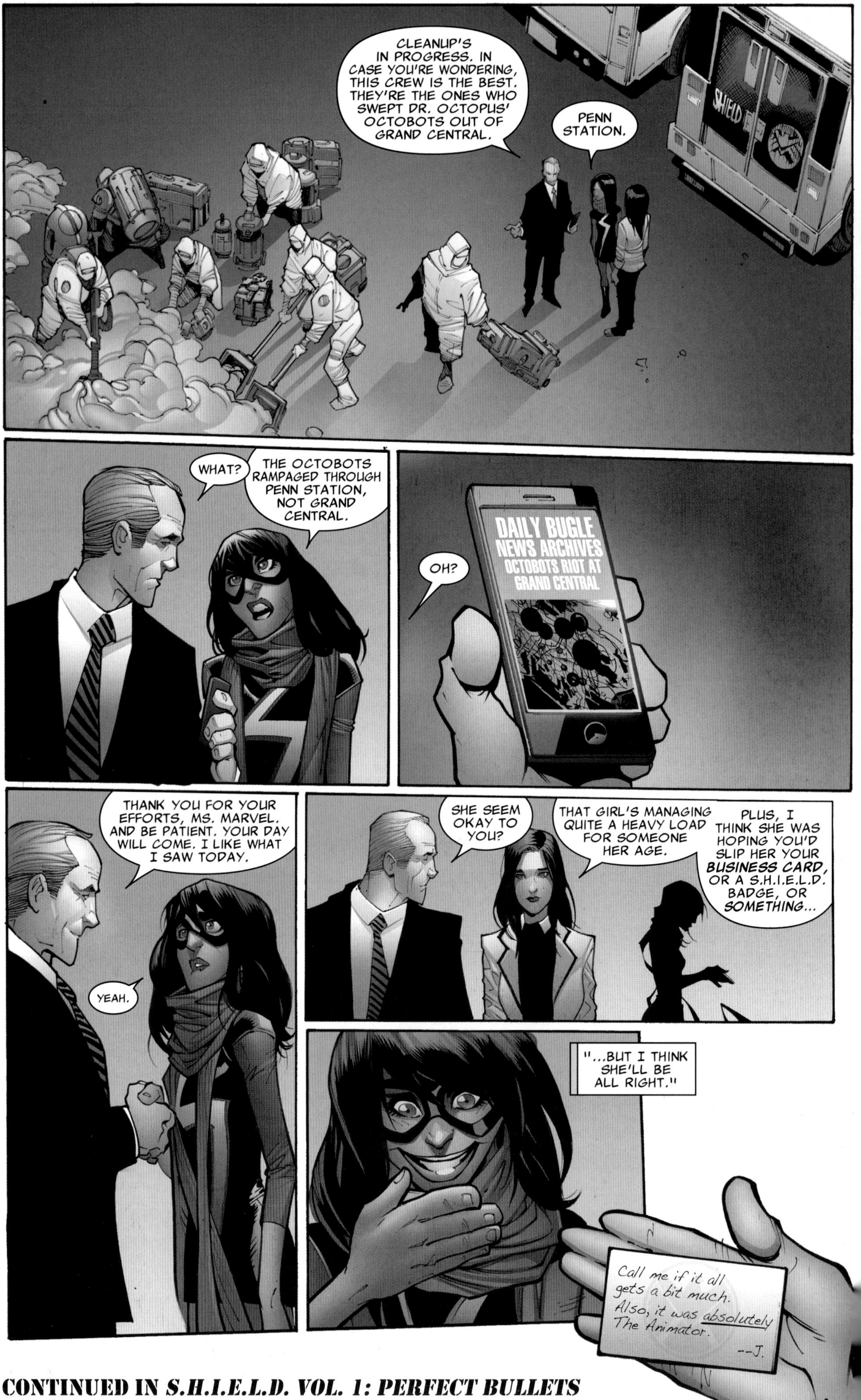
CLEANUP'S IN PROGRESS. IN CASE YOU'RE WONDERING, THIS CREW IS THE BEST. THEY'RE THE ONES WHO SWEPT DR. OCTOPUS' OCTOBOTS OUT OF GRAND CENTRAL.
PENN STATION.
SHIELD
WHAT?
THE OCTOBOTS RAMPAGED THROUGH PENN STATION, NOT GRAND CENTRAL.
OH?
DAILY BUGLE
NEWS ARCHIVES
OCTOBOTS RIOT AT GRAND CENTRAL
THANK YOU FOR YOUR EFFORTS, MS. MARVEL. AND BE PATIENT. YOUR DAY WILL COME. I LIKE WHAT I SAW TODAY.
YEAH.
SHE SEEM OKAY TO YOU?
THAT GIRL'S MANAGING QUITE A HEAVY LOAD FOR SOMEONE HER AGE.
PLUS, I THINK SHE WAS HOPING YOU'D SLIP HER YOUR BUSINESS CARD, OR A S.H.I.E.L.D. BADGE, OR SOMETHING...
"...BUT I THINK SHE'LL BE ALL RIGHT."
Call me if it all gets a bit much. Also, it was absolutely The Animator. --J.

CONTINUED IN *S.H.I.E.L.D. VOL. 1: PERFECT BULLETS*

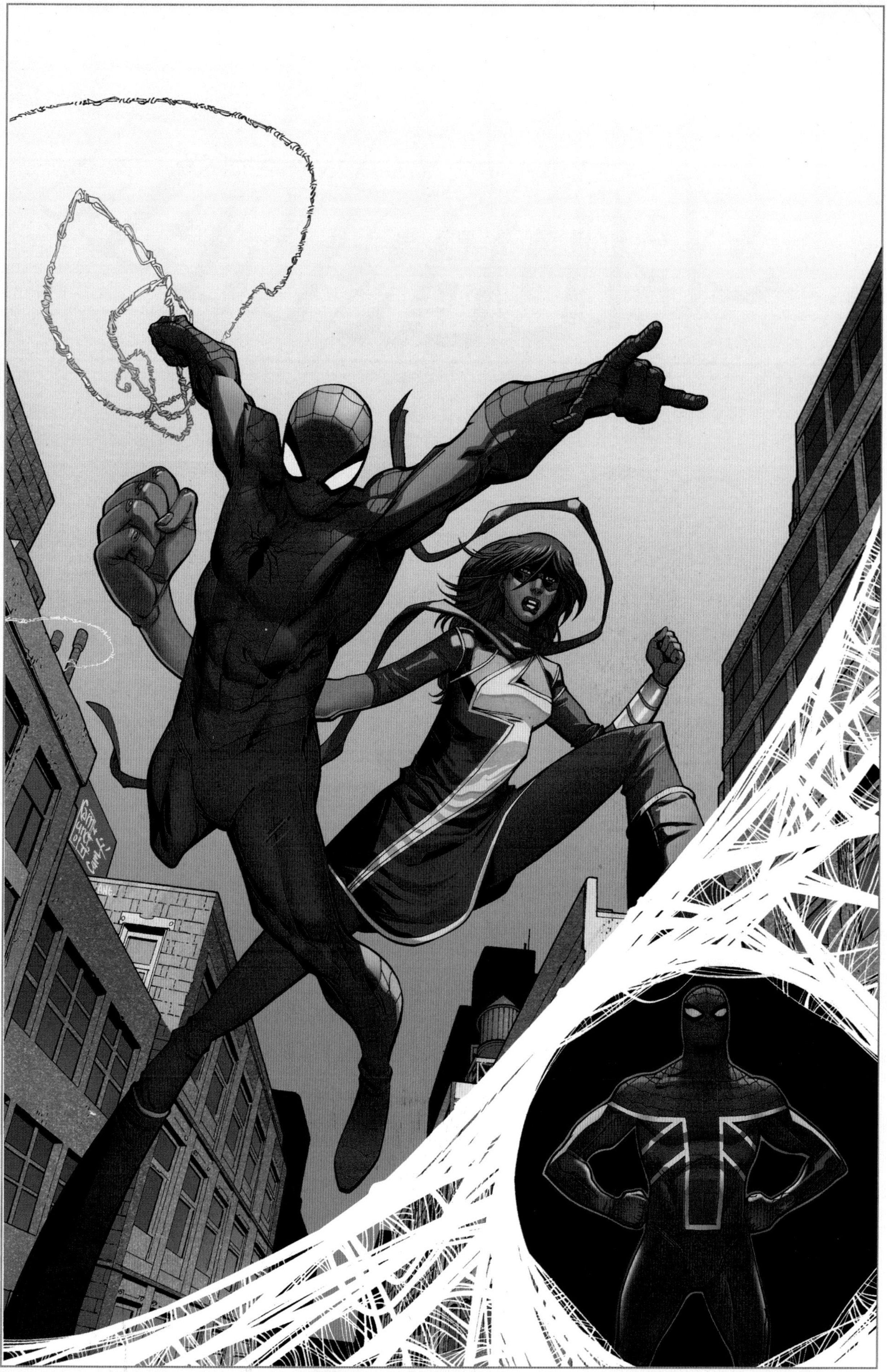

AMAZING SPIDER-MAN #7

Years ago, high school student PETER PARKER was bitten by a radioactive spider and gained the speed, agility, and proportional strength of a spider as well as the ability to stick to walls and a spider-sense that warned him of imminent danger. After learning that with great power there must also come great responsibility, he became the crime-fighting super hero…

the AMAZING SPIDER-MAN

After swapping his mind into Peter's body, one of Spider-Man's greatest enemies, DOCTOR OCTOPUS, set out to prove himself the SUPERIOR SPIDER-MAN. He also completed Peter's PhD, fell in love with a woman named Anna Maria Marconi, and started his own company, "Parker Industries." But in the end Doc Ock realized that in order to be a true hero, he had to sacrifice himself and give control of Peter's body back to Peter.

Peter recently found out that someone else, Cindy Moon A.K.A. SILK, was bitten by his radioactive spider giving her similar powers to Peter. And that's not the only thing they have in common.

GREAT. NOT ONLY HAVEN'T I FOUND MY FAMILY, NOW I CAN'T FIND NETSCAPE!

PETE, COULD YOU GIVE ME A HAND?

UH, SURE.

TRIBECA.
THE APARTMENT OF PETER PARKER, ANNA MARIA MARCONI... AND, APPARENTLY, CINDY MOON.

9:23 A.M.

UH-OH.

HERE, CINDY. FACEBOOK BARELY EXISTED LAST TIME YOU WERE ONLINE, BUT IT'S THE MOST POPULAR WAY TO...STAY...

...CLOSE...

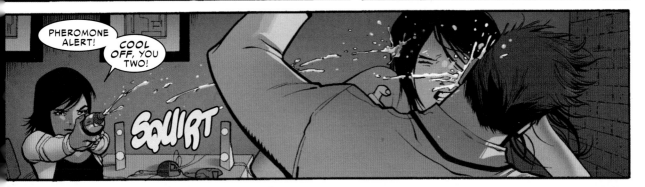

PHEROMONE ALERT! COOL OFF, YOU TWO!

SQUIRT

9:46.

BEHAVE!

9:58.

DOWN!

10:06.

THAT'S ENOUGH, ANNA!

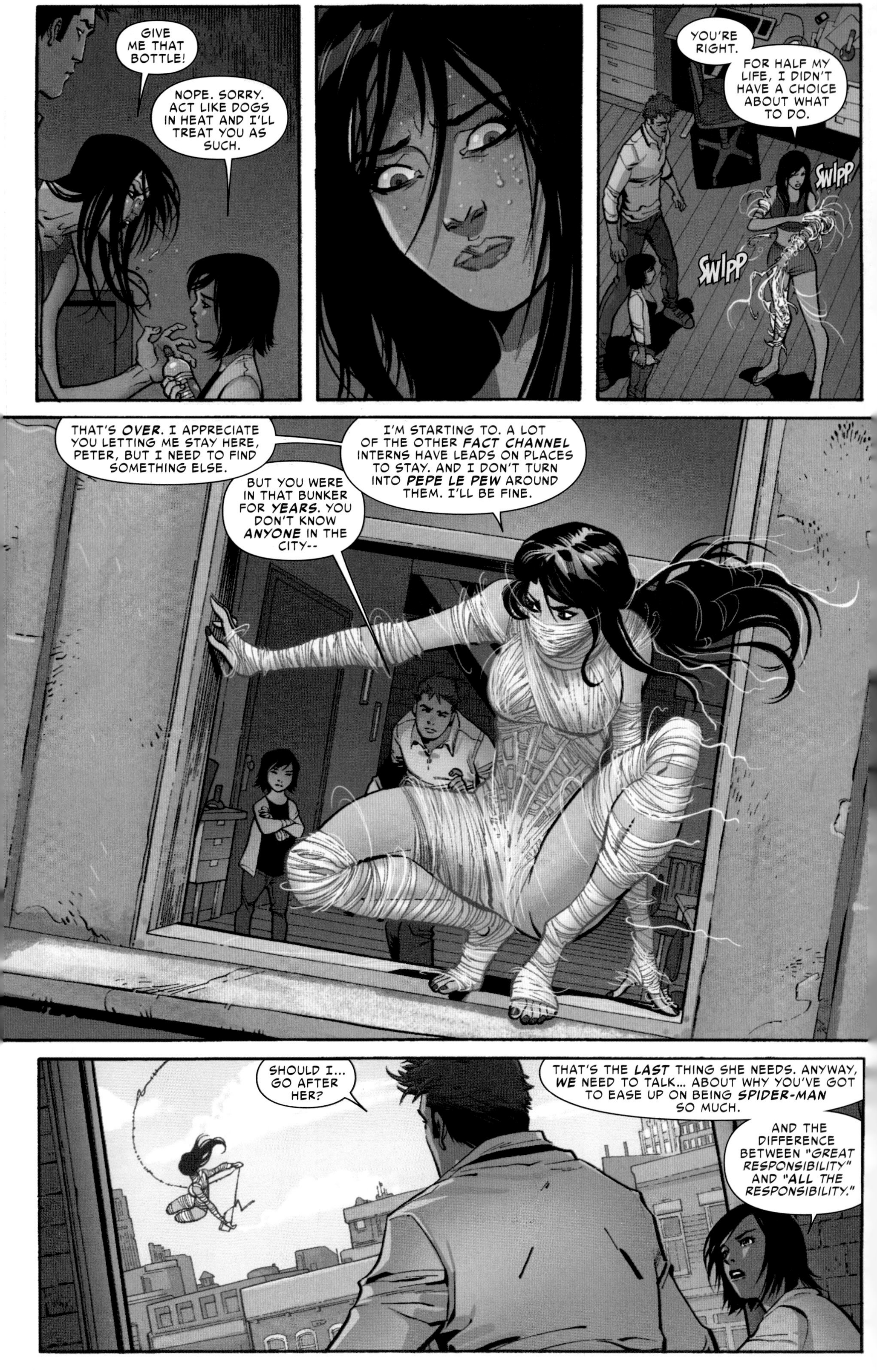
GIVE ME THAT BOTTLE!
NOPE. SORRY. ACT LIKE DOGS IN HEAT AND I'LL TREAT YOU AS SUCH.
YOU'RE RIGHT.
FOR HALF MY LIFE, I DIDN'T HAVE A CHOICE ABOUT WHAT TO DO.
SWIPP
SWIPP
THAT'S OVER. I APPRECIATE YOU LETTING ME STAY HERE, PETER, BUT I NEED TO FIND SOMETHING ELSE.
BUT YOU WERE IN THAT BUNKER FOR YEARS. YOU DON'T KNOW ANYONE IN THE CITY--
I'M STARTING TO. A LOT OF THE OTHER FACT CHANNEL INTERNS HAVE LEADS ON PLACES TO STAY. AND I DON'T TURN INTO PEPE LE PEW AROUND THEM. I'LL BE FINE.
SHOULD I... GO AFTER HER?
THAT'S THE LAST THING SHE NEEDS. ANYWAY, WE NEED TO TALK... ABOUT WHY YOU'VE GOT TO EASE UP ON BEING SPIDER-MAN SO MUCH.
AND THE DIFFERENCE BETWEEN "GREAT RESPONSIBILITY" AND "ALL THE RESPONSIBILITY."

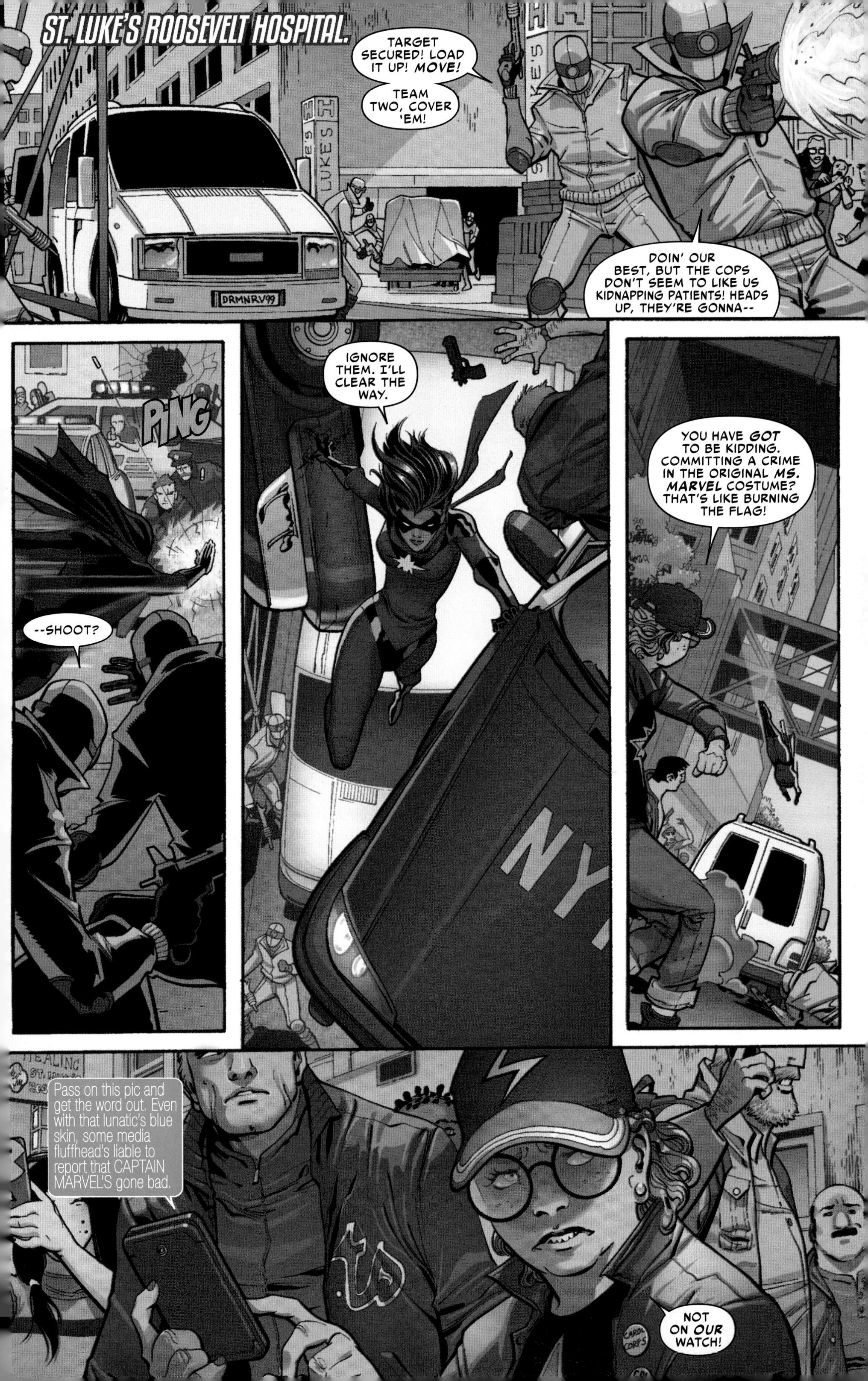
ST. LUKE'S ROOSEVELT HOSPITAL.
TARGET SECURED! LOAD IT UP! MOVE!
TEAM TWO, COVER 'EM!
DRMNRV99
DOIN' OUR BEST, BUT THE COPS DON'T SEEM TO LIKE US KIDNAPPING PATIENTS! HEADS UP, THEY'RE GONNA--
PING
--SHOOT?
IGNORE THEM. I'LL CLEAR THE WAY.
NY
YOU HAVE GOT TO BE KIDDING. COMMITTING A CRIME IN THE ORIGINAL MS. MARVEL COSTUME? THAT'S LIKE BURNING THE FLAG!
Pass on this pic and get the word out. Even with that lunatic's blue skin, some media fluffhead's liable to report that CAPTAIN MARVEL'S gone bad.
NOT ON OUR WATCH!
CAROL CORPS

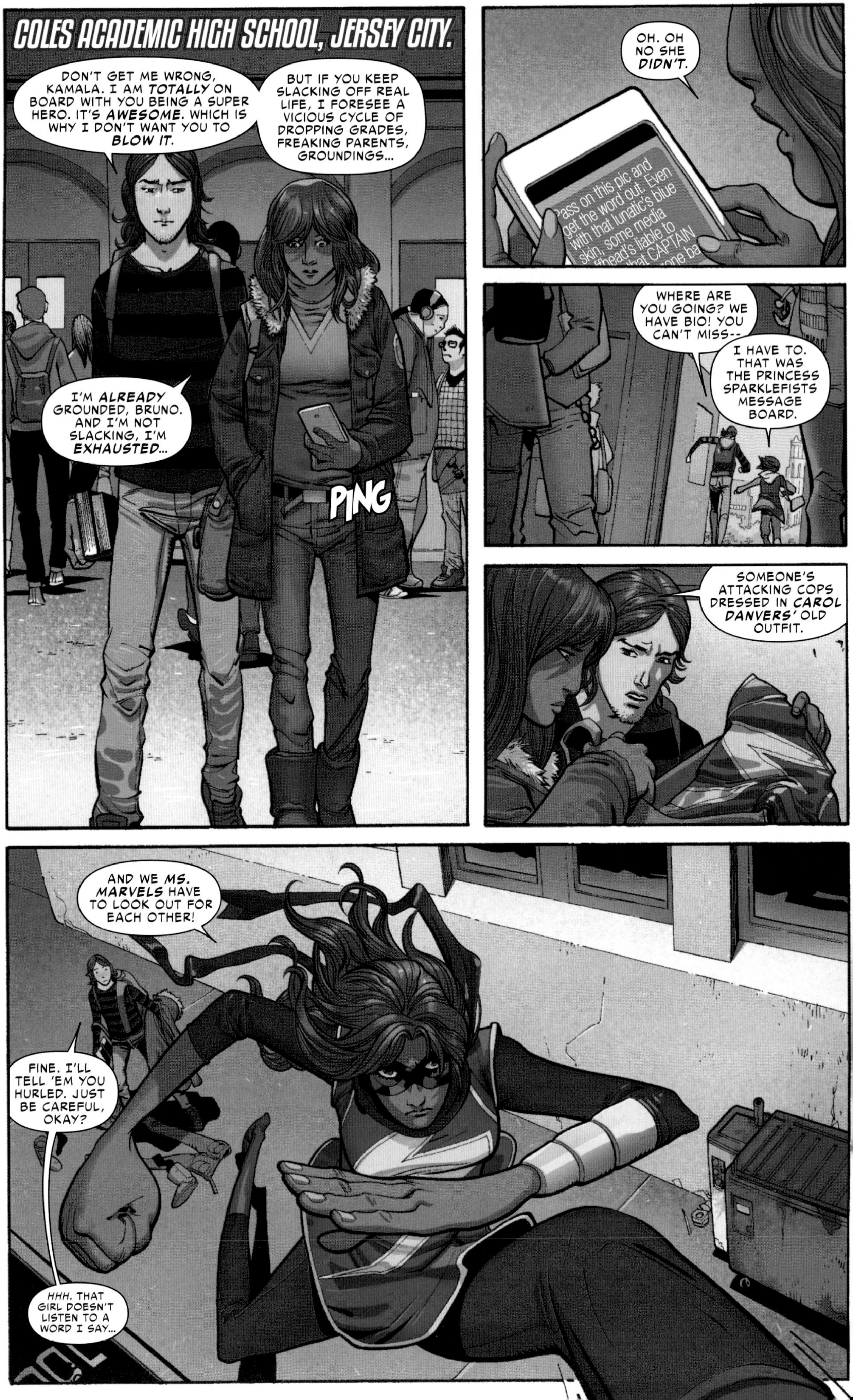
COLES ACADEMIC HIGH SCHOOL, JERSEY CITY.
DON'T GET ME WRONG, KAMALA. I AM TOTALLY ON BOARD WITH YOU BEING A SUPER HERO. IT'S AWESOME. WHICH IS WHY I DON'T WANT YOU TO BLOW IT.
BUT IF YOU KEEP SLACKING OFF REAL LIFE, I FORESEE A VICIOUS CYCLE OF DROPPING GRADES, FREAKING PARENTS, GROUNDINGS...
I'M ALREADY GROUNDED, BRUNO. AND I'M NOT SLACKING, I'M EXHAUSTED...
PING
OH. OH NO SHE DIDN'T.
Pass on this pic and get the word out. Even with that lunatic's blue skin, some media
WHERE ARE YOU GOING? WE HAVE BIO! YOU CAN'T MISS--
I HAVE TO. THAT WAS THE PRINCESS SPARKLEFISTS MESSAGE BOARD.
SOMEONE'S ATTACKING COPS DRESSED IN CAROL DANVERS' OLD OUTFIT.
AND WE MS. MARVELS HAVE TO LOOK OUT FOR EACH OTHER!
FINE. I'LL TELL 'EM YOU HURLED. JUST BE CAREFUL, OKAY?
HHH. THAT GIRL DOESN'T LISTEN TO A WORD I SAY...

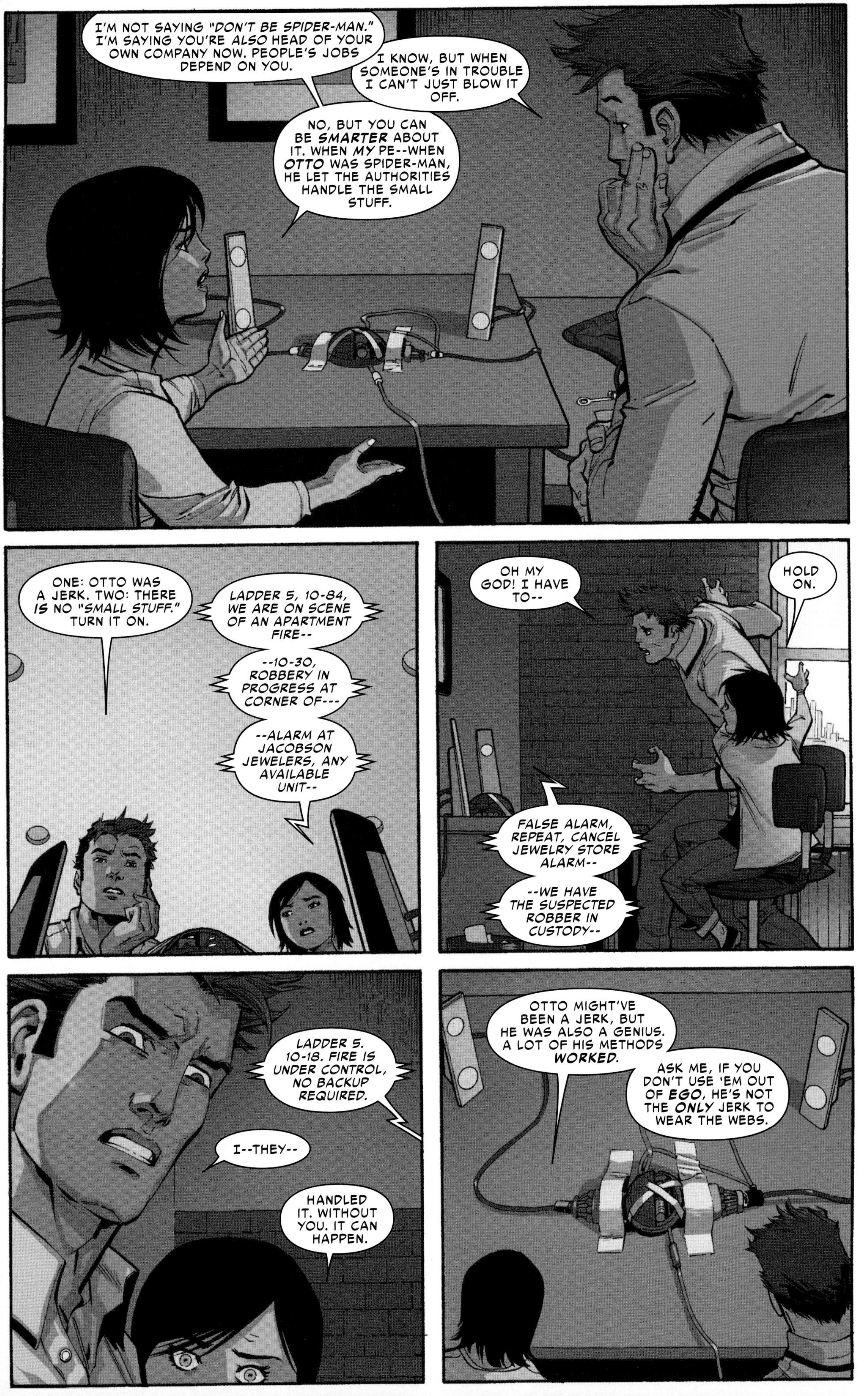
I'M NOT SAYING "DON'T BE SPIDER-MAN." I'M SAYING YOU'RE ALSO HEAD OF YOUR OWN COMPANY NOW. PEOPLE'S JOBS DEPEND ON YOU.
I KNOW, BUT WHEN SOMEONE'S IN TROUBLE I CAN'T JUST BLOW IT OFF.
NO, BUT YOU CAN BE SMARTER ABOUT IT. WHEN MY PE--WHEN OTTO WAS SPIDER-MAN, HE LET THE AUTHORITIES HANDLE THE SMALL STUFF.
ONE: OTTO WAS A JERK. TWO: THERE IS NO "SMALL STUFF." TURN IT ON.
LADDER 5, 10-84, WE ARE ON SCENE OF AN APARTMENT FIRE--
--10-30, ROBBERY IN PROGRESS AT CORNER OF---
--ALARM AT JACOBSON JEWELERS, ANY AVAILABLE UNIT--
OH MY GOD! I HAVE TO--
HOLD ON.
FALSE ALARM, REPEAT, CANCEL JEWELRY STORE ALARM--
--WE HAVE THE SUSPECTED ROBBER IN CUSTODY--
LADDER 5. 10-18. FIRE IS UNDER CONTROL, NO BACKUP REQUIRED.
I--THEY--
HANDLED IT. WITHOUT YOU. IT CAN HAPPEN.
OTTO MIGHT'VE BEEN A JERK, BUT HE WAS ALSO A GENIUS. A LOT OF HIS METHODS WORKED.
ASK ME, IF YOU DON'T USE 'EM OUT OF EGO, HE'S NOT THE ONLY JERK TO WEAR THE WEBS.

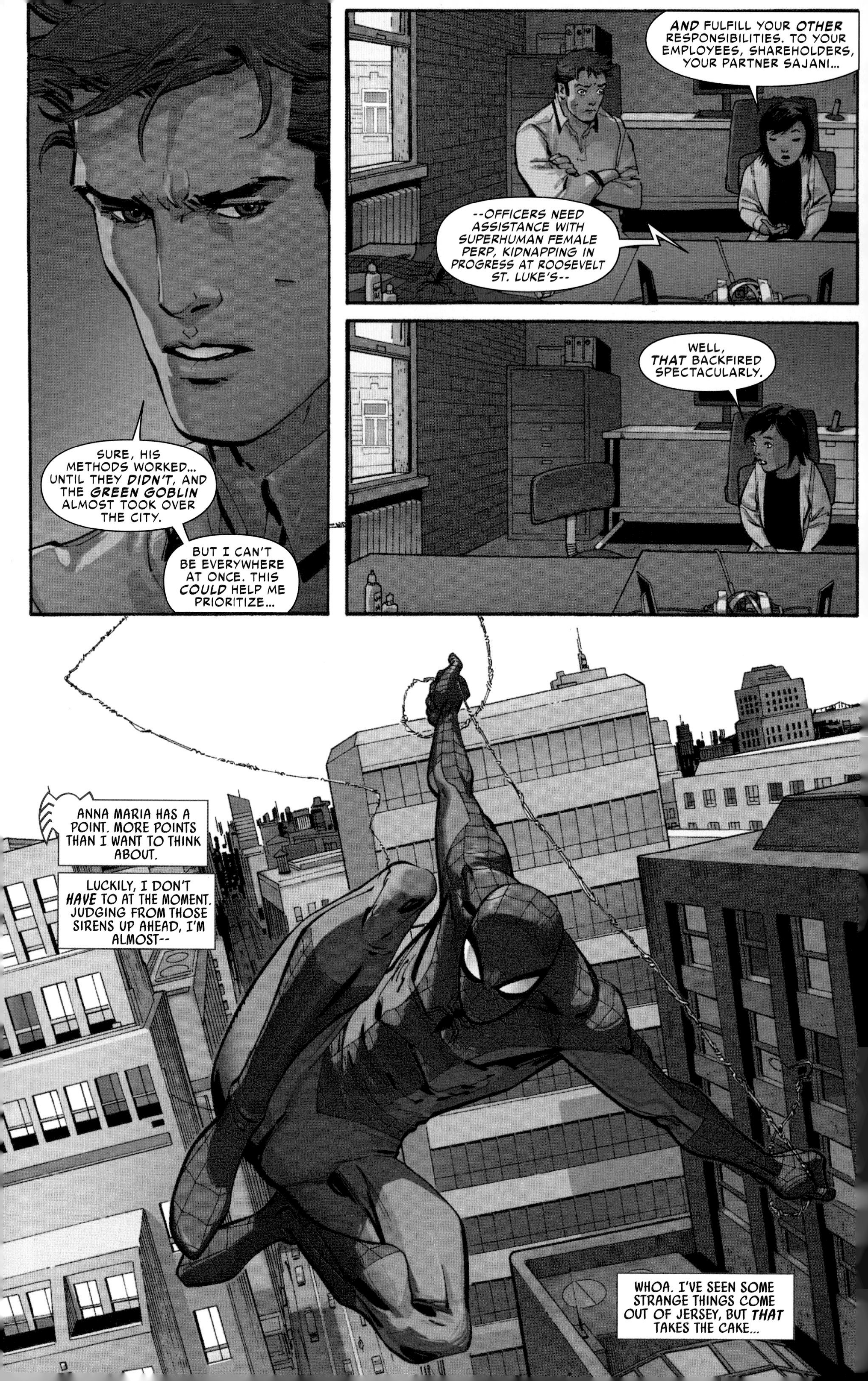
SURE, HIS METHODS WORKED... UNTIL THEY DIDN'T, AND THE GREEN GOBLIN ALMOST TOOK OVER THE CITY.
BUT I CAN'T BE EVERYWHERE AT ONCE. THIS COULD HELP ME PRIORITIZE...
AND FULFILL YOUR OTHER RESPONSIBILITIES. TO YOUR EMPLOYEES, SHAREHOLDERS, YOUR PARTNER SAJANI...
--OFFICERS NEED ASSISTANCE WITH SUPERHUMAN FEMALE PERP, KIDNAPPING IN PROGRESS AT ROOSEVELT ST. LUKE'S--
WELL, THAT BACKFIRED SPECTACULARLY.
ANNA MARIA HAS A POINT. MORE POINTS THAN I WANT TO THINK ABOUT.
LUCKILY, I DON'T HAVE TO AT THE MOMENT. JUDGING FROM THOSE SIRENS UP AHEAD, I'M ALMOST--
WHOA. I'VE SEEN SOME STRANGE THINGS COME OUT OF JERSEY, BUT THAT TAKES THE CAKE...

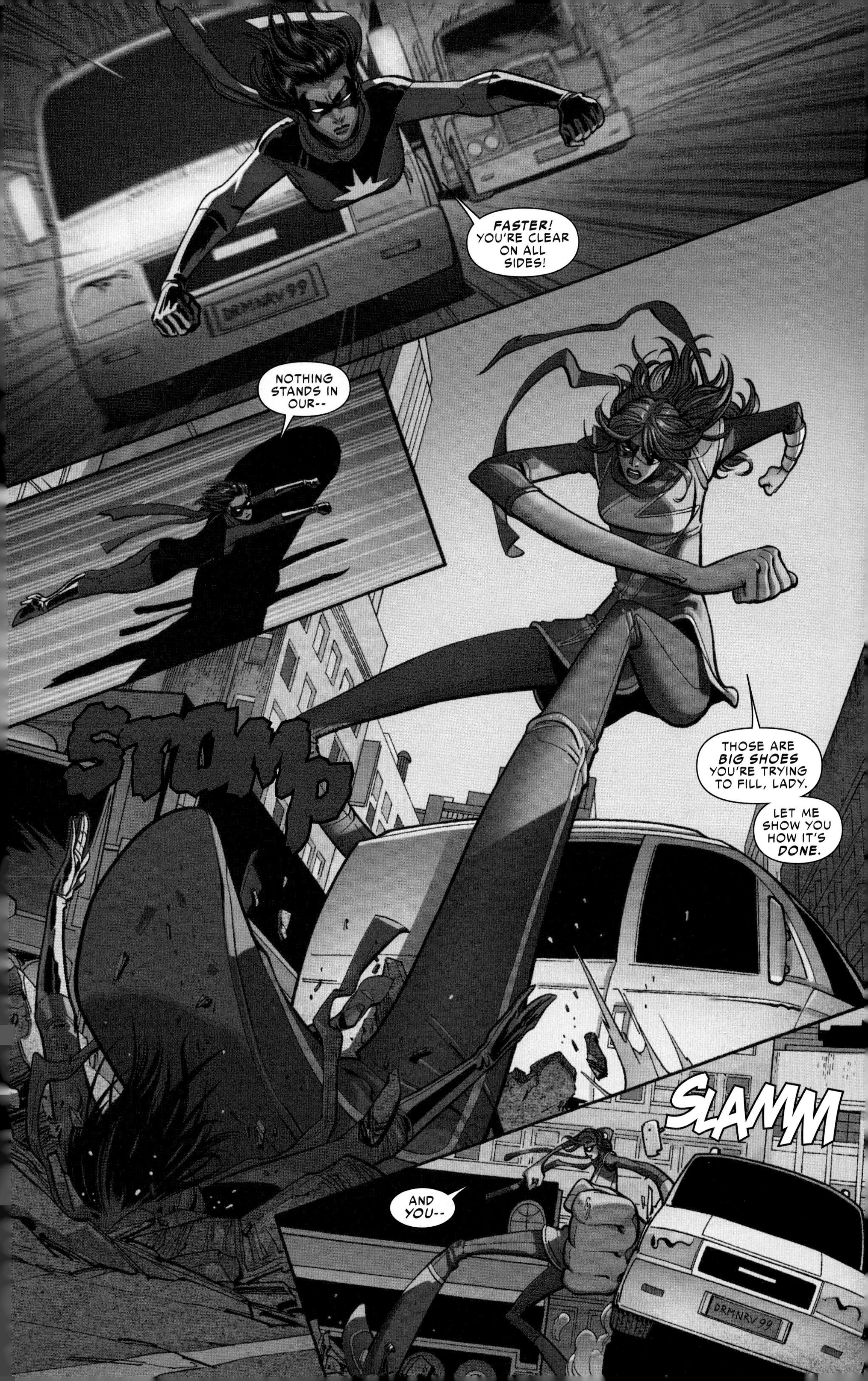
FASTER! YOU'RE CLEAR ON ALL SIDES!
DRMNRV 99
NOTHING STANDS IN OUR--
STOMP
THOSE ARE BIG SHOES YOU'RE TRYING TO FILL, LADY.
LET ME SHOW YOU HOW IT'S DONE.
SLAMM
AND YOU--
DRMNRV 99

OH, NO! STILL GETTING USED TO MY STRENGTH AT THIS SIZE...

SKREEE

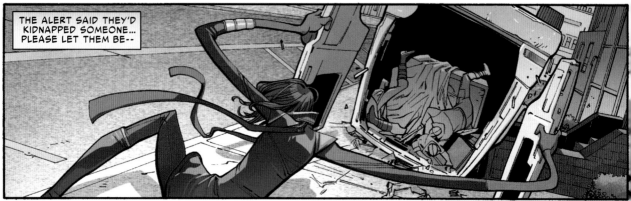

THE ALERT SAID THEY'D KIDNAPPED SOMEONE... PLEASE LET THEM BE--

A COCOON? AND IT LOOKS FAMILIAR.

LIKE THE ONE I CAME OUT OF WHEN I GOT MY POWERS...

HELLO? CAN YOU HEAR ME IN THERE?

I--I DON'T KNOW IF IT'S SAFE TO MOVE YOU--

DON'T HURT YOUR PRIMITIVE HUMAN BRAIN.

LET ME.

WHRAMM

GUHH--

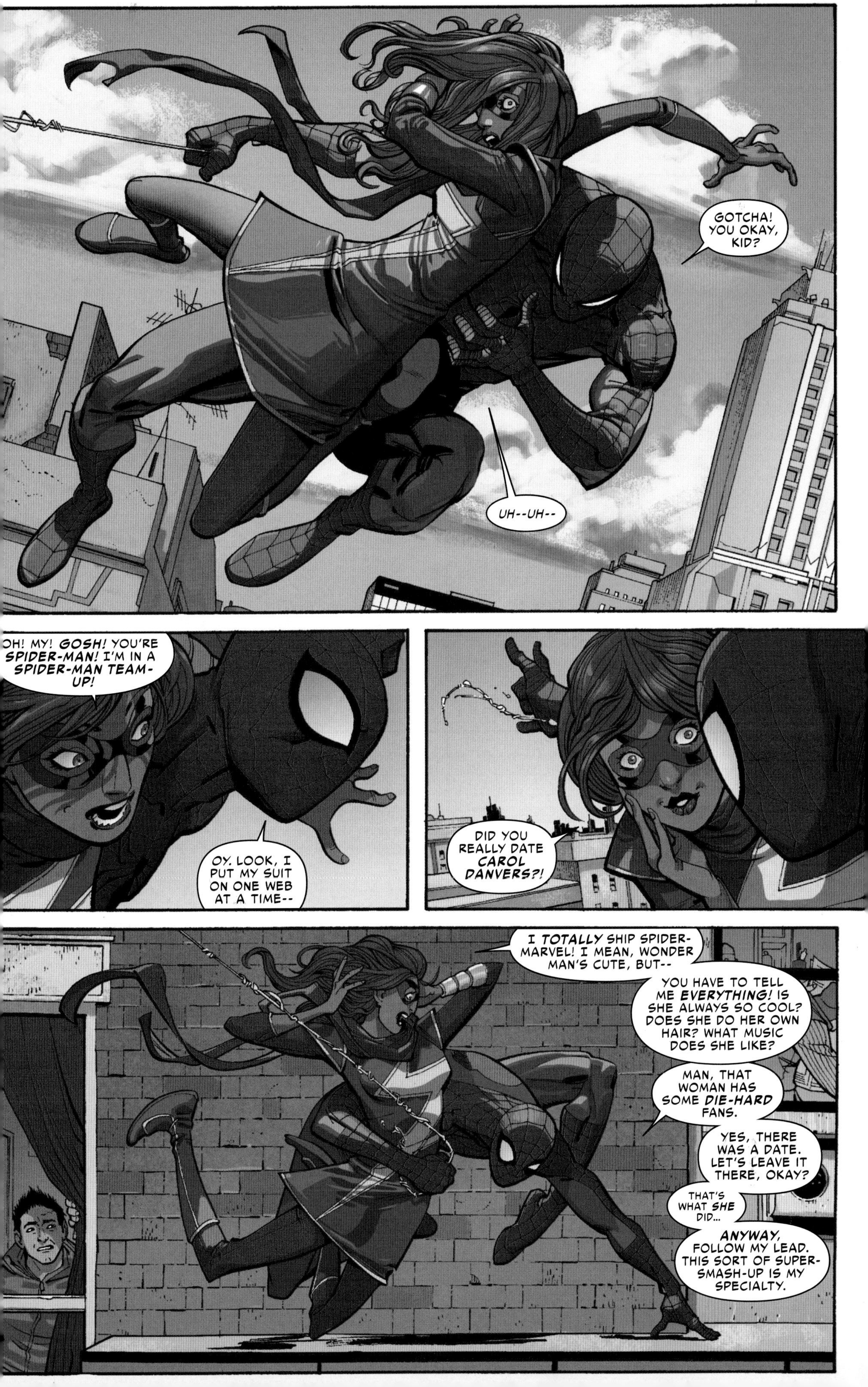
GOTCHA! YOU OKAY, KID?
UH--UH--
OH! MY! GOSH! YOU'RE SPIDER-MAN! I'M IN A SPIDER-MAN TEAM-UP!
OY. LOOK, I PUT MY SUIT ON ONE WEB AT A TIME--
DID YOU REALLY DATE CAROL DANVERS?!
I TOTALLY SHIP SPIDER-MARVEL! I MEAN, WONDER MAN'S CUTE, BUT--
YOU HAVE TO TELL ME EVERYTHING! IS SHE ALWAYS SO COOL? DOES SHE DO HER OWN HAIR? WHAT MUSIC DOES SHE LIKE?
MAN, THAT WOMAN HAS SOME DIE-HARD FANS.
YES, THERE WAS A DATE. LET'S LEAVE IT THERE, OKAY?
THAT'S WHAT SHE DID...
ANYWAY, FOLLOW MY LEAD. THIS SORT OF SUPER-SMASH-UP IS MY SPECIALTY.

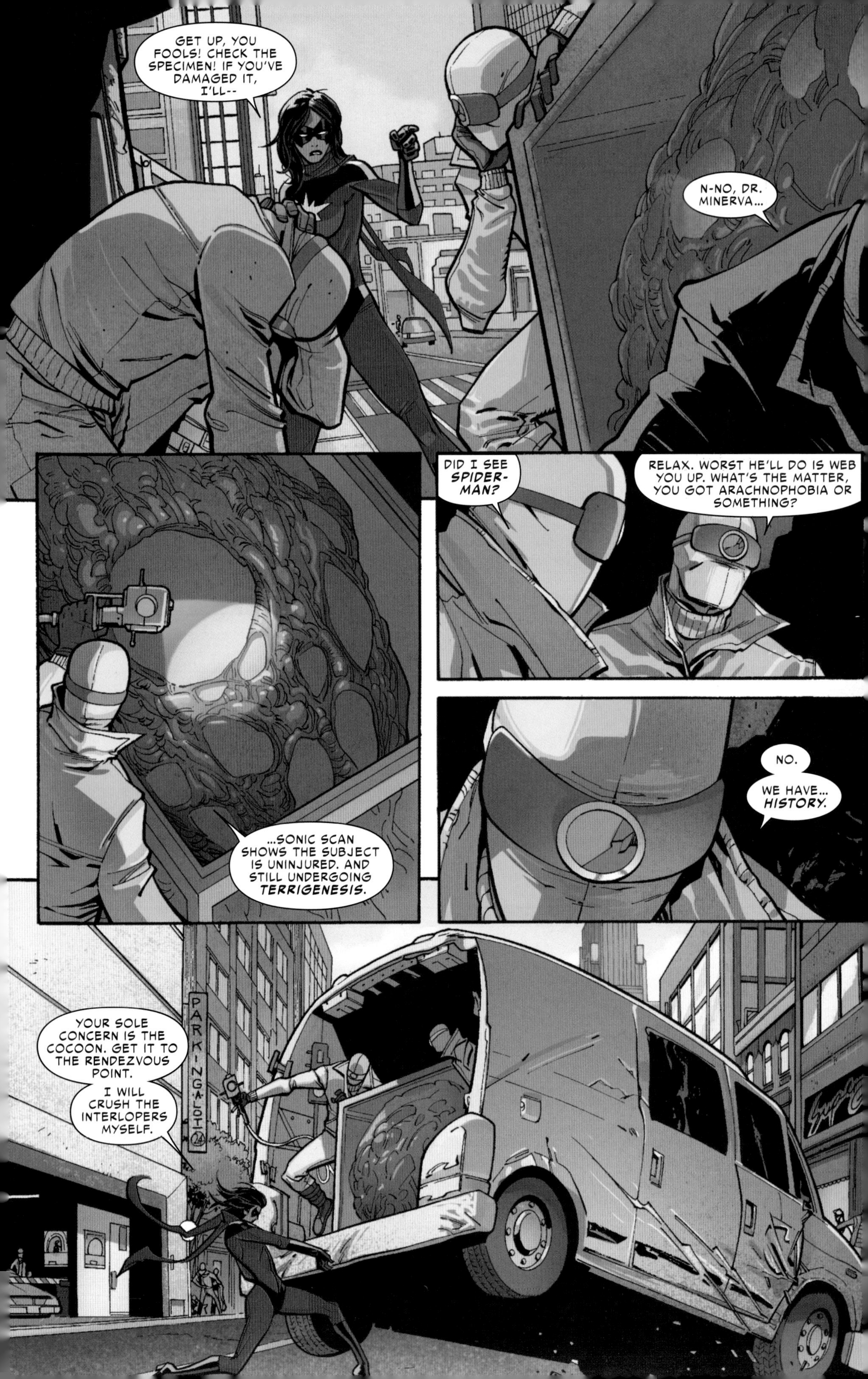
GET UP, YOU FOOLS! CHECK THE SPECIMEN! IF YOU'VE DAMAGED IT, I'LL--
N-NO, DR. MINERVA...
...SONIC SCAN SHOWS THE SUBJECT IS UNINJURED. AND STILL UNDERGOING TERRIGENESIS.
DID I SEE SPIDER-MAN?
RELAX. WORST HE'LL DO IS WEB YOU UP. WHAT'S THE MATTER, YOU GOT ARACHNOPHOBIA OR SOMETHING?
NO.
WE HAVE... HISTORY.
YOUR SOLE CONCERN IS THE COCOON. GET IT TO THE RENDEZVOUS POINT.
I WILL CRUSH THE INTERLOPERS MYSELF.
PARKING LOT
24

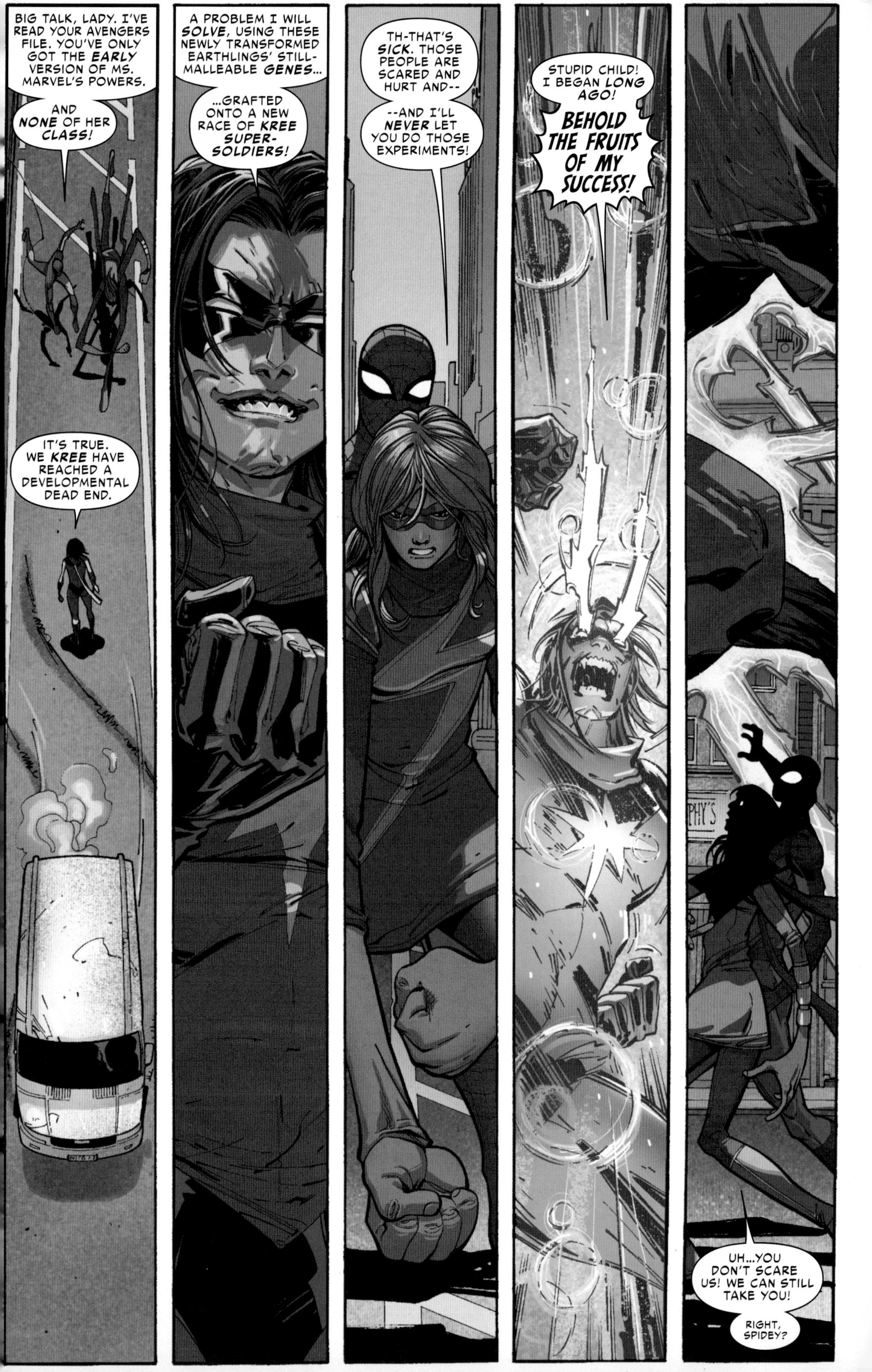
BIG TALK, LADY. I'VE READ YOUR AVENGERS FILE. YOU'VE ONLY GOT THE EARLY VERSION OF MS. MARVEL'S POWERS.
AND NONE OF HER CLASS!
IT'S TRUE. WE KREE HAVE REACHED A DEVELOPMENTAL DEAD END.
A PROBLEM I WILL SOLVE, USING THESE NEWLY TRANSFORMED EARTHLINGS' STILL-MALLEABLE GENES...
...GRAFTED ONTO A NEW RACE OF KREE SUPER-SOLDIERS!
TH-THAT'S SICK. THOSE PEOPLE ARE SCARED AND HURT AND--
--AND I'LL NEVER LET YOU DO THOSE EXPERIMENTS!
STUPID CHILD! I BEGAN LONG AGO!
BEHOLD THE FRUITS OF MY SUCCESS!
UH...YOU DON'T SCARE US! WE CAN STILL TAKE YOU!
RIGHT, SPIDEY?

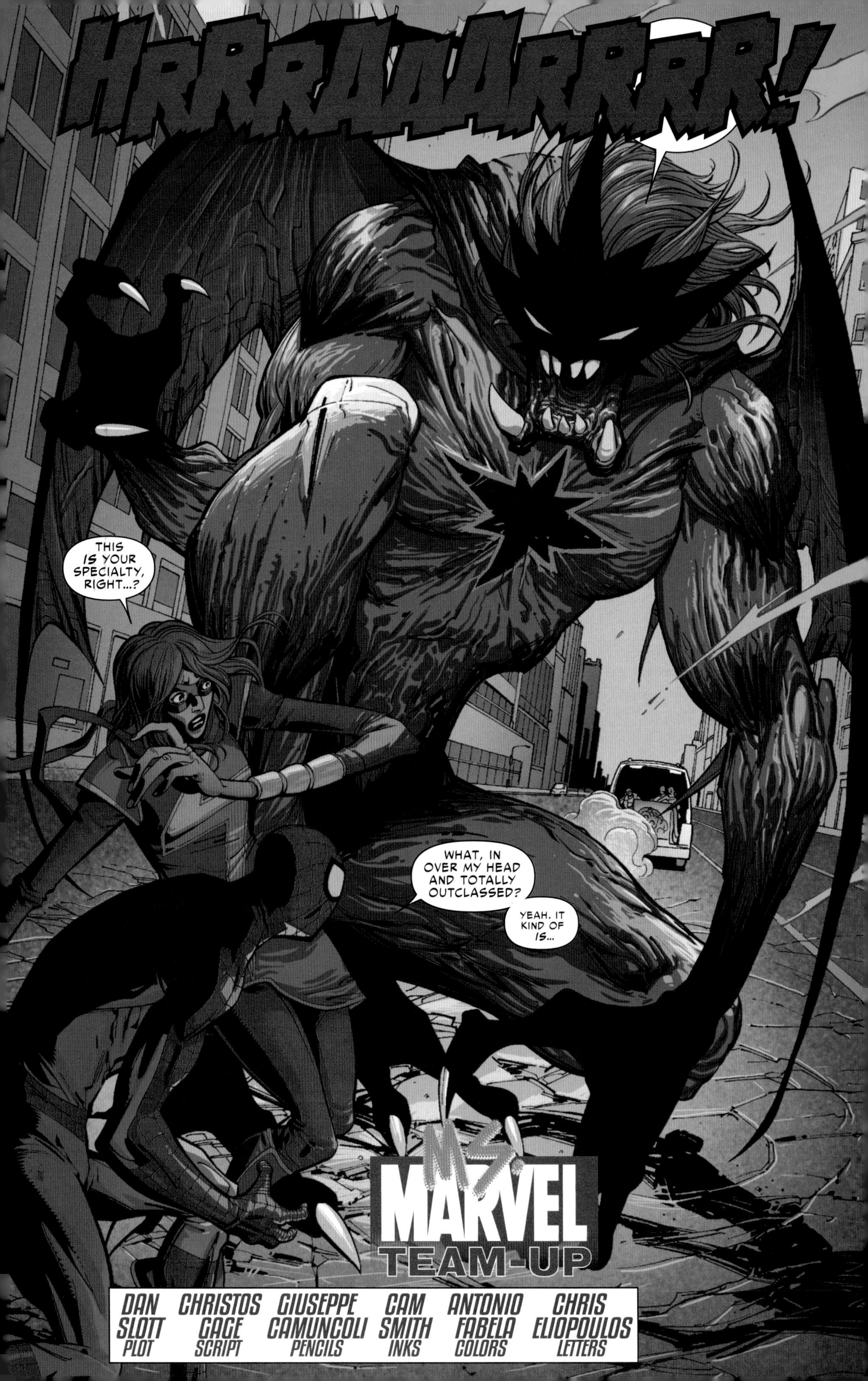
HRRRAAARRRR!
THIS IS YOUR SPECIALTY, RIGHT...?
WHAT, IN OVER MY HEAD AND TOTALLY OUTCLASSED?
YEAH. IT KIND OF IS...
MS. MARVEL TEAM-UP
DAN SLOTT PLOT
CHRISTOS GAGE SCRIPT
GIUSEPPE CAMUNCOLI PENCILS
CAM SMITH INKS
ANTONIO FABELA COLORS
CHRIS ELIOPOULOS LETTERS

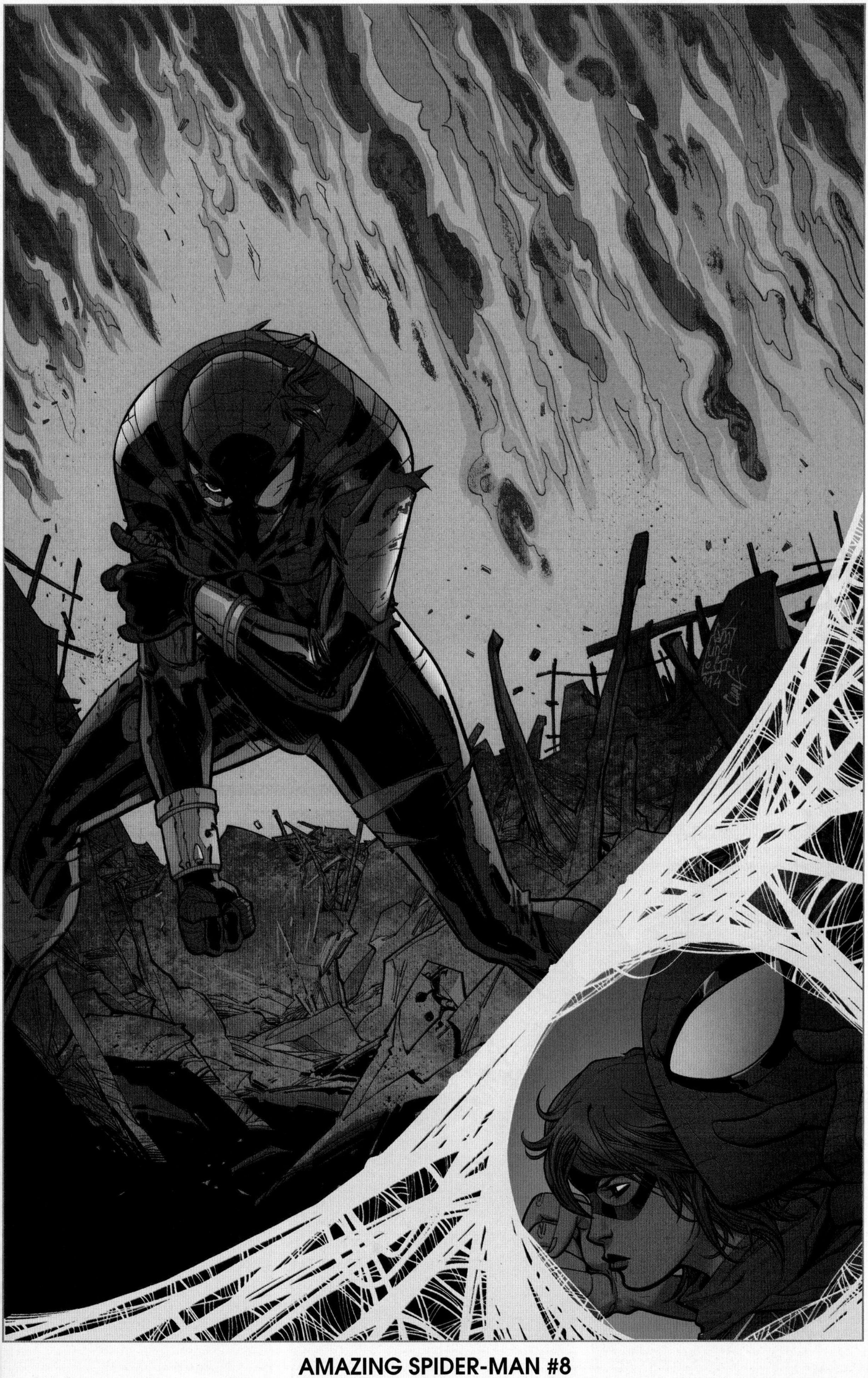

AMAZING SPIDER-MAN #8

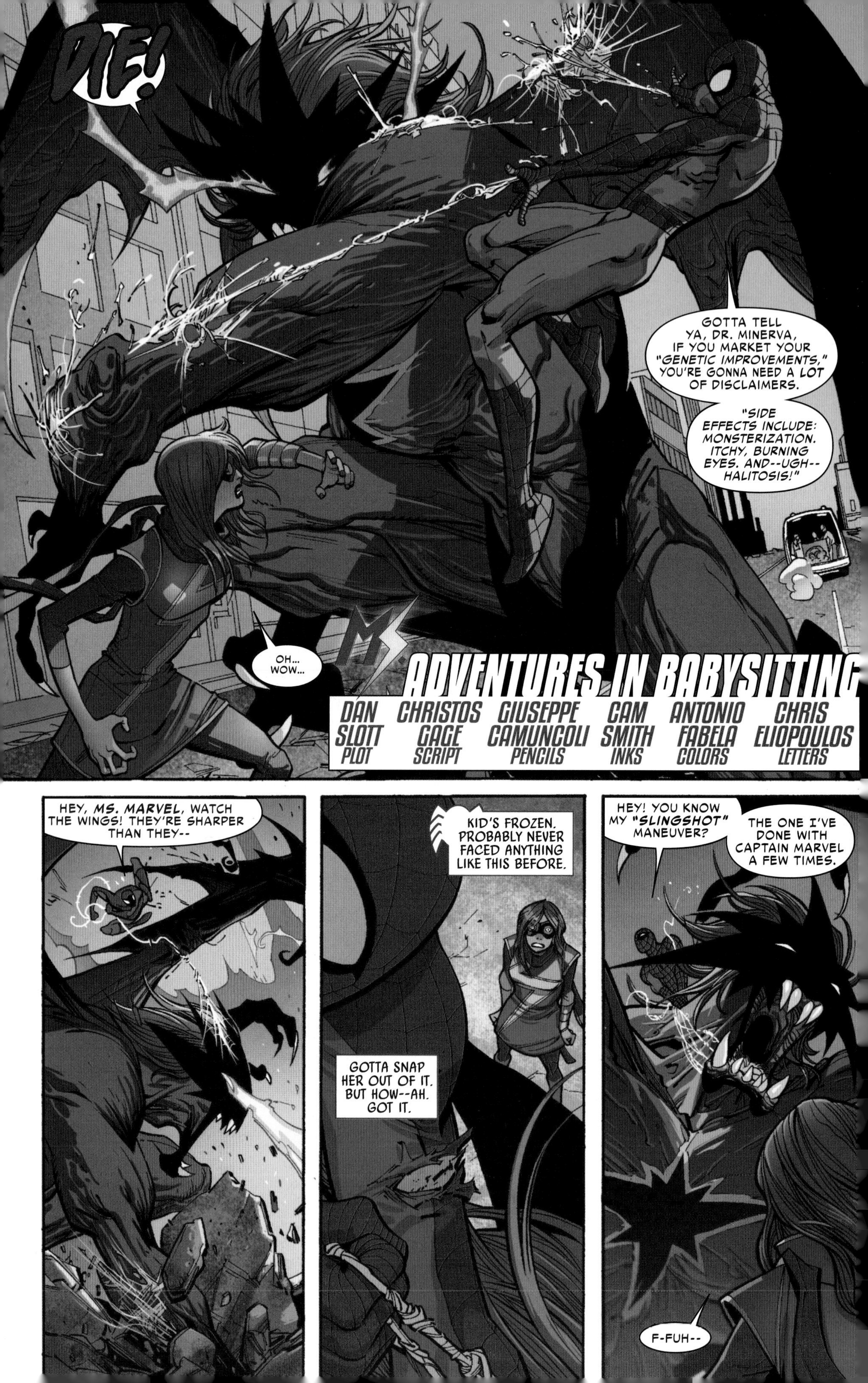
DIE!
GOTTA TELL YA, DR. MINERVA, IF YOU MARKET YOUR "GENETIC IMPROVEMENTS," YOU'RE GONNA NEED A LOT OF DISCLAIMERS.
"SIDE EFFECTS INCLUDE: MONSTERIZATION. ITCHY, BURNING EYES. AND--UGH--HALITOSIS!"
OH... WOW...
MS.
ADVENTURES IN BABYSITTING
DAN SLOTT PLOT
CHRISTOS GAGE SCRIPT
GIUSEPPE CAMUNCOLI PENCILS
CAM SMITH INKS
ANTONIO FABELA COLORS
CHRIS ELIOPOULOS LETTERS
HEY, MS. MARVEL, WATCH THE WINGS! THEY'RE SHARPER THAN THEY--
KID'S FROZEN. PROBABLY NEVER FACED ANYTHING LIKE THIS BEFORE.
GOTTA SNAP HER OUT OF IT. BUT HOW--AH. GOT IT.
HEY! YOU KNOW MY "SLINGSHOT" MANEUVER?
THE ONE I'VE DONE WITH CAPTAIN MARVEL A FEW TIMES.
F-FUH--

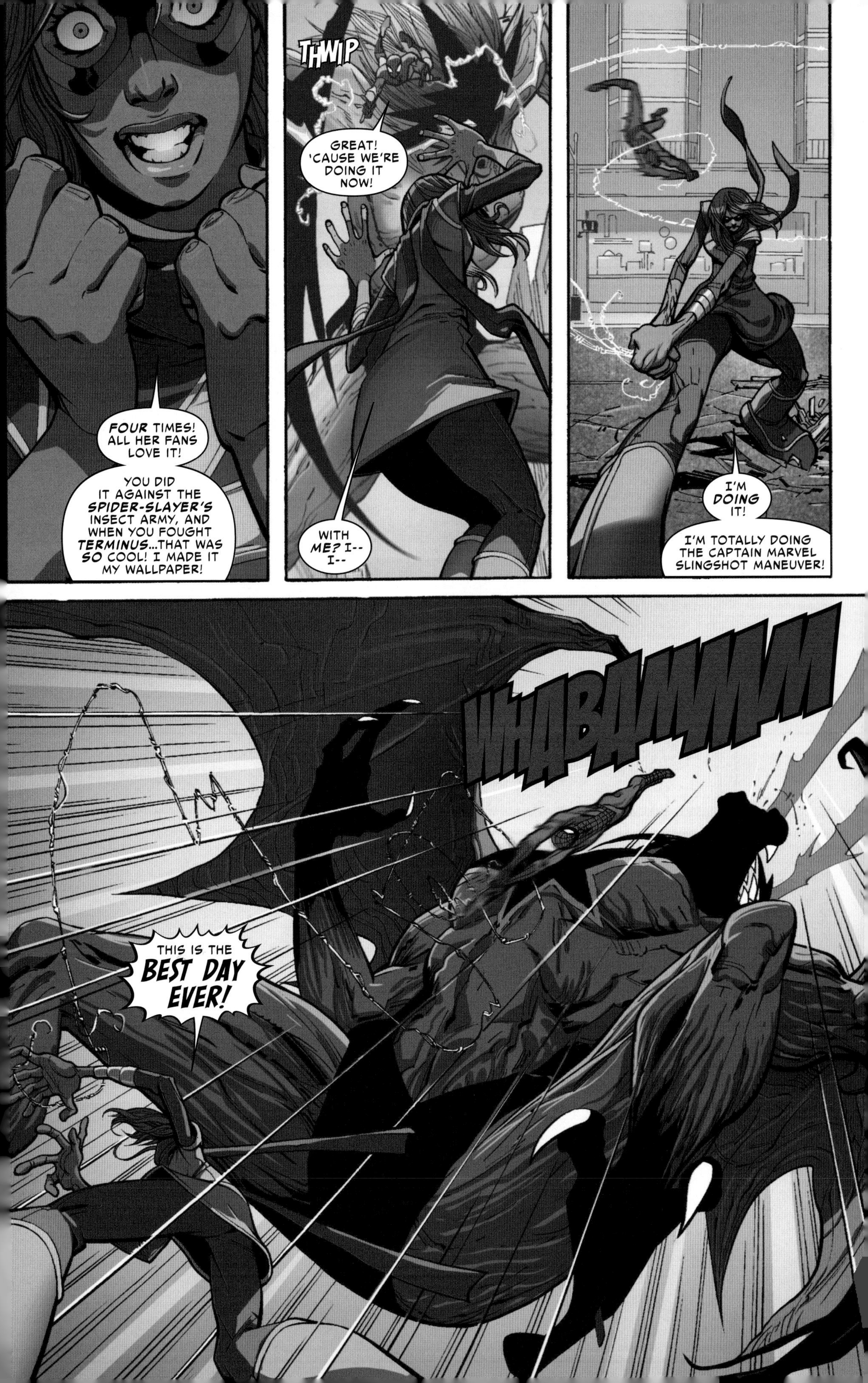
FOUR TIMES! ALL HER FANS LOVE IT!
YOU DID IT AGAINST THE SPIDER-SLAYER'S INSECT ARMY, AND WHEN YOU FOUGHT TERMINUS...THAT WAS SO COOL! I MADE IT MY WALLPAPER!
THWIP
GREAT! 'CAUSE WE'RE DOING IT NOW!
WITH ME? I-- I--
I'M DOING IT!
I'M TOTALLY DOING THE CAPTAIN MARVEL SLINGSHOT MANEUVER!
WHABAMMM
THIS IS THE BEST DAY EVER!

AWESOME! WHAT'S NEXT, SPIDEY? *OOH!* LET'S FASTBALL SPECIAL!

EASY THERE, SLUGGER. WE'RE NOT GOING FOR THE KNOCKOUT, WE'RE GOING FOR THE *WIN.*

MINERVA WANTS THAT COCOON. WE GET IT, GAME OVER! SO LET'S GO!

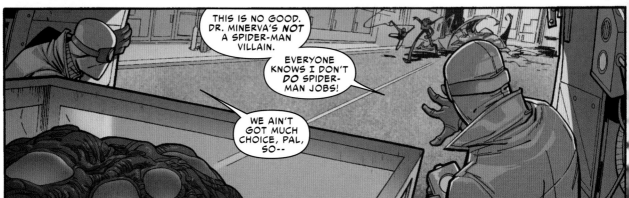

THIS IS NO GOOD. DR. MINERVA'S *NOT* A SPIDER-MAN VILLAIN.

EVERYONE KNOWS I DON'T *DO* SPIDER-MAN JOBS!

WE AIN'T GOT MUCH CHOICE, PAL, SO--

BASH

--UHH!

WAIT! I THINK I CAN MODIFY THE SONIC SCANNER INTO A WEAPON.

JUST NEED A MINUTE. BEEN A WHILE...

YOINK!

NO! THEY WERE AFTER THE *COCOON!*

FIGURE THAT OUT ALL BY YOUR--

HEY, NEW KID. THERE'S A TIME TO BANTER--

--AND A TIME TO *RUN!*

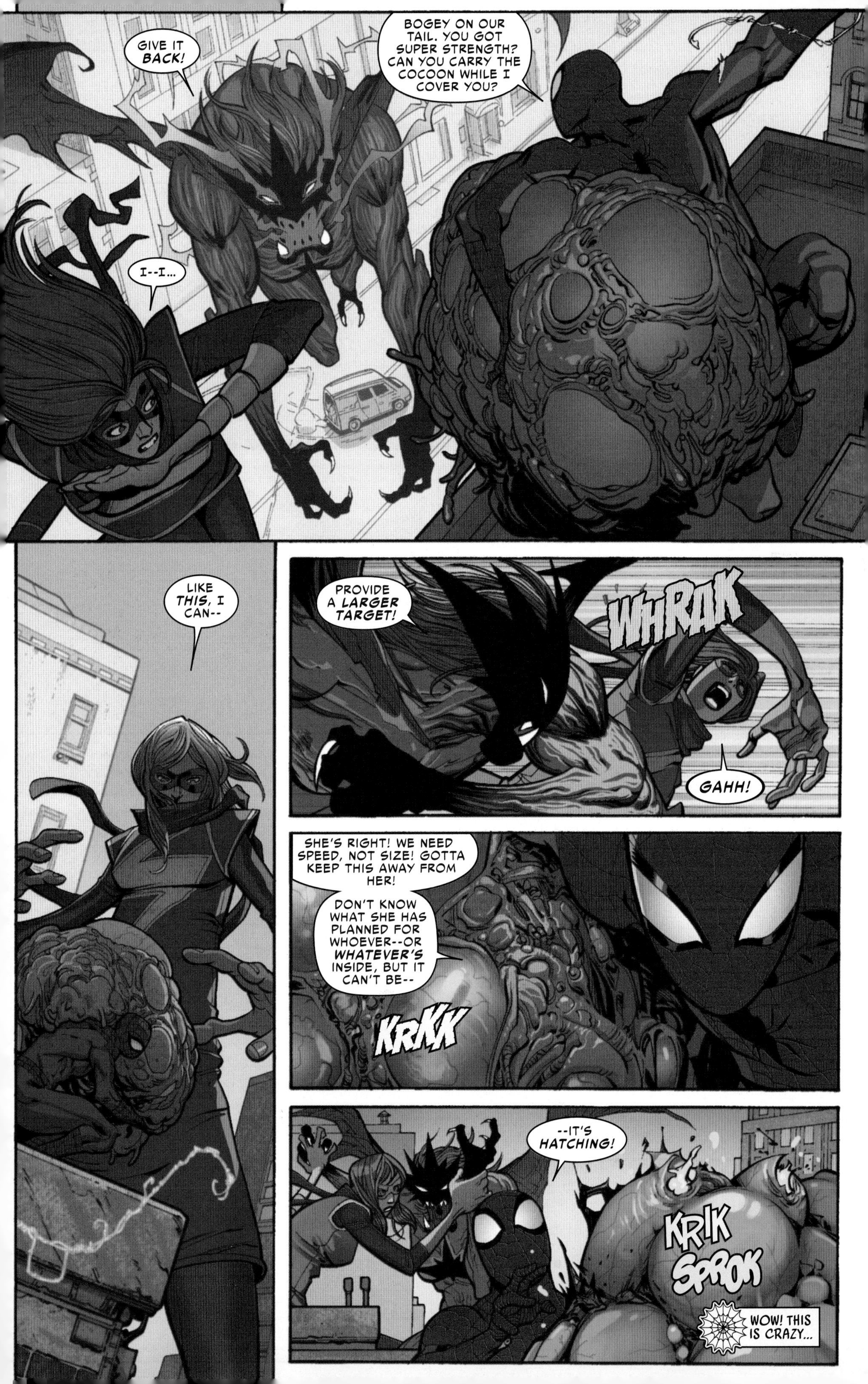
GIVE IT BACK!
BOGEY ON OUR TAIL. YOU GOT SUPER STRENGTH? CAN YOU CARRY THE COCOON WHILE I COVER YOU?
I--I...
LIKE THIS, I CAN--
PROVIDE A LARGER TARGET!
WHRAK
GAHH!
SHE'S RIGHT! WE NEED SPEED, NOT SIZE! GOTTA KEEP THIS AWAY FROM HER!
DON'T KNOW WHAT SHE HAS PLANNED FOR WHOEVER--OR WHATEVER'S INSIDE, BUT IT CAN'T BE--
KRKK
--IT'S HATCHING!
KRIK
SPROK
WOW! THIS IS CRAZY...

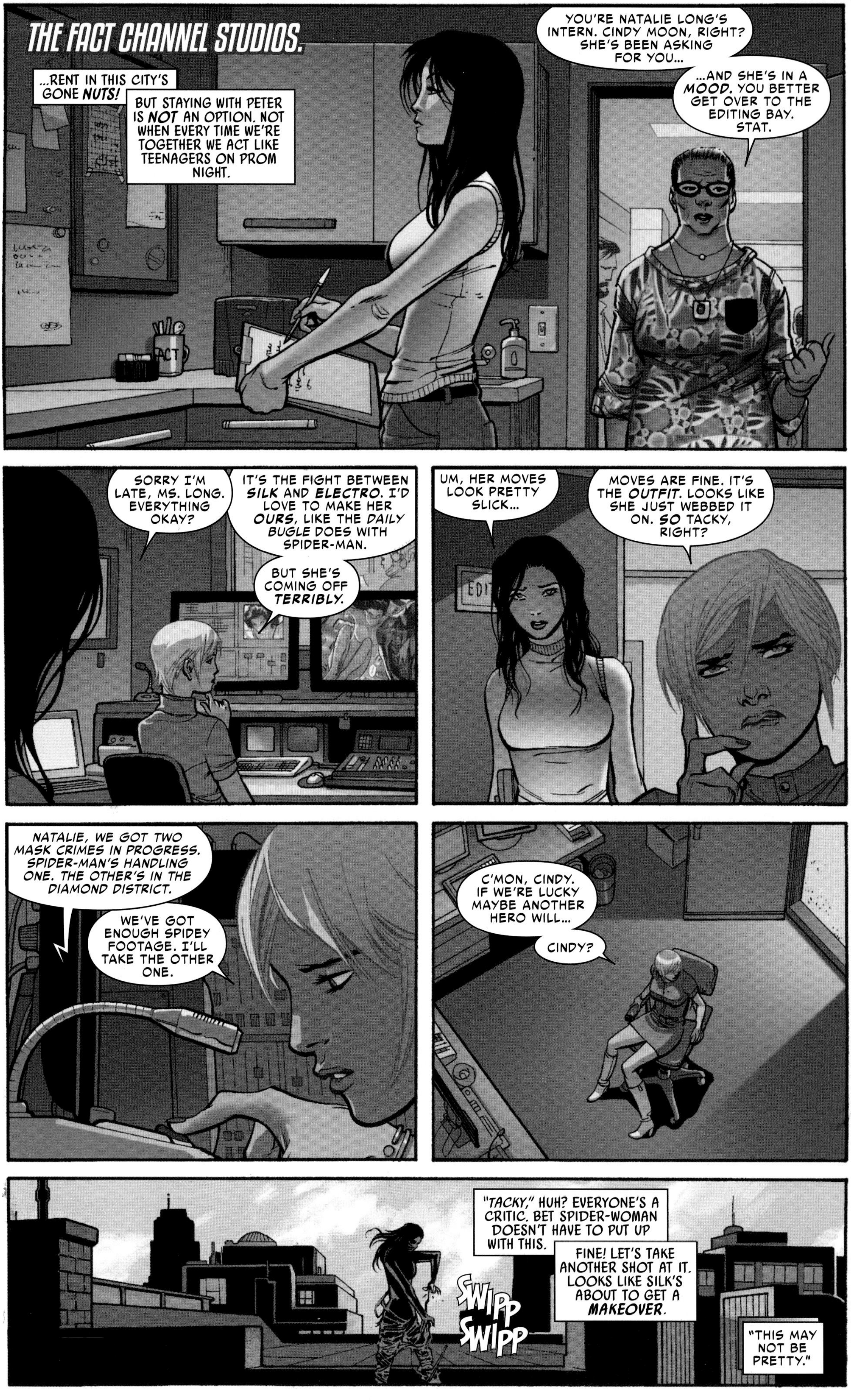
THE FACT CHANNEL STUDIOS.
...RENT IN THIS CITY'S GONE NUTS!
BUT STAYING WITH PETER IS NOT AN OPTION. NOT WHEN EVERY TIME WE'RE TOGETHER WE ACT LIKE TEENAGERS ON PROM NIGHT.
YOU'RE NATALIE LONG'S INTERN. CINDY MOON, RIGHT? SHE'S BEEN ASKING FOR YOU...
...AND SHE'S IN A MOOD. YOU BETTER GET OVER TO THE EDITING BAY. STAT.
FACT
SORRY I'M LATE, MS. LONG. EVERYTHING OKAY?
IT'S THE FIGHT BETWEEN SILK AND ELECTRO. I'D LOVE TO MAKE HER OURS, LIKE THE DAILY BUGLE DOES WITH SPIDER-MAN.
BUT SHE'S COMING OFF TERRIBLY.
UM, HER MOVES LOOK PRETTY SLICK...
MOVES ARE FINE. IT'S THE OUTFIT. LOOKS LIKE SHE JUST WEBBED IT ON. SO TACKY, RIGHT?
EDIT
NATALIE, WE GOT TWO MASK CRIMES IN PROGRESS. SPIDER-MAN'S HANDLING ONE. THE OTHER'S IN THE DIAMOND DISTRICT.
WE'VE GOT ENOUGH SPIDEY FOOTAGE. I'LL TAKE THE OTHER ONE.
C'MON, CINDY. IF WE'RE LUCKY MAYBE ANOTHER HERO WILL...
CINDY?
"TACKY," HUH? EVERYONE'S A CRITIC. BET SPIDER-WOMAN DOESN'T HAVE TO PUT UP WITH THIS.
FINE! LET'S TAKE ANOTHER SHOT AT IT. LOOKS LIKE SILK'S ABOUT TO GET A MAKEOVER.
SWIPP SWIPP
"THIS MAY NOT BE PRETTY."

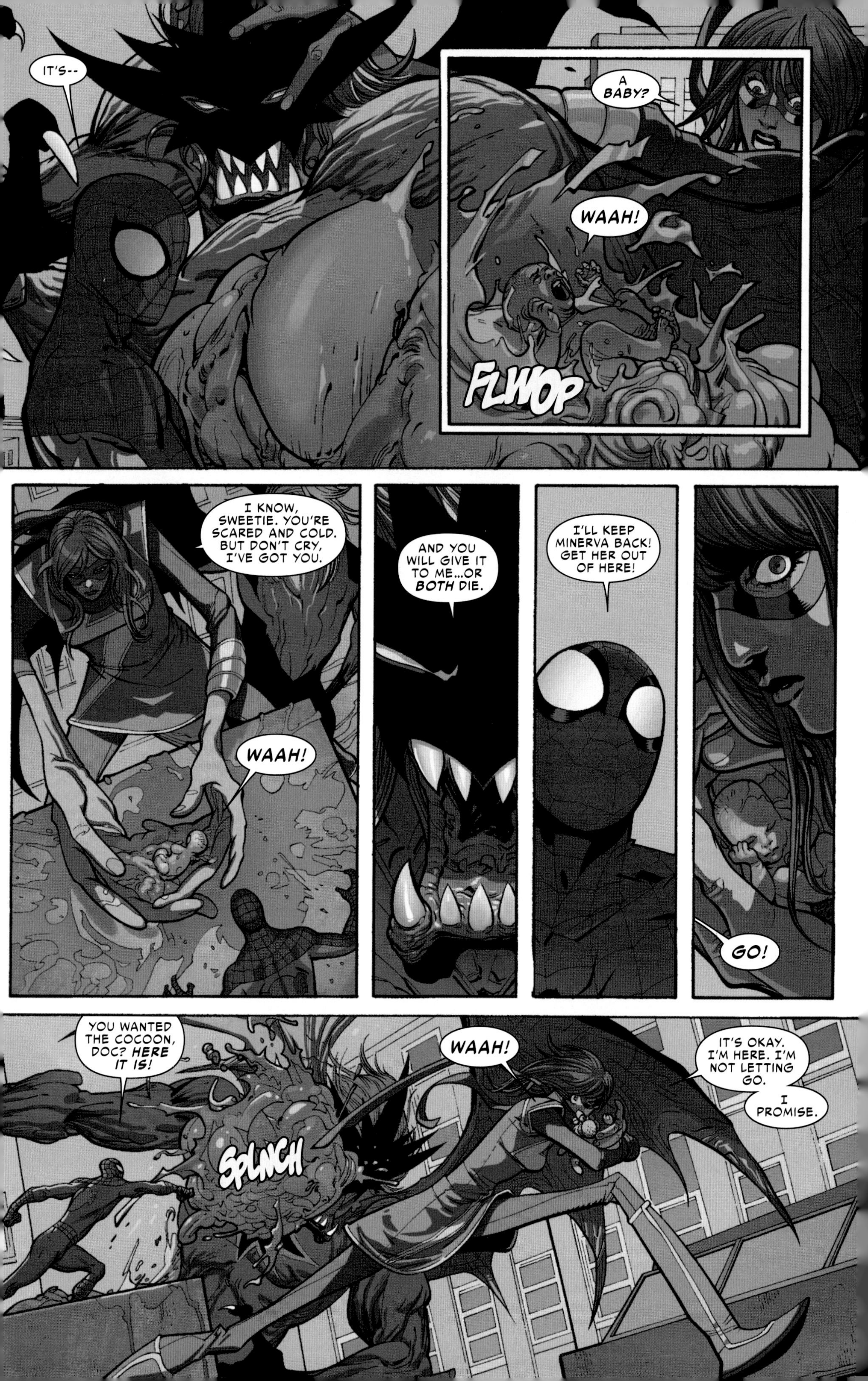
IT'S--
A BABY?
WAAH!
FLWOP
I KNOW, SWEETIE. YOU'RE SCARED AND COLD. BUT DON'T CRY, I'VE GOT YOU.
WAAH!
AND YOU WILL GIVE IT TO ME...OR BOTH DIE.
I'LL KEEP MINERVA BACK! GET HER OUT OF HERE!
GO!
YOU WANTED THE COCOON, DOC? HERE IT IS!
SPLNCH
WAAH!
IT'S OKAY. I'M HERE. I'M NOT LETTING GO.
I PROMISE.

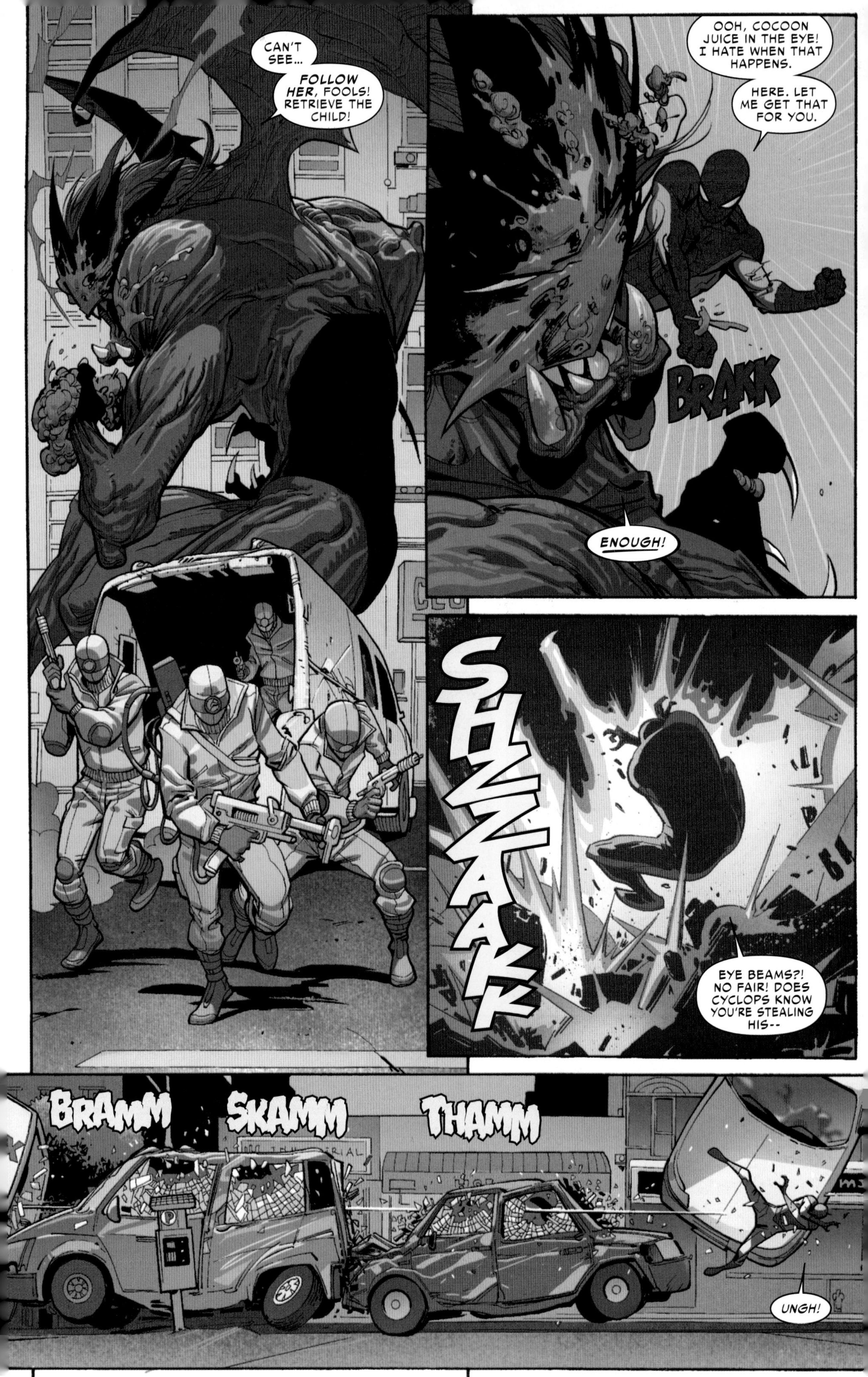
CAN'T SEE... FOLLOW HER, FOOLS! RETRIEVE THE CHILD!
OOH, COCOON JUICE IN THE EYE! I HATE WHEN THAT HAPPENS.
HERE. LET ME GET THAT FOR YOU.
BRAKK
ENOUGH!
SHZZAAKK
EYE BEAMS?! NO FAIR! DOES CYCLOPS KNOW YOU'RE STEALING HIS--
BRAMM
SKAMM
THAMM
UNGH!

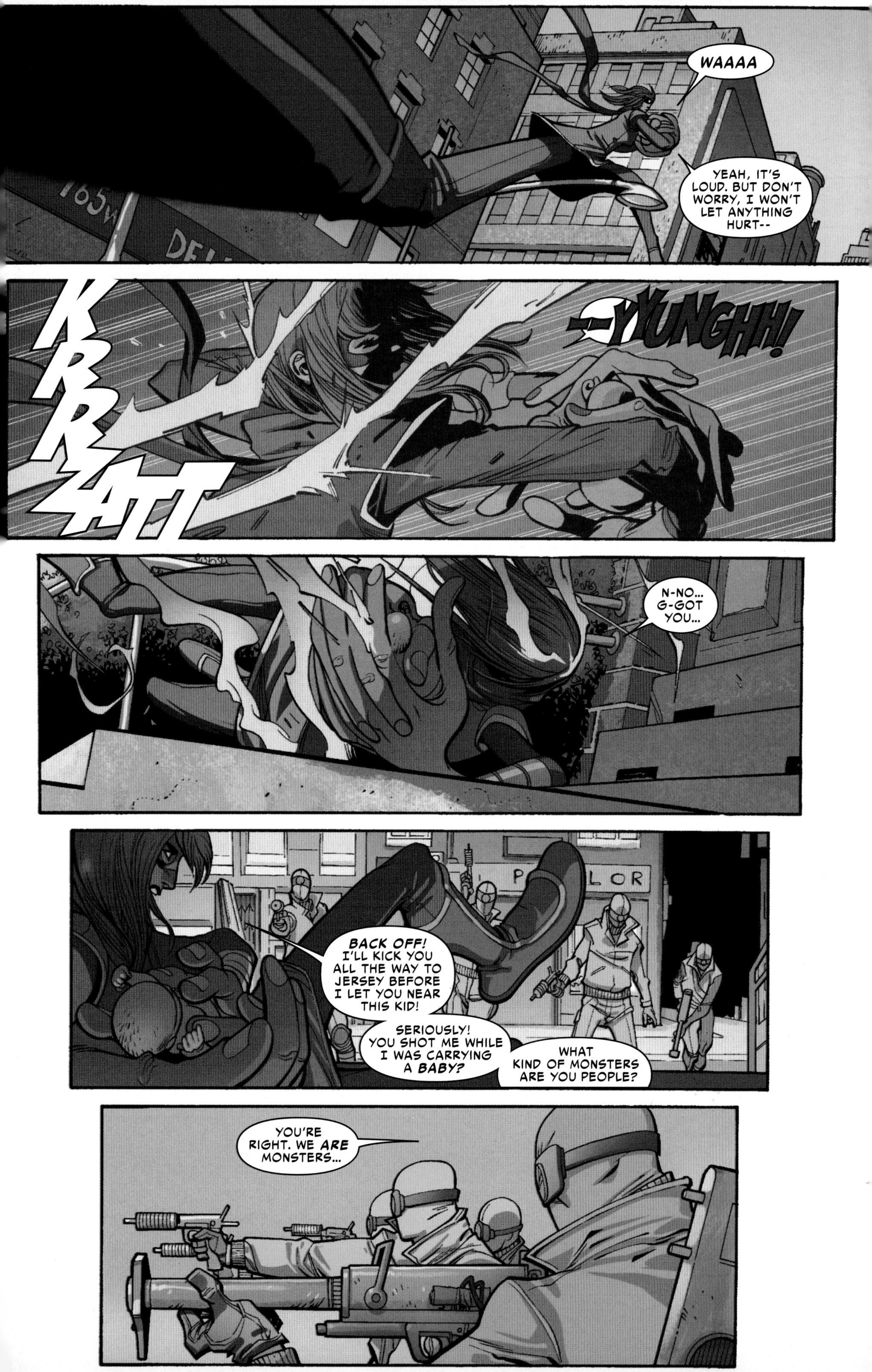
WAAAA
YEAH, IT'S LOUD. BUT DON'T WORRY, I WON'T LET ANYTHING HURT--
KRRZATT
--YYUNGHH!
N-NO... G-GOT YOU...
P LOR
BACK OFF! I'LL KICK YOU ALL THE WAY TO JERSEY BEFORE I LET YOU NEAR THIS KID!
SERIOUSLY! YOU SHOT ME WHILE I WAS CARRYING A BABY?
WHAT KIND OF MONSTERS ARE YOU PEOPLE?
YOU'RE RIGHT. WE ARE MONSTERS...

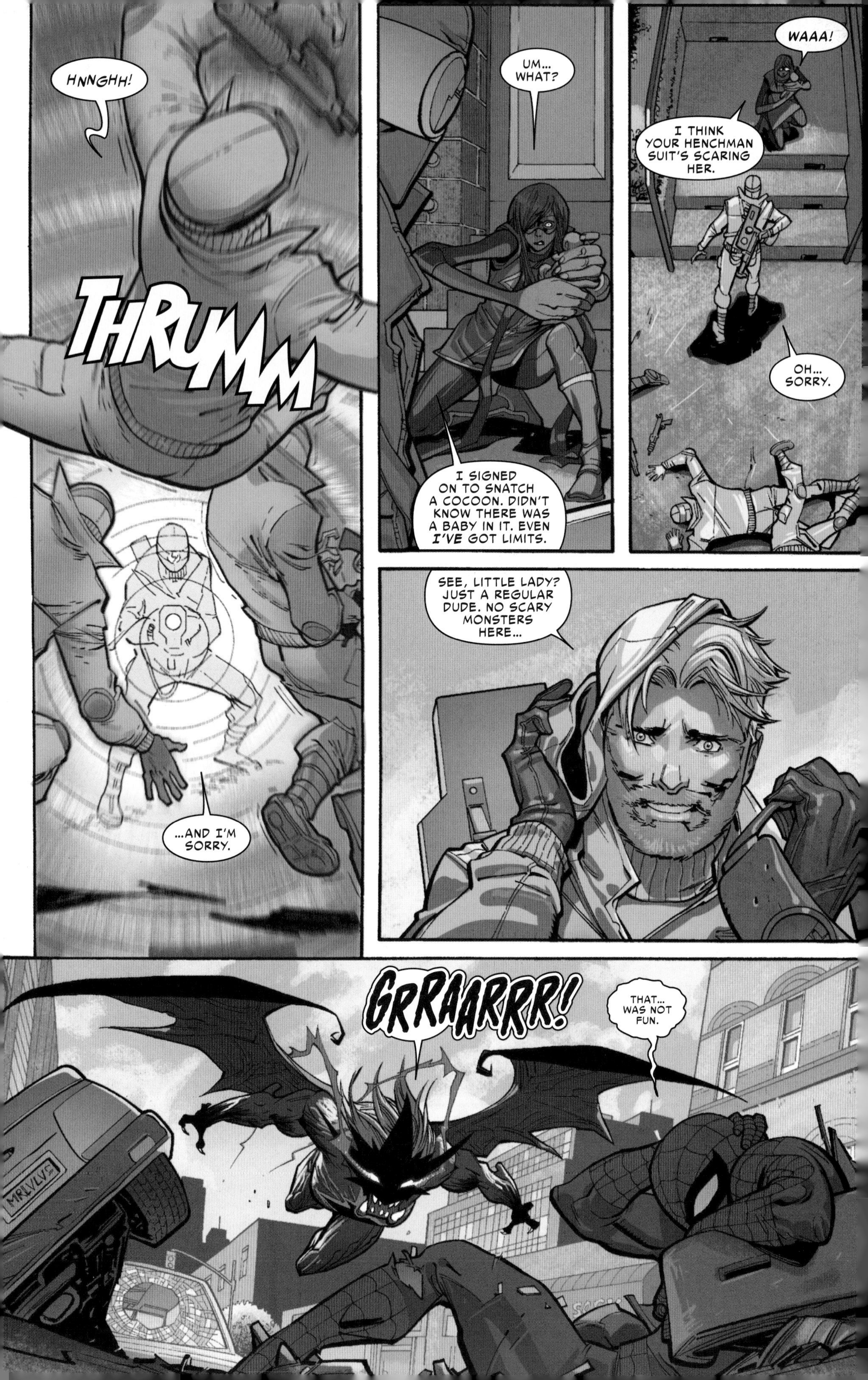
HNNGHH!
THRUMM
...AND I'M SORRY.
UM... WHAT?
I SIGNED ON TO SNATCH A COCOON. DIDN'T KNOW THERE WAS A BABY IN IT. EVEN I'VE GOT LIMITS.
WAAA!
I THINK YOUR HENCHMAN SUIT'S SCARING HER.
OH... SORRY.
SEE, LITTLE LADY? JUST A REGULAR DUDE. NO SCARY MONSTERS HERE...
GRRAARRR!
THAT... WAS NOT FUN.

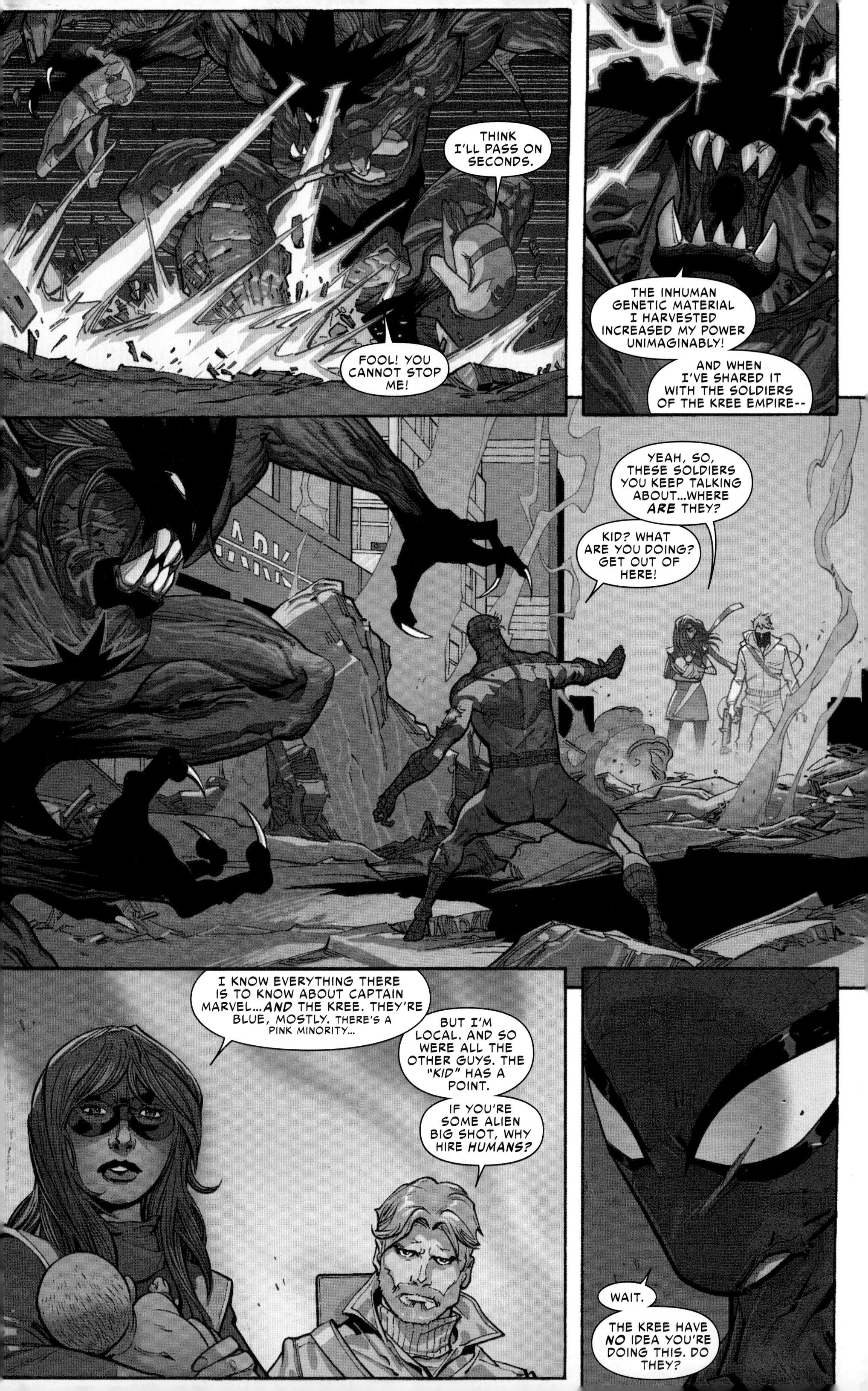
THINK I'LL PASS ON SECONDS.
FOOL! YOU CANNOT STOP ME!
THE INHUMAN GENETIC MATERIAL I HARVESTED INCREASED MY POWER UNIMAGINABLY!
AND WHEN I'VE SHARED IT WITH THE SOLDIERS OF THE KREE EMPIRE--
YEAH, SO, THESE SOLDIERS YOU KEEP TALKING ABOUT...WHERE *ARE* THEY?
KID? WHAT ARE YOU DOING? GET OUT OF HERE!
I KNOW EVERYTHING THERE IS TO KNOW ABOUT CAPTAIN MARVEL...*AND* THE KREE. THEY'RE BLUE, MOSTLY. THERE'S A PINK MINORITY...
BUT I'M LOCAL. AND SO WERE ALL THE OTHER GUYS. THE "*KID*" HAS A POINT.
IF YOU'RE SOME ALIEN BIG SHOT, WHY HIRE *HUMANS?*
WAIT.
THE KREE HAVE *NO* IDEA YOU'RE DOING THIS. DO THEY?

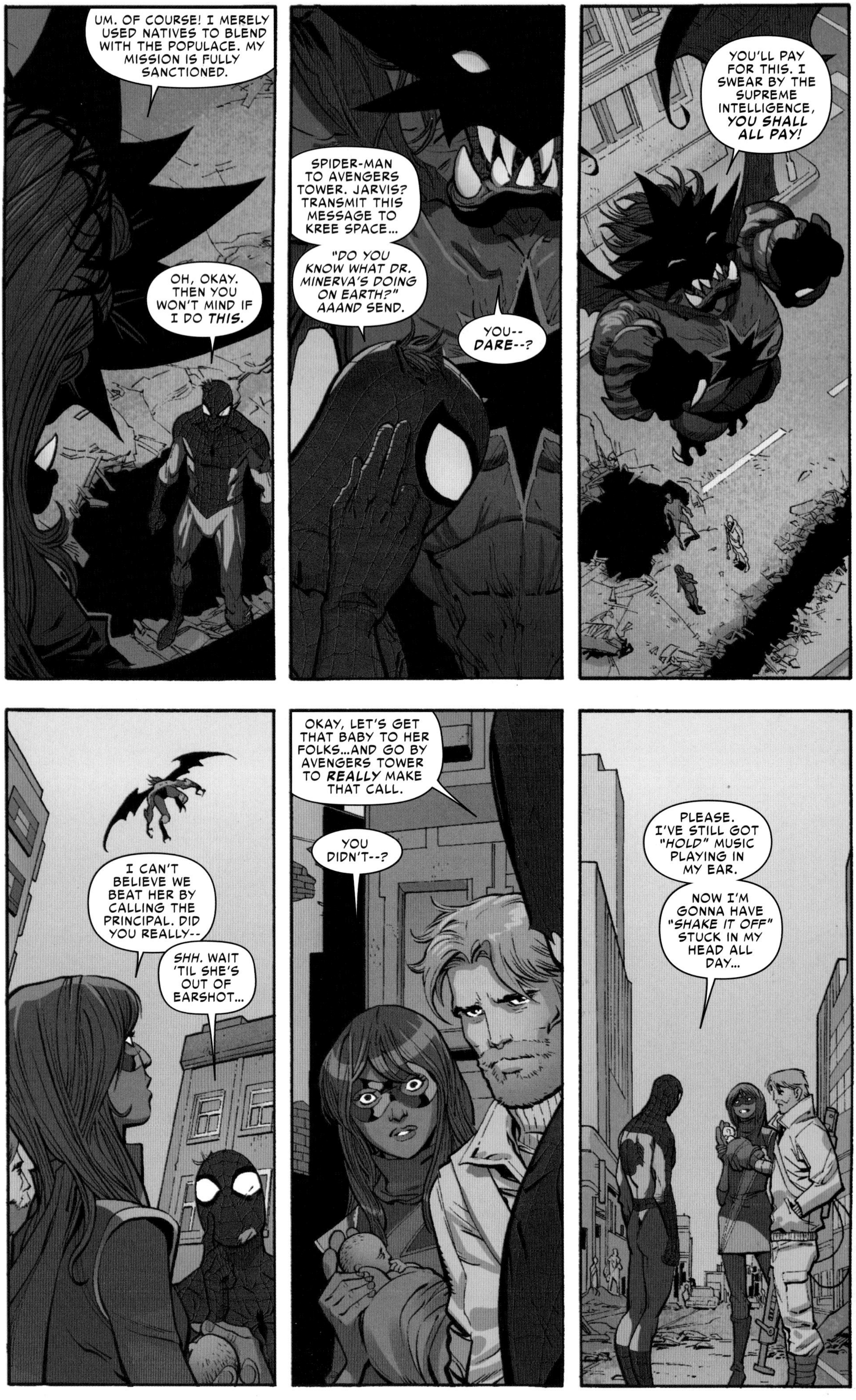
UM. OF COURSE! I MERELY USED NATIVES TO BLEND WITH THE POPULACE. MY MISSION IS FULLY SANCTIONED.
OH, OKAY. THEN YOU WON'T MIND IF I DO *THIS*.
SPIDER-MAN TO AVENGERS TOWER. JARVIS? TRANSMIT THIS MESSAGE TO KREE SPACE...
"DO YOU KNOW WHAT DR. MINERVA'S DOING ON EARTH?" AAAND SEND.
YOU-- *DARE*--?
YOU'LL PAY FOR THIS. I SWEAR BY THE SUPREME INTELLIGENCE, *YOU SHALL ALL PAY!*
I CAN'T BELIEVE WE BEAT HER BY CALLING THE PRINCIPAL. DID YOU REALLY--
SHH. WAIT 'TIL SHE'S OUT OF EARSHOT...
OKAY, LET'S GET THAT BABY TO HER FOLKS...AND GO BY AVENGERS TOWER TO *REALLY* MAKE THAT CALL.
YOU DIDN'T--?
PLEASE. I'VE STILL GOT *"HOLD"* MUSIC PLAYING IN MY EAR.
NOW I'M GONNA HAVE *"SHAKE IT OFF"* STUCK IN MY HEAD ALL DAY...

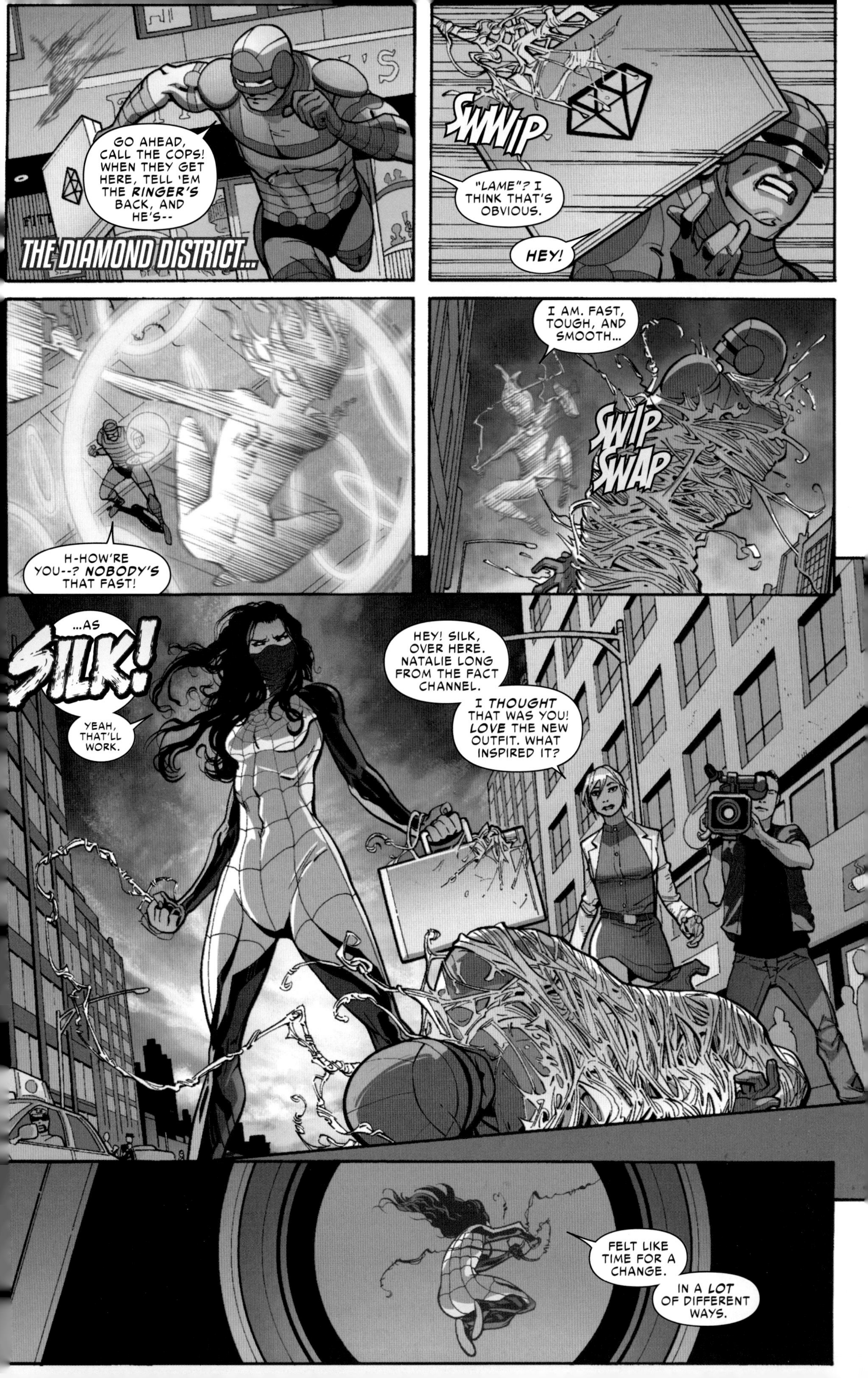

GO AHEAD, CALL THE COPS! WHEN THEY GET HERE, TELL 'EM THE RINGER'S BACK, AND HE'S--
THE DIAMOND DISTRICT...
SWWIP
"LAME"? I THINK THAT'S OBVIOUS.
HEY!
H-HOW'RE YOU--? NOBODY'S THAT FAST!
I AM. FAST, TOUGH, AND SMOOTH...
SWIP SWAP
...AS
SILK!
YEAH, THAT'LL WORK.
HEY! SILK, OVER HERE. NATALIE LONG FROM THE FACT CHANNEL.
I THOUGHT THAT WAS YOU! LOVE THE NEW OUTFIT. WHAT INSPIRED IT?
FELT LIKE TIME FOR A CHANGE.
IN A LOT OF DIFFERENT WAYS.

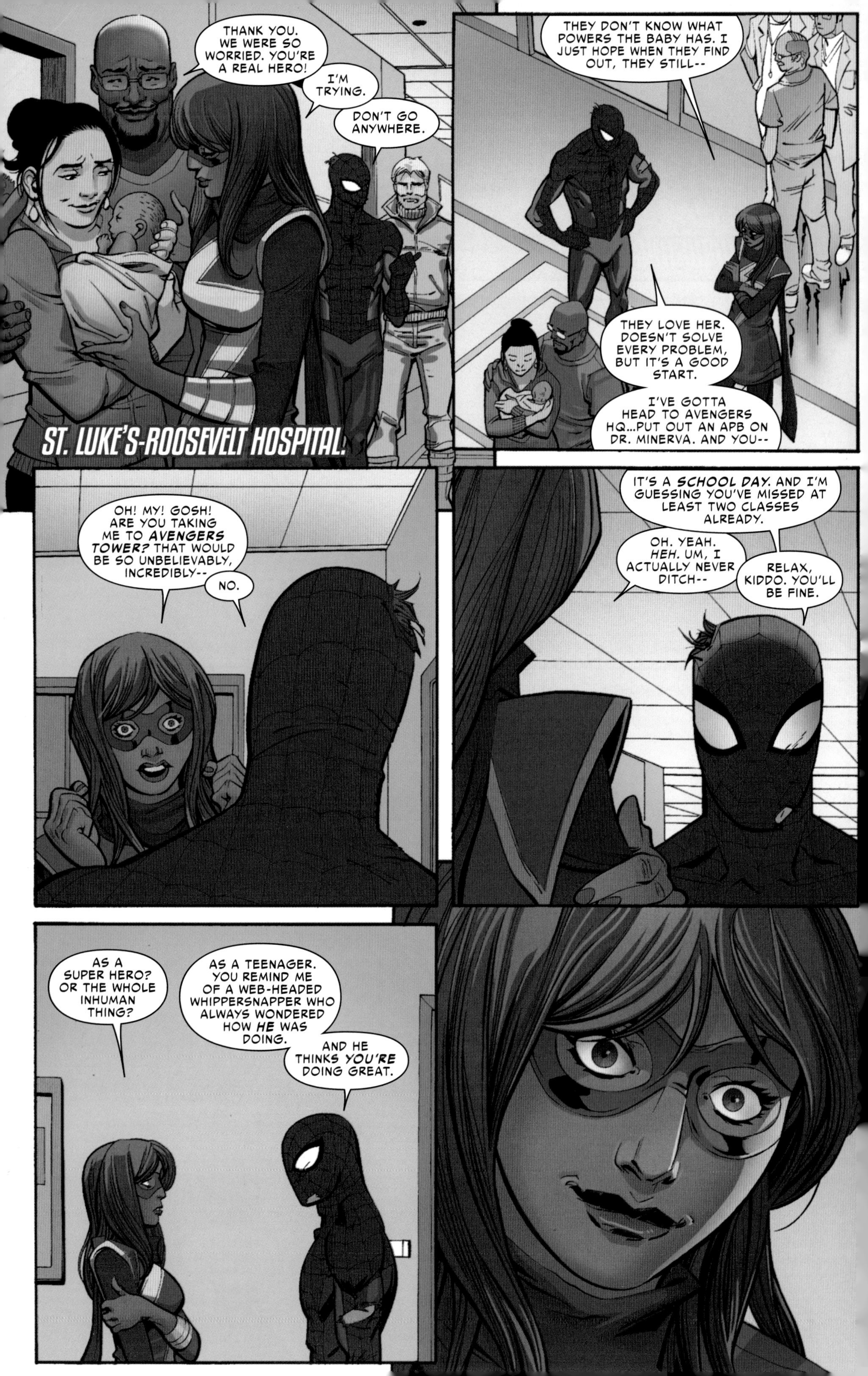
THANK YOU. WE WERE SO WORRIED. YOU'RE A REAL HERO!
I'M TRYING.
DON'T GO ANYWHERE.
ST. LUKE'S-ROOSEVELT HOSPITAL.
THEY DON'T KNOW WHAT POWERS THE BABY HAS. I JUST HOPE WHEN THEY FIND OUT, THEY STILL--
THEY LOVE HER. DOESN'T SOLVE EVERY PROBLEM, BUT IT'S A GOOD START.
I'VE GOTTA HEAD TO AVENGERS HQ...PUT OUT AN APB ON DR. MINERVA. AND YOU--
OH! MY! GOSH! ARE YOU TAKING ME TO AVENGERS TOWER? THAT WOULD BE SO UNBELIEVABLY, INCREDIBLY--
NO.
IT'S A SCHOOL DAY. AND I'M GUESSING YOU'VE MISSED AT LEAST TWO CLASSES ALREADY.
OH. YEAH. HEH. UM, I ACTUALLY NEVER DITCH--
RELAX, KIDDO. YOU'LL BE FINE.
AS A SUPER HERO? OR THE WHOLE INHUMAN THING?
AS A TEENAGER. YOU REMIND ME OF A WEB-HEADED WHIPPERSNAPPER WHO ALWAYS WONDERED HOW HE WAS DOING.
AND HE THINKS YOU'RE DOING GREAT.

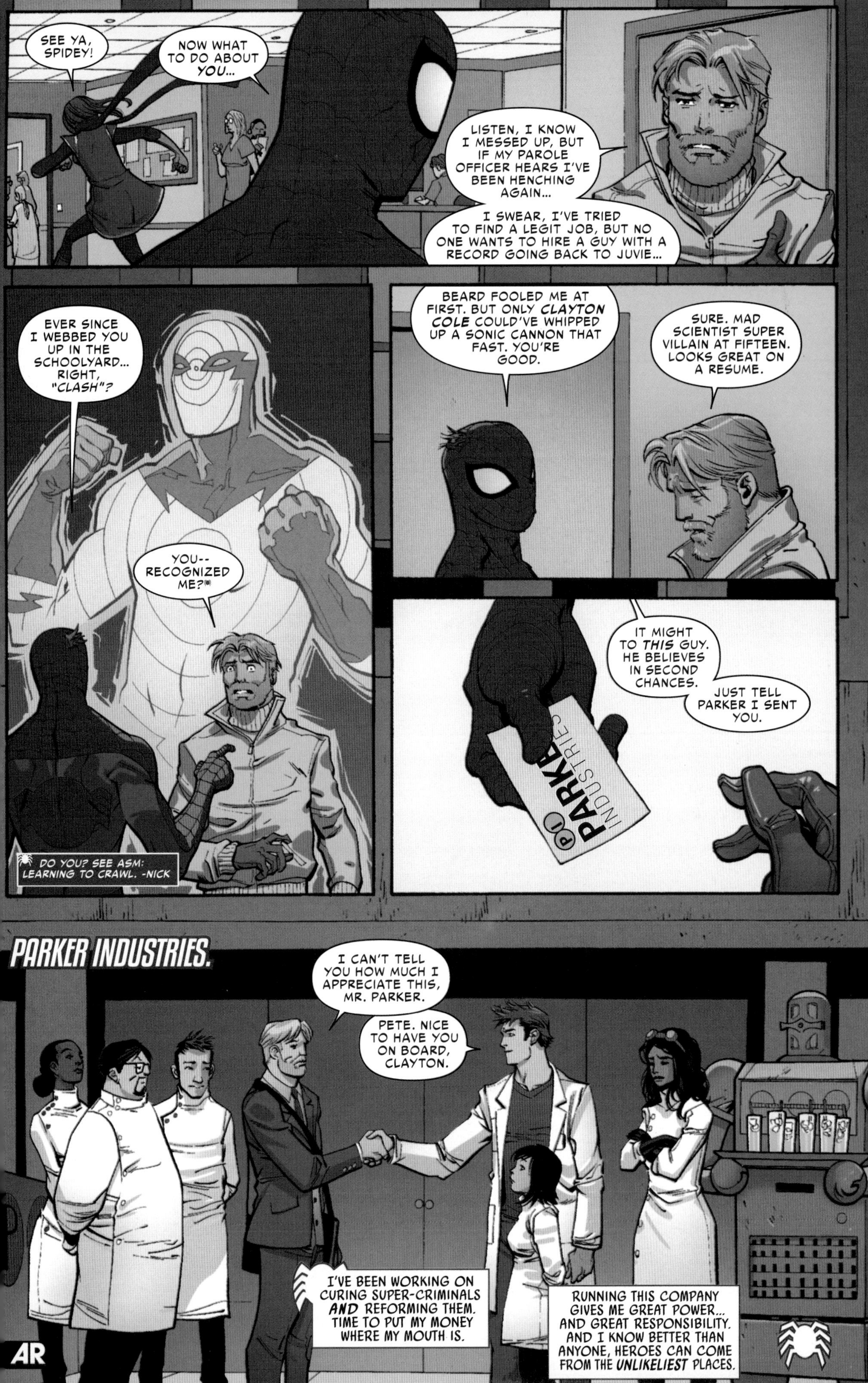
SEE YA, SPIDEY!
NOW WHAT TO DO ABOUT YOU...
LISTEN, I KNOW I MESSED UP, BUT IF MY PAROLE OFFICER HEARS I'VE BEEN HENCHING AGAIN...
I SWEAR, I'VE TRIED TO FIND A LEGIT JOB, BUT NO ONE WANTS TO HIRE A GUY WITH A RECORD GOING BACK TO JUVIE...
EVER SINCE I WEBBED YOU UP IN THE SCHOOLYARD... RIGHT, "CLASH"?
YOU--RECOGNIZED ME?*
*DO YOU? SEE ASM: LEARNING TO CRAWL. -NICK
BEARD FOOLED ME AT FIRST. BUT ONLY CLAYTON COLE COULD'VE WHIPPED UP A SONIC CANNON THAT FAST. YOU'RE GOOD.
SURE. MAD SCIENTIST SUPER VILLAIN AT FIFTEEN. LOOKS GREAT ON A RESUME.
IT MIGHT TO THIS GUY. HE BELIEVES IN SECOND CHANCES.
JUST TELL PARKER I SENT YOU.
PI PARKER INDUSTRIES
PARKER INDUSTRIES.
I CAN'T TELL YOU HOW MUCH I APPRECIATE THIS, MR. PARKER.
PETE. NICE TO HAVE YOU ON BOARD, CLAYTON.
I'VE BEEN WORKING ON CURING SUPER-CRIMINALS AND REFORMING THEM. TIME TO PUT MY MONEY WHERE MY MOUTH IS.
RUNNING THIS COMPANY GIVES ME GREAT POWER... AND GREAT RESPONSIBILITY. AND I KNOW BETTER THAN ANYONE, HEROES CAN COME FROM THE UNLIKELIEST PLACES.
AR

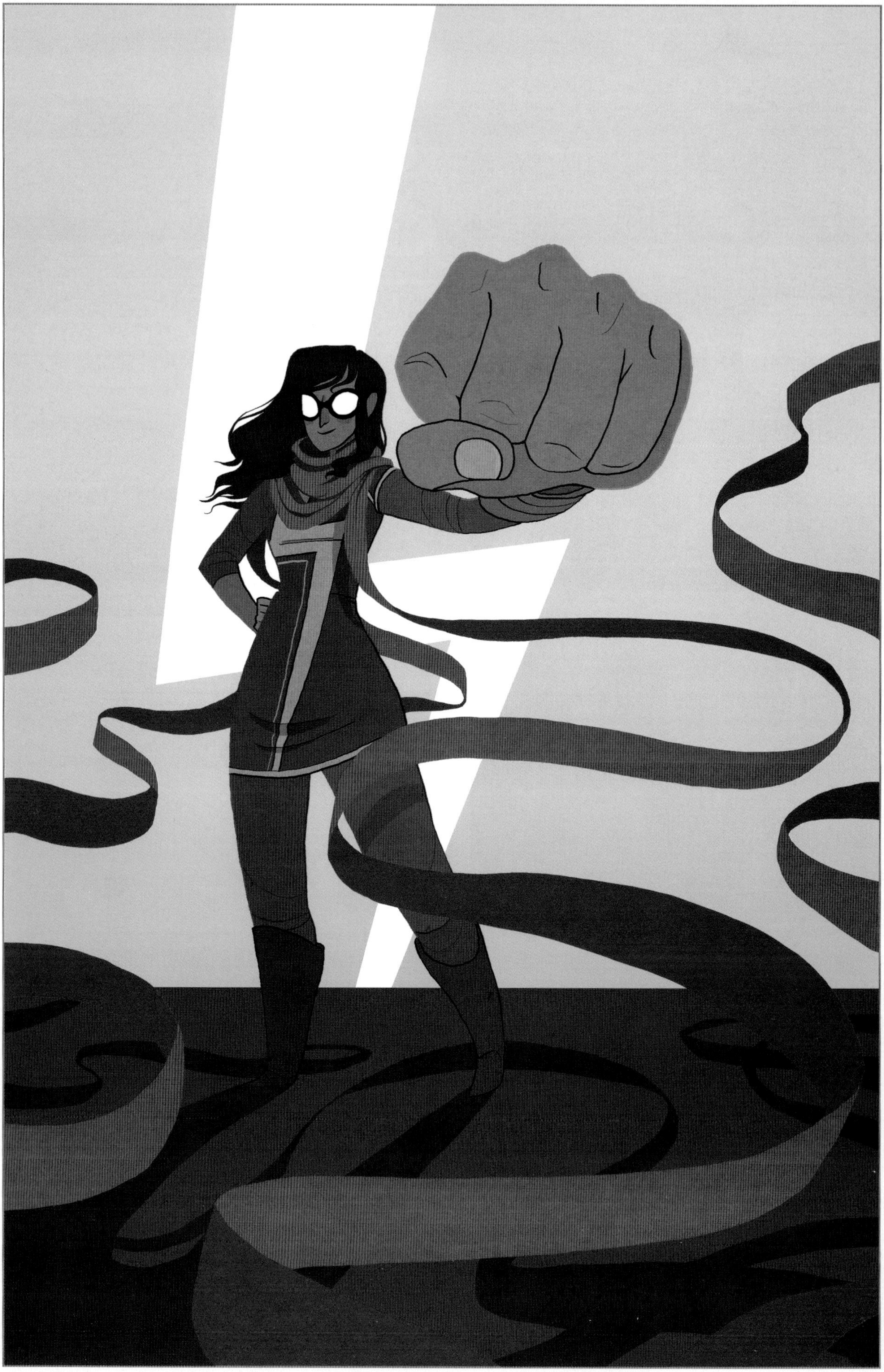

MS. MARVEL #13 WOMEN OF MARVEL VARIANT
BY NOELLE STEVENSON

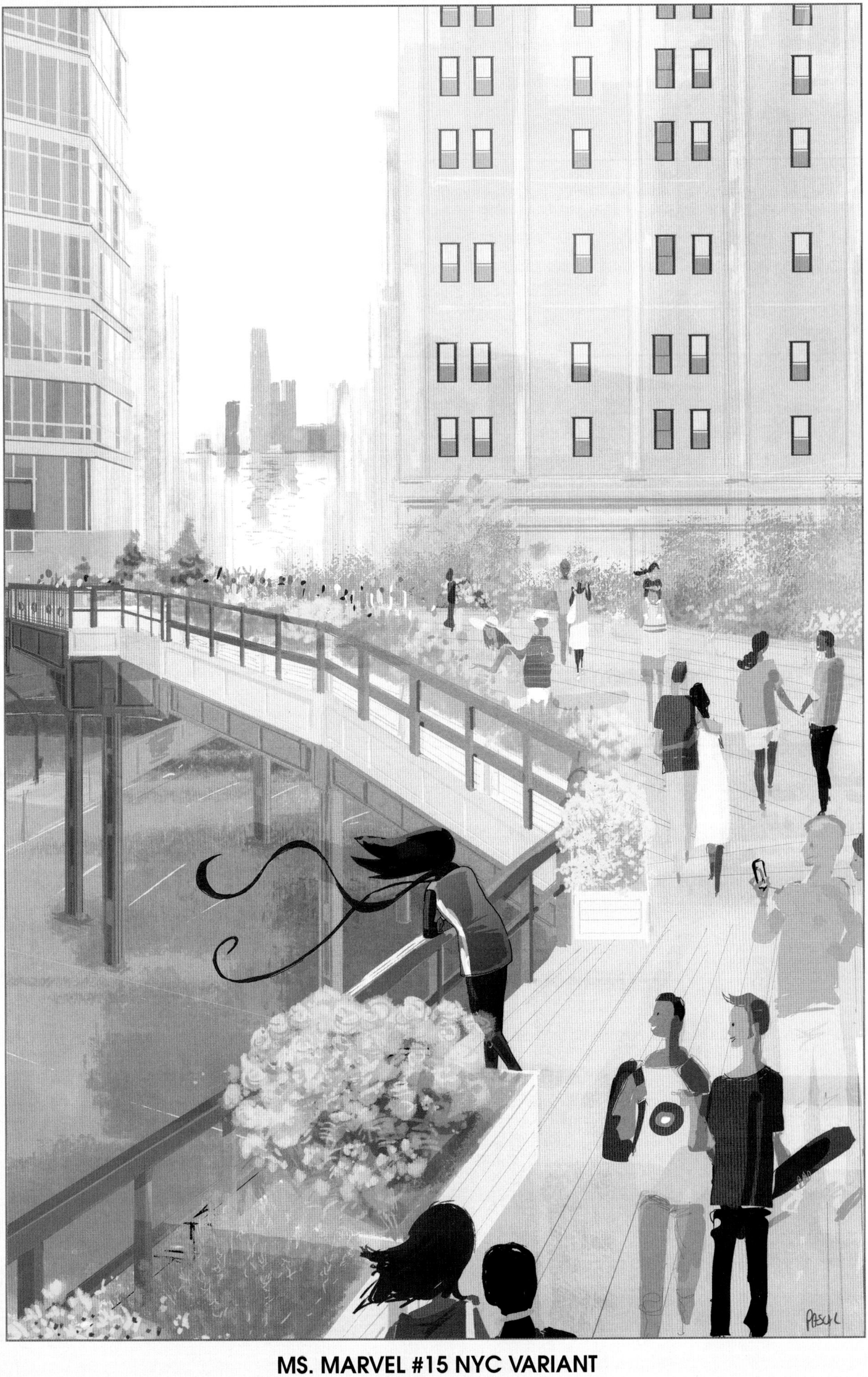

MS. MARVEL #15 NYC VARIANT
BY PASCAL CAMPION

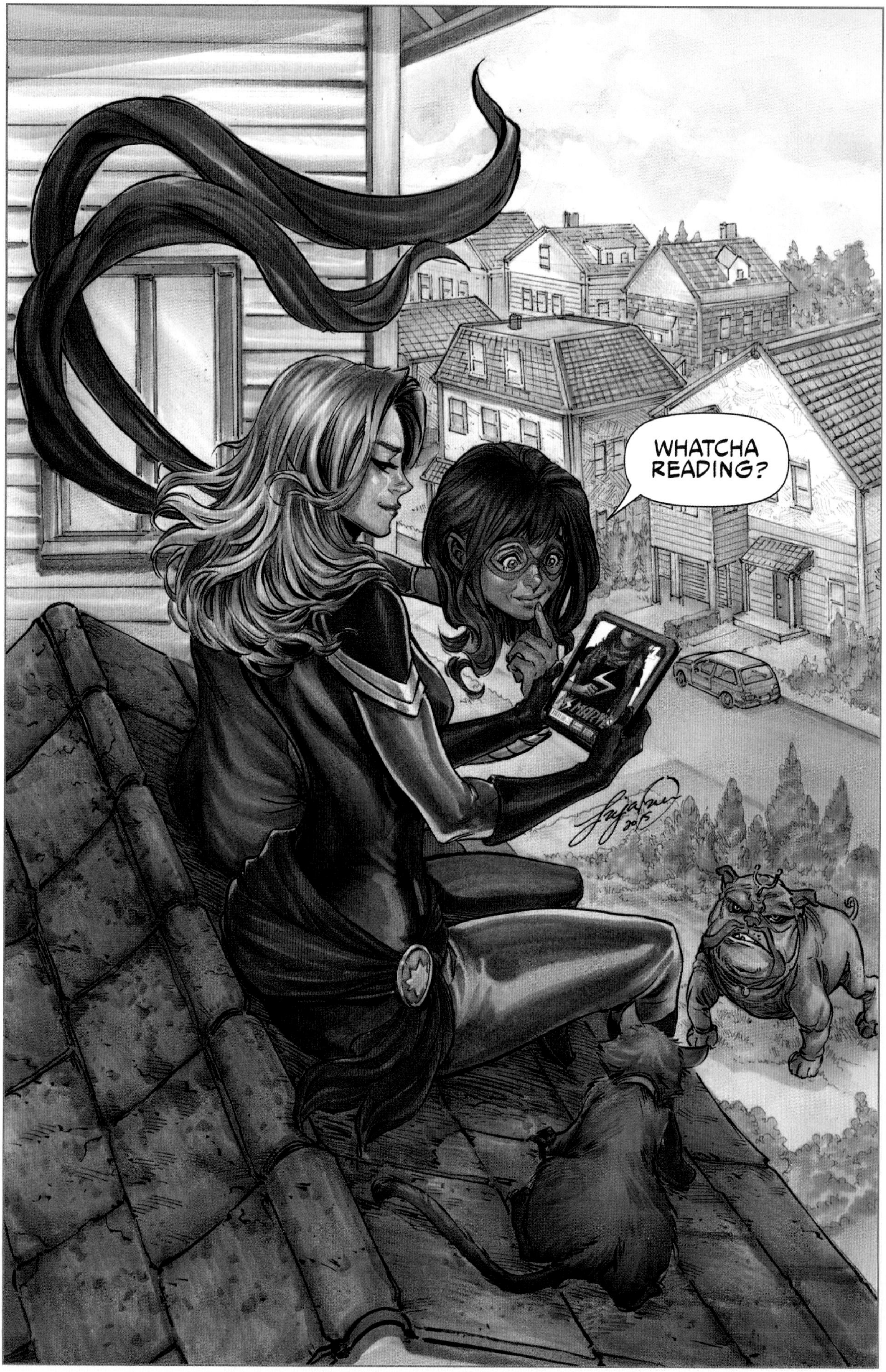
WHATCHA READING?

MS. MARVEL #17 VARIANT
BY SIYA OUM

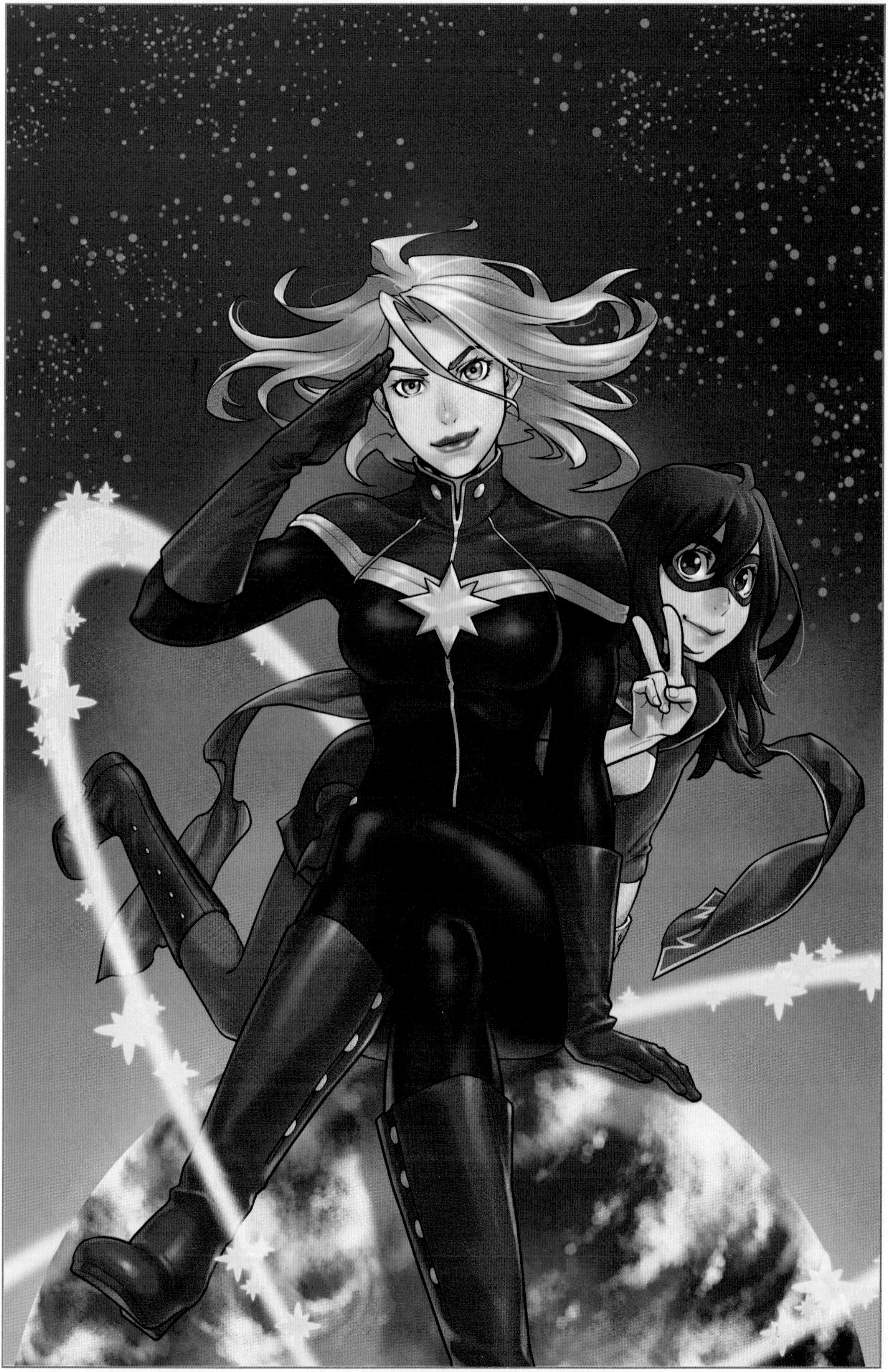

MS. MARVEL #18 MANGA VARIANT
BY RETSU TATEO

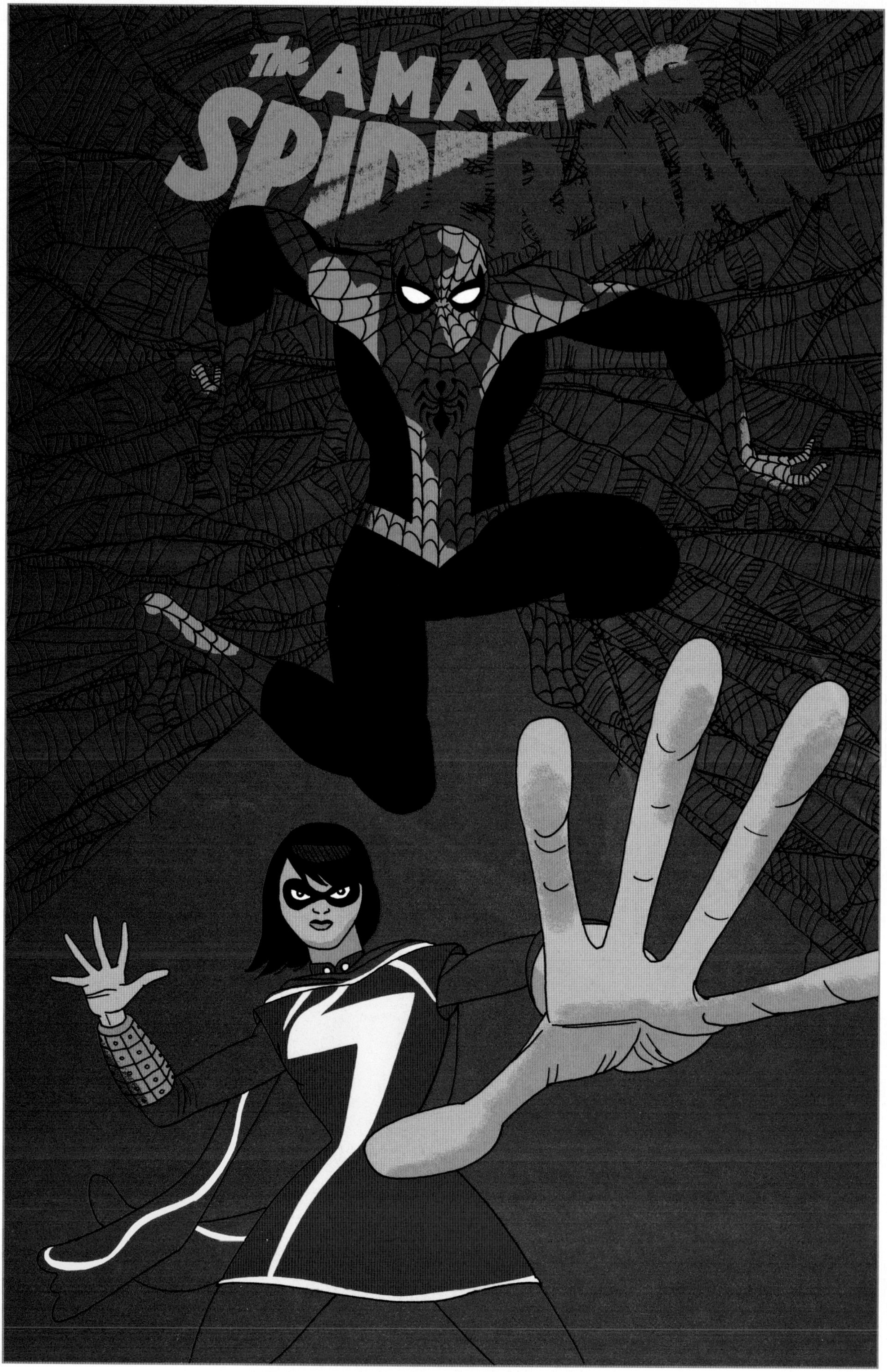
The AMAZING
SPIDER-MAN

AMAZING SPIDER-MAN #7 VARIANT
BY JAVIER PULIDO

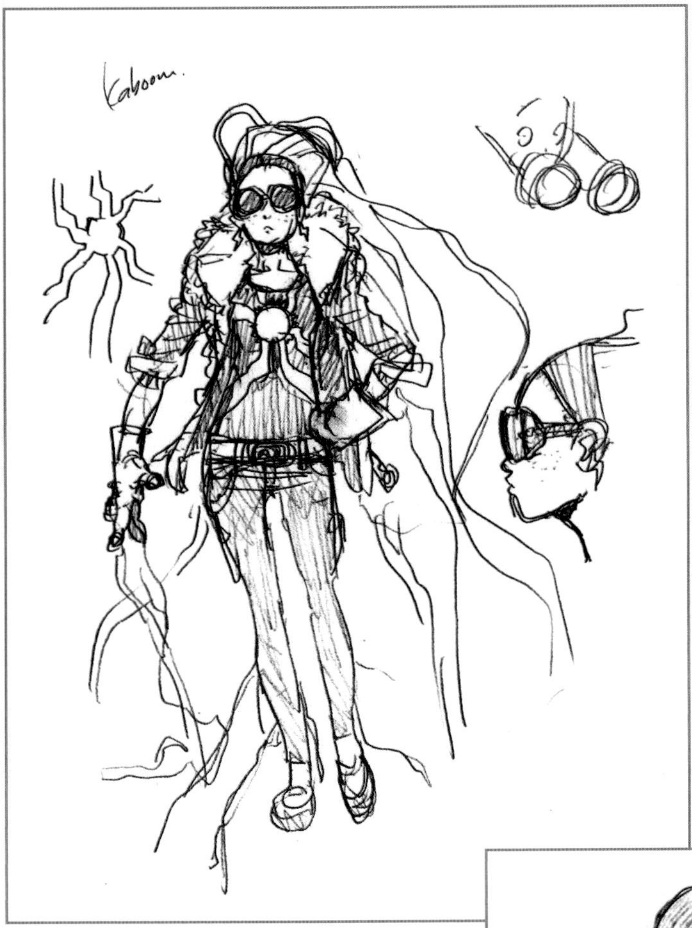
Kaboom.

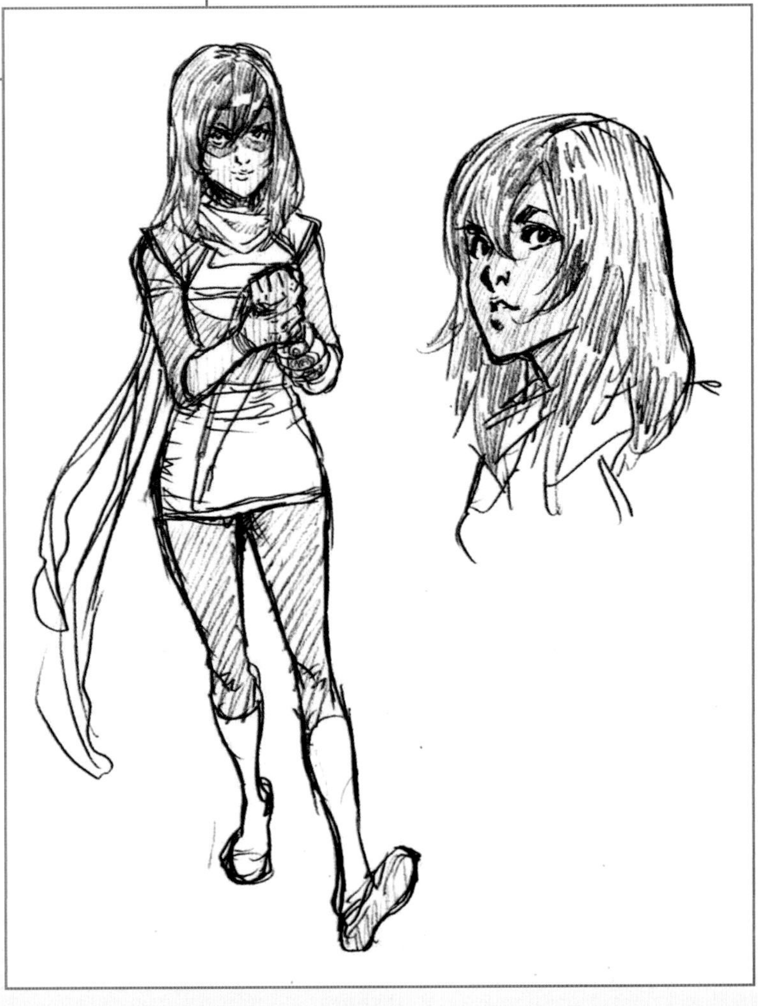

art process by takeshi miyazawa & ian herring

#13, page 1

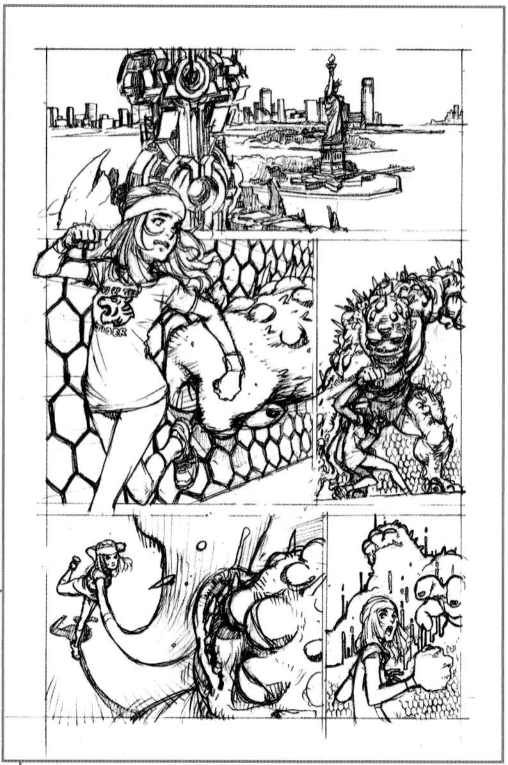

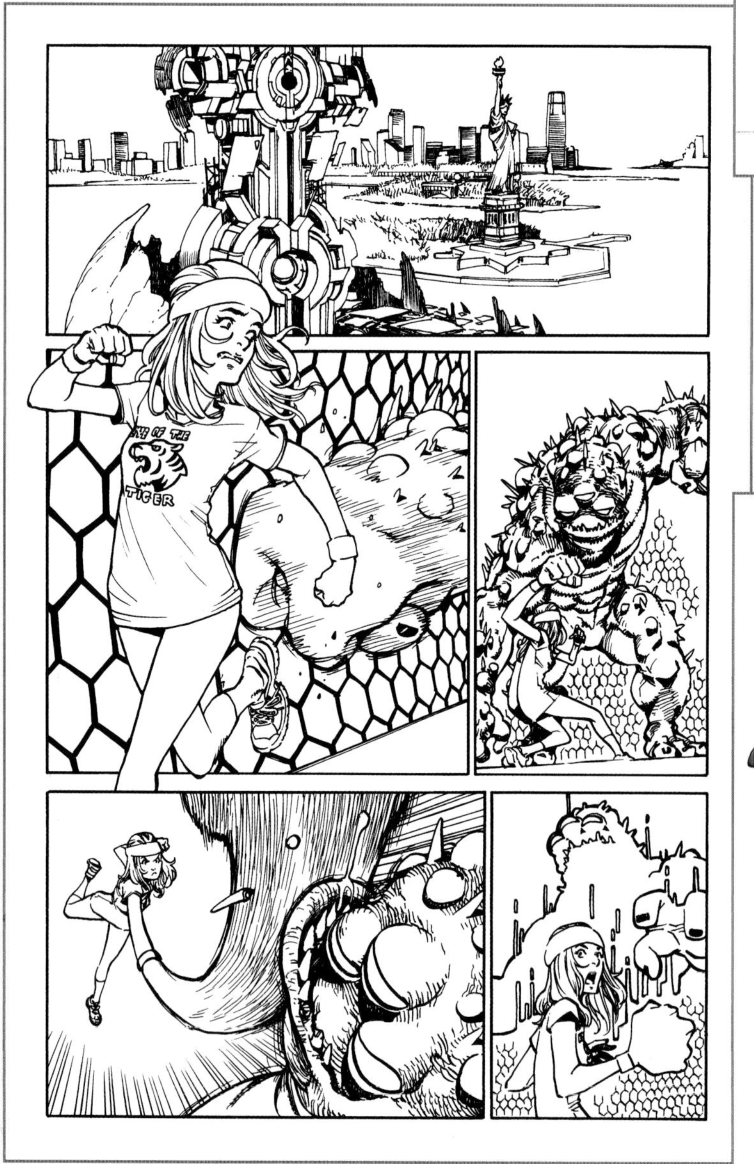
TIGER

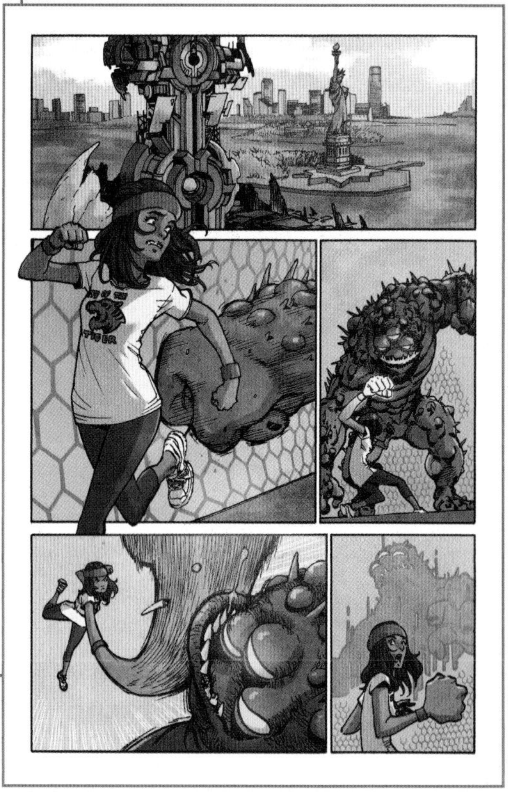

#13, page 13

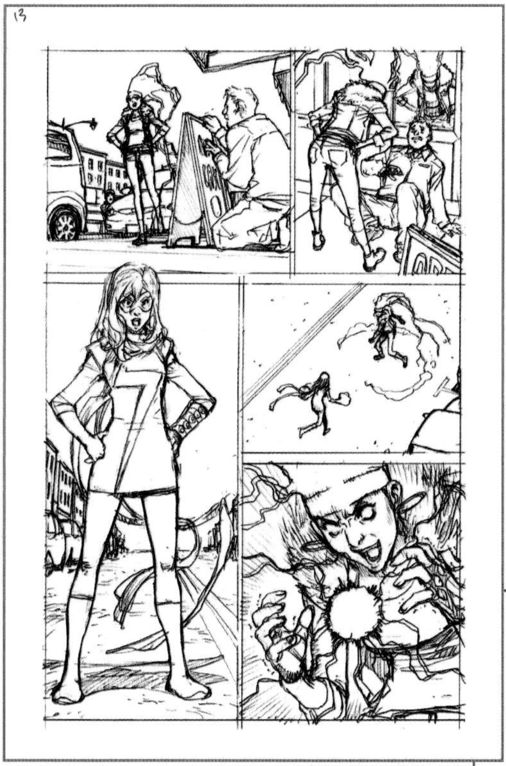

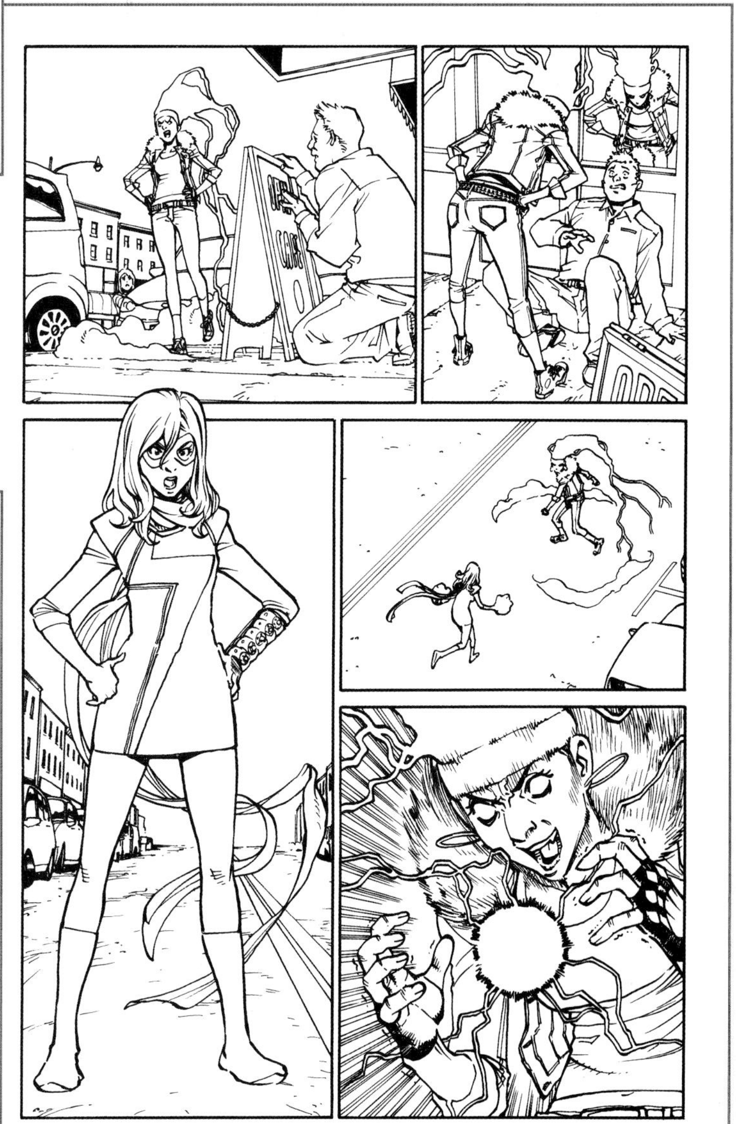

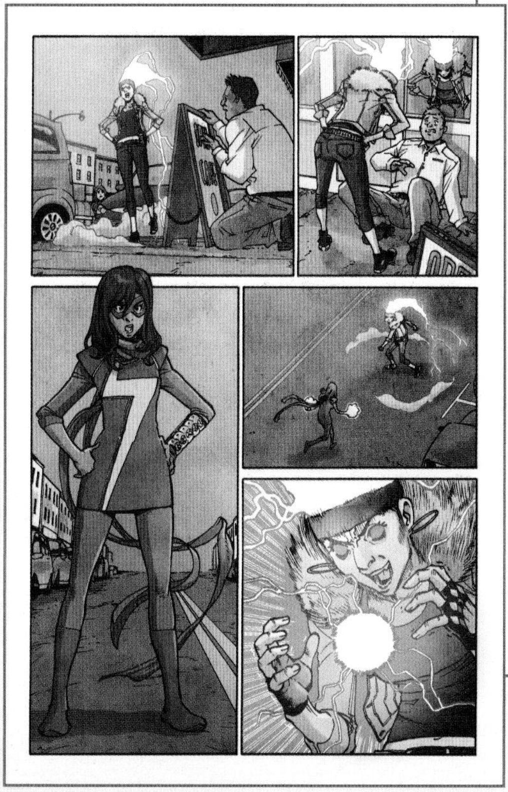

#15, page 5

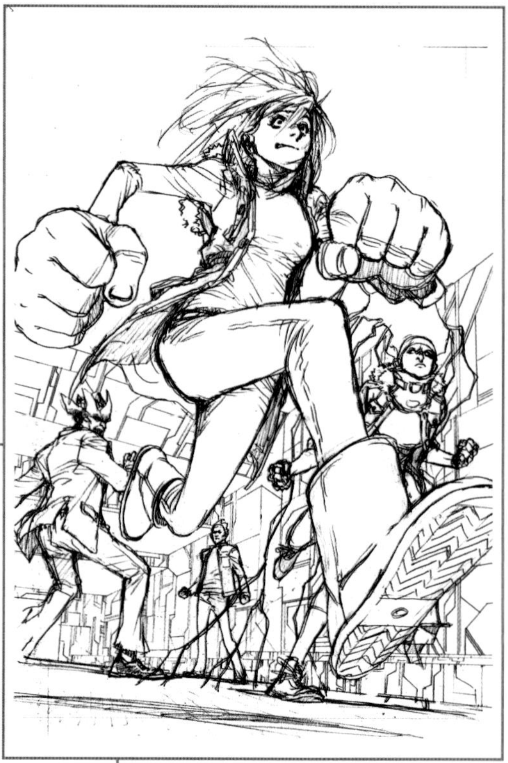

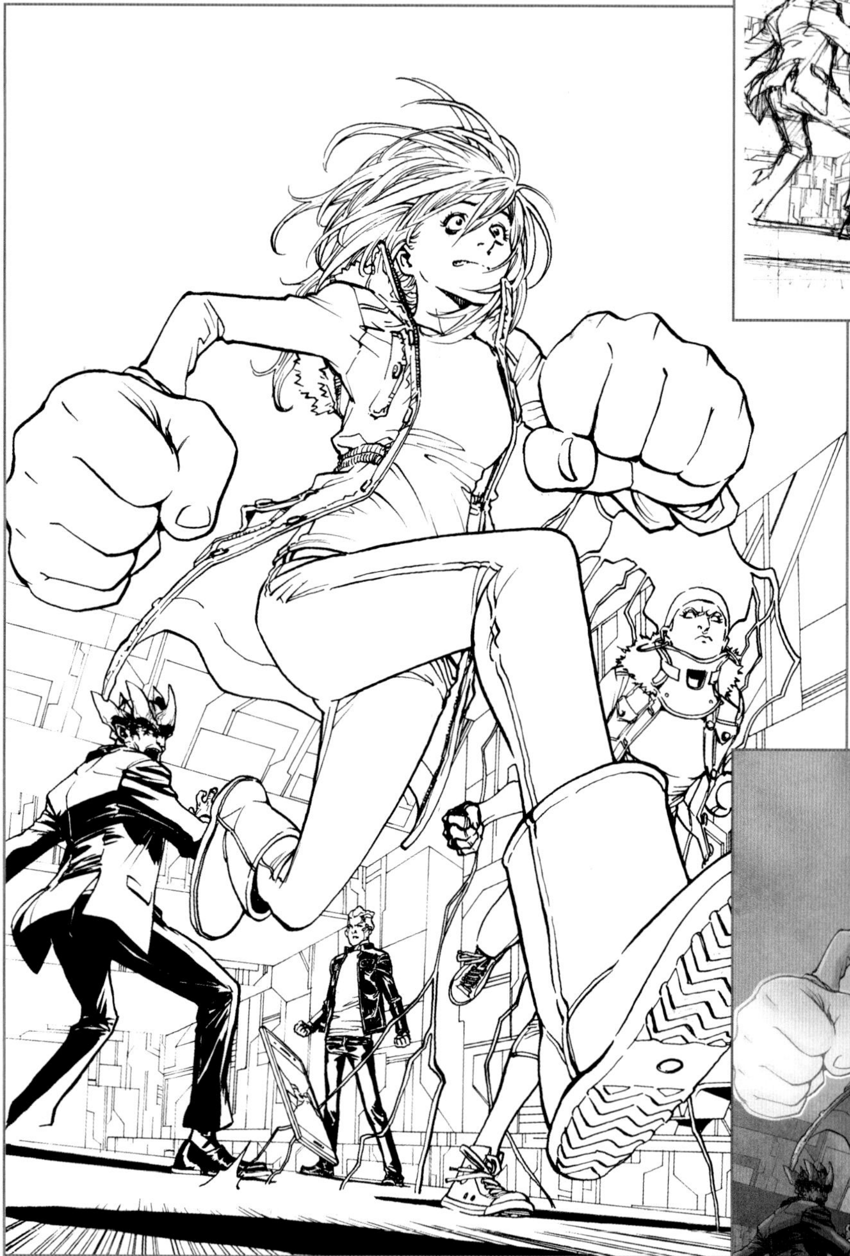

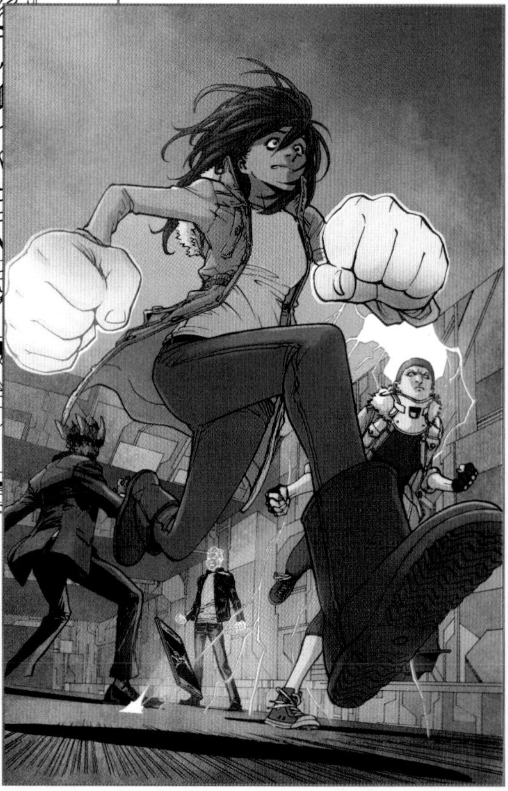